# Building Acc[...] Systems Using

## Access2000

James T. Perry, Ph.D.
The University of San Diego School of Business

Gary P. Schneider, Ph.D., CPA
The University of San Diego School of Business

**South-Western College Publishing**
Thomson Learning™

Australia • Canada • Mexico • Singapore • Spain • United Kingdom • United States

Building Accounting Systems Using Access 2000 by Perry and Schneider

Acquisitions Editor:  Rochelle Kronzek
Marketing Manager:  Dan Silverburg
Production Editor:  Marci Dechter
Manufacturing Coordinator:  Doug Wilke
Internal Design:  Joe Devine
Cover Design: Paul Neff Design
Cover Photographer: © 1999 PhotoDisc, Inc.
Production House:  Cover to Cover Publishing, Inc.
Printer:  R. R. Donnelley, Crawfordsville

Printed in the United States of America
5  03 02

For more information contact South-Western College Publishing, 5191 Natorp Blvd., Mason, Ohio, 45040 or find us on the Internet at http://www.swcollege.com

**For permission to use material from this text or product, contact us by**
• **telephone:  1-800-730-2214**
• **fax:  1-800-730-2215**
• **web:  http://www.thomsonrights.com**

**Library of Congress Cataloging-in-Publication Data**
Perry, James T.
    Building accounting systems : using Access 2000 / James T. Perry, Gary P. Schneider.
      p. cm.
    ISBN 0-324-01593-3
    1. Accounting--Data processing. 2. Transaction systems (Computer systems)
  I. Schneider, Gary P. II. Microsoft Access.

HF5679 .P4194 2000
657'.0285'57565--dc21

                                                                        00-021222

This book is printed on acid-free paper

To Nancy C. Perry and Cathryn A. Cosby

# PREFACE

**TO THE STUDENT**

Traditional methods of recording economic events and accumulating accounting information have given way to database technology in today's accounting information systems. As we write this fourth edition of *Building Accounting Systems*, we find that organizations increasingly depend on databases that include accounting and other operating data for mission-critical information. Accounting information systems—or the accounting views of enterprise-wide databases—contain much of the information managers use to make decisions and control operations. These databases also store the information that accountants use to prepare the formal accounting reports, such as year-end financial statements, that organizations issue to external users. As a professional accountant, you will play a central role in ensuring that the accounting systems you use, audit, and help design will deliver timely, accurate, and complete information. This book will help you learn how to perform that role effectively.

This text describes how database management systems provide design tools that information systems professionals and accountants can use to build accounting systems. The text begins by explaining how database systems are a part of your everyday life, then helps you develop a basic understanding of the theory and practice of relational database management systems. With that foundation, the book then shows you how to build the elements of accounting systems using Microsoft Access, one of the most widely available database management software packages for personal computers.

The book begins by explaining how to use the Windows operating environment. It then reviews the history and theory of relational database systems, and describes practical uses of Microsoft Access. The book explains accounting transaction cycles and shows you how to use the database theory and tools you learned in the earlier chapters to build accounting system elements for each of the four main transaction cycles: revenue, purchase, payroll, and production.

Chapter 1 provides a firm grounding in the fundamentals of the Windows 95/98/NT/2000 operating systems. This chapter may be a review for some of you;

for others, this will be your first hands-on introduction to the Windows operating system. Chapter 2 introduces Microsoft Access database management software. You will learn the basics of using tables to store information, displaying database contents, finding answers to questions with database queries, using forms to enter data, and printing database reports. Chapter 3 presents a concise, yet thorough, introduction to database theory. You will learn how to use normalization rules to structure your data in ways that avoid redundancy and data loss. This chapter also introduces user views and entity-relationship modeling. Additionally, you will learn the differences between database accounting systems and double-entry bookkeeping systems, and the advantages of the database approach. You will learn how to classify business activities by level of complexity. You will also learn to identify the business activities that occur in the four main transaction cycles we use in this book. Finally, you will learn how to perform basic database operations that enable you to locate subsets of table rows or columns and to collect information from several related database tables. In Chapter 4 you create several tables and queries—tasks for which we provide step-by-step guidance. You will be happy to know that you can perform all of these database functions *without writing a single line of program code*. When you have finished Chapter 4, you will have the database skills you need to create both tables and queries—the fundamental database building blocks that deliver data to the remaining basic accounting system components. Chapter 5 provides an in-depth discussion of designing and creating Access forms and reports. You will learn how to create forms based on one table and multiple tables. Similarly, you will learn how to design and create reports using the Access Report Wizard and how to manually create reports based on queries.

Chapters 6 through 9 of the book apply database concepts and techniques to the specific challenges of building accounting information systems. In Chapter 6, you will begin your walk through the accounting transaction cycles with the revenue cycle. For example, you will learn how to use tables and forms to record sales and cash collections. Chapter 7 shows database applications in the purchase cycle, which include creating purchase orders, recording the receipt of goods ordered, and paying vendors. In Chapter 8, you will build the database elements that businesses use to handle the many details of payroll accounting. You will learn how to combine records of time worked with employee information to calculate gross pay, deductions, and net pay. Chapter 9 describes the production cycle and shows you how to build accounting database elements that track materials, labor, and overhead costs into production using job order cost accumulation examples. The chapter also explains how you can extend these examples to build process, hybrid, and activity-based cost accounting databases. Chapter 10 shows you how to add "icing" to the database "cake" with enhancements to the database elements you created in the preceding chapters. These enhancements include custom buttons for simplifying database operations and custom menus that replace the Access default menu.

We hope you will become an active participant as you read the text and work through the step-by-step examples. You will best retain what you have read by working through the book on a computer. To reinforce your learning, we have included three types of review questions at the end of each chapter:

• Multiple-choice questions, which refresh your memory about key points in the text.

• Discussion questions, which are more general and can provide a basis for interesting small group discussions of the topics.

• Problems, which require you to use Access to create your own accounting databases or extend the examples in the text.

By studying the text carefully, working through the examples, and using the end-of-chapter materials to reinforce your knowledge, you will learn how to use database management software to design and build accounting systems that deliver timely, accurate information to managers and financial statement users.

**TO THE INSTRUCTOR**

Many accounting professors feel that the accounting information systems course is the greatest teaching challenge in the curriculum. One of our goals in writing this book was to help make your job of teaching accounting systems easier. Accounting practice has evolved from manual journals and ledgers to database accounting systems—even in very small firms. At the same time, many introductory accounting courses have shifted to financial statement user and managerial decision-maker orientations from the more traditional preparer orientations. Despite this decreased emphasis on the mechanics of accounting in the introductory courses, accounting majors still need to understand how accounting systems record, classify, and aggregate economic events. This book gives you a powerful tool that can help you give your students a solid introduction to database principles *and* valuable hands-on experience in constructing accounting systems. By using Microsoft Access—object-based software that features an intuitive graphic user interface—this book vastly reduces the amount of class time you must spend on nonaccounting systems matters. The text's step-by-step instructions can reduce your time and drudgery in the computer lab. The time you do spend with students in class or in the computer lab will not be wasted on mundane "click here and then click there" instructing because we have filled this book with detailed instructions and examples to save you that kind of work.

We are convinced that there are at least as many different ways of teaching the accounting systems course as there are professors teaching it. Therefore, this book was designed to be flexible. In a junior- or senior-level course, the book can effectively supplement any accounting information systems text currently on the market. Most of these texts are organized around transaction cycles that are identical or similar to the transaction cycles we use in this book. Adopters of this book's earlier editions have used it successfully with many different accounting information systems texts. Some instructors have used this book as the main course text, supplementing it with readings from the current literature on internal control and systems design. Instructors have incorporated the book into their courses in various ways. Some cover all or part of the book in class. Others assign the book as a series of computer lab assignments or as outside reading.

Many accounting systems courses include some type of systems design project. A number of instructors have used earlier editions of this book as an effective springboard for such projects. Students can extend the book's examples or use them as analogs for the real-world systems they design and build in their projects. Students will feel better prepared to take on the challenge of a systems design project after they have experienced successes with creating the example accounting systems in this book.

Although we designed this book to meet the needs of the undergraduate accounting major systems class, it is flexible enough to be used in other settings. Many community colleges now offer a computer accounting course. This book would serve well as either the main text or a supplement in such a course. Instructors of graduate accounting systems courses may wish to assign this book as a project for those students who lack undergraduate systems course work or for students whose undergraduate systems exposure is dated. Instructors of information systems auditing courses at the graduate level have also found the book to be a useful supplement in those courses.

The book includes a number of features that will make your teaching easier:

- A concise introduction to database theory that includes thorough discussions of normalization and entity-relationship modeling.

- An exposition of the database approach to accounting systems that includes a comparison to double-entry bookkeeping procedures.

- Step-by-step instructions in all chapters that guide the student through each example.

- Numerous figures that show the computer screen at key points in each task and that show finished forms and printed reports.

- A Companion CD that contains tables, files, queries, forms, reports, and other information to help students complete the exercises and follow along with the examples in the text.

We have taken special care to include database tables, forms, queries, and reports so that students can use any chapter independently of other chapters. You will find that many of the tables include comprehensive examples of significant size. By including these very large tables, we hope to give students an experience that resembles working with real-world databases.

An Instructor's Manual is available to adopters that includes detailed lecture suggestions for each chapter and solutions to all end-of-chapter questions and exercises. The Instructor's Manual also includes an Instructor's CD, which contains solutions to all computer exercises in the form of Microsoft Access tables, forms, queries, and reports. The Instructor's CD also contains the text of the Instructor's Manual, in both Microsoft Word and Adobe PDF formats, to help you create customized lecture notes, transparencies, and presentation software slide shows for classroom use. We have also included digital movies, created with HyperCam, that illustrate each step of the in-text exercises throughout all chapters of the book. To play a movie, you simply double-click on a movie file. Your Windows media player automatically plays the movies. We have tested the HyperCam format movies on Windows 95, 98, NT, and 2000 systems.

## ORGANIZATION OF THE BOOK

The text contains ten chapters. The first five chapters introduce the Windows 95/98/NT/2000 operating systems, Microsoft Access, and basic database modeling. The next four chapters show students how to use the database theory and tools from the earlier chapters to build functional accounting system database elements. Chapter 10 describes advanced features of Microsoft Access, including automating database procedures and validity-checking features with custom-built Visual Basic for Applications (VBA) code.

Chapter 1 is an overview of Windows 95/98/NT/2000 and emphasizes fundamental operations such as launching programs, examining object properties, and manipulating windows. This chapter will help students who are computer novices attain sufficient Windows proficiency to use any Windows database management product. Chapter 2 familiarizes students with the Microsoft Access database management system. All major database elements are discussed, including tables, queries, forms, and reports. Chapter 3 presents a brief history of databases; describes the requirements for databases to be in first, second, and third normal forms; and describes how database accounting differs from double-entry bookkeeping and why firms are using database accounting systems. Chapter 3 also identifies firms as service, merchandising, or manufacturing; discusses the transaction cycle elements that exist in each type of firm; and gives students sufficient grounding in database theory to create well-designed, anomaly-free databases. Chapter 4 provides students with hands-on experience in building database tables and queries. Chapter 5 contains a thorough discussion about designing and building Access forms for data entry, data viewing, and Access reports to supply management with hard copy output. Building on a foundation of tables and queries, the forms and reports discussion provides the capstone Microsoft Access experience needed to completely understand the role of a database management system in producing accounting objects.

The next four chapters of the book show students how to apply the tools and techniques from the first five chapters to the specific tasks of building accounting system elements. We use four transaction cycles to organize these four chapters:

revenue, purchase, payroll, and production. Each of these four chapters begins with a description of an example company and an entity-relationship diagram of its data model. The data model feature is new in this edition. We included it in response to requests from many users of previous editions.

We define the revenue cycle to include cash receipts and the purchase cycle to include cash disbursements. Chapter 6 shows students how to track customer information, sales, and cash receipts in the revenue cycle. In Chapter 7, students get to see the purchase cycle as a mirror image of the revenue cycle. They learn how to track vendor information and record purchase orders, receipt of goods ordered, and cash disbursements. Chapter 8 presents students with a straightforward payroll system example that they can easily extend to accommodate greater levels of complexity. Chapter 9, which covers the production cycle, shows students how to track materials, labor, and overhead costs in a job order cost accumulation system. Chapter 9 also explains how students can extend these job order examples to build process, hybrid, and activity-based cost accounting database systems.

Chapter 10 concludes the book with instructions for enhancing database systems with command buttons and custom menus. These enhancements require the student to write macros and VBA code; however, we provide step-by-step instructions that make this a pleasant exercise. Even the most computer-phobic accounting student should find writing these short code snippets tolerable.

## PATHS THROUGH THE BOOK

The chapters need not be assigned in sequence. You can follow several paths through the book. If your students are familiar with whichever of the Windows (95/98/NT/2000) operating environments you will be using, you can skip Chapter 1 or assign it as review reading. Chapters 2, 3, 4, and 5 should be assigned in order, since Chapters 4 and 5 integrate the Chapter 2 introduction to Microsoft Access with the Chapter 3 treatment of database principles and their application to accounting systems.

Many instructors will want to cover all four of the transaction cycle chapters, assigning Chapters 6, 7, 8, and 9 in sequence. Some instructors prefer to focus on one or two transaction cycles each semester. Chapter 6, the revenue cycle, and Chapter 7, the purchase cycle, are ideal candidates for such a focus. You can go directly to Chapter 8 from Chapter 5 if you wish. Chapters 8 and 9 are independent of each other, but students will find these chapters easier if they have first worked through Chapter 7. Although Chapter 9 includes a brief introduction to cost accounting concepts, most students will find the material in this chapter to be somewhat difficult if they have not already had a cost accounting course.

We made Chapter 10 the last chapter because some instructors may wish to omit it. The chapter includes advanced database software techniques that students can use to enhance the accounting systems that they build. If your students are comfortable with Windows productivity software such as word processors or spreadsheets—particularly if they have written macros or VBA code—then you should be able to assign Chapter 10 any time after Chapter 5. None of the book's other chapters require students to have mastered the material in Chapter 10, so you may wish to cover this material at the end of the course if time permits.

## ABOUT THE AUTHORS

Jim Perry is a Professor of Management Information Systems at the University of San Diego School of Business. He is the co-author of over twenty-seven textbooks and trade books and over a dozen articles on computer security, database management systems, multimedia delivery systems, and chief programmer teams. Jim is a charter member of the Association for Information Systems. He holds a Ph.D. in computer science from the Pennsylvania State University and a Bachelor of Science in mathematics from Purdue University. Jim has worked as a computer security consultant to various private and governmental organizations, including the Jet Propulsion Laboratory. He was a consultant on the Strategic Defense Initiative ("Star Wars") project and served as a member of the computer security oversight committee.

Gary Schneider is an Associate Professor of Accounting and Information Systems at the University of San Diego School of Business. The author or co-author of eleven books, Gary has written widely on accounting and systems topics. His work has appeared in a number of journals including the *IS Audit & Control Journal*, *Interfaces*, and the *Journal of Information Systems*. Gary is active in the American Accounting Association and has served as editor of its *Accounting Information Systems and Technology Reporter*. He has provided training and consulting services to a number of major clients, including AlliedSignal, the Gartner Group, and Qualcomm. In 1999, he was named a Fellow of the Gartner Institute. Gary holds a Ph.D. in accounting from the University of Tennessee, an MBA in accounting from Xavier University, and a BA in economics from the University of Cincinnati. He is a CPA and practiced public accounting in Ohio for fourteen years before undertaking his academic career.

## ACKNOWLEDGMENTS

Creating a successful book is always a collaborative effort between authors and publisher. We work as a team to provide the best book possible. We want to thank the following reviewers for the insightful comments and suggestions they gave us on this and previous editions: A. Faye Borthick, Georgia State University; Severin Grabski, Michigan State University; Mary R. Scott, Grambling State University; and Jerry D. Siebel, University of South Florida. We would also like to thank the many professors who have used previous editions in their classes and have provided us with valuable insights and suggestions for this edition. Students in accounting information systems classes at the University of San Diego and at Georgia State University have used various versions of the manuscripts for this and previous editions of the book. We appreciate the many helpful suggestions these students provided. In particular, we want to thank former students Pamela S. Drotman and Steven French for their help with technical editing and data generation tasks. Our special thanks goes to Dorene De Turi, who has done an excellent job producing the digital movies for the Instructor's Companion CD.

The authors especially want to acknowledge the work of the professionals at South-Western College Publishing. We thank David L. Shaut for his initial interest in and continual support of this project. Dave recognized an emerging need for this kind of book before any other publisher. We extend special thanks to Richard K. Lindgren, Rochelle Kronzek, Marcella Dechter, Dan Silverburg, and the other members of the Accounting Team at South-Western. We appreciate the care and attention to detail with which everyone at South-Western handled the development and production of this edition. We especially want to acknowledge Martha Wagner, the South-Western sales representative who enthusiastically encouraged and supported our proposal for the first edition of this book.

Finally, we want to express deep appreciation to our spouses, Nancy Perry and Cathy Cosby, for their remarkable patience as we worked both ends of the clock to complete this edition of the book on a very tight schedule. We also thank our children for tolerating our absences from their lives while we were consumed with the work of revising and updating this book.

If you would like to contact us about the book, we would enjoy hearing from you. We welcome comments and suggestions that we might incorporate into future editions of the book. You can e-mail book-related messages to us at **debit@acusd.edu**. For the latest information about *Building Accounting Systems* and related resources, please visit our Web site at **http://www.swcollege.com/ perry.html**.

## TRADEMARK LIST

The following trademarks and registered trademarks appear in this book:

1. Microsoft, Windows, Access, Word, Excel, Exchange, Internet Explorer, FoxPro, Paint, Office, and The Microsoft Network are registered trademarks of Microsoft Corporation. Any reference to Microsoft Windows, Access, Word, Excel, Exchange, Internet Explorer, FoxPro, Paint, Office, or The Microsoft Network refers to this note.

2. Adobe is a registered trademark of Adobe Systems Incorporated. Any references to Adobe refer to this note.

# CONTENTS

**2**            **INTRODUCTION TO MICROSOFT ACCESS    51**

**3**                  DATABASES AND ACCOUNTING SYSTEMS   111

**5**                                      **ACCESS FORMS AND REPORTS    219**

## 8            PAYROLL CYCLE   387

# 1 WORKING WITH WINDOWS

OBJECTIVES

This chapter presents an overview of the Microsoft Windows environment available on millions of microcomputers around the world. For those unfamiliar with Windows, you will learn the skills essential for working with it. Everything in this chapter applies to Windows 95, Windows 98, and Windows NT unless specifically noted. Those of you who are familiar with Windows will probably discover some new techniques while reading this chapter. Several key Windows features are presented. In particular, you will learn how to:

- Understand what objects are found on the desktop.
- Open, close, maximize, and minimize windows.
- Launch an application using the Start button.
- Use a dialog box.
- Exit an application.
- Use Explorer to manage files and programs, and to launch a program.
- Create folders in Explorer.
- Get help on the current application.
- Launch multiple applications and switch between them.
- Pass data between Windows programs.
- Create and use desktop shortcuts.
- Modify the Start menu.
- Relocate the Taskbar.
- Exit Windows.

**AN OVERVIEW OF WINDOWS**

Windows provides a convenient work surface from which you can run applications, manage files, and run your business. By simply clicking the Start button and

1

selecting a program, you can launch Microsoft Word, Microsoft Access, or any of the thousands of Windows programs available. One significant advantage of using Windows is that you can run more than one program at the same time. For instance, you could be writing a memo to your sales manager using your favorite word processing program, Word. When you are ready to summarize last month's sales figures, you can quickly switch to Excel, your tried and true spreadsheet program, to review the sales figures found in last quarter's spreadsheet. Switching between applications is as easy as clicking a button.

Another advantage of Windows is that transferring data between Windows programs is easy. Suppose you want to mail letters to customers in a particular state—Washington, for example—informing them about a special, limited time product promotion. You create Word documents for each customer in Washington containing details about the promotion. This might be a daunting task if you actually typed each letter. However, you know that Word can use Windows tools to retrieve information from an Access database containing your customers' names and addresses. Microsoft Word and Microsoft Access work seamlessly together to deliver database information to Word documents on demand. With Windows, Word, and Access, it is simple to create a form letter for each customer as well as mailing labels. Figure 1.1 shows an example of a Word document (bottom), a sheet of Avery 5160 mailing labels, and an Access database (right) that dynamically supplies customer addresses to both forms. This is an example of Windows information sharing between applications employing Dynamic Data Exchange (DDE).

Another way that applications can share information is called Object Linking and Embedding, or OLE. Newer than DDE, OLE actually embeds a *copy* of the data into another document. For instance, you could place a copy of the customer database, or a subset of it, into a Word document. In this example, the Word document is the *container* and the Access database, supplying the database information to the document, is known as the *server*. (You will see this container/server relationship illustrated throughout this text.)

Because of its ease of use and the advantages mentioned, Windows is a well-established standard among PC users. In the sections that follow, you will learn the most important features of Windows—those skills and techniques essential to thrive in today's business world.

## Starting Windows

Windows automatically executes after your computer is turned on and has successfully completed some hardware tests. You will first see some introductory screens, and then the Windows desktop will appear. Depending on how you have set up Windows, you may be asked to type a user name and password. If asked to do so, follow the steps outlined in the following section.

## Logging On to Windows

If your computer is in a school or corporation, you may be required to log on to Windows. After starting Windows, you will see the Windows logo on the screen fol-

mailing
labels

database
records

form
letter

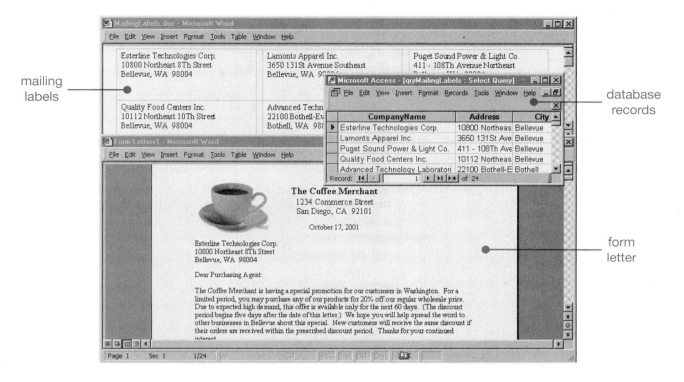

**Figure 1.1**   Linking database information to Word documents.

lowed by a dialog box requesting that you enter your user name and password in order to gain access to the computer. (Windows NT and Windows 2000 ask you to press Ctrl+Alt+Del prior to logging in.) You may simply enter your last name and a password assigned by your instructor or supervisor. Check with your instructor or the lab supervisor. The actual process of logging on is simple once you know your user name and password. Type your user name and press Tab to place the cursor in the Password text box. Type your password and press Enter to complete the Windows log-on process. Within a few moments the Windows desktop is displayed.

## What's on the Desktop

Windows uses the *desktop* metaphor whereby the computer screen simulates one's desktop upon which rest icons and other objects. Everything on the desktop is an *object*, meaning it is a thing having properties or characteristics. Examples of objects on the desktop include My Computer, Network Neighborhood, and so on. You can even add *shortcuts* to programs, printers, and documents. Figure 1.2 shows an example of a Windows desktop. Keep in mind that your desktop may look different because it may contain a different number of objects that are arranged in different ways. However, our figure is representative of the major elements found on the desktop.

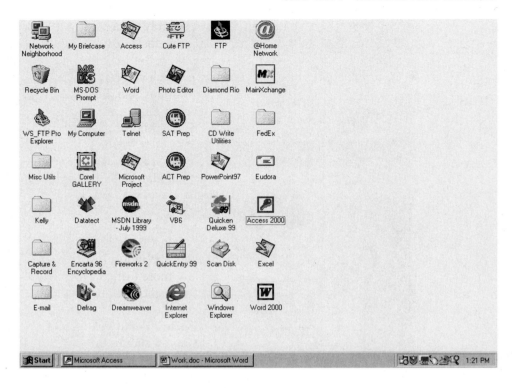

**Figure 1.2**  Windows desktop example.

Your desktop may contain the My Computer icon. My Computer is the entrance to all the disk drives and files on your computer. Through My Computer you can examine the floppy disk drive, hard drives, CD drives, and the system configuration.

The Recycle Bin icon holds files and folders that have been deleted. Anything in the Recycle Bin can either be recovered or removed permanently. Once objects have been removed, they cannot be restored.

On your desktop may be the Internet icon. It provides a convenient way to access the World Wide Web (WWW) using Microsoft's full-featured Internet Explorer. Navigating the WWW couldn't be simpler, because WWW uses a page metaphor to display information.

Desktops can also contain My Briefcase. This icon provides a way to keep various copies of your files synchronized and up to date whether you are working on the road, at home, or in the office. When you are finished working on a file on your laptop computer, for instance, you can use My Briefcase to update the file on your main computer when you get back to the office. Files are automatically and nearly effortlessly maintained so that you needn't worry about which file is the latest version and which file should be deleted.

The *Taskbar* is the gray area that normally rests on the bottom of your screen. (You can move the Taskbar to the top or sides of the screen if you wish, and you can even hide it until it is needed.) Windows Taskbar contains the Start button (see Figure 1.2), which you can use to quickly find a file or start a program; buttons representing programs that are currently running; and the task tray. Two programs are currently running, and the buttons on the Taskbar indicate their names: Microsoft Word and Microsoft Access. The *task tray* contains small icons representing programs that are always in memory. For example, the task tray shown in Figure 1.2 shows several icons representing programs to schedule regularly run system tasks, guard against computer viruses, and other important programs. The task tray also displays the current time.

## Using the Mouse

Before we examine Windows further, it is important to understand how to use the essential pointing device, the mouse. Although you can use Windows without a mouse, it is considerably more difficult. Five terms, describing different ways to use the mouse, occur throughout this text: *point, click, right-click, double-click,* and *drag.*

When we ask you to "point to Programs" or "point to Find in the Start menu," we simply mean you should move the mouse pointer so that its tip is directly over the desired object on the screen. Pointing in Windows frequently opens displays, menus, or submenus.

When you are instructed to "click the mouse" or "click," press and release the left mouse button. If you are to "click on the ... button" shown onscreen, move the mouse pointer to that element and then press and quickly release the left mouse button once. Select an item onscreen by moving the mouse pointer (the arrowhead) to the item and clicking once with the left mouse button. After you select an item, you can perform various activities. For example, you can move an icon from one place on your desktop to another after you have selected it.

The action of right-clicking is similar to clicking except that you use the right mouse button. For example, if you wanted to learn about a desktop icon's properties, you would first right-click the icon to display a shortcut menu.

Frequently, we will ask you to *double-click* some object on the Windows work surface. When you double-click an icon representing a program, that program is activated. To double-click, quickly click the left mouse button twice. If you don't click rapidly enough, you will simply select the object twice, not activate it.

Another way to use the mouse is to *drag* an object. In a word processing program, for example, you might want to move a sentence from one place to another. You can do this by dragging it. To drag any object, select the object (click it), press and hold down the left mouse button, and move the mouse. It takes a little practice, but you will master it quickly. Dragging is useful in several circumstances. For instance, you can enlarge a window by dragging its border or corner. You can also reduce or enlarge a Windows help frame by dragging a border toward or away from the opposite border.

## BECOMING MORE FAMILIAR WITH WINDOWS

### Anatomy of a Window

Most windows contain the same elements. The window that opens when you double-click My Computer is typical (see Figure 1.3). A window has a frame or border that defines the outer edges of the window. The My Computer window shown can be sized—that is, the window can be stretched or shrunk by dragging any edge. In the lower right corner is the *size grip*, which is a special handle to make obvious to the user how to resize a window. Along the window's top is a *Title bar* containing the name of the application, current topic, or current document. The current application, My Computer, is displayed in this case. When a window is active, its Title bar is a darker color than the Title bars of other windows.

**Figure 1.3**   Components of a window.

On the extreme left of the Title bar is a *control icon*, which can be opened to manipulate the window with the keyboard. You can close a window by double-clicking its control icon, though you will find it far easier to use the mouse for most actions. Three window buttons appear on the right end of each window's Title bar. These are called the Minimize, Maximize/Restore, and Close buttons. You click the *Minimize* button (the button that looks like a dash) to remove the window from view (the program remains running). If the window does not fill the screen, like ours in Figure 1.3, then the middle button, called the *Maximize* button, causes the window to fill the screen when the button is clicked. If the window is already maximized, then the middle button looks like two overlapping windows and is called the *Restore* button. When you click Restore, the window is reduced to less than full screen. You use the *Close* button in the upper right corner of a window to close the window with one click. If the window represents a program, rather than a group, then clicking the Close button terminates execution of the application.

Below the Title bar is the menu bar. Clicking any of the menu items displays a pull-down menu, which contains commands that you can select. If you click the Control Panel's Edit menu, for instance, you will see the pull-down menu shown in Figure 1.4. A list of commands is associated with each menu of any Windows program. When you select a menu, its pull-down menu is displayed. You can select a menu either by clicking it with the mouse or by pressing the Alt key and the letter underlined in the menu name. For example, notice that the letter E in the Edit menu (see Figure 1.4) is underlined. Pressing Alt and E simultaneously displays the Edit menu. Throughout the text, we use a standard notation to indicate keys that are pressed simultaneously. For example, Alt+E connotes pressing and holding the Alt key and pressing and releasing the letter E to invoke the Edit menu. The key that follows Alt varies depending on the menu to be selected.

**Figure 1.4**  A typical Windows pull-down menu.

When you want to execute one of the commands in a pull-down menu, simply point to it. The selection bar highlights the command that the mouse points to. To execute a highlighted command, simply click the mouse. Alternately, you can use the arrow keys to move up and down the pull-down list of commands. You can press Enter to execute the highlighted command. A third way to invoke a command is to press the underlined letter corresponding to the desired command.

Press the letter *A* to execute the Edit menu Select All command, for example. Some commands are inapplicable in certain situations. Whenever a command cannot be selected from a menu, it is *dimmed* (light gray). The Cut, Copy, Paste, and Paste Shortcut commands are dimmed in Figure 1.4. All other commands are bold (for example, Select All).

Along the window's bottom edge is the status bar. The status bar displays useful information about the window such as the number of objects it holds or a description of a command you have selected when the window contains a running application.

When there is more information than can be displayed in the window, *scroll bars* automatically appear on the right and bottom window edges. By sliding the scroll boxes or using the scroll arrows, you can pan the window up, down, left, or right to see otherwise hidden parts of the object within the window.

## Manipulating Windows

Like the other sections that follow, this section actively involves you in learning several Windows features. You will manipulate program and document windows in several ways, including moving and sizing them. To help you learn and reinforce these Windows skills, we ask you to follow up your reading and actually practice each task being described. There are two types of activities in which you can participate as you read: *try it* tasks and *exercises*. Try it tasks are smaller, more easily accomplished computer activities that take only a few moments to complete. For example, a try it task might be to minimize, maximize, and restore a window; or it might be a description of how to switch between Microsoft Access and Windows Explorer using the Taskbar. We use the words *Try it* to mark a paragraph describing these types of activities. If the task comprises several steps, the individual steps are not numbered. *Exercises* are more comprehensive activities that are central to some ongoing and important process or project that is being described in a chapter. Exercises typically consist of two or more numbered steps whose completion helps you achieve some important goal. An example of an exercise is the series of steps that illustrate how to launch several Windows applications, open document windows in each application, and copy information between open windows. Such an exercise strongly reinforces how to implement information sharing between, for example, Access and Word—an essential task in business.

### Try it

Let's learn a little about the computer you're using. Double-click the My Computer icon (see Figure 1.2). What happens if you click a desktop icon only once? You simply select the icon. To activate it, double-click. The My Computer window will open, displaying icons representing hardware on your computer and your network similar to Figure 1.3. Maximize the My Computer window. Right-click the icon representing drive C. The *shortcut menu* is displayed. Locate Properties in the menu (near the bottom of the list) and click it. A tabbed dialog box, showing the properties of the selected object, is displayed. Click the General tab, if necessary, to go to the page containing a pie graph. It illustrates how much space is either occupied or available on drive C. After you have had a chance to examine the display, click the question mark button, called *What's This?* Notice that the mouse pointer changes to an arrow with a question mark attached to its right side. After clicking What's This? you can move to any object and click it to obtain context-sensitive help. Move the mouse pointer down to the pie graph and click it. A brief explanation of the clicked object (the chart in this case) is displayed (see Figure 1.5). Click the help box to make it disappear. Finally, click the Close button on the dialog box to close it. Click the Close button on My Computer to close it. The desktop reappears. Moving windows about the desktop, changing their size, and closing them is intuitive in Windows. We'll direct you through some fundamental window manipulation activities next.

What's This? button

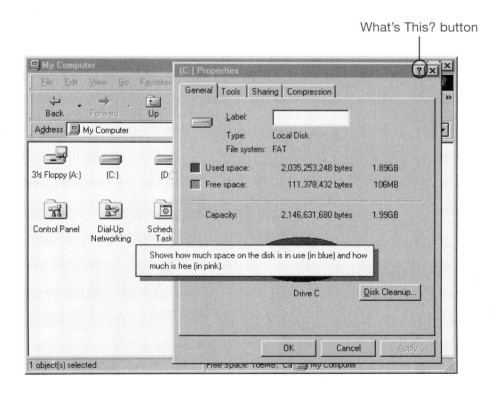

**Figure 1.5** Obtaining help with the What's This? button.

*Try it*

Open the My Computer window again (double-click its desktop icon). Maximize the window, if necessary, so that it fills the screen (click the Maximize button, which looks like a small rectangle). Restore the window so it occupies only part of the work surface by clicking the Restore button (the icon that looks like two overlapping windows or rectangles located in the top right corner of the window). Make the window virtually disappear by pressing the Minimize button (the button in the top right corner of the My Computer window that contains a narrow line or dash). Where did the My Computer window go? When a program is minimized, a button representing it—called a *Taskbar button*—is placed on the Taskbar. The window disappears but its Taskbar button remains. By clicking a program's Taskbar button, you can switch from one program to another. Restore the My Computer window by clicking the Taskbar button labeled My Computer. You can change the size of a window that is not maximized. Click and drag the My Computer window's size grip away from its opposite corner to increase the window's size. Similarly, drag the size grip towards its opposite corner to reduce the window's size. There are an infinite number of window sizes you can create this way. Moving a window to a different part of the screen is also easy. Simply click and drag the window's Title bar to move the window anywhere you want. Move the My Computer window to the top left of your screen. Then, move it so it is approximately in the center of your screen. Finally, close the My Computer window.

## Getting Help

Help is available in all Windows programs in a variety of ways. Context-sensitive help provides help for almost every object on the screen. Microsoft products have help screens that are actually Web pages. That is, help for Microsoft products including Windows and Microsoft Access are formatted as Web pages complete with hyperlinks that take you to related information when you click them. You have already used What's This? to obtain information about an object on the screen. *ToolTips* are another form of context-sensitive help. ToolTips are small pop-up banners that appear when you hover the mouse over an object, such as a toolbar button, briefly. See for yourself.

*Try it*

Move the mouse pointer over the Start button, which is located at the left end of the Taskbar. After a second or two, a ToolTip appears indicating you should "Click here to begin." Likewise, you can see the date if you move the mouse pointer to the time display located in the task tray.

Windows programs supply explicit help through a Help menu. Extensive help is available on the computer. The Windows Help system provides search features, as well as contents and indexing capabilities. An excellent way to see Help in action is to try it yourself. Windows help, available from the Start button (you will learn more about the Start button in the next section) is an excellent choice. Read the following exercise and then perform the steps.

## EXERCISE 1.1: GETTING SPECIFIC HELP

1. Click the Start button (the Start button is explained fully in the next section). The *Start menu* is displayed.
2. Click the Help menu item on the Start menu.
3. The Windows Help dialog box opens.
4. Select the Index tab.
5. Type *formatting* into the text box because we want help on formatting disks.
6. The help system highlights the topic *formatting disks* (see Figure 1.6).
7. Click the Display button to view detailed help about formatting disks. The right panel in the Help dialog box describes how to format a disk.
8. Click the Close button after reading the help information. That will close and re-move the pop-up box.

**Figure 1.6**   Locating help on formatting disks.

## THE START MENU

The Start button, located on the left end of the Taskbar, provides the major access point for programs, documents, and other objects. The Start menu is displayed when you click the Start button, and it is a cascading menu. That is, its submenus cascade—logically flow from—the main menu items.

## Opening the Start Menu

Opening the Start menu is easy. Simply click the Start button to display its menu items (see Figure 1.7). Standard menu items found on the Start menu are Programs, Documents, Settings, Find, Help, Run, and Shut Down. Some of the menu items have right arrows. These arrows indicate that the menu item leads to a submenu, which opens when you merely point to the menu item by moving the mouse over the item and pausing briefly.

**Figure 1.7**   The Start menu.

## The Programs Menu Item

The Programs menu item cascades to reveal program items and program group items. Only executable items are found in the Programs menu, not data or other non-executable objects. Programs include the MS-DOS prompt as well as Windows Explorer and other application programs. When you point to a group item, further entries are revealed. For example, Accessories is a group item that contains the usual collection of standard Windows groups and programs (see Figure 1.8). You simply point to Accessories and then select a program or group item from the cascaded menu. You can close each of the cascading menus in turn by selecting a menu item from a previous menu. Similarly, you can close all menus except the Start menu by moving the mouse pointer to one of the Start menu items that doesn't cascade, such as Run or Help.

**Figure 1.8**   Displaying submenus of the Start menu.

Windows provides keyboard alternatives to the mouse. For instance, you can press Ctrl+Esc to open the Start menu. Once open, the Start menu items can be selected by using the arrow keys. The up and down arrow keys move up and down an open menu, and the right and left arrow keys move to a cascading menu or the previous menu, respectively. Press the Alt key to close all open menus.

### Try it

Point to the WordPad program (but don't run it). Open the Start menu and move the mouse pointer to Programs. Pause and the cascade menu opens. Next, move to the right and point to Accessories. Move the mouse pointer down the menu items to WordPad. Finally, close all menus.

## The Documents Menu Item

The Documents menu item displays a list of the 15 objects you have most recently used. If you worked on an Access database named *accounts payable.mdb* and then opened Microsoft Word to write a letter you later saved as *New accounts.doc*, then those two document names would appear in the Documents menu item list. The Documents menu facilitates returning quickly and easily to the items you have recently worked with. For example, you return to your computer after a day's absence, start Windows, click the Start menu button, point to Documents, and then select the document you want to work with. (In this context, the word *document* refers to a variety of objects, including a word processing document, a spreadsheet, a database, or a graphic image.) This reinforces the notion that you focus on the object that you want to work with, rather than worrying about which program or tool is required to load and manipulate the document—the document "knows" what program is needed to operate on it. This is called *document centric* and is orthogonal to the older Windows 3.1 notion of *tool centric* in which one first located the program needed to view or change a document and then loaded the document once the program was operational.

### Try it

See what documents people using your computer have recently used. Click Start and point to Documents. The cascade menu will reveal the document names, or *empty* if the list has been erased. (You will learn how to erase the Documents list later.)

## The Settings Menu Item

The Settings menu item allows you to change global Windows settings and options. It contains three menu items: Control Panel, Printers, and Taskbar. Control Panel contains icons representing a large number of system settings you can change and actions you can take. For example, you can add or remove programs from the Control Panel group, change your monitor's display characteristics, or alter the date and time. Clicking the Printers item takes you to a group that adds, deletes, or modifies printers available to your system. Taskbar allows you to modify the structure and contents of the Start menu and provides a way to change selected properties of the Taskbar. You could choose to hide the Taskbar or hide the clock, which is customarily displayed in the task tray on the right end of the Taskbar.

## The Find Menu Item

Having a document-centric system like Windows aids your productivity; however, it is not useful if you cannot locate the document you want. That's when the Find menu item goes to work. You can use Find to locate files or folders on any disk drive, including floppy drives. In addition, you can find files or folders on any computer on any network to which your computer is attached. If you have opted to use Microsoft Network, you can locate files on that on-line service as well. If you cannot find a file on your hard disk, you can invoke the Find menu item to search through every file on your hard drive.

### Try it

See if you can find where the Windows file called *msaccess* is located. Search for it. Click the Start menu, point to Find, and choose Files or Folders. When the Find All Files dialog box is displayed, type *msaccess* in the Named text box and ensure that the Look in text box contains *My Computer*. If it does not, then click the list box drop-down list arrow, scroll to the top of the list, and click My Computer. Finally, ensure that the Include subfolders checkbox is checked. Click the Find Now button to start the search process. Windows begins searching for any files or folders that begin with *msaccess*. Shortly, several files are displayed in the search results window. After you have reviewed the names, click the dialog box's Close button.

## The Help Menu Item

The Help menu item, which you used earlier, provides systemwide help at the click of a button. Select Help whenever you want to find more information on a Windows topic. Product-specific help is best obtained through the Help menu of the product itself, because software product manufacturers supply rich help content along with their programs. If you want help on Microsoft Access, it is best to seek help from the Help menu within Access. Help on creating Windows shortcuts—a topic that is common across applications—can be found by using the Start menu Help menu item.

## The Run Menu Item

The Run menu item provides a way to run a program by simply typing the program's name and pressing Enter. Often, people use the Run command to launch infrequently used programs that might not be represented on the Start menu or its submenus. When you want to launch a program from the Run menu item, click Start, choose Run, and enter the program's name, including the full path, in the Open text box. If you don't know the program's exact location on the disk, you can choose the Browse button and search through folders until you locate it. Or you can use Find to locate the program. If you use the latter method, then you can double-click the program within the search results list to execute it. If you find yourself using the Run command frequently for a particular program, consider placing the program in the Programs menu item or placing on the desktop a *shortcut* to the program (we will show you how to do that later in this chapter).

## The Shut Down Menu Item

It is incorrect to simply turn off your computer when you are finished using Windows. In fact, Windows requires you to follow a simple procedure to shut down your computer. Doing so protects files and other data from being corrupted or saved improperly. In short, never turn off your computer while Windows is running! The Shut Down menu item provides a one-step Windows exit procedure. To shut down Windows prior to system power off, choose the Start menu and click Shut Down. A dialog box containing your options is displayed (see Figure 1.9). Choose the option "Shut down the computer" if you want to turn off your computer for an extended period (more than a few hours). If you want to restart (also known as rebooting your computer), then the "Restart the computer?" option is available. Choosing "Restart the computer in MS-DOS mode" exits Windows and leaves you at the DOS prompt.

Use caution. If you are using a computer in a laboratory of several computers, you probably should not shut down the computer. Always check with your instructor or an available lab assistant before selecting the shut down option. If you merely want to restore the computer desktop to its original state before leaving the lab, then select the option "Restart."

**Figure 1.9**　The Shut Down Windows dialog box.

## WORKING WITH PROGRAMS AND DATA

WordPad is a word processor that comes with Windows (95, 98, NT). We will describe and use WordPad to help illustrate several mouse and keyboard techniques that can be used in other Windows products. (The term *Windows products* is used to differentiate between products designed specifically to run under Windows as opposed to programs that are designed for older, DOS-based systems.) Methods used here can be duplicated with, for example, Microsoft Access—the Windows relational database system featured in this text.

Perhaps the best way to get better acquainted with the Windows environment is to go through a complete cycle: launching a program, opening a document, altering some of the document's text, and printing the final result. We show you that process in the paragraphs that follow. WordPad, a close relative of the full-featured Microsoft Word, is featured here.

## Launching Applications Directly

The following exercise guides you through the process of executing (sometimes called *launching*) the WordPad program. Subsequent exercises continue the cycle to its conclusion—a finished letter ready for mailing.

### EXERCISE 1.2: LAUNCHING AN APPLICATION

1. Click the Start button.
2. Point to Programs in the Start menu.
3. Point to Accessories in the menu that cascades from Programs.
4. Locate the WordPad menu item and click it once. If necessary, maximize the WordPad window. WordPad opens and displays an empty document.

Next, you will use a menu to open a document and then make a change to it. Doing this gives you practice using a typical Windows application menu. To read a document from a disk or CD into the WordPad window, you *open* a document. Open is a command found in the File menu of almost any Windows application.

First, let's discuss a few disk-naming conventions we will use throughout the text. The exact names of your internal hard disk, floppy disk(s), and CD drives vary depending on the configuration of your computer, so we adopt the following disk names to keep things simple and consistent. We refer to your floppy drive as drive A, though it could be drive A or B. We assume you have at least one hard drive, which we refer to as drive C (though you may have more than one). Finally, drive D refers to the CD-ROM drive. So simply remember: Drive A—floppy disk drive, drive C—hard disk drive, drive D—CD-ROM.

To prepare for the next exercise, place the Companion CD, which came with your text, into the CD-ROM drive D. If your CD-ROM drive is E, for example, simply substitute E whenever we refer to drive D. Note: If an AutoPlay dialog box automatically opens shortly after you insert your CD-ROM, Windows is trying to help. It thinks you want to install new software from the CD. Simply click the dialog box Close button to remove the dialog box and proceed to the next exercise.

EXERCISE 1.3: OPENING A DOCUMENT

1. With WordPad still open, click the File menu to display its menu items. Note that you can also press Alt+F to pull down the File menu.
2. Click Open or move to Open with the arrow keys, then press Enter. The Open dialog box appears. Dialog boxes require you to supply additional information and, occasionally, make decisions by clicking various check boxes, option buttons, and other objects within the dialog box. A list of file names (if any) found on one of the available disk drives is displayed in the File Name list box. Notice, however, that only files with .doc extensions are displayed. Those files are stored in a form compatible with both WordPad and Word.
3. Click the arrow on the Look in drop-down list box and select the CD-ROM drive (drive D or E). A list of ten folders called Ch01 through Supplement appears.
4. Double-click the Ch01 folder to open it (see Figure 1.10).
5. Open the file *FallWashPromotion.doc* by double-clicking it. The *FallWashPromotion.doc* document is placed into the WordPad document window.

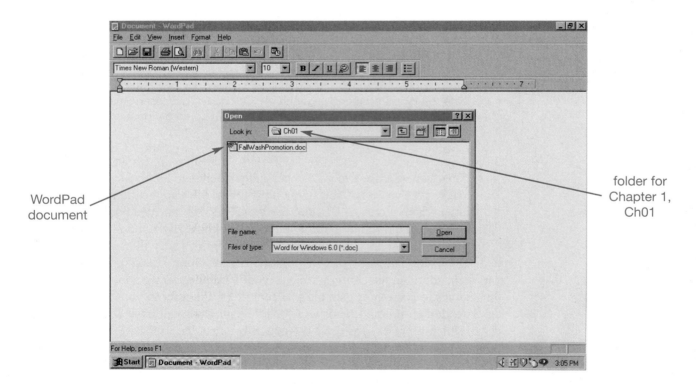

**Figure 1.10**   Open dialog box.

The document you see in WordPad is a letter to selected customers of The Coffee Merchant. It will be mailed to customers in the Washington state area promoting, as you can see, a special sale for a limited time. The letter now displayed in WordPad is used to illustrate a few typical Windows operations and WordPad procedures.

WordPad's Edit menu commands are similar to those found in other Windows products such as Excel or Word. With the *FallWashPromotion.doc* document still visible, let's locate and replace the two placeholder-phrases *company-city* and *company-state* with an actual customer's city and state. There's no need to replace the other placeholder tags that you see in the inside address right now. We just want you to briefly experience a typical replace operation.

### EXERCISE 1.4: SEARCH AND REPLACE

1. Select the Edit menu (click Edit or press Alt+E).
2. Select the Replace command (notice the shortcut key combination Ctrl+H invokes replace without first selecting the Edit menu).
    The *insertion point*, a blinking vertical bar, is in the leftmost position in the Find what text box. The insertion point indicates where typed characters will appear.
3. In the Find what text box of the Find dialog box type *company-city* and press Tab to move to the Replace with text box. (The characters in the Find what text box are often called the *search string*.)
4. In the Replace with text box enter the replacement string—those characters that replace any or all occurrences of the search string, company-city. Type *Seattle* in the Replace with text box.
    Because the search string is long enough to be unique, there's no need to check either of the check boxes (Match whole word only or Match case). Figure 1.11 shows the completed Replace dialog box.
5. Click the Replace All button to replace all occurrences of company-city with Seattle.
6. Click OK when the search ends.
7. Repeat steps 3 through 6, entering *company-state* in step 3 and *Washington* in step 4.
8. Click the Close button to return to the document.

The last exercise in this series illustrates how to print a document. The techniques shown are nearly identical for most Windows products. The Print command is normally found in the File menu.

### EXERCISE 1.5: PRINTING PAGES AND EXITING

1. Click the File menu to display its commands.
2. Select Print (click the Print command). The Print dialog box will be displayed.

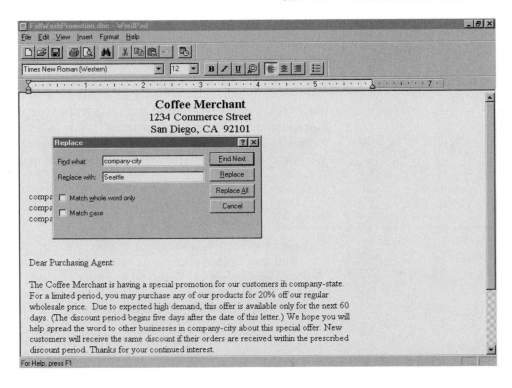

**Figure 1.11**   Replace dialog box.

3. Click the Pages option button found on the left side of the dialog box. The bullet to the left of Pages is darkened, marking it as the current choice among the three Print Range options.
4. Type *1*, press Tab, and type *1* again because we want to print only page 1. The completed dialog box is shown in Figure 1.12.

## Launching an Application from a File

Launching a program by double-clicking a data file defines the concept of a document-centric system, which we mentioned earlier. In contrast, the previous section illustrated how to open WordPad and then open a document found on the Companion CD. This roundabout method exemplifies the old *program-centric* approach to microcomputer computing. You will find the document-centric approach much faster, efficient, and error-free. In this section, we introduce you briefly to this faster method. Instead of directing you to a program and then a file to be manipulated by a program, we'll simply tell you the name of a data file on the Companion CD and ask you to find the data and launch the program that created it. Two questions come to mind. First, how does one find the file—especially considering the size of the CD and the number of files it contains? Second, what

**Figure 1.12**  Print dialog box.

program must be launched in order to view or modify the data file? You'll see that the answer to question one is that you let the system search the entire Companion CD for you. Question two's answer is that the system automatically associates a program with a data file as long as the file has a recognized *secondary name* (or extension, as it is sometimes called).

Let's try this approach to computing: find a file and load its associated program. The next two exercises show you how to do that. In the first exercise, you will use a very helpful program called Find. Find locates files and directories by name on any disk drive. Suppose you know that a particular file is stored on the Companion CD, but you cannot remember where. All you remember is part of the file name—the first part of the file name is *Olympic* and has something to do with the Olympic games.

EXERCISE 1.6: FINDING A FILE

1. Click the Start button to display the Start menu.
2. Point to Find. The Find submenu is displayed.
3. Click Files or Folders, indicating you want to search for a file (or folder).
    The Find: All Files dialog box displays.
4. Type *Olympic* in the Named text box.
    This is the partial file name that the Find program will attempt to locate.
5. Ensure that your Companion CD is the CD drive. Then, click the drop-down arrow on the Look in text box and click your CD drive (D in our examples). If the search turns up nothing, then select My Computer from the drop-down list in the Look in text box. That causes Find to search *all* of your disk drives, including floppy disk drives and Zip drives.

6.  Click the Find Now button to begin the search. (Keep the Find window open because you are going to use it again shortly.)

Within a short time, the Find program locates and displays all file or folder names it found that match, completely or partially, the file name you specify. Figure 1.13 shows it found only one file on the CD, *OlympicHostCountries.wri*.

**Figure 1.13**   Locating a file using Find.

Now that you have found the file, you want to modify it. Suppose you don't know what program was used to create the file. That's okay, because the file name extension (or secondary name) is usually associated with a particular program. Files ending with .xls, for example, are Microsoft Excel files. Similarly, files ending with .mdb are Microsoft Access database files. You don't have to know these facts in order to invoke the program that created the file. The system remembers *associations* like those—file name extensions and their related programs. The next exercise shows you how simple it is to execute the program associated with the file that the Find program just located.

EXERCISE 1.7: LAUNCHING A PROGRAM FROM A DATA FILE

1.  Make sure the Find window is still available and displaying the located file, *OlympicHostCountries.wri*.

2. Double-click the file name *OlympicHostCountries.wri* located in the list of located files.
3. WordPad, a Windows-supplied word processing program, is launched and the Olympic document is displayed in a WordPad document window. The document lists information about the modern Olympics including the host countries and participant information.
4. Personalize the document by inserting your name in the upper right corner: Move the insertion point to the top of the document and press Enter twice to open up two new lines. Then press Tab several times to move to the right in the new, first line and type your name. (The font may be too large for your liking. In that case, select your name, select Format, Font, and select a smaller point size.)
5. Print the document using Print from the File menu.
6. Close the Find program, but leave WordPad running, because you will use it in the next section.

The preceding exercise illustrates how easy it is to launch a program from a document. This illustrates the meaning of the term *document centric*. That is, you don't have to first load the program and then load the document. Instead, simply locate the document (*document* is used here to mean any file including a database, spreadsheet, or word processed document) you want to work with and double-click its name. That loads the required program—the one that is associated with the document.

## Switching Between Applications

Windows is a *multitasking* operating system, which means it is capable of running more than one program at a time. You probably will find that it is most convenient to have several programs running and at the ready simultaneously. Perhaps you are working with accounts receivable files with Microsoft Access and also writing letters to customers using Microsoft Word or WordPad. To appreciate how handy the multitasking capabilities are, you have to experience it. Windows multitasking is smooth and intuitive. To illustrate how easy it is, you will start another program and practice switching between programs. Then you will learn how simple it is for two applications to share information.

EXERCISE 1.8: LAUNCH ANOTHER PROGRAM

1. Make sure that WordPad is still running.
2. Open the Start menu and select Programs.
3. Select Accessories.
4. Locate Paint in the Accessories cascade menu of programs.
5. Click Paint to launch it.

Paint is a graphics creation program supplied with Windows. After a brief pause, the Paint window appears as shown in Figure 1.14.

Figure 1.14   Paint and WordPad programs running simultaneously.

Now two programs are loaded and available simultaneously—WordPad and Paint. Examine the Taskbar (usually located at the bottom of your screen, though you can drag it to any of the four edges of your screen). Two Taskbar buttons represent both programs. Program Taskbar buttons provide a convenient way to switch back and forth between programs, especially when programs are minimized and thus not visible. There are three ways to move from one running program to another. Each method operates slightly differently, and you may eventually select a favorite way to switch between applications. The first method uses the Taskbar to switch between tasks.

EXERCISE 1.9: USING THE TASKBAR TO SWITCH BETWEEN PROGRAMS

1. Ensure that WordPad and Paint are still running.

2. Switch to WordPad, which is probably obscured by Paint's window at the moment, by clicking the WordPad button on the Taskbar. The WordPad window becomes active.
3. Switch back to Paint by clicking its Taskbar button.

Another equally effective way to move to another program that is running is to use the keystroke shortcut Alt+Tab. The next exercise shows you how.

EXERCISE 1.10: USING ALT+TAB TO SWITCH BETWEEN PROGRAMS

1. Press and hold down the Alt key and tap and release the Tab key. With the Tab key released, continue holding down the Alt key for a moment. Windows displays in the middle of the screen a marquee of running programs. A border surrounds the program icon that will be displayed if you release the Alt key (see Figure 1.15).
2. Practice moving the border between the two program icons by tapping the Tab key as you continue to hold down the Alt key.
3. Release the Tab key when the border is on the Paint icon and then release the Alt key to move to that program.

**Figure 1.15**   Using Alt+Tab to move between running programs.

Using the Alt+Tab key sequence is convenient for touch typists because it allows you to switch quickly between programs.

Occasionally, you may want to minimize all open windows on the desktop so that you can move to one of your desktop *shortcuts*—the icons that represent programs. Minimizing all open windows is simple. Simply right-click the Taskbar (place the mouse in any unoccupied area of the Taskbar—avoiding any Taskbar buttons) and select *Minimize All Windows* from the context menu. Knowing this method can save you time when the desktop is filled with several windows and you want a clear shot at the desktop.

The next section briefly describes how to share information between Windows applications. The particular method, called *object linking and embedding*, or *OLE* for short, simplifies producing mailing labels in Word from a subset of your customers' addresses in an Access database, for example.

## Sharing Data Among Applications

Data from one program can be shared with another. In this simple but typical example, you will create a graphic in Paint and transfer the graphic to a WordPad document. The combined data—a graphic inside a document—is known as a *compound document*.

### Try it

First, make sure that WordPad and Paint are still running. If not, launch both by clicking Start, point to the Programs menu item, point to the entry Accessories in the cascading menu, and click WordPad to load it. Repeat the preceding, if necessary, to load the Paint program. Switch to Paint using the Taskbar and load the graphic file *WeRecycle.bmp* found in the Ch01 folder on your Companion CD. Click the Select tool (the dashed rectangle) and click and drag the dashed line so that it just encompasses the graphic. Then, select Copy from the Edit menu to place the graphic on the Clipboard. Next, you will send the graphic over to the WordPad document using Copy and Paste operations. Switch to WordPad and load (execute File, Open) the file called *RecycleLetter.wri*, which is also found in the Ch01 folder on your Companion CD. Insert a blank line at the top of the document where the graphic will be placed. Choose Paste from WordPad's Edit menu. The graphic is pasted into the document. If you wish, you can print the document. Figure 1.16 shows the completed compound document. When you are finished, close both the WordPad and Paint applications.

What is important to remember from the preceding example is that you pass information between Windows applications by *copying* from one application—placing the object on the Clipboard—and then *pasting* the object into the recipient (container) document. This works for virtually all Windows-compliant programs, including Access, Excel, and Word.

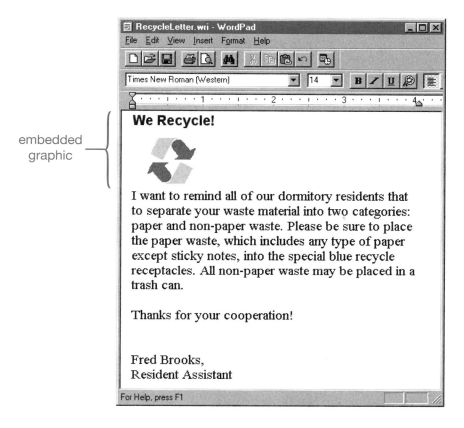

embedded
graphic

**Figure 1.16** Graphic embedded in a WordPad document.

## USING WINDOWS EXPLORER

Windows provides an advanced browser and file manager called Windows Explorer, though most experienced users simply call it Explorer. Explorer allows you to perform file management duties, open and close documents, and run programs. In fact, you may find that Explorer is the interface you use most often, because it is frequently more convenient to find a file and work with it by using Explorer. By default, Windows Explorer is found in the Programs group of the Start menu. It may be located elsewhere on your institution's computers, but it is easy to find.

### Try it

Launch Windows Explorer so that you can see its interface. Click the Start button, then point to the Programs item. Finally, click the Windows Explorer item to start Explorer. (You can also launch Explorer by right-clicking the Start button and selecting *Explore* from the shortcut menu. This is probably the most convenient method.)

The Folders pane, also known as the *Tree* pane, presents a tree structure of your entire computer system including desktop objects. Each branch of the tree can be expanded or collapsed, as you desire. In the right panel is the *Contents* pane, displaying the folders, files, and other objects found in the folder that is selected and open in the Tree pane.

Normally, Explorer displays a view of your computer system beginning with your desktop—the "root" of the hierarchical or tree structure of files and devices. Emphasizing the outline structure of your disk file structure, each folder displayed can contain files and other folders. Figure 1.17 shows a typical Explorer window with folders and files.

**Figure 1.17**   Typical Explorer window showing folders and files.

The lines in the Folders pane emphasize the relationships between folders and the folders and files that they contain. Notice the plus and minus signs at the intersection of horizontal and vertical lines in the Folders pane. A small box with a plus sign—called the *Expand* button—indicates that the object contains other objects and can be expanded to reveal further detail. Likewise, boxes with minus signs are called *Collapse* buttons. Clicking a Collapse button implodes the structure, revealing less detail.

## Opening Drives, Files, and Folders

The Contents pane can show only one level of detail at a time, so you must click the Expand button on the particular drive or folder until you reach the particular file or folder you are looking for. Suppose, for example, that you want to see what is on the Companion CD. Using Explorer, you can "walk" down through each of the folders and files, noting what files are stored in which folders. Practice expanding and collapsing folders in Explorer.

### Try it

If Explorer is not running, start it (click the Start button, point to Programs, and click Windows Explorer). In the Folders pane, click the icon representing the C drive. Reveal more information about the C drive by clicking its Expand button. Your display should resemble Figure 1.17, though the exact folder and file names on your disk differ from the figure. Open the folder named *Windows* on the C drive. You may have to use the Folders pane scroll bar to move down the hierarchy of folders until the Windows folder appears. Click the Windows folder to reveal in the Contents pane the first level of folders and files in the Windows folder. Note, the Folders pane never displays file names. File names are displayed only in the Contents pane.

The preceding exercise illustrates the fundamental way you explore the disks and their contents. If you want to look at the contents of your Companion CD, then you simply click the D drive icon—the drive we are assuming is your CD—and look at the Contents pane. If you are curious about how much space is used on your disk drive and how much is left, you can use this shortcut: right-click the drive icon in the Folders pane. Then, click the Properties item on the shortcut menu that is displayed. The Properties dialog box is displayed showing a three-dimensional representation of your disk in two colors. One color represents the amount of space used; the other is the space free. Click OK to close the dialog box.

## Formatting a Floppy Disk

One of the useful activities you can perform while running Explorer is formatting a disk. In particular, you can format your floppy disk, because it is highly unlikely you will want to format your hard disk(s) and you cannot format your Companion CD, which contains files, databases, and data critical to this textbook. You will want to save your database files, temporary files, and other documents you develop while reading this book and working on assignments. The logical place to save information, especially while working in a university computing laboratory, is on a floppy disk. Although the capacity of a floppy is limited, it is very portable. A floppy disk is a convenient way to transport your work from your own computer to a central computer laboratory and back. So let's learn how to format a new floppy disk, just in case you purchase an unformatted disk.

You may already know that formatting a floppy disk prepares it for first-time use. Unformatted disks have no magnetic marks identifying the beginning and ending of tracks and sectors on the disk. Tracks and sectors are the "grooves" in which all data is stored. Tracks, concentric rings on a disk, hold data. The blank spaces between concentric rings separate individual tracks. Windows Explorer can format disks quickly and easily. Once formatted, a disk can be used and reused repeatedly without ever being formatted again. You can also format a disk after it has been used. But be aware that the formatting process erases any data that may be present on the disk. This next exercise formats a new disk so that you can use it later in the text to store data. If you have a formatted disk containing valuable data, then do not do this exercise if you want to keep the data. On the other hand, this is a good opportunity to format any new disks you have just purchased.

EXERCISE 1.11: FORMATTING A DISK WITH EXPLORER

1. Launch Windows Explorer, if necessary.
2. Place a floppy disk in drive A.
3. In the Folders pane of the Explorer window right-click the drive A icon (not the Expand button). (If drive A is not visible in the Folders Pane, then slide the Folders Pane scroll button to the *top* of the scroll bar. The icon for Drive A will come into view.)
4. Click the Format item in the pop-up menu.
5. Select *Full* in the Format type group.
6. Select the *No label* and *Display summary when finished* options.
7. Click the Start button to begin formatting the floppy disk. Shortly, a summary dialog box is displayed indicating the total storage capacity of your disk.
8. Click Close twice—once to close the dialog box and a second time to close the Format dialog box.
9. Close Explorer. (You will use it soon in the next section, so you may wish to leave it running if you will be continuing with your reading.)

## Creating Folders

Folders, like their physical counterparts in filing cabinet systems, are a convenient way to store and organize your files and other folders. Folders provide a way to partition and separate one group of project files from another. For instance, you may find it convenient to keep each chapter's homework, databases, and other work in its own folder whose name clearly indicates which chapter's material is stored therein (for example, a folder named Chapter 1). The next exercise guides you through this process using Windows Explorer. To prepare for this exercise, place a floppy disk in drive A. You may want to use the disk you formatted in the previous exercise. Then complete the following exercise.

EXERCISE 1.12: CREATING FOLDERS WITH EXPLORER

1. Ensure Explorer is running and switch to it by clicking its button on the Taskbar.
2. Place a formatted floppy in drive A.
3. Click the drive A icon in the Explorer Folders pane.
4. Select File and point to New.
5. Click Folder from the cascade menu. A folder called New Folder is created and displayed in the Contents pane.
6. With the folder called "New Folder" still highlighted, type the folder's new name: *Chapter 2*. Press Enter.
7. Click the Expand button on drive A to display the new folder both in the Folders and Contents panes. Figure 1.18 shows the new folder in place.
8. Click the Explorer's Close button to terminate the program.

**Figure 1.18**    Creating a folder.

Now you know how to make new folders in which you can store files or other folders. Perhaps the most important subtlety in creating a folder is to ensure you have selected the appropriate folder or disk *before* creating a new folder. New folders are created *below* the folder or disk currently selected in the Folders pane. That is, if you wanted to create a folder labeled Chapter 3 along side the Chapter 2 folder, then first select the drive A icon. If Chapter 2 is highlighted in the Folders pane, then a new folder would be created as a *subfolder* of Chapter 2.

## Copying, Moving, Naming, and Deleting Files

The problem with opening and using Access databases that are stored on your Companion CD is that Access prefers to open databases in a mode called read/write, whereby database records can be both read from the database and written back to it. Unless you have special software and you are "burning" a new CD, you cannot write data to a CD. You can read any data you wish from a CD. However, when you open a database on your CD, Access displays a warning dialog box instructing you that you cannot make any changes to your data. We have a simple solution to this dilemma.

Your Companion CD contains several databases, tables, and other objects that you will use as you read this textbook and work on the problems. In order for you to both read and write to Access databases, you will be asked to copy files from the Companion CD to your computer's hard drive or to your floppy disk. Then, you will be asked to alter the *Read-only* file property so that the database can be both read and modified. Having done these two activities, you can operate normally on the copy of the database because it is on a standard disk and is available for both reading and writing. That's why we want you to pay especially close attention to this section where we demonstrate using Explorer to copy a file from the Companion CD to another disk. In the following exercise, you will copy the file *Ch02.mdb* from the CD to the folder you just created, Chapter 2, on your floppy disk. In preparation for the exercise, launch Windows Explorer, if necessary, insert the floppy disk you formatted in the preceding exercise in drive A, and insert your Companion CD into the CD drive.

EXERCISE 1.13: COPYING A FILE FROM YOUR COMPANION CD TO A DISK

1. Prepare the Folders pane display by locating the drive A icon and clicking its Expand button so that the Chapter 2 folder is displayed in the Folders pane.
2. Scroll down the Folders pane display, locating the icon for your CD. Click it and click its Expand button so that the folders beginning with Ch01 are displayed.
3. Click the Ch02 folder in the Folders pane. The contents of the folder, some file names, are displayed in Explorer's Contents pane.
4. Locate the file *Ch02.mdb* in the Contents pane, click it, and then drag it from the Contents pane to the Folders pane.
5. If disk A is not visible near the top of the Folders pane, continue dragging by moving the mouse to the top of the Folders pane. It will move, revealing drive A.
6. Continue dragging the file until the dimmed file name, which represents the mouse, is directly over the Chapter 2 folder in the Folders pane. The folder will be highlighted when the mouse is properly situated.
7. Release the left mouse button, dropping the file into the folder.

When you drag and drop a file from one disk to a different disk, the default action is to *copy* the file. However, if you drag and drop a file from one folder on a disk to another folder on the *same* disk, the default action is to *move* the file. You can have more control over the action by right-clicking the selected file to drag it (we call this action right-drag for short). When you drop the file into its destination folder, a pop-up menu is displayed from which you can choose either to copy or move the file by clicking which action you'd like. Figure 1.19 shows the pop-up menu displayed when you right-drag a file.

**Figure 1.19**   The pop-up menu displayed after right-dragging a file.

Moving a file from one place to another is a cut and paste operation. The easiest way to move a file is by right-clicking it and then dragging it from one location to another. When you release the right mouse, a pop-up menu is displayed. From the menu you can select Move. Perhaps the fastest way to copy or move a file from one place to another is as follows:

• Locate and select (click) the file to be copied (the *source* file).

• Press Ctrl+C (to copy) or Ctrl+X (to move).

• Locate the target folder in Explorer's Folders pane and select the folder (the *target*).

• Finally, press Ctrl+V to paste the file into the target folder.

Entire files or a collection of files can be copied or moved from one folder to another using copy or cut and paste keystrokes identical to those you use when copying objects between programs and the Clipboard.

Eventually, files and folders are no longer useful to you and must be deleted. The folder and file you created on disk A—the folder called Chapter 2 and the file *Ch02.mdb*—have been used for demonstration purposes and you no longer need them. You can delete them. Deleted objects can be recovered once deleted if you act within a reasonable time. Windows places deleted files and folders in a special folder called the *Recycle Bin* where they remain until you empty the bin. Once you empty the Recycle Bin, you cannot recover them. That is, when you empty the Recycle Bin, Windows physically removes them from the disk. Let's see how to delete files and folders.

### Try it

Open Windows Explorer, place your floppy disk in drive A, and select drive A in Explorer's Folders pane. Click the Expand button, if necessary, to reveal the folder called Chapter 2 in the Folders pane. Select that folder in the Folders pane. The Contents pane reveals the file (a database) named *Ch02.mdb*. With the mouse positioned over the file name, right-click the file. A pop-up menu opens containing items including Cut, Copy, Delete, and Properties. Click the Delete menu item and click Yes when the confirmation dialog box is displayed. The file is automatically placed in the Recycle Bin.

You delete folders in the same way as files. The consequences of deleting a folder can be more significant than deleting one or more files, however. When you delete a folder, you also delete any files and folders it may contain. Make sure that the folder to be deleted contains only files and folders that you are sure you want to delete. Delete a folder by selecting it in Explorer and dragging it to the Recycle Bin. (This may require you to reduce the Explorer's window so that the Recycle Bin and window are simultaneously visible.)

Whenever you feel the urge, you can empty the Recycle Bin, permanently removing all files it contains. Simply right-click the Recycle Bin and select the option titled *Empty Recycle Bin*. Then click the Yes button.

Restoring previously deleted files is simple. Right-click the Recycle Bin, select the file(s) to be restored, and then select Restore from the File menu. Any selected files are restored and placed in their original locations.

### Try it

Minimize Windows Explorer and locate the Recycle Bin on the desktop. Double-click the Recycle Bin icon, then locate and select the file *Ch02.mdb*. Select Restore from the File menu. The document is placed back in the Chapter 2 folder on your floppy disk.

Windows provides several helpful keystroke shortcuts for selecting files. While using Windows Explorer, for example, you can press and hold Ctrl and click file names to select noncontiguous files. Hold Shift and click the first and last of a group of contiguous files (those files whose names appear in sequence next to one another) to select the whole group. Besides these tried and true methods, you can drag the mouse pointer across Explorer's Contents window, creating a rectangular dashed line. Any file names the line touches will be selected when you release the mouse pointer. Try it yourself.

You can rename a folder or file by right-clicking it and then selecting *Rename* from the pop-up menu. Then you can type the object's new name. You can cancel the pop-up menu and choose to take no action by clicking anywhere outside the menu. Another, perhaps simpler, way to rename a file or folder is to select it and then press F2. Or you can *slowly* click twice (do not double-click) a file or folder name. A vertical, blinking cursor appears at the end of the object's name. You can retype the name or use the arrow keys to move the cursor left or right to make small changes in the name. Practice clicking slowly twice to master the procedure. If you are too quick, you'll end up launching the application that is associated with the file whose name you double-clicked. Stick with one of the other renaming techniques if you have difficulty using the two-click method.

## Setting File and Folder Properties

Files and folders have hidden attributes or properties that both limit actions you can take on the objects and display information about the objects. Which properties are available and can be altered depends on the type of object. Files and folders have a common set of properties that are accessible from Windows Explorer either by right-clicking the object or selecting Properties from Explorer's File menu. Some objects such as Excel spreadsheet files and Word documents have additional properties—summary information and statistics—that reveal additional details such as the date when the object was created and last altered. Four properties that all file types and folders have in common are called Archive, Read-only, Hidden, and System. Of these, only two are important to us—the properties Read-only and Hidden.

A file or folder whose Read-only property is set cannot be easily erased. Worse, database files, which you will use throughout this book, will not open properly if their Read-only attributes are set. (We use the term *set* to mean "has the value of yes" or "is enabled.") When you delete a file whose Read-only attribute is set, Windows displays a dialog box asking you to reaffirm your intention to delete one or more objects. Setting a file's Hidden property makes it invisible in Explorer. Hiding files is useful when you want to reduce screen clutter by eliminating some file names from displaying while using Explorer. The next exercise shows you how to clear (remove) a file's Read-only property, thus ensuring you can alter its contents and then save it back to its original file.

EXERCISE 1.14: CLEARING A FILE'S READ-ONLY PROPERTY

1. Navigate to drive A in the Folders pane and select the folder Chapter 2, which contains the file *Ch02.mdb* you copied in Exercise 1.13.
2. In Explorer's Contents pane, right-click the file *Ch02.mdb* and select Properties from the pop-up list. The Properties dialog box is displayed.
3. Clear the Read-only check box by clicking it if necessary. (If the box has a check mark, clicking it will erase the check mark—clear it). Notice that the Apply button, dimmed prior to your action, is now available (see Figure 1.20).
4. Finally, click OK to affirm the change and return to Explorer.

**Figure 1.20**   Clearing a file's Read-only property.

## Launching a Program from Explorer

As you become more comfortable with Windows, you likely will use Explorer as your default work surface for beginning your Access database work. Because most files are associated with an application, it is usually simplest to launch Explorer, locate the database file you want to work with, and then launch Access by double-clicking the file. This is a simple, efficient approach to starting a program *and* opening a file to work on. You have practiced this once already, in Exercise 1.7, *Launching a Program from a Data File*. In that exercise, you located a file with Find and then double-clicked the file name to launch WordPad. You can do the same thing in Explorer. When you locate with Explorer the database file you want to open, simply double-click its name to launch Microsoft Access. You might want to try this on your own with one of the many database files we have supplied on your Companion CD. Remember, however, to first copy the database file to your floppy disk or, better yet, to a temporary file on drive C. Then double-click the file in Explorer to run Access and open the database file.

Generally, the pattern you should follow in working with our supplied database files is to first copy the particular chapter's database file to drive C, your computer's hard drive, so that the database can be opened to both read database information as well as alter the data. This way, you will be able to make needed database modifications as you read the text and see the effects of your changes. Of course, you can open the Companion CD databases directly on the CD, but Access allows you to read the data only. You cannot post any changes to the database stored on the CD.

## Exiting Explorer

Exiting Explorer is child's play. You can either choose Close from the File menu or click the Close button located in the upper right corner of the Explorer window. If you haven't closed Explorer yet, do so now using either method. The Windows desktop reappears (or another application if any are still running). Make sure all running applications are closed so that you have a clear view of the desktop.

## CUSTOMIZING WINDOWS

You can customize the Windows desktop to make it more efficient for you to use and to provide the kind of detail you like. Some customization features, such as desktop shortcuts, will yield large time savings while other changes you make simply establish the desktop—your virtual office space—as uniquely yours. Windows also provides accessibility options, which make Windows easier to use for those with physical impairments. Nearly anyone can find several good reasons to customize the Windows desktop. Only those in a university computer laboratory environment will find it counterproductive to alter the appearance and functionality of the desktop because the customized desktop cannot be saved in that situation.

Different people who use a single computer may wish to customize the desktop to their liking, changing the background wallpaper, the number and types of icons on the desktop, and so forth. *User profiles* save each user's uniquely customized desktop so that no one user affects the settings of another. Which desktop environment is selected is determined by the *user name* provided. Details of how to enable tracking multiple users on a single machine are beyond the scope of this chapter.

## Creating and Using Shortcuts

A *shortcut* is an icon representing a program or other object and providing a quick way to access a particular object. The Start menu items, for example, are shortcuts to programs. This can be confusing to users new to Windows, but the distinction is important. A shortcut is analogous to a telephone number found in a typical address book. The telephone number is a shortcut to the real person who (you hope) answers the phone when you call. Like a telephone number, a shortcut can be deleted without deleting the actual object—usually a program—to which it points. Shortcuts inherit the same icon as the object to which they point, so it is sometimes difficult to distinguish between them. However, shortcut icons also contain a small arrow, which distinguishes the shortcut icon from the icon actually representing a program or other object.

The most common reason to create a desktop shortcut is to provide quick access to frequently used applications. There is practically no limit to the number of shortcuts you can create and place on the desktop, but we advise restraint. If you create too many shortcuts, the desktop can become cluttered and unreadable and you are almost back to where you started—unable to find a particular application or other object quickly. On the other hand, you may want to create shortcuts for lots of objects and then later cull the collection to the 20 percent of the shortcuts you use 80 percent of the time (the often observed "20/80" rule). In any case, it is simple enough to delete unwanted shortcuts later. Let's see how to create desktop shortcuts by creating one of your own. Bear in mind that your university computer laboratory may be set up to prevent this type of desktop customization. It can't hurt to try, though.

EXERCISE 1.15: CREATING A DESKTOP SHORTCUT

1. Close any open applications so that the desktop is clearly visible.
2. Right-click any blank area of the desktop.
3. Select New.
4. Select Shortcut from the submenu that appears.
5. Click the Browse button.
6. Navigate to the WordPad program file, which is found in the Accessories folder of the Program Files folder on drive C.
7. Select the WordPad file (*Wordpad.exe*) and click the Open button. The Create Shortcut dialog box appears, and the complete directions to the program, called the path, appear in the Command Line text box (see Figure 1.21).
8. Click Next.
9. Type *WordPad* in the text box and click Finish.

The shortcut appears on the desktop. The shortcut icon matches WordPad's icon in every respect except that an arrow appears in the lower left corner. This identifies the icon as a shortcut (see Figure 1.22).

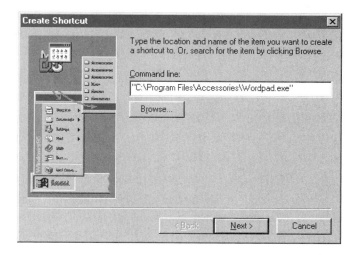

**Figure 1.21**  Create Shortcut dialog box.

**Figure 1.22**  WordPad shortcut.

Use folders on the desktop to group shortcuts if your desktop becomes too cluttered. This way, you can find a shortcut by opening the folder containing related shortcuts. Creating a desktop folder follows the same basic procedure as the first three steps of the preceding exercise. That is, right-click any blank desktop area, select New, and then select Folder. Finally, type the folder's name and press Enter to finalize the operation. The folder's name appears below the desktop folder. Then, you can drag shortcuts from the desktop and drop them into the folder. Because the desktop is both the source and destination of the operation, the shortcut is *moved* to a folder by default when you click, drag, and then drop it. To remove an object from a desktop folder and place it back on the desktop, double-click the folder to open it and then drag the object from the open folder onto the desktop. Delete a folder by selecting it and pressing the Delete key. Click Yes to confirm the delete operation.

## Placing Shortcuts on the Start Menu

The Start menu can be customized like other Windows objects. One of the things that speeds access to programs is to place on the Start menu shortcuts to the programs you use a lot. Then, when you click Start, a favorite program is immediately accessible from the shortcut. Plan a bit here, though. The real estate available on the Start menu is limited, so restrict what you place there to your most often used programs. Remember, too, if you are working in a university computing laboratory, you probably will not be able to customize the Start button. The following exercise explains how to place a shortcut to Microsoft Access on the Start menu.

### *Try it*

Locate the Microsoft Access program file called *Msaccess.exe*. Drag the file name directly to the Start button and drop it there. The first question is how do you find the Access file object? Use the Find command on the Start menu to search for it. Click Start, click Find, and select Files or Folders. In the Named box type *msaccess.exe* and make sure that drive *My Computer* is indicated in the Look in text box. Then, click the Find Now button. Shortly, the file name is displayed in the text box at the bottom of the dialog box. Select the name in the Name column of the Find dialog box and drag it to the Start button. Windows creates a shortcut to Access on the Start menu. Click Start and locate the shortcut at the top of the Start menu (see Figure 1.23).

**Figure 1.23**　Access shortcut on the Start menu.

## Removing Start Menu Items

Objects including shortcuts can be removed from the Start menu. You may want to remove the Start menu shortcut to Microsoft Access you just created. Removing an item is only slightly more involved then adding an item to the Start menu. The Settings item on the Start menu is the doorway to removing a shortcut. Perhaps the simplest way to understand this process is to actually remove a shortcut. If you followed our suggestion above and added a shortcut to the Start menu, then try the following exercise to remove the item. Otherwise, simply read on as we list the steps needed.

EXERCISE 1.16: REMOVING A SHORTCUT FROM THE START MENU

1. Click the Start menu and select the Settings menu item. Three submenus are displayed: Control Panel, Printers, and Taskbar.
2. Select Taskbar. The Taskbar Properties sheet is displayed.
3. Select the Start Menu Programs tab.
4. Click the Remove button. The Remove Shortcuts/Folders dialog box is displayed (see Figure 1.24).
5. Navigate, using the scroll box if necessary, to the item *Msaccess.exe*. (You may want to click the Programs group Collapse button to reveal the shortcut at the end of the list.)
6. Select the object *Msaccess.exe*, click Remove, and click Close.
7. Click OK on the Taskbar Properties dialog box to close it.

**Figure 1.24** Remove Shortcuts/Folders dialog box.

There's a slightly faster way to display the Taskbar Properties sheet. Simply right-click any *gray* area of the Taskbar (a gray area is any Taskbar area that is not occupied by a program button or the Status area). Then choose Properties from the pop-up menu. Remember this time-saver when you deal with the Start menu or the Taskbar.

## Clearing the Start Menu Documents Window

The Documents menu displays the names of the last 15 documents that you accessed. For instance, the document *FallWashPromotion.doc* appears in the Documents window if you opened that document recently. Similarly, if you open a database, the name of that database is placed in the Documents menu. When the number of document names exceeds 15, the oldest name is removed from the bottom of the list and the newest name is placed on the top. The Document window provides a quick way to return to a document you were working with recently—whether it is a Word document, Access database, or Notepad memo. This ability reinforces the notion of a document-centric system that we introduced earlier in this chapter. For example, if you wanted to work with the *FallWashPromotion.doc* document again, the fastest way to load WordPad and the document is to locate *FallWashPromotion.doc* in the Documents menu and click the name. WordPad is launched and the letter is opened automatically.

Take a moment to look at the Documents menu on your computer to see what names appear there: Click the Start button and then select Documents.

Sometimes people are sensitive about document names appearing in the Documents window. For instance, suppose you had just worked on a letter named *IncomeTaxesDue.doc* containing sensitive tax and income information. You certainly do not want an unauthorized person reading the document. It may be best to eliminate the name from the recently used names stored in the Documents menu. Clearing the names from that list is a matter of remembering a few keystrokes. The next exercise illustrates the required steps.

EXERCISE 1.17: CLEARING THE DOCUMENTS MENU

1. Right-click the Taskbar.
2. Select Properties from the pop-up menu.
3. Select the Start Menu Programs tab of the Taskbar Properties dialog box (see Figure 1.25).
4. Click the Clear button. The document names are cleared from the Documents menu and the Clear button is dimmed.
5. Click the Taskbar Properties Close button to remove the dialog box.

Now if you examine the Start menu Documents menu items, you will see a single item indicating that the list is empty. Emptying the Documents menu does

clear document
names

**Figure 1.25** Clearing document names from the Documents menu.

not prevent someone from accessing your documents, but it does prevent someone else from knowing what documents you accessed recently.

## Customizing the Taskbar

Some people prefer to have the Taskbar out of sight until needed. Others like the Taskbar placed in a different location on the desktop. Like the Start menu, the Taskbar can be customized to suit your needs. We show you how to alter both the location and behavior of the Taskbar. However, we want to remind you to be considerate of others who may use the computer after you are done. Anyone using a public-access computer such as a college laboratory computer expects to find shortcuts and Start menu items in a familiar order. Change the Taskbar all you want, but be sure to return the computer to its original state prior to leaving the laboratory. If you hide the Taskbar, the next student who uses the computer may not know how to make the Taskbar reappear. Be sure to clear the Auto hide Taskbar property before leaving the computer.

Relocating the Taskbar or altering its size is the most obvious change you can make to it. To change the height of the Taskbar, move the pointer to the upper edge of the Taskbar. When the pointer changes to a double-headed arrow, drag the upper border towards the center of the screen to widen the Taskbar. Similarly, drag the top edge of the Taskbar towards the edge of the screen to make the Taskbar very narrow but not quite invisible. Try altering the Taskbar's size. Widen it to almost half the height of the screen, and then restore it to its standard height.

Changing the location of the Taskbar from its default position at the bottom of the screen is a straightforward procedure. Simply drag the Taskbar to one of the four edges of the screen to place it in that position.

### *Try it*

Click any empty area of the Taskbar and drag it to the top of the screen. Notice that the Taskbar snugs itself up against the top of the display, and desktop icons automatically shift down slightly to accommodate the Taskbar. Drag the Taskbar to the right or left side of the desktop. Again, desktop shortcuts move out of the way accordingly.

Sometimes the Taskbar is unneeded and/or is using up valuable screen space. You can hide the Taskbar until you need it by setting its Auto hide property. To change the Taskbar's display behavior, bring up the Taskbar Properties sheet (right-click an empty area of the Taskbar and then select Properties). Click the Taskbar Options tab of the Taskbar Properties sheet that appears. Check the Auto hide check box and click OK to set the new property (see Figure 1.26). The Properties sheet closes, and the Taskbar will move off the screen until you move the cursor near the Taskbar's former location. Experiment yourself. Set the Auto hide property and then move the cursor near the edge of the screen where the Taskbar usually appears. The Taskbar reappears. Move the pointer away from the

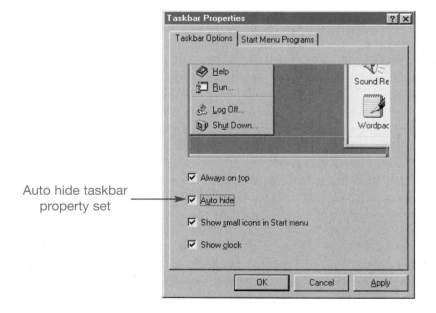

Auto hide taskbar
property set

**Figure 1.26**   Setting the taskbar's Auto hide property.

edge of the screen, and the Taskbar slips out of sight. Clearing the Auto hide property reverses this behavior. Bring the Taskbar into sight, right-click in a blank area, select Properties, and clear Auto hide on the Taskbar Options tab. Finally, click OK to establish the Taskbar characteristics.

Another property, Show Clock, determines whether the time is displayed on the Taskbar. Clearing it removes the clock. Setting it displays the clock.

You probably noticed the Apply button on the Taskbar Properties sheet. It behaves differently from the OK button. Clicking Apply establishes the properties you have selected but leaves the Properties sheet open. You can make additional Taskbar changes if you wish. Clicking OK establishes the properties you have selected and closes the Properties sheet, precluding further property changes until the sheet is reopened.

## RESTARTING WINDOWS

You may need to restart Windows because an error occurs that causes the keyboard to freeze, Windows indicates that an error has occurred and instructs you to restart, or you may need to log off your network and reconnect as a different user. The first two cases are infrequent and require you to simply restart Windows but not necessarily reinitialize the entire machine. The latter case, logging on as a different user, is useful for several reasons. Whenever you restart Windows, you are asked to specify your username and password. If your computer is on a network, you must also provide a username and password to log onto the local area network. The network and Windows usernames and passwords can be the same to simplify the task of connecting to both the network and Windows. To focus our discussion on Windows itself, let's assume for a moment that your computer is not connected to a LAN (Local Area Network). Why then are a username and password required or even useful on a stand-alone Windows computer? One major reason is that Windows can accommodate and keep track of multiple users' desktop preferences with usernames. This way, several people, each with a self-assigned username, can log on to a particular computer. Then, Windows restores the user's desktop icons, Start menu settings, and other work environment information for each identified user. Preserved desktop settings and environment are saved in *user profiles*. User profiles provide customized desktop configurations that allow people using the computer to work most efficiently. Forcing everyone who uses a particular computer to use a fixed set of shortcuts does not aid creativity or efficiency.

## EXITING WINDOWS

If you are using a computer in a computer laboratory, chances are that you will not want to exit Windows. Doing so will require the next user to restart Windows or the computer from scratch. Avoid exiting Windows in this situation. However, you will want to occasionally take a break and turn off your computer. Always exit Windows *before* turning off your computer. Windows often has some clean up work to do before you can safely turn off your computer. You could lose valuable data or programs if you do not follow this admonition. Shutting down or exiting Windows is straightforward. Here's how. Click the Start button on the Taskbar and then select the Shut Down option. The Shut Down Windows dialog box appears containing several options from which to choose. Select *Shut down* and then click OK to initialize the shut down process. Shortly, your screen will display a message indicating that it is safe to turn off your computer. The exact wording of the message depends on whether you are using Windows 95, 98, or NT Workstation.

## SUMMARY

This chapter describes the Windows (95, 98, and NT) environment. You have launched Windows, logged on to Windows, examined what is on the desktop, and used the mouse. You have learned how to use a typical Windows dialog box, and what menu items are found in the Start menu. You understand how to launch programs directly from the Start button Programs menu item. Using the more intuitive document-centric approach, you launched applications by selecting the programs they manage. You learned how to share data between running programs by embedding a Paint graphic inside a WordPad document. You learned how easily you can switch from one program to another by using the program buttons located on the Taskbar.

After working with the Windows interface, you examined Windows Explorer. You opened disk drives, folders, and files; formatted a floppy disk for first-time use; created a folder on your floppy disk; and copied files from the Companion CD to your floppy disk. Using Explorer, you discovered how to delete and rename files, how to set selected file properties, and how to launch applications from associated data files.

You discovered that shortcuts are a very convenient and flexible Windows feature. You used existing shortcuts and learned how to create your own desktop shortcuts. You found that you could place shortcuts on the Start menu to provide quick, global access to your most often used programs. You learned that the Document menu's list of recently accessed files provided automatic and fast access to items you recently worked on. We illustrated how to clear the Document menu's list to eliminate the file names from prying eyes. Moving the Taskbar to other edges of the screen, you realized yet another way to customize the Windows desktop. Finally, you learned how to exit Windows and shut down the computer.

# QUESTIONS AND PROBLEMS FOR REVIEW

## MULTIPLE-CHOICE QUESTIONS

1. Using the mouse, how do you execute a program whose shortcut is displayed on the desktop?
   a. click the program's shortcut
   b. double-click the program's shortcut
   c. right-click the program's shortcut
   d. select Execute from the shortcut's pop-up menu
2. You can click the _____ button and then move to any object on the screen and click the mouse to obtain context-sensitive help about the clicked object.
   a. Help
   b. What's This?
   c. Properties
   d. Find
3. If you want to work on a file called *MyResume.doc* but have forgotten where on your computer it is filed, the fastest way to locate the file is to
   a. use Windows Explorer.
   b. select Help from the Start menu.
   c. select Locate from the Start menu.
   d. select Find from the Start menu.
4. The Settings item found on the Start menu contains several menu items including Printers, Taskbar, and
   a. My Computer.
   b. Control Panel.
   c. Shut Down.
   d. My Network.
5. To switch between Windows programs, you can either use the Taskbar or the keystroke combination
   a. Alt+Esc.
   b. Ctrl+Alt.
   c. Alt+Tab.
   d. none of the preceding.
6. Using Windows Explorer, you can copy a file from one folder to another by
   a. dragging and dropping the selection to the target folder.
   b. pressing Ctrl+C to copy the source file(s), selecting the target folder, then pressing Ctrl+V.
   c. executing Copy and then Paste from the Explorer Edit menu.
   d. all of the preceding will work.

7. Shortcuts
   a. can be created for applications but not for documents or other files.
   b. are found only on the desktop.
   c. cause the program to be deleted when the shortcut is deleted.
   d. are frequently created to provide quick access to often-used applications.
8. Which of the following statements is true?
   a. Start menu items are permanent.
   b. The Taskbar is always visible somewhere on the screen.
   c. Only one application at a time may be running under Windows.
   d. User Profiles enable desktop settings of different users to be preserved.
9. You can minimize all open windows, revealing the desktop by
   a. clicking the Minimize button on the Taskbar.
   b. right-clicking the Taskbar and selecting *Minimize All Windows*.
   c. double-clicking the Taskbar.
   d. setting the Auto hide Taskbar property.
10. When you exit Windows,
   a. Windows performs some housekeeping chores before shutting down.
   b. you can safely turn off your computer after told to do so by Windows.
   c. the next user must restart Windows before logging on.
   d. all of the preceding are true.

## DISCUSSION QUESTIONS

1. Describe in a few sentences how you would use Windows Explorer. Start by explaining the structure of the Windows Explorer panels. What types of operations can you do on files?
2. Briefly explore and describe at least five applications contained in the Accessories folder (Start, Programs, Accessories).
3. Describe two ways to create a shortcut to a program or document.
4. Describe the ways to get help on Windows in general. How would you get help with cut and paste if you were using WordPad? Describe the steps you would follow.
5. Describe some of the ways you might be able to take advantage of Windows ability to work with multiple programs and data.

## PROBLEMS

1. Using WordPad, write a short, two-paragraph summary of the main points covered in one of your recent classes. For instance, write about your latest accounting information systems class lecture. Be sure to include your name on the document so you can easily identify it. After you have created the document, save it on your floppy disk. Then print the document.

2. If you have a new, unused floppy disk, use Windows Explorer to format your disk. In addition, label the new disk with your last name. Next, using either the new disk or one that already has information on it, use Windows Explorer to create two folders called *Notes* and *Homework* on your floppy disk.

3. Create a new company logo using Microsoft Paint. The logo should contain at least your company's name. Try the Airbrush, Brush, Line, and Pencil tools. Change colors. Be creative. This might be your future company's logo, after all! Choose 256 Color Bitmap in the Save as type list box. Save the graphic on your disk in any folder as the file *MyLogo.bmp*. Launch the WordPad program. Start the document by embedding your logo into the new document, and then write some text on the lines below your logo. Save the document as *MyLogo.wri* on your floppy disk and print the document. Be sure your name is either in the logo or near the top of the typed material so that you can easily distinguish your output. Finally, close both Paint and WordPad.

4. Launch the following programs, one after the other: WordPad, Paint, Notepad, and Windows Explorer. Minimize all applications so they are buttons on the Taskbar. Right-click a program's Taskbar button and select Close from the pop-up menu to stop and unload the program. Repeat the program-exiting process for all remaining programs. How many ways can you think of to exit the programs you launched?

5. Learn about Windows by consulting Help. Select Help from the Start menu, select the Index tab of Help, and type *Copying files*. Click the Display button to display the first of several Windows help panels. Click a topic in the secondary window, Topics Found, and then click the Display button. Print any help topic of interest that you find by clicking the Options button and then clicking Print.

# 2 INTRODUCTION TO
## MICROSOFT ACCESS

## OBJECTIVES

This chapter describes the Microsoft Access database management system in detail. You will use predefined databases to browse data, use Microsoft Access menus, and create several types of information forms. The purpose of this chapter is to bring you up to speed in using Access. If you have used Access extensively, then you can skip this chapter. Important topics covered in this chapter include:

- Starting and exiting Access.
- Understanding the Access work surface icons.
- Using the Access objects, including tables, queries, forms, and reports.
- Opening and displaying database tables.
- Retrieving information with queries.
- Modifying tables' contents with action queries.
- Creating and using forms to display and query tables and databases.
- Designing and using database reports.

We feature a small, fictitious stock brokerage firm to illustrate how organizations use databases to manipulate and store crucial business information. The brokerage firm must maintain a record of each client's portfolio of stocks, bonds, etc. Among the important information stored is client information (such as name and address) and portfolio information (such as the stock purchased, purchase date, and number of shares bought). As we work with the database package in this chapter, we will reveal various information items kept by the stock brokerage firm. More importantly, this chapter demonstrates that a relational database system can be built to track and maintain critical business information and economic events.

## INTRODUCTION

Modern computer-based systems, including most accounting systems, have a database system. An accounts receivable program, for example, frequently stores its information in a special system known as a database. The information is subsequently extracted, summarized, and displayed by a program especially adept at storing, organizing, and quickly retrieving facts stored in a database. Such systems are known as *database management systems*.

## What Is Access?

You will study and use one such database management system written for microcomputers, called Microsoft Access. Produced by Microsoft Corporation, Access is the most popular database management system for Windows. Once you learn the fundamentals of Microsoft Access, you will be able to create your own accounting systems with this powerful database system. (We usually use the shorthand term "Access" in this textbook rather than the longer term "Microsoft Access.")

## What Is a Relational Database?

Access is a *relational* database management system. Briefly, a relational database system is founded on the rules, created and published by Dr. E. F. Codd, that collectively define a relational database management system. Of the several database management system types, the relational database management systems are the most widely accepted and easiest to use. We will uncover some of Codd's rules for relational database systems in Chapters 3 and 4 and elsewhere in the text.

The fundamental storage entity for a relational database system is easy to visualize—it is a two-dimensional object having rows and columns called a *table*. A table holds data, and each row corresponds to one instance of data. Each of a table's columns corresponds to a different characteristic, called an *attribute*. For example, consider a table holding employee information. A particular row of the table represents an individual employee. There are as many rows in an employee table as there are employees in the company, division, or department. The employee table's columns might hold data such as employees' first names, last names, hire dates, social security numbers, genders, birth dates, and so on. Each column holds only one "fact." For instance, a given column always contains employees' hire dates and nothing else; another column holds only employees' last names.

A database often is comprised of more than one table. For instance, the employee table might be only one of several tables that collectively describe a company's employees, their skills, and their complete productivity histories. Almost always, more than one table is used to store information. A collection of tables that are related and collectively describe an entity is known as a *database*. You can imagine that an accounts receivable database contains many tables that are related to one another: a customer table, a salesperson table, an inventory table (you sell goods from inventory), and so on. Although most databases contain several tables, the terms *database* and *table* frequently are used interchangeably. The term for a database consisting of only one table is *flat file*.

Most databases used in business and government are large, and they often consist of hundreds of tables. We will not subject you to such a large system in our examples or exercises. However, our databases do contain more than one table and some of those tables have several hundred rows. Manipulating several, larger tables will give you an idea of what real corporate databases entail. The reason for using multiple tables to represent related information will become clear as you continue to read.

To better understand the concept of tables and their relationships, begin by launching Access and looking at a few tables we have prepared.

## Starting Access

Your first exercise in this chapter is to launch Access. First, launch Windows if necessary. Access is usually stored with other Microsoft Office products. Locate Access, whose file name is *Msaccess.exe*, with Windows Explorer. If you have difficulty, then use Find in the Start menu and search for the file name. Once you find it, you can launch Access directly from the Find dialog box.

### EXERCISE 2.1: STARTING MICROSOFT ACCESS

1. Locate the Microsoft Access program. You may wish to use Explorer or the Find menu item on the Start menu and search for *msaccess.exe*.
2. Execute Access (double-click the Access program icon). Shortly, the Microsoft Access dialog box is displayed. It contains three option buttons from which you can choose: Blank Access database; Access database wizards, pages, and projects; and Open an existing file.
3. Click the option Open an existing file and then click the OK button.
4. The Open dialog box is displayed (see Figure 2.1). Normally you would locate the database to be opened and then click the Open button. In this case, you won't specify a particular database.
5. Click the Cancel button.
6. The Open dialog box closes, revealing the Access Startup window behind it.

The Startup window is the principal workspace. All Access windows are opened in the Access Startup window, and they are wholly contained in it. Each type of Access window you will encounter appears in its own window. Tables are always displayed in a Table window. Forms, described in the section *Using Forms* in this chapter, are viewed in a Form window, and so on. Each window has its own

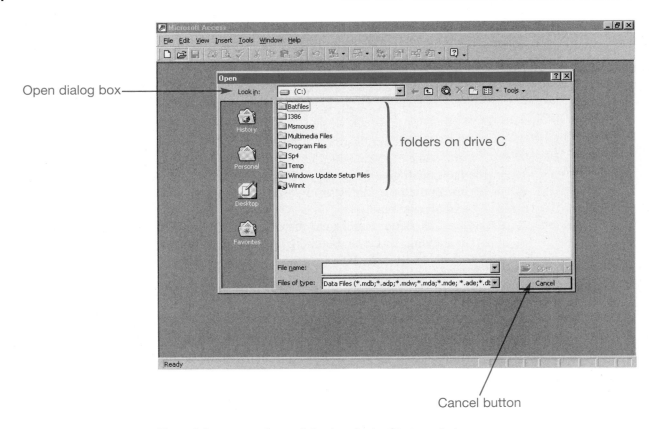

**Figure 2.1** Access Open dialog box in the Startup window.

distinct commands and functions that apply only to that type of window. You will see these windows and the commands contained in them when we discuss each type of window. Take a moment to examine the Access window (see Figure 2.1 if you are not using the computer right now).

   Along the top of the window are the Title bar and the Minimize, Restore, and Close buttons. Just below the Title bar is the Startup window menu bar, containing the File, Tools, and Help menus. Below the menu bar is the Database toolbar, displaying buttons appropriate for the current window. When you move the mouse over toolbar buttons, their names appear after a short delay. Simultaneously, a brief explanation about the selected toolbar button appears in the status bar located along the bottom of the Startup window.

## Finding Help

It is important to know how to get help when you get stuck or would just like to know more about a particular aspect of Access. Let's see what help is available on creating forms. Make sure the Access Startup window is visible and active, and then do the following exercise.

EXERCISE 2.2: OBTAINING HELP

1. Select Microsoft Access Help from the Help menu.
2. Click the Index tab.
3. Type *form wiz* in the text box found near the top of the dialog box and then click the Search button. (Notice that you do not always have to spell the entire word or phrase for Help to recognize it.)
4. Select Create a form from the list of choices in the Choose a topic panel. Help about creating forms is displayed.
5. Select Create a form on my own, which is found in the right panel (see Figure 2.2).
6. After you have examined the help screen for a moment, close it by clicking the Close button on the Help title bar.

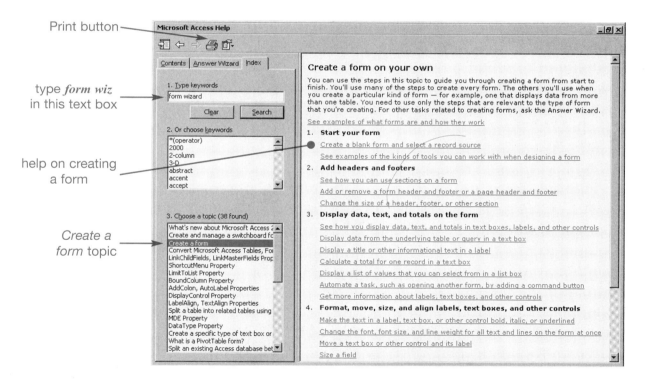

**Figure 2.2** Obtaining help.

## Printing Help

Occasionally, you may wish you could write down some especially important information you found in Help. Like all Windows products, help screens can be printed. By printing a few of the important help screens, you can have a handy reference within easy reach—even if you aren't near a computer. Printing help information is simple. Once you have located the help screen you want to print, click the Help page Print button (see Figure 2.2), then select the correct printer and click OK. The help screen information is printed. If you wish, you can continue to other screens and print them in the same way. That is all there is to it. (Print the Create a form help screen you located in the preceding exercise to ensure that you understand the help-printing process.)

## Exiting Access

After completing all of your database work, you should always exit Access. This signals Access to do its housekeeping chores such as posting any changes you have made to your database on your disk, closing other information sources, and returning to Windows. If you simply press Alt+Tab, for instance, to jump to Windows—leaving Access running—you run the risk of losing important information. You exit Access by selecting Exit from the File menu found on the Access menu bar. Access quickly closes any open databases and returns to Windows.

## EXAMINING THE ACCESS ENVIRONMENT

The Access Startup window's toolbar icons change as you move to other parts of Access. Toolbar buttons that are applicable in a particular window appear in color. Inapplicable buttons are dimmed.

## Access Work Surface

The Startup window has menus whose names and functioning are like those of other Windows products. Through the File menu, for instance, you can open files (database files in this case) and exit Access. In addition, the File menu contains commands to create a new database and open any hidden windows. The two File menu commands most often used are New and Open. Executing New allows you to create a database, whereas executing Open makes available an existing Access database. Figure 2.3 shows the screen display after selecting the Open command.

After you locate and then open one of the available databases, Microsoft Access displays a Database window within the Microsoft Access window. The Database window is the central control point from which all database activities are conducted. Figure 2.4 shows the Database window for one of the databases, Ch02, found on your Companion CD.

The File menu changes once a Database window is open. Additional File menu commands that become available include Get External Data, Close, Save, Save As, Export, Page Setup, Print Preview, Print, Send To, and Database Properties. These important commands allow you to import data from other sources, close the current database, save the database, save the database under a new name or export it to another data type, alter database properties, and perform standard Windows print activities. You will use some of the File menu commands as you read this text and work through its examples.

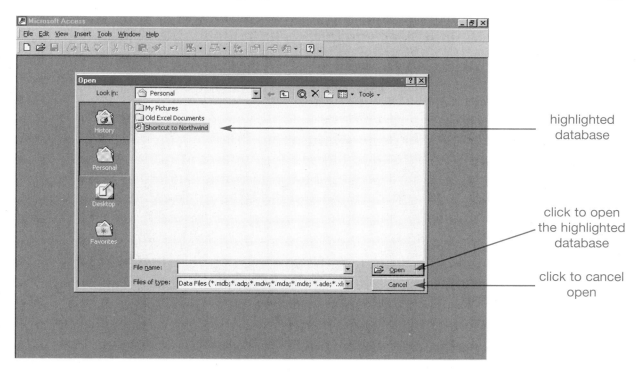

**Figure 2.3** Preparing to open a database.

Other menus on the menu bar include Edit, View, Insert, Tools, and Window. The Edit menu contains familiar commands such as Cut, Copy, and Paste as well as Create Shortcut, Delete, and Rename. The latter three commands allow you to create a desktop shortcut to any database object, delete an object, or rename an object.

The View menu lets you display different types of objects in the Database window. You can select Tables, Queries, Forms, Reports, Pages, Macros, or Modules from the Database Objects menu item, for instance. Or you can select those objects by clicking their names in the Objects bar on the left side of the Database window. Another group of commands—Large Icons, Small Icons, List, Details, and Arrange Icons—provides alternative views of the objects in the Database window. The Properties command displays summary information about a table or other database object. The Code and Debug commands open Code and Debug windows, respectively. You use the Toolbars command to display or hide one or more of the several special toolbars.

The Insert menu contains commands to insert tables, forms, queries, and other database objects into the current database. AutoForm and AutoReport create a new form and a new report based on the currently selected table or query. We will use these commands in this text.

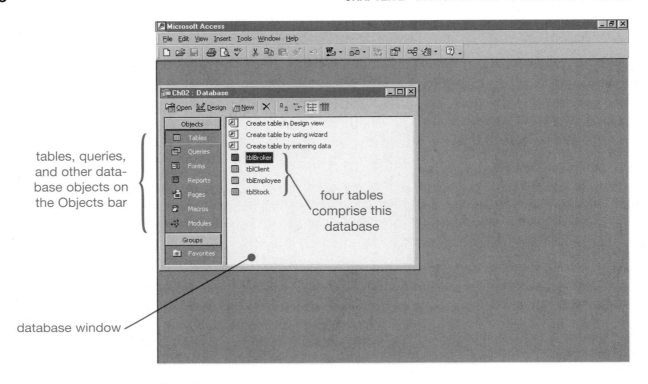

tables, queries, and other database objects on the Objects bar

four tables comprise this database

database window

**Figure 2.4**   Database window.

The Tools menu contains Spelling and AutoCorrect commands; Relationships, which lets you establish relationships between tables; Security, to keep your database secure; and Options, which allows you to set database-wide default values and conditions. There are other commands in the Tools menu, but they are beyond the scope of this text.

The Window menu contains six commands. (If you see fewer than six commands, then click the double arrow at the end of the drop-down list to reveal all of them.) They are Tile Horizontally, Tile Vertically, Cascade, Arrange Icons, Hide, and Unhide. Tile Horizontally and Tile Vertically arrange all Access windows so that they do not overlap one another. The orientation depends on which of the two you choose. Cascade presents windows so that only the title bar of each open but inactive Access window is displayed. The active window is placed on top. When Access windows are reduced to icons, the Arrange Icons command lines up the icons along the bottom edge of the Access window in the same order as it found them. Finally, the Hide command hides the active window from view, whereas the Unhide command reveals a hidden window. Figure 2.5 shows an example of several database tables. Two tables and the Database window are cascaded, and one table is reduced to an icon. It is in the lower left corner of the Access window. (Later in this chapter you will look more closely at each of these three tables.)

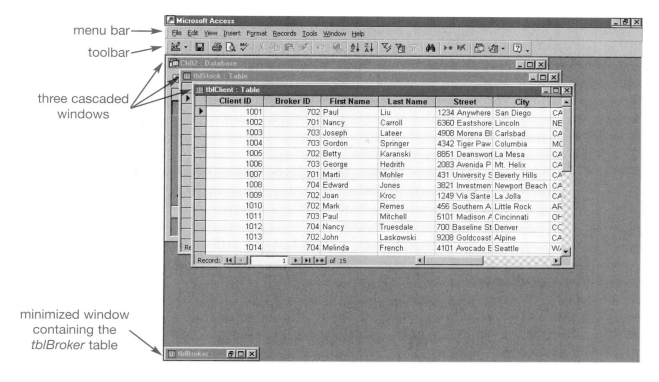

menu bar

toolbar

three cascaded
windows

minimized window
containing the
*tblBroker* table

**Figure 2.5** Icons and cascaded windows.

Help is the rightmost menu on the Database window. Clicking Help displays a standard Help menu. We have presented an overview of the Help menu already, so we will not discuss it further.

Look at Figure 2.5 again. Notice the several toolbar icons. Those icons represent shortcuts to commands accessed from the menu bar. The toolbar buttons that are unavailable in a particular situation are dimmed. Buttons that are not dimmed may be clicked to rapidly accomplish various tasks. The buttons provide a shortcut to menu commands; they do not replace the menu commands. You will use both the buttons and menus to create and modify various database objects as you read through this text.

## Access Objects

Access provides many ways to store, display, and report your data. The structures and methods you employ to store and display your data are called *objects*. Access objects include tables, queries, forms, reports, pages, macros, and modules. This text tells you how to use these objects, placing emphasis on the first four of them—tables, queries, forms, and reports. This section presents an overview of four of these seven important types of objects and shows how each can be used in building accounting information systems. Chapter 10 describes the sixth and seventh types, macros and modules. Sections that follow use tables, queries, forms, and reports we have already created to illustrate further how information is organized and retrieved with a database system located at the heart of an accounting information system. At various points in the chapter, we ask you to create some tables, queries, forms, and reports for a small system. First, let's see what these objects are that are the building blocks of a database management system that you will be using to build your accounting information systems.

**TABLES.** *Tables* are the fundamental storage structures for data, a company's information resource. Like spreadsheet models you have seen, tables are two-dimensional objects with columns and rows. Each row contains all available information about a particular item. (We will use the term *record* interchangeably with *row*.) All rows contain exactly the same number of columns, though not every column of every row necessarily has a value. Sometimes an entry is empty—database folks say the entry is *null*. Consider a table holding employee information. A small company having 50 employees could store employee data—name, date of birth, hire date, etc.—in a 50-row table. Each employee column would be a particular information *field*. (The terms *field* and *column* are used synonymously in this and other texts.) Each column contains one type (or category) of information. For instance, one column contains each employee's hire date, another column holds each employee's last name, and yet another column holds each employee's birth date. Figure 2.6 shows an example of a small Access table that stores employee data. The main difference between this employee table and one you are likely to see in industry is size—most employee tables contain hundreds, if not thousands, of rows. Additionally, employee data usually consists of many columns—not just five. This example is purposefully small so you understand the principles of database tables without the added complexity of large volumes of data.

Observe that each column holds only one type of data—an important rule to keep in mind when you create your own tables. Each row contains information about an employee, and only one employee's data is stored in a given row. As you can see, several types of data can be stored in a table: text, memo, number, date/time, currency, and hyperlink. Access tables can also hold other types of data including AutoNumber (generating a unique number), Yes/No, and OLE objects.

At the top of each column is the column's name, called an *attribute*, that uniquely identifies a column. Each row corresponds to one of the employees. A row is indivisible. That is, the data in a row remains with the row, even if the rows are sorted or displayed in a different order. Though the rows are unordered, they can be organized into a more meaningful arrangement whenever necessary. This is one of the advantages of a relational database system: the order of rows in a table is unimportant. In other words, you do not have to be worried about inputting data into a table in an orderly way. No row is more important than another.

each column holds a
different characteristic
about the row it describes

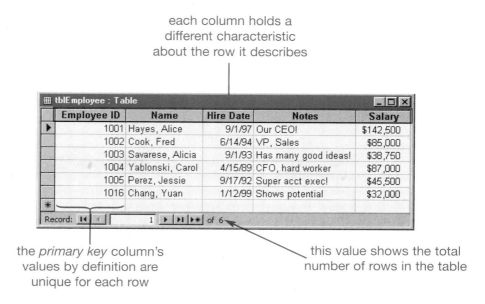

the *primary key* column's
values by definition are
unique for each row

this value shows the total
number of rows in the table

**Figure 2.6**   Example table containing employee data.

Similarly, the columns are placed in an arbitrary order left to right. Is there some arcane rule that states columns must be arranged in a particular order? No. We have designed the Employee table so that the employee identification number is first, but no other implicit meaning or significance exists in the columns' arrangement. (Though it is not necessary to put all rows' unique identifier column first, it is customary and convenient.) You can rearrange columns so that the Salary field is second, the Notes field is last, and so on. This is another advantage of relational databases: the order of table columns is unimportant. The field *Employee ID* contains mutually unique values. No two employees share the same identification number. This type of field is called a table's *primary key*. You will learn more about primary keys later.

**QUERIES.**   There are several types of queries, but the most common query is called a selection query. A *selection query* is a question you can ask about your database. (Because selection queries are the most common, they are simply called queries.) For instance, a query is "How many employees earn more than $50,000?" or "What customers' invoices are over 60 days past due?" Queries are especially helpful for combining information from several related tables into a single, cohesive result. Also, queries provide a way to reduce the data volume by returning and displaying only the subset of table rows in which you are interested. You can use queries to summarize data, displaying only the aggregate results (for instance, the sum of all outstanding invoices in the accounts receivable file). Other types of queries can be used to insert new data into a table, delete unwanted data from a table, or change values in a table. Using Access queries, you can select which tables are the subjects of your questions, designate the columns you would like to see, and specify which table rows are to be returned.

The query result, called the *dynaset*, is displayed in a Query window. Figure 2.7 shows an example of a query's design and its dynaset, each in its own window. Notice the query design window: only the columns appearing in the *query grid* are displayed in the dynaset—the result of executing an Access query. Check marks (✔) in the query grid Show row prescribe which columns are displayed in the dynaset, and the expression **>50000**, called a *selection criterion*, filters the rows. That is, selection criteria restrict the rows that are returned to those that meet the conditions specified by the criteria—in this case, rows whose Salary field is greater than $50,000.

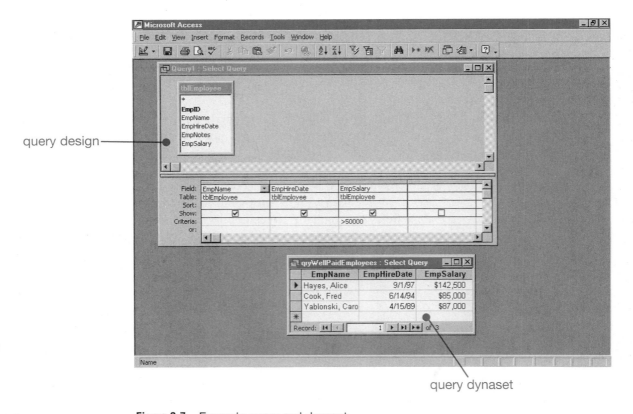

**Figure 2.7**   Example query and dynaset.

**FORMS.** Frequently, it is better to work with table data one row at a time. Tables are not an intuitive interface for many people, especially those who are not accustomed to working with databases. Access forms solve this problem. *Forms* let you see the data from a table in a format that is easier to understand. You can see one row or many rows of a table. Figure 2.8 shows an example of a form displaying the Employee table data in an attractive and intuitive layout.

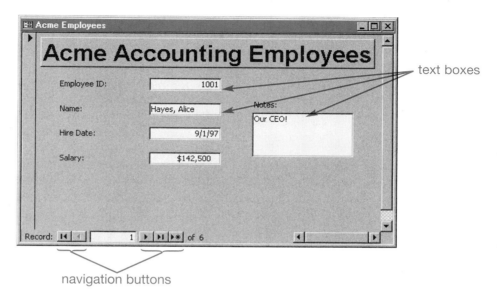

**Figure 2.8**  Example form displaying an Employee table row.

As you can see, a form may be an easier way to view and change data stored in your databases. One of several records is displayed. You can move to the next or the previous record, or the first or last record, by clicking the navigation buttons, which are located in the lower left corner of the window. You can move directly to a specific record by pressing F5, typing a record number, and pressing Enter. The single, right-pointing arrow button moves one record at a time, displaying the next record in the form. The right-pointing arrow button with a vertical line to its right moves directly to the last record. The opposite actions take place for the left-pointing navigation buttons.

**REPORTS.** Imagine showing several people in a meeting a financial statement displayed on your notebook computer's screen. That would be awkward and unprofessional. Hard copy output—a report—is a better solution. That way, the report can be distributed to an assembled group easily. Access provides a comprehensive report-producing facility.

Access reports are often the main output or result produced by a database system. While it is important to store accounts receivable information in a database and to query that database for answers, a far more important activity is to produce a printed output. For instance, you might want a list of all receivables over 60 days past due. If there are more than a few, a printed report is the most useful output. You can scan the list, marking accounts that deserve special attention. You can also make copies of a hard copy output for distribution to appropriate departments and managers.

You can use Access's report design features and tools to customize a report to look any way you would like. A report can display data from one table or from several tables that have been linked together. Figure 2.9 is an example of a simple report employing a drop shadow around the title, a graphic (a company logo), bold column headings, and sorted employee names from the Employee table. The simple report is easy to create, and the results are professional looking. An equivalent report produced using a programming language such as COBOL would require a few hundred lines of code and would require far more than the few minutes it takes to create the same report with Access.

## Employee Report

| Ident Number | Name | Hire Date | Salary |
|---|---|---|---|
| 1016 | Chang, Yuan | 1/12/99 | $32,000 |
| 1002 | Cook, Fred | 6/14/94 | $85,000 |
| 1001 | Hayes, Alice | 9/1/97 | $142,500 |
| 1005 | Perez, Jessie | 9/17/92 | $45,500 |
| 1003 | Savarese, Alicia | 9/1/93 | $38,750 |
| 1004 | Yablonski, Carol | 4/15/89 | $87,000 |

**Figure 2.9**  Example report.

Sections that follow describe the process of using and creating tables, queries, forms, and reports. We encourage you to participate in the exercises, because the remainder of the chapter is much more interactive. You will learn the most if you duplicate the steps we present and actually use and create the objects that we do. To help you in this process, we have supplied many of the required tables, queries, forms, and reports so that you can try them out. In addition, you will create a few of your own.

**WORKING WITH DATABASES AND TABLES**

The foundation of any database system rests on its tables. Tables hold the data that is transformed into information. In this section you will learn how to use tables that we have provided, create your own tables, modify the order in which table columns are displayed, and link tables together.

**Important Note:** Before you work on the tables found on your Companion CD, you should first copy the database from the Companion CD to the hard disk, drive C, of the computer on which you are working (Exercise 1.13). Remember to clear the copied file's Read-only attribute (Exercise 1.14). Do these two activities *before* beginning your work session. That way, you will be able to make changes to your tables, queries, and other objects stored in the databases we supply with the textbook. You should avoid using databases directly from your Companion CD because Access limits your activities to "read-only." That means you cannot make any changes either to the structure of tables or other objects, and you cannot alter the data stored in the tables. When you have completed your work on a database, simply copy the database from your hard disk to a floppy disk. That way, you can transport your database work from one machine to another if necessary. (All database files in this textbook are designed to *individually* fit on one floppy disk.)

The only database you need to copy from the Companion CD for this chapter is found in the folder called *Ch02*. The database is called *Ch02.mdb*. Copy this file to your hard disk now, before you start working with the database. We will assume from this point on that you have copied each chapter's database(s) from the CD to drive C prior to working through a chapter. (Recall from Chapter 1 that you can use Windows Explorer to copy files from one place to another.) At the end of each work session—after you copy your database file to a floppy disk—you may want to erase the database from the hard disk. Simply locate the file on the hard disk with Explorer, select it, and press the Delete key to remove the database. You always have the original database file on your Companion CD, whose contents cannot be erased.

Before you work on your database with Access, be sure to tell Access where to find your database objects. This simple procedure is called *opening a database*. We describe this process next.

**Opening a Database**

Whether you are using a stand-alone computer (one not connected to a network of computers) or a computer in a laboratory on a local network, you must first open a database. A *database* is a collection of objects that are related, including tables, queries, forms, reports, macros, and modules. Access stores all the objects of a particular database within one file. Access fetches and stores information in whichever database is open, but only one database may be open at one time.

All exercises in this text refer to the *Companion CD* that comes with this text. (You used the CD-ROM in an exercise in Chapter 1.) We have segregated files of all types needed for each chapter into separate databases so that you can isolate all changes and activities by chapter. Here is how the disk directories are set up. All files needed for Chapter 2 are found in the directory Ch02 (C-h-zero-two), all files needed for Chapter 3 are found in the directory Ch03, and so on. Whenever you are working with a chapter, you can locate databases and files in the associated chapter directory on your Companion CD. The next exercise shows you how to open a database that has been copied to drive C from your Companion CD so the data is available to Microsoft Access.

### EXERCISE 2.3: OPENING A DATABASE

1. Launch Access by double-clicking the Access icon (locate it, if necessary, using the Start menu Find command as you did in Chapter 1). The Microsoft Access dialog box displays.
2. Click the option button Open an existing file, if not selected, and then click OK.
3. Click the Look in drop-down menu and select drive C. Folders and file names found on drive C are displayed in the list box (see Figure 2.10).
4. In the large list box displaying folder names and file names, select *Ch02.mdb* and click the Open button. (Alternately, you can double-click the database file name to open it.) Microsoft Access displays the Ch02 Database window (see Figure 2.11).

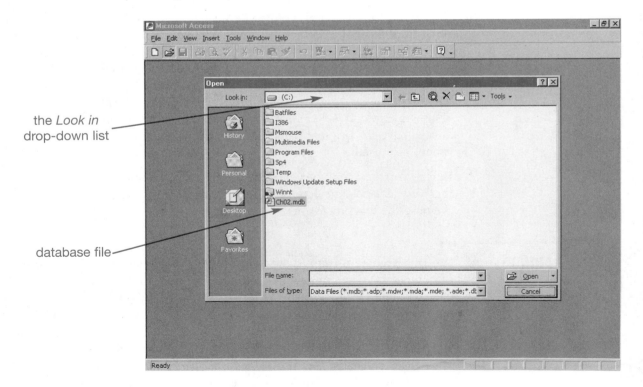

the *Look in* drop-down list

database file

**Figure 2.10**   Open Database dialog box.

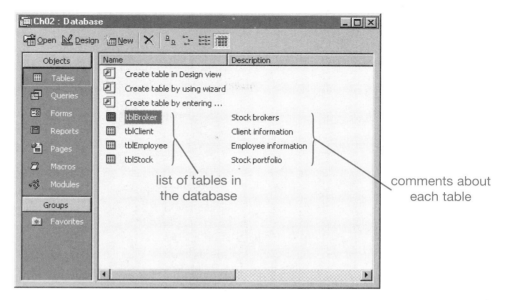

**Figure 2.11** Database window.

The Database window displays the names of all tables in the database. There are other objects held in the database including queries, forms, and reports. The names of forms in this database can be seen if you click Forms on the Objects bar. Likewise, you can see all queries by clicking Queries. If the table objects show icons or show more information, then your view setting has been changed. If your table list match doesn't match the list in Figure 2.11, select the Details command from the View menu. Now the two should look alike.

## Looking at Your Data through Different Windows

Access provides several ways to view your data. You can inspect your data in a Table window, which displays data in columns and rows called a *Datasheet view*—just like a spreadsheet's data. Or you can use a Form window to display one or more rows in a nontabular format. Forms provide an attractive way to view and change data, because they can be designed to resemble paper forms with which you are already familiar. (You can also view a form in Datasheet view.) Alternately, you can view your data in a report format with the Report window. The Report window provides a preview of a printed report so that you can review it as you would a hard copy report prior to printing it.

Because each view is found in a separate window, you can display several different windows simultaneously. Figure 2.12 shows both a Table window and a Form window of the Employee table. Because the Form window is active (notice the Form window Title bar is darker), the menu bar and toolbar are the ones used in a Form window.

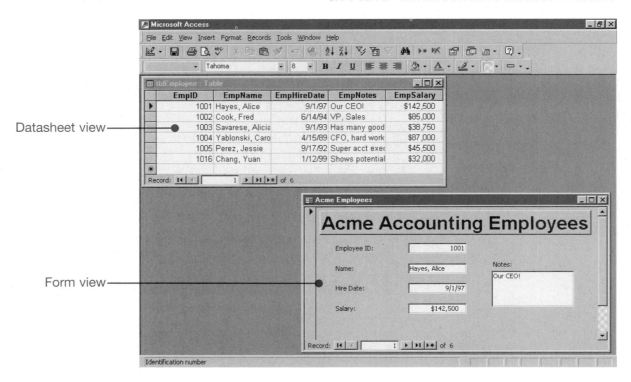

Datasheet view

Form view

**Figure 2.12** Two views of the same data.

One of the databases found on the Companion CD contains information about a fictitious stock brokerage firm. This small database consists of three related tables: Broker (*tblBroker*), Client (*tblClient*), and Stock (*tblStock*). We follow the object naming convention that all tables begin with the prefix *tbl* followed immediately by the rest of the object name. Queries begin with *qry* and the rest of the object name, forms begin with *frm* and the rest of the object name, and reports begin with *rpt* and the remainder of the name. (For simplicity, we refer to the tables in the text without their prefixes.) The Broker table contains information about four of the brokerage firm's employees, all stockbrokers. Client contains the names, addresses, and other data about selected brokerage clients. The Stock table lists the stocks currently held by each customer whose name is in the Client list. Of course, all of these tables are smaller than corresponding tables in a real brokerage house. We want you to comprehend the *process* of extracting meaningful information from the data, not marvel at the *size* of the database. It is easier to understand database concepts if we use several small tables. Client, for instance, contains 15 rows, one for each customer. Broker contains 4 rows, which contain a few facts about the brokers. Finally, the Stock table contains 173 rows. Whenever a customer purchases an individual stock, that transaction is recorded and saved in the Stock table.

You may be interested in more details about what these three tables contain. Details about each of the brokerage firm tables are revealed as we describe fundamental Access operations and procedures in this chapter. We begin by examining the use of Access tables, the elemental building block of all database applications.

## Opening a Table

The Table window is one way to view your data. When you open a table, the menu bar and toolbar change to menus and icons that are appropriate for table operations. You can better understand this process if you open an existing table and experience firsthand how some of the toolbar buttons and menus operate. In preparation for the exercise that follows, execute Access and the Ch02 database you have copied to drive C. If you forget how to open a database, review the previous exercise to refresh your memory. Now you are ready to follow the steps in the next exercise to open one of the tables on your disk.

### EXERCISE 2.4: OPENING A TABLE

1. Click Tables in the Object bar to display the list of tables in the Ch02 database.
2. Double-click the table *tblClient* found in the list of tables. (Alternatively, you can select *tblClient* and click the Open button in the Database window.) The Client table is displayed in Datasheet view (see Figure 2.13).

Take a moment to examine the Client table. Notice the Datasheet navigation buttons located in the Navigation bar found at the bottom edge of the Table window. The Database window may be visible behind the table and slightly to its left. Below the Access Title bar is the Table window menu bar. The menu bar's contents vary depending on what type of window is active (Table, Form, etc.). Below the menu bar is the toolbar. The contents of the toolbar vary with the active window. The Table Datasheet toolbar, shown in Figure 2.14, is displayed when a Table window is active and you are viewing a Datasheet (a table). The Form Design toolbar is displayed when the Form Design window is active.

Some Datasheet toolbar buttons are familiar, because they are similar to those found in other Windows products. They include the Print, Print Preview, Cut, Copy, and Paste buttons, which are on the left side of the toolbar. The Print button is a familiar icon that you can click to print a table. With the mouse pointer hover briefly over the Print button. When you pause the mouse pointer over a toolbar button, you will see that text, called a *ToolTip*, appears just below the button. The ToolTip displays the toolbar button's name.

Binoculars on the toolbar are used to search the table for particular values. Other toolbar buttons allow you to modify the table's design (Design view), sort the table into ascending or descending order, apply filter criteria to select particular records, and create forms and reports from the table. You will use some of these latter buttons later in this chapter.

*tblClient* table
among the collection
of tables

Datasheet view
of *tblClient*

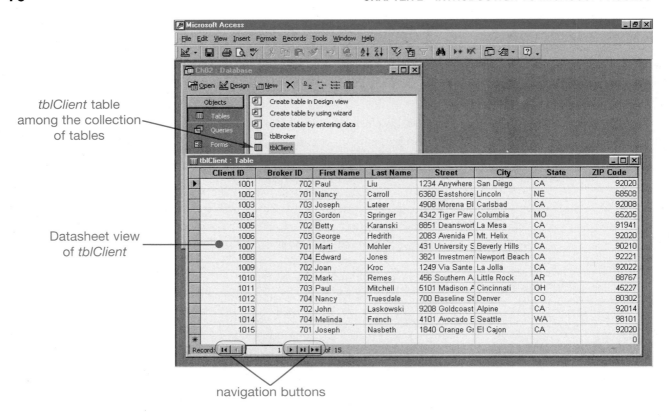

navigation buttons

**Figure 2.13**  The Client table (*tblClient*).

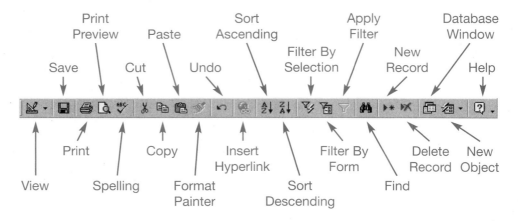

**Figure 2.14**  Table Datasheet toolbar.

When a horizontal scroll bar appears along the bottom of the Table window, it indicates that some table columns are out of view. The scroll bar works like any other Windows scroll bar: drag the scroll box to the right and the window pans to the right; click the scroll arrows and the window shifts for each click in the indicated direction. Vertical scroll bars appear whenever any rows of the table cannot be seen, as is frequently the case. The vertical scroll bar, located on the right side of the Table window, operates similarly to the horizontal scroll bar.

## Moving Around a Table

When you open a large table, only the first few rows are displayed. There are several ways to move through a table so that its rows are displayed in the Table window. You can select one of the movement choices from the Go To selection of the Edit menu: First, Last, Next, Previous, or New Record. You can also use the keyboard: the up arrow, down arrow, PgUp, and PgDn keys move up one row, down one row, up one screen, and down one screen, respectively. Perhaps the easiest way to scroll through a table's rows is to use the navigation buttons (see Figure 2.13). Left to right, they move to the top of the table, up one row, to a specific numbered record, down one row, to the last record in the table, or add a new row to the table. The last button opens a new record, which is placed immediately following the last record in the table. The New Record button is a convenient way to add a new record to a table. Try the navigation buttons. With the Client table still displayed in a Table window, first go to the top of the database. Then click the Last Record navigation button to go to the last record (we use the term *record* interchangeably with the term *row*).

Notice that the dark *row pointer* rests in one row of the *record selector column* found to the left of the table's leftmost column (see Figure 2.13). As you move around the table with the navigation buttons, the record selector moves to another row. Pressing the right and left arrow keys moves the cursor to a different column in the same row.

## Searching for a Value in a Column

Searching for a particular record in a table based on the value of one of its columns is straightforward. Though nearly all the data is visible in this small Client table example, most corporate tables contain thousands and hundreds of thousands of rows. Finding a particular client's record in such a large table would be extremely difficult without a database system. Let's imagine that the Client table contains many rows and you want to find a client whose name begins with the letters "Lasko" but you do not remember the exact spelling. Your task, in the next exercise, is to locate the client's record. If necessary open the table *tblClient* in the Ch02 database.

EXERCISE 2.5: SEARCHING FOR A ROW CONTAINING A PARTICULAR VALUE

1. With the *tblClient* datasheet displayed, click the topmost name in the Last Name column. That moves the cursor to the column to be searched.

2. Click the Find button (it looks like a pair of binoculars) and type *Lask** in the Find What text box. Be sure to include the asterisk, a wildcard, following the last letter.
3. Click the More>> button to reveal additional Find options.
4. Select Down from the Search drop-down list.
5. Click the Find Next button to start the search process. The arrow is moved in the record selector column to the row containing the name *Laskowski*, and the matching name is highlighted. (You may have to close the Find and Replace dialog box to see the highlighted Last Name entry.)
6. Close the Find dialog box.
7. Move the record pointer to the first record in the *tblClient* table by using the appropriate navigation button.

Try a few other search operations. For instance, locate the record whose City column contains "Seattle." What happens if there is no match? A dialog box is displayed indicating the search was unsuccessful.

## Changing a Table's Display Characteristics

You can change the visual properties of any table you are viewing. For instance, you can move columns left or right in a table, alter individual column widths, and remove the grid lines that separate the rows and columns. You can change a table's display properties by selecting an entire column and then right-clicking (clicking the right mouse button) the table column selected. Even though you may change a table's display characteristics, you are *not* changing the table's structure or contents. For instance, if you move the ClientName column to the left of its current position, the underlying table, Client, is unaffected. Only the *display* characteristics of the Client table are affected. (Access gives you the opportunity to save a table's display characteristics permanently when you close the table.)

Let's change two display properties for the Client table temporarily. The next exercise moves the ClientName column to the first column, just to the right of the record selector column. You will also make one other visual change: You will optimize the widths of all columns so no data is obscured. Before starting the exercise, make sure Access is loaded, the database Ch02 is open, and the Client (*tblClient*) datasheet is displayed. Maximize the Table window so you can see more of the table.

EXERCISE 2.6: CHANGING A TABLE'S DISPLAY CHARACTERISTICS

1. Move the pointer to the First Name *field selector* (column heading). When the mouse pointer is over the column heading, it changes to a down-pointing arrow. (When the pointer is within the data column, it changes to an I-beam shape.)

2. Click and drag the mouse to the right until both the First Name and the Last Name columns darken.
3. Click inside either darkened column's field selector and drag to the leftmost position in the table. Then, release the left mouse button. (The columns remain darkened after you release the mouse.)
4. With the columns still selected, right-click the mouse in the First Name column. A pop-up menu appears.
5. Select Column Width... from the list of pop-up menu choices.
6. Click the Best Fit button. The column resizes to the smallest width that will display both the column label and the widest column entry.
7. Move the mouse to the Last Name column field selector, which is no longer darkened. When the mouse changes to a down-pointing arrow, click and drag it across all columns to select them. Release the mouse.
8. With all columns except First Name darkened (selected), position the pointer on the right border of any darkened field selector and double-click the mouse to produce the best fit width for all the selected columns.
9. Click anywhere in the table to deselect the columns. Figure 2.15 shows the reformatted *tblClient* datasheet.

two name columns moved to the leftmost position

| First Name | Last Name | Client ID | Broker ID | Street | City | State | ZIP Code |
|---|---|---|---|---|---|---|---|
| Paul | Liu | 1001 | 702 | 1234 Anywhere Street | San Diego | CA | 92020 |
| Nancy | Carroll | 1002 | 701 | 6360 Eastshore Drive | Lincoln | NE | 68508 |
| Joseph | Lateer | 1003 | 703 | 4908 Morena Blvd | Carlsbad | CA | 92008 |
| Gordon | Springer | 1004 | 703 | 4342 Tiger Paw Lane | Columbia | MO | 65205 |
| Betty | Karanski | 1005 | 702 | 8851 Deansworthy Street | La Mesa | CA | 91941 |
| George | Hedrith | 1006 | 703 | 2083 Avenida Picante | Mt. Helix | CA | 92020 |
| Marti | Mohler | 1007 | 701 | 431 University Street | Beverly Hills | CA | 90210 |
| Edward | Jones | 1008 | 704 | 3821 Investments Heights Dr. | Newport Beach | CA | 92221 |
| Joan | Kroc | 1009 | 702 | 1249 Via Sante Fe | La Jolla | CA | 92022 |
| Mark | Remes | 1010 | 702 | 456 Southern Accent Way | Little Rock | AR | 88767 |
| Paul | Mitchell | 1011 | 703 | 5101 Madison Avenue | Cincinnati | OH | 45227 |
| Nancy | Truesdale | 1012 | 704 | 700 Baseline Street | Denver | CO | 80302 |
| John | Laskowski | 1013 | 702 | 9208 Goldcoast Drive | Alpine | CA | 92014 |
| Melinda | French | 1014 | 704 | 4101 Avocado Blvd | Seattle | WA | 98101 |
| Joseph | Nasbeth | 1015 | 701 | 1840 Orange Grove | El Cajon | CA | 92020 |

Record: 1 of 15

**Figure 2.15**  Changing a table's display characteristics.

We are finished with this exercise and do not want to permanently change the Client datasheet display characteristics, so close the table by clicking its Close button. A dialog box opens. It informs you that the layout for Client has changed and asks whether you want to save the new layout. Choose No to discard the table display changes you have made.

## Sorting Table Rows

Often, you can locate a record or group of records more quickly if the table is sorted. For instance, it is somewhat difficult to scan the Client table, as small as it is, and determine quickly whether a client named Toadvine is among the last names in your client list. You can imagine how difficult searching for clients by name would be for a much longer client list containing thousands of records, especially when the records are not sorted by name. The Client table is already sorted on one of its fields, Client ID.

There are two ways to sort any table. One way is to perform a *quick sort* to organize the table on a single column. Another way is to create and apply a *filter*, which allows you to accomplish more complex, multicolumn sort operations. No matter which method you choose, the table returns to its original order once it is closed.

Some tables are automatically organized because they have *key* field(s). Client, for instance, is organized on the Client ID field because that field was designated a primary key field when the table was constructed. (Primary key fields ensure that tables contain only one record for a particular key field value.) You will sort the Client table into ascending name order in the next exercise. In preparation for the exercise, ensure that Access is still running and that the Ch02 database is open. Click Tables in the Object bar of the Database window to display the list of tables in Ch02. Then, open the Client table (*tblClient*).

EXERCISE 2.7: SORTING A TABLE

1. With the Client table displayed in Datasheet view, click anywhere in the Last Name column.
2. Execute Records, Sort, Sort Ascending (or click the Sort Ascending button on the toolbar). The datasheet is sorted into order by clients' names. Do not close the table yet.

Another way to sort a table is to create an *Advanced Filter/Sort*. When you do, you can select multiple table sort columns (for instance, ascending order by State and then ascending order by City within each State). You can select column names from a list, place each sort column into a sort grid, and select either an Ascending or Descending sort order for each column. Once you create an Advanced Filter/Sort, you apply it by clicking the Apply Filter button found on the toolbar (it is the unembellished funnel). You redisplay the datasheet in its original order by selecting Remove Filter/Sort from the Records menu. Experiment a bit with these. They can do no harm, because the table's actual record order is unaffected. Only a datasheet's displayed row order is changed.

After you are done experimenting with sorting, close the Client table by clicking the Table window Close button. When the dialog box appears asking if you want to save the changes to the design of the table, click the No button. The Database window becomes active. Be careful not to click the Access *application* Close button, because the entire application will close and you will have to restart Access.

## Printing a Table

Printing a database table could not be easier. Merely select the table (it need not be open in a window to print its contents) or display the table in a Table window and select Print from the File menu. You can also click the toolbar Print button. However, be aware that you cannot control the number of pages or other print parameters if you use the toolbar Print button. Clicking the button starts printing the table immediately. We suggest you always select Print from the File menu to maintain greater control over the content and volume that you want printed.

When you select Print from the File menu, a Print dialog box appears (see Figure 2.16). You can choose to print all pages or a range of pages. Select a page range by entering From and To page numbers. Normally, you need only one copy of the report. However, if multiple copies are needed, simply alter the value in the Number of Copies text box. When you are ready to print the table, click the OK button. Otherwise, click the Cancel button to nullify the print process and return to the Table window.

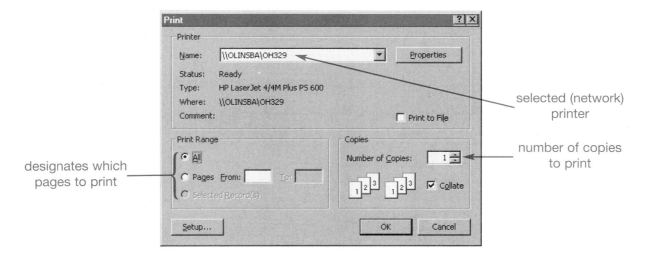

designates which pages to print

selected (network) printer

number of copies to print

**Figure 2.16**  Print dialog box.

A printed table is created using a default format. The table's contents are printed in columns with horizontal and vertical table grid lines. Today's date appears in the upper right corner of the report, and the table's name appears centered above the table. At the bottom center of the page is a page number.

The table report is functional but far from beautiful. Access provides tools for producing boardroom-quality reports replete with fonts, specialty features such as underlining and boldface, etc. Later in this chapter we describe how to create and use Access reports. Table printouts are quick and easy to produce and allow you to quickly check values in various columns.

Printing information about the *structure* and *definition* of any table is a bit more complicated. Click Tools, point to Analyze, and then select Documentor. Check the box corresponding to the name of the object(s), *tblClient*, for instance (see Figure 2.17). Click OK. Then, select Print from the File menu to print detailed information such as properties, relationships, permissions, data names, data types, and sizes. A printed copy of a table's definition provides good system documentation.

click other tabs to select
additional objects

**Figure 2.17**   Using Documentor to print table structure information.

## QUERYING A DATABASE

One of the real power capabilities of relational databases is the ability to ask questions that return interesting and meaningful answers derived from a database. Relational database systems make asking questions particularly easy, and Access is no exception. A *query*, the usual name for a question, can be simple or complex and can involve only one table, dozens of tables, or even hundreds of tables. In a query, you specify which tables are involved in the data retrieval operation, which columns are to be retrieved, which records are to be returned, how to sort the returned rows, and what calculations should be performed. The result is also a table. Relational database systems are *closed* systems, because queries use tables as input and return tables as answers. Simply stated, you put tables in and get tables out. A very important distinction between tables and queries, though both appear similar, is that tables are the only database objects that actually hold data. Queries *do not* hold data. They are merely stored definitions that extract and display data from tables when they are run.

The most frequently used type of queries are called *selection queries*, because they *retrieve* rows from tables. There are other types of queries that do not retrieve answers. Instead, they alter tables—insert new records into a table, delete existing records from a table, update data in one or more columns of a table, or create new table columns. All of the examples and discussion in this section illustrate selection queries. The section called *Creating Action Queries* describes the other types of queries that alter table data.

What are examples of the kinds of information you could retrieve with a query and why not simply print a table? Consider a larger version of the Client table. Suppose it contained information on over 14,000 clients and your supervisor wants to know how many clients are located in California. Or perhaps another manager wants to know how many clients are served by broker number 701. You probably would not print a 14,000-row client table and then manually look for the answers. That could take hours and be fraught with error and frustration. To compound the problem of sifting through data, the File Print command does not allow you to regulate which rows or which columns are printed.

Queries allow you flexibility in deciding which rows and columns of a table should be printed and provide an easy way to sift through large volumes of data. That is, queries provide a simple way to ask questions that return subsets of table rows, columns, or both. Access uses a query method called *Query by Example*, or *QBE*. Queries are formulated by giving Access an example of the result you want, and Access uses that model to return a result in a special, table-like structure called a *dynaset*. Let's look at an example.

## Using a Query

Suppose you are a stockbroker and you want a list of all your California clients. Furthermore, you want the list sorted by city. Because you are planning to mail literature to those customers, you want to see the clients' name and address fields (including zip code). However, you do not need to see the clients' identification numbers nor their assigned brokers' numbers. To extract the needed information, you would create the query by opening a Query window and showing Access an example of what you want. Figure 2.18 shows both a Query window and the resulting dynaset.

Let's try running the preceding query just to see how the question formation process works. The query shown in the Query window of Figure 2.18 has been saved in the Ch02 database under the name *qryCaliforniaClients*. By using the *qry* prefix on all query names, we can easily distinguish queries from other database objects.

**A note about naming objects:** We follow the convention that query names have the prefix *qry* followed by the query name. No object name contains embedded

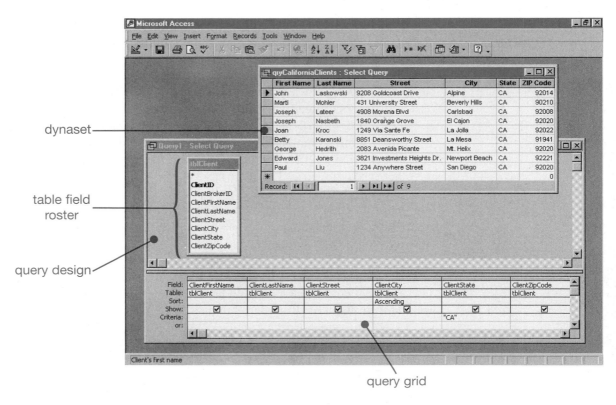

**Figure 2.18**   A query design and resulting dynaset.

blanks. Blanks in names can be troublesome and should be avoided. For instance, the name *qryNewCustomers* is preferred to the name *qry New Customers*, with blanks between the words. Squash the separate words together and distinguish them by using initial capital letters for each word (except the prefix).

With that in mind, we show you how to use an existing query. In the next section we will build a new query from scratch. Set the scene before doing the next exercise: launch Access, if necessary, and ensure that database Ch02 is open. Then complete the following exercise to open and run a query.

EXERCISE 2.8: RUNNING A QUERY

1. Click Queries in the Objects bar of the Database window to display a list of the queries stored in the Chapter 2 database, *Ch02.mdb*.
2. Double-click the query *qryCaliforniaClients*. (Double-clicking a database object's name is a fast way to open it in nondesign view. Alternatively, you can click the

query name and then click the Open button.) Shortly, a dynaset appears displaying the query's result.

3. After you have examined the results, click the Query window Close button.

The preceding dynaset displays clients living in California, sorted by city. Candidate rows are drawn from a table called *tblClient*. If you are a bit curious about how the query is structured, you can click the toolbar Design View button. It is the leftmost icon on the toolbar and displays a ruler and a triangle.

## Creating a One-Table Query

You create new queries using the Query By Example method. For instance, suppose you want to see a list of all customer invoices that are over 60 days past due. Printing or displaying the Invoice table would not be the answer, since all invoices would be printed. What you want is to sift through all the invoices and display only those whose invoice date is older than 59 days.

You create a query by clicking on Queries in the Object bar of the Database window and then clicking the New button. When the query grid is displayed, you write a query that tells Access to search through the Invoice table for all invoices more than 59 days old. Rows that satisfy the age condition will be displayed. Queries that restrict which rows are returned (by using some criteria) use a relational database operation called *selection*. (You specify which rows to *select*.)

Let's go through the process of creating a simple selection query that searches the *tblStock* table, returning a portion of the rows. In the exercise that follows, we will create a query that lists all stock transaction information for the client whose number is 1015. One table holds all the information we want: *tblStock*. Prepare for the exercise by closing all open windows except the Ch02 Database window. Then complete the exercise.

EXERCISE 2.9: CREATING A ONE-TABLE QUERY

1. Click Queries in the Database window to display the list of queries.
2. Click the New button in the Database window. The New Query dialog box is displayed.
3. Select Design View, if necessary, from the list and then click OK. The Show Table dialog box is displayed (see Figure 2.19).
4. Select the Stock table (*tblStock*), and then choose the Add button. Microsoft Access adds the Stock table to the query.
5. Click the Close button to indicate that no more tables are to be part of the query definition. The Show Table dialog box is closed. Now you can select the fields (columns) to be displayed.
6. Drag the asterisk (*) field from the *tblStock* field list to the first cell in the Field row of the Query By Example (QBE) grid. The asterisk stands for all fields in the

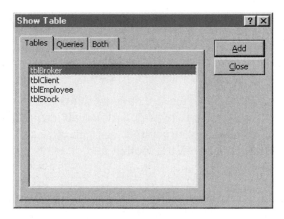

**Figure 2.19**   Show Table dialog box.

table. Dragging the asterisk saves time; you avoid dragging individual fields to the QBE grid, but you lose control over the left-to-right placement of fields.

7. Drag the ClientID field from the *tblStock* field list to the second cell in the Field row of the QBE grid. (A shortcut is to double-click the field name in the list of fields to place it in the next available Field row cell of the QBE grid.) Notice that the check boxes in the Show row are checked, which means the data for that column will be displayed in the dynaset.

8. Click the Show row check box under the ClientID column to clear (erase) it. There's no need for ClientID to be displayed twice, but we want to select only rows containing a particular value for ClientID. Therefore we include, but do not display, a separate column to hold selection criteria.

   Next, we limit the search for records to those that satisfy our criteria: rows whose ClientID is 1015. That is, we want only client 1015's rows displayed in the dynaset, not all rows. We limit rows by entering the example value 1015 in the Criteria row of the ClientID column in the QBE grid.

9. Point to the cell in the Criteria row that is under the ClientID column, click the cell, and type *1015*

   Figure 2.20 shows the completed query definition.

10. Click the Datasheet View button on the toolbar (it is the grid-looking icon left-most in the toolbar). The dynaset appears shortly with the results of this query (see Figure 2.21).

You will be creating more queries, so you can leave the Query window open. Or you can close the database and continue at another time.

## Saving a Query

Queries can be executed periodically to produce current lists of clients, spare parts, invoices over 60 past days due, etc. Always save queries so that you do not

QBE grid
Show row

selection criteria

**Figure 2.20** One-table query, Design view.

only rows with 1015 for ClientID
are selected for the dynaset

**Figure 2.21** One-table query dynaset.

have to recreate them. By saving a query, you can later rerun it to obtain accurate, timely information about data that changes over time. Note that you cannot save the dynaset, because it is not an object. It merely displays data from the underlying table that pass the criteria test. (You can create a special query, called a Make-Table query, which can save the dynaset as a table. We explore this and other special query types later in this chapter.)

### Try it

You save a new query by selecting either Save or Save As from the File menu and then entering a query name in the Query Name text box. Click OK and the query is saved. Let's check it out by saving the current query. Select the Save command from the File menu. The Save As dialog box appears. Type the name *qryClient1015* in the Query Name text box. Click OK. The query is saved in the Ch02 database in the Queries window with the name *qryClient1015*. We have saved the query in your database under the name *qryClient1015Stock* on your Companion CD in case you choose not to.

For any existing query you may have altered, the procedure to save it is almost the same. Simply select Save from the File menu, and the query will be saved under the existing name in your database. Keep in mind that if there are several query windows open simultaneously, only the *active query*—the one whose window is active—is saved.

## Sorting the Results

Normally, Access displays a dynaset—the result of a selection query—in order by the primary key of the underlying table. (For instance, the *tblClient* table's key column is ClientID.) If the table searched by the query has no primary key, then the dynaset's rows are displayed in no particular order. However, you can specify your own sort requirements so that dynaset rows will be in a more meaningful order. You select a sort order by selecting either Ascending or Descending beneath the appropriate column(s) in the QBE grid Sort row.

### Try it

Display in Design view the query *qryCaliforniaClients* and click in the Sort row beneath the first column. Select either Ascending or Descending from the drop-down list. Continue, if necessary, selecting other columns to the right in the QBE grid. You can select Ascending or Descending for any number of columns, but the leftmost column having the Sort row cell filled is the *primary* sort column. The significance of other sort columns are determined by their *relative position* in the QBE sort grid, left to right. You may wish to drag one or more columns to the left to enhance their influence on the final sort order. Better yet, you can add columns to the right specifying sort orders for each column. Clear the Show check box of any duplicate columns so they are used to sort but are not displayed in the dynaset.

## Using More Complex Selection Criteria

Suppose the manager of the stock brokerage firm wants to know the number of stock transactions and the volume of each purchase that occurred in her office during the month of January. She is considering sending most of her brokers on vacation for January if activity is sufficiently low during that month. Let's see how we could answer that question with a query.

To answer the preceding request, a query is formulated that returns all Stock table rows for which the value in the Date column is greater than 12/31 of the previous year *and* less than 2/1 of the current year. The criteria clearly involves two conditions—two different dates. Furthermore, both conditions must be true for a row to be returned in the Answer table. For situations like this, the criteria must use an *AND* operator. In fact, you can use the AND operator in the criteria whenever you select rows based on a range of values for a single column of a table. Let's create a new query to select all rows representing January 2001 stock purchases.

For this query we need not list all columns of the Stock table, because the manager is interested only in gross numbers of transactions, their volume, and the price of each trade. It is sufficient to list only the client identification number (ClientID), the purchase date (Date), number of shares purchased (Volume), and the purchase price (Price) columns. We are using the projection operation. A *projection* operation is one in which a subset of a table's columns is displayed. In this example, we include a subset of the Stock table's columns in the dynaset returned by the query. Projection is one of the important operations available with relational database systems such as Access. Close all windows except the Database window in preparation for the next exercise.

### EXERCISE 2.10: WRITING SELECTION CRITERIA USING AN "AND" OPERATOR

1. Click Queries in the Objects bar of the Database window and then click the New button.
2. Select Design View in the New Query dialog box and click OK.
3. Double-click the *tblStock* table from the list shown in the Show Table dialog box and click the Close button. (Double-clicking a table's name is a fast way to add it to a query.)
4. Click ClientID in the *tblStock* field list and then hold down the Ctrl key and click, in turn, the following fields: PurchDate, PurchVolume, and PurchPrice. Release the Ctrl key.
5. Click inside any of the selected fields in the field list and drag the list to the first cell in the Field row.
6. Release the mouse. When you release the mouse, the four fields are placed in separate Field row cells in the QBE grid.
7. Click the Criteria cell below the PurchDate column and enter the following selection criteria: *>#12/31/00# And <#2/1/01#*. Be sure to include the > and < symbols and be sure to surround the date constants with the # symbols.

8. Click the Datasheet View button to see the results of your query (see Figure 2.22).
9. When you are finished, click the Query window Close button to close it.
10. Click No when you are asked if you want to save the newly created query. The query is saved as *qryJanuaryStockPurchases* on your Companion CD in the Ch02 database.

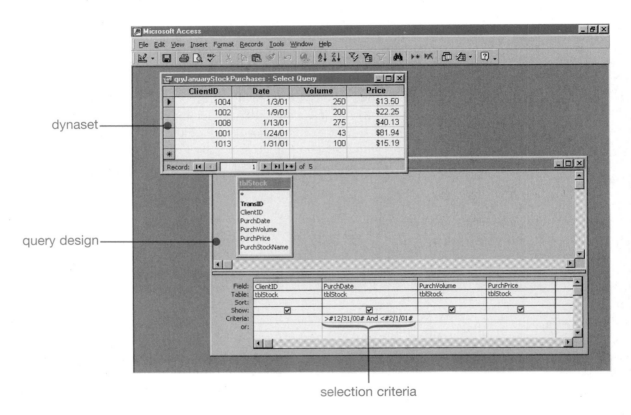

**Figure 2.22**    Selection and projection operations in an AND query.

Look carefully at the expression in the QBE grid in Figure 2.22 in the Criteria row of the Date column. That expression is used to filter rows, selecting only those rows whose Date value falls within the specified range.

Three new symbols and a logical operator are introduced in the criteria. The *And* separates two expressions. This indicates that the conditions to its left and right must be met simultaneously. In other words, rows are displayed only if the Date value is later than December 31, 2000 *and* before February 1, 2001. Pound signs (#) enclose each date value. Embedding dates in # symbols ensures that Access recognizes the enclosed values as dates rather than arithmetic expressions.

An alternate way to write an expression having the same effect is the criterion: Between *#1/1/01# And #1/31/01#*. Most people prefer to use this form instead.

You probably are already familiar with the greater than (>) and less than (<) symbols. These are just two of the *comparison* operators that bracket the date range. A complete list of comparison operators is given in Figure 2.23. Among the *logical* operators is "And." The list of logical operators is given in Figure 2.24.

| Operator | Meaning |
|---|---|
| < | Less than |
| > | Greater than |
| = | Equal to |
| <= | Less than or equal to |
| >= | Greater than or equal to |
| <> | Not equal to |

**Figure 2.23**    Comparison operators.

| Operator | Meaning |
|---|---|
| And | Conditions on both sides must be true for the statement to be true. Otherwise, the statement is false. |
| Or | The statement is true if a condition on either side is true or if both conditions are true. Otherwise, the statement is false. |
| Not | A unary operator, it negates the logic it precedes. |

**Figure 2.24**    Logical operators.

When you want to use criteria on two or more fields simultaneously, you place those conditions under the respective column names in the query image. For instance, suppose you want to list all stock purchases made by a particular client in a particular month of a given year, which involves a combination of queries similar to those you created in previous exercises.

### Try it

Modify the preceding query—*qryJanuaryStockPurchases*—to answer your new question. Click the Criteria row in the ClientID column and type *1008*. Running the new AND query returns rows whose ClientID value equals 1008 *and* whose Date column value is any day in January 2001. The value 1008 is an *exact match* criterion, whereas the Date criterion is a *value range* criterion. What you have learned is that AND queries involving different fields of a table are created by entering all of the criteria in the same Criteria row of the QBE grid.

# Creating Selection Criteria Using the OR Operator

You are likely to encounter queries similar to the following: "Which clients have purchased either item A or item B? Locate those purchase transactions and list them." Another example is a request like this one: "List all client records whose stock purchase price is less than $3.50 or whose stock name is *Microsoft*, regardless of purchase price." Both of the preceding questions involve two conditions, either of which is reason enough to list the record. That is, the criteria are called OR conditions. Unlike AND conditions in which *all* conditions must be true to select and return a row to the dynaset, only *one* of the conditions must be true for a row to be returned.

How do you form a query involving OR conditions? Let's examine the latter example in the previous paragraph and see exactly what is needed to form a query. Two independent criteria are involved. There are two basic ways to formulate OR criteria, depending on whether the criteria concern one field or different fields. If two different fields are involved (stock price and stock name, in our example), then you create a query containing two Criteria rows—one row for each condition. If a criterion involves only one field, then you can place alternate acceptable values in one field, separating them with the word *Or*.

The next exercise uses the first method, since two different fields are involved. Close any open Access windows, but leave the Ch02 Database window open.

EXERCISE 2.11: FORMING AN "OR" QUERY

1. Click Queries in the Database window to ensure you are about to create a query, not a table, form, or some other object.
2. Click the New button.
3. Select Design View in the New Query dialog box and click OK.
4. Double-click the *tblStock* table in the Show Table dialog box, and then click the Close button to close the Show Table dialog box.
5. Drag the asterisk (*) from the *tblStock* field list to the first cell in the Field row of the QBE grid.
6. Drag the PurchPrice and PurchStockName fields from the field list to the second and third cells in the Field row.
7. Clear the check boxes under the PurchPrice and PurchStockName columns so they are not displayed. (They will be displayed anyway because you dragged all fields to the Field row when you placed the asterisk in the first cell.)
8. Click the first Criteria row under the PurchPrice column in the QBE grid, press Shift+F2 to enlarge the Criteria cell (this action is called "invoking the Zoom window"), and type the criterion *<3.5*
9. Click the OK button to close the Zoom window.
10. Click the second Criteria row under the PurchStockName column. Type the expression *Microsoft* (either lower- or uppercase is fine). Access automatically

surrounds text with double quotation marks. Access ignores capitalization when searching for matches.

Now each Criteria row specifies an independent selection criterion. Each will return a table row whenever its one criterion is satisfied. Thus, both criteria contribute to the dynaset. However, when a row satisfies both criteria, only one copy is inserted into the dynaset.

11. Click the Datasheet View button to see the query results.

The dynaset, whose rows are in TransID order (because TransID is the queried table's primary key), is shown. Figure 2.25 shows both the query and the returned dynaset. (Normally, you can see either the query or the dynaset, since they are opposite sides of the same "coin." We have created a second query so you can see both at once.)

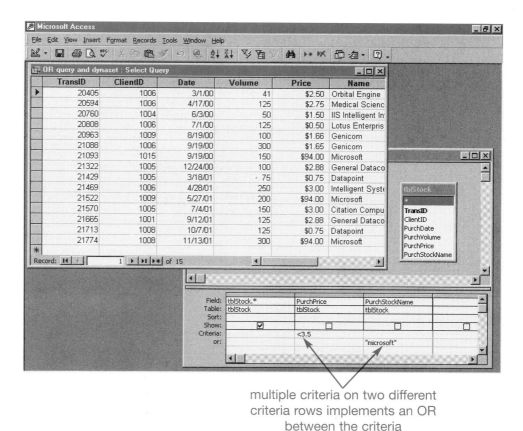

multiple criteria on two different criteria rows implements an OR between the criteria

**Figure 2.25** OR query and dynaset.

Notice that to form an OR query you have as many Criteria rows in the query grid as there are independent selection criteria. Each row contains characters, a value, or an expression below a single column. When OR conditions involve only one field, there is an alternate way to write the criteria. For instance, suppose you want to display Stock table rows for anyone who has purchased either Microsoft or Biogen stock. Because both criteria involve the same field, StockName, you can write both criteria in one query image row, separating the criteria with the reserved word *OR* (either uppercase or lowercase):

"Microsoft" Or Like "Biogen*"

Normally, when dealing with character fields in a table, capitalization is significant. However, Access ignores capitalization and locates matching rows based on spelling alone. Character matching rules vary from one database product to another, however. Be sure to experiment with it first. *BIOGEN* in a query may not match *Biogen* in the database if you are not using Microsoft Access.

The asterisk following the word *Biogen* is one of the *wildcard* characters, which can stand for none or for any number of letters. This allows a match on a string such as *Biogen, Inc.*, *BIOGEN LTD*., and so on. The asterisk can be used on either or both ends of any query string. Whenever you use a wildcard with a character string, Access automatically inserts the word *Like* ahead of it. Of course, the order of the strings separated by OR does not matter.

What would happen if you formed a query with only one row and placed the expression <3.5 beneath PurchPrice and placed MICROSOFT beneath PurchStockName? No rows would be returned in the dynaset, because no table rows satisfy both criteria *simultaneously*. The latter query is an example of specifying AND criteria. Simply stated, each Criteria row states conditions that must all be satisfied before any rows are selected by that particular criteria for inclusion in the dynaset. Of course, if there are other Criteria rows, they too may select rows to be retrieved. You should try the AND criteria as described above with Price and StockName values. Verify that no rows are returned for the data we have supplied.

## Including Expressions in a Query

For most applications, it is useful to calculate values that are not stored in the database. Accounting applications are a good example. For instance, brokers keep a watchful eye on their larger accounts. One measure of a client's account size is the total purchase price of each stock a client owns. However, the Stock database does not record that value. There are two approaches to solving this problem, one is correct and the other is wholly incorrect.

An incorrect solution would be to create a new *tblStock* table column that holds the total purchase price of a stock. While this might be an acceptable solution when using a spreadsheet product, doing this with a database can lead to inconsistencies in the database and trouble later on. Why? Suppose that the total purchase price is calculated as the product of the PurchPrice and PurchVolume columns (that is, purchase price is the product of price per share and the number of shares purchased). Suppose further that a mistake is discovered in transcribing the volume purchased for a particular transaction. Instead of recording 200 shares, someone recorded the transaction as 100 shares. Later the error is discovered and rectified.

Even though the PurchVolume value is corrected in the database record for a particular errant transaction, there is a danger that the total purchase price is not. Unlike a spreadsheet, a field value in a database row does not change automatically when other values on which it depends are changed. Here's an important rule covering this situation: *Never store in a table any value (field) that is functionally dependent on two or more fields in the record*. That's a simplification of a rule that will be described in Chapter 3, but it merely states you shouldn't store in a database a value you can calculate or derive from the database.

So, what is the correct way to arrive at the total purchase price for each stock for every customer? The correct way is to include an *expression* in the query QBE grid to calculate the desired value dynamically—each time the query is executed. Instead of having you go through the process of creating such a query, we have provided an example for you to simply execute. You will find a query containing a calculation stored as *qryStockValue* in your Ch02 database on the Companion CD.

### Try it

Click Queries in the Objects bar of the Database window. Then double-click the query *qryStockValue*. The query displays rows from the *tblStock* table as well as each transaction's total value. Examine the query in Figure 2.26 as well as the dynaset showing the retrieved and calculated results.

Click the Design View button and examine the query. Pay particular attention to the expression in the Field row. (You may have to click the horizontal scroll bar to bring the field into view.) The expression *Total: [PurchPrice]\*[PurchVolume]* is placed in the Field row. The expression computes total stock purchase price for each row in turn and creates a new column in the dynaset. The word *Total* followed by a colon and a space designates the name (also called an *alias*) for the column that appears in the dynaset (otherwise, the expression is the column label). The expression variables *[PurchPrice]* and *[PurchVolume]* reference table field names and get their values from the columns Price and Volume, respectively.

### Printing Dynasets

To print a query's resulting dynaset, first display the dynaset (click the Datasheet View button if necessary). Before printing, always check the dynaset to make sure it contains the results you expected. Occasionally, you may pose a query that is too broad and encompasses too many database records. Or perhaps you inadvertently omitted a needed column. Always preview the query's result first. Print it only when you are satisfied.

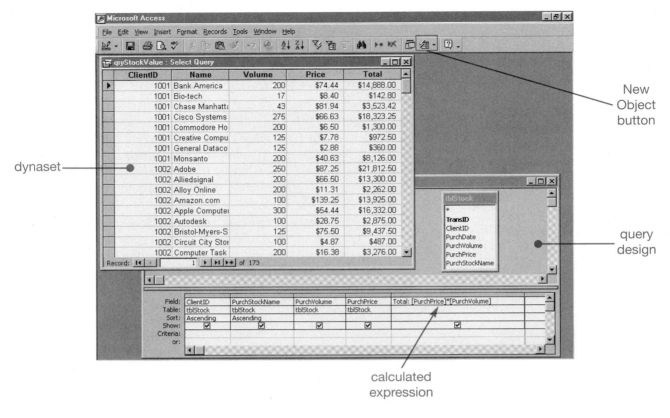

**Figure 2.26**   Calculating values with a query.

Print the dynaset by choosing Print from the File menu. The familiar Print dialog box, shown earlier in Figure 2.16, appears. Make any selections necessary, perhaps limiting the range of pages to print, and then click OK to proceed. That's all there is to printing the results of a query—you simply print the dynaset.

## Printing Query Definitions

You can document an object—a table, query, and so on—by printing its definition. It is very helpful to print the definitions of all your queries, because these serve as documentation for your evolving system. You might want to keep a notebook with a special section devoted to all query definitions for each database.

Printing a query's definition is a little tricky. Here's a brief overview of the steps to print the documentation for the *qryStockValue* query. Open the Query window by clicking Queries in the Object bar of the Database window. Select the Tools menu. Then, choose Analyze and Documentor. The Documentor dialog box is displayed. Click the Queries tab. All of the query names are displayed along with check boxes. Click the *qryStockValue* check box and any other queries whose definition you want to print (Figure 2.27). Finally, click OK to preview the definition report. If you are satisfied with the report preview, select Print from the File menu to print the query definition report.

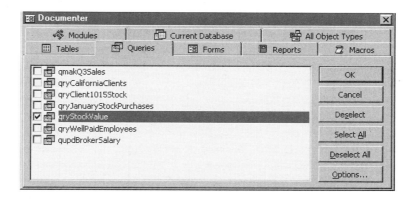

**Figure 2.27**    Preparing to print a query's definition.

## CREATING ACTION QUERIES

Besides selection queries, you can create another type of Access query called an *action query*. Action queries provide a powerful means to make changes to a database's tables. Action queries can create a new table, remove records from an existing table, update one or more fields of an existing table, and add new records to an existing table. Action queries resemble selection queries such as those discussed in the previous section. The major difference is that they *alter* the database in some way, not merely display results from the database. Action queries include make-table, update, delete, append, and crosstab.

With a make-table query, you can retrieve a subset of rows from one or more tables and save the dynaset as a table. Perhaps you want to concentrate on the smaller table, or you want to export the smaller table to Excel to analyze it further. Update queries allow you to change existing database information. You can create or run an update query to increase all programmers' hourly pay rates by 8 percent, for instance. A delete query selects and removes records from one or more tables. You could run a delete query to purge records of clients who have not contacted your office in over two years. With an append query, you can add new records to an existing table. Finally a crosstab query summarizes and combines data from more than one source to present a compact, spreadsheet-like result. You might use a crosstab query to sum stock sales by broker for the first quarter of 2001—a statistic that is not apparent by observing tables alone. We will present a concise description of how to create and run four of these action query types next.

## Make-Table Query

You can create a new table from existing tables by using a make-table query. Suppose you want to create a new table containing only third quarter 2001 stock sales transactions from the *tblStock* table. The new table has the same structure, but contains only July, August, and September transactions. You could create a make-table query to deliver the information in two steps. First, create a selection query based on the *tblStock* table that retrieves all columns but only those rows whose transaction date falls between 7/1/01 and 9/30/01. Then, turn the selection query into a make-table query and run it to create the desired table.

## Try it

Click Queries in the Object bar of the Database window and click the New button to create a new query. Select Design View and click OK when the New Query dialog box is displayed. Add the table *tblStock* and then close the Show Table dialog box. Drag all fields from the *tblStock* field roster to the Field row of the QBE grid. Drag another copy of the PurchDate field to the QBE grid. Clear the Show box corresponding to the second copy of PurchDate. In the Criteria row beneath the second copy of PurchDate, enter the selection criteria *Between #7/1/01# And #9/30/01#* and select Datasheet from the View menu to preview the new table. Select Design from the View menu to return to the Design view window. Now, for the new part! In the Design view window, select Make-Table Query from the Query menu. The Make-Table dialog box is displayed. Enter a new table name—the name of the table you will be creating—*tblThirdQuarterSales*—and click OK. You can save the make-table query and run it later, or you can run it now. (We have included this query on your Companion CD as *qmakQ3Sales*.) Save the query first: select Save from the File menu and name the query *qmakThirdQuarterSales*. (The prefix *qmak* indicates the query is a make-table query.) Finally, you can run the query to create a new table. In Design view, select Run from the Query menu. A warning is displayed indicating "You are about to paste 15 row(s) into a new table." Click Yes to approve creating the new table. If you run the make-table query, you will find a new table when you click Tables in the Object bar of the Database window. Of course, you can delete the table (you may want to save the query, however) by selecting the table, choosing Delete from the Edit menu, and clicking Yes when asked to confirm the deletion. You can also right-click the table and select Delete from the pop-up menu.

## Update Query

With update queries, you can make changes to many records in a table. You can update one field, or you can simultaneously update several. Update queries alter individual table fields, replacing them with new values. For instance, suppose we are sensitive to gender equity and want to make a mid-year adjustment to female brokers' salaries. We determine that they should receive a 5 percent raise. (Their male counterparts will have to wait an additional six months to qualify for a raise.) An update query is what's needed to make mass changes to the table containing brokers' salaries. Of course, our table is small, but this is an example of the kind of database change that would be laborious if it were done manually, one record at a time. The following activity leads you through making an update query. You can choose to actually create and run the query, or you can simply run the one we have created called *qupdBrokerSalary*.

### Try it

Create a selection query of the records to be updated, placing in the QBE grid only the fields to be updated or used for criteria. In this case, place only the *tblBroker* fields BrokerSalary and BrokerGender in the QBE grid. (Salary will be updated, but Gender is used to select which rows' salary values are updated.) In the Criteria row, type *F* below the QBE BrokerGender column. Before proceeding, view the affected records to ensure your selection criteria are in good shape. Select the Datasheet View button to view the selected records. Switch back to Design view and continue. Select the Update Query command from the Query menu. Notice that the QBE grid changes. A new "Update To" row is added. In the Update To row beneath the BrokerSalary column type the expression *[BrokerSalary]*1.05* (be sure to enclose BrokerSalary in square brackets). Figure 2.28 shows the completed update query prior to execution. You can run the query to update the BrokerSalaries fields of the *tblBroker* table by selecting Run from the Query menu or by clicking the Run button on the Query Design toolbar.

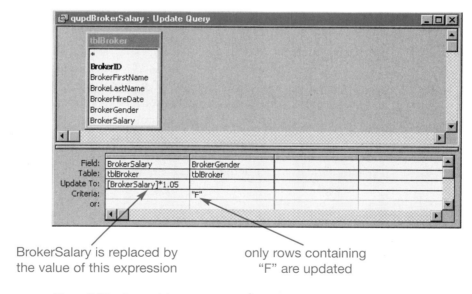

**Figure 2.28** An update query example.

Bear in mind one extremely important fact about updating database tables. An update operation *cannot be reversed with an Undo command—there is no undo*. You can undo some update operations by formulating a new update query to restore updated values, but many update operations are irreversible. For instance, suppose you choose to update the location field of an employee's work address to "New York" for all employees whose city is currently Indianapolis. This will effectively move all Indianapolis employees to New York. However, you cannot easily reverse the change if other employees already are listed as living in New York. That is, it is not a matter of changing the City field of New York back to Indianapolis, because some are New Yorkers who were never located in Indianapolis in the first place! Always select Datasheet View before running an update query to check the scope of your changes.

## Delete Query

A delete query is used to delete records from tables. It is *not* used to delete entire tables. To delete an entire table, not just the records it contains, you click Tables in the Database window, select the table, and press the Delete key. The entire table, plus data, is removed from the database. Deleting records is a much subtler activity. Suppose, for instance, that you want to remove from the *tblStock* table all transactions that occurred on or before December 31, 2000. In other words, you want to "clear the books" for a new year, 2001. A delete query with the proper selection criteria will do the trick. First create a selection query and then examine its Datasheet view to ensure that proper records will be deleted when the query is transformed to a delete query. To create a delete query from a selection query, ensure the query is displayed in Design view and then select Delete Query from the Query menu.

Once you have properly defined a delete query, all that is left is to run it. Figure 2.29 shows an example of a delete query that removes from the table *tblStock* all stock transactions that occurred before 2001. The delete query, called *qdelOldTransactions*, is stored in your database, Ch02. Notice that the only fields that are needed in the QBE grid are those that are being used for criteria. In this example, only the PurchDate field is required, because that is the sole criteria—the purchase transaction date. Remember, though, that the entire record will be deleted.

## Append Query

You use an append query to add records from a table or query to the end of another table. For instance, you would use an append query to create a comprehensive employee table containing all employees in all divisions. The table *tblEmployee*, for instance, represents only one division of a larger company. By creating an append query, you can add other divisions' employee records to the *tblEmployee* table.

To create an append query, simply create a selection query including fields from the source tables that are in the target (destination) table *and* any fields that are used as criteria. In the Criteria row of the query, establish the conditions that are used to select records from the other table to append to the current table (for

delete criteria

**Figure 2.29** A delete query example.

instance, only division 1 and division 2 employees). View the potential new records by clicking the Datasheet View button. Then, switch back to Design view and select Append Query from the Query menu to turn the selection query into an append query. When prompted for the target table name by the Append dialog box, enter the target table's name or select it from the Table Name drop-down list. Click OK to complete the query definition. Figure 2.30 shows an example in which a fictitious division's employee records are to be appended to the *tblEmployee* table.

## USING FORMS

A form provides a convenient, less cluttered work surface through which you can enter or alter information in your tables. A form can display information from one or more tables. Additionally, a form can display information from a query (that is, the query's dynaset).

One of the advantages of using a form to enter or change data is that the form can look like a paper form with which you or your clients are already familiar. When the form on the screen mimics a paper form, those using the form will intuitively know what information goes where, and they usually feel more comfortable with a familiar interface. Entering data directly into a table can be more confusing and error-prone, especially for anyone not familiar with databases in general or Access in particular. Another advantage of a form is that you can enforce a medley of validation checks on values that are entered in a table through a form.

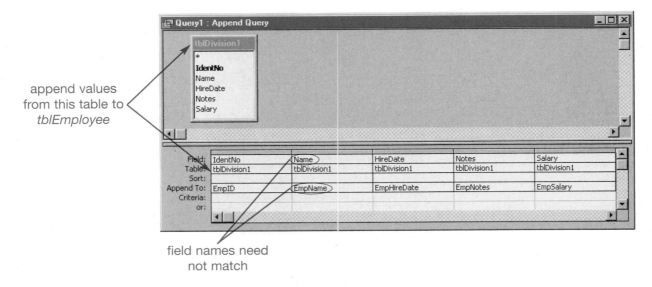

append values from this table to *tblEmployee*

field names need not match

**Figure 2.30**   An append query example.

## Viewing a Table through a Form

So that you understand a form better, we have created one that displays information from the Client table (*tblClient*), which is shown in Figures 2.13 and 2.15. The form is found on your Companion CD and is called *frmClient*. (All forms on the Companion CD have the prefix *frm*.) Work through the next exercise to open a Form view of the *tblClient* table.

EXERCISE 2.12: OPENING AND USING A FORM

1. Close all open windows except the Database window. (This isn't necessary, but it reduces screen clutter.)
2. Click Forms in the Objects bar of the Database window to display all forms in the Ch02 database.
3. Double-click the form *frmClient*. The Client form appears (see Figure 2.31).

All fields from the Client table (Figure 2.13) appear in a pleasant arrangement in the form in Figure 2.31. Familiar navigation buttons appear along the bottom edge of the Form window. Those buttons perform the usual actions: move to the top of the table, move up one row, and so forth. Look at the 15 records one at a time by clicking the Next Record button at the bottom of the Form view window. After you have moved to the last record, click the First Record navigation button to display the first record. Notice that the form displays records in order by

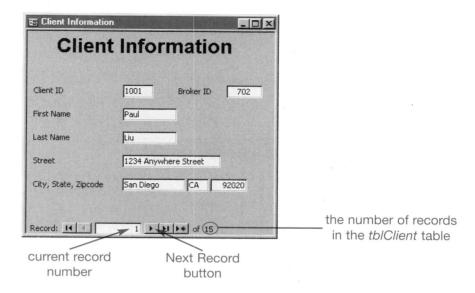

the number of records
in the *tblClient* table

current record
number

Next Record
button

**Figure 2.31**   A client form.

ClientID. The form is built from the *tblClient* table whose primary key, ClientID, maintains the table (and thus the form) rows in order by the ClientID field. If you want rows displayed in the form in name order, you could create a query that returns rows sorted on ClientLastName (specify Ascending in the QBE grid under ClientLastName). Then you can build a form based on the query. We illustrate a query-based form in the next section.

Several interesting design elements have been employed in the Client form so that it is at once intuitive and attractive. Along the top is a simple title, in Arial typeface, that identifies the form. Each form field is labeled and arranged on the form in a logical order. In the upper left part of the form is the client's identification number. It is entered first. Below it are the client's name and address. Notice that wherever information is supplied from the table—data to be changed or viewed—it is contained in a box frame that appears sunken. (You can change that, of course.) This helps the user visually separate labels from data.

## Viewing a Query through a Form

Forms can be created for saved queries as well as tables. It makes no difference whether the form displays a table's contents or a query's contents. Figure 2.32 shows a form that displays a subset of the fields from the *qryStockValue* query, which is shown in Figure 2.26. Unlike the previous form, this one has no Minimize or Restore buttons available in the form's Title bar. Notice that the Form window status line displays the current record and the total number of records. In this case, the total number of records depends on how many rows are selected by the query upon which the form is built. It is likely that you will create and use many forms based on queries. The form shown in Figure 2.32 is stored on your Companion CD in the Ch02 database as *frmStockValue*. Try it out yourself.

no minimize or maximize button is available

record count

**Figure 2.32**  Form based on the query, *qryStockValue*.

## Creating a Form Quickly

When you want to enter data into a table one record at a time, your best work surface may be a form. We illustrate how easy it is to create a functional and attractive form by simply choosing a table and clicking a button. Let's create a simple form for the *tblBroker* table (on your Companion CD) through which we can observe or alter information. First, switch to the Database window (the fastest way is to click the Database Window button on the toolbar). Then, create an *AutoForm* by completing the steps in the following activity.

### Try it

Click Tables in the Object bar of the Database window to display a list of the Ch02 table names. Highlight the table name *tblBroker* in the list of tables. Click the New Object button (see Figure 2.26) on the toolbar and select AutoForm from the drop-down list. A Form window is displayed containing your newly created form (see Figure 2.33). The Form window Title bar contains the table name by default. You can change it later if you want. Leave the Form window open, because you will save the form in a few moments. That's all there is to creating a form from a table. You probably agree with us that the form is attractive and functional. We show you how to modify and enhance a form in Chapter 5. For now, simply save the new form on your copy of the database.

**Figure 2.33** Broker form.

## Saving a Form

You can save a form design either by executing Save or Save As from the File menu. Then you supply the form's name. Let's save the form in your hard-drive copy of the database.

### Try it

With the newly created Broker form still displayed, select Save in the File menu. Type the name *frmBrokerAutoForm* in the Form Name: text box of the Save As dialog box. Click OK to complete the form save operation. Click the form's Title bar Close button to close it.

The form is saved in your C drive copy of the current database, Ch02. We have also saved the form in the Ch02 database on your Companion CD. It is called *frmBroker*.

## Editing Data with a Form

It is often easier to alter data in a table using a form. Because only one table row is usually displayed on the form, you are less likely to make mistakes. Editing table data through a form is simple. While looking at a form in Form view (not Design view), you click the field that you want to change and make any needed changes. Let's try editing a record in the Broker table with the form. In preparation, make sure the Broker form is displayed in the Form view window. Then, complete the following exercise.

EXERCISE 2.13: EDITING DATA WITH A FORM

1. Move to the record for David Vickrey (press PgUp or PgDn or use the navigation buttons if necessary).

2. Press Tab to move to the Hire Date field. (The entire value is highlighted if you use Tab or the arrow keys to move to the selected fields.)
3. Type the correct hire date, *7/5/88*
4. Click the Form window's Close button to close the form.

Changes to a particular record are not posted (saved) to the table until you move to another record or close the database. Simply click one of the navigation buttons on the form to store the changed record in the table. Go back to the record you changed to verify that the new hire date value has been saved. Keep in mind that the form merely displays table data. The form, itself, is not changed. Only the table data is actually changed. Changed data is automatically saved for you, and you need not save a form again unless you change the form's design.

## Querying a Database with a Form

When you are looking for a particular record in a table containing many records, there's no better way to locate it than by using a form. You can load a form and then use the command *Filter By Form* or *Filter By Selection*. Additionally, you can create a more complex search using the *Advanced Filter/Sort* tool. To illustrate this process, let's use the Filter By Form command to locate all the stocks purchased by client 1013. You can imagine the daunting task this would be if you had to visually examine every row in the *tblStock* table looking for all a given client's transactions. Naturally, you wouldn't do it that way. Instead, you would request Access to apply a *filter*—another term for applying selection criteria so that only a subset of records is displayed—and retrieve only records of interest. Let's try it. In preparation, open your copy of the Ch02 database, if necessary.

EXERCISE 2.14: FILTERING DATA THROUGH A FORM

1. Click Forms in the Object bar of the Database window to display the existing form names.
2. Double-click *frmStockValue* to open that form.
3. Select the Records menu, point to the Filter menu item, and then select Filter By Form. Notice that a down-pointing arrow appears on the ClientID data field and that the menu has changed. The ClientID has changed into a drop-down list box from which you can choose one of the unique ClientID values retrieved from the *tblStock* table ClientID column.
4. Click the ClientID drop-down list box arrow to reveal the collection of ClientID values (see Figure 2.34).
5. Choose 1013 from the list. The ClientID field displays the value 1013.
6. Select Apply Filter/Sort from the Filter menu found on the menu bar. The first of several client 1013 records is displayed in the form. Notice that the indicator (filtered) appears just to the right of the navigation buttons. This indicates the form is displaying a subset of the underlying table (a filtered view), not all the records.
7. Use the navigation buttons to scroll through a few of the records.

8. When you are done, select Remove Filter/Sort from the Records menu or click the Remove Filter button (the funnel in Figure 2.34) found on the toolbar. The Remove Filter toolbar button is renamed Apply Filter when not engaged. You can toggle the filter on and off by clicking the button on and off.
9. Close the form.

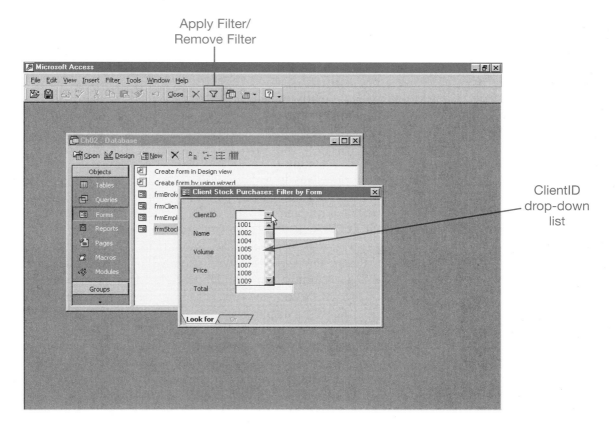

**Figure 2.34**   Filter By Form example.

You can choose to filter by any form field. Repeat steps 1 through 3 and select the field by which you want to filter. Then, clear the other fields, otherwise other field values will further restrict the records that are retrieved. Try it yourself. See if you can display in the *frmStock* form information about clients who own Microsoft stock.

Using Filter By Selection works almost the same way. When you choose Filter By Selection, it filters records shown in the form based on the currently selected data. To Filter By Selection, select a field or part of a field in a form and then click Filter By Selection. Only records matching the selected value are displayed in the form.

## Printing a Form

Though forms are best suited for onscreen work, they can be printed. To print one record, open the form, locate the record, and click the File menu Print command. (If you click the toolbar Print button, *all* forms begin printing—something you probably do not want to do.) When the Print dialog box is displayed, click the *Selected Record(s)* option button, and click OK. You will notice that neither the form's Title bar nor its navigation buttons appears on the printout.

Printing a range of records is an equally straightforward process. Select Print from the File menu, click the Pages option button, enter the beginning and ending page numbers in the two page range boxes, and click OK. Table rows are printed in the format of the displayed form. However, you probably will not want to print more than a few records this way. There is a better way to print larger amounts of information from tables. An Access report is the most efficient way to design and produce tabular output of the records in a table or a query result. Access reports are introduced next.

## DESIGNING REPORTS

Producing reports could not be much easier than the click of a button or two. Frequently, you will want either to preview a report onscreen or to produce a printed report, which you can pass around at a meeting or keep as a permanent record. Access reports are just that—reports. You cannot enter data or edit data in a report. Reports range from simple, utilitarian designs to professional-looking reports replete with attractive typefaces, drop shadows, and graphics.

## Previewing a Report

Reports typically display information from a table, a collection of related tables, or a query. We have created a report from the query you examined earlier (Figure 2.26). Though a lot can be gained from looking at the query's results onscreen, it is even more useful to have a printed report. The report you are about to preview and then print has some added features that make the information delivered by the query *qryStockValue* (Figure 2.26) more understandable and useful. First, let's learn how to open a stored report definition and preview the report prior to actually printing it. Switch to the Database window (click the Database Window button on the toolbar). Then complete the following exercise to display a report.

EXERCISE 2.15: LOADING AND PREVIEWING A REPORT

1. Click Reports in the Objects bar of the Database window. A list of available reports appears.
2. Click the report named *rptClientStocks* and click the Preview button. A preview of the report will be displayed in the Print Preview window.

3. Click the Maximize button to display the whole window and use the scroll bars to pan the report. Click the mouse to zoom out and zoom in. Figure 2.35 shows the report preview.
4. Close the report if you wish, or continue examining the report by following the directions in the paragraph that follows.

| Client ID | Stock Name | Volume | Price | Total Price |
|-----------|------------|--------|-------|-------------|
| **1001** | | | | |
| | Bank America | 200 | $74.44 | $14,888.00 |
| | Bio-tech | 17 | $8.40 | $142.80 |
| | Chase Manhattan | 43 | $81.94 | $3,523.42 |
| | Cisco Systems | 275 | $66.63 | $18,323.25 |
| | Commodore Holdings | 200 | $6.50 | $1,300.00 |
| | Creative Computers | 125 | $7.78 | $972.50 |
| | General Datacomm | 125 | $2.88 | $360.00 |
| | Monsanto | 200 | $40.63 | $8,126.00 |
| | | | | $47,635.97 |
| **1002** | | | | |
| | Adobe | 250 | $87.25 | $21,812.50 |
| | Alliedsignal | 200 | $66.50 | $13,300.00 |
| | Alloy Online | 200 | $11.31 | $2,262.00 |
| | Amazon.com | 100 | $139.25 | $13,925.00 |
| | Apple Computer | 300 | $54.44 | $16,332.00 |
| | Autodesk | 100 | $28.75 | $2,875.00 |
| | Bristol-Myers-Squib | 125 | $75.50 | $9,437.50 |
| | Circuit City Stores | 100 | $4.87 | $487.00 |
| | Computer Task Group | 200 | $16.38 | $3,276.00 |
| | Digital Link | 50 | $9.87 | $493.50 |

**Figure 2.35**   Previewing a report.

Use the Report window's scroll bars to move around the displayed page. To move to another page, use the navigation buttons in the lower left corner of the Print Preview window. You can also use the arrow keys and the PgUp and PgDn keys to move around the report. Take a few moments to try out the page navigation buttons. Go to the last report page, and then go back to the first. There is a brief pause as Access moves to a particular page and repaints the Print Preview window. Experiment with printing a report page. Select Print from the File menu, click the Pages option, enter a page range to print, and click OK to start the printing process. Close the report by clicking the Close button in the upper right corner of the Print Preview window. The Database window for Ch02 is redisplayed.

Now that you have seen an example of a report based on a query and how to preview and print it, let's create a simple report. It is based on the *tblClient* table.

## Creating a Report Quickly

Creating a report from a table is similar to creating a form from a table. You select a table name in the Database window, click the New Object toolbar button, and select AutoReport from the drop-down list. A default-format report appears. In the following exercise you will create an AutoReport based on the Client table.

EXERCISE 2.16: CREATING A REPORT QUICKLY

1. Click Tables in the Object bar of the Ch02 Database window.
2. Click *tblClient* from the list of tables (highlight its name, but do not open the table).
3. Click Insert on the menu bar and then click AutoReport. The default style report is displayed in a Print Preview window (see Figure 2.36).

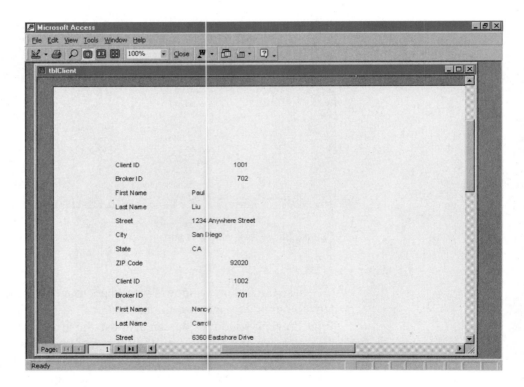

**Figure 2.36**　Typical AutoReport-style report.

By default, an AutoReport-generated report contains each table field arranged vertically, one above the other, with the numeric data fields right aligned and the character fields left aligned. You can easily change any of these elements or remove them. However, you must display the report in Design view to make structural changes to any report.

Click the Close button located on the Print Preview toolbar (or select Design View from the View menu). The report's design is displayed in the Design view window. Figure 2.37 shows the Client report's design.

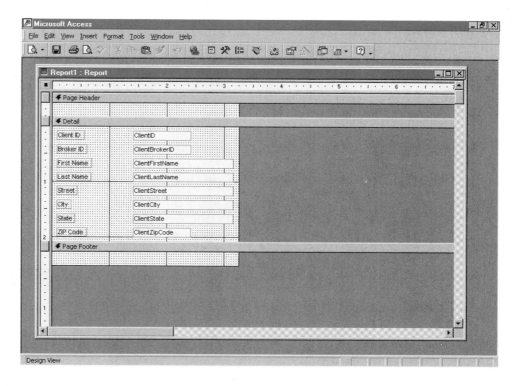

**Figure 2.37** Report design.

In the Design window, you can change a report in many ways. For instance, you can remove a report field by selecting it with the mouse and then pressing the Delete key after the square selection handles appear surrounding the field. If you make a mistake, remember you can use the Undo command (Undo Delete in this case) in the Edit menu.

**Saving a Report**    Reports are saved like any other objects described in this text—by selecting the Save or Save As command from the File menu.

EXERCISE 2.17: SAVING A REPORT

1. Select the Save As command from the File menu. The Save As dialog box appears.
2. Type *rptClientTest* in the upper text box, labeled *Save Report 'Report1' To:* That label is the report's name, and it is listed along with the other Report objects in the database.
3. Click OK to complete the save operation.

**SUMMARY**

You have learned a great deal about database systems in general and the Access database system in particular. You understand what a relational database is and why it is the best choice for dealing with related sets of information. Tables are the building blocks of a database system and consist of columns and rows.

Tables can be manipulated in several ways to produce the result you want. Table rows can be maintained in order when a table has a primary key. The navigation buttons in the Table window facilitate moving to various rows in a table. You can move a column in a table to another position by dragging its heading left or right. This alters the table's display characteristics but does not actually alter a column's position in the stored table.

In addition to tables, Access contains other objects including queries, forms, and reports. Queries, or questions, use the Query by Example method to pose questions about the data stored in one or more tables. Able to retrieve a subset of rows or columns, queries narrow the search for relevant information to just those elements of interest. You learned how to create queries using simple criteria as well as more complex expressions involving comparison operators. You created AND criteria in which two or more conditions must be simultaneously true. You saw that OR criteria are created by placing conditions on two or more rows of the query model. Besides selection queries, you learned how to create a variety of action queries, which alter the database's tables.

Forms provide a simpler interface to tables, because only one row at a time is displayed. You used a form and created a quick form from a table. Forms can be made to look like paper forms encountered in a business. When a form resembles an existing paper one already in use, the computer form is rather intuitive and easy to use. You learned that by merely clicking a form entry and typing, you can change a table's data. When you move to a new record, the change is then posted to the table. And you learned that you can filter data through a table, thereby restricting which table rows are shown in a form.

Finally, you got a brief look at the hard copy output facility of Access: the report. First, you previewed an existing report. Then, you created an AutoReport for a table. Reports provide a way to print and summarize information from one or more tables in a pleasant-looking format. Reports are output only. You cannot change a table's contents with a report.

This chapter has given you the fundamental tools to begin using Access to build systems. In Chapter 3, we introduce more formal foundations of relational database management systems. In that chapter you will learn about some rules and techniques that will help you design and build accounting information systems using tables, which are well-suited for the purpose.

# QUESTIONS AND PROBLEMS FOR REVIEW

## MULTIPLE-CHOICE QUESTIONS

1. Access is a(n) _____ database management system.
   a. algebraic
   b. flat file
   c. strictly Windows-based
   d. relational
2. Access help screens
   a. are only available when no Access table windows are open.
   b. can be printed for handy reference.
   c. only give information about Windows in general.
   d. are for advanced uses beyond the scope of this text.
3. The structure holding the result of a query is called the
   a. primary key.
   b. open query.
   c. dynaset.
   d. relational operator.
4. _____ are the fundamental storage structures for data.
   a. Forms
   b. Spreadsheets
   c. Tables
   d. Queries
5. A _____ is a question you can ask about your data in tables.
   a. help command
   b. query
   c. form
   d. request
6. You can examine your data in which of the following structures?
   a. table
   b. form
   c. report
   d. all of the above

7. A query can involve
   a. one table.
   b. two tables.
   c. three tables.
   d. all of the above.
8. An example of a logical operator that can be placed in a selection criteria of a query when you want two conditions to be true at once is
   a. but.
   b. nor.
   c. and.
   d. none of the above.
9. _____ provide a convenient, less cluttered work surface through which you can enter or alter table information.
   a. Forms
   b. Reports
   c. Conditional operators
   d. all of the above
10. Reports
    a. are output only—no table data can be altered with a report.
    b. can be used to change a table's information.
    c. can only be printed.
    d. all of the above.

## DISCUSSION QUESTIONS

1. Describe the Access work surface icons, discuss their uses, and tell how they differ from the menu commands.
2. Discuss when it is advantageous to view your data in a Table window and when a Form window is better. Explain your reasons.
3. List the steps necessary to open and display database tables.
4. Discuss why you would use database queries to retrieve information.
5. Describe the different ways to design a database report and discuss the possible situations where you might use these different designs.

## PROBLEMS

**Note:** Before doing any of the following exercises, first copy *Ch02.mdb* from your Companion CD to the hard drive of the computer on which you are working. Then, clear the copied database's Read-only file attribute (see Chapter 1, Exercise 1.14, *Clearing a File's Read-Only Property*). Having done that you can complete each exercise using the copy of the Companion CD database.

1. Sort the *tblClient* table on the ClientState and ClientCity fields so that the rows are in order first by state (A to Z) and then city (A to Z) within each state. Print the sorted table directly from the Table window.

2. Create and execute a query based on the *tblClient* table that displays which clients are assigned broker 702. Display only the columns ClientFirstName, ClientLastName, ClientID, and ClientBrokerID (in that order, left to right). The query should sort the rows into descending order by the clients' names (like a telephone book listing does). Print the resulting dynaset.

3. Run the query *qryClient1015Stock* found in the query list for the Ch02 database. It produces a list of client 1015's stock purchases in ascending order by transaction identification number. Change the sort order of the rows so that the query returns rows in Price order (low to high). Print the dynaset. Then modify the sort order so that the dynaset is sorted in descending order (high to low) by the Volume column. Print the dynaset. Can you combine these sort criteria so that the dynaset is sorted first in descending order by Volume and then in ascending order by Price within matching volumes? Try it. Print the third dynaset. Remember to write your name on all three printed dynasets.

4. You can create an AutoForm from a query in exactly the same way you do from a table. Create an AutoForm for the query called *qryStockValue* in the query list for the database Ch02. Begin by selecting the query from the list. Click the AutoForm button. When you are done, save the form design under the name *frmAutoForm*. Turn in a printed copy of the first two pages of the form. Remember to write your name on the output.

5. Create an AutoReport report for the *tblStock* table found in the Ch02 database. Print only the first two pages of the report. Print your name on the report. If you feel adventuresome, try adding a label containing your name in the report in either the report header or the page header.

# 3 DATABASES AND ACCOUNTING SYSTEMS

## OBJECTIVES

This chapter introduces database accounting systems and compares them to the double-entry bookkeeping systems with which you are already familiar. It also explains how accountants break down business activities into transaction cycles and how database accounting systems use those transaction cycles as organizing themes. This chapter covers the theoretical foundations for database accounting systems and contains practical examples of applying database theory. You will learn about the connection between accounting systems and database systems, why a relational database system is the best choice for capturing accounting information, and some of the theory and history of relational database management systems. Just enough theory is provided to aid you in creating efficient, optimal database objects, but the discussion avoids presenting more database theory than you need. In this chapter, you will learn about:

- Differences between double-entry bookkeeping and database accounting systems.
- Advantages and disadvantages of database accounting systems.
- Business activity classifications.
- Transaction cycles.
- The relationship between accounting systems and database systems.
- A brief history leading to the development of database management systems.
- Functions of database management systems.
- Theory and application of relational database management systems.
- The structure of database objects that store accounting events.
- Why it is important to optimize tables using normalization procedures.
- Performing database selections, projections, and joins.

This chapter will help you understand the differences between double-entry bookkeeping and database accounting. The information about business activity classifications and transaction cycles will provide a framework that will help you apply your knowledge of Microsoft Access to the task of building accounting database components.

This chapter introduces you to a classic accounting application involving processing and maintaining invoice data that illustrates the principles we discuss. The fictitious company, a coffee bean and tea wholesaler called The Coffee Merchant, purchases whole-bean coffees and teas at international auctions and sells the coffees and teas to a variety of coffee roasters.

Let's start by examining briefly the connection between accounting and database systems. That is, how did accounting come to embrace relational database management systems?

## INTRODUCTION

Most accounting students learn the mechanics of accounting for economic transactions using the tools of manual double-entry bookkeeping such as journals and ledgers. This chapter begins with a discussion of the differences between database accounting systems and manual double-entry bookkeeping systems. We then explain the advantages and disadvantages of using a database approach to building accounting systems.

The chapter's discussion of business activity classifications then introduces three levels of complexity that accountants use to classify firms. These classifications will help you understand when to incorporate particular database features into your accounting database system designs. Finally, the chapter describes transaction cycles, which provide a way for accountants and others to classify economic events into related categories.

Many students have learned how to use Microsoft Access as a software application but have not learned much of the database theory that is essential for creating complex applications such as accounting systems. Chapters 4 and 5 describe how to use database software to build accounting system elements for a specific transaction cycle, Chapter 6 presents a revenue cycle system, and Chapters 7 through 9 describe purchase, payroll, and production cycles, respectively. In these chapters, we describe details of the database table fields and show you how to create forms, queries, and reports to accomplish accounting tasks in two major transaction cycles.

## DATABASE ACCOUNTING SYSTEMS

Much of the current interest in using databases for accounting systems arose as businesses saw the advantages of relational databases such as Microsoft Access for all their information processing needs. Rather than maintain separate files and programs for each business function, firms are trying to consolidate their data and data-handling operations. Some firms have created enterprise-wide databases that store all of the firm's information in one system.

## Events-Based Theories of Accounting

Over the past thirty years, researchers such as William McCarthy and George Sorter have developed and refined various events-based approaches to accounting theory. Their work provides a solid theoretical underpinning for accountants' increasing use of relational databases to perform accounting tasks. These events-based approaches argue that accountants should strive to store all relevant attributes of economic events in a readily accessible form. Relational database software, such as Microsoft Access, provides a tool that accountants can use to accomplish that objective.

## Double-Entry Bookkeeping vs. Database Accounting

For many years, double-entry bookkeeping provided an excellent method for recording transactions. It satisfied accountants' need to capture the essence of each transaction. When double-entry bookkeeping was first developed over five hundred years ago, the costs of gathering and storing information were very high. Recording transactions with pen and paper was a time-consuming task. Double-entry bookkeeping gave accountants a valuable tool that quickly identified essential elements of transactions. Therefore, double-entry bookkeeping let businesspersons capture and store key attributes of transactions in a highly aggregated form. This helped keep the cost of information gathering and storage at affordable levels. Also, the debit-credit balancing check provided an important internal control feature in manual accounting systems.

### Try it

If you would like to see how far we have come in replacing manual accounting systems with database systems, go to your local office supplies store and try to find a pad of two-column accounting paper. If you have trouble finding it, ask a salesperson for help. He or she will probably look up the product's location—in the store's computerized inventory database.

Computerized transaction processing has released accountants from the limitations and drudgery of manual accounting systems. Using computers, we can now capture a wide variety of information about each transaction quite easily. For example, supermarkets and other retail stores routinely read bar codes at checkout stations to capture the date and time of purchase, the identity of the item purchased, the store location, the checkout station number, and the cashier number. Even more important is that they obtain all of this information with one quick swipe!

Technologies such as bar code readers and optical scanners have played a major role in reducing the cost of acquiring and storing multiple attributes of each economic event. To see more clearly how double-entry bookkeeping and database accounting differ, let's consider a simple sales transaction. Most sales transactions begin when a customer sends a purchase order. If the firm receiving the purchase order has the goods in stock and finds the customer's credit to be acceptable, the firm ships the ordered goods and invoices the customer. A double-entry bookkeeping system would record this transaction for the selling firm with the following journal entry:

| Date | Account | Debit | Credit |
|------|---------|-------|--------|
| *Date* | *Accounts Receivable* | *Amount* | |
| | *Sales* | | *Amount* |
| | *Explanation* | | |

Note that this journal entry includes five items of information:

• Transaction date

• Names of the accounts debited

• Names of the accounts credited

• Transaction amount

• Explanation of the transaction

In a general journal entry such as the one shown above, the explanation might contain the name of the customer. Firms that use specialized journals and subsidiary ledgers can store one additional information item, the customer's name or account code. For example, if the above journal entry had been posted to a subsidiary ledger, the record keeping process would store the customer's name or account code in the subsidiary ledger. If the sale had been recorded in a specialized sales journal instead of in a general journal as shown above, the format would differ. For example, the account names might be implied by the transaction appearing in the sales journal rather than being explicitly stated; the information recorded would be the same in both cases. To summarize, a double-entry bookkeeping system records five or six transaction attributes and records one of them, the amount, twice.

Now let's consider how a relational database accounting system might handle the same transaction. A database accounting system would record the transaction in a set of database tables similar to those that appear in Figure 3.1.

The database system shown in Figure 3.1 stores some attributes of the sales transaction in the Sales table, which appears in the figure as *tblSales*. We use the "tbl" prefix in this book to indicate that the Access object is a table. We use similar prefixes for other Access objects, including "frm" for forms, "rpt" for reports, and "qry" for queries.

Note, however, that many other attributes of the sales transaction are stored in the seven other tables that appear in Figure 3.1. A database accounting system

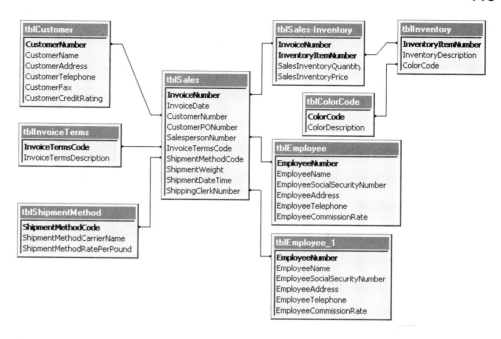

**Figure 3.1**   Sales transactions stored in a database accounting system.

can store many more attributes of the sales transaction than a journal entry can store. Note that this database accounting system for sales information stores these attributes in an atomic form, scattered throughout the tables. In Chapter 2 you learned a number of rules for designing effective database tables that store information attributes in multiple tables, yet allow the information to be pulled back together when needed. One of these rules requires you to establish a primary key for each table. The primary key consists of one or more fields in each table that provides a unique identifier for each row in the table. The primary key fields of the tables in Figure 3.1 are shown in bold type.

The database system shown in Figure 3.1 stores 10 transaction attributes in the *tblSales* table and a virtually unlimited number of attributes in the other tables. For example, if the invoice included 20 items, the *tblSales-Inventory* table would store 40 attributes (20 item quantities and 20 item prices) for the transaction. Contrast this with the information stored in the double-entry bookkeeping journal entry. The journal entry does not even tell you how many items were on the invoice, much less tell you anything about those items.

Not only does the database accounting system store many more attributes than the double-entry bookkeeping system, it does so efficiently. A key feature of relational database software such as Microsoft Access is that it allows table designs that reduce or eliminate the storage of redundant information. For the sales information database in Figure 3.1, let's examine what is stored in each table, how the tables are linked, and how we might extract information from this sales system.

The primary key of *tblSales* is the InvoiceNumber field. The other attributes of the sale that are stored exclusively in this table include the invoice date, the customer's purchase order number, the shipping weight of the items sold, and a shipping date-time stamp. The other five fields in *tblSales* are foreign key fields. Access, like many other relational database software packages, uses links between primary key fields and corresponding foreign key fields in other tables to maintain the connections among information attributes. The foreign keys in Figure 3.1 show the links from *tblSales* to other tables that contain information about sales.

Foreign key links help accountants avoid recording information more than once. For example, the first foreign key field in *tblSales* is CustomerNumber, which links *tblSales* to *tblCustomer*. Instead of storing customers' names, addresses, and other information in *tblSales* repeatedly for every invoice, this database design lets you store customer information once for each customer and link it to individual sales by including just one field, the CustomerNumber field, in *tblSales*.

The other foreign keys in *tblSales* are SalespersonNumber, InvoiceTermsCode, ShipmentMethodCode, and ShippingClerkNumber. The InvoiceTermsCode links each sale to a table of invoice terms, such as cash, 2/10 net 30, 1/15 net 30, or net 30. If these terms were entered directly in *tblSales*, each input clerk might enter them differently and corrupt the sales database. The ShipmentMethodCode performs a similar error-control function.

### Try it

With several other members of your class, see how many different logical ways you can record the names of the shipping firms with which you are familiar. You might be surprised at how many variations you can create.

The SalespersonNumber and the ShippingClerkNumber foreign key fields contain the identification numbers for these two employee participants in sales transactions. Although Figure 3.1 shows *tblEmployee* twice to accommodate these two links, the firm has only one Employee table.

The primary key of *tblSales*, InvoiceNumber, participates in a link to *tblInventory* as part of the primary key in *tblSales-Inventory*. Since this primary key includes two fields, it is called a composite primary key. As you may know from your previous work with Microsoft Access, the only way to link two tables that have a many-to-many relationship is through a relationship table. In a sales transaction, each invoice can have many inventory items. Also, each inventory item can appear on many different invoices. In this sales system, *tblSales-Inventory* is the relationship table that models the many-to-many relationship between *tblSales* and *tblInventory*. Its composite primary key includes two fields that link to the primary keys of the two tables that participate in the relationship.

Note that the database system records directly only some of the items that the double-entry bookkeeping system records. The database system records directly the date of the sale, the customer number, and the nature of the transaction as a sale. The database system does not record directly the transaction as an element of accounts receivable. Since sales transactions constitute the left side of the accounts receivable account, storing information about sales in the tables that appear in Figure 3.1 is sufficient in a database accounting system.

To calculate the amount of a particular invoice—the amount that the double-entry bookkeeping system recorded twice in the journal entry—an accountant using a database system would run a query that links *tblSales* with *tblSales-Inventory* and *tblShipmentMethod*. The query would obtain the SalesInventoryQuantity and SalesInventoryPrice for each InventoryItemNumber in *tblSales-Inventory* for the InvoiceNumber. The query would also obtain the ShipmentMethodRatePerPound from *tblShipmentMethod* and the ShipmentWeight from *tblSales*. The query would then multiply the SalesInventoryQuantity by the SalesInventoryPrice for each InventoryItemNumber and multiply the invoice's ShipmentWeight by the ShipmentMethodRatePerPound for the ShipmentMethodCode on the invoice. Finally, the query would sum these products to determine the amount of the invoice.

Although database theory argues against storing calculated fields in relational databases, accounting databases sometimes store intermediate calculation results such as this invoice amount calculation. Accountants violate the strict database rules to increase processing efficiency when the database must handle large amounts of repetitive transaction data. Accountants do this reluctantly and avoid storing calculated fields whenever possible.

The database approach can do anything that double-entry bookkeeping can do and more. Accountants can use the database tables in Figure 3.1 to calculate invoice amounts and generate the same accounts receivable records and financial statement amounts that they could with journals and ledgers. The real power of using relational databases to store accounting information arises when managers need specific information that they did not know they would need when the system was created. For example, if a manager wanted to know how many green-colored inventory items were sold during March of last year, the journals and ledgers of double-entry bookkeeping would be virtually useless. Using our database accounting system for sales, however, we could quickly provide the manager with an answer that includes number of items and sales in dollars. We could even offer to generate subtotals by customer or geographic location for both number of items and sales in dollars.

### Try it

Examine Figure 3.1 carefully. Identify interesting facts about the firm's sales and sales-related activities that you might find or calculate by searching the database tables and combining the information attributes they contain.

As you can see, relational databases record far more information for each transaction than a traditional double-entry bookkeeping system can record. A database accounting system also provides a flexible web of information relating a firm's economic events to each other. In the next two sections, we discuss some of the advantages and disadvantages of using database management systems in accounting applications.

## Advantages of Database Accounting Systems

Manual double-entry bookkeeping systems can be very efficient; however, computer implementations of double-entry bookkeeping use a flat file processing design. In manual systems, the dual nature of the accounting debit and credit model provides a built-in error correction mechanism. In automated systems, this same duality is inefficient and serves no real control purpose.

Database accounting systems store data only once. This feature leads to a number of advantages over flat file double-entry accounting systems. A database accounting system can:

- Reduce data storage costs
- Eliminate data redundancy
- Eliminate data inconsistencies
- Avoid duplicate processing
- Ease add, delete, and update data maintenance tasks
- Make data independent of applications
- Centralize data management
- Centralize data security

Database accounting systems offer greater flexibility in extracting data than flat file double-entry accounting systems. This flexibility leads to other advantages. For example, a database accounting system can:

- Ease report modifications and updates
- Provide *ad hoc* query capabilities
- Facilitate cross-functional data analysis
- Permit multiple users simultaneous data access

Database accounting systems also provide data entry and integrity controls as part of the database management system. Accounting systems designers can embed these controls into the structure of the tables as they create them, which eliminates the need to program controls into every application that uses the tables' data.

Because a database stores data only once, the storage costs will be lower than for a flat file system that requires redundant storage. By avoiding the need to store data in multiple locations throughout the system, a database accounting system prevents users from creating data inconsistencies. For example, when a customer address changes, a database accounting system needs to make the change only once, in the Customer table. Every application that uses customer addresses—which may include invoicing, billing, sales promotions, marketing surveys, and sales summaries—automatically begins using the updated address from the Customer table as soon as it is entered. Data inconsistencies can be a source of many potentially embarrassing problems for businesses. Since data is entered only once, the tasks of adding, deleting, and updating records can be accomplished more efficiently. By avoiding data redundancy, a database approach also ensures that the data items used in accounting applications will have the same field names, field lengths, and data types as other applications.

Centralizing data management and security lets businesses fix responsibility for these functions on one person or group. By concentrating this activity, a database approach enables the person or persons responsible for data management and security to develop valuable expertise in this function. When a firm adopts a database approach to managing its data, it usually hires a database administrator. The database administrator holds ultimate responsibility for the specifications and structure of all database tables in the information system. The database administrator is also responsible for enforcing security, making backups, and coordinating contingency plans for emergency situations.

Having the best collection of data in the world will not do managers any good if they cannot access it. A major advantage of database accounting systems is that they facilitate users' access to accounting data. By providing intuitive, graphically based report generators, database management software such as Microsoft Access allows accountants to easily change the structure and format of their reports.

One of the most difficult challenges of designing any accounting system has always been the task of creating reports. Designers found it very hard to anticipate every report that accountants and managers using the system might ever want because they had to do it before the system even existed. The powerful query languages built into Access and other database management systems make this task much easier. Queries let users ask database accounting systems for information by combining data tables and performing calculations in ways the systems' designers never imagined. Further, these user-designed queries and reports can access more than accounting data. For example, tables containing marketing and production information can be combined with accounting information tables to create truly cross-functional reports. This *ad hoc* querying and report-generating capability is one of the key advantages of using an accounting system built with relational database software.

Finally, database accounting systems implement many important data input and data integrity controls at the database level. In Chapters 4 and 10, you will learn how to create accounting data tables that include validity checks, existence checks, reasonableness checks, and limit controls for the sales and purchases cycles of accounting systems. By implementing these controls as part of the database, you avoid the need to include the controls in every application that uses the data.

## Disadvantages of Database Accounting Systems

Despite the long list of advantages outlined in the previous section, database accounting systems do have some disadvantages. The increased functionality of a database system does not come free—the higher price tag for a database system can include costs for items such as:

- Greater hardware requirements
- The database software itself
- Employing a database administrator

Although centralizing management and security control functions in a firm can be advantageous, such centralization can create drawbacks such as:

- The system operation becomes critical
- Incorrect data entry corrupts many users' work
- Territorial disputes over data ownership may arise

One last disadvantage that accountants occasionally note, a disadvantage that is more psychological than real, is accountants' distrust of single-entry accounting systems in general. Double-entry bookkeeping is so pervasive in accounting education and practice that most accountants automatically question and fear anything else.

The increased cost of a database accounting system is often offset by reduced needs for data storage and reduced programming costs. The elimination of data redundancy in a database system reduces the data storage capacity required. Since the data table structures can include many data entry and integrity controls, application programming is simplified—and simpler programming takes less time and costs less money.

The centralization of data and security control is a double-edged sword. Centralization puts all of a firm's information eggs in one basket, and that increases risk. However, it also allows a focusing of resources on contingency planning, security, backup, and recovery that can actually reduce risk levels.

Many firms have decided that the advantages offered by database accounting systems outweigh the disadvantages. Most new accounting system implementations are built using relational database systems. We expect this trend to continue as database management software becomes less expensive, more capable, and easier to use.

## BUSINESS ACTIVITY CLASSIFICATIONS

Different businesses require different kinds of accounting information systems. The size of a business determines part of its accounting information requirements. Larger businesses process more transactions and require greater computing capacity than smaller businesses. However, dollar volume alone is not always a good indicator of the kind of information systems a firm needs. The complexity of a firm's business activities also has a significant effect on its accounting system design. Accountants classify the complexity of firms' business activities using three broad categories: service, merchandising, and manufacturing. Not all businesses fit neatly into one of these categories, but the categories provide a good beginning reference point when considering accounting information system options.

## Service Firms

Service firms comprise the simplest form of business activity. They provide their customers or clients a service for which they charge a fee. Service firms' accounting information systems track revenues and expenses only; they do not need to track inventory information because service firms do not have inventory. Examples of service firms include:

- Accounting firms
- Advertising agencies
- Barbershops
- Entertainers
- Interior decorators
- Law firms
- Management consulting firms
- Physicians
- Realtors
- Trucking companies

You can see the simplicity of service firm accounting system requirements by examining the income statement in Figure 3.2.

This income statement shows revenues and expenses. The expenses are shown in one list; they are not broken down into categories of expenses. The most important information that most service firms must track is information about revenues. Some service firms also need detailed information about their expenses, including salaries paid to employees.

## Merchandising Firms

Merchandising firms are the next step up in complexity from service firms. The goal of merchandising firms is to buy goods at a low enough cost and sell those goods at a high enough price to earn a margin that will cover other expenses and provide a profit. Examples of merchandising firms include:

- Computer stores
- Department stores
- Discount merchandise chains

**Example Service Firm
Income Statement
Year Ended December 31, 2001**

| | | |
|---|---:|---:|
| Revenue | | $353,150 |
| | | |
| Expenses: | | |
| Advertising | $ 42,170 | |
| Depreciation | 27,640 | |
| Insurance | 9,420 | |
| Salaries | 94,210 | |
| Rent | 106,400 | |
| Other | 62,180 | 342,020 |
| | | |
| Net income | | $ 11,130 |

**Figure 3.2**  Example Service Firm income statement.

- Food markets
- Hardware stores
- Health food stores
- Mail-order merchandisers
- Office supply stores
- Shoe stores
- Wholesalers

Merchandising firms' accounting information systems must track revenues and expenses, just like service firms' systems. However, the single largest expense for merchandising firms is the cost of goods that they have sold. A merchandising firm's income statement devotes a separate section to the cost of goods sold calculation. Because firms often buy goods in one period and sell those goods in the next period, their accounting systems must also track inventory. Figure 3.3 contains an example of a merchandising firm's income statement.

Note how the merchandising firm's income statement uses beginning and ending inventory in the cost of goods sold calculation. You should recall from your earlier accounting courses that the purchases amount shown on this income statement is net of purchase returns and allowances and includes freight on incoming inventory shipments. Merchandising firms track detailed information about their sales and expenses. Many merchandising firms maintain comprehensive records of which products were sold along with the locations and dates the

**Example Merchandising Firm**
**Income Statement**
**Year Ended December 31, 2001**

| | | |
|---|---:|---:|
| Sales | | $822,370 |
| | | |
| Cost of goods sold: | | |
| Beginning finished goods inventory | $ 59,530 | |
| Purchases | 472,930 | |
| Less: Ending finished goods inventory | (63,240) | 469,220 |
| | | |
| Gross profit | | $353,150 |
| | | |
| Selling and adminstrative expenses: | | |
| Advertising | $ 42,170 | |
| Depreciation | 27,640 | |
| Insurance | 9,420 | |
| Salaries | 94,210 | |
| Rent | 106,400 | |
| Other | 62,180 | 342,020 |
| | | |
| Net income | | $ 11,130 |

**Figure 3.3** Example Merchandising Firm income statement.

products were sold. Some merchandising firms even record the times at which products were ordered and shipped.

## Manufacturing Firms

The most structurally complex type of firm is the manufacturing firm. In addition to the activities that merchandising firms undertake, manufacturing firms produce the goods that they sell. Examples of manufacturing firms include:

- Automobile manufacturers
- Canneries
- Construction firms
- Farmers
- Machine tool manufacturers
- Meat packers
- Oil refineries

- Pharmaceutical firms
- Restaurants
- Steel mills

All manufacturing firms engage in similar types of activities even though they create and sell a wide variety of products. Manufacturing firms must engage in activities such as:

- Purchasing raw materials and labor
- Incurring other manufacturing costs
- Processing the raw materials, labor, and other manufacturing costs into finished goods
- Selling the finished goods

A manufacturing firm's accounting information system must track information about all four of these activities. Therefore, a manufacturing firm's system must track the service and merchandising firm activities of purchasing and selling and must bear the additional burden of tracking acquisition costs through the production activity. Figure 3.4 contains an example of a manufacturing firm's income statement.

The manufacturing firm's income statement reflects the increased complexity of its activities. The merchandising firm's *Cost of goods sold* section has expanded to include the three manufacturing costs: direct materials, direct labor, and manufacturing overhead. These costs, adjusted by beginning and ending work-in-process inventories, are shown on the income statement in Figure 3.4 as the *Cost of goods manufactured*. The cost of goods manufactured was $472,930. The cost of goods manufactured is analogous to purchases on a merchandising firm's income statement.

Manufacturing firms are not the only firms using manufacturing accounting systems today. Many service and merchandising firms now use accounting systems based on the manufacturing systems model. For example, many law firms now use a manufacturing-style job-order cost accounting system that treats each case as a separate job. Service firms have found it useful to track details about key business processes using accounting systems that were originally designed for manufacturing applications.

Now that we have seen how the different levels of complexity in the three business activity categories affect a firm's income statements and cost-accumulation procedures, we can discuss accounting information system requirements for each category. These accounting information system requirements are often expressed in terms of transaction cycles.

## TRANSACTION CYCLES

Most accounting information systems and auditing textbooks are organized around business cycles. Some authors refer to these cycles as transaction cycles

**Example Manufacturing Firm**
**Income Statement**
**Year Ended December 31, 2001**

| | | | |
|---|---|---|---|
| Sales | | | $822,370 |
| | | | |
| Cost of goods sold: | | | |
| Beginning finished goods inventory | | $ 59,530 | |
| Cost of goods manufactured: | | | |
| Beginning work-in-process inventory | $ 44,900 | | |
| Direct materials: | | | |
| Beginning inventory | $ 26,270 | | |
| Purchases | 98,910 | | |
| Less: Ending inventory | (28,360) | 96,820 | |
| Direct labor | | 153,460 | |
| Manufacturing overhead | | 210,600 | |
| Less: Ending work-in-process inventory | | (32,850) | 472,930 |
| Less: Ending finished goods inventory | | | (63,240) | 469,220 |
| | | | |
| Gross profit | | | $353,150 |
| | | | |
| Selling and adminstrative expenses: | | | |
| Advertising | | $ 42,170 | |
| Depreciation | | 27,640 | |
| Insurance | | 9,420 | |
| Salaries | | 94,210 | |
| Rent | | 106,400 | |
| Other | | 62,180 | 342,020 |
| | | | |
| Net income | | | $ 11,130 |

**Figure 3.4** Example Manufacturing Firm income statement.

or accounting cycles. This framework, structuring accounting systems around cycles rather than financial statement accounts, is consistent with a database approach to accounting systems. A diagram of commonly used transaction cycles appears in Figure 3.5.

You can see how the transaction cycles relate to each other in Figure 3.5. In the revenue cycle, firms sell finished goods for cash or the promise to pay cash. This cash enters the financial cycle. In the financial cycle, firms obtain cash by issuing equity and debt securities. They also pay dividends on the equity securities and the interest and principal repayments on debt securities in the financial cycle.

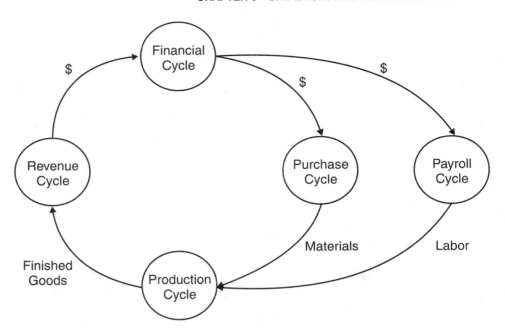

**Figure 3.5**  Transaction cycles.

Cash flows out of the financial cycle and into the purchase and payroll cycles. In the purchase cycle, the firm exchanges cash for materials, supplies, and other expenses related to providing products or services to its customers. In the payroll cycle, the firm exchanges cash for salaries and related labor costs. The production cycle converts materials, labor, and other acquired resources into finished goods, completing the cycle.

These exact cycle definitions are not universally accepted. For example, some accountants and systems designers include payroll activities in the purchase cycle since both payroll and purchase cycles culminate in writing a check. However, most accounting information systems texts treat payroll separately because payroll transaction processing is more complex and requires tables and calculations that the purchase cycle does not require. You may also see the revenue cycle divided into separate sales and cash receipts cycles. Similarly, the purchase cycle can be divided into separate purchase and cash disbursement cycles.

A firm may not have all of the transaction cycles depicted in Figure 3.5. For example, service and merchandising firms usually do have a production cycle. The purchase cycle in a merchandising firm acquires finished goods for resale; the purchase cycle in a manufacturing firm acquires raw materials and other resources for production. In many service firms, the purchase cycle is relatively unimportant, since revenue tracking is more important to those firms.

Most accounting information systems courses avoid extensive treatment of the transactions specific to the financial cycle because these transactions are few in number. However, auditing classes do spend significant time on financial cycle transactions because they are unusual and often involve large dollar amounts. The transactions that occur only in the financial cycle, such as stock issuances and large borrowings, are interesting but do not require highly complex information processing systems in most firms because of their infrequent occurrence.

Some accounting systems books describe a general ledger or financial reporting transaction cycle. When a firm uses database accounting, its financial reporting activities do not require it to record a separate set of transactions. These reporting activities merely query and summarize the data that the firm stores as it conducts its revenue, purchase, payroll, and production activities. Therefore, we do not treat financial reporting as a separate cycle in this book. The remainder of this chapter provides a brief introduction to the revenue, purchase, payroll, and production cycles.

## Revenue Cycle

The revenue cycle includes all sales and cash collection activities. The three main transactions that we must record in the revenue cycle are customer orders, sales, and customer payments. We must also record the shipment of goods if it occurs separately from the sales transaction. The revenue cycle accounting system must be able to generate documents and reports that include:

• Sales order reports

• Invoices

• Shipping documents

• Remittance advices

• Cash receipts summaries

• Sales analyses

• Balances owed by customers

Manufacturing, merchandising, and service firms all have similar revenue cycles. They all sell goods or services to customers and they all expect customers to pay them. A typical revenue cycle database would include the following data tables:

• Cash receipt

• Customer

• Finished goods inventory

• Sales

• Sales order

• Salesperson

The database design would also include necessary relationship tables, such as a Sales-Finished Goods Inventory table. We will explain how to build revenue cycle tables, forms, queries, and reports in Chapter 6.

## Purchase Cycle

A manufacturing firm's purchase cycle includes all activities related to ordering raw materials from vendors, receiving the materials ordered, and paying for the materials. A merchandising firm's purchase cycle includes the activities related to ordering, receiving, and paying for goods acquired for resale. If a service firm has a purchase cycle system, it will record the purchase of materials incidental to providing services, such as office supplies. The main transactions that we must record in the purchase cycle are purchase orders, receipt of goods ordered, and payments to vendors. The purchase cycle accounting system must generate documents and reports that include:

- Purchase orders
- Receiving reports
- Checks
- Backorder reports
- Purchase summaries
- Goods received summaries
- Balances owed to vendors

The details included in the purchase cycle tables will vary depending on whether the firm is service, merchandising, or manufacturing; a typical purchase cycle database would include the following data tables:

- Cash disbursement
- Purchase order
- Raw materials inventory
- Raw materials inventory receipt
- Vendor

The database design would also include necessary relationship tables, such as a Purchase Order-Raw Materials Inventory table. We will explain how to build specific purchase cycle tables, forms, queries, and reports in Chapter 7.

## Payroll Cycle

The payroll cycle includes the system elements needed to calculate employees' gross pay, deductions, and net pay. The payroll cycle must comply with a complex set of government regulations. The payroll cycle is closely related to the human resources management system in all firms—some firms have even integrated the two systems. The main transactions that occur in the payroll cycle are employees earn pay, the employer makes payments to employees, and the employer makes payments of payroll taxes and taxes withheld from employees' pay to various governmental entities. The payroll cycle must generate documents and reports that include:

- Employee time reports
- Employee commission reports
- Checks
- Payroll registers
- Employee earnings records

Manufacturing, merchandising, and service firms all have similar payroll cycles since they all have employees. A typical payroll cycle database would include the following data tables:

- Cash disbursement
- Employee
- Time worked

## Production Cycle

A manufacturing firm's production cycle converts raw materials and labor into finished goods. The production cycle accounting database must record the use of materials and labor in production and record the allocation of manufacturing overhead costs to units produced. Merchandising and service firms do not have a production cycle. The production cycle's main transactions are all cost flows and include:

- Materials inventory costs flow into production.
- Labor costs flow into production.
- Overhead costs are allocated to production.
- Total production costs flow into finished goods inventory.

The production cycle accounting system must generate documents and reports that include, for example, bills of materials and job cost reports. A typical production cycle database for a job-order manufacturing system might include the following data tables:

- Finished goods inventory
- Job
- Raw materials inventory
- Time worked

## ACCOUNTING INFORMATION SYSTEMS AND DATABASE SYSTEMS

Historically, accounting information has been captured in special ledgers and journals. Information about credit sales, for instance, would be recorded in a sales journal. Strict rules regarding how and where accounting information is recorded have been followed throughout time. Whenever management wanted to see an income statement, they could produce it with relative ease. Likewise, it was relatively easy to retrieve a balance sheet and other standard reports, because accounting systems were designed to produce those reports. Today's business world, however, requires more than the standard accounting reports for companies to be competitive and lean. Some reports cannot be obtained easily, if at all, using traditional double-entry accounting software. For example, it would be difficult for a manufacturer to obtain data about total monthly inventory spoilage from a traditional accounting system. Other valuable aggregations of data that provide pictures of a company's current financial or labor situation are not easily obtained with conventional accounting systems. Conventional aggregation methods provided by accounting systems have made valuable data inaccessible, except for the preparation of traditional financial reports.

Today, however, many modern accounting systems use a different approach. Database reports are steadily replacing traditional accounting reports. Advances in accounting practice and the advent of both inexpensive and widely available computer hardware and database management software have accelerated the move toward capturing accounting information in database systems. *Events accounting* consists of storing data about an economic event, such as a cash sale or receipt of a purchase order, in one or more database tables. Events accounting goes beyond merely recording the aggregate numbers associated with the event. Information recorded about an economic event can include who was involved (e.g., the customer's name), why the event occurred, when the event occurred, and what resources were affected by the event.

Events-based accounting systems avoid preconceived notions and implicit assumptions about how the information captured is to be aggregated, output, or used. Rather, the responsibility for gleaning information from accounting event data falls on the shoulders of the decision maker. An inventory manager, for example, can create (or request the creation of) a report to display current stock levels and the percentage change in stock levels from the previous month.

This is a significant change from accounting information systems that made use of the debit and credit method of recording transactions in a highly aggregated form. If managers need information from the accounting system to help make crucial decisions, they simply request the data they need and then review the resultant report. Managers and other decision makers need no longer rely exclusively on the standard financial statements and other reports produced by traditional accounting systems. Although some of the standard statements help managers make enterprise-wide decisions, much information is masked by the inherent aggregation that takes place in traditional accounting systems.

What you are studying here are accounting information systems implemented using database management systems. Because database management systems can store anything you want to record, they provide a wealth of information. Much useful business information can be gleaned from the data stored in a database's tables. As an emerging accounting information systems expert, you are on the leading edge of this significant shift to more useful accounting systems.

Next we discuss evolution of the database management systems and present some advantages and disadvantages of using database systems. We begin with a brief look at what software business tools were available before the advent of database systems.

## DATABASE MANAGEMENT SYSTEMS

Database management systems (DBMSs) are valuable to business enterprises because they provide the software to store, retrieve, and modify crucial business data. DBMSs can be very cost effective, even though the software is usually more expensive for large, mainframe computers. Assuming that a database system is an efficient way to manage both corporate and small business data, why is it cost effective? The next section briefly describes data management and reporting prior to the advent of database management systems. Subsequent sections describe the general capabilities of database management systems—what core services they typically provide—and the advantages and disadvantages of using database management systems.

## Pre-DBMS Data Acquisition and Reporting

In those adventurous years before the availability of modern database management systems, corporate data acquisition and reporting was far different from today. Let's suppose we have traveled back in time to the late 1960s, when the Beatles were still performing together and parents were convinced that long haircuts on young men were a sign of declining morality in the United States. Further, assume you are responsible for ensuring that business information about The Coffee Merchant's customers is kept on the corporate computer. The Coffee Merchant, a small coffee wholesaler, has a medium-sized minicomputer on-site. The data processing department has a staff of computer programmers and support personnel to supply all the company's data processing needs.

*Flat files* are data files containing information that is not explicitly linked to other information files. Flat files formed the core of business information processing. For instance, the accounts receivable department kept customer names and addresses in one file. When purchase orders were received, someone entered the coffee and tea order information into other flat files kept on disk. An orders file contained purchase order data such as the items ordered, quantity requested of each item, and whether the purchase was subject to tax—goods acquired for resale are not taxable until they are sold to a retail customer. Accounts payable kept its own set of files, which contained the names and addresses of vendors to which they owed money, invoice numbers, purchase order numbers, and similar information items.

Standard, frequently requested reports were readily available. These reports summarized data held in the files. When a manager wanted to see the latest sales figures for the previous month, he could place a request with the data processing department. The requested report would be on his desk by the next morning. Finding the current stock levels on all coffees and teas was a typical request that could be satisfied easily. Again, the data processing department would process the management request, run a program that accessed the appropriate files, and produce the report. This was typically how reports were generated for standard, traditional requests.

Requests for custom or unusual reports were a different matter altogether. Although standard reports could be produced by scheduling and running programs written for that purpose, unusual report requests had to be custom-designed and written. For example, suppose the procurement office wanted to compare the inventory levels of the 20 most popular coffees and teas with the same period the previous year. Such a report would require programmers to design and write a custom program. When a special request was received, a system analyst determined what files contained the information used in the report. The analyst would also provide a program design. After the design was approved by the user(s), one or more programmers wrote the program that would read the files, manipulate and summarize the data, and print a report. Programmers frequently wrote the program in COBOL, a high-level programming language still in wide use today. It was not unusual for a requested custom report to take several weeks before it was delivered to the requesting manager! Keeping a large pool of systems analysts and programmers on staff to supply the data processing needs of the company was expensive. Time is money, and managers could ill afford to wait weeks for critical reports.

Other problems abounded in pre-DBMS days. Those problems included the creation of outdated and redundant data. Many departments and individuals created and maintained their own computer files, which duplicated information that was kept in the master files. They would do this so they could access and examine data with their own programs quickly, rather than waiting for the overworked data processing department to respond. Duplicate data files led to occurrences of data redundancy and to data inconsistency.

In many firms, the marketing department kept its own files, sorted by zip code, of large customers in order to send them advertising and promotional mailings. The marketing department hired a bright young programmer to maintain these "best customer" files, and that programmer would write programs to produce mailing labels from those files. Problems occurred when the independently maintained customer list fell out of date. Although the master list of customers was kept current by the data processing department using the purchase orders received from customers each month, the marketing department did not have access to the updated data. Their customer list gradually became so out of date—old customers moved, and new customers were gained—that it was eventually useless.

You can begin to see the types of problems that arose when businesses used separate information systems. A wall existed between the information consumers and the information itself. That wall was the data processing department, a necessary element in the information request and receipt cycle. Departments coped with unresponsive data processing departments by spawning separate islands of information that were independently maintained. These separate information islands created data redundancy and data inconsistency. In short, much time and money was expended to store and retrieve business data on computers before the arrival of database management systems and accounting information systems based on them.

## Functions of a Database Management System

A database management system is a sophisticated file management system that can store and manage different types of records within one integrated system. Using a database management system's tools, a database administrator can create a sophisticated system that maintains company records, generates invoices, and in general keeps track of all a company's transactions. A *database* is the physical implementation of a particular set of records, and the database management system controls access to those records. A *relational* database management system, one of three classical models of database management systems, consists of tables containing data whose contents are related to one another through the data content of the tables. The capabilities that a database management system provides in development of an information system are the following:

- Efficient data maintenance: storage, update, and retrieval
- User-accessible catalog
- Concurrency control
- Transaction support
- Recovery services
- Security and authorization services
- Integrity facilities

One of the most important abilities of a database management system is its capacity to store, update, and retrieve data. Unlike a flat file system, you need not write and run a special program to store new data in a database. Likewise, when you want to extract information from various data files that are maintained by the DBMS, you can formulate a relatively simple report request in the database system's language. You need not enlist the support of a programmer to write lengthy and complicated programs to extract information. Besides, the DBMS hides all the file storage details from the user. Instead, the user is presented with an uncomplicated view of the data that the DBMS maintains.

## Advantages of Database Management Systems

Some of the advantages that a database management system provides should be clear from the preceding material. DBMSs have other advantages over the old file and programmatic access methods. Many larger database systems provide each user with an individual view of the database. Also known as a *subschema*, a view is a pseudo table that appears to the user to be the real table. It is a definition stored in the database that can extract information from one or more tables and exclude selected rows and columns from being displayed. For instance, a manager might have a view of the database that displays employee data for the employees who report to the requesting manager, but no others. Views are implemented by database systems and provide a measure of security.

Data independence is another advantage of a database management system. The term *data independence* refers to a database management system's ability to hide the details of the physical storage of information from application programs that use the data. To extract information from a database, you merely request information by name and supply conditions that limit which rows are selected. The database system is responsible for translating the information request into data access statements that the database system can understand.

Changes to the structure of a database can be made transparently to the users. This is important because table designs can change over time and it becomes necessary to make changes to the internal structure of one or more tables. Frequently, table structure changes are made to provide significantly shorter database access times. When structure changes occur, using database views can mask those changes since database *views* restrict what various users can retrieve from the database. The views mimic users' old perceptions of the affected tables' contents, and the database structure change causes no changes to users' access techniques or methods. On the other hand, imagine the degree to which programs would be affected in a flat file system if just a few changes were made to the structure of the files they access. Programmers would have to spend a great deal of time changing all the programs that reference the files whose structure was changed. In large systems it can be very difficult to find all programs that reference a particular file or set of files.

Finally, database systems help users share data with each other. Because corporate data is centrally stored, everyone has access to the same information and that information is always current and consistent, because there is only one copy of it. There are no duplicate versions of inconsistent data, as was often the case in the years prior to the advent of database management systems.

## Disadvantages of Database Management Systems

The principal disadvantage of a database management system is that it can occupy a large amount of expensive disk storage space. You should consider the cost of disk storage when determining whether a database system is cost effective. Though database systems can occupy more than ten times the space required to hold the same data in flat files, DBMSs can still be a good value. Disk storage costs are much lower than the cost of maintaining data in flat files. Programming costs have gone up rapidly in the last 15 years, but prices of hardware such as disk drives have dropped sharply.

Larger database systems often require additional people such as a database administrator to keep the system running smoothly. Other database experts may be hired to handle the information needs of the company. With few exceptions, these added costs are far less than the cost of not using a database management system. Of course, smaller businesses using PC-based database management packages such as Microsoft Access can often avoid these additional personnel costs. In such cases, only the additional disk space cost is a factor in the decision.

## RELATIONAL DATABASE MANAGEMENT SYSTEMS

Database management systems can be implemented by following one of three data models in widespread use today. A *data model* is an abstract representation of a database system providing a description of the data and methods for accessing the data managed by the database. The three models in use are the *hierarchical* model, the *network* model, and the *relational* model. Throughout most of the late 1960s and early 1970s, most databases used the hierarchical or network model. IBM's IMS database system, prevalent in the 1970s, is a prominent example of a hierarchical database management system. A DBMS that is an example of a network model is Cullinet's IDMS/R. However, things changed rapidly in the 1970s. Dr. E. F. Codd, then an IBM Fellow, introduced the relational model for database systems. Since that time, this model has evolved somewhat, but the number of database systems based on the relational model has exploded. Today, the relational model is the overwhelming choice for database systems running on all kinds of computers, from PCs to mainframes.

The relational model provides several significant advantages over the hierarchical and network models. In the relational model, the logical and physical characteristics of the database are distinct; this provides users with a more intuitive view of the data. Using the relational model requires very little training. The relational model includes more powerful retrieval and update operators that allow complex operations to be executed with concise commands. Perhaps most importantly, the relational model provides powerful tools to let analysts know when a database has inherent design flaws.

The advantages of the relational model overwhelm the disadvantages of using database systems. From this point on in the text, when we refer to a database management system, we specifically mean a *relational database management system*, or *RDBMS*.

## Database Objects

Based on sound mathematical principles, the relational model is rooted in mathematical set theory, the theory of relations, and first-order predicate logic. (Don't bail out now! We will avoid deep theoretical discussions and do not expect you to read about or understand the mathematical underpinnings of the relational model.) The model defines the conceptual view that the user has all of the objects contained by the database system. Both the data objects and the relationships between them are represented as a collection of related tables. In fact, all data—including the database table definitions and object information—exists only in tables. This provides a simple, consistent view of the database.

A relational database is a collection of relations. The primary structure in a relational model database is a relation. A table is an example of a relation. For that reason, you will often see the terms *relation* and *table* used interchangeably—although database purists disagree with this casual treatment of the terms. A table, or relation, consists of rows and columns, similar to a matrix or spreadsheet. Each row is technically called a *tuple*, though we prefer to use the less formal term *row*. Each column is formally known as an *attribute*, but we will often use the term *column*. Other terms used frequently in database textbooks for relation, tuple, and attribute are file, record, and field, respectively. Figure 3.6 summarizes these three sets of terms.

| Formal Term | Less Formal Term | Data Processing Term |
|---|---|---|
| relation | table | file |
| tuple | row | record |
| attribute | column | field |

**Figure 3.6**   Three sets of database terms.

You may have used spreadsheet software in some of your other accounting courses. A spreadsheet page resembles a database table in several ways. For example, a spreadsheet page has columns and rows. The columns in a spreadsheet page often have titles that describe the content of the columns. You might want to think of database tables as a special form of spreadsheet pages. The difference is that database tables must adhere to very strict rules. The most important properties of database tables include the following:

• The entries in each column of any row must be single valued.

• Each attribute (column) in a table has a distinct name, called the attribute name.

• Every entry in a column contains a value for that column only, and the values are of the same data type.

• The order of the rows is unimportant.

• The order (position) of the columns in relation to each other is unimportant.

• Each row is unique; it differs from all other rows in the table.

The preceding table (relation) properties are very important. Later in this chapter, we will discuss each of these in practical terms, giving examples. Figure 3.7 shows an example relation that is one of the several tables constituting The Coffee Merchant's database. Because the table is large, only a few rows are shown and only four of the ten columns are displayed—just enough for you to get the idea.

The Customer table contains hundreds of rows, in no particular order, representing the current and potential Coffee Merchant customers. Because the row

**Figure 3.7** The Customer relation, *tblCustomer*.

order is unimportant in a RDBMS, there is no implied meaning that one customer is more important than another. All you can tell from the row order is that the identification number field, called CustomerID, is in ascending order. For relational databases, a row's identity is determined by its content, not its location within a table.

## Primary and Foreign Key Attributes

The table that appears in Figure 3.7 contains ten columns. Six of these attributes appear in Figure 3.7: CustomerID, CompanyName, Contact, Address, City, and State. However, there is no theoretical reason to list the columns in that order. We have chosen to place the primary key column, CustomerID, as the first table column. Though Access does not require the primary key column to be first, most database designers follow this convention. We could, for example, place the Contact column in the second column, followed by the State and City columns.

Within each column you can see the attribute values for each row. For instance, the row identified as CustomerID 30121 contains "Fairfield Communities Inc." in its CompanyName value and "Best, F. Stanley" in its Contact value. Each row may store a different value for each attribute. In particular, the CustomerID value is unique for each row. This satisfies the rule that each row must be unique. A row is unique if any one of its columns is unique.

Every relation must have a primary key that uniquely identifies each row in the table. The primary key can include one or more columns. When the primary key includes more than one column, the individual column values need not be unique, but the combined column values must be unique.

Every row in a RDBMS must be distinct from all other rows in that table, or else it cannot be retrieved easily. This is one of the fundamental rules of a relational database management system. To ensure uniqueness, a primary key is designated for a table. A primary key, as mentioned previously, is a column (or group of columns) that uniquely identifies a given row. Therefore, the system can distinguish one record (row) of a table from another. In the *tblCustomer* table, for instance, the CustomerID column—the customer's identification number—uniquely identifies a row. Thus CustomerID is the primary key for the *tblCustomer* table.

Another important table field is a foreign key. A *foreign key* is an attribute in one table that matches the primary key field of another table. Figure 3.8 shows two of The Coffee Merchant tables used to retrieve invoice data from the set of tables constituting the database. Many database designers use the same field name for related primary key and foreign key columns to indicate the two columns tie together two tables. For example, the foreign key CustomerID in the table *tblInvoice* is related to the identically named field in the table *tblCustomer*. Although many database designers do follow this naming practice, Microsoft Access and other database management software packages do not require it.

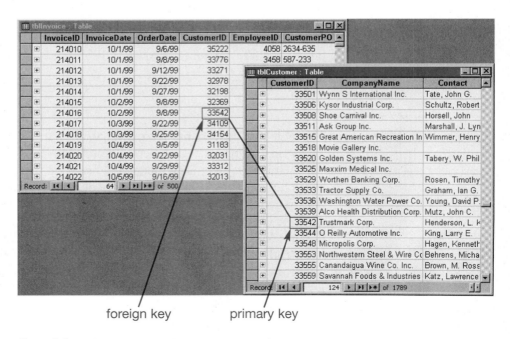

foreign key          primary key

**Figure 3.8**  Primary key and foreign key relationship.

The CustomerID column in the Invoice (*tblInvoice*) table is a foreign key, because it references a primary key found in one row of the *tblCustomer* table. Foreign key/primary key associations are important in establishing connections between related tables. Connecting two or more related tables based on their matching primary/foreign keys is a fundamental relational database operation called *join*. You will learn more about the join operation later in this chapter.

## Schema of a Relation

The *schema* of a relation for the Customer table is the relation's name and its attributes. Some database designers also call this set of information a *table structure*. A compact representation of the schema for the *tblCustomer* table, using the reduced number of columns in this illustration, can be written like this:

Customer(<u>CustomerID</u>, CompanyName, Contact, Address, City, State)

where the table's attributes are enclosed in parentheses following the table name. In this notation, an underline indicates the primary key column(s). This is not the only way to write this schema, but it is one you will find in common use in many books on database design and in many accounting information systems textbooks. Though not shown here, a line appearing over one or more fields indicates the field is a foreign key.

## Data Dictionary

Relational database systems have a data dictionary. A data dictionary is a collection of tables containing the definition, characteristics, structure, and description of all data maintained by the RDBMS. In other words, there is no external definition of the data structures, names of tables, column names, column data types, and so on. Instead, all the information is stored in special tables accessible by either the database administrator or the object's owner.

Other than table descriptions, the data dictionary stores view definitions, object owner names, database login names (for minicomputer and mainframe database systems), and passwords. Fields in the data dictionary are automatically changed whenever an object's structure is changed. For example, if you delete a column from a table and rename another table, both operations cause changes to the data dictionary entries. A row in a table holding other tables' column names is deleted when you delete a column, and a row containing table names is updated when you rename a table (actually, several tables are affected by a rename operation). Having a data dictionary makes the job of the database management system and the database administrator more efficient, because all information needed about the system is self-contained.

Unfortunately, Microsoft Access does not provide a facility that automatically creates a data dictionary table. You can create a data dictionary in a separate Access file, but it will not automatically update itself when you change the elements of the database.

## The Coffee Merchant Tables

To understand how accounting information can be organized in a database system, let's look at an example. Several of the tables contained in the *Ch03.mdb* database, which is stored in the Ch03 folder on your Companion CD, include invoice data for customers of The Coffee Merchant. Figure 3.9 shows schema for each table used in the invoicing subsystem of The Coffee Merchant's database.

| | |
|---|---|
| tblCountryName | (CountryID, CountryName, ExportCoffeeBags, ExportTeaPounds) |
| tblCustomer | (CustomerID, CompanyName, Contact, Address, City, State, ZipCode, PhoneNumber, FaxNumber, CreditLimit) |
| tblEmployee | (EmployeeID, EmployeeFirstName, EmployeeLastName, EmployeeWorkPhone, EmployeeTitleID, EmployeeCommRate, EmployeeHireDate, EmployeeDOB, EmployeeGender, EmployeeNotes) |
| tblEmployeeTitle | (TitleID, Title) |
| tblInventory | (InventoryID, ItemID, Caffeinated, Price, OnHand) |
| tblInventoryDescription | (ItemID, Name, BeverageType, Flavored, CountryID, Comments) |
| tblInvoice | (InvoiceID, InvoiceDate, OrderDate, CustomerID, EmployeeID, CustomerPO) |
| tblInvoiceLine | (InvoiceID, InventoryID, Quantity, UnitPrice, Discount) |
| tblSalesTaxRate | (StateAbbreviation, StateName, TaxRate, Population, LandArea) |

**Figure 3.9**   Schemas of tables in the invoicing system.

When bits of data from each of these tables are combined in the proper way, we can build and print an invoice. The *tblCustomer* table contains vital information about each customer. Each customer is assigned a primary key—a sequence of integers beginning with any number is sufficient—so that a customer can be uniquely identified. The Invoice table, *tblInvoice*, contains a history of invoices sent out by The Coffee Merchant. Each row is identified by the primary key, InvoiceID, and it holds each customer's invoice date (InvoiceDate), order date (OrderDate), customer identification number (CustomerID), identification number of the associated salesperson (EmployeeID), and the customer's original purchase order number (CustomerPO). Of course, an invoice shows more details than these held in the Invoice table *tblInvoice*, but those additional details (such as the customer's address) are contained in *tblCustomer*, which is linked to the Invoice table on the CustomerID attribute—the primary key in *tblCustomer* and a foreign key in *tblInvoice*. Figure 3.10 shows a Datasheet view of some *tblInvoice* rows.

Order lines contain details about individual items ordered by the customer and included on the current invoice such as quantity ordered, unit price, and discount. These order line details are not stored in the Invoice table. Instead, those details are stored in three other tables: *tblInvoiceLine*, *tblInventory*, and *tblInventoryDescription*. Figures 3.11, 3.12, and 3.13 show sample rows from each of these tables. The *tblInvoiceLine* table may appear to be a bit unusual at first glance. It contains only five attributes: two fields that make up its composite pri-

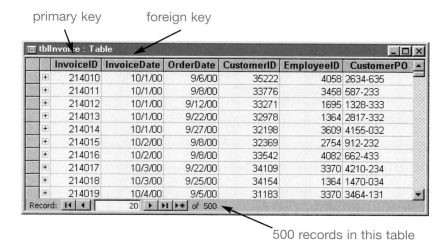

**Figure 3.10**   Example rows in the Invoice table, *tblInvoice*.

**Figure 3.11**   Example rows in the Invoice Line table, *tblInvoiceLine*.

mary key and three other fields that contain information about the items on each invoice. These information items include the quantity ordered, the quoted unit price (which can vary for a given product depending on the customer), and the discount percentage for each item on each invoice. A composite primary key consists of more than one attribute. In this table, InvoiceID and InventoryID combine to form the composite primary key. These two attributes identify the invoice and each inventory item number that will appear on a line of that invoice. The *tblInventory* and *tblInventoryDescription* tables store information about the coffees and teas available from The Coffee Merchant. Only a few of the over 100 items stored in primary key          foreign key

**Figure 3.12**  Example rows in the primary Inventory table, *tblInventory*.

primary key                                    foreign key

**Figure 3.13**  Example rows in the secondary Inventory table, *tblInventoryDescription*.

the inventory tables are shown in Figure 3.12. InventoryID identifies each inventory item uniquely, and other characteristics about the inventory item are found collectively in the *tblInventory* and *tblInventoryDescription* tables.

From the tables shown here, how can you obtain the extended price, subtotal, and other important values that normally appear on an invoice? The answer is that you have Access calculate those values when it prints the invoice. Calculated values need not and should not be stored in tables. Because they can be calculated by multiplying each invoice line's quantity and price attributes, there is no need to store the calculated fields. In addition, you will learn shortly that it is undesirable to store values in a table that can be calculated from other table fields. Thus, the data in these four tables plus the Customer table, *tblCustomer*, contain all of the information needed to produce invoices for The Coffee Merchant.

Now that you understand the details included in The Coffee Merchant's database tables, you can learn about normalization. We will use The Coffee Merchant tables to illustrate our discussion of the reasons for and the definition of normalized tables.

## Normalization

Unlike the past, when data was stored in flat files, we have learned that it is important to think carefully about where individual pieces of data are stored. We try to design a database carefully so that its attributes are stored in the proper tables. The process of determining the correct location for each attribute is called *normalization*. Another way of thinking about normalization is this: normalizing a database is storing data where it uniquely belongs. What might happen if we choose to ignore normalization? Unnormalized databases can lead to redundant, inconsistent, and anomalous information being stored in tables—precisely the problems that led us to use relational databases in the first place.

There are many ways to arrange the invoice system attributes in sets of tables. Some arrangements are better than others. A particular subset of the ways that attributes can be organized into tables is called a *normal form*, and the basis of this arrangement is called normalization theory.

Researchers have identified seven normal forms. Like layers of an onion, each normal form is completely compliant with the rules of the normal forms that it contains—for example, a table that is in third normal form is automatically in first and second normal form. The rules applied to achieve each normal form are successively more stringent. The least restrictive is called the *first normal form* (abbreviated as 1NF). Following that form are the *second, third, Boyce/Codd, fourth, fifth,* and *Domain/Key* normal forms. Most accounting systems require use of only the first three normal forms. Tables in third normal form are better than tables in second normal form. Likewise, tables in second normal form are better than tables in first normal form. The goal of the normalization process is to start with a collection of tables (or relations), apply normalization, and arrive at an equivalent collection of tables in a higher normal form. The process is repeated until all tables are in third normal form (3NF).

**FIRST NORMAL FORM.** A table that contains a repeating group is called an *unnormalized* table. The relational model requires that all tables be in first normal form. To achieve this, repeating data must be removed from the table and stored elsewhere. For example, suppose that an invoice table held each invoice line for all invoices in the arrangement shown in Figure 3.14.

Notice that for each invoice in the Invoice table, there are several inventory item numbers, quantities, unit prices, and discounts. For instance, invoice number

| InvoiceID | InvoiceDate | CustomerID | InventoryID | Quantity | UnitPrice | Discount |
|-----------|-------------|------------|-------------|----------|-----------|----------|
| 214010 | 10/1/99 | 35222 | 1184 | 18 | $6.90 | 5% |
|  |  |  | 1192 | 17 | $13.30 | 10% |
|  |  |  | 1195 | 17 | $3.90 | 0% |
|  |  |  | 1209 | 14 | $6.20 | 15% |
|  |  |  | 1237 | 17 | $10.90 | 5% |
| 214011 | 10/1/99 | 33776 | 1104 | 19 | $5.30 | 5% |
|  |  |  | 1133 | 8 | $7.90 | 0% |
|  |  |  | 1137 | 15 | $7.00 | 15% |
|  |  |  | 1197 | 2 | $7.10 | 0% |
|  |  |  | 1211 | 10 | $14.70 | 15% |
| 214012 | 10/1/99 | 33271 | 1127 | 17 | $4.50 | 0% |
|  |  |  | 1129 | 5 | $8.40 | 0% |
|  |  |  | 1189 | 14 | $5.30 | 15% |
|  |  |  | 1203 | 12 | $8.10 | 15% |
|  |  |  | 1249 | 2 | $11.90 | 0% |
| 214013 | 10/1/99 | 32978 | 1139 | 10 | $5.30 | 15% |
|  |  |  | 1198 | 17 | $8.10 | 5% |
|  |  |  | 1208 | 14 | $4.50 | 15% |
|  |  |  | 1216 | 19 | $7.20 | 5% |
|  |  |  | 1229 | 5 | $12.90 | 0% |
|  |  |  | 1249 | 5 | $11.90 | 0% |
| 214014 | 10/1/99 | 32198 | 1170 | 6 | $44.50 | 10% |

*(repeating group — brackets mark the item rows for invoices 214010, 214011, 214012, and 214013)*

**Figure 3.14**   Example table containing repeating groups.

214010 contains five items; each item corresponds to an invoice detail item on a printed invoice. The schema for this table is:

> tblInvoice (<u>InvoiceID</u>, InvoiceDate, CustomerID,
> InventoryID, Quantity, UnitPrice, Discount,
> InventoryID, Quantity, UnitPrice, Discount, …)

where the ellipsis indicates that InventoryID, Quantity, UnitPrice, and Discount can repeat any number of times—as many times as there are items listed on a single invoice.

If we want a table in first normal form, we cannot store repeating groups (multiple values) in one table column, and we do not want to store a variable number of {InventoryID, Quantity, UnitPrice, Discount} quadruples in each row. Instead, we can collect together all quadruples in repeating groups, remove them from the existing Invoice table, and place them in the rows of a new table. This requires that an additional column be added to the new table linking the rows of the newly formed table with the original Invoice table. An example of the structure of the two tables conforming to first normal form is this:

> tblInvoice(<u>InvoiceID</u>, InvoiceDate, OrderDate, CustomerID, EmployeeID,
> CustomerPO)
> tblInvoiceLine(<u>InvoiceID</u>, <u>InventoryID</u>, Quantity, UnitPrice, Discount)

The new table, *tblInvoiceLine*, contains five columns. The first two columns, InvoiceID and InventoryID, combine to form the new table's primary key. This is a *composite primary key* because the primary key includes two attributes. Also, we have inserted three new fields into *tblInvoice* to conform to the Invoice table stored on your Companion CD.

**SECOND NORMAL FORM.** Tables in first normal form can be placed into a relational database system, but in most cases first normal form is not good enough. Such tables are prone to several problems. Let's look at an example. Figure 3.15 shows an example of some rows of the *tblCustomer* table in first normal form (vastly different from the actual *tblCustomer* table stored in Ch02 on your Companion CD). The schema for this table is:

tblCustomer(CustomerID, CompanyName, PhoneNumber, Contact, InvoiceID, Total)

The *tblCustomer* table contains customer information including the customer identification, company name, telephone, and contact person. The last two columns indicate the customer's invoice number and amount. The two table columns, CustomerID and InvoiceID, form the table's primary key. Both are needed to access a row.

| CustomerID | CompanyName | PhoneNumber | Contact | InvoiceID | Total |
|---|---|---|---|---|---|
| 30125 | Alamo Group Inc. | (210) 555-1483 | Maul, Duane A. | 214480 | 306.80 |
| 30139 | Cavco Industries Inc. | (602) 555-6141 | Golkin, David | 214123 | 225.11 |
| 30139 | Cavco Industries Inc. | (602) 555-6141 | Golkin, David | 214460 | 315.10 |
| 30174 | Thomas Nelson Inc. | (615) 555-9079 | Harber, L. H. | 214390 | 491.96 |
| 30174 | Thomas Nelson Inc. | (615) 555-9079 | Harber, L. H. | 214418 | 185.95 |
| 30206 | Matlack Systems Inc. | (302) 555-2760 | Gordon, W. Phil | 214334 | 218.39 |
| 30212 | Lilly Industries Inc. | (317) 555-6762 | Choong, Jerry | 214117 | 152.20 |
| 30221 | Mcdonald & Co. Investments Inc. | (216) 555-2368 | Bianco, Andrew R. | 214249 | 297.34 |
| 30225 | Krause S Furniture Inc. | (510) 555-6208 | Woltz, Neil G. | 214087 | 260.15 |
| 30228 | F N B Corp. Pa | (412) 555-6028 | Fancher, William R. | 214284 | 98.35 |
| 30231 | Everest & Jennings Internation | (314) 555-7041 | Gray, Robert R. | 214036 | 270.60 |
| 30231 | Everest & Jennings Internation | (314) 555-7041 | Gray, Robert R. | 214256 | 165.96 |
| 30258 | Lcs Industries Inc. | (201) 555-5666 | Lebuhn, Eugene | 214230 | 895.25 |

**Figure 3.15**  Example rows of the Customer table in first normal form (1NF).

Several potential problems exist with the proposed 1NF Customer table. Suppose that the *tblCustomer* table is the only place in which customer information such as address or name is placed. What happens when you want to add a new customer and that customer has paid for an order in advance? That is, can we add a customer to the *tblCustomer* table without first generating an invoice? No, unfortunately we cannot! If we did, then the InvoiceID value would be empty. When an attribute is empty, or has no value, it is *null*. The InvoiceID attribute cannot be null, because relational database rules do not allow the primary key, or one of its components, to be null. This situation is known as an *insertion anomaly*.

Consider this scenario. Cavco Industries pays for its two invoices, numbers 214123 and 214460 (see Figure 3.15, second and third rows), bringing its amount due to zero. The two rows corresponding to Cavco Industries are removed from *tblCustomer*. Not only are the two invoices removed, but the customer's identification number, name, phone, and contact person are deleted as well. So the deletion has a wider effect than desired—you lose knowledge of the customer entirely. Your mailing list is being destroyed! This predicament is known as a *deletion anomaly*.

Finally, the *tblCustomer* table shown in Figure 3.15 contains a great deal of redundant information. For instance, the company identification number, name, phone number, and contact person are repeated for each new invoice that is issued for a particular customer. The customer name *Cavco Industries Inc.* is entered twice, as is *Golkin, David*, the contact person. It is pure luck that both the company name and contact person's name have been spelled correctly both times. And what if you want to change the company name? You must find all occurrences of the name in the database and change each one. What a time-consuming task that could be! This small example illustrates that tables in first normal form usually contain a great deal of redundant data.

Altering a table's structure and changing it into second normal form can prevent these anomalies. A table (relation) is in *second normal form* (2NF) if it is in first normal form and none of the nonkey attributes depend on only one portion of the primary key. That is, second normal form requires that each nonkey attribute depend on the entire primary key, not just part of it. This rule applies only when you have a composite primary key—one consisting of more than one table column.

The attribute Total in the *tblCustomer* table in Figure 3.15 violates the 2NF definition. The value of Total is determined by the partial primary key InvoiceID. We say that Total is *functionally dependent* on InvoiceID, because a particular value of InvoiceID determines a single value of Total. On the other hand, Total does not depend on the attribute and partial primary key CustomerID, because the total invoice amount varies from invoice to invoice; no relationship exists between Total and a particular customer. On the other hand, the attributes CompanyName, PhoneNumber, and Contact each functionally depend on the partial primary key CustomerID. These two sets of functional dependencies are shown in Figure 3.16.

The arrows lead from a primary key to another attribute. For instance, the arrow leading from CustomerID to CompanyName means that CustomerID *determines* CompanyName (or CustomerID is a *determinant* of CompanyName). It is clear that we can correct this problem by breaking *tblCustomer* into two tables. Of course, we must note the relationship between these two tables by including an extra attribute—a foreign key—linking both tables (*joining* them in database

**Figure 3.16** Functional dependencies in the Customer table.

parlance) on the CustomerID key. *tblCustomer* and its related *tblInvoice* table in second normal form could be restructured this way:

tblCustomer(<u>CustomerID</u>, CompanyName, PhoneNumber, Contact)
tblInvoice(<u>InvoiceID</u>, CustomerID, Total)

where we have included in *tblInvoice* the CustomerID field as a foreign key to *tblCustomer*, thus associating these two tables.

**THIRD NORMAL FORM.** The design goal for relational databases is to create tables that are in third normal form. A table is in *third normal form* (3NF) if it is in second normal form and all transitive dependencies have been eliminated. A *transitive dependency* exists in a table if attribute B determines attribute C, and attribute C determines attribute D.

You have probably heard an expression that can help you understand and remember the difference between 2NF and 3NF. Part of the phrase used to swear in witnesses who are about to take the stand in a trial goes roughly like this: ". . . to tell the truth, the whole truth, and nothing but the truth." The second normal form is analogous to "the whole truth" part of the phrase—each attribute depends on the *whole* primary key. Similarly, the third normal form is analogous to "and nothing but the truth"—each attribute depends *only* on the primary key and on no other attribute in the relation. For example, consider the Invoice table shown in Figure 3.17.

The Invoice table's primary key is InvoiceID. Because only one customer may be assigned a particular invoice number (the value in the InvoiceID field), the invoice number uniquely determines the invoice date, order date, customer identification number, employee identification number, and company contact person. There are no repeating groups in the table. Therefore, it is in first normal form. Furthermore, it is in second normal form because all attributes depend on the single-attribute primary key. How about third normal form? Are all attributes functionally dependent on only the InvoiceID attribute? The answer is no. There is a transitive dependency. The InvoiceID determines the CustomerID value. CustomerID, in turn, determines the Contact column. Figure 3.18 shows the dependency in the Invoice table.

| InvoiceID | InvoiceDate | OrderDate | CustomerID | EmployeeID | Contact |
|---|---|---|---|---|---|
| 214010 | 10/1/99 | 9/6/99 | 35222 | 4058 | Shaffer, Shaun P. |
| 214011 | 10/1/99 | 9/8/99 | 33776 | 3458 | Olbrych, Fred H. |
| 214012 | 10/1/99 | 9/12/99 | 33271 | 1695 | Yocam, William C. |
| 214013 | 10/1/99 | 9/22/99 | 32978 | 1364 | Swift, Scott C. |
| 214014 | 10/1/99 | 9/27/99 | 32198 | 3609 | |
| 214015 | 10/2/99 | 9/8/99 | 32369 | 2754 | Gosa, Myron E. |
| 214016 | 10/2/99 | 9/8/99 | 33542 | 4082 | Henderson, L. Keith |
| 214017 | 10/3/99 | 9/22/99 | 34109 | 3370 | Pirie, Thomas R. |
| 214018 | 10/3/99 | 9/25/99 | 34154 | 1364 | Ammerman, Donnie l |
| 214019 | 10/4/99 | 9/5/99 | 31183 | 3370 | Dykstra, Bruce A. |

**Figure 3.17**  Invoice table in second normal form (2NF).

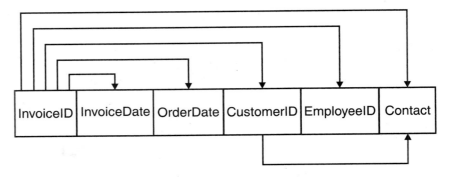

**Figure 3.18**  Transitive dependencies in the Invoice table shown in Figure 3.17.

The arrows above the attributes (represented by boxes) show the dependencies that exist between attributes and the table's primary key. Those relationships are fine. However, the arrow below the boxes shows a transitive dependency between CustomerID (the determinant) and Contact. The easiest way to remove the offending dependency is to create another table containing at least the determinant attribute (CustomerID, in this case) and all dependent attributes (Contact, in this example). Once the transitive dependency is excised, the table will be in 3NF. Of course, the field CustomerID becomes a foreign key to link the invoice to individual customer information. The new tables could be structured as follows to bring them into compliance with 3NF:

　　　　tblInvoice(<u>InvoiceID</u>, InvoiceDate, OrderDate, CustomerID, EmployeeID)
and
　　　　tblCustomer(<u>CustomerID</u>, Contact)

Third normal form enforces an informal rule stating that a table should store one fact and one fact only. Prior to decomposing *tblInvoice* into two separate tables, it housed two facts: one fact about invoices (InvoiceDate, OrderDate, etc.) and one fact about customers (Contact). After two tables are created from a single table, each new table's structure (shown previously) holds only one fact.

**TABLE RELATIONSHIPS.** You have learned that the process of normalizing a database's tables usually produces several additional tables. Yet the relationships between associated tables is maintained by the foreign key to primary key links. There are three fundamental types of relationships between related tables: one-to-one (1—1), one-to-many (1—M), and many-to-many (M—M). The capital letter *M* indicates *many* records. Knowing about these three is important in understanding how to reconstruct information from data stored in constituent tables. Recall that rows from two tables are joined when the foreign key in one table's row matches the primary key in another table. That's the way we synthesize information from disparate tables.

One-to-one relationships usually indicate unnecessary tables in the database design. You can usually combine tables with a one-to-one relationship into one table. Exceptions to this general rule can occur. For instance, the Customer table could have a one-to-one relationship with *tblCustomerNotes*, which might hold supplementary information about a few of The Coffee Merchant's customers. Because only a few customers have notes in the *tblCustomerNotes* table, you do not want to allocate an additional column for an occasional note. This would waste storage space. So *tblCustomerNotes* would contain the foreign key CustomerID and a Notes column. CustomerID would serve both as the primary key for the *tblCustomerNotes* table and as a foreign key into the parent *tblCustomer* table. The following notation shows this relationship conveniently:

$$\text{tblCustomer } ^1\!\!\longrightarrow\!\!^1 \text{ tblCustomerNotes}$$

Databases often contain tables that have one-to-many relationships with each other. There are several examples in The Coffee Merchant's database. Look again at Figure 3.8. Consider the relationship between the *tblCustomer* table and the *tblInvoice* table. Each customer can have as many unpaid invoices as The Coffee Merchant permits (or none). On the other hand, an invoice row in the *tblInvoice* table can be associated with one and only one customer in the *tblCustomer* table. The relationship between the *tblCustomer* table and the *tblInvoice* table is said to be a one-to-many relationship (in that direction—customer to invoice). Although it is technically correct to talk about "many-to-one" relationships, most database designers indicate the "one" side of the relationship first and use the "one-to-many" phrasing. A one-to-many relationship is shown this way:

$$\text{tblCustomer } ^1\!\!\longrightarrow\!\!^M \text{ tblInvoice}$$

Finally, consider the relationship between invoices and the coffee and tea items found on individual invoice lines. Various coffees and teas can appear on the many lines of a single invoice. An invoice might contain a line for 10 pounds of Kona coffee and another line for 5 pounds of Zimbabwe. Similarly, the coffee and tea items in The Coffee Merchant's inventory can appear in several invoices. For example, many different invoices might include Kona coffee. This type of relationship between the Invoice table and Inventory table is called a many-to-many relationship. We depict this type of relationship as follows:

$$\text{tblInvoice } ^{M}\text{———————}>^{M} \text{ tblInventory}$$

Many-to-many relationships can be difficult to represent and maintain in a relational database system. Most database designers create a new table to represent the M—M relationship. The table is called a *relationship* table or a *junction* table, and it combines attributes from the tables that participate in the M—M relationship. The relationship table makes the connection between the two tables by converting the M—M relationship into two 1—M relationships. The relationship table in The Coffee Merchant's database is called Invoice Line (*tblInvoiceLine*); it preserves the relationship between invoices (*tblInvoice*) and inventory (*tblInventory*). You can represent this three-table relationship for the M—M relationship as:

$$\text{tblInvoice } ^{1}\text{————}>^{M} \text{ tblInvoiceLine } ^{M}<\text{————}^{1} \text{ tblInventory}$$

Thus, it is always possible to break a many-to-many relationship between two tables into two one-to-many relationships by using an intermediate relationship table. The following are some general rules governing relationships among tables.

1. Primary keys must not be null.
2. Create a foreign key from the primary key on the one side of the 1—M relationship.
3. Many-to-many relationships are handled by creating an additional table—the *relationship table*—that consists entirely of the parent tables' primary keys. (The relationship table can contain other columns as well.)
4. Most one-to-one relationships indicate unnecessary tables in the database design. Normally, you should merge the two tables. Exceptions occur when there are just too many columns in one table, or one group of fields is used far more frequently than another group. Then, you can consider separating them into different tables for efficiency's sake.

## Fundamental Relational Database Operations

Relational database management systems provide several important and fundamental retrieval operations. Among the most significant are select, project, and join.

**SELECT.** The select operator chooses a set of rows from a table. Rows are selected based on a set of qualifying factors, often called *selection criteria*. A new, virtual table is created by the select operation. There are several ways to implement a selection operation. Some RDBMSs such as Access provide a Query By Example (QBE) graphical interface, in which you can choose example elements to specify selection criteria and check the attributes to be displayed.

Figure 3.19 shows a selection operation and the resulting dynaset, another table. The query selects rows from a smaller version of an Employee table. Rows are selected in which the HireDate is after a particular date. Notice that the result returns all columns of the original table satisfying the selection criterion. The result is a table, because queries in relational database systems always deliver answers in table form.

**Employee table:**

| ID | Name | Comm | HireDate | BirthDate | Gender |
|----|------|------|----------|-----------|--------|
| 1301 | Stonesifer | 5% | 07/06/96 | 03/10/66 | F |
| 1364 | Pruski | 4% | 12/01/00 | 01/26/79 | M |
| 1528 | Pacioli | 6% | 08/26/95 | 05/06/50 | M |
| 1695 | Nagasaki | 4% | 01/28/00 | 04/10/77 | M |
| 2240 | Stonely | 15% | 11/05/88 | 05/03/61 | F |
| 2318 | Hunter | 8% | 11/16/93 | 01/26/54 | F |
| 2754 | Kahn | 5% | 05/14/97 | 05/29/61 | M |
| 3370 | Kole | 9% | 02/08/92 | 03/23/63 | M |
| 3432 | English | 8% | 10/01/93 | 02/14/56 | F |
| 3436 | Gates | 6% | 04/11/95 | 03/09/54 | M |
| 3458 | Morrison | 15% | 12/13/89 | 07/04/56 | F |
| 3609 | Chang | 5% | 09/16/97 | 03/30/77 | F |
| . . . | . . . | . . . | . . . | . . . | . . . |
| 4112 | Goldman | 11% | 12/24/90 | 03/05/62 | M |

**Result of selection operation: HireDate > 1/1/97**

| ID | Name | Comm | HireDate | BirthDate | Gender |
|----|------|------|----------|-----------|--------|
| 1364 | Pruski | 4% | 12/01/00 | 01/26/79 | M |
| 1695 | Nagasaki | 4% | 01/28/00 | 04/10/77 | M |
| 2754 | Kahn | 5% | 05/14/97 | 05/29/61 | M |
| 3609 | Chang | 5% | 09/16/97 | 03/30/77 | F |

**Figure 3.19** Select operation.

**PROJECT.** The project operator returns a subset of columns from one or more tables. Columns retrieved are a result of the user indicating them, not as a result of specifying a selection criterion. Figure 3.20 shows an example of a projection of the Name and Gender columns of our example Employee table shown previously in Figure 3.19. Notice that a projection operation does not specify which *rows* are retrieved. Projections indicate only which *columns* are retrieved in the result. Of course, you can combine the selection and projection operations in one query to produce both a row and column subset of a table.

Employee table:

| ID | Name | Comm | HireDate | BirthDate | Gender |
|----|------|------|----------|-----------|--------|
| 1301 | Stonesifer | 5% | 07/06/96 | 03/10/66 | F |
| 1364 | Pruski | 4% | 12/01/00 | 01/26/79 | M |
| 1528 | Pacioli | 6% | 08/26/95 | 05/06/50 | M |
| . . . | . . . | . . . | . . . | . . . | . . . |
| 4057 | Bateman | 9% | 02/16/92 | 05/01/58 | M |
| 4058 | Halstead | 5% | 06/16/96 | 12/22/73 | F |
| 4082 | Flintsteel | 11% | 03/21/90 | 08/22/58 | F |
| 4112 | Goldman | 11% | 12/24/90 | 03/05/62 | M |

Projection:

| Name | Gender |
|------|--------|
| Stonesifer | F |
| Pruski | M |
| Pacioli | M |
| . . . | . . . |
| Bateman | M |
| Halstead | F |
| Flintsteel | F |
| Goldman | M |

**Figure 3.20** Project operation.

**JOIN.** Arguably the most important relational database operation is the join operation. It provides the ability to pull together data from associated tables into a single, virtual table. Usually, you join two tables together using a common attribute found in both tables. This is the role of the foreign and primary keys. In the most common form of the join operation, one table's foreign key value is used to locate a matching primary key in another table. Then the selected data from the matching rows in both tables are combined. That is, rows of one table are concatenated with (placed next to) rows of the second table for which the common attribute matches.

For instance, suppose we want to join a slightly altered Employee table with the employee title information found in a table on your Companion CD called *tblEmployeeTitle*. In the Employee table is a number, which stands in place of an actual job title. The number is used so that the title is not misspelled when it is entered over and over in the Employee table. *tblEmployeeTitle* contains the numbers and actual job titles associated with the numbers. Normalization has produced the two tables, rather than a single table with repeating job titles, which would violate 3NF rules. The tables are joined on title number columns found in both tables. In the Employee table, this column is called *EmployeeTitle*, although the Caption property setting for that field has been shortened to *TitleID*. The *TitleID* column in *tblEmployeeTitle* is the primary key and contains a corresponding title field, *Title*. Joining the two tables in TitleID produces the result shown in Figure 3.21. Note that the join column *does not* have to have the same name in both tables. In the illustration, TitleID is a foreign key in the *tblEmployee* table, whereas TitleID is the primary key in the *tblEmployeeTitle* table. Joining is a matter of matching foreign key and primary key values. The join illustration in Figure 3.21 is an example of the most common type of join. It is called an *equijoin*, because rows from the two tables are concatenated on matching join column values, and the join column appears only once in the result.

**tblEmployee**

| ID | Name | TitleID | HireDate | Gender |
|----|------|---------|----------|--------|
| 1301 | Stonesifer | 2 | 07/06/96 | F |
| 1364 | Pruski | 1 | 12/01/00 | M |
| 1528 | Pacioli | 2 | 08/26/95 | M |
| 1695 | Nagasaki | 1 | 01/28/00 | M |
| 2240 | Stonely | 3 | 11/05/88 | F |
| 2318 | Hunter | 2 | 11/16/93 | F |
| 2754 | Kahn | 2 | 05/14/97 | M |
| 3370 | Kole | 2 | 02/08/92 | M |
| 3432 | English | 2 | 10/01/93 | F |
| 3436 | Gates | 2 | 04/11/95 | M |
| ... | ... | ... | ... | ... |
| 4082 | Flintsteel | 3 | 03/21/90 | F |
| 4112 | Goldman | 3 | 12/24/90 | M |

**tblEmployeeTitle**

| TitleID | Title |
|---------|-------|
| 1 | Sales Trainee |
| 2 | Sales Associate |
| 3 | Senior Sales Associate |
| 4 | Sales Manager |
| 5 | Senior Sales Manager |
| 6 | Division Sales Manager |
| 7 | Regional Manager |
| 8 | Division Manager |
| 9 | National Sales Manager |

**Result of join operation:**

| ID | Name | TitleID | HireDate | Gender | Title |
|----|------|---------|----------|--------|-------|
| 1301 | Stonesifer | 2 | 07/06/96 | F | Sales Associate |
| 1364 | Pruski | 1 | 12/01/00 | M | Sales Trainee |
| 1528 | Pacioli | 2 | 08/26/95 | M | Sales Associate |
| 1695 | Nagasaki | 1 | 01/28/00 | M | Sales Trainee |
| 2240 | Stonely | 3 | 11/05/886 | F | Senior Sales Associate |
| 2318 | Hunter | 2 | 11/16/93 | F | Sales Associate |
| 2754 | Kahn | 2 | 05/14/97 | M | Sales Associate |
| 3370 | Kole | 2 | 02/08/92 | M | Sales Associate |
| 3432 | English | 2 | 10/01/93 | F | Sales Associate |
| 3436 | Gates | 2 | 04/11/95 | M | Sales Associate |
| ... | ... | ... | ... | ... | ... |
| 4082 | Flintsteel | 3 | 03/21/90 | F | Senior Sales Associate |
| 4112 | Goldman | 3 | 12/24/90 | M | Senior Sales Associate |

**Figure 3.21** Join operation.

Another join operation type combines rows from two or more tables on the join column, but rows that do not match on the join column are included in the result. This type of join is called an *outer join*. Outer joins are useful for creating reports such as a list of employees that have made no sales or a list of students who have not signed up for a particular class.

There is no practical limit to the number of tables that may be joined. For instance, one of the results we can produce with a join operation are invoices. An invoice is created by a query that joins five of The Coffee Merchant's tables whose schemas are shown in Figure 3.9. Tables joined to form an invoice are connected in pairs on common columns, but not all on the same columns. For instance, the *tblCustomer* table can be joined to the *tblInvoice* table via their common column, CustomerID. Continuing, the *tblInvoice* table can be joined to the *tblInvoiceLine* table (individual invoice lines) over the join column InvoiceID, an attribute found in both tables. The Inventory table, *tblInventory*, is joined to *tblInventoryDescription* to link the names of each invoiced item. *tblInventory* is joined to *tblInvoiceLine* on the common column InventoryID. Figure 3.22 illustrates how the join columns of all involved tables are connected to form the single result—a dynaset. All of the joins shown in Figure 3.22 are equijoins.

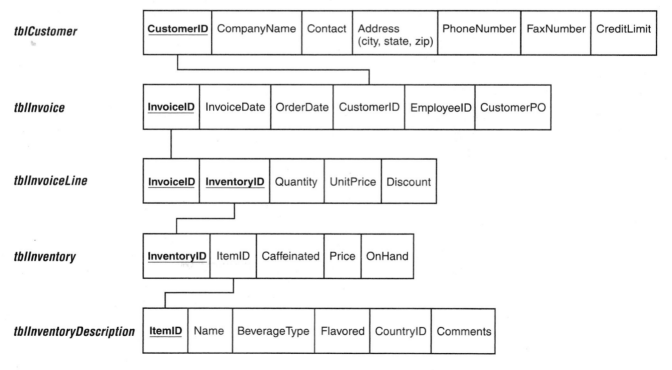

**Figure 3.22**   Joining tables with primary key/foreign key relationships.

## INTRODUCTION TO DATABASE DESIGN

A well-designed database that accurately models an enterprise's operations is crucial to the success of any database system designed to maintain accounting information. On the other hand, a badly designed database that is supposed to represent a company's business can be worse than using no system at all. In the worst cases, information can be misrepresented, difficult to find, or completely lost.

One very important aspect of database design is carefully choosing the rows and attributes that you want to include in each table. This activity, often referred to as *modeling*, can be accomplished using any of several methods. We introduce you to two of these methods in this section. The first method we offer draws information from existing business documents. The other method, called entity-relationship (abbreviated E-R) modeling, is described in the context of The Coffee Merchant's invoice system.

## Creating User Views and Relations

One way to approach designing database objects to represent a business organization is to use existing documents as a starting point. For instance, we can look at a current customer invoice facsimile used before the database accounting system was implemented. The first step in designing database objects to replace paper forms is to list all the information found on the document and to assign names to the attributes. Next, identify functional dependencies, if any. Then, the entities (tables) can be created by selecting which attributes belong in which tables. Finally, apply normalization rules to the tables to ensure that all tables (entities) conform to third normal form.

The first step, listing potential attributes from an existing document, is relatively straightforward. Attribute names may not be exactly right the first time, but they provide a starting point. Figure 3.23 shows a list of potential attribute names. Of course, there are other possible attributes that have been omitted from the list such as Ship Date, Item Quantity Backordered, and Item Quantity Shipped. We have omitted these to keep the example simple yet sufficient to illustrate the modeling process.

| | |
|---|---|
| CustomerContactPerson | ItemExtendedPrice |
| CustomerName | ItemName |
| CustomerNumber | ItemNumber |
| CustomerPhone | ItemPrice |
| CustomerAddress | ItemQuantity |
| InvoiceDate | OrderDate |
| InvoiceNumber | OrderNumber |
| InvoiceTotalAmount | SalesTax |
| ItemDescription | ShippingCharges |

**Figure 3.23** A list of possible attribute names.

Next, we identify functional dependencies. You can make good guesses as to which attributes determine the value of other attributes. Don't worry about making a mistake. Errors will be uncovered when you show your design to the people that will be using the system. Figure 3.24 shows an example of a dependency list. Dependent attributes are listed below the attributes that determine them.

CustomerNumber:
    CustomerName
    CustomerPhone
    CustomerContactPerson
    CustomerAddress

InvoiceNumber:
    InvoiceDate
    CustomerNumber
    OrderDate
    OrderNumber
    ShippingCharges
    InvoiceTotalAmount
    SalesTax

InvoiceNumber, ItemNumber:
    ItemQuantity
    ItemExtendedPrice

ItemNumber:
    ItemDescription
    ItemPrice
    ItemName

**Figure 3.24**  Tentative dependency list.

After making initial assignments of attributes, you may discover that the CustomerName depends on the InvoiceNumber, not on the CustomerNumber, in cases in which the shipping address varies from the usual customer address (a case we disallow in our example). You may determine that the price charged to a customer depends on the CustomerNumber, not the ItemNumber. The latter is true when a customer is given a price reduction based on volume or other factors contributing to a "most favored" status. Finally, results depending on fields of the database such as InvoiceTotalAmount, SalesTax, and ShippingCharges should not be stored in the database at all. Why? Because doing so would violate second normal form rules. SalesTax, for instance, depends on additional attributes besides InvoiceNumber. A change in the unit price of an item would not be reflected in

SalesTax (or InvoiceTotalAmount) automatically. As the last step in this process, you develop a revised list of attributes that conform to third normal form. The attributes upon which each group depends constitute the relation's primary key, and each table's attributes are the primary key and the attributes listed below the primary key. The latter list of corrected dependencies is left as an exercise for the student (Hint: See Figure 3.9).

## Developing Entity-Relationship Models

Another popular modeling technique is called *entity-relationship (E-R) modeling*. Introduced by P. P. Chen in 1976, E-R modeling has gained wide acceptance as a graphical approach to database design. Space limitations restrict us to introducing the topic and showing only a few examples of its use in designing The Coffee Merchant's database. For an in-depth discussion of E-R modeling, consult any database management text.

Database designers often use three terms to describe a company's information: entities, relationships, and attributes. *Entities* are objects found in the company (nouns such as invoice, purchase order, or sales receipt). *Relationships* describe the way in which distinct entities interact or are related to one another. *Attributes* describe the entities and relationships.

In the E-R model, diagrams represent entities and relationships. The diagrams contain three symbols: rectangles, diamonds, and lines. Rectangles represent entities and diamonds represent relationships. Lines are the connections between the two. A digit or letter above the line indicates the *degree* of the relationship: one-to-one, one-to-many, or many-to-many. Figure 3.25 shows an example of an E-R diagram for The Coffee Merchant's invoice system.

At first, the E-R model dictated that both entities and relationships could have attributes. Attributes are listed near the relationship or entity they represent. An attribute name is attached to a line leading from the entity or relationship to the attribute. Chen later suggested a slight change to the E-R approach. The altered E-R representation proposed that only entities can have attributes, not relationships. A problem arises using the refined E-R methodology when representing many-to-many relationships. In this case, a new entity—shown with a diamond within a rectangle—is used to redraw two entities as three. The new entity reduces the relationship to three entities having a 1—M degree relationship on one side and an M—1 degree relationship on the other side (see Figure 3.26). 1—M signifies that one record from the table on one side *may* have many related records in another table (the other side of the relationship). For instance, an invoice statement has a 1—M relationship to the items on the invoice: one invoice has many possible invoice lines. Students have a many-to-many relationship with classes: a student can take many classes, and a class contains many students.

The newly created entity in the middle is implemented in a database as a *relationship table*, comprising the primary keys of the two entities on either side of it. This type of relationship is seen between an invoice and the inventory items that

**Figure 3.25** Entity-relationship diagram.

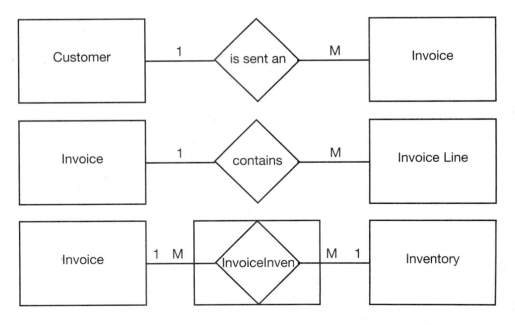

**Figure 3.26** Revised entity-relationship diagram.

appear on invoice lines. Similarly, students and classes they take are another example of a many-to-many relationship.

After the E-R diagrams are complete, they can be combined into a single E-R diagram. This process is called *view integration*. For larger systems the process is started by placing the most often used entity in the center of the diagram. Then lines connect the related entities as in the original diagrams. From these entities you can identify tables. For each entity, one table is created. Primary keys for each table must be identified next. The relationships between entities, exemplified by lines connecting the entities, are maintained by foreign key/primary key linkages between tables. That is, a line from one entity to another is implemented by a key in one table (a foreign key) that matches one or more primary keys in the other table. In the case of a 1—M relationship, the "one" side of the relationship has a foreign key matching possibly several rows on the many side of the relationship.

When a many-to-many relationship exists in the E-R diagram, such as the relationship between *tblInvoice* and *tblInventory*, a third table is created. Often called a *relationship* table (or *bridge* entity), it contains the primary keys from both tables. In other words, the InvoiceInven table in Figure 3.26 contains the primary key from the *tblInvoice* table and the primary key from the *tblInventory* table. Once the relationship table is created, the three tables have a pair of one-to-many relationships. Both relationship tables and the tables to which they are related can be constructed easily. However, representing many-to-many relationships with only two tables can lead to problems, and you should avoid that by using a relationship table.

A table can also be related to *itself* in a special case in which rows of a table are related to other row(s) in the same table. A typical example is an employee table in which the primary key, EmployeeID say, identifies employees and a "supervisor" column contains foreign keys pointing to each employee's supervisor. Supervisors are in the same table and are, after all, employees themselves. A parts inventory is another example. Some parts comprise several other parts, all appearing in the same inventory table. When rows of a table are related to rows in the same table, the relationship is called *recursive*.

The last step in view integration is to normalize the individual tables. For best results, all tables should be at least in third normal form to avoid the anomalies mentioned previously in the section describing normalization.

**SUMMARY**

In this chapter, you learned about database accounting systems, business activity classifications, transaction cycles, database management systems, database tables, relationships between tables, and database design. You learned why double-entry bookkeeping was an excellent system for organizing manual data gathering and storage tasks for many years, but you also learned that database accounting systems can offer significant advantages over computerized double-entry book-keeping systems. Most firms today have concluded that the advantages of database accounting systems outweighed their disadvantages. The discussion of business activity classifications showed you how to categorize firms as manufacturing, merchandising, and service businesses. You then learned how these classifications can help you match particular database features to accounting applications. The chapter discusses transaction cycles and the characteristics of database accounting systems for the revenue, purchase, payroll, and production cycles.

This chapter also introduced database management systems and their application to accounting information. Database management systems are found at the heart of many accounting systems and provide several advantages over nondatabase approaches to managing data. High on the list of advantages are cost savings resulting from the centralization of all data management functions and the enforcement of data integrity and consistency by the database system. Relational database management systems provide the needed capabilities to represent accounting information. Data maintenance with a RDBMS does not require a programmer's help. Usually, people can learn to insert and delete database records, and can even learn to query database systems with little previous experience. Valuable accounting information can be retrieved, and it is not limited to a standard set of accounting reports. You can tailor the output to your needs.

Among the key points in this chapter is the importance of representing table objects in normalized form. First, second, and third normal forms have been described. First normal form precludes repeating groups; second normal form goes further to require that all table attributes be dependent on the table's entire primary key, not just part of it. Third normal form assumes all the characteristics of second and first normal forms. In addition, third normal form tables must not contain attributes that depend on other nonkey attributes. Though other normal forms go beyond third normal form, the latter is sufficient for our needs. Tables in third normal form avoid anomalies that can destroy the accounting information credibility.

# QUESTIONS AND PROBLEMS FOR REVIEW

## MULTIPLE-CHOICE QUESTIONS

1. A double-entry bookkeeping system records each transaction
   a. twice.
   b. as an abstraction.
   c. in a relational database.
   d. on the day it occurs.

2. The events-based approach to accounting theory
   a. classifies businesses in terms of their complexity.
   b. requires validity checks on all accounting events that are entered into the database.
   c. supports the use of relational database accounting systems.
   d. supports the use of double-entry bookkeeping systems.
3. Database systems store data only once. This feature
   a. makes *ad hoc* queries possible.
   b. eliminates data inconsistencies.
   c. facilitates cross-functional data analysis.
   d. allows multiple users to have simultaneous data access.
4. One disadvantage of database accounting systems is that they
   a. make data more dependent on applications.
   b. often require duplicate processing.
   c. can be more expensive to install and operate.
   d. fail to adequately control data entry errors.
5. The term *cost of goods manufactured* on a manufacturing firm's income statement is analogous to
   a. cost of goods sold on a merchandising firm's income statement.
   b. revenue on a service firm's income statement.
   c. purchases on a merchandising firm's income statement.
   d. gross profit on a merchandising firm's income statement.
6. A time worked table would normally appear in a
   a. payroll cycle application.
   b. revenue cycle application.
   c. production cycle application.
   d. both a and c.
7. The purchase cycle includes
   a. manufacturers' ordering and receipt of raw materials.
   b. merchandisers' ordering and receipt of goods for resale.
   c. both a and b.
   d. none of the above.
8. A table's primary key field
   a. is always stored in one table column.
   b. is always referenced by a foreign key in another table.
   c. guarantees that each row is unique.
   d. can sometimes be empty or null.
9. When you retrieve related information from two or more tables in a database, that operation is called what?
   a. join
   b. selection
   c. criteria
   d. projection

10. How are many-to-many relationships represented in a relational database system?
   a. by four tables, each having a one-to-one relationship with one another
   b. by three tables, one of which is a relationship table containing primary keys from each original table
   c. by combining two tables having the many-to-many relationship into a single table
   d. many-to-many relationships must be eliminated entirely, without creating any other tables

## DISCUSSION QUESTIONS

1. Why is double-entry bookkeeping better suited to manual accounting systems than to computerized accounting systems?
2. What prevents accountants from using a database model to automate a double-entry bookkeeping system?
3. In which of the business activity classifications described in this chapter would you include a hospital? Why?
4. Discuss the problems with storing data in two different places. What can this lead to?
5. What is a primary key and why is it so important in a relational database management system?

## PROBLEMS

1. Describe the tables that a grocery store would use in its revenue cycle. Be sure to include all necessary relationship tables and foreign keys.
2. Assume you are working for a manufacturing firm that operates 14 factories, each with 16 departments. What tables would you add to those listed in this chapter for the payroll cycle to track employee time worked by factory and department?
3. Redraw Figure 3.5 for a merchandising firm.
4. Discuss the inherent problems of storing an employee's age as one of the attributes of a table. Discuss alternative solutions that would not cause inaccuracies in the database.
5. Suppose you are designing a database that contains information about university classes, students enrolled in classes, and instructors teaching various classes. The Catalog table lists all the courses that the university can offer. The Classes table describes the classes offered during the semester and includes names of students currently enrolled in each class offered. The Students table contains one record for each student enrolled in the university. The Instructor table contains information about instructors including their names, phone numbers, and office telephone numbers. Discuss the relationship between the

Instructor table and the Classes table. Is the relationship 1—1, 1—M, or M—M? Describe the relationship between the Students table and the Classes table. Finally draw a diagram showing the tables Catalog, Classes, Instructors, and Students and how they might be linked. Use Figure 3.22 as a model of how to represent the tables. You do not need to list more field names than the primary and foreign key fields in each table's representation.

# 4 TABLES AND QUERIES

## OBJECTIVES

This chapter extends the knowledge you gained in Chapters 2 and 3 with detailed information about Microsoft Access. Several hands-on exercises and special Try it exercises reinforce the material in this chapter. You will learn about creating and altering tables and a wide variety of queries. Throughout this chapter, exercises emphasize Microsoft Access techniques critical to building accounting information systems. Like Chapter 2, this chapter is application oriented and contains very little theory; however, we emphasize *employing* the theory we presented earlier. In this chapter you will learn how to use two important types of Access objects, tables and queries. In particular, you will learn how to:

- Reset the Tables and Queries toolbars to their original configuration.
- Define a table's structure.
- Enter data into a table.
- Alter a table's structure.
- Set a table's field properties.
- Join tables and establish referential integrity checks between them.
- Create queries involving a single table.
- Create queries for tables with a many-to-many relationship.
- Create queries involving multiple tables, derived column values, and expressions.
- Create queries with an outer join relationship to reveal hidden information.
- Create parameter queries.

We continue using The Coffee Merchant's tables as the backdrop application in this chapter. All the tables and queries mentioned in Chapter 3 have been copied to the Ch04 folder on the Companion CD. For all exercises and examples in this chapter, we assume that you have inserted the Companion CD in your CD drive, copied the database *Ch04.mdb* to your hard disk, turned off the database file's read-only attribute, started Microsoft Access, and opened the Ch04 database. If not, then please be sure to do so before doing the exercises in this chapter.

## ACCESS OBJECTS

The term *Access objects* refers to the several ways you can store and display information in your tables. Like most database systems, Access provides a rich variety of objects for your use. Beginning with the most fundamental, objects include tables, queries, forms, reports, pages, macros, and modules.

### Tables

All database information is stored in one or more tables comprised of rows and columns. A row contains all the information about a particular item in the table. Also called a record, a row's columns contain individual values for each attribute that characterizes the row. For instance, The Coffee Merchant's *tblCustomer* table contains a row for each current or potential customer. Columns in the Customer table hold information about ten different attributes of a customer record.

Each column can contain only one data type. Though the exact names of these data types vary from one RDBMS to another, they are all drawn from a small, common set. Data types constrain the type of information that can be entered into a column. Access supports the data types listed in Figure 4.1. Of the listed types, you will probably use the AutoNumber, Currency, Date/Time, Text, and Number data types most frequently.

### Queries

A query is a question you ask about one or more tables in your database. You use queries to locate and display a subset of the rows of a table, combine information from several tables into a single result, or perform calculations on fields. You can also use queries to make massive changes to a table, delete data from a table, or insert rows into a table. These latter queries are known as *action queries*.

Access uses the popular Query By Example (QBE) method in which you select one or more tables to query and then check off the columns you would like to see. By placing values or expressions below particular column names, you can limit the rows that are retrieved. These values or expressions are called selection criteria. By using the appropriate selection criteria, you can, for instance, list all customers who live in the Midwest. Or you can compute the total value of all outstanding invoices based on an invoice table or tables. Queries are used to reduce the amount of information that is displayed, summarizing it and giving it meaning.

### Forms

Forms provide a simpler way of looking at the data in a table one row at a time. You can look at a great deal of information or only a small amount. Data displayed in a form is exactly the same data found in a table. The only difference is that you

| Data Type | Description and Use |
|---|---|
| Text | Holds characters—anything you can type on the keyboard. Data cannot be used in calculations. Employee names and inventory descriptions are examples. A text field can hold up to 255 characters. |
| Memo | Lengthy, variable-length text and numbers for comments or explanations. A memo field can contain up to 65,535 characters. |
| Number | Numeric data that can be used in calculations (unlike identification numbers, which are not used in calculations). Set the FieldSize property to define the specific Number type. Do not use Number type data for calculations involving money; use Currency for these calculations. |
| Date/Time | Holds date or time information. Several formats are available, or you can establish a custom format. |
| Currency | Holds monetary data of up to 19 significant digits (15 to the left of the decimal point and 4 to the right). Currency fields are formatted to display a currency symbol and two decimal places. Use currency to avoid rounding errors in financial calculations. |
| AutoNumber | A unique sequential number that is automatically generated by Access. Numbers no longer needed are retired. The AutoNumber data type is often used for primary keys, because it guarantees unique values. |
| Yes/No | Yes/No, True/False, or On/Off are all examples of legitimate field values. Choose the Yes/No data type when only two values are possible (gender or invoice paid, for example). |
| OLE Object | Contains objects from another Windows application such as a picture, graph, or spreadsheet. When you double-click an OLE object, the program that created the object is launched so you can modify or view the OLE object. OLE objects occupy large amounts of space. |
| Hyperlink | Text or combinations of text and numbers constituting a World Wide Web hyperlink address. |
| Lookup Wizard | Creates a field that provides the mechanism to automatically look up a value from another table or list of fields by using a combo box or list box control. |

**Figure 4.1**  Access data types.

can format and enhance the data's appearance in a form. Figure 4.2 shows a form displaying data from The Coffee Merchant's Employee table.

A form is especially useful for nonexperts who must enter or change data in a table. Data entry is also much easier when using a well-designed form. Helpful aids, such as drop-down lists or radio buttons, can be embedded in a form.

**Figure 4.2**  Example form.

Drop-down lists, for example, are helpful when you encounter an entry whose possible values are limited but not known to the user. By making a list available, you can choose one of a select set of values by simply clicking your choice. When you move to another row the changed information is automatically posted to the underlying table.

Form navigation buttons make moving around the data easy. You can move to the first or last row in a table, up or down one row at a time, or to a particular row. You can customize a form so that it precisely matches an existing paper form, making the computerized version less intimidating and more familiar to those who are computer novices. You will learn about forms in Chapter 5.

## Reports

While forms provide an excellent way to view and alter data in one or more tables, reports are superb for providing boardroom-quality printed, detailed, and summary information. You can sort, group, and summarize results. Reports can contain subtotals, totals, averages, and counts, all attractively printed. Like other reporting tools, you can include report headers and footers and page headers and footers. You can also create mailing labels using the Access report facility.

Like forms, reports can take advantage of Access' many design tools, including graphic import, lines, boxes, and text, to name a few. Data can be drawn from several tables and combined in one report. Figure 4.3 shows an example of a simple report that can be quickly and easily produced with Access. You will learn about reports in Chapter 5.

## Pages

A data access *page* is a special Web page designed to allow you to view and work with data from the Internet or an intranet—data that is stored in a Microsoft Access

# Employees Grouped by Title

| Title | Name | ID | Hire Date | Birth Date | Gender |
|---|---|---|---|---|---|
| Sales Trainee | | | | | |
| | Nagasaki, Ted | 2695 | 1/28/00 | 4/10/77 | M |
| | Pruski, Kevin | 1364 | 12/1/00 | 1/26/79 | M |
| Sales Associate | | | | | |
| | Bateman, Giles | 4057 | 2/16/92 | 5/1/58 | M |
| | Chang, Annie | 3609 | 9/16/97 | 3/30/77 | F |
| | Ellison, Larry | 3700 | 4/18/94 | 12/12/54 | M |
| | English, Melinda | 3432 | 10/1/93 | 2/14/56 | F |
| | Gates, William | 3436 | 4/11/95 | 3/9/54 | M |
| | Halstead, Whitney | 4058 | 6/16/96 | 12/22/73 | F |
| | Hunter, Helen | 2318 | 11/16/93 | 1/26/54 | F |
| | Kahn, Phillipe | 2754 | 5/14/97 | 5/29/61 | M |
| | Kole, David | 3370 | 2/8/92 | 3/23/63 | M |
| | Pacioli, Luca | 1528 | 8/26/95 | 5/6/50 | M |
| | Stonesifer, Patti | 1301 | 7/6/96 | 3/10/66 | F |
| | Watterson, Barbara | 3943 | 10/10/93 | 5/1/61 | F |
| Senior Sales Associate | | | | | |
| | Ballmer, Steve | 3692 | 5/16/85 | 7/13/44 | M |
| | Flintsteel, Hillary | 4082 | 3/21/90 | 8/22/58 | F |
| | Goldman, Ted | 4112 | 12/24/90 | 3/5/62 | M |
| | Manispour, Sharad | 4029 | 12/18/90 | 2/4/69 | M |
| | Minsky, Barbara | 4012 | 10/13/90 | 4/12/59 | F |
| | Morrison, Alanis | 3458 | 12/13/89 | 7/4/56 | F |
| | Shoenstein, Brad | 3892 | 9/5/90 | 3/6/55 | M |
| | Stonely, Sharon | 2240 | 11/5/88 | 5/3/61 | F |

**Figure 4.3**  Example report.

database or a Microsoft SQL Server database. Additionally, the data access page can contain data from other sources such as a Microsoft Excel worksheet.

You design all your data Access pages in Design view; the collection of page designs is found in the Pages collection of the database. When you design a data access page, the page is actually stored as a separate file outside Access, and Access automatically adds a shortcut to the file in the Pages collection of objects in the Database window. Often, data access pages are a convenient way to consolidate and group information that is stored in a database and then publish summaries of the data on the Internet. Data access pages also allow you to view, add, and edit records.

A data access page is connected directly to a database. When users display the data access page in Microsoft Internet Explorer, they are viewing their own copy of a page. Thus, if each user filters, sorts, or changes the way the database displays, that affects only their copy of the data access page. However, any changes a user makes to the database—by deleting records, editing fields, or adding data—do affect the database. The changes are available to anyone viewing the database through Access or through data access pages on the Web. A clear advantage of data access pages, a facility not available prior to Access 2000—is that remote users with an Internet connection can view and manipulate an Access database without having Microsoft Access installed, though they must have a Microsoft Office license to do so. Figure 4.4 shows a page generated from Access. It behaves just like an Access form (discussed in Chapter 5).

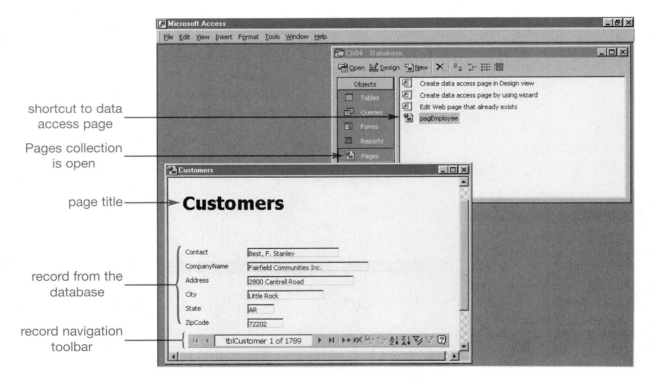

**Figure 4.4** Viewing a database record with Internet Explorer.

## Macros and Modules

*Macros* are Visual Basic codes that can be executed at the click of a button or when a form is opened. They define one or more actions that you want Access to perform in response to a particular event. Macros are frequently attached to objects located on a form, but you can write stand-alone code segments that can be invoked by a wide variety of objects in your applications. For example, you can write a small macro to check the value of an entry after the user moves to the next form field. If the field fails a value range test performed by the macro, then the macro can display an error message and move back to the erroneous field. We will illustrate macros in Chapter 10.

A *module* is an object containing custom procedures that you code using Visual Basic. Modules provide a finer degree of control and flow that allow you to write code that recognizes and traps errors—something macros cannot do. Modules are stand-alone, global objects that can be called into action from anywhere within your Access application. Defining modules means the code can be reused by all of your forms, scripts, and other libraries. You will learn about modules in Chapter 10.

## Separating Tables from Other Objects

Whether or not you are developing an application for a client server environment, you may find it convenient to separate an application's tables from queries, forms, reports, and other database objects. Doing so allows you to store tables in one database and related, nontable objects in another database. You can then create queries, forms, reports, macros, and modules based on linked tables. A *linked table* is stored in a file outside the open database from which Microsoft Access can access records. You can perform all the normal database operations on linked tables except altering their structure. That is, you can insert, delete, update, and view records in linked tables.

Why would you bother to separate tables—the only database object storing data—from other database objects? The single most important reason to separate tables from the other application objects is to provide application development independence. As a developer, you can continue to improve and develop the queries, forms, and reports embedded in one of the two application database files. Then, when you replace a client's application with the newest version of the database application you have been independently developing, you simply supplant the database containing the queries, forms, reports, macros, and modules with the new one. The database containing only tables remains unchanged. This way, your client's ever-changing tables are not affected, and the client can continue processing using the database. This method allows you to transparently update software without affecting the firm using your database software. Figure 4.5 shows a graphical representation of table/object separation.

## WORKING WITH TABLES

We have described tables in Chapters 2 and 3. Here we show you how to alter an existing table's structure, and how to modify a table whose rows are related to another table. Prohibiting removal of a parent table row until all the rows in another

**Figure 4.5** Separating tables from other database objects.

table referring to the parent table are first removed is called *referential integrity.* This is an important feature provided by most relational database management systems. Referential integrity can be enforced, and we will show you how on one of the existing tables for The Coffee Merchant. In this section we show you how to add and delete columns from a table and how to forge a permanent link between related tables. First, let's see how to add and delete table columns.

One of the important tables in the evolving invoice subsystem contains customer names, addresses, and telephone numbers (and other fields) collected from both customers and people who merely expressed an interest in receiving a catalog. Besides periodically sending out promotional material to selected members of the customer "list," customer information appears in the "Ship to," "Sold to," or "Bill to" areas of invoices. The Coffee Merchant sample Customer table is somewhat large (over 1,700 rows), but it is small when compared to the customer database of a company such as Microsoft. The Coffee Merchant Customer table, called *tblCustomer*, is stored in the database called *Ch04.mdb*. The database is found on your Companion CD in the Ch04 folder. We have loaded *tblCustomer* with several rows so you can experience manipulating a non-trivial table. All of the data is real, including company names and addresses. The telephone numbers and contact persons have been randomized sufficiently to protect the privacy of individuals. You will notice that the telephone area codes are correct and correspond to the city in which the business is located.

In the next several sections we want you to create a table from scratch and enter data into it. Rather than have you be mere observers of our data, you will be involved with the entire process, from start to finish, of designing your own table. Doing so prepares you to create quality databases after you finish reading this book and working its exercises. That's why it is instructive for you to build and fill at least one of the tables so that you experience the process. If you have trouble, the Companion CD contains all the tables and other objects for The Coffee Merchant. The next section begins the process by describing how to create a mini-version of the Customer table. The section afterward describes the step-by-step process of filling (called *populating*) your table.

## Defining a Table's Structure

From here on in the chapter, you will be doing a lot of work with the Ch04 database. If you have not already done so, copy the database from your Companion CD to the hard drive on your computer. Insert your Companion CD in the drive and copy the file *Ch04.mdb* from the Ch04 folder. Remember to turn off the read-only attribute on the *Ch04.mdb* file after you have copied it to your hard disk. Once the database has been copied to your disk, you can remove the Companion CD and store it for safekeeping. Every change you make to the database will be made to the copy of the database you just created on your hard disk. Of course, you will want to save your database to a floppy disk to preserve the work you have done to that point. (As you know, you cannot write the database file back to the Companion CD.)

Prepare for the first exercise in this chapter using Access by launching Access. Next, select Open from the File menu and then locate and select in the Open dialog box database *Ch04.mdb*. Follow the steps in the next exercise to create an example Customer table that is a much smaller version of the *tblCustomer* table already stored in the Chapter 4 database.

EXERCISE 4.1: CREATING THE CUSTOMER TABLE STRUCTURE

1. Make sure the Tables collection in the Database window is open, and then click the New button to open the New Table dialog box.
2. Select Design View from the list of choices and click OK to get started. In the upper part of the Table window in Design view are columns in which you can enter a field name, data type, and description for each field. You will do this next.
3. Type *CustomerID* in the first row of the Field Name column in the Table dialog box. Press Tab to move to the Data Type column. Most database experts agree that column names should *not* contain embedded spaces. Some database

systems disallow spaces, so your table and database cannot be ported to or used by those systems. Always follow the Hungarian notation in which words are given initial capitalization and concatenated to form an object name.

4. Type *N* in the Data Type column (click the list box to see a list of all Access data types). Press Tab to move to the Description field.

5. Type the description *Customer identification number.* (The Description field text appears in the status bar on the left side whenever the cursor is positioned on the corresponding field during data entry. It helps you remember the purpose of the field.)

6. Click the Primary Key button on the toolbar or select Primary Key from the Edit menu. (The Primary Key toolbar button displays a small key. Move the mouse over it, pause, and the ToolTip "Primary Key" is displayed confirming you have selected the correct button.) Access places a small key symbol to the left of the field name indicating that CustomerID is the table's primary key. If you need to select multiple columns for a composite primary key, simply hold down the Ctrl key and click the row selectors to the left of the fields' names. Then click the Primary Key toolbar button. Press Tab to move to the next row to define the next customer column.

7. Type *CompanyName* in the Field Name column and press Tab. Text is the suggested data type. That is fine. However, the default length, 50, is too large. You will change it in the next step.

8. Click the Field Size property in the Field Properties list found in the lower half of the dialog box. (You can press F6 to move to the Field Properties panel and back.) Type *25* in the Field Size cell.

9. Click the Description column in the Company field row and type *Company name.* Press Tab to move to the next row in the Table dialog box.

10. Type *PhoneNumber*, select the Text data type, change the default data length (Field Size property, lower panel) to *8*, and type the description *Telephone number.* Press Tab to move to the next row.

11. Type *LastContactDate*, type *D* to select the Date/Time data type, and type the description *Date of last contact* in the Description column. Press Tab to move to a new row.

12. Type *CreditLimit* in the Field Name column, select the Number data type, and type the description *Credit limit.* Press Tab to move to the next (and last) row.

13. Type *Notes* and type *M* to select the Memo data type. In the Description field type *Miscellaneous notes*

14. Save the newly defined table: select Save from the File menu. The Save As dialog box is displayed (see Figure 4.6). (Your field names, types, and descriptions should match those shown in Figure 4.6. If not, simply click in the incorrect cell and change it.)

15. Type *tblMyCustomer* in the Table Name text box and then click OK. Access saves your newly created Customer table, *tblMyCustomer*, in the Ch04 database.

16. Click Close in the File menu to close the table. (Alternatively, you can click the Close button on the table's Title bar to close its Design view.)

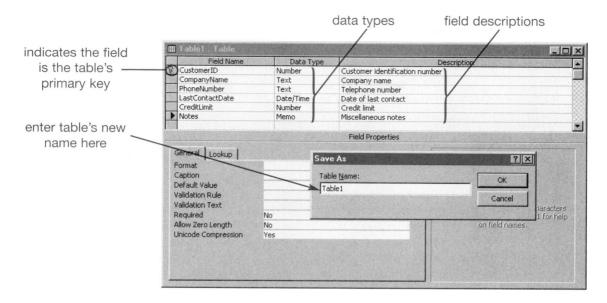

**Figure 4.6**   Defining a table's structure and saving it.

Be sure you save your new table with the name *tblMyCustomer*, not *tblCustomer*. This is a safety feature. This way you still have the original table *tblCustomer*, which is on the Companion CD, for use in the textbook's exercises.

Next, let's enter some data into the table *tblMyCustomer*. This will give you experience entering, altering, and saving data.

## Populating a Table

When you *populate* a table, you are simply placing data into a table whose structure already exists. Entering data into a table is straightforward. First, ensure that *Ch04.mdb* is open. Then, locate *tblMyCustomer* in the Tables objects of the Database window. Double-click the *tblMyCustomer* table name to open it in Datasheet view. Maximize the Table window so that you can see the full table. Next, you will enter the first customer record. Exercise 4.2 uses three different methods to move to the next field: pressing Tab, clicking the next field, and pressing Enter. Select the one that suits you best.

EXERCISE 4.2: ENTERING A RECORD INTO A TABLE

1. In the CustomerID field, type *3001* and press Tab to move to the CompanyName field.
2. Type *Experience Coffee* in the CompanyName field. Move to the PhoneNumber field by clicking the cell just under the PhoneNumber field name.

3. Type *555-1233* in the PhoneNumber field. Press Enter to move to the next column, LastContactDate.
4. Type *5/23/2001* in the LastContactDate field. Press Tab to move to the CreditLimit column.
5. Type *4000* and press Tab to move to the last column, Notes.
6. Type *This is a good customer* in the memo field.

Don't press any keys for a moment. Do you notice the small pencil symbol in the row selector button of the table? This indicates that a record's contents have been changed but not yet posted to the table. You post changes to a table simply by moving to another table record. You will do that in a moment.

If you make a mistake anywhere while entering data, simply use the arrow keys to move left or right in the field, or use the Backspace or Delete keys to delete information. Pressing a key inserts the letter into the field at the insertion point indicated by the cursor. To correct a value in a field to the left of the current field, press Shift+Tab repeatedly until the cursor arrives at the field to be changed. To display the blinking insertion point, simply press F2. Then you can use the arrow keys to move the insertion point within a field. Pressing Tab or Shift+Tab moves to another cell and selects the entire value.

Next, enter the remaining *tblMyCustomer* table data by completing Exercise 4.3. When you move to a new row, the previous row is stored on disk. The last record you enter in a table is saved when you close the table or you close the entire database. Alternatively, you can simply press the up arrow key to move to a previous record to save the latest record.

EXERCISE 4.3: ENTER THE REMAINING *TBLMYCUSTOMER* TABLE DATA

1. With the *tblMyCustomer* table still displayed, click in the CustomerID column of the second table row.
2. Enter the remaining table rows. Figure 4.7 shows all customer table rows. Refer to it as you enter the remaining customer records. You can enter anything you like (or nothing) in the Notes field of each customer record. That's entirely up to you.
3. After you enter the last customer's information, click the Table window Close button to close the table. The last row of the *tblMyCustomer* table will be posted automatically to the database.

## Adding a Column to a Table

If you create and use a table and later—perhaps much later—discover you have left out an important column or two, you can add one or more new columns to ta-

| CustomerID | CompanyName | PhoneNumber | LastContactDate | CreditLimit |
|---|---|---|---|---|
| 3101 | Experience Coffee | 555-1233 | 5/23/01 | 4000 |
| 3122 | Gourmet Grinder | 555-7826 | 9/14/00 | 1000 |
| 3245 | La Jolla Expresso | 555-3919 | 7/9/01 | 5500 |
| 3658 | Starbucks Coffee | 555-5561 | 9/14/00 | 15000 |
| 3702 | Kensington Coffee Company | 555-6153 | 12/16/00 | 1000 |
| 3824 | Intermezzo Espresso Bar | 555-8282 | 8/5/01 | 7500 |
| 3961 | Just Bean Counters | 555-9646 | 3/15/01 | 2500 |

**Figure 4.7**   Contents of the example customer table, *tblMyCustomer*.

bles at any time. You can add a column to a table either in Datasheet view or Design view. Adding a column in Design view is the best way, because you can add a column and define all of its characteristics in one window—the Design View window. On the other hand, you can add a column more quickly in Datasheet view.

The Coffee Merchant's Division Location table (*tblDivisionLocation*) contains the city and state in which each of The Coffee Merchant's divisions is located. It is useful to place often-repeated character strings such as cities or organization names in their own table along with a unique identification number. Then you can refer to the cities with a number in place of the long string in the original table. Among other advantages, this prevents you from misspelling "Cincinnati" or other city names when they occur frequently in a table's columns. This is the purpose of the *tblDivisionLocation* table. A related column, yet to be placed in the *tblEmployee* table, will contain a number that is related to the company division number found in the *tblDivisionLocation* table. Your next job will be to add a new table column to *tblEmployee*—a division number column—which is a foreign key field linked to the primary key of the *tblDivisionLocation* table. A *foreign key* is a column whose values match similar values in another table's primary key column. A foreign key column in one table *always* corresponds to a primary key column in another table. Once the *tblEmployee* and *tblDivisionLocation* tables are linked together through their primary key/foreign key pairs, you will be able to determine the city and state in which each employee and each employee's division are located.

Each employee row should have an entry indicating which division the employee works for. Adding or deleting a column in a table is called *altering* the table's structure. Do not confuse this activity with adding or deleting *data* in a table's columns.

The next exercise shows you how to add a column to a table. In particular, you will add a column called *EmployeeDivisionID* to the *tblEmployee* table. This column is a foreign key to the *tblDivisionLocation* table.

EXERCISE 4.4: ADDING A COLUMN TO THE EMPLOYEE TABLE

1. Click Tables in the Database Objects bar if necessary. Select *tblEmployee*, and click the Design button. Maximize the Table window to display all columns.
2. Select the entire EmployeeTitleID row by clicking its row selector button. Press the Insert key. (Alternatively, you can select Row from the Insert menu.) A new, empty row is added to the table's structure.
3. In the new row, select the Field Name cell, type *EmployeeDivisionID*, and press Tab to move to the Data Type column.
4. Type *N* because the EmployeeDivisionID field will hold a number.
5. Select the Description field and type the description *Identification of the division for which this employee works* to document the field's use.
6. Select the Caption property box in the Field Properties panel and type *Division ID* (with an embedded space). The Caption property text is displayed in place of the column's name in forms, reports, and Datasheet views of tables.
7. Select Save from the File menu. This saves the revised *tblEmployee* table structure.
8. Click the Design view Close button.

To complete this operation, you need to place data in the newly created EmployeeDivisionID column. This is relatively easy. Make sure you fill in the field for each employee row, because the next exercise will use the EmployeeDivisionID column values to establish a connection to the *tblDivisionLocation* table.

EXERCISE 4.5: PLACE VALUES IN THE EMPLOYEEDIVISIONID COLUMN

1. Open the *tblEmployee* table in Datasheet view and click any entry in the Phone column.
2. Select Records, Sort, Sort Ascending to sort the table low to high on the telephone number.
3. Select the topmost Division ID cell corresponding to employee David Kole and type *101* into the cell.
4. Repeat step 3 for the next five employees. The first six employees all work in division 101.
5. Type the value *102* in the next six Division ID cells, indicating that employees Sharad Manispour through Whitney Halstead work in Division 102. (Hint: After entering the value 102 once, use Copy/Paste to rapidly paste the next five entries.)
6. Type *103* for the next six employees' Division ID attributes—employees whose names are Kevin Pruski through Luca Pacioli. (Remember to speed up data entry by pasting—Ctrl+V—copies of the same field into successive rows' cells.)
7. Finally, type *104* for the remaining four employees—Ellison through Flintsteel.

8. Close the table (click the Datasheet view Close button) and click No when you are asked if you want to save changes to the design of the table. (We are not interested in preserving the *view* of the table in sorted order, even though the table is not actually sorted.)

Keep the following distinction in mind. A table's design has to do with its structure—the number and characteristics of its columns, not the columns' contents. You have changed the table's contents just now and those changes are automatically posted to the table. Remember to save any table structural changes by executing the Save command in the File menu.

## Deleting or Renaming a Table Column

It is easy to remove unwanted columns from any table or to give one or more columns a new name. Though you don't need to delete table columns right now, you should learn how to do it. You can delete a column while viewing a table in either Datasheet view or Design view. It is equally easy to delete a column in either view. To delete a table's column in Design view, click Tables in the Database Objects bar, select a table, and open it in Design view. Click the row selector to the left of the column you want to delete and click the Delete button. Remember to click the Save button (or File, Save) to post the changed table structure to your database. To delete a table column in Datasheet view, right-click the column's field selector, select Delete Column from the pop-up menu, and click Yes when a dialog box asks if you want to permanently delete the column. In Design view, any attribute rows that are below the deleted field are moved up to close the gap. In Datasheet view, any columns to the right of the deleted column move left to close the gap left by the deleted column.

You may decide that a column name no longer makes sense or is otherwise inappropriate. Renaming a column is straightforward. You can change a table column's name either in Datasheet view or Design view. In Datasheet view, simply double-click the column's selector, type a new name, and press Enter. The new name replaces the name originally assigned. Also, the renamed field's Caption property is deleted. (You will learn about field properties later in this chapter.) To rename a table column in Design view, first display the table in Design view. Next, click the Field Name cell that you want to change and type over the old name with its replacement. Finally, click Save in the File menu to store the altered table.

## Moving a Table Column

Although the order of columns in a table has no importance whatsoever, you can rearrange table columns so they appear in a different order in Datasheet view. Just like other table structure alteration operations mentioned here, you can rearrange table columns either in Datasheet view or Design view. We think that this is easiest to accomplish in Datasheet view. To move a column or a group of contiguous columns, you begin by selecting the columns. Click the field selector of the column you want to move. To select adjacent columns, click a column field selector and move the mouse to adjacent columns without releasing the mouse. In either case, one or more columns is selected. Click and hold the mouse in the field selector again and drag the column(s) to their new location. Release the mouse button to "drop" the selected columns into their new locations. Click Save in the File menu to save the altered table structure in the database.

## Establishing Referential Integrity

Access provides a way to enforce *referential integrity* whereby defined relationships between tables are maintained permanently and automatically. For example, referential integrity rules prevent you from adding a record to a related table if there is no associated record in the primary table. Additionally, the rules prevent you from deleting or changing records in a primary table that would result in orphan records in a related table. Suppose you want to enforce referential integrity between the Invoice table (*tblInvoice*) and the related Invoice Line table (*tblInvoiceLine*). Once you tell Access to enforce referential integrity rules between two tables, you cannot delete an invoice from the parent Invoice table unless there are no related invoice line items in the Invoice Line table. As you work more with Access, you will gain a deeper understanding of how referential integrity works to preserve a kind of "parent/child" relationship between tables falling under the integrity protection rules.

In the next exercise, you will do your work in the *Relationships* window, a window that displays linkages between tables for a given database. You define permanent linkages—primary key to foreign key relationships—to make forming multiple-table queries easier. You can also choose whether or not the Relationships window displays none, some, or all intertable relationships. To illustrate just how this works, you will establish referential integrity between the Employee table (*tblEmployee*) and the Division Location table (*tblDivisionLocation*). This will ensure that a division in the table *tblDivisionLocation* cannot be deleted until all employees (*tblEmployee*) have been reassigned to a new division or first removed completely.

EXERCISE 4.6: ESTABLISHING REFERENTIAL INTEGRITY

1. Close all windows except the Database window.
2. Select Relationships from the Tools menu (or click the Relationships button on the Tables toolbar). A Relationships window opens. It may appear empty initially.
3. Select Show Table from the Relationships menu (or click the Show Table button on the toolbar). A Show Table dialog box is displayed.
4. Select the Tables tab, if necessary.
5. Double-click the *tblEmployee* table to add it to the Relationships window (see Figure 4.8).

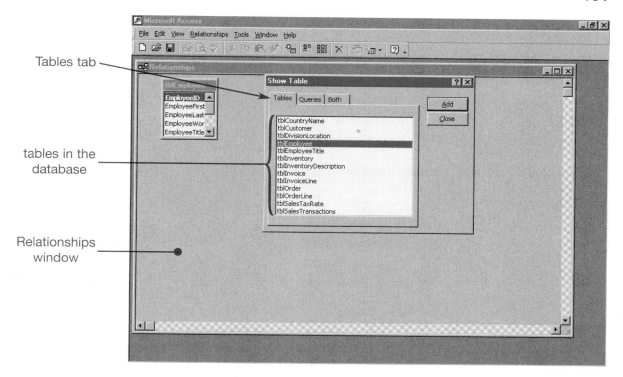

Tables tab

tables in the database

Relationships window

**Figure 4.8** Show Table dialog box.

6. Select *tblDivisionLocation*, click the Add button to display that table's field roster in the Relationships window, and click the Close button. No more tables are to be added at this time. The two tables and their attribute names are displayed in the Relationships window. (You may want to drag the bottom border of *tblEmployee* to reveal all of its attributes. Drag the right border of *tblEmployee* to reveal the longer field names.)

   Next, let's show the primary key to foreign key connection between the two tables.

7. In the Relationships window click the DivisionID field in *tblDivisionLocation* and drag and drop the field onto the EmployeeDivisionID field in *tblEmployee* (see Figure 4.9).

8. Click the Enforce Referential Integrity check box to select this option. A check mark is placed in the check box (see Figure 4.10).

9. Click the Create button to establish referential integrity between the two tables.

10. Finally, click the Relationships window Close button and click Yes when you are asked "Do you want to save changes to the layout of 'Relationships'?" This preserves the newly established relationship and the referential integrity constraint. Figure 4.11 shows the line in the Relationships dialog box before you close it. On one end of the line is the number 1, indicating the primary key side of the relationship. On the other side is the symbol for infinity, which indicates

the foreign key side of the relationship. The infinity symbol means that several records can be related to a single record in the "parent" table.

the mouse pointer changes shape when you drag a field from one table field list to another

click and drag the DivisionID field to the *foreign key* in *tblEmployee*

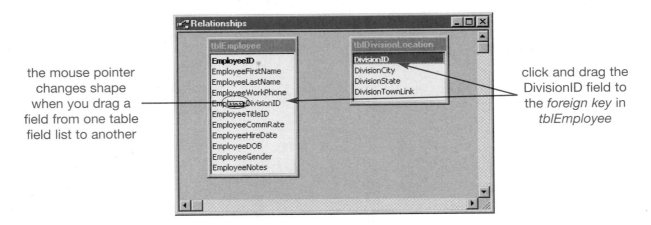

**Figure 4.9**  Establishing a link between related tables.

primary key field name from *tblDivisionLocation*

foreign key field name from *tblEmployee*

Enforce Referential Integrity check box

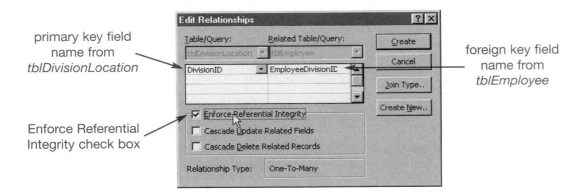

**Figure 4.10**  Enforcing Referential Integrity in the Relationships dialog box.

When you join two tables in the Relationships window as illustrated here, their Datasheet view is slightly different from the way it appears before the tables are joined. A new column called the *expand indicator* appears in the first column of each table that is explicitly linked to another table. The indicator displays either a plus sign (+) or minus sign (–). When viewing a linked table in Datasheet view, you can click the expand indicator attached to any row to view any related records. The next exercise illustrates how to view related records in the *tblEmployee* and *tblDivisionLocation* tables.

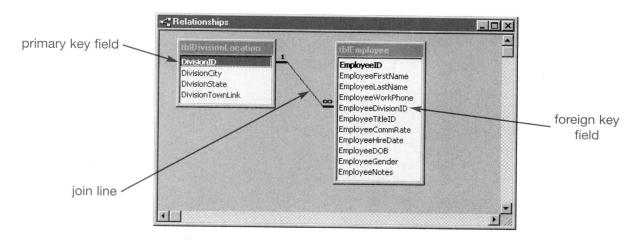

**Figure 4.11**  A join line connects two tables.

EXERCISE 4.7: DISPLAYING RELATED TABLES WITH THE EXPAND INDICATOR

1. Open the *Ch04.mdb* database, if necessary, and close all windows except the Database window.
2. Select Tables from the Database Objects bar and double-click *tblDivisionLocation* to open it. The table opens in Datasheet view (the default view when you double-click a table name).
3. Click the expand indicator of the first *tblDivisionLocation* row, which corresponds to DivisionID 101. A portion of the Employee table opens, revealing which employees work in that division (see Figure 4.12). Notice that the expand indicator, normally a plus sign, changes to a minus sign. The minus sign indicates that the related table rows are open. Of course, if no rows are related to the row whose expand indicator you click, then no related *tblEmployee* rows are displayed.
4. After you examine the results, click the *tblDivisionLocation* expand indicator to close the rows of *tblEmployee*.

Any table rows revealed when you click an expand indicator are called a *subdatasheet*. Not all rows in *tblDivisionLocation* have a subdatasheet. For example, no employees are currently working at the Knoxville, Tennessee plant. You can add rows to subdatasheets that are open by simply entering data in the open row at the end of the table—next to the new row indicator. If you add a row to the *tblEmployee* table subdatasheet, Access automatically fills in the foreign key field value for EmployeeDivisionID—the value that corresponds to that group of related rows.

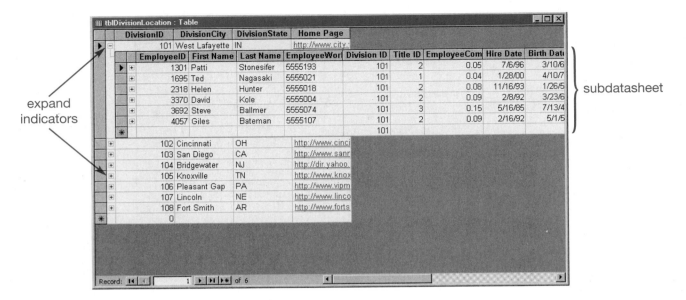

**Figure 4.12**   Clicking the expand indicator reveals related records.

**Try it**

Click the expand indicator corresponding to Knoxville in *tblDivisionLocation*. An empty row is returned. This indicates no employee currently is assigned to that location.

## Editing and Removing Intertable Relationships

You can remove or edit an existing relationship between pairs of tables by a procedure similar to the preceding one. For example, you can remove referential integrity checks between *tblEmployee* and *tblDivisionLocation* by opening the Relationships window, right-clicking the line connecting the two tables, selecting Edit Relationship, and clearing the Enforce Referential Integrity check box. This edits the relationship between the tables, but does not remove it. Removing a relationship is equally easy. Open the Relationships window (choose Relationships from the Tools menu), click the line that connects the two tables, then press the Delete key. Similarly, you can right-click the line connecting the tables and select Delete from the pop-up menu that appears. In either case, the connecting line disappears along with the explicit relationship definition. Whenever you change a relationship by editing or removing it, be sure to select Save from the File menu to preserve the relationship changes.

## Setting Field Properties

You can customize each field of a table by setting its specific properties. Each field has property settings that affect the way the field looks and behaves. These property settings are found in the Field Properties panel, which is visible when you display a table in Design view (see Figure 4.6). When you set one or more properties for a particular field, those properties are enforced wherever the field appears subsequently—including queries, forms, and reports. The number and type of properties vary slightly depending on the field's data type you select. A field whose data type is numeric, for instance, has a Decimal Places property, whereas a Text field does not. Similarly, a text type field has a Field Size property, but a date type field does not. All together, there are 45 distinct properties available. We will discuss a few of the most important properties here. You can learn about other field properties by pressing F1 to obtain online help. Next, you will learn about several important properties. We present these in the same order as they appear from top to bottom in the Field Properties panel. After we explain key properties, we present exercises that show you how to set Field Properties values.

**FIELD SIZE.** The Field Size property allows you to specify the length of text and number fields. Text fields can be from 0 through 255 characters long. The default Field Size for text fields is 50. Number fields have sizes varying from a single-byte integer (Byte), to two integer sizes (Integer or Long Integer), and two floating point number sizes (Single or Double). The size of a text field limits how much information you can enter. Specifying a numeric field size restricts fields to a particular magnitude and to either integer numbers or real numbers (numbers containing decimal places).

**FORMAT.** You can use the Format property to customize the way number, dates, times, and text appear when they are printed or displayed. For example, you can set the EmployeeCommRate—employees' commission rates—Format property to *percent* and the Decimal Places property to *2* so that a value such as 0.057 will display as 5.70% in the table, queries, forms, or reports—wherever the field is referenced. The Format property uses different settings for different data types. Consult Access help for details about the several format choices.

**INPUT MASK.** The Input Mask property makes data entry easier and allows you to control the values that users can enter. For example, an Input Mask for a date field can indicate exactly what you expect the user to enter and prevent all keystrokes except digits: __/__/__. It is frequently easier to use the Input Mask Wizard to help you create an Input Mask.

**CAPTION.** The Caption property provides an alternative field name—an alias—that appears in various views. Field captions specify the heading for the field in a table's Datasheet view or a query's Datasheet view. When a field appears in a report or form, the table's caption appears as the field's label. The Caption property is a string expression that can contain up to 2,048 characters. If you do not specify the Caption property value, then the table's Field Name appears wherever the field is referenced.

**DEFAULT VALUE.** The Default Value property specifies a value that is automatically entered in a field when you create a new record. For example, if you are entering the names and addresses of members of your Chicago area club or organization, you can set the default value for the City field to Chicago. When anyone adds a new record to the table, "Chicago" automatically appears in the City field. You can either accept this value or enter the name of a different city. Set the Default Value property whenever you can identify a field whose contents are often a particular value.

**VALIDATION RULE AND VALIDATION TEXT.** The Validation Rule property specifies the requirements for data entered into a record or field. When anyone attempts to enter data that violates the Validation Rule setting, you can use the Validation Text property to specify the message to display. The Validation Rule and Validation Text properties go hand in hand. For example, suppose you want to restrict the values that users can enter in the annual salary field of an employee table. Simply enter into the salary field Validation Rule property the expression *Between 15000 and 87500* to limit the values users can enter to that range. The Validation Text property is a character string that displays when a user violates the Validation Rule for a particular field. The text is merely a character string up to 255 characters that indicates the nature of the error. For example, the salary field Validation Text "Valid salaries values are $15,000 to $87,500" indicates to the user the probable error.

**REQUIRED.** The Required property specifies whether a value is required in a field. If this value is set to Yes, then whenever you add a new record to a table, you must enter a value in the field. You might want to specify that the LastName field always has a value for each record. When a field's Required property is set to Yes and you are entering a new record, Access will not permit you to go to the next record if any required fields are empty (called *null* by database people).

**INDEXED.** The Indexed property has the value of Yes or No. When a field's Index property is Yes, Access performs a special operation on that field—called generating an index—to speed searches on the field. Fields that have an Index property value of No do not have associated indexes. While any nonindexed field can be searched, indexed field searches are much faster. Primary key fields are always indexed. You might want to index a LastName field of a table if you anticipate frequent searches by last name. In a small table, there is no noticeable difference between indexed and nonindexed field searches. In large tables—tables with 50,000 rows for instance, the search times between indexed and nonindexed fields is significant.

To illustrate how to set properties, you will set the field properties of two fields of the *tblEmployee* table. The fields are EmployeeWorkPhone and EmployeeCommRate. The employee phone numbers should be restricted to seven digits (assume the phones are all on a corporate system in which you can call any division without first entering a telephone area code). Furthermore, you want the hyphen between the first three digits and the last four digits inserted automatically. That will save time whenever anyone enters a telephone number and will ensure that the hyphen is placed in the correct position. The caption "Phone" is better than the default column name that displays, "EmployeeWorkPhone." So you will set the EmployeeWorkPhone field Caption property to display a more concise field name.

Several property changes will be made to the commission rate field, called EmployeeCommRate. The commission rate is a small number, so you will indicate its Field Size is Single to accommodate small numbers with decimal places. Set the format so that the commission rate is displayed in percentage format with two decimal places. For example, the value 0.0895 displays as 8.95% in Datasheet view. You will change the Caption property so that the commission rate column displays the heading "Rate" instead of the default and awkward heading "EmployeeCommRate," the column's Field Name. New employees and management personnel earn no commission, so you want to set the default value for the commission field to zero percent. Lastly, you will establish a valid range of commission rates so that no one can mistakenly enter an unreasonable commission rate such as 45 percent. A Validation Rule will validate all newly entered commission rates, and an appropriate Validation Text message will display when the commission rate is invalid.

Let's start with an exercise to set three employee phone field properties: Field Size, Input Mask, and Caption. To prepare for this exercise, ensure that *Ch04.mdb* is open and close all windows except the Database window. Then do the following exercise.

EXERCISE 4.8: SETTING FIELD PROPERTIES
FOR THE EMPLOYEEWORKPHONE FIELD

1. Open the table *tblEmployee* in Design view.
2. Click anywhere in the EmployeeWorkPhone row and then press F6 (a shortcut) to move to the Field Size property in the Field Properties panel.
3. Type *7* in the Field Size property.
4. Click in the Input Mask field and type *000\-0000;1;_* (three zeroes, a backslash, a hyphen, four zeroes, a semicolon, the digit 1, another semicolon, and an underline character). We explain these symbols following the exercise.

5. Click in the Caption property and type *Phone*
6. Click Save in the File menu to save your table design changes. A warning dialog box opens and displays the ominous message "Some data may be lost."
7. Click the Yes button in the dialog box. No data will be lost.
8. Close the Design view window.

The Input Mask property symbols require some explanation. The zeroes in the Input Mask mean that a digit is required in the given digit position. A backslash indicates that the character that follows the backslash, a hyphen in this case, is a literal character and not an operator such as subtraction. The first semicolon ends the first part of the Input Mask. The value 1 between the semicolons indicates that the hyphen in any entered phone number will not be stored in the field—only the seven digits of the phone number. The second semicolon ends the second part of the Input Mask. Finally, the third part of the Input Mask specified the character that Access displays for the space where you should type a character in the Input Mask. In other words, an underline appears in the Phone field wherever no digits appear.

### Try it

To see how the Phone field mask operates, open *tblEmployee* in Datasheet view. Then, drag across the digits of the Phone field of any employee and press Delete to erase the current phone number. Notice that the Phone field displays a series of underlines separated by a hyphen. Next, type *5557777* (without entering a hyphen). Notice that the digits 555 are placed before the hyphen and the remaining four digits are placed after the hyphen. Close the Datasheet view window.

EXERCISE 4.9: SETTING FIELD PROPERTIES
FOR THE EMPLOYEE COMMISSION FIELD

1. Open *tblEmployee* in Design view and click in any column of the EmployeeCommRate row.
2. Press F6 to move to the Field Size property in the Field Properties panel.
3. Click the Field Size drop-down list arrow and click *Single*.
4. Click the Format property, click the drop-down list arrow, and click *Percent*.
5. Click the Decimal Places property, drag the mouse to select the current entry, and type *2* to select two decimal places.
6. Click the Caption property and type *Rate*. Observe the comment in the right portion of the Field Properties panel. It has helpful information about the selected property.
7. Click the Default Value property and type *0*

8. Click the Validation Rule property and type *between 0 and 0.15* to indicate the range of valid commission rates. Be sure the second value is 0.15, not 15. A value of 15 means 1500%, which is an unreasonable commission rate! (When you move to another property field, notice that Access changes the expression by capitalizing the words "Between" and "And.")

9. Click the Validation Text property and type *Commission rates range from 0% to 15%*, the message that is displayed when a new, invalid commission rate is entered. Figure 4.13 shows *tblEmployee* in Design view and the new properties you set in this exercise.

10. Click Save in the File menu. A dialog box opens and displays a warning indicating that data integrity rules have changed and that existing data may not be valid. Click No to bypass the validity check for existing data. The warning occurs because you have established criteria for the commission rate field—criteria that were not in place when some records were entered. Access recognizes that existing commission data may fall outside the acceptable range. We know the data is fine.

11. Click Datasheet View in the View menu. Notice the EmployeeCommRate column has a new caption—Rate. Observe that the commissions are formatted with a percentage sign and two decimal places.

12. Close the Datasheet view window.

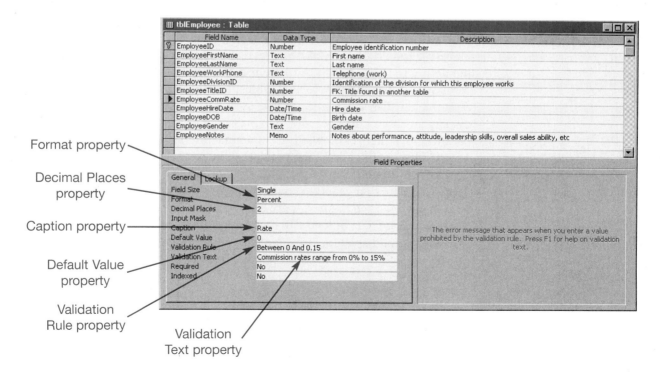

**Figure 4.13** Setting *tblEmployee* field properties.

Check out the new commission rate validation software. Go to the bottom of *tblEmployee* in Datasheet view and enter a new EmployeeID number in the empty row. Continue entering information in the row. When you reach the Rate column, type *0.55* and move to another field. What happens? Type in the valid commission rate, *12%*. Move to a new row to post the new row to the table. Delete the new employee row you just added: click in any field in the row you just added and press the Delete Record button on the Datasheet view toolbar. Click the Yes button to confirm the record-delete operation.

Be careful whenever you set both a field's Default and Validation Rule properties. They can come into conflict with each other if you aren't careful. For instance, suppose you set the Default value of a field to 2 and subsequently type the Validation Rule *Between 3 And 25*. Clearly, the default value is not in the range of allowed values set forth by the Validation Rule property. That conflict can occur inadvertently when you skip the field and Access attempts to insert the default value, 2, into the field—violating the Validation Rule.

## CREATING AND USING QUERIES

A database's ability to retrieve selected rows and columns from tables lies at the heart of its information retrieval ability. Managers seeking information about employees can retrieve rows and columns from an employee table, but information gathering would be limited if retrieval were restricted to a single table. Without the ability to select which rows are retrieved and without the ability to select information from multiple, related tables, a database's retrieval capabilities would be no better than those of a flat file system. Further, suppose someone wants to display an entire customer table in an attempt to locate all customers from Idaho, or inventory items supplied by manufacturers from California or Oregon. Manually scanning a list for candidate table rows satisfying those criteria would be time-consuming, frustrating, and error-prone.

There are two general classes of queries you can use: action queries and selection queries. *Action queries* are queries that allow you to change insert, create, or delete sets of data in your database. *Selection queries* are queries that allow you to retrieve and display data from one or more tables or queries. Chapter 2 introduced you briefly to both of these query types. In this section, we will focus on selection queries.

Selection queries pose questions to the database. Unlike tables, which hold information, queries actively search specified tables and return answers to your questions. For instance, you can use a query to return a list of all employees in the San Diego branch office in order by department and last name within department. A query can be used to list all invoices that are over 30 days past due. Although you can do a lot of work with datasheets—including sorting, updating, filtering, and printing—you will quickly find that manually manipulating a table's Datasheet view is restrictive. Queries provide you with a convenient way to filter, sort, and manipulate data. Furthermore, you can store the query so that you can repeat the operations on one or more tables. For instance, you can create a query to scan an airline reservation system's database and display the names of passengers on TWA flight 711 from Memphis to Los Angeles. By creating a query to perform the actions of searching the flight data, extracting passengers' names for a particular flight, and sorting them in name order, you automate the multi-step information retrieval process. When you run the stored query next week, the same query (a stored definition) returns a completely new result. The result is called a *dynaset*, which is a temporary table. Called a *closed set*, relational database queries examine, on input, tables and then produce, as output, a table-structured result.

Relational database systems differ in how they deliver a query facility to users. Some systems use a widely accepted RDBMS interface language called Structured Query Language (SQL). Other systems use an interface called Query By Example (QBE). Microsoft Access provides both, but most people use QBE because it is both easier to learn and straightforward to use.

Perhaps the most important feature of queries is their ability to join tables together. Related tables can be linked in a query. Then you can apply selection criteria to eliminate unwanted data and sort it on any number of fields. For example, suppose you wanted to query The Coffee Merchant tables. You might write a query to list the names and addresses of all customers whose invoices are more than 30 days past due. Two tables, *tblCustomer* and *tblInvoice*, are joined on their linking fields—their CustomerID column. The query's selection criteria limit retrieved rows to those whose InvoiceDate value is more than 30 days ago.

Building queries is not difficult. Here is an overview of the steps. The chapter provides you with a lot of practice using these steps to build actual queries to retrieve information. The steps to creating and saving a database query are:

• Select Queries in the Objects bar of the Database window and click New.

• Select Design View from the list and click OK.

• Add the table(s) to be included in the query.

• Drag the fields you want returned in the dynaset to the QBE grid.

• Enter selection criteria so that Access returns only rows that match the criteria.

• Open the query in Datasheet view to see the query's results.

• Select Design view, if necessary, to revise the query to achieve the results you want.

• Save the query if you want to rerun it later.

When you build queries involving more than one table, you follow the same basic steps outlined above except that you select additional tables for the query design. Tables cannot be arbitrarily selected to form a query. They must be related to one another. You can either indicate the relation of one table to another as you design the query, or you can establish a more permanent relationship between tables in the Relationships window. Before continuing, take a moment to look at all the intertable relationships already established for your Ch04 database. Figure 4.14 shows nearly all the tables in your database and the relationship between each pair. Take a moment to study the figure.

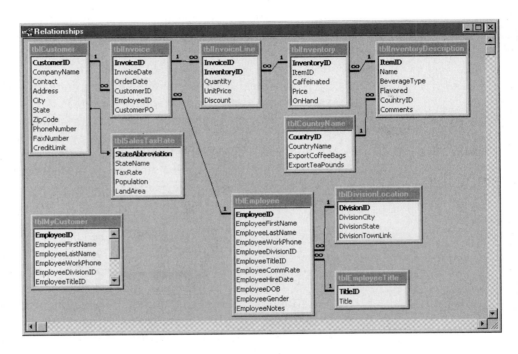

**Figure 4.14**   Relationships among tables.

Tables related to one another contain a line that connects the primary key of one table to a foreign key of the related table. For all tables in *Ch04.mdb*, the relationships are one-to-many (1—M). For example, *tblCustomer* (upper left corner of Figure 4.14) is on the "one side" of a one-to-many relationship with *tblInvoice*. That means that for each customer record in the Customer table, there may be zero, one, or several related customer invoice records. The line connecting the tables indicates the "one" side of the relationship with the digit 1 above the line next to the primary key. Similarly, Access displays the symbol for infinity to indicate the "many" side of the relationship next to the table's foreign key. Of course, any given table may be related to several other tables in the database. For example, *tblEmployee* has established relationships with two other tables, *tblDivisionLocation* and *tblEmployeeTitle*. You must explicitly establish any relationships between tables yourself. You must either create a relationship in the Relationships window where relationships persist when you create new queries, or you must create the relationship each time you create a query. Unless the name of a primary key in one table matches the foreign key of another, Access will not automatically forge a relationship between table pairs.

We introduce queries by starting with a single-table query—a query whose data is retrieved from one table. Then, you will build more complex queries involving some rows and some columns of a single table. Finally, you will build queries that draw data from many related tables.

## Retrieving Selected Rows from a Table

A query is the best way to examine a large table and select a group of records from it. A one-table query is easy to construct, and it whittles down to a manageable size the list you look at. We will illustrate a one-table query with the *tblInventoryDescription* table. It contains several important product descriptors including the beverage type (the allowed values are only *c* or *t*, which stand for coffee and tea) and whether or not the coffee or tea is flavored (yes/no). Other descriptors include the country of origin (an identification number pointing to the *tblCountryName* table) and lively comments about the particular coffee bean or tea leaf. Figure 4.15 shows some of the rows of the Inventory Description table.

**Figure 4.15** Some rows of the *tblInventoryDescription* table.

Inventories without quantity or back-order values for each inventory item are not very helpful. A related table, *tblInventory*, holds additional inventory information such as unit price and quantity in stock. (See Figure 4.14.) Together, the *tblInventory* and *tblInventoryDescription* tables supply all the inventory information for our small example. The two tables have a one-to-many relationship because each coffee listed in the *tblInventoryDescription* (for example, Jamaican Blue Mountain) can have both decaffeinated and caffeinated choices. In reality, the "many" side of the relationship, *tblInventory*, has at most two entries for every named coffee or tea. When necessary, we join the two tables on their common fields—both named ItemID in this case.

Let's create a simple query to locate and display all unflavored coffees whose beans are described as "hard bean" in the inventory. (Hard bean coffees are grown at higher altitudes than others and generally yield a better coffee.) Start from the Database window and click Queries in the database window Objects bar. Then, click the New button on the Database window, select Design View from the list, and click OK to begin the query creation process. (When creating queries, it is often easier to *not* use the Query Wizards.) Then, do the following exercise.

EXERCISE 4.10: CREATING A ONE-TABLE QUERY

1. Select the *tblInventoryDescription* table from the list presented in the Show Table dialog box, click the Add button to add it to the query, and click the Close button.
2. Drag the fields ItemID, Name, Comments, BeverageType, and Flavored from the *tblInventoryDescription* field roster to the first through fifth cells in the Field row of the QBE grid.
3. Clear the Show check boxes under BeverageType and Flavored in the QBE grid, because you do not want to display these fields in the result—they are in the query so we can use them to specify criteria.
4. Enter three selection criteria in the Criteria row:
   • under the Comments column type *Like "\*hard bean\*"* (including the quotation marks and asterisks at both ends of the string),
   • under the BeverageType column type *"c"* (with the quotation marks),
   • and under the Flavored column type *no* (letter case does not matter, but *do not* place quotation marks around this criterion or any other Yes/No criterion).
5. If you omit quotation marks when entering character string data, Microsoft Access automatically surrounds the data with quotation marks. Because the two selection criteria are in the same Criteria row of the QBE grid, both criteria must be true for a row to be returned. This is a classic AND criteria.
6. Select Datasheet View from the View menu to see the query results (dynaset).

Your dynaset should look like the one shown in Figure 4.16. We have saved this query as *qryHardBeanCoffee* on your Companion CD, so you need not save yours. Simply close the query without saving it.

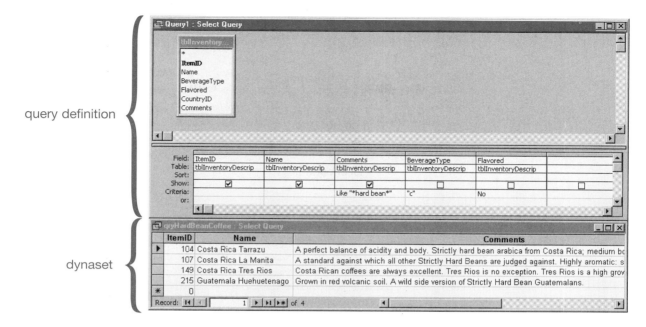

**Figure 4.16** One-table query definition and dynaset.

What if we wanted to see all inventory items that were either not flavored *or* are coffees? We would then place one criterion on one Criteria row and the other criterion on the "or" row just below the Criteria row of the QBE grid. (This type of query is a classic OR question.) Figure 4.17 shows the OR query and part of the result. As indicated in the status line, the query returned many rows—all unflavored beverages (tea or coffee) and all coffees (flavored or not).

## Working with a Dynaset

Access returns query results in a dynaset. Similar to a table in behavior and structure, a dynaset is only temporary. It is replaced every time another query is run. For most queries, you can alter information displayed by the dynaset while in Datasheet view simply by typing in new information. The new information is placed in the appropriate row and column of the underlying table. Thus, dynasets present live, updateable views of underlying table data. Some dynasets are not updateable, and Access will warn you when you attempt to update data through one of the non-updateable dynasets. Most of the dynasets presented in this textbook are updateable.

You can alter the appearance of the dynaset so that the rows are arranged differently, the columns are displayed in a different order, or the columns are formatted in a special way. The next section illustrates how easy it is to make changes to the dynaset.

query definition
(Design view)

independent
criteria are on
separate rows

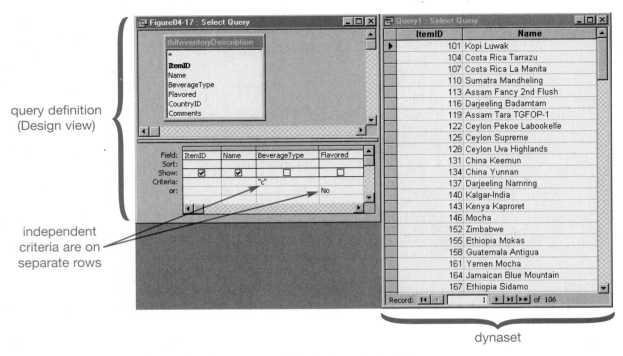

dynaset

**Figure 4.17**   Query with multiple, independent criteria.

**PRODUCING SORTED QUERY RESULTS.** Suppose you want to re-arrange dynaset rows so they are displayed in a more useful form. For instance, the list of coffees and teas shown in Figure 4.15 would be easier to use if it was arranged in name order. Sorting dynasets is easy. By default, Access displays dynaset records in ascending order on the table's primary key, if it has one, whether or not the primary key is displayed in the dynaset. Creating a query to sort data in other ways is particularly useful. For example, a list of employees in order by their last and first names is particularly handy when you want to look up someone on a printed list. We'll show you how to sort the dynaset next.

Suppose you want to list all flavored teas in stock in order by their names. First, you would construct a one-table query based on the *tblInventoryDescription* table. In the QBE Field row you might include the fields ItemID, Name, Flavored, and BeverageType. Only ItemID and Name would have their Show check boxes marked. Flavored and BeverageType would contain the criteria values *Yes* and *t*, respectively, to retrieve only flavored teas (both criteria must be met). How about the sorting part of it? Simple! Follow along in the next paragraph and try it.

**Try it**

Open in Design view the query *qryFlavoredTea*, which selects flavored teas in the dynaset. To sort the dynaset on Name, click the Sort row under the Name column—

the attribute by which you want the rows sorted—and select Ascending from the drop-down list (or type *a*). Select Datasheet View from the View menu to see the dynaset. Notice that the rows are in Name order beginning with *Apricot* and ending with *Vanilla with Vanilla Bean*.

You can specify a sort order for more than one column. Access sorts by the leftmost field first followed by the next sort field to the right, and so on. Therefore, you should arrange the columns you want to sort, relative to each other, from left to right in the QBE grid. Note that the sort columns do not have to be the first group of columns in the QBE grid. You can sort by fields whose Show check box is cleared and thus does not display, though the reasons seem obscure at this point. We will explain later why this may be necessary.

**ALTERING THE ORDER AND SIZE OF COLUMNS.** You can alter the order of the dynaset table columns. The dynaset columns' order is established by the query. For instance, the first field whose Show box is checked in the QBE grid is the first column in the dynaset, but you can alter the dynaset's column order either by altering the query's design or by altering the dynaset's column ordering after it is displayed. The former method is the best way.

To rearrange query columns, display the query in Design view and move the mouse pointer to the column selector of the field to be moved. (The column selector is the area just above the field name.) When the mouse pointer is on the column selector, it turns to a down-pointing arrow. Click the column. The entire column is darkened, indicating you have selected it. (Be careful not to move the mouse.) Release the mouse but keep it poised over the column selector. Next, click and drag the column to its new location. A rectangle appears below the pointer, indicating you are about to move the column. Finally, release the mouse when the column is in its new location. A vertical bar appears as you drag the column, which indicates where the column would reside if you were to release the mouse. When you do release the mouse, columns to the right of the vertical bar move to the right, making room for the new column to be dropped in place.

If necessary, you can enlarge individual columns by moving to the column selector area of a column so the mouse is over the right line of the column selector. When the mouse changes from a down-pointing arrow to a double-headed arrow, drag the right edge to the right to enlarge the column, or drag it to the left to shrink the column.

Both column order and column size can be changed in the dynaset—that is, after executing a query. When the query is displayed in Datasheet view (dynaset), you can move columns or change their size following the procedures outlined in the preceding paragraphs. You can move the cursor to a dynaset column and then select Column Width from the Format menu. The Column Width dialog box is displayed (see Figure 4.18). Click the Best Fit button to size the column so it is just wide enough for the widest entry. (The shortcut for Best Fit is to move the cursor to the right edge of the column selector and then double-click the pointer after it changes to a double-headed arrow.) You can also size multiple columns at once. Drag the mouse across all the column selectors to select multiple contiguous columns. Move the mouse to the right column line of any one of the selected columns. When it changes to a double-headed arrow, double-click the pointer to optimize the column width.

manually set
column width

click to set column(s)
to a standard width

click to select
optimal fit

**Figure 4.18**   Column Width dialog box.

**ALTERING COLUMN DISPLAY PROPERTIES.** Like other dynaset characteristics, column display formats can also be changed. First, display the query in Design view. Then move the mouse to the Field row in the QBE grid of the column whose format you want to change. When you right-click a column, a pop-up menu displays several choices. Click the Properties selection. A Field Properties dialog box opens. You can experiment with changing characteristics such as Format yourself. For instance, try changing the format of the ItemID dynaset column so the data is displayed in Currency format. After you are done experimenting, there is no need to save the altered query.

## Saving a Query and Printing Dynasets

**SAVING A QUERY.** You should save queries that you anticipate using more than once. Save a query by selecting Save from the File menu with the query displayed in either Design or Datasheet view. The query design is saved in the database on your disk under the name you type (if it is a first-time save operation) in the Query Name text box. If the query has been saved before, it is simply saved under the original name, replacing the older copy.

**PRINTING DYNASETS.** Printing query results simply means that you print the dynaset displayed in the Datasheet view. You can select the stored query name and print it, or you can open the query and view it. In either case, you select Print from the File menu (or click the toolbar Print button) to print the dynaset. When the Print dialog box displays, make any necessary adjustments to the page range to print (or print all pages), and click OK to give final authority to print the table.

Note that you do not have any control over the page headers or footers. Table and dynaset outputs are somewhat "raw" and undisciplined, especially when you compare them to Access reports.

## Dealing with Many-to-Many Relationships

The relationship between *tblInvoice* and *tblInventory* is many-to-many. Any particular invoice can contain several items drawn from inventory. From another perspective, any particular inventory item (for example, Kona coffee) may be found in several invoices. Recall that whenever an M—M relationship exists between two tables, you must create a *relationship* table. Minimally, the relationship table contains primary keys from both the *tblInvoice* and *tblInventory* tables for every item on a particular invoice and all invoices.

There are as many rows in the relationship table as there are invoice line items for all invoices. We have removed invoice lines from the *tblInvoice* table and placed them in the *tblInvoiceLine* table (see Figure 4.14). Matching the invoice number with the InvoiceID attribute of *tblInvoiceLine* can retrieve all the items of a particular invoice. InvoiceID is the primary key of the *tblInvoice* table, whereas the attribute InventoryID in *tblInvoiceLine* is the primary key in *tblInventory*. Thus, InventoryID in *tblInvoiceLine* is a *foreign key*. The other attributes in the relationship table are Quantity, UnitPrice, and Discount. Quantity is the amount invoiced for a particular item (coffee or tea) for a given invoice line. UnitPrice is the price charged for this item. It can be different from the Price column stored in the *tblInventory* table. The Discount field holds the percentage discount for a line item on a particular invoice. Discounts vary from customer to customer and from one time of the year to another. The two *tblInvoiceLine* table attributes, InvoiceID and InventoryID, form a *composite primary key*, because they are both required to form a primary key for the relationship table called *tblInvoiceLine*.

If you encounter other tables having a many-to-many relationship, which cannot be handled easily by a RDBMS, the remedy is simple. Create a relationship table containing a composite primary key that is formed from the primary keys of the two tables having the M—M relationship—just like we have done with the *tblInvoiceLine* table. Once a relationship table is in place, then both of the original tables have a 1—M relationship with the relationship table. In other words, the relationship table provides the "glue" connecting two tables in a one-to-many relationship.

## Producing Queries Involving Multiple Tables

We created the various tables for The Coffee Merchant to normalize them in order to avoid problems such as data redundancy and data inconsistency, and to reduce data entry errors. Data is found in several related tables, and we need a way to connect the tables to retrieve information not found in a single table. When we connect tables together, we are *joining* them. Related tables are joined together by indicating which columns are common to the tables to be joined. For instance, we could join the *tblCustomer* and *tblInvoice* tables on the common column CustomerID found in each table. Though these columns have the same name, they do not need to. It is often simpler to remember the join columns by naming them identically.

**JOINING RELATED TABLES.**  Linking two or more tables is not difficult. You connect a table's primary key to another's foreign key to explicitly indicate how tables are linked. In many cases, Access can automatically determine how tables are linked when tables to be linked (*joined* is the preferred term) have identically named fields or they have been joined permanently via the Relationships window. If Microsoft Access does not create join lines for you automatically, you can join tables manually.

You join tables manually by creating a query and adding all the related tables to the query in the Show Table dialog box. Then you can create a join line between each table pair by selecting the primary key field in one table and dragging it to the equivalent foreign key field in the other table. Of course, you can join tables by performing the preceding actions in the Relationships window. Once you join tables in the Relationships window, you never need to do so inside individual queries. Access remembers table-to-table relationships that you create in the Relationships window until you explicitly delete them.

**CREATING CONDITIONAL QUERIES.**  Queries containing conditions are very useful. A *condition* provides a way for you to specify a range of values, or minimum and maximum values, for a field. For example, suppose you would like to locate all inventory items that are back-ordered. The coffee buyer is preparing to order more coffee and tea from the ranches around the world. One of the important questions that the buyer must answer is which products are back-ordered. In The Coffee Merchant system of tables, a product is back-ordered when the OnHand field in *tblInventory* is *negative*. In order to make intelligent product buying decisions, the buyer needs to know the product identification number, product name, and back-order volume column values. From that listing, he or she can order the correct quantity and types of products from the various suppliers.

To answer the buyer's question, we must construct a query involving two tables that are to be joined. The tables are *tblInventory*, the Inventory master table, and *tblInventoryDescription*. We will use a special operator called a comparison operator to create the selection criterion in a new query. A *comparison operator* is a special symbol that compares one value to another. The comparison operators are shown in Figure 4.19. In particular, we will use the less than (<) comparison operator in the selection criterion of the exercise that follows. We begin presenting you with more condensed exercise steps by combining several separate steps into one numbered step.

| Operator | Meaning |
|----------|---------|
| < | Less than |
| <= | Less than or equal to |
| > | Greater than |
| >= | Greater than or equal to |
| = | Equal to |
| <> | Not equal to |
| Between | Test for a range of values where two extreme values are separated by the And operator |
| In | Test for "equal to" any member in a list |
| Like | Test a text or memo field to match a pattern string |

**Figure 4.19** Comparison operators.

EXERCISE 4.11: CREATING A TWO-TABLE
QUERY THAT USES A COMPARISON OPERATOR

1. Create a new query joining the tables *tblInventory* and *tblInventoryDescription*: click Queries on the Database window Objects bar, click New, select Design View, click OK, add the two tables from the Show Table dialog box, and close the Show Table dialog box. Access automatically links the tables on their common field, ItemID, because we previously defined the relationship between them in the Relationships window.
2. Drag the columns ItemID (from *tblInventory*), Name, BeverageType, and OnHand to the Field row of the QBE grid. (You can double-click field names in the field roster to automatically place them in the next available column of the Field row.)
3. Click in the Criteria row of the OnHand column and type <*0* (the less than symbol followed by zero).
4. Select Datasheet View from the View menu to display the dynaset. Figure 4.20 shows both the query design and the resulting dynaset. Your screen may be arranged differently, but the dynaset should show the same rows as the figure. (This query is named *qryStockOut* on your Companion CD.)
5. After observing the result, click the Datasheet view Close button and click No when you are asked if you want to save changes to the query.

**USING WILDCARDS IN CRITERIA.** A *wildcard* character allows you to find information when you are unsure of the complete spelling of an alphanumeric field. Used with the Like operator (see Figure 4.19), the wildcard characters define positions that can contain any single character, a single number, or zero or more characters in a text string match pattern. There are three Like wildcard characters available in Access. They are shown in Figure 4.21. Here's an example of

**Figure 4.20** Two-table query using a comparison operator.

how you can use them. Suppose you want to check The Coffee Merchant's stock for any beverages whose name contains the word *chocolate* (for example, Dutch Chocolate). You are interested in how much is available, if any. You can use the * (asterisk) wildcard character and the partial word *choc* to return any beverages whose Name field contains *choc* anywhere within it.

The preceding query involves two tables, *tblInventory* and *tblInventoryDescription*. The key search criterion is the wildcard expression *\*choc\**. This criterion is placed in the Criteria row just below the Name column in the QBE grid. (After you type the preceding expression, Access automatically surrounds it with double quotation marks and precedes the entire phrase with *Like*.) The asterisk preceding *choc* indicates that any word, phrase, or character string can appear before the word—or none at all. Similarly, the asterisk following *choc* indicates that any characters may follow the word—or none at all. That

| Wildcard Character | Meaning | Example Pattern Matches |
|---|---|---|
| ? | Any single character | *b?lk* matches balk or bulk |
| * | Zero or more characters | *\*or* matches door, floor, and matador |
| | | *or\** matches ordinary, order, and organize |
| | | *\*or\** matches bored, category, and fluoride |
| # | Any single digit | *6#4* matches 604, 644, and 664 |

**Figure 4.21** LIKE wildcard characters.

is, the search criterion requests any rows in which the partial word *choc* is found anywhere within the name. Figure 4.22 shows a query and the resulting dynaset.

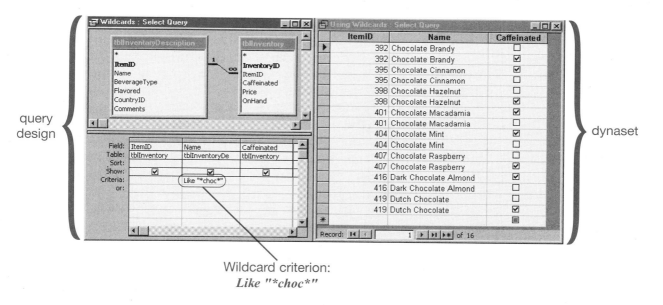

query design

dynaset

Wildcard criterion:
*Like "\*choc\*"*

**Figure 4.22** Query using a wildcard in its criteria.

**USING LOGICAL OPERATORS IN QUERY CRITERIA.** Some other useful operators helpful in forming selection criteria are called logical operators. *Logical operators* provide a way of bonding two comparison or wildcard criteria. There are several logical operators, but the ones used most often are AND, OR, and NOT. Using the AND operator, you can specify a condition in which two criteria must be true simultaneously. For example, suppose you want to examine the invoices issued during the first week in November 2000. A temporary employee was used to process the invoices that week, and you heard that some invoices were handled incorrectly. You can use the AND operator to bound the range of invoice dates you want to inspect. Specifically, you write the criterion expression *>=#11/1/00# And <=#11/7/00#* in the Criteria row below InvoiceDate in the QBE grid. This selection criterion states a range of acceptable invoice dates. The range encompasses dates that are greater than or equal to November 1, 2000 *AND* (simultaneously) less than or equal to November 7, 2000. (The # characters always surround dates so that Access doesn't confuse dates with arithmetic expressions. Do not mistake this use of the pound sign with the wildcard character used to match a single digit.) Thus the criterion limits rows from the Invoice table to invoices issued during the first week. An equivalent and simpler way of writing the preceding criterion using the Between comparison operator is *Between #11/1/00# And #11/7/00#*. Any dates between or matching the two dates satisfy the criteria.

## Performing Calculations with Queries

Recall that in Chapter 3 we emphasized the importance of omitting from a table information that can be calculated or derived from other columns in the table. For instance, good database design and normalization rules preclude the inclusion of a column of extended prices in any of The Coffee Merchant's invoice tables. This is because the extended price is calculated from the fields Quantity, UnitPrice, and Discount stored in *tblInvoiceLine*. Because the extended price can be calculated, it should not be stored in the table. Why? Suppose the extended price is stored in *tblInvoiceLine* along with Quantity, UnitPrice, and Discount. What if someone discovers a mistake in the Quantity or UnitPrice values in one or more invoices? Changing either renders the extended price value inaccurate. Database experts say that the database is *inconsistent*.

That leads us to this question: How do you produce the extended price and other useful calculated results? One answer is that you include any calculations in a query. Access allows you to write expressions that sum, average, and count values as well as write expressions that involve the arithmetic operators, fields, summary operators (we will discuss these in the next section), numeric constants, and comparison operators. The arithmetic operators are the familiar ones: +, -, *, and /, and you have been introduced to comparison operators. You reference other query or table fields by enclosing their names in brackets. To compute a result and display it in a query, you simply write an expression in its own Field row cell.

Let's write an expression to see exactly how to calculate results and display them in a dynaset. In the next exercise, we will join the *tblInvoiceLine*, *tblInventory*, and *tblInventoryDescription* tables and display invoice line items for invoices in the database. The query you will construct displays the extended price, among other columns, using the following formula:

[Quantity]*[UnitPrice]*(1-[Discount])

(Always surround field names with brackets when you include them in expressions.) For example, if someone ordered 20 pounds of a particular coffee priced at $10.00 per pound and received a discount of 5 percent, then the extended price would be:

20*10*(1-0.05)

(Though the Inventory table, *tblInventory*, contains a price field, Price, for each item carried, customers may or may not be charged that *suggested* price. The actual price charged is stored in UnitPrice, an invoice line field [*tblInvoiceLine*], and may vary from one customer to the next.) The extended price that is calculated by the preceding expression is $190.

EXERCISE 4.12: WRITING EXPRESSIONS IN QUERIES

1. Close all windows except the Database window.
2. Create a new query, adding the tables *tblInvoiceLine*, *tblInventory*, and *tblInventoryDescription* to it. Access will draw join lines connecting the three tables on their respective primary and foreign keys. Close the Show Table dialog box.
3. Drag the fields InvoiceID, ItemID, Name, UnitPrice, Quantity, and Discount to the first six Field row cells in the QBE grid (in the order listed).
4. Click in the Sort row beneath the InvoiceID column in the QBE grid, click the drop-down list box arrow, and select Ascending from the drop-down list box. This will list the invoices in ascending order by invoice number.
5. Click in the seventh cell in the Field row, the first empty cell in the Field row of the QBE grid, and press Shift+F2 to open a Zoom dialog box. A Zoom dialog box opens a larger area in which you can see the entire expression as you type it.
6. Type the following expression. When you are done, click OK to close the Zoom dialog box and then press Enter.

*Extended Price: [Quantity]*[UnitPrice]*(1-[Discount])*

7. Right-click the cell containing the preceding expression and select Properties from the pop-up menu that appears.
8. Select Format and then select Currency from the drop-down list (see Figure 4.23). Doing this will format the calculated expression to display the result rounded to two decimal places and will include a currency symbol and commas (if necessary).
9. Select Datasheet View from the View menu to see the dynaset (see Figure 4.24). We have saved the query as *qryInvoiceLineItem* on the Companion CD.
10. Close the query without saving it (or save it under a name different from the preceding one) once you are finished examining the results.

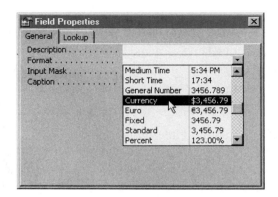

**Figure 4.23**    Formatting a query's calculated column.

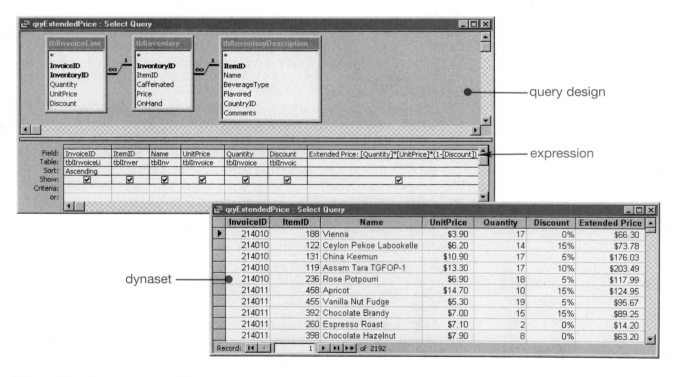

**Figure 4.24**    Query design and dynaset with calculated column.

Step 6 of Exercise 4.12 illustrates how you write an expression—the product of three fields: Quantity, UnitPrice, and Discount—in Access. Whenever you refer to Access table field names, always enclose them in brackets. Otherwise,

Access becomes confused. *Extended Price* is an alias for the field. It precedes the expression. To rename a column (an expression in this case), simply begin with the new name (it can be several words) followed by a colon and a space. Then write the expression. If you omit an alias in an expression, Access assigns a unique, default field name such as *Expr1* or *Expr12*. Access-assigned field names are neither particularly attractive nor informative.

## Grouping and Summarizing Data

Summary information can reveal situations that are not obvious from examining detailed data. Access provides several functions that produce aggregate information for data groups or an entire table. Figure 4.25 lists seven of the most important aggregate functions along with a brief description of what each function does. Of the listed functions, the most useful to those of us in the accounting profession are Avg, Count, Max, Min, and Sum.

| Function | Meaning |
|----------|---------|
| Avg | Computes a field's average value (ignores null fields) |
| Count | Counts the number of non-null (empty) items in a field |
| Max | Computes largest value in a field |
| Min | Computes smallest non-null value in a field |
| Sum | Computes the total of all items in a field |
| StDev | Computes the standard deviation of non-null values in a field |
| Var | Determines the variance of non-null values in a field |

**Figure 4.25**  Access aggregate functions.

Sometimes you will want statistics for all rows of a table or joined set of tables. At other times, however, you will need summary statistics on smaller groups of records. For instance, it may be revealing to know the total number of pounds of each type of coffee and tea ordered each month. This would disclose the more popular choices. Or, the accounts receivable department might be interested in a statistic such as the average elapsed days, by customer, between the time invoices are sent and their corresponding payments are received. When summary information is calculated for several sets of rows, that calculation involves *grouping*. Grouping information simply means forming groups of rows that share some common characteristic such as having identical values for a client name, customer identification number, invoice number, or other attribute.

Frequently, the summary functions are used in queries (but they can also be used in forms and reports). To compute an average of a numeric field in a query, simply click the Totals toolbar button. Access adds a new row to the QBE grid, called the *Total* row. When the row appears, type Avg in the Total row beneath the field whose values you want to average. Then, run the query. You can compute multiple summary statistics on a particular field as long as you include multiple copies of the field name in the QBE grid Field row.

In the next exercise, you will try out a summary function and learn how to meld two character fields into one field by *concatenating* them. Let's try some of the summary functions. You will join together three tables so that you can compute and display the total sales grouped by salespersons' names. In other words, you want to know how much each salesperson sold. The three tables involved in the query are *tblEmployee*, *tblInvoice*, and *tblInvoiceLine*. The fields required to form the query summarizing sales are all found in just two tables—*tblEmployee* and *tblInvoiceLine*. However, the relationship between *tblEmployee* and *tblInvoiceLine* is many-to-many. Because Access cannot link many-to-many tables together directly, the *tblInvoice* table serves as a "bridge" table that restructures the M—M relationship into two 1—M relationships.

Whenever you want to combine text fields from a table into a single field, you simply write an expression containing the two fields separated by the symbol for ampersand, &. Suppose you want to produce a listing of employees for a telephone book listing their last name, a comma, a blank, and their first name. Combine text fields in a single cell of the Field row in a query to get the desired result. For instance, the following expression provides the required single text field:

Name: [LastName] & ", " & [FirstName]

The ampersand adds one string onto another. In this case, the previous expression is "adding" three text strings together, back to back. This is a handy tool to keep in mind whenever you need to combine disparate fields from a table into a single field in a query, report, form, or web page.

Prepare for this exercise by closing all windows except the *Ch04.mdb* Database window. Click Queries on the Database window Objects bar.

EXERCISE 4.13: USING SUMMARY FUNCTIONS IN A QUERY

1. Create a new query (select Design View from the New Query dialog box), add the three tables *tblEmployee*, *tblInvoice*, and *tblInvoiceLine* to the query, and close the Show Table dialog box.
2. Select Totals from the View menu to insert in the QBE grid a new row called Total. (You can also click the Totals button on the Design view toolbar.)
3. In the first cell in the Field row enter the following expression, which combines the two name fields together, separated by a blank. Be sure to place a space between the two quotation marks.

*Name: [EmployeeFirstName] & " " & [EmployeeLastName]*

(You can place a blank on either side of the two ampersand symbols, but you don't have to. Access will do that for you automatically after you move to another cell in the QBE grid.)

4. Click the Show box in the first column so that a checkmark appears in it. This causes the employee name field to display when you run the query.

5. In the second cell in the Field row enter the following expression to compute and display sales totals, including any discount applied for each customer.

*Sales: [Quantity]\*[UnitPrice]\*(1-[Discount])*

You may want to press Shift+F2 to produce a larger view of the cell in the Zoom dialog box. The larger display makes it easier to see the whole expression. When you are finished writing the expression in the Zoom dialog box, click OK to close the Zoom dialog box.

6. Click in the QBE grid Total row beneath the second cell—the expression you just typed—and select the Sum function from the drop-down list (click the list box to display the list of summary functions).

7. Click in the QBE grid Sort row beneath the second cell and select Descending from the drop-down list. You want to see the sales summary sorted from highest sales total to lowest.

8. Set the format of the second cell, the expression, to Currency by right-clicking the Field row cell containing the expression, selecting Properties, and selecting Currency from the drop-down list in the Format box of the Field Properties dialog box.

9. Close the Field Properties dialog box.

10. Select Datasheet View from the View menu to see the results. Figure 4.26 shows both the query design and its dynaset.

11. Select File, Save, and then type *qryTotalSales* to name and save the new query.

The dynaset calculates total sales for 19 salespersons. The top 10 performers appear in the figure. Switch back to the query Design view in preparation for a little experiment. (*Do not* close this query yet.) Can Microsoft Access compute the grand total of all invoices that are in the database? In other words, is it possible to sum all the sales amounts for all the invoices by using a query? The answer is yes. As a matter of fact, you can make a simple change to the query you created in the preceding exercise to yield the grand total.

**Try it**

Display the previous query in Design view. Move the mouse pointer just above the Field row of the Name field (an expression) in the QBE grid. When the pointer changes to a solid, dark, down-pointing arrow, click it to select the entire Name column. Press the Delete key to delete that column. Select Datasheet View from the concatenated fields form a single name    total sales

Total row    expressions

**Figure 4.26**    Sorted sales totals for each employee created with the Sum aggregate function.

View menu to see the grand total of all invoices in the database. Your altered query should display a single row with the value of $176,729.37—the current total of all invoices stored in the system. Close the Datasheet view window. Click No in response to the dialog box that asks if you want to save the query's design, because you want to preserve the original query you created in Exercise 4.13.

Keep the following in mind whenever you use the summary functions. Place the summary function in the field for which the computation is to be performed (beneath an expression in our previous example). Rename a summary column when desired by typing the new name, a colon, a space, and then the field name. (This technique works equally well to create aliases for fields, too.)

## Using an Outer Join in a Query

Often in joining two tables, you find that one or more rows in one table do not have matching rows in the other table. Knowing this may be important for someone. For example, a sales manager would want to know if there are any salespersons who have sold nothing during a particular period. There are examples of hidden information in your databases, too. In your *Ch04.mdb* database, for example, it is not apparent which cities have no employees simply by performing a standard join of the *tblEmployee* and *tblDivisionLocation* tables on matching primary and foreign keys. Instead, you produce this kind of information by using an *outer join*, which lists *all* rows from one table and only matching rows from another table.

The next exercise shows you how to create an outer join. The exercise uses as its starting point the query you created in Exercise 4.13 called *qryTotalSales*. You will modify the join properties for both of the existing joins to form an outer join. (The query's two joins are called *inner joins*.) The new query, when completed, will reveal the names of people who sold nothing in addition to those that did. Prepare for the exercise by copying *qryTotalSales* in the Queries collection of the Database window. (Simply click *qryTotalSales* and press Ctrl+C and Ctrl+V to cut and paste the query. Then type *qryOuterJoin* to name the new query.) Follow the steps in the following exercise.

EXERCISE 4.14: CREATING AN OUTER JOIN QUERY

1. Open *qryOuterJoin* in Design view.
2. Double-click the join line between the field lists of *tblEmployee* and *tblInvoice* in the upper part of the Query window. The Join Properties dialog box opens. If you double-click on the gray area and not on the join line, the Query Properties dialog box opens. If that is the case, close the Query Properties dialog box and place the tip of the mouse arrow directly on the join line and try again.
3. Select the second option in the dialog box (see Figure 4.27) and click OK. You should now see an arrow on the join line pointing from the *tblEmployee* field list to the *tblInvoice* field list, indicating you have asked for an outer join with all records from *tblEmployee* regardless of whether or not corresponding records are found in *tblInvoice*.
4. Repeat steps 2 and 3 for the join line between the field lists of *tblInvoice* and *tblInvoiceLine*.
5. Display the query in Datasheet view. Notice that the Sales column is empty for Melinda English, Giles Bateman, and Brad Shoenstein. That means that they have no records in the *tblInvoiceLine* table, which means they have no sales for the period.
6. Display the query in Design view, move to the criteria row beneath the Sales column, and type *Is Null* into the Criteria cell. That reduces the Datasheet view to those employees who did not report sales for the period. Figure 4.28 shows both the query design and the dynaset.
7. Save and close the query.

## Designing and Using a Parameter Query

So far you have seen and created queries containing selection criteria directly in the design grid of the Query window. However, you can create a special type of query that allows you to specify selection criteria when you *run* the query. Known as a *parameter query*, it prompts you to enter the selection criteria just before running the query. The advantage of a parameter query over conventional queries is versatility. For example, you could create and run a query that lists all customers

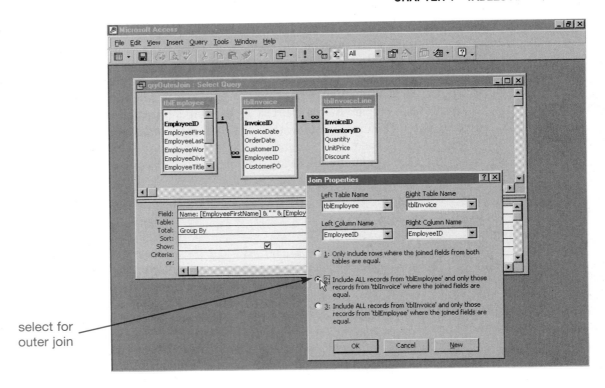

**Figure 4.27**   Creating an outer join.

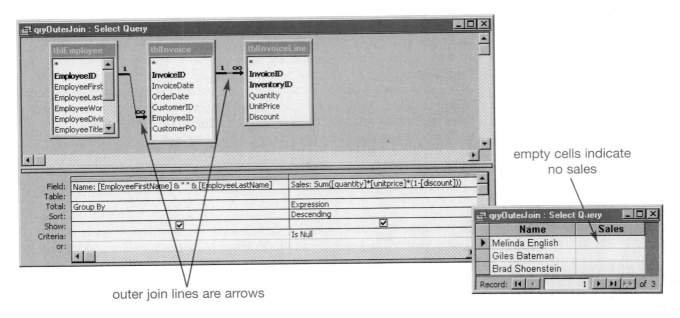

**Figure 4.28**   Using "Is Null" to display rows with empty fields.

that live in Minnesota. Using the query to pass information to a report (Chapter 5), Access could create a form letter you mail to all Minnesota residents. When the northwest sales region decides to run a similar promotion, they can revise the Minnesota query, substituting "Oregon" for "Minnesota" in the criteria row to extract those residents. Imagine creating 50 such queries simply to generate a listing for each of the U.S. states. Creating those queries would be time-consuming, and your database would be filled with 50 copies of a query whose basic forms are identical except for the criteria each contains.

A single parameter query can be used in place of the 50 individual queries. The only action required by a user running the query is to type the state name or abbreviation when prompted by Access. One query does the work of many. You can extend the use of parameter queries to an unlimited number of other accounting applications. A parameter query provides a perfect way to extract a group of invoices for varying time periods. Simply create a parameter query with two parameters—the beginning and ending dates for the billing period—and anyone can retrieve invoices from the date ranges a user enters when the query begins execution. Further, you can imagine a simple search engine query that retrieves a sales tax rate from a table when a user types the state name or state abbreviation. Simply enter the state name and the query returns the sales tax rate for that state.

The best way to understand parameter queries is to build one. Let's create a parameter query that displays a list of customers, retrieved from the table *tblCustomer*, for any state that the user wishes. When you run the query, you are prompted to enter a two-character state abbreviation. The query then retrieves addresses for customers in that state. In preparation for the next exercise, open *Ch04.mdb*, close all windows except the Database window, and click Queries on the Objects bar. Follow the exercise steps to create and save a parameter query.

EXERCISE 4.15: CREATING A PARAMETER QUERY

1. Create a new query by clicking New, select Design View from the list in the New Query dialog box, select and add the table *tblCustomer*, and close the Show Table dialog box.
2. Double-click the following fields found in the field roster in this order: CompanyName, Address, City, State, and ZipCode. Access places each field in the Fields row of the QBE grid.
3. Type *[Enter a two-character state abbreviation:]* into the Criteria row in the State column. This sequence of characters, enclosed in beginning and end brackets, defines a parameter.
4. Select Datasheet View from the View menu to test your new parameter query before you save it. An Enter Parameter Value dialog box appears.
5. Type *ne* in the Enter Parameter Value text box. This indicates you want to display addresses for Nebraska customers (see Figure 4.29). Recall that the capitalization of search strings doesn't matter. Lowercase "ne" will match table entries such as "Ne" or "nE."

6. Click OK to test the query. If you constructed the query correctly, Access will display a list of 11 companies—all from Nebraska, of course (see Figure 4.30).
7. Select Save from the File menu and type *qryParameter*, then click OK to save the query under the name you entered.
8. Close the Datasheet view window.

enter criteria

parameter in criteria row of QBE grid

**Figure 4.29**   A parameter query design and run-time prompt.

| CompanyName | Address | City | State | ZipCode |
|---|---|---|---|---|
| Commercial Fec | 2120 South 72N | Omaha | NE | 68124 |
| Lincoln Telepho | 1440 M Street | Lincoln | NE | 68508 |
| Data Document | 4205 South 96T | Omaha | NE | 68127 |
| Firstier Financia | 1700 Farnam St | Omaha | NE | 68102 |
| Lincoln Telecom | 1440 M Street | Lincoln | NE | 68508 |
| Inacom Corp. | 10901 Malcolm | Omaha | NE | 68154 |
| Richman Gordm | 12100 West Ce | Omaha | NE | 68144 |
| Buckle Inc. | 2407 West 24Tl | Kearney | NE | 68847 |
| Mfs Communica | One Internationa | Omaha | NE | 68131 |
| Valmont Industr | P.O. Box 358 | Valley | NE | 68064 |
| First National of | One First Natior | Omaha | NE | 68102 |

Record: 14 ◄  1 ► ►I ►* of 11

**Figure 4.30**   A parameter query dynaset.

**SUMMARY**

This chapter has emphasized using Access to create tables and queries. You have learned how to create table structures, enter data into tables, and set limits on the type and size of information that one can enter into a table. In addition, you learned how to establish referential integrity between tables. We have stressed the importance of specifying primary keys when constructing tables. Tables, you learned, hold all of the data in a database system. Queries, on the other hand, access one or more tables to produce combined results that display related data fields from several tables. You know how to write and save queries that involve both single and multiple tables. Queries can contain expressions comprised of comparison operators, arithmetic operators, example elements, and wildcard characters. Using queries, you can focus on the data elements important to you. Finally, you learned that parameter queries are quite versatile and can provide varied results depending on what criteria you enter when you run queries.

## QUESTIONS AND PROBLEMS FOR REVIEW

### MULTIPLE-CHOICE QUESTIONS

1. If you want to list all male employees in the Accounts Receivable department, which object would you use to reduce the possible results to just the requested persons?
   a. table
   b. form
   c. query
   d. report
2. If you wish to add a column to an existing table, you must
   a. first enter Edit mode.
   b. display a table in Design view.
   c. change the table's Datasheet view properties.
   d. disable referential integrity checks.
3. A query involving more than one table must indicate how the tables are related to each other by
   a. minimizing them.
   b. displaying their property sheets.
   c. linking them.
   d. drawing link diagrams.
4. You can design a table's salary field to automatically restrict legitimate values by entering an expression in the field property called
   a. Field Size.
   b. Default Value.
   c. Validation Text.
   d. Validation Rule.

5. You can link two tables permanently, so that any new queries involving the tables automatically link them, in which window?
   a. Query design
   b. Relationships
   c. Datasheet
   d. Table design

6. The comparison operator meaning "is not equal to" is what?
   a. <=
   b. <>
   c. <=>
   d. \=

7. The QBE grid contains a(n) _____ row.
   a. Field
   b. Table
   c. Sort
   d. all of the above

8. Access supports two classes of queries. They are called
   a. Action and Field.
   b. Selection and Referential.
   c. Selection and Action.
   d. Active and Passive.

9. You can add special functions that allow you to group and summarize numeric data. An example is the Sum function. Collectively, these functions are known as _____ functions.
   a. summary
   b. table
   c. aggregate
   d. equijoin

10. What is the general name for a query that prompts you for criteria values to filter dynaset rows when you run the query?
    a. filter query
    b. criterion query
    c. update query
    d. parameter query

## DISCUSSION QUESTIONS

1. Discuss the advantage(s) of providing a data validity check in the Validation Rule field property. What might happen if you omitted validation rules from text fields, and how could that affect the integrity of your database tables?

2. Explain why referential integrity is so important when dealing with a database, such as The Coffee Merchant's, involving several related tables. Give a scenario in which the lack of referential integrity could cause problems. Be specific.

3. Discuss the problem with storing an extended price (an invoice item quantity multiplied by an item's wholesale or retail price) in the *tblInvoiceLine* table. Why could you not simply add a column called ExtendedPrice to the Invoice Line table?

4. Discuss the advantages of an outer join query. Give an example, different from the one used in the textbook, of using an outer join to display information from two tables related in a query with an outer join. What role does the expression "Is Null" play in outer join queries?

5. Suppose the table *tblStudents* contains the first and last names of students and that *tblClassRosters* contains the list of students enrolled in each class in the university. Discuss the relationship between *tblStudents* and *tblClassRosters*. Is it 1—1, 1—M (or vice versa), or M—M? Are there any problems representing the relationship of these two tables to one another?

## PROBLEMS

1. List the first name, last name, commission rate, and gender of all male employees from the Employee table (*tblEmployee*) whose commission rate is at least 7 percent. Sort the rows in ascending order by last name. Print the dynaset. Be sure to write your name on the output before you turn it in.

2. Create a query to list the ItemID, OnHand, and Name values for all inventory items whose on-hand amount is between 1 and 139 pounds, inclusive. Sort the result in descending order by the OnHand value. Print the dynaset. (You should have fewer than a dozen rows in the dynaset.)

3. Create and run a query that retrieves all teas whose inventory price is at least $16.00. List only Name, BeverageType, and Price in the dynaset. Sort the list into ascending order by Name. Print the dynaset and write your name and course section number on your paper.

4. Write and execute a query based on the *tblInventoryDescription* and *tblCountryName* tables that lists all products that originate from either Ethiopia or Kenya. List the name of the coffee or tea (Name from *tblInventoryDescription*) and the country name (in that order). Give the CountryName column an alias of *Country*. Sort the dynaset rows by the Country column in ascending order. Print the dynaset and write your name on it.

5. Create and run a query that displays all employees from the Employee table (*tblEmployee*) who have the title *Senior Sales Associate* (*tblEmployeeTitle*). In the dynaset only display each qualifying employee's last name and gender (in that order). Sort the dynaset by gender and then by last name within gender groups. (The sort will group females and then males and then sort them by last names within the group.) Print the resulting dynaset. Remember to write your name on the output.

6. You want to examine the invoices issued in November 2000 in order by date. You are interested only in general information. To answer this question, form

a query that joins The Coffee Merchant tables *tblInvoice* and *tblCustomer*. Display the company names, invoice dates, and invoice numbers (InvoiceID) for invoices issued only during the period 11/1/00 through and including 11/30/00. Sort the dynaset in ascending order by invoice date and then by company name among the same invoice dates. Print all pages. Save the query. (Figure 4.14 contains the schemas of all tables for The Coffee Merchant.)

7. Create a query joining tables *tblInventoryDescription* and *tblCountryName*. Display with the query the columns (in this order left to right) Name, BeverageType, CountryName, and Comments. Include only the countries of Kenya and Costa Rica in your results. Sort the rows by country name. Print the resulting dynaset. Reviewing the output, which of the two countries displayed produces more coffee varieties?

8. Write a query that displays the five most densely populated states in the United States. Use criteria to eliminate the District of Columbia. Include in the dynaset the long state name, the short state name, and the calculated field, density. Assign the column alias *Density* to the population density column. Format the Density column so it displays two decimal places. Sort the dynaset in descending order by Density. (Hints: *tblSalesTaxRate* contains state names, populations, and area—in square miles—of each state. Density is, of course, the measure of the number of people per square mile. Right-click the blank area above the QBE grid to locate and set the Top Values property of the Query Properties so that only the top five results are displayed.)

9. Create a query that produces invoice information from The Coffee Merchant's tables: *tblInvoice*, *tblInvoiceLine*, *tblEmployee*, *tblCustomer*, *tblInventory*, and *tblInventoryDescription*. Display the following columns: InvoiceID, ItemID, Quantity, UnitPrice, Discount, InvoiceDate, OrderDate, CustomerID, EmployeeLastName, CompanyName, and PhoneNumber. Write the expression for extended price Quantity*Price*(1-Discount), and rename the resulting column Extended Price. Format the Extended Price column to display a dollar sign and two decimal places—the Currency format. After you have completed the query's design, run it. Use Page Setup to print in landscape instead of the default, portrait. The output is very long, so print only the first three pages. Write your name on the first page of the output.

10. The boss has decided to split the table *tblInventoryDescription* into teas and coffees, dropping the "beverage" field in the process. Write two make-table queries to split the table, making a coffee-only table called *tblCoffee* and a tea-only table called *tblTea*. Run the make-table queries and then print the two tables.

# 5 ACCESS FORMS AND REPORTS

## OBJECTIVES

This chapter extends the knowledge you gained by providing detailed information about Microsoft Access forms and reports. You will learn about the advantages of using forms and reports, and about defining and using accounting forms and reports. Throughout this chapter, exercises emphasize Microsoft Access techniques critical to building accounting information systems. Like the chapters before it, this chapter is application oriented and contains very little theory. Exercises actively engage you in using the theory you learned earlier to create typical accounting forms and reports. In particular, you will learn how to:

- Put forms to work in a variety of accounting applications.
- Create a form replete with formatted fields and aesthetic enhancements.
- Add label, text box, and list controls to a form.
- Build forms and associated subforms from queries and tables.
- Examine the details of a report's structure.
- Produce a grouped data report.
- Design and print reports ranging from one-table reports to more complex multiple-table reports employing summary information.

We continue using The Coffee Merchant's database system as the backdrop application in this chapter. All the tables, but no queries, that you used in Chapter 4 have been carried over to the *Ch05.mdb* database found in the Ch05 folder on your Companion CD. For all exercises and examples in this chapter, we assume that you have inserted the Companion CD in the CD-ROM drive, copied the database

*Ch05.mdb* to your hard disk, removed the database's read-only protection, started Microsoft Access, and opened the Ch05 database. If not, then please be sure to do so before doing the exercises in this chapter.

## CREATING AND USING FORMS

A form displays information from one or more tables in an easily understood, attractive format on a computer screen. Unlike a Table window, a Form View window can show one row of a table at a time. One advantage of a form over a Datasheet view of a table is that a form can be sculpted to look like any of a company's paper forms. When database forms match paper forms, the computer forms are almost always intuitive and familiar to those using them. And because the computer forms look familiar, they are not intimidating to new computer users. Forms are the primary interface between users and database applications. As far as your users know, forms *are* the application—not the tables and other objects that are behind the scenes. Forms can be used to store information and pass it from one form to another or from one phase of your application to the next.

Forms can have a plain but functional design, or they can be elaborate, with drop-down lists, built-in help, attractive field designs, graphics, and buttons that activate predefined activities when users click them. Forms, like queries, do not store any information. They simply display information retrieved from one or more tables. Data exhibited in a form can be retrieved from a single table or from multiple tables joined on a common key field. Forms can also display data directly from a query of arbitrary complexity. Any of the queries we created in the previous section could be the basis of a form.

## Putting Forms to Work

Forms provide a convenient way to control application flow and organize your database application. Using command buttons on a form, you can create macros (see Chapter 10) or code (called VBA) that automates all major database procedures. When a user clicks one of the buttons, it activates a procedure such as producing a report or displaying invoices. Forms can contain a special code that runs when a specific event occurs. For example, you can easily create a code, stored with one of your forms, that performs a specific action when someone clicks a button, opens a form, or moves to a particular text box on a form.

Forms are a particularly attractive and effective way to control the data users enter into a database. For example, you could create a special form for entering new information into an invoice table. The new form contains control information that prevents a user from entering an already-assigned invoice ID number or entering an unreasonable value for a unit cost field. You can provide these types of data consistency checks as part of the logic of a form that are far more versatile and robust than the elementary table property checks provide. Figure 5.1 shows an example of an inventory input form.

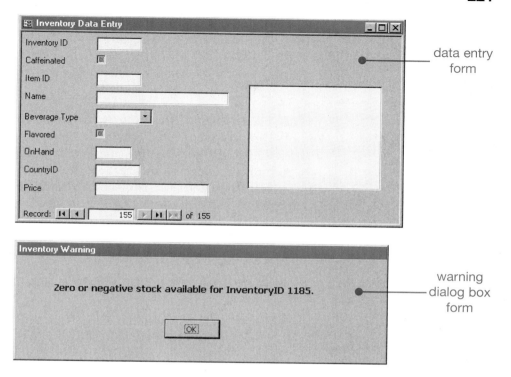

**Figure 5.1** Example of two ways to use forms.

Forms are by far the most widely used interface for entering, editing, and checking database information. You can use forms to add, change, or delete information from one or several tables at once. Forms allow you to lock selected table fields to prevent their alteration. Other options allow forms to fill in values with default and calculated values based on other entries the user makes.

Creating forms that display the progress of a database application is an effective way to communicate with the user. During a particularly lengthy database update process, for example, you can display a form that contains a progress chart indicating how far along the update operation is. Forms are the favored way to display informative messages such as warnings or error conditions in various parts of the database. For example, a form can simply display the message "Ordered item, ID number 123445, is now out of stock." when you ship the last of an inventory item. Figure 5.1 shows an example warning dialog box—a form. Notice the warning dialog box has no close button and no control menu.

Although forms are designed primarily for viewing on a screen, you can print them. An invoice form can serve the dual role of input and output. Data entry personnel can use a form to enter invoice information, and accounts receivable personnel can use the same form to generate individual invoices to mail to customers. The differences between the input form and the printed form may be slight. An input form may have different headers and footers—one for the customers and one for the company's data entry personnel.

## Viewing Form Types

You can create several different types of forms either manually or by using the Form Wizard. Normally, the Form Wizard is your best choice for creating most forms—at least until you become comfortable with forms.

A form can contain several sections, or subdivisions. These include the Page Header and Page Footer sections, Form Header and Form Footer sections, the Detail section, and any number of Group Header and Group Footer sections. Headers or footers for each of the preceding sections can appear independently of each other. That is, a Page Header may appear in a form but no Page Footer. Similarly, a form may contain a Group Header listing the department to which a list of employees belongs but no Group Footer. As you have probably guessed, Page Headers and Footers occur at the beginning and ending of each page, respectively. Likewise, a Form Header appears at the top of each form and a Form Footer appears at the bottom of each form—regardless of whether a form is displayed or printed. The Detail section contains information from the database and labels to identify individual items. Typically, information in the Detail section is variable, because the information there is obtained from queries and tables in the database. Figure 5.2 shows an example of a form containing Header, Detail, and Footer sections. Unless you see a multipage printout of forms, it is difficult to distinguish a form's Page Header from a Form Header.

A form type that is particularly useful for browsing through several records at once is a continuous form. A *continuous form* displays several records simultaneously on one form. The form resembles a spreadsheet, because labels appear at the top of each field and row selectors appear on the left side of each record. Figure 5.2 is an example of a continuous form showing all of the fields of several employee records. To view the remaining records, you click the scroll bar on the right side of the form or you can click the record number box and navigation buttons in the lower left portion of the form.

Forms designed to display a lot of information are usually designed as *multiple-page forms*. Multiple-page forms contain too much information to be displayed on a single screen. Thus, they group information into page-sized pieces. A user simply scrolls down the form to view its other parts. There are many examples of multiple-page forms in use. An employee form might contain many text boxes with name, address, date of birth, and similar information in the first screen-sized form piece. Lower in the form could be a large text box containing the employee's resume, a salary history, and other longer text passages.

Periodically in a database application it is helpful to have a window that remains the topmost window on the Windows desktop. Known as a *pop-up form*, the form might display an opening statement the first time you open a database file,

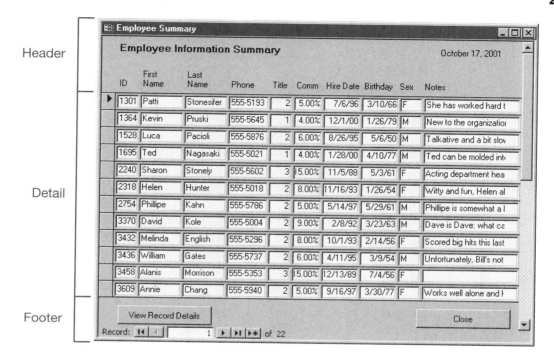

**Figure 5.2**  Example form with Page Header, Detail, and Page Footer sections.

or the pop-up form might provide users with information about the person who developed the database application. Unlike most windows, a pop-up window remains the topmost window, regardless of which other windows you make active on your desktop. This is especially useful to ensure that the database user reads the important information found in the pop-up form. Pop-up forms always contain a button—usually labeled OK—that closes the window. A special version of a pop-up form is called a modal form. A *modal form* is one that requires a response before the user can continue working on any other part of the application. A modal form might provide a stern warning about some action that is about to occur, or it may simply list critical information. In either case, a modal window will not let you click and make active any other window in the database application. Modal windows really get your full attention, and you should use them sparingly. Figure 5.3 shows an example of a pop-up form. (Of course, it would be impossible for you to determine if a form is modal simply by examining a textbook figure.)

A *subform* is especially useful when you want to display information on the "many" side of a one-to-many relationship. For example, a subform is a perfect way to display invoice lines that make up a larger form that is the entire invoice. An invoice's main form displays customer information while a subform displays details about the line items. You will see several examples of this form/subform

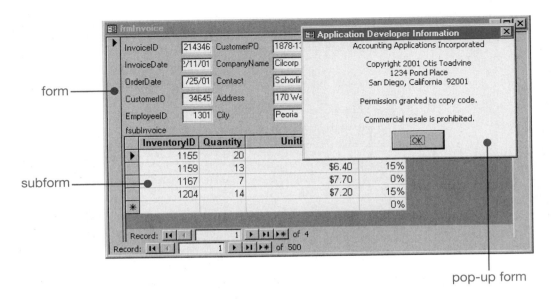

form

subform

pop-up form

**Figure 5.3**  A pop-up form displays information about an application's developer.

relationship in this chapter—particularly when you create invoice forms by following this chapter's exercises. Figure 5.3 shows a form and subform example.

We begin our exploration of forms and their utility by creating a rather simple form from a single table. Then we will create a form whose data is derived from multiple related tables. The last form will be created from a query.

## Building a Simple Form

It is much easier to enter data and alter data in the Customer table using a form. The next exercise shows you how to create an *AutoForm* from the Table window. Subsequent exercises will enhance the form's appearance. First, start with a clean slate. Launch Access if necessary and open your copy of *Ch05.mdb*. Close any open windows except the Database window. Then create a form by doing the steps in the following exercise.

EXERCISE 5.1: CREATING A FORM FROM A TABLE

1. Click Tables in the Objects bar of the Database window and select the table *tblCustomer*. You do not need to open it to perform the remaining steps in this exercise, but you can if you wish.
2. Select AutoForm from the Insert menu. Access quickly builds a form and a related subform (see Figure 5.4).
3. Save the newly created form by selecting Save from the File menu and typing *frmMyCustomer* in the Form Name text box of the Save As dialog box. Click OK

to store the form in the database. (The string *frm* is the customary form name prefix—one of the database world's rules that is equivalent to accounting's "GAAP.")

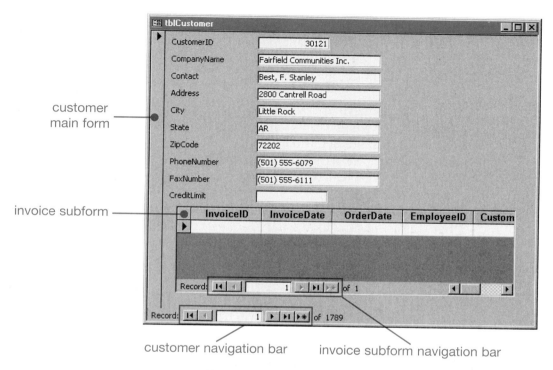

**Figure 5.4** AutoForm generated for the table *tblCustomer*.

Notice that the first row of *tblCustomer* is displayed along with an empty row in the subform beneath the main customer record. Two rows of navigation buttons appear. The top row of navigation buttons moves the record pointer through invoices that are stored in *tblInvoice* and are related to the *tblCustomer* table. The lower row of navigation buttons moves from one customer record to another. Whenever you move to a new customer, the associated invoice rows change to those of the new customer. Click the Next Record navigation button for the customer—the lower set of navigation buttons—and view different customers' information and invoice records. Click the Last Record navigation button to view the last customer's information. Click the toolbar View button and select Design View to examine the form's *design*. Close the form. Click Forms on the Objects bar to see the new form's name, *frmMyCustomer*.

Whenever you want to create a form to enter or examine data in a table, the easiest way is to first create an AutoForm-style form for a table. Subsequently, you can alter the default form to suit your needs, making it more attractive and functional. One of the fundamental operations you will use in the Form Design window is moving and sizing fields and other form objects. To move an object, you first select it and then drag it to its new location. When you select an object, small square handles appear around it. Passing the pointer over any of the object's handles causes the pointer to change shape. By dragging a handle, you can enlarge or shrink the object by dragging the handle away from or towards the object, respectively.

You can move several objects at once by selecting them and dragging the entire group. As with other Windows programs, you select multiple objects by holding down the Shift key while clicking each object in turn. Alternatively, you can simply drag the mouse so that the dashed line touches or surrounds all objects you wish to select. When you release the mouse, handles appear around all the objects that you selected.

Let's rework the default form you created previously—first by changing the title. Ensure that the form *frmMyCustomer* is displayed in Design view. Click the Maximize button on the Form window to make it as large as possible.

EXERCISE 5.2: ALTERING A FORM'S TITLE

1. Select Form Header/Footer from the View menu. Form Header and Form Footer sections are added to your form.
2. Select Toolbox from the View menu to display the toolbox on the work surface (see Figure 5.5). You can also display the toolbox by clicking the Toolbox button found on the Design View toolbar—it has a hammer and wrench on it. You can move the toolbox anywhere on the screen by dragging its Title bar, or you can drag it to the top, left, right, or bottom of the screen to dock it there.
3. Click the Label button to add a title to the form; move the mouse to the upper left corner of the form header, and drag it down and to the right until the outline is approximately 0.25" by 2.0". Release the mouse. An empty label appears in the Form Header section of the form.
4. Type the label *Coffee Merchant Customers* in the label box. Click outside the label box to see the text.
5. Remove the toolbox from the screen by clicking its Close button.
6. Right-click the label box in the Form Header and select Properties from the shortcut menu. (Alternatively, you can click the Properties button on the Design View toolbar.)
7. Click the Format tab.
8. Scroll to the Text Align property, near the end of the list of properties, and type *Center* (or select it from the drop-down list) in the Text Align box.
9. Type *14* in the Font Size property to indicate you want a point size of 14. Close the property sheet by clicking its Close button.

Select Objects → / ← Control Wizards
Label → *Aa* ← Text Box
Option Group → ← Toggle Button
Option Button → ← Check Box
Combo Box → ← List Box
Command Button → ← Image
Unbound Object Frame → ← Bound Object Frame
Page Break → ← Tab Control
Subform/Subreport → ← Line
Rectangle → ← More Controls

**Figure 5.5** Access toolbox.

10. If the title is not entirely visible in its text box, move the mouse to the right-edge sizing handle. When the pointer turns to a double-headed arrow pointing left and right, drag the sizing handle until the entire title is visible.
11. Select Form View from the View menu to see the altered form.
12. Close and save your form.

Your revised form, called *frmMyCustomer*, should resemble the one shown in Figure 5.6. We have saved it as *frmCustomer* on your Companion CD.

## Using a Form

By using a form-based interface to a database, you will realize that data entry with a form is more intuitive and easier than entering data directly into a table. We have created a simple form called *frmOrder* (remember to use the prefix *frm* for all your form names) that will introduce you to the look and feel of a typical form. The form *frmOrder* found on the Companion CD provides a convenient work surface to enter new orders into the tables comprising the order database. The form provides all the requisite mechanisms to automatically place order information into two tables called *tblOrder* and *tblOrderLine*. Furthermore, the form supplies a helpful table lookup feature in two key locations: the Customer No. (customer identification number) field and the Sales Rep. (sales representative) field.

A table lookup field is helpful to anyone entering information with which he or she is not familiar. For instance, if you do not know a customer's number—a normal situation—you can click the *combo* box (a combination of a text box and

form header

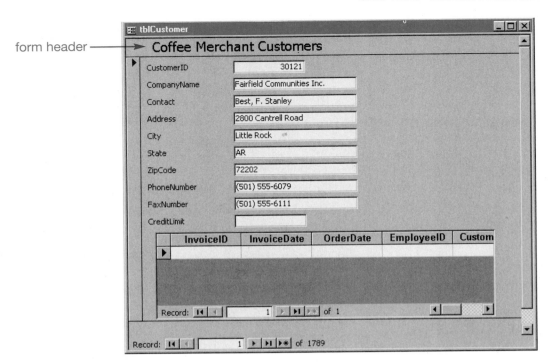

**Figure 5.6**　Customer form with a form header.

a list box) to display customer names. When the cursor is on the customer number entry, you can click the down-pointing arrow to peruse the list of existing customer numbers and names. Similarly, you can look up a sales representative's name by clicking the *list* box arrows associated with the field. Let's enter one order into the system using the order form.

Prepare for the next exercise by launching Access, if necessary, and by closing all windows except the Database window. Click Forms on the Objects bar and double-click *frmOrder* found in the list of forms. The Order Entry form opens. Follow the steps in the next exercise to enter and save information in an existing order entry table.

EXERCISE 5.3: USING THE ORDER ENTRY FORM

1. Type *5678* into the Order Number field. Press Tab to move to the next field.
2. Enter a date in the form mm/dd/yy (for example, type *7/18/01*) into the Order Date field. Press Tab to move to the next field.
3. With the cursor in the Customer field, click the combo box arrow on the right side of the field to display a list of customer numbers and names (see Figure 5.7).

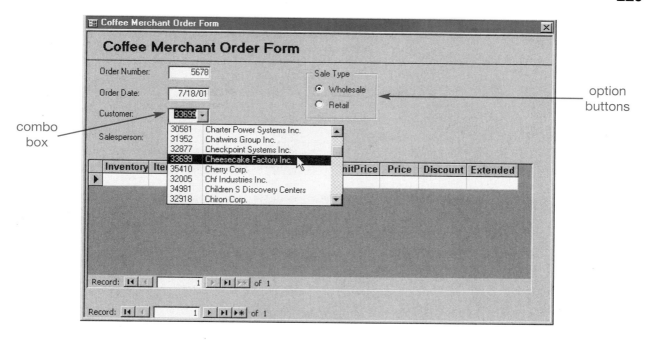

**Figure 5.7** Using a combo box to select a customer.

4. Scroll through the list of customers until the company name *Cheesecake Factory Inc.* appears. Click that name. After you select the name, its corresponding customer number is inserted into the field and thus the underlying table.

5. Click the down arrow on the Salesperson combo box and select (click) the name *English, Melinda*.

6. Press Tab to move to the Sale Type option group. Click the Retail option button. Option buttons within a group are mutually exclusive due to their behavior: clicking one button deselects any other previously selected option button in the group.

7. Click the Inventory column in the first row of the subform. This is another way to move the focus in a form. (The *focus* is the active field on a form into which you can type or press the spacebar.)

8. Type *1128*, press Tab, and type *20* in the Quantity column. Press Tab to move to UnitPrice.

9. Type *8.5* and press Tab twice. The cursor moves to the next row in the subform. Notice that the ItemID, Name, and Price are automatically inserted into the form; the extended price is calculated and inserted also. Discount takes on its default value, 0.00, if you do not enter a value.

10. Continue entering values into the subform, using Figure 5.8 as a guide. In addition to entering Inventory, Quantity, and UnitPrice values for each row, remember to type *5%* and *15%* (type the percent sign) in the Discount column for the last two entries, respectively. (What happens if you type 15 in the Discount

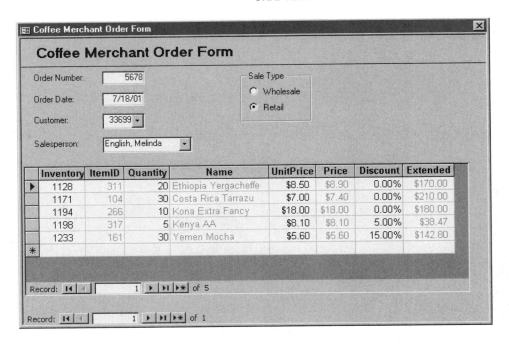

**Figure 5.8**   Completed order entry form.

column—without typing a trailing percent sign—and then press Enter? Try it. It won't hurt anything.)
11. Click the Form view Close button to cease entering values or continue on with the Try it examples.

### Try it

You may not have noticed that there are helpful hints available called *ControlTips* that display when you hover the cursor over a field in the form. *Hovering the cursor* simply means that you move the mouse pointer over a control and pause (but do not click the mouse). After a brief pause, a tip displayed in a yellow box appears. Hover over the Order Number, Order Date, and Customer fields and observe their ControlTips.

If you want to try the form again, first clear it by clicking the Next Record navigation button located at the bottom of the form. Whenever you move to another record, Access automatically posts the current data to various tables. Then Access clears the form to make way for new data. When you are done entering information, click the form's Close button. Don't be concerned that you might lose data. Microsoft Access automatically posts any newly entered data to the database when you move off the current record or close the form.

You have used a Table window's navigation buttons to view the data in a table. Similarly, you can examine all the data in the Order form—from multiple tables—through a form. Assuming you have entered additional orders, you can click the First Record button to go to the first order you entered, or click the Last Record button to go to the last order entered in the system. Other navigation buttons work in a familiar way.

Editing data couldn't be simpler. In a Form View window, click on any field you would like to change and type the change. For form fields using lookup tables (fields having list boxes or combo boxes), click the arrow near the field to display the list of values; then enter a new value or select one of the displayed entries. It is best to use a lookup table when available, especially for noncontiguous values such as sales representative identification numbers. As budding form designers, you should incorporate lookup tables for fields whose values are limited to a specific and small list of acceptable values. This saves much frustration and confusion on the part of form users.

With forms, you can view particular records or groups of records using either the Filter By Form or Filter By Selection techniques. When you filter objects, you are restricting what is displayed to some subset of the total objects available. Filtering records being viewed through a form is no different. You simply specify the criteria—similar to query criteria—that are used to restrict your view of the records and then select Apply Filter/Sort from the Filter menu. Records are displayed in the usual way in the form, but you will notice that only a select group of records are available. The total number of records in the filtered set are indicated to the right of the navigation buttons at the bottom of the form. Try it yourself.

### Try it

Display the form *frmCustomer* found on your Companion CD. Notice that there are 1,789 customer records. All are available for viewing. Next, click the Records menu, select Filter, and select Filter By Form from the Filter cascade menu. Let's see how many customers from California there are in the database—and who they are. Click the State form field and type *CA* in either uppercase or lowercase letters. Select Apply Filter/Sort from the Filter menu. (Be careful to not click Advanced Filter/Sort. That will have a different consequence.) Access reveals that there are 196 customers in California (see Figure 5.9). Use the navigation buttons to go to the next record and the last record. Select Remove Filter/Sort from the Records menu. The form indicates all records in the table are available again. Close the form, *frmCustomer*. If a Save dialog box appears, click the No to All button.

Filter By Selection works in almost the same way as Filter By Form. You select a field, such as City, which has an entry by which you would like to filter and then

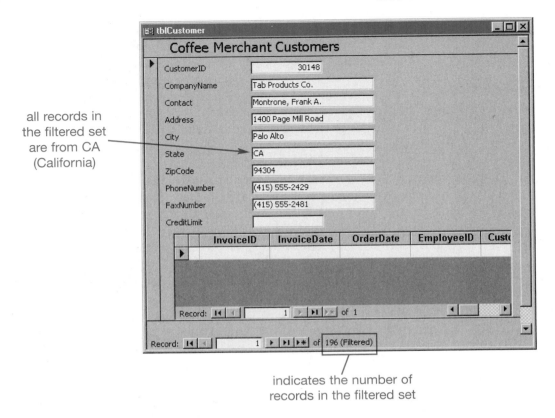

all records in
the filtered set
are from CA
(California)

indicates the number of
records in the filtered set

**Figure 5.9**   Filter By Form example.

choose Filter By Selection from the Records menu. Only records whose fields match that of the selected field are displayed.

### Try it

Display in Form view the form *frmCustomer*. Move to the first customer in the Customer table, Fairfield Communities Inc. Click the City form field and drag the cursor across the entire city name to select it. Let's see how many other customers we have in the selected city of Little Rock. Click the Records menu, select Filter, and select Filter By Selection from the Filter cascade menu. Access indicates that currently there are six customers in Little Rock. Select Remove Filter/Sort from the Records menu. The form indicates all records in the table are available again. Close the *frmCustomer* form.

You can do more with Filter By Form and Filter By Selection. However, those details you will have to discover on your own. We have a lot more to cover on other topics, so we'll move on.

## Creating a Multitable Form and Subform

Many forms involve more than one table. The Coffee Merchant's Order form is an example of a multitable form, because data such as the order number, order date, and sales representative number are stored in a table called *tblOrder*. Details about the items ordered (item ID and quantity ordered) are stored in another table called *tblOrderLine*. The Inventory table, *tblInventory*, is also referenced by The Coffee Merchant's Order form, although no new inventory items can be entered via the form. Finally, the *tblCustomer* table is consulted to locate and display customer numbers in the Customer field. Four tables are joined and referenced by The Coffee Merchant's Order form.

Although using The Coffee Merchant's Order form is an informative exercise, you will benefit much more from *building* a form from scratch. Once you create a form, it is only a short time until you will be designing elaborate forms for your own applications. Figure 5.10 shows you an example of a multitable invoice review and data entry form that displays data from several of The Coffee Merchant's tables. That form has the look of the finished form we are striving for in this section. When finished, your form should start to resemble the one in Figure 5.10.

**Figure 5.10**   Example invoice review and data entry form.

The invoice form that you will build in this section is actually two forms: a main form and a subform. The main form displays one record from the *tblInvoice* table. Simultaneously, the subform displays several related records that are the individual items that are listed on the invoice. Information on the subform includes item number, item name, quantity ordered, unit price, discount, and extended price. Subform information is synthesized by a query supplied on the CD-ROM called *qryInvoiceLineItem*.

## Creating a Form Containing a Subform

Access allows you to create forms and reports that use data found in more than one table or query. The best way to create a main form and its subform is to use a Form Wizard. The following exercise outlines how to create an invoice form. Prepare for the next exercise by closing all open windows except the Database window and clicking Forms in the Objects bar of the Database window.

EXERCISE 5.4: CREATING AN INVOICE FORM AND SUBFORM

1. Click the New button on the Forms collection of the Database window. Access displays the New Form dialog box.
2. Select Form Wizard from the list of form choices and type *qryInvoiceMain* in the list box found just above the Cancel button. (When creating forms with subforms, it is normally best to use the Form Wizard.) You base the top half of the form on the table or query that contains the data to appear on the main form (the data on the "one" side of the one-to-many relationship). In this case the main form will contain customer invoice information. The subform will contain invoice detail lines with products, quantities, prices, etc.
3. Click the OK button to begin the form-building process. The first of several Form Wizard dialog boxes is displayed.
4. Click the chevron button (">>") to move all fields on the Available Fields list onto the Selected Fields list. The latter list contains the fields that will be displayed on the form.
5. Add the subform fields to the form: click the drop-down list arrow beneath the Tables/Queries list box to display the queries and tables in the database.
6. Locate *qryInvoiceLineItem* in the list and click it. The query-supplied fields appear in the Available Fields list (see Figure 5.11).
7. Click the chevron button to move all the subform fields onto the Selected Fields list.
8. In the Selected Fields list, locate and select the field called *qryInvoiceLineItem.InvoiceID*.
9. Click the less than button—the one displaying "<"—to remove the extra InvoiceID field, moving it from the Selected Fields list back onto the Available Fields list. (Alternatively, you could select each field in turn, clicking the ">" to place each onto the Selected Fields list. The way we suggest here is faster.)
10. Click the Next button to proceed to the next step.
11. When the dialog box appears asking you how you want to view your data, click the Next button to accept the suggested default.
12. Select the suggested Datasheet layout for your subform by clicking the Datasheet option button. Click Next to go to the next step.

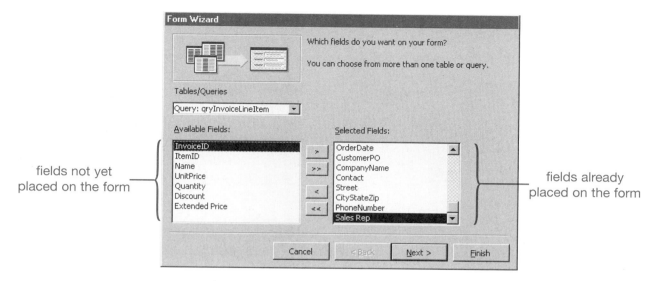

Figure 5.11    Selecting main form and subform fields.

13. Select the suggested "Standard" style (near the bottom of the list) and click the Next button. Be careful on the last Form Wizard dialog box: change the form and subform names by altering them in the text boxes. If you do not do it here, it is more difficult to do later.
14. In the Form text box type *frmInvoice2* and in the Subform text box type *fsubInvoice2*. (Be sure to enter the prefix *fsub* for the subform. This prefix indicates a form is a subform and is the accepted standard for naming subforms.)
15. Click the "Open the form to view or enter information." option button, if it is not already selected.
16. Click the Finish button to conclude the form-building process.

Access takes a few moments to build both the form and subform and then opens it for your use (see Figure 5.12). Scroll through the records to experience how the form works. Occasionally, you may want to scroll through the subform to display all the invoice items for a particular invoice. Keep in mind that the outermost set of navigation buttons page through whole invoices, while the inner set skip from line to line on invoice details in the subform.

**Modifying a Subform's Column Widths and Labels**

Some of the subform's fields are not sufficiently wide. Consequently, some fields are completely visible while others are not. For example, notice in Figure 5.12 that the Extended Price column, which is the rightmost field of the subform, is not visible. Similarly, the UnitPrice column seems far too wide. Let's modify the widths of some subform columns so that they are just large enough to display their

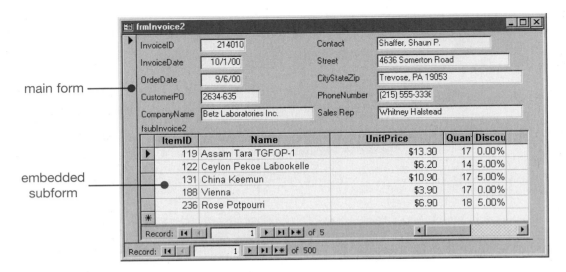

main form

embedded
subform

**Figure 5.12**   Main form and embedded subform created by the Form Wizard.

information but not too large. Then, we will change the subform column label
from *UnitPrice* to *Price*. The next exercise shows you how to accomplish these
tasks. Prepare for this exercise by closing all windows except the Database window. Next, click Forms on the Database window Objects bar to display the list of
forms in your database. (Notice *frmInvoice2* and *fsubInvoice2* are among the list
of forms.)

EXERCISE 5.5: MODIFYING A SUBFORM'S COLUMN WIDTHS AND LABELS

1. Double-click the subform *fsubInvoice2* to open it. If necessary, select Datasheet
   View from the View menu so the information is displayed as a datasheet, not a
   form.
2. Alter all the columns to an optimal width: move the mouse to the leftmost column label, ItemID. When the mouse turns to a down-pointing arrow, drag it to
   the right until all columns are selected. (Selected columns are displayed in black.)
   Release the mouse button.
3. Move the mouse to any border between two columns in the label area or move it
   to the rightmost border of the rightmost label. When the mouse pointer changes
   to a double-headed arrow with a vertical line dissecting it, double-click the
   mouse. All columns change size, adjusting to the smallest width that is wide
   enough to display the largest values or column labels.
4. Click anywhere to deselect the columns. Now the columns display the widest
   values in the column without truncating them. If you wish to further customize individual column widths, you can do so by dragging the line to the right of a column's label when the mouse pointer is a double-headed arrow. Dragging the

right column line to the right widens the column; dragging to the left narrows the column.
5. Display the table in Design view: select Design View from the View menu.
6. Double-click the UnitPrice field in the Detail section of the form to display its property sheet. (If you find this difficult—double-click timing is everything—then right-click the field and select Properties from the pop-up list.)
7. Click the property sheet tab labeled *Other*, double-click the value displayed in the Name property, and type *Price* to replace the UnitPrice name.
8. Click the property sheet Close button.
9. Close the *fsubInvoice2* subform (click the form's Close button) and click Yes when asked if you want to save the changed design.

What you have learned here is that to resize subform fields displayed as a datasheet, simply resize the table fields. This automatically causes the fields to display in their new widths in any subforms constructed from the changed tables.

You will do additional work on this form, but it is always a good idea to preserve the partially complete work. This way, you don't risk losing a large amount of work if something should happen to the power to your computer.

There are several controls on the forms with which you are working. *Controls* are all the objects that appear on forms or reports. For example, the label *InvoiceID* is a control as is the field displaying the value 214010 in the InvoiceID field. There are three general types of controls in Access: bound controls, unbound controls, and calculated controls. A *bound control* has as its data source a field in a table. The invoice date field in Figure 5.12 is a bound control. An *unbound control* has no data source and is used to display a title or label on forms and reports. It does not change from one record to the next. The invoice date label (*InvoiceDate*) in Figure 5.12 is an example of an unbound label. A *calculated control* has as its data source an expression rather than a table field. The Extended Price field is an example of a calculated control. Access database users and developers use the term *control* frequently when referring to objects on forms or reports.

## Altering a Subform's Column Formats

When you want to alter an item's property such as its display format, you summon the item's property sheet and make the necessary changes. You use the property sheet to set, view, or change the properties of a table, query, form, report, or controls on forms and reports. Available in the Design view of a Table, Query, Form, or Report window, the property sheet is displayed whenever you click the Properties button on the toolbar. It remains on the work surface, even when you select other controls or objects, until you close it. You can also display the property sheet for a selected object by right-clicking the mouse and then choosing Properties from the pop-up menu.

The next exercise illustrates how to change the display properties of two numeric values found in *fsubInvoice2*. Currently, the Price and Extended Price columns display their values in currency format. This may not be desirable in some situations. Let's change the display format for the columns to eliminate the currency symbols. Prepare for the next exercise by opening the subform, *fsubInvoice2*, in Design view.

EXERCISE 5.6: CHANGING A COLUMN'S DISPLAY CHARACTERISTICS

1. Select both the UnitPrice and Extended Price controls (*not* their labels) in the Detail section by holding down the Shift key and then clicking each one. (Be careful to not *move* the controls as you click them. If you accidentally do move them, then simply click Undo in the Edit menu.)
2. Click the Properties button on the toolbar. The property sheet appears with the Title bar displaying *Multiple selection*, which indicates more than one object will be affected.
3. Click the Format tab. The group of properties associated with the way data appears when displayed are called Format properties.
4. Click the Format property text box, click its list box arrow, and locate and click Standard (see Figure 5.13).
5. Close the property sheet.
6. Close and save the subform (click the subform's Close button and click the Yes button to save the changed subform).

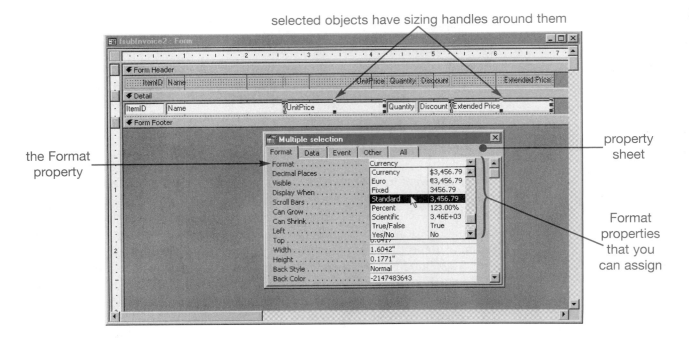

**Figure 5.13**   Changing objects' properties.

If you want to verify the property changes you just made, then simply open the form in Form view. Observe that currency symbols no longer appear in either the Price or the Extended Price fields. Figure 5.14 shows the altered invoice form and subform.

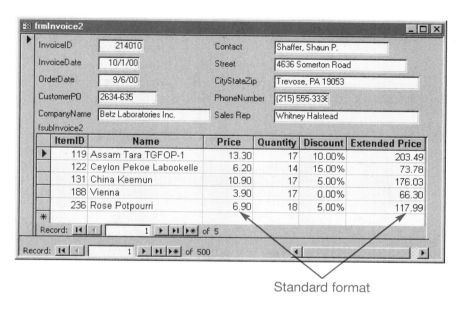

Standard format

**Figure 5.14** Altered invoice subform and form.

## Rearranging Form Fields

You can easily rearrange controls on a form by selecting them and then dragging them to a new location. For example, you can move the CompanyName control closer to the customer's address controls on the right side of the form. You move controls by displaying the form or subform in Design view. Then, after you click the bound control, you can move the mouse over the selected control. When the mouse pointer changes to a small hand, click and drag the bound control and its attached unbound control (its label) to a new location. If you want to move a group of controls, simply Shift-click each of them and then move them as a group. To deselect controls, simply click outside the selected control or group of controls.

If a subform's data is not fully visible because the form is not wide enough (a likely case), click the View button and select Design View, click the subform frame to select it, and drag the right border handle to the right to widen the entire frame. (You may have to switch back and forth between Design view and Form view until you have adjusted the subform frame to your liking.) Though your form does not exactly match our Invoice form, it is very close. Only a few embellishments remain to make them identical. You can do that on your own, if you want to practice the techniques.

## Printing a Form

Usually, you do not print forms to produce printed output. However, printing one page of a form is a good way to keep track of all the forms you have developed for any accounting system. Printing a form is probably the easiest task of all. First, select and open in Form view the form you want to print from the list on the Forms sheet of the Database window. Optionally, you can use the form navigation buttons to display a particular record, or you can simply print the first record displayed. In either case, select Print from the File menu. When the Print dialog box opens, click the "Selected Record(s)" option button so that Access prints only one form (see Figure 5.15). Click OK to start the print process. If your form is wider than can be accommodated by the current print setup, you will receive a warning similar to the one shown in Figure 5.16. In that case, click the Cancel button to close the warning dialog box and click Page Setup in the File menu. Next, click the Page tab and click the Landscape option button. That should fix the print problem.

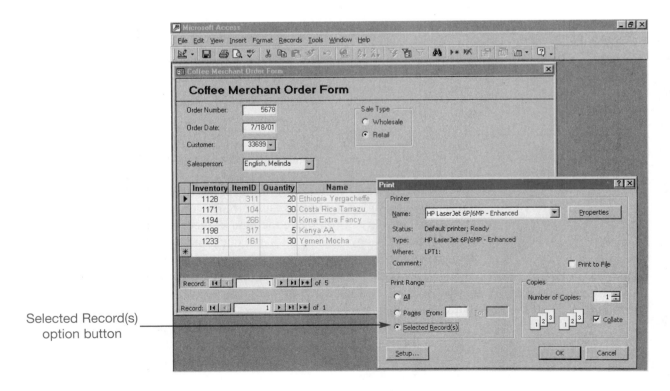

Selected Record(s) option button

**Figure 5.15** Printing a single form.

**Figure 5.16** Print width warning dialog box.

You can print properties, permissions, and design information for database objects, including your forms' designs. Printing the design characteristics of your database objects helps you document your database's design and the accounting application you develop. Select Tools, Analyze, Documentor. Then, check the objects for which you want printed definition information. Click OK and the report is formulated and displayed in the Object Definition window. If you decide to print the report, simply click the Print button on the toolbar. If not, click the Close button on the toolbar to discard the report and return to the Database window.

### Try it

Close all windows except the Database window. Select Tools, click Analyze, and click Documentor. Click the Forms tab of the Documentor dialog box and click the check box to the left of the form *frmInvoice2*. Click OK. Access takes a second or two to construct a report and display it in the Object Definition window. Examine the report. Click the Zoom button on the toolbar and click inside the Object Definition window to alternately zoom in and then zoom out. Close the Object Definition window after you are done and close the *Ch05.mdb* database. Take a break if you wish.

When you want to see a comprehensive list of information from one or more tables, then printing forms is not adequate. Instead, you need a report. Reports and how to produce them are described next.

## BUILDING AND PRINTING REPORTS

Reports provide the mechanism to produce high-quality printed database information. While you can use a form for viewing or altering information in the database, you cannot enter or alter information in a report. Reports are strictly for output. Like forms, reports are based on information found in tables or supplied by queries. Unlike forms, reports allow you to group information from one table. With forms, you must join two or more tables to group information by using a form/subform combination.

## Using Reports

Reports are used in accounting database applications to provide hard copy output that compares, summarizes, and subtotals data found in customer and billing data. An Access report can produce printed output such as shipping labels, purchase orders, bill of materials lists, or invoices that mimic paper-only forms used by businesses. Producing mailing labels from database customer records using Access reports can save money for larger mailings because Access can sort the output into zip code order. When you group mail by zip code, the U.S. Postal Service provides lower postage rates.

## Using Report Wizards

Microsoft Access provides two ways to create reports. You can create a report from scratch, starting with a blank form, or you can use a Report Wizard. We believe that you will prefer using Report Wizards because the process is easier and faster than creating a report from scratch.

Report Wizards offer several styles of reports, including Columnar AutoReport, Tabular AutoReport, Chart Wizard, and Labels Wizard. The AutoReport Wizards create preformatted, single-column (Columnar) or multicolumn (Tabular) reports with very little involvement from you.

You invoke a Report Wizard from the Database window after clicking Reports on the Objects bar and then clicking the New button on the Reports page. Of course, reports get their data from tables or queries. So, you must designate the table or query that produces the data that is placed in the report. Next, you select one of the report types, such as Report Wizard, from the list displayed in the New Report dialog box. Once you click OK, an Access Wizard guides you through the process of creating a report—step by step. Simply follow the Report Wizard's dialog boxes and respond to its questions. When you click the Finish button in the last step of the Wizard-guided report creation process, Access quickly builds an attractive report that it displays in the Print Preview window.

## Examining a Report's Anatomy

The Report window has three views: Design view, Print Preview, and Layout Preview. Design view is used to change the layout and design of a report. Print Preview is used to check all the data and its appearance in the report. Layout Preview is used to inspect the font, layout, and general appearance of the report. Design view is where you will spend most of your time, because you create and modify the report's layout here. A printed report is simply a matter of placing selected data from the database into the proper predefined locations in the report and printing the merger.

All reports are based on data supplied by tables or queries. An Access report is divided into *sections*, which appear at particular places when the report is printed. There are seven different types of sections, but a report does not have to include all seven sections. Each section appears once in Design view. When you print a report, some sections are repeated as needed. Figure 5.17 shows an example of a report's design.

**Figure 5.17** Report sections.

The Detail section is required in each report. However, the other sections are optional, thus you can omit them. Beginning at the very top of the report is the Report Header section. It is printed once at the beginning of the report. The Page Header's contents are printed at the top of every page. The Group Header's contents are printed every time the grouping field value changes. Contents of the Detail section are printed for each record selected from the underlying table(s) or queries. The Group Footer prints at the end of each group. The Page Footer prints at the bottom of each page. The Report Footer prints on a page at the end of the report.

## Creating a Tabular-Style Report with a Report Wizard

In many ways, creating a report resembles creating a form. Designing a report, including its field layouts, headings, and other details, occurs in the report Design View window. When you want to see the report replete with data—a facsimile of the printed report—you click the Print Preview button on the toolbar. We introduce report creation by showing you how to build and print a tabular-style, one-table report.

Let's experiment with the Employee table. It is a good one to start with. Suppose we want a printed list of employee names and other information sorted by the employees' last names. All the requisite information is found in one table, *tblEmployee*. Follow the steps in the next exercise to create a report with the help of the Access Report Wizard. As usual, prepare by clearing the work surface: open *Ch05.mdb*, and close all Access windows except the Database window.

EXERCISE 5.7: CREATING A REPORT

1. Click Reports in the Database window Objects bar and click the New button.
2. Select Report Wizard, which is found in the upper panel of the New Report dialog box.
3. Click the drop-down arrow to display all the database's tables and queries, click *tblEmployee* in the list of tables and queries, and click OK to start the Report Wizard. A new dialog box is displayed in which you choose which fields will appear on the report.
4. From the Available Fields list, double-click the following fields, one at a time, to move them onto the Selected Fields list: EmployeeID, EmployeeLastName, EmployeeHireDate, EmployeeDOB, and EmployeeGender (see Figure 5.18). Click the Next button when you have entered all fields. (You can also select a field and press the ">" button to move a field onto the Selected Fields list, but it is faster to double-click the names.)

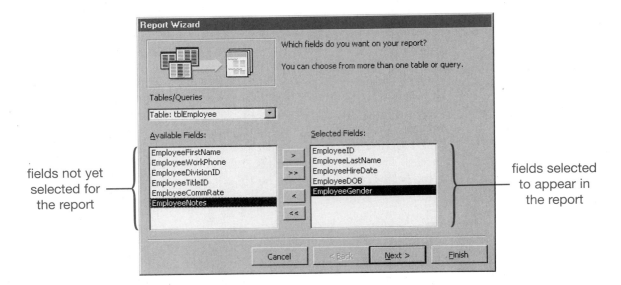

fields not yet selected for the report

fields selected to appear in the report

**Figure 5.18**   Selecting fields for a report.

5. The Report Wizard displays several more dialog boxes. The next one asks if you want to create a grouping level. Because you do not want to for this report, click Next without making any changes.

6. The next dialog box asks if you want to sort the report records. Because we want the report to display the employee information in name order, click the drop-down arrow next to the first sort box and select *EmployeeLastName* from the list of report fields. Click the Next button to proceed.

   **Note:** If you discover you have made a mistake on an earlier Report Wizard dialog box, you can simply click the Back button repeatedly until you reach the dialog box containing the mistake. Make any changes and then click the Next button to return to where you left off.

7. Ensure that the Tabular option (in the Layout option group) and the Portrait option (in the Orientation option group) are selected. Also ensure that the "Adjust the field width so all fields fit on a page." check box is checked. Click the Next button.
8. Select the Formal report style and press the Next button.
9. Type *Coffee Merchant Employees* in the text box. Click the Finish button to finalize your choices and generate your report.
10. After reviewing the report preview, click the Design View button on the toolbar to view the report's design. Finally, click the Design view Close button to close and save the report.

   **Note:** The report title that you entered in step 9 is also used to name the report. That is not a good feature of Access reports. You should rename the report *rptMyEmployee* immediately after you save it. To rename a report, select the report from the list of reports, press F2, type *rptMyEmployee*, and press Enter. You can rename any object that way. We have saved this report as *rptEmployee* on your Companion CD.

Access creates the report and displays it in Print Preview (see Figure 5.19). The report lists employee records in name order. Did you notice that some report column labels such as *Last Name*, *Hire Date*, and *Birth Date* are different from their table column names? The reason for this is that we included less cryptic names for them in the Caption property of the table design when we created the *tblEmployee* table. (To verify this, examine the Employee table in Design view and pay particular attention to the Caption property as you select field names in the upper portion of the Design view.) Print the report, if you wish, by selecting Print from the File menu.

## Modifying a Report Field's Data Alignment

You can enhance the appearance of a control's data or label by adjusting its alignment (its Text Align property). Some of the data columns in the Employee report do not line up well with their column labels. For example, the column label EmployeeID is far to the left of the actual identification number column values. Similarly, the Gender data values appear misaligned when compared to their column label. You can alter the *alignment* of labels (unbound controls) or data (bound controls) to achieve the effect you want. Briefly, we will illustrate how to alter the

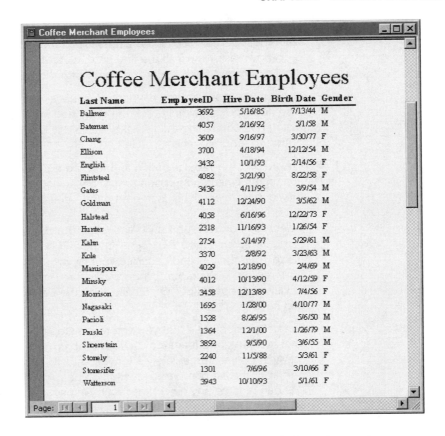

**Figure 5.19**   Print Preview window showing a tabular-style report.

data alignment in the next exercise. Prepare for the exercise by displaying your newly minted Employee report, *rptMyEmployee*, in Design view. Then follow the steps in the next exercise to alter the data alignment of several report column data controls.

EXERCISE 5.8: ALTERING REPORT CONTROLS' DATA ALIGNMENT

1. Move the cursor to the Detail section and select the EmployeeID and EmployeeGender bound controls: hold down the Shift key and click each one in turn. Be careful to not *move* the controls when you select them. (It is very easy to do that.)
2. Select Properties from the View menu (or click the Properties button found on the toolbar) to display the property sheet.
3. Click the Format tab to reveal that collection of format-related properties.
4. Scroll the property list until near its bottom, click the Text Align property text box, and click the Text Align list box arrow to reveal the alignment choices.

5. Select Center from the four alignment choices (see Figure 5.20).
6. Close the property sheet and select Save from the File menu to save your design changes.
7. Click the Design window Close button.

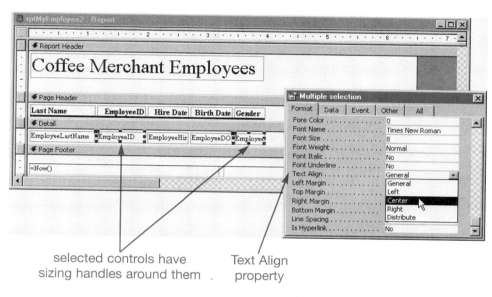

selected controls have
sizing handles around them

Text Align
property

**Figure 5.20** Altering the alignment property of multiple controls.

## Deleting Controls and Report Sections

Because the *rptMyEmployee* report is short—only one page long—there is no need for a Page Footer section. It contains a single control that displays the current page number, which is unnecessary in a one-page report. Deleting a report section—the Page Footer section in this case—is straightforward, so we will skip a formal exercise and simply describe the steps in the following Try it paragraph. Before eliminating the Page Footer section, you must first remove all its controls. There are three controls in the Page Footer section: two calculated controls and an unbound control.

### Try it

Display *rptMyEmployee* in Design view. Using the horizontal scroll bar, move to the left edge of the report and locate the control in the Page Footer section containing the Access function =*Now( )*. Select it (handles appear around it when it is selected) and press the Delete key to remove it. In a similar way, remove the second control that resides in the Page Footer. Move to the right edge of the report and locate the

Page Footer control containing the expression =*"Page " & [Page] & " of " & [Pages]*. Select the control—a rather long expression—and press Delete to remove it. Finally, select the thin line (the unbound control) that appears near the top of the Page Footer section. Press Delete to remove it. Once all controls in a section are gone, you remove the section by dragging up the bar below the section. In our case, you move the mouse to the *bottom* of the Page Footer section until it turns into a double-headed arrow, dissected by a small horizontal line, pointing up and down. Then drag the arrow up until the Page Footer section is eliminated. Release the mouse button. Click Save in the File menu to save the altered report. Close the Design View window after you save the report.

In the step you executed above prior to saving the report, you reduced the height of the Page Footer section to zero. That removes it. Removing *both* the Page Header section and the Page Footer section is even simpler. Simply click Page Header/Footer in the View menu to remove the checkmark to its left. The two sections are removed simultaneously, and any controls in both are removed automatically.

## Saving and Printing a Report

You should save any reports that you anticipate running periodically. On the other hand, you need not save any reports that are used only once. You can save a report in Design view or Print Preview: select Save from the File menu. For new reports, you must supply a name before Access will save the report definition in the database.

Reports exist to be printed, so let's print this report. You can print a report from either the Design View window or the Print Preview window. Before actually printing a report, you may want to check and alter some global report settings such as margin settings, page orientation (portrait or landscape), or paper size. You alter any of those settings by clicking the Setup button in the Print dialog box or by clicking Page Setup in the File menu. You should print the report *rptMyEmployee* so you have a copy of its final form. We will not be using this report further, so you can either save it or delete it from the database.

Is it possible to produce a report similar to *rptEmployee* or *rptMyEmployee* but sort the rows into order by division location and by employee names within each division? The answer is yes—by using the Report Wizard to form report groups. You learn how to do this next.

## Producing a Grouped Data Report

You learned that either tables or queries can be the basis of any forms you create. The same is true for reports. When you base a report on a query, you can alter the query's selection criteria, save the query, run another report, and produce different report results. For example, we could create a query that selects invoices that are 30 days past due, base a report on that query, and then run and print the report. Printing a list of invoices that are 31 to 60 days past due would then be easy.

Simply modify the existing query to select rows whose invoice date is 31 to 60 days ago, save the modified query, and rerun the report. Alternatively, you could create a parameter query that prompts you for the value of "days past due" and run the report after the query processes your input.

Building a report that lists employees and their division locations involves information from at least two tables: *tblEmployee* and *tblDivisionLocation*. There are two general approaches to producing the report. One way is to first create a query that joins the two tables and then create a report based on the query. The other way is to create a report, with the help of a Report Wizard, by including all the tables involved and let the Report Wizard join the tables. The latter approach produces a report through the use of a "behind the report" query. A *behind the report* query is one that is stored inside the report's definition and is not available for general use in the Queries collection. When you create a specialized report whose query will not have widespread use, the latter report method is preferable. That's what we will illustrate here. In preparation for the next exercise, close all windows in *Ch05.mdb* except the Database window.

EXERCISE 5.9: CREATING A GROUPED DATA REPORT WITH A REPORT WIZARD

1. Select Report Wizard, which is found in the upper panel of the New Report dialog box.
2. Click the drop-down arrow to display all the database's tables and queries, click *tblEmployee* in the list of tables and queries, and click OK to start the Report Wizard. A new dialog box is displayed in which you choose which fields will appear on the report.
3. From the Available Fields list, double-click the following fields, one at a time, to move them onto the Selected Fields list: EmployeeLastName, EmployeeID, EmployeeHireDate, EmployeeDOB, and EmployeeGender.
4. Click the Tables/Queries drop-down arrow to display the database's tables and queries once again and click the entry Table: *tblDivisionLocation*. You may have to use the scroll bar to locate the table, which is just above the entry *tblEmployee* in the drop-down list.
5. From the Available Fields list, double-click DivisionCity and then click the Next button to move to the next step in the report-building process.
6. The Report Wizard asks how you want to view your data. Click the choice *by tblDivisionLocation* listed in the left panel. That causes Access to group the report's rows by city (see Figure 5.21). Click the Next button to move to the next step.
7. The dialog box requests whether or not you want additional grouping levels. Because you do not, click the Next button to move to the next step.
8. The next dialog box asks if you want to sort the detail records. Click the drop-down arrow next to the first sort box and select EmployeeLastName from the list of report fields. Click the Next button to proceed.
9. Ensure that the Stepped option (in the Layout option group) and the Portrait option (in the Orientation option group) are selected. Also ensure that the

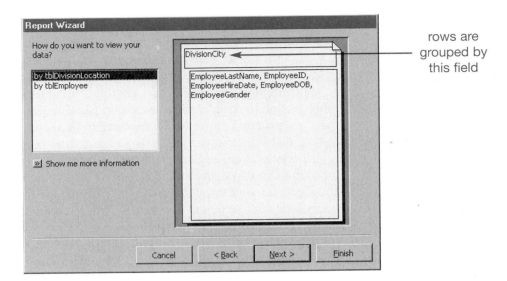

**Figure 5.21**   Selecting a grouping field.

"Adjust the field width so all fields fit on a page." check box is checked. Click the Next button.

10. Select the Formal report style and press the Next button.
11. Type *Employees by Location* in the text box. Click the Finish button to finalize your choices and generate a preview of your report.
12. After reviewing the report preview, click the Design View button on the toolbar (*not* the Close window button) to view the report's design. Finally, click the Design view Close button to close and save the report.

Remember that the report is saved under the name you typed for the report title—a nonconforming database object name. Be sure to rename the report *rptEmpLoc*. For your convenience, we have placed the report on your Companion CD. It is called *rptEmployeesByLocation*. Examine that report, or print it if you wish.

A *Group Footer* is displayed just after the grouping element, the employee's city in our example, changes. Currently, our report does not have a Group Footer because, for one thing, we have no numeric fields whose sums or averages need to be displayed after a complete group is printed. Let's add a Group Footer to see how it's done.

### Try it

Display the report in Design view and select Sorting and Grouping from the View menu. When the Sorting and Grouping dialog box appears, click the drop-down arrow to the right of the DivisionID row. Click DivisionCity from the drop-down list. (This will group and sort entries by city name rather than city identification number.) Click the row selector to the left of the entry DivisionCity to select it. Then double-click the Group Footer list box located below in the Group Properties area. This will change the value from "No" to "Yes," which means that a Group Footer will be displayed (see Figure 5.22). Close the Sorting and Grouping dialog box. Notice the new Group Footer section in the report.

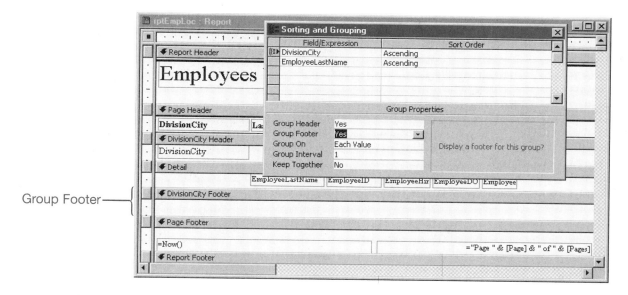

**Figure 5.22**   Inserting a Group Footer into a report.

A *page break* causes the printer to skip to the top of a new page. You can place a page break in any section of a report. For instance, you can place a page break in the Group Footer section. That way, Access prints each city and the employees located in it on a separate page.

### Try it

Go ahead and place a page break in the *rptEmployeesByLocation* report so that each group prints on a new page. First, display *rptEmployeesByLocation* in Design view. Insert a page break: display the toolbox (click the Toolbox toolbar button if needed), click the Page Break button, and move the mouse to the left side of the report within the Group Footer section. Click the mouse to drop the page break into the report's Page Footer section (see Figure 5.23). Close the toolbox. Save the report again and print the first two pages to examine the changes you made to the report. Close the report but leave the Database window open. We are done changing the design of the *rptEmployeesByLocation* report.

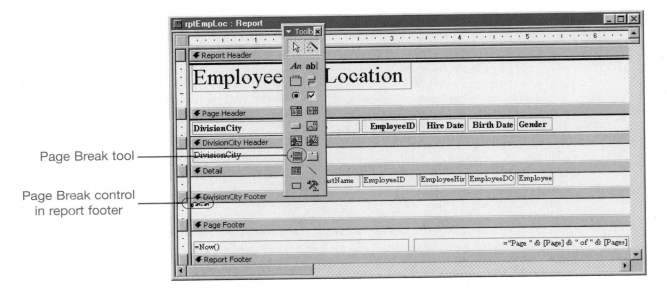

**Figure 5.23**   Report design containing a Page Break control.

## Building Reports with Queries and Expressions

We will next design a report that produces invoices. You will participate and help build the invoice report, and we will help. We merely outline some of the easier procedures, however. You are familiar with all of the steps needed to build the Invoice report except for a few. These we will carefully explain in individual exercise steps. We begin with the query—one that you have not seen before—that joins six tables to assemble all the fields we need for an industrial strength invoice.

Figure 5.24 shows the query that will produce the fields needed for each invoice. The QBE grid columns have been narrowed so that you can see several of the Field row entries, though most fields are out of view. Before continuing, please open the query, which is the foundation of our Invoice report, and study it briefly. The query is saved on your Companion CD as *qryInvoiceReport*. Observe how the tables are joined.

The *tblCustomer* and *tblInvoice* tables are joined on the column CustomerID. The table *tblInvoice* is joined to the table *tblInvoiceLine* on the col-

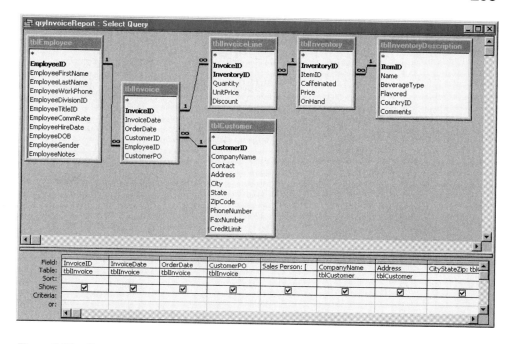

**Figure 5.24** Query to select fields for an invoice report.

umn InvoiceID found in both tables. Other joined tables are *tblInvoice* to *tblEmployee* on the column EmployeeID, *tblInvoiceLine* to *tblInventory* on the column InventoryID, and *tblInventory* to *tblInventoryDescription* on the key column ItemID. Thus, the six tables are joined by five sets of primary key to foreign key pairs. Figure 5.25 shows a typical invoice that we would like to produce with Microsoft Access. The report produces one customer invoice per page and is ready to be mailed to customers.

We begin by generating the initial report using the Access Report Wizard. However, before you proceed, examine this brief list of the steps needed to create the Invoice report from the *qryInvoiceReport* query:

- Use the Report Wizard, which will automatically group data on the InvoiceID value, to produce the initial report with data supplied solely from the query *qryInvoiceReport*.

- Move selected report fields from the Page Header into the InvoiceID Group Header.

- Move selected report fields from the Report Header into the Page Header.

- Delete the Report Header, Report Footer, and Page Footer sections.

# Invoice

| | |
|---|---|
| **Invoice Number:** | 214010 |
| **Invoice Date:** | 10/1/00 |
| **Order Date:** | 9/6/00 |
| **Customer PO #:** | 2634-635 |
| **Sales Person:** | Whitney Halstead |

**The Coffee Merchant**
**5998 Alcala Park**
**San Diego, CA 92110**

**Sold to:**

Betz Laboratories Inc.
4636 Somerton Road
Trevose, PA 19053

| Item # | Qty | Description | Price | Discount | Extended |
|---|---|---|---|---|---|
| 119 | 17 | Assam Tara TGFOP-1 | $13.30 | 10% | 203.49 |
| 122 | 14 | Ceylon Pekoe Labookelle | $6.20 | 15% | 73.78 |
| 131 | 17 | China Keemun | $10.90 | 5% | 176.03 |
| 188 | 17 | Vienna | $3.90 | 0% | 66.30 |
| 236 | 18 | Rose Potpourri | $6.90 | 5% | 117.99 |

| | |
|---|---|
| **Subtotal:** | $637.59 |
| **Sales Tax:** | 0.00 |
| **Shipping:** | 20.75 |
| **Invoice Total:** | $658.34 |

**Figure 5.25** First page of the invoice report.

- Create expressions in the InvoiceID Footer that calculate the invoice subtotal, sales tax (if any), shipping, and invoice total amounts for each invoice.

- Add miscellaneous graphics and other labels as needed to embellish the invoice.

## Creating the Report's First Draft

It is almost always best to create the first draft of a report with the Report Wizard. Creating a report with no help is difficult work, and the Report Wizard is sophisticated and resourceful. The Wizard determines we need a report with groups because the data is produced from a query whose tables are joined in a chain of several one-to-many relationships. That's just what we want. In particular, we want all the invoice detail lines—the item name, quantity, price, discount, and total price—in any given invoice grouped by invoice number.

Let's begin building the first version of the Invoice report. Ensure that the database *Ch05.mdb* is open. Click Reports in the Database window Objects bar. Then follow the steps in the following exercise to create the initial draft of the Invoice report.

EXERCISE 5.10: USING THE REPORT WIZARD

1. Click the New button on the Database window, select Report Wizard, and click the drop-down arrow on the list box to display the names of tables and queries in your database. Click *qryInvoiceReport*, and then click OK.
2. Make these choices (and click the Next button as needed) as you go through the remaining Report Wizard steps:
   - Select all available fields from the query to appear on the report.
   - Choose to view data with the "by tblInvoice" group.
   - Select no other grouping levels.
   - Sort your records in ascending order by the ItemID field. On the sort field step, click the Summary Options button and check the box under the Sum column of the Extended row to sum that field for both detailed and summary fields (see Figure 5.26). Click OK to confirm your choices.
   - Accept the Stepped report layout in Portrait orientation.
   - Select the Formal report style.
   - Type the report title *Invoice* in the text box on the last dialog box.
3. After reviewing the draft report, close it and its Design window.
4. Rename the report by selecting Invoice from the list of reports, pressing F2, and typing *rptInvoiceCut1*. This name allows you to keep each successive, improved version so you can compare and contrast them.
5. Reopen the *rptInvoiceCut1* report in Design view.

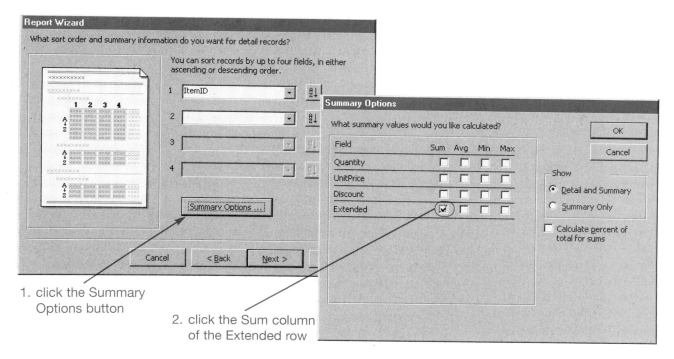

1. click the Summary Options button

2. click the Sum column of the Extended row

**Figure 5.26** Report Wizard Summary Options choices.

Figure 5.27 shows the initial report in Design view. Notice that we have removed the rulers and grid lines. While viewing a report in Design view, you can remove the rulers or the grid lines by clicking Ruler or Grid in the View menu. The check mark beside the Ruler choice or the Grid choice is removed, indicating they won't display. These items are toggle commands: select either one again to reestablish them.

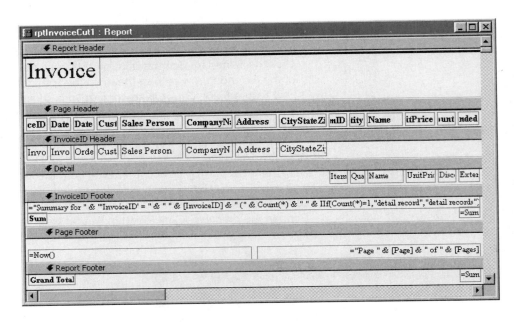

**Figure 5.27**    Initial Invoice report layout.

## Rearranging and Deleting Report Fields

The next step is to move selected text fields from the Page Header section to the InvoiceID Header section. Follow the discussion as we outline how to rearrange fields. All the fields in the Page Header will be either moved or eliminated. First, we must make room in the InvoiceID Header section. Drag the bottom of the InvoiceID Header section—just above the Detail bar—down until the InvoiceID Header section is about two inches tall. Then, select all fields in the Page Header section (they are all labels). Remember that you first press and hold the Shift key and then click each field in turn to select all of them. (Be careful to not accidentally move them as you click.) Drag the selected fields down into the InvoiceID Header area and release the mouse. Click anywhere to deselect the items. In the Page Header, delete the two horizontal lines (select each and press Delete). Move the large label *Invoice* and its attendant horizontal line from the Report Header section to the Page Header section.

Move the ItemID, Quantity, Name, UnitPrice, Discount, and Extended text labels down so that they are just above the bar labeled Detail and about one inch in from the left edge of the report border. With those six controls still selected, move the pointer to the right side of any one object and double-click its side handle to enlarge all labels so their full names are visible. (Label controls are bold, whereas you notice that bound controls displaying field values are not bold.) In a similar way, select the Detail section bound controls and spread them out from one another a bit. With all Detail section controls selected, drag any one of the bound controls' right selection handles to enlarge all selected controls. Delete the labels *CompanyName*, *Address*, and *CityStateZip*. Be careful to not delete the bound controls of the same name! They contain the actual customer information.

Continue to rearrange bound and unbound controls. Do not worry when the labels and associated bound controls do not line up horizontally or vertically. You can fix that later. For now, simply rearrange objects so their approximate location matches Figure 5.25. Eliminate the very long character string in the InvoiceID Footer and the label *Sum*, leaving in place only the expression *=Sum([Extended])*. (The expression sums the extended prices from each invoice line's extended price, yielding the subtotal.) Using Figure 5.25 as a guideline, rearrange each of the Group Header labels and bound controls so they resemble the layout shown. Switch to Print Preview periodically to see how the data and labels line up and to ensure bound controls are wide enough to display the data.

The Coffee Merchant's name and address shown in Figure 5.25 are bold, 12 point, Times New Roman typeface. Create them by opening the toolbox and dragging three labels to the Group Header section, change the Format properties of all three using the property sheet, and type the name and address information you see. Below The Coffee Merchant's address is the customer's address. It consists of four bound controls referring to the fields *CompanyName*, *Address*, and *CityStateZip*, which are all supplied by the query. The latter is a concatenation of the three *tblCustomer* fields City, State, and ZipCode. The expression found in the query that "glues" these three fields together is:

[City] & ", " & [State] & " " & [ZipCode]

The ampersands are character string operators that "add" one group of characters to the end of another. Once your design is fairly close to Figure 5.25, select Save As from the File menu, type *rptInvoiceCut2*, and click OK to save your new report design.

Next, you can simplify the report by eliminating the Report Header, Report Footer, and Page Footer. These contain unneeded lines and summary information—information that is unsuitable for our Invoice report. It is simple to eliminate entire report sections, and you don't need to remove any fields from the sections beforehand. Remove the Report Header and Footer first by clicking the Report Header/Footer selection in the View menu. Click Yes when the warning dialog box appears. Because you want to retain the Page Header, you cannot use the same technique to eliminate the Page Footer. Instead, simply delete all controls in the Page Footer. This removes the Page Footer itself because nothing prints there or below that band.

## Modifying Existing Labels

Notice in Figure 5.25 that the label to the left of the invoice number is *Invoice Number:* (with a colon), not the original label taken from the field name, *InvoiceID*. It is easy to alter labels. Click the label you wish to change once and the entire label is selected. Click a second time (do not double-click the label) and an insertion point style cursor is placed in the string so you can add and delete characters. If you find the activity of clicking twice slowly a bit difficult to master, you can use an alternate technique. Double-click the label to bring up its property sheet. Then click the property sheet's Format tab and type in the Caption property text box the corrected label. You can close the property sheet or leave it open. Leaving it open makes it simpler to change other labels' Caption properties. Change all labels in the InvoiceID header to match Figure 5.25. Now is a good time to save your design. A lot of work has gone into the invoice since you last saved it. Select Save As from the File menu and type *rptInvoiceCut3,* which indicates this is version three of the report design.

## Creating Calculated Fields

Writing an expression involving arithmetic operators, numeric or character constants, table field names, and report objects creates a *calculated control*, the third major type of control. For example, the query *qryInvoiceLineItem*, which supplies information to a form, contains an expression that forms the product of the Quantity, UnitPrice, and Discount fields. You can create calculated controls, or expressions, in forms and reports also. For example, Subtotal, Sales Tax, Shipping, and Invoice Total in Figure 5.25 are calculated fields. They are not values stored in tables, because that would violate normalization rules and quickly lead to inconsistent data.

Because the Subtotal, Sales Tax, Shipping, and Invoice Total fields are calculated, their values change with each invoice printed or displayed on the console. The Report Wizard automatically created the Subtotal report field in the InvoiceID Footer when you selected Summary Options and checked Sum for the Extended field. The calculated control computes the sum of the Extended Price fields for every invoice. Let's rename the Subtotal calculated control so we can refer to it by an appropriate name in subsequent calculated controls, such as the Invoice Total control's expression. Other fields such as Sales Tax and Invoice Total will reference the field holding the summation of Extended Price. Here is how you rename an existing control—assigning it a new internal name that other controls can reference.

*Try it*

With *rptInvoiceCut3* open in Design view, click the field in the InvoiceID Footer that sums the Extended Price field. Display its property sheet (select Properties from the View menu). Select the tab labeled *Other*. Type *ctlSubtotal* in the Name property text box, replacing the current entry. Close the property sheet. That assigns the control a new and meaningful name.

Prefixes such as *ctl* identify the source of the value—a report control, not a table field. Assigning objects names such as *ctlSubtotal* or *ctlSalesTax* accomplishes two important things. First, the names document the meaning of the fields you create on a design document (report or form). Second, names are mnemonic and easy to remember when you construct other calculated expressions.

Creating a new field that contains an expression is straightforward. The next two exercises explain how to create the *ctlSalesTax* and *ctlShipping* calculated controls that are placed just below the Subtotal field in the InvoiceID Footer. First, create more room in the InvoiceID Footer so that it can accommodate the additional fields. Move the mouse to the bottom edge of the footer. When the pointer changes to a double-headed arrow, drag the bottom edge of the InvoiceID Footer down so that it is approximately two inches high.

EXERCISE 5.11: CREATING A SIMPLE SALES TAX CALCULATED CONTROL

1. Display the latest version of the invoice report (*rptInvoiceCut3*, for example) in Design view, display the toolbox, and click the toolbox Text Box tool. (Hover the mouse pointer over a tool for a second or two and a ToolTip displaying the tool's name will appear.)
2. Move the mouse to a position just below the subtotal control in the InvoiceID Footer and drag the mouse to create a control that is the same size as the *ctlSubtotal* control. When you release the mouse, an unbound text box control appears on the form.
3. Display the new control's property sheet and change the control's name: type *ctlSalesTax* in the Name property. (Remember, click the Other tab to locate the Name property.)
4. Click the property sheet Format tab, select the Format property, and type *Standard* (or select it from the drop-down list).
5. Click the Data tab in the property sheet.
6. Click anywhere inside the Control Source text box and then click the Build button that appears at the right side of the Control Source property. (The Build button has three dots, called an ellipsis, on it.) The Expression Builder dialog box opens.
7. Because our customers are wholesale customers, we will not charge sales tax (a simplifying assumption). In the Expression Builder box, type *=0* and then

click OK to close the dialog box. (Notice that Access expressions resemble Excel spreadsheet expressions. They begin with an equal sign and are followed by an arbitrarily complex expression, though just a constant in our example here.)

8. Edit the label control to the left of the sales tax control: click it twice and type *Sales Tax:*

9. Click outside the sales tax label and then click the label to reselect it.

10. Click the Format tab and change the label's Text Align property to Right. (The Text Align property is far down in the list of Format properties. Use the scroll bar to locate it.) Click outside the label to deselect it.

Leave the property sheet and toolbox open for the expression you will build in the next exercise. Next, let's construct the expression to calculate the shipping cost. To keep things relatively uncomplicated, assume that it costs $0.25 per pound to ship everything, regardless of the size of an order. The number of pounds is determined by summing the Quantity bound control (Quantity is recorded in pounds). The next exercise builds the shipping cost control expression.

## EXERCISE 5.12: CREATING A SHIPPING CALCULATED CONTROL

1. Display the Invoice report in Design view and click the Text Box tool in the toolbox. (Hover the mouse pointer over the toolbox's objects so ToolTips reveal which tool is the Text Box button.)

2. Move the mouse to a position just below the sales tax control, *ctlSalesTax*, in the InvoiceID Footer and drag and release the mouse to create a control that is approximately the same size as the *ctlSubtotal* control.

3. Click the property sheet's Other tab and type *ctlShipping* in the Name property to change the control's name.

4. Click the property sheet Format tab, select the Format property, and select Standard.

5. Click the property sheet Data tab, click inside the Control Source property text box, and click the Build button (labeled with the ellipsis).

6. Type the expression *=0.25\*Sum([Quantity])* to calculate shipping costs (see Figure 5.28).

7. Click OK to close the dialog box.

8. Type the text *Shipping:* into the label control and right-align it. Place the label control to the left of the calculated control, *ctlShipping*.

Click the Print Preview button to verify that the subtotal, sales tax, and shipping values are correct. Click any of the navigation buttons to verify other invoices display correct values for the three controls you have created so far. Switch back to Design view to complete the remaining work on your report. If you

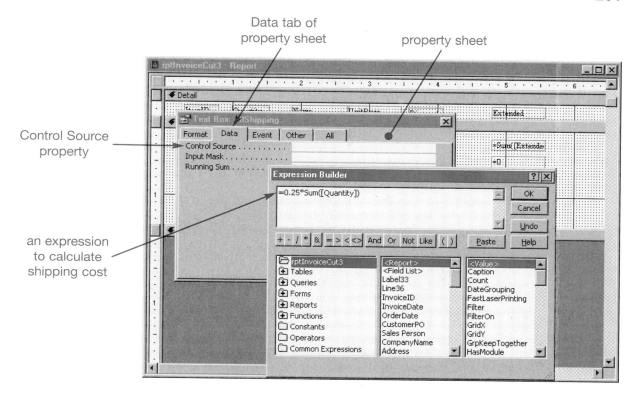

**Figure 5.28**  Writing an expression for a calculated control.

haven't already, create a label to the left of the subtotal calculated control and type the text *Subtotal:* in the label.

Following the two previous exercise examples, create the Invoice Total calculated control. Name it *ctlInvoiceTotal,* type the expression

$=[ctlSubtotal]+[ctlSalesTax]+[ctlShipping]$

for the Control Source, and choose the Currency format. Edit and right-align the label to the left of the Invoice Total control, typing *Invoice Total:* for its Caption property. Though labels attached to text boxes are bold by default, you can bold other controls' contents by selecting the control(s) (Shift-click if more than one) and then changing the Font Weight property (found on the Format sheet) to Bold. Save the report once again to preserve your work.

## Aligning and Sizing Fields

It is important to know how to align report controls (fields) and size them so that your report looks professional. Up to this point you have not been concerned with how labels and data are aligned. For instance, we have ignored the fact that the

Extended label in the InvoiceID Header appears far to the left of the actual prices in the detail lines below it. A simple exercise will illustrate how to align one column of values. Once you have aligned and sized one column, you can repeat the same steps for other labels and values. In preparation for the next exercise, ensure that the report *rptInvoiceCutx*, where *x* is the number corresponding to your latest version of the report, is displayed in Design view.

### EXERCISE 5.13: ALIGNING AND SIZING MULTIPLE FIELDS

1. Select the following six objects: the label control Extended in the InvoiceID Header, the bound control Extended in the Detail section, and the four calculated controls *ctlSubtotal*, *ctlSalesTax*, *ctlShipping*, and *ctlInvoiceTotal*. Release the mouse when all six objects are selected. Quick tip: Select all the objects by clicking above the topmost label and then drag down and through the objects. Keep the rectangle outline narrow so you do not "touch" other objects (see Figure 5.29).
2. With the six objects selected, select the Format menu and then select Size, to Narrowest. All six objects are resized to match the narrowest of them all.
3. Align all objects on the right by selecting the Format menu and then Align, Right. All objects snap into vertical alignment on the rightmost object of the six.
4. Click outside the objects to deselect them.

rectangle touches controls to be selected simultaneously

**Figure 5.29**    Selecting multiple objects in different report sections.

Repeat the preceding four steps for the label control/bound control pairs ItemID, Quantity, UnitPrice, and Discount. However, do not narrow the Name column, because it displays sometimes-long names of coffees and teas. Instead, size the Name label and value controls by executing Format, Size to Widest. The Name label in the header widens to match the values in the Detail section. If necessary, you can widen both controls later to accommodate long descriptions.

Finally, place a Page Break control near the bottom of the InvoiceID Footer, below all existing InvoiceID Footer controls. Be sure to place the page break far enough down so that it will fall below the Shipping and Invoice Total controls. Save your report one more time.

Preview your Invoice report in the Report window. Your screen should resemble the one shown in Figure 5.25. There are several small embellishments you need to add to spruce it up, but you can fine tune your invoice any time you wish. So that you will have a good base from which to understand this report, we have saved the complete Invoice report and named it *rptInvoiceReport* on your Companion CD. You can improve on your design, or you can study ours.

## SUMMARY

This chapter has emphasized using Access to create and modify forms and reports. You crafted forms for several tables that display a friendlier, more intuitive interface between the form user and the database. You learned how to add columns to forms and how to change the properties of fields on the form.

You have gained a lot of knowledge about Access reports in this chapter. You built a tabular-style report using a Report Wizard. You learned that reports can receive their data from both tables and queries. One of the reports you built contained a query. You also created an invoice report that tied together six of The Coffee Merchant's tables with a query. Various report headers and footers were described including Group Headers and Footers, and you added calculated controls to the Group Footer that computed invoice subtotals, sales tax, shipping, and total invoice values. Having read this chapter, you can design and use Access forms and reports. Now that you have read the first five chapters, you are ready to apply your knowledge to build richly featured accounting database systems that serve the needs of your users.

## QUESTIONS AND PROBLEMS FOR REVIEW

### MULTIPLE-CHOICE QUESTIONS

1. While displaying the property sheet of a control on a form, you can change the control's
   a. size.
   b. font size.
   c. orientation.
   d. position.
2. One advantage of using a query as the foundation of a report is that
   a. a query is the only way to join multiple tables.
   b. different reports can be run from a query by changing the query's selection criteria and rerunning the report.
   c. tables cannot be used to create a report.
   d. a query is protected from unauthorized access.
3. A report can be used to
   a. change data in a table.
   b. print information found in one or more tables.
   c. input information into multiple tables.
   d. none of the preceding can be accomplished with a report.
4. What is the expression to form a subtotal of a control called Extended Price?
   a. =Sum(Extended Price)
   b. =Sum[Extended Price]
   c. =Sum([Extended Price])
   d. Sum[Extended Price]
5. Information that is unsorted can be organized into related groups in a report by
   a. creating a Page Footer.
   b. creating a Sort Footer.
   c. creating a calculated field.
   d. creating a Group Header or Footer.
6. You can align objects that lie in different sections or bands of a report. After selecting the objects to be aligned, you execute what?
   a. Format, Size All
   b. Format, Align
   c. Format, Snap to Grid
   d. View, Align
7. When you use the Report Wizard, the report name is also used as the
   a. report section.
   b. report title.
   c. report footer.
   d. report bound control.

# 6 REVENUE CYCLE

## OBJECTIVES

Revenue cycle activities include accepting orders from customers, recording sales, invoicing customers, recording cash received from customers, and maintaining records of these events. In this chapter, you will learn how to use Microsoft Access to design tables, queries, forms, and reports that can help you:

- Create and maintain customer records.
- Create and maintain finished goods inventory records.
- Record sales orders.
- Record sales/shipment information.
- Print invoices.
- Record payments received from customers.
- Summarize and report cash receipts information.

## INTRODUCTION

This chapter describes the revenue cycle elements of accounting information systems. We illustrate many of these components using example data for the Pipefitters Supply Company, a merchandising firm. The revenue cycle includes those activities related to the sale of goods or services. Whether firms are manufacturers, merchandisers, or service businesses, their revenue cycles are similar. For example, manufacturing and merchandising firms sell products to customers; service firms perform services for customers. In both cases, customers place orders for the product or service that they are purchasing. The selling firm then ships the product or performs the service. At this point, the selling firm will send the customer an invoice that shows details of the sale. Customers then, pursuant to the terms stated on the invoice, usually pay the amount due shown on the invoice. Some customers will pay on receipt of a monthly statement that lists all of the invoices for that month. The practice of paying the statement amount once each month is a holdover from the days when running batch computer processes or manually writing checks was a cumbersome ordeal. Most businesses now find it more convenient to print checks daily and, therefore, pay from invoices rather than from monthly statements.

In addition to handling orders, invoices, and incoming payments, the revenue cycle accounting system must maintain a permanent record of customer information and provide tools for updating and revising that customer information. As we discussed in Chapter 1, a key feature of database accounting systems is their ability to store much more information about each transaction than a traditional double-entry system stores. To take full advantage of this feature, users must be able to access the revenue cycle information stored in the system to perform sales and cash flow analyses. Users must also be able to perform update and maintenance tasks on finished goods inventory information. Finally, the revenue cycle system should give financial accountants the information they need to create ledgers, journals, and financial statements.

Copies of all tables, forms, queries, and reports that appear in this chapter are included in the *Ch06.mdb* database on your Companion CD. Feel free to copy that file to your hard drive and experiment with it as you work through this chapter. Remember to remove the read-only attribute from the file after you have copied it as you learned in Exercise 1.14. Note, however, that the step-by-step instructions for this chapter assume you are working in your own Access file. For example, if you follow our instructions to save the customer table and you are working in the *Ch06.mdb* file, Access will display a message asking if you want to replace the existing customer table with the new one you have created.

## PIPEFITTERS SUPPLY COMPANY REVENUE CYCLE INFORMATION

Pipefitters Supply Company accepts orders over the telephone, via fax, and by mail. When an order arrives, one of the salespersons enters it as a sales order. The sales order includes the customer's name and a list of the inventory items that the customer wishes to purchase. This inventory list includes the quantity of each inventory item and the price at which Pipefitters is currently selling the item. When the order is ready to ship, Pipefitters completes an invoice and records the sale. Sometimes, some of the inventory items a customer has ordered are not in stock. In those cases, Pipefitters will ship partial orders. Customers are expected to pay their invoices within 30 days. Most customers do pay on time; however, some customers make partial payments over two or more months.

The data model for Pipefitters includes five entities: customer, sales order, sale, inventory, and cash receipt. Each customer may have many sales orders, many sales, and many cash receipts. Sales order, sale, and cash receipt, however, can each have only one customer. Sales orders and sales can each have many inventory items, and each inventory item can appear on many sales orders and many sales. The data model for Pipefitters, showing these five entities and the one-to-many and many-to-many relationships among them, appears in Figure 6.1.

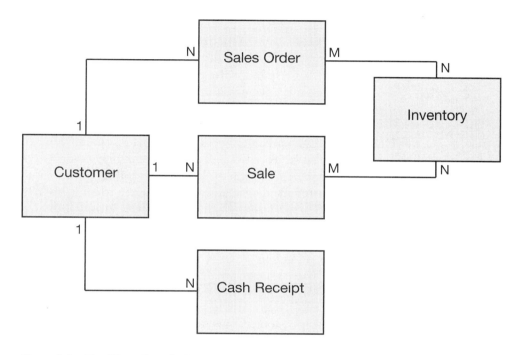

**Figure 6.1**   Pipefitters Supply Company revenue cycle data model.

This chapter will show you how to build elements of the accounting system for Pipefitters' revenue cycle. The design will include five tables for the entities and two additional tables to model the many-to-many relationships. You will learn how to create forms to enter data into these tables efficiently. You will also learn how to create queries and reports that extract information about revenue cycle activities.

---

**CUSTOMER INFORMATION**

Customers are the lifeblood of any business; therefore, accounting system database tables must include many details about each customer. At a minimum, firms want to know where their customers are located, what they have purchased, and when they purchased it. Businesses also want to track when their customers pay and the amounts of the individual payments. Some businesses do not record information about their customers' identities. For example, businesses such as retail stores, fast-food restaurants, and amusement parks seldom record individual customers' names and addresses. Customers of these businesses pay cash and would not tolerate the time it would take to record their identities. These businesses do, however, keep careful records of customer traffic by day, hour, and location. Increasingly, these types of firms are developing ways to obtain information about their customers' identities. Many supermarket chains now offer their customers an identification card that gives them a discount on merchandise. The discount is the price that these supermarket chains are willing to pay to obtain customer identity information.

Customer information appears on many documents that businesses create and use. Invoices, shipping documents, and end-of-month account statements require customer names and addresses. For example, the marketing department might want a list of customers that includes the name and telephone number of customer contact persons or a set of mailing labels for a particular group of customers. To ensure that customer information is consistent wherever it is used, many firms keep all customer information in one database table. Any document or report that includes customer information obtains it from that table. If, for example, a customer moves to a new location, the customer's address needs to be changed only once. A relational database accounting system stores customer information in a *customer table*.

## The Customer Table

The first table in the revenue cycle that we will describe is the Customer table. The Customer table provides a central location for storing all information about each customer. This makes adding, deleting, displaying, or changing customer information easy and efficient. The Customer table needs a primary key field that uniquely identifies each row in the table and exists for every row.

Firms use a variety of coding schemes to create customer numbers that will have these characteristics. For example, some firms use alphanumeric codes that combine the first four letters of the customer name with the first four digits of the customer address to create a unique customer number. To ensure that each CustomerNumber is unique, many firms assign a sequential number to each new customer. A sequential number scheme gives each new customer a number that is one greater than the largest customer number that currently exists. In Exercise 6.1, you will begin creating a customer table, called *tblCustomer*. In this exercise, you will open a new table and create its primary key field, CustomerNumber. Pipefitters uses a five-digit sequential numbering scheme for its customer numbers that they have designed to start with a customer number of 10001 and accommodate up to 89,999 customers.

EXERCISE 6.1: CREATING *TBLCUSTOMER* AND THE CUSTOMERNUMBER FIELD

1. Start Microsoft Access, click Tables in the Objects bar, then click the New button in the Database window.

2. Double-click Design View in the New Table dialog box.
3. Type the name of *tblCustomer's* first field, *CustomerNumber*, and press Enter. When you press Enter, the first row in the Data Type column changes into a combo box and the Field Properties list appears in the bottom pane of the Table window.
4. Click the Primary Key button on the toolbar to make the CustomerNumber field the primary key for *tblCustomer*. A small key symbol appears in the row selector box to the left of the first row in the Field Name column and the Indexed property sets itself to Yes (No Duplicates).
5. Since you will not be using the CustomerNumber field in any calculations, you can set its data type to Text. The Data Type combo box contains *Text* as its default selection.
6. Press Tab to accept the Text default selection. You can use the Description column to store a description of the CustomerNumber field if you wish. The Description column is a built-in documentation tool that is especially useful for storing explanations of complex or potentially confusing fields. Next, you can set the remaining properties of the CustomerNumber field.
7. Press F6 to switch to the Field Properties pane. The cursor will highlight the default Field Size value of 50. Type *5* in the Field Size column to replace the default selection.
8. Press the Tab key three times and type *Customer Number* (including the space between words) as the field's Caption property.

This Caption property setting will cause *Customer Number*, rather than the field's name, *CustomerNumber*, to appear as the default text for form and report controls that reference the field. Creating a useful Caption property setting can be a real time saver when you are building reports and forms that use table fields.

The panel on the right side of the Field Properties pane provides detailed instructions for each step in the property-setting process. Figure 6.2 shows the new Customer table with the CustomerNumber primary key field and the caption setting in Design view.

Another important table property is the Validation Rule property. The Validation Rule property provides a useful internal control feature at the table level. You can use this property to limit the values that a user can enter for a table field. This feature can help prevent data entry errors. For example, CustomerNumber is a five-digit field. The Validation Rule property lets you limit data entered into the field to numbers that are exactly five digits long. In Exercise 6.2 you will set the validation properties for the Customer table.

EXERCISE 6.2: SETTING THE VALIDATION PROPERTIES FOR *TBLCUSTOMER*

1. Press the Tab key twice or click the Validation Rule property box to select it.

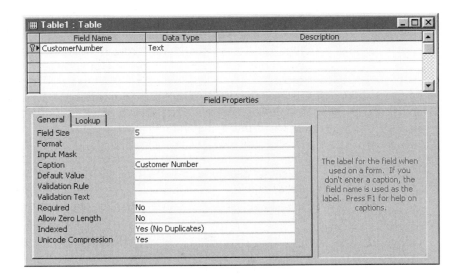

**Figure 6.2**   The CustomerNumber field in *tblCustomer*.

2. Type the expression *Like "#####"* in the Validation Rule box to prevent a user from entering anything other than exactly five digits in the CustomerNumber field. For example, this Validation Rule would prevent a user from entering *JTP46* (which contains nondigit characters) or *9244* (which contains four, not five, digits) in the CustomerNumber field. You can make this data input internal control feature even more useful by entering Validation Text to accompany the Validation Rule.
3. Press Tab to move the cursor to the Validation Text property box.
4. Type *Invalid entry. You must enter a Customer Number of exactly five digits.*

    The text you enter as a field's Validation Text property will appear in an error message dialog box whenever a user attempts to enter a CustomerNumber value that violates the Validation Rule. Figure 6.3 shows the Table window with all of the property settings you have created for the CustomerNumber field.

    Since the CustomerNumber field is the primary key of *tblCustomer*, Access will require that a unique value be entered for each record before saving it. Therefore, you do not need to specify a value in the Required property. Setting the Required property to Yes for a primary key field does not alter the database's behavior. The Validation Rule property setting will override the Allow Zero Length property.

    The Indexed property was automatically set to Yes (No Duplicates) when you made CustomerNumber the table's primary key in Exercise 6.1. Access automatically sets the Unicode Compression property to Yes. Unicode compression

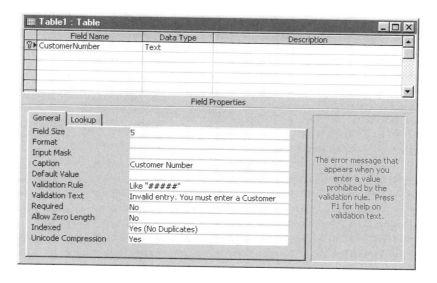

**Figure 6.3** Property settings for the CustomerNumber field.

reduces the amount of disk space that text and memo fields require for storage, so most database designers leave the property set to the default setting.

In Exercise 6.3 you will create the remaining nine fields in the Customer table. These fields will store customer names, addresses, telephone numbers, and other valuable information about customers. Note that the address is stored in multiple fields. Placing, for example, customer city, state, and zip code information in separate fields helps users more easily search and select records from the database on values of those elements.

EXERCISE 6.3: CREATING THE REMAINING FIELDS IN *TBLCUSTOMER*

1. Type *CustomerName* in the second row of the Field Name column and leave its Data Type set to Text. The appropriate size for CustomerName will vary from firm to firm, but you should set it to accommodate the longest customer name you anticipate. For this example, set the CustomerName Field Size property to *25*. When you use the CustomerName field in forms and reports, the context will usually indicate that you are referring to a *customer* name. Select the Caption property and set it to *Name*. Of course, the Caption property only sets the default, so if you need to clarify the label in a particular form or report, you can change the control's text in that form or report. Note that this firm's customers are business entities. If the customers had been individuals, you might have stored the customer name by creating separate fields for CustomerFirstName, CustomerMiddleInitial, and CustomerLastName.

2. Enter *CustomerAddress1* and *CustomerAddress2* fields with property settings that are similar to those of the CustomerName field. The CustomerAddress2 field lets the table accommodate customers with a second address line, such as a suite or office number. In the sample form, we set the Caption property to *Address* for both of these fields.

3. Enter *CustomerCity* as a Text Data Type with a Field Size property of *25*, then set its Caption property to *City*

4. Enter *CustomerState* as a Text Data Type with a Field Size property of *2*, then set its Caption property to *State*

5. Enter *CustomerZipCode* as a Text Data Type with a Field Size property of *10* to accommodate the U.S. Postal Service's five-digits-plus-four ZIP Code format, then set its Caption property to *Zip Code*

6. Enter *CustomerTelephone* as a Text Data Type and a Field Size property setting of *14*, then set its Caption property to *Telephone*

7. Enter *CustomerCreditLimit* in the next open row of the Field Name column. Type *Currency* over the default Data Type setting of Text. Currency is a number Data Type that displays dollar signs automatically. Selecting a Currency Data Type automatically sets the Format property to Currency and the Decimal Places property to Auto. You will not see these settings until you press F6 or click in the Field Properties pane of the Design view window. To restrict credit limit amounts to integer values, change the Decimal Places property to *0*. Set the Caption property to *Credit Limit*

8. Enter *CustomerPrimaryContact*. Use your own judgment in setting the Data Type, Field Size, and Caption properties for this field.

---

**Try it**

Another way to choose a field's Data Type is to click the combo box button and select one of the choices that appear in the drop down list. For example, you could have chosen Currency in step 7 of the previous exercise by clicking the Data Type cell and selecting Currency from the list.

---

You now have a complete set of fields in *tblCustomer* that Pipefitters can use to store their customer data. Recall that you used the validation properties to control data entry in the CustomerNumber field. The validation properties check the entire contents of a field when it is entered. Access provides another way to control data entry that uses the Input Mask property. This property checks each character as you enter it. An input mask will not permit a user to enter any characters that violate the input mask rules for a field. Unfortunately, the Input Mask property does not allow you to customize the error message that appears when an entry is incorrect. You should carefully consider whether to use the Input Mask property or the Validation Rule property for a particular field.

The CustomerState field is an excellent candidate for an input mask, since all U.S. state abbreviations are two capital letters. In the following exercise, you will create an input mask that controls the data entered into the CustomerState field so that it conforms to the U.S. Postal Service's abbreviation convention.

EXERCISE 6.4: CREATING A CUSTOM INPUT MASK FOR CUSTOMERSTATE

1. Select the CustomerState field by clicking it in the Field Name column that appears in the top pane of the Table window.
2. Type >LL in the Input Mask property box.

The > symbol converts lowercase letters to uppercase letters. For example, if a user enters the letters *oh*, the input mask converts them to *OH*. The *LL* placeholders in the expression limit the entry to two letters. Entering any other value, a number or punctuation symbol for example, will generate an error message.

Using an Input Mask property setting for the CustomerZipCode field also works well. The CustomerZipCode Field Size property setting of 10 provides enough characters to use the U.S. Postal Service's five-digits-plus-four Zip Code format. This format is so common that Access includes an Input Mask Wizard that can create an appropriate input mask for you. When you select the Input Mask property box, a button with an ellipsis label, called the Build button, appears to the right of the Input Mask box. Clicking the Build button starts the Input Mask Wizard, which can create input mask templates for zip codes and other commonly used fields.

EXERCISE 6.5: USING THE INPUT MASK WIZARD FOR CUSTOMERZIPCODE

1. Select the CustomerZipCode field by clicking it in the Field Name column that appears in the top pane of the Table window.
2. Click the Input Mask property box.
3. Click the property's Build button to open the Input Mask Wizard. A Microsoft Access dialog box appears informing you that you must save the table before proceeding. Save the table with the name *tblCustomer* and open the Input Mask Wizard dialog box, which appears in Figure 6.4.
4. Select Zip Code from the list of Input Mask names and click the Next button.
5. Click the Next button to accept the default placeholder character, the underscore.
6. Click the option button to indicate that you want to store the field with the symbols in the mask (this changes the data storage default of not storing the hyphen so that Access does store the hyphen as part of the field contents), then click the Next button.
7. Click the Finish button to return to the Table window. The Wizard will create the Input Mask property setting of 00000\-9999;0;_ for the CustomerZipCode field.

Input Mask property settings includes three parts; each part is separated by a semicolon. The first part contains the template. The Zip Code template includes

**Figure 6.4**   Using the Input Mask Wizard to select a Zip Code setting.

the placeholder *00000*, which requires the user to enter five digits in this field. The backslash character tells Access to recognize the next character, a hyphen, as itself. When a character that has a special meaning in an expression is used as itself, it is called a *literal*. The *9999* placeholder permits, but does not require, the user to enter another four digits. The *0* in the second part of the setting, between the first and second semicolon, tells Access to store the hyphen along with the digits in the CustomerZipCode field. The third part of the setting makes the underscore character the default placeholder that will appear in CustomerZipCode field controls on data entry forms.

You can use the Input Mask Wizard to set the CustomerTelephone field's Input Mask property to the predefined Phone Number setting that appears at the top of the list in the Input Mask Wizard dialog box shown in Figure 6.4. In our example database on the Companion CD, we elected to store the telephone numbers with the input mask characters (the hyphen, space, and parentheses that are used in U.S. telephone numbers and area codes).

### Try it

Note that we used a number of different characters in the Input Mask properties of the fields in *tblCustomer*. If you would like to review a complete list of characters that you can use in customizing Input Mask properties, use the Microsoft Access on-line help feature. Select Help, Microsoft Access Help from the menu, click the Index tab, and type *input mask*. Click the Search button, then double-click the words "InputMask Property" that appear in the Choose a Topic dialog box. This help topic includes a complete list of available characters and explains how to use them in the Input Mask property's syntax. Click the Close button to close the Microsoft Access Help dialog box.

At this point, you can either close the Table window or open the table in Datasheet view to enter data. If you close the window, a dialog box will appear and ask you if you would like to save your changes. To open the table in Datasheet view, click the first toolbar icon. This icon toggles between Datasheet view and Design view for tables.

If you open the table in Datasheet view, you may notice that the toolbar at the top of the screen has changed; it has become the Datasheet toolbar. This toolbar provides buttons that can help you perform data entry, editing, and viewing tasks. You may also notice that the title of each table column in Datasheet view is the Caption property value you set. The *Ch06.mdb* database on your Companion CD includes a *tblCustomer* table with sample data that you can use to populate your table instead of entering data yourself.

## The Customer Information Form

You could enter customer information in *tblCustomer* while it is open in Datasheet view. However, the number and size of the fields in the table makes this a difficult task. Depending on your screen resolution, only six or seven of the table's ten fields will be displayed in the Datasheet view window. Entering customer information in Datasheet view requires that you scroll back and forth to enter all ten field values for each record. In this section, you will learn how to create a form for *tblCustomer* that will make entering, changing, and deleting customer information much easier.

You can create a form for *tblCustomer* by using the AutoForm procedure. Access offers several ways to activate AutoForm; perhaps the easiest is to use the Insert menu. First, make sure you have selected Table objects in the Database window and have selected *tblCustomer*. Then choose Insert, AutoForm from the menu as shown in Figure 6.5.

AutoForm examines the selected table and creates a form that accommodates many of the table's field characteristics. AutoForm is quick, easy to run, and often creates a usable form. Even when it does not create an ideal form, it often creates a form that you can edit to meet your specific needs. The results of the AutoForm action appear in Figure 6.6. Note that the form shown in the figure is bound to the version of *tblCustomer* included on the Companion CD that contains a number of customer records. Your form will not show any data unless you have entered or copied data into your Customer table object.

Although AutoForm did a good job of creating a usable form, you can improve the appearance of the form and enhance its usefulness. You will learn how to do this in the next exercise. As you follow these instructions, remember that you should try to develop your own sense of what makes a form useful. Your forms do not need to look exactly like the forms we show in this book.

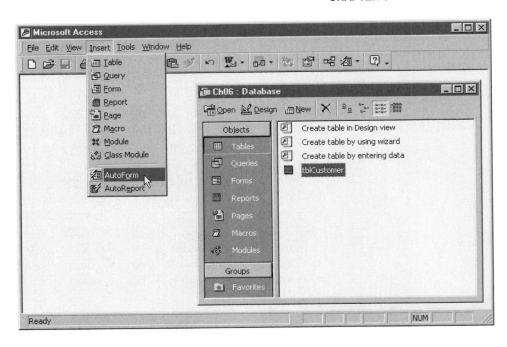

**Figure 6.5**   Selecting AutoForm from the menu for *tblCustomer*.

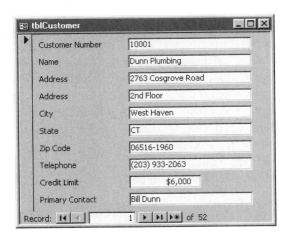

**Figure 6.6**   The AutoForm-generated Customer Data Entry form.

EXERCISE 6.6: IMPROVING THE CUSTOMER DATA ENTRY FORM

1. To modify the form, you will need to work in Design view. To enter Design view while the new form is displayed, click the Design View toolbar button or select

View, Design View from the menu. You can click and drag the edges of the form to make all of the form's controls visible.

2. Select the CustomerNumber label by clicking the box in its upper-left corner—the mouse cursor will change to a hand with a pointing index finger—and carefully drag the label toward the CustomerNumber text box control to its right. Only leave one or two grid dots exposed between the label and the text box control.

3. Select all of the label controls. You can do this by holding down the Shift key as you click each control or you can click and drag a marquee around the controls. Select the menu command Format, Align, Right to right-justify the label controls.

4. Click the Align Right text formatting toolbar button to align the label text within the controls.

5. Click the Bold text formatting toolbar button to format the labels as bold text.

6. Drag the left edge of the CustomerNumber control label (it is the widest label) far enough to the left to expose all of its text.

7. Right-click the CustomerCreditLimit control and select Properties. In the Properties sheet, click the Format tab and change the Text Align value from General to Left. (You may have to scroll the properties to expose the Text Align property.)

8. With the Properties sheet still open, select the form by choosing Edit, Select Form from the menu or clicking the small gray box in the upper-left corner of the form.

9. Click the Format tab in the Properties sheet and change the value of the Caption property from *tblCustomer* to *Customer Information*. You can also change the value of the Record Selectors property from Yes to *No*, the value of the Dividing Lines property from Yes to *No*, and the value of the Scroll Bars property from Both to *Neither*. Close the Properties sheet.

10. Adjust the widths of the bound controls to accommodate the longest possible field contents.

This last step may require some trial and error adjusting. You can use the Form View and Design View toolbar buttons to switch between the two views. Note that as you switch back and forth, the form changes size because the Design View rulers and the Detail section indicator bar disappear when you open the form in Form view.

### Try it

You cannot eliminate the Detail section bar from the Design View window, but you can remove the rulers. Select View, Ruler from the menu. Note that this action operates as a toggle; if you repeat the action, the rulers will reappear. This little trick works in the Design View window for reports, too.

You can make additional adjustments to the form's look to satisfy your own sense of aesthetics. Figure 6.7 shows a finished version of the Customer

Information form. To save the Customer Information form, select File, Save As from the menu or press Ctrl+S and enter *frmCustomer* as the new name for the form in the Save As dialog box. Click OK to save it. You can close your Customer Information form with the menu command File, Close. The form is saved in the Forms section of the database. To see the form, click the Forms tab.

**Figure 6.7**   The finished Customer Information form in Form view.

## Maintaining Customer Records

Now that you have created a Customer table to store customer information and a form that makes using that table easy, you can efficiently and effectively maintain customer records. First, you will want to create records for new customers. Second, you will occasionally delete customer records you no longer need. Third, you will need to update the table as customers move, get new telephone numbers, and change other information that you have entered in *tblCustomer*.

You will want to keep your file of customer information current. Remember, one advantage of using a relational database model for an accounting system is that you only need to add, delete, or change information in one place. For customer information, *tblCustomer* is that place.

To use *frmCustomer* to add customers to *tblCustomer*, open the form by clicking the Forms tab in the Database window and double-clicking *frmCustomer*. To enter customer information, just begin typing. Press Enter after typing the information into each control field. Notice how the Input Mask and Validation Rule properties that you set for *tblCustomer* help you avoid data entry errors in the CustomerNumber, CustomerState, CustomerZipCode, and CustomerTelephone fields.

After entering all of the information for a customer, press Enter to go to the next record. After you have entered a number of customers, you can move backward and forward through the table using the PgUp and PgDn keys or the navigation buttons at the bottom of the form.

Deleting records from *tblCustomer* is a dangerously easy operation. Open the Customer Information form by clicking the Forms tab in the Database window and double-clicking *frmCustomer*. To delete a record, move to that record using the navigation buttons at the bottom of the form, then choose Edit, Select Record from the menu. Press the Delete key to delete the record (if you are using the database supplied on the Companion CD, it will not permit you to delete customer records because of integrity constraints that we have built into that database). Microsoft Access gives you a warning message that asks you to confirm the deletion. This deletion is not reversible. You can delete individual fields in a record using the Delete key while you are in Form view. Individual field deletions are reversible by selecting Edit, Undo Delete before you move to another field. After you move to another field, you can reverse *all* field deletions in the current record by selecting Edit, Undo Current Field/Record from the menu or pressing Esc. If you want to reverse changes you have made to a field *and* changes to other fields in the record, press Esc twice. All other deletions are permanent.

Deleting records in accounting databases is an action you will always want to consider carefully. Data in accounting tables is usually related to data in other tables. For example, if you examine a record in a Sales Order table, it will contain a customer number. The only place you will find that customer's name and address is in the related Customer table. If someone has deleted that customer's record in the Customer table, you may never find out who the customer was!

Keeping existing customer records current to reflect address changes, new telephone numbers, and other changes is an easy and straightforward task using *frmCustomer*. Open the Customer Information form by clicking the Forms tab in the Database window and double-clicking *frmCustomer*. Use the navigation buttons at the bottom of the form to move to the customer record that you want to change. The Input Mask and Validation Rule property settings for *tblCustomer* will limit any changes you make to field contents, just as though you were entering data for the first time.

### Try it

You can move through the individual fields of the displayed record by using the Enter or Tab keys. The Shift+Tab key moves backward through the record. The up and down arrow keys also move the cursor through the form.

## Useful Variations on the Customer Information Form

The Customer Information form you just created is an attractive, functional data entry screen. However, you can improve its usefulness by adding more features to the form. For example, you could use the Command Button tool in the Toolbox to create buttons on the form that would make it easier to use.

**Try it**

Open *frmCustomer* in Design view. Click the Toolbox toolbar button and ensure that the Control Wizards Toolbox tool is depressed. Then click the Command Button tool. Draw a new command button on the form to open the Command Button Wizard. The first Command Button Wizard dialog box provides three categories of buttons that might be useful on this form. The Record Navigation Category includes buttons that can help users navigate the table more easily. The Record Operations category includes buttons that can help users add, delete, and undo changes to records more easily. The Form Operations category includes buttons that perform other form operations and filter database records. Click Cancel to close the Command Button Wizard dialog box. Select and delete the command button.

In accounting databases, you will often want to create separate forms for entering and modifying different portions of each record. By restricting users' access to particular fields, you can increase the internal control strength of your system. For example, you may want only the credit department to be able to set and modify customers' credit limits. You could then create two versions of the Customer Information form, one for general data entry and the other for the credit department.

In the general data entry version of the form, you can prevent access to the CustomerCreditLimit control by changing its properties. You can remove a control from the form's tabbing sequence and prevent it from being selected or edited. To indicate to users that they cannot change the field, you can modify the control's appearance by changing its Back Color property to the light gray color of the form background. In Exercise 6.7 you will learn how to modify the CustomerCreditLimit control's properties to accomplish these objectives.

EXERCISE 6.7: PREVENTING EDITS OF THE CUSTOMERCREDITLIMIT FIELD

1. Open the Customer Information form in Design view by clicking the Forms object button in the Database window, selecting *frmCustomer*, and clicking the Design button.
2. Right-click the CustomerCreditLimit control and choose Properties to open its Properties sheet.
3. Click the Data tab and change the Enabled property to *No*, then change the Locked property to *Yes*
4. Click the Other tab and change the Tab Stop property to *No*
5. Click the Properties sheet's Format tab, select the Back Color property, then click the Build button that appears to the right of the property box. You can make your color selection from the dialog box that appears. If you prefer, you can enter the number of the light gray color, *12632256*, directly into the Back Color property box.

6. Change the Special Effect property to *Flat* and the Border Style property to *Transparent*
7. Close the Properties sheet and display the form in Form view.


The CustomerCreditLimit control now blends in with the form's background, suggesting to users that they will not be able to select or change a customer's credit limit. Try to enter the field you have protected. You will find that you cannot select the field by clicking it, tabbing into it, or using the arrow keys to move to it. You can save this form in the current database by switching to Design view and selecting File, Save As and entering *frmCustomerGeneral* as the new name for the form in the Save As dialog box. Click OK to save the form.

Just as you do not want the persons that enter and edit customer information to be able to access the credit limit field, you will also want to prevent persons in the credit department from changing customer attributes such as name and phone number. To create a version of this form for the credit department, you can change the properties of every control on the form *except* CustomerCreditLimit. To do so, complete Exercise 6.8.


## EXERCISE 6.8: CREATING A CREDIT DEPARTMENT VERSION OF THE CUSTOMER FORM

1. Open the Customer Information form in Design view by clicking the Forms tab in the Database window, selecting *frmCustomer*, and clicking the Design button.
2. While holding down the Shift key, click each control except CustomerCreditLimit, then click the Properties toolbar button to open a Properties sheet for all the selected controls.
3. Click the Data tab and change the Enabled property to *No*, then change the Locked property to *Yes*
4. Click the Other tab and change the Tab Stop property to *No*
5. Click the Properties sheet's Format tab and change the Back Color property to the light gray color of the form background, *12632256*
6. Change the Special Effect property to *Flat* and the Border Style property to *Transparent*
7. Choose Edit, Select Form from the menu. Click the Format tab on the Properties sheet and change the form's Caption property to *Customer Information - Credit Department*
8. Close the Properties sheet.
9. You can save this form in Design view by selecting File, Save As and entering *frmCustomerCreditDepartment* as the new name for the form in the Save As dialog box. Click OK to save the form.
10. Switch to Form view to see the effects of your changes.

Now you have a Customer table that contains information about customers. The table relates each piece of information to a particular customer through the CustomerNumber primary key field. All information about a particular customer appears in one row of the Customer table. You also have built two versions of a form that facilitate entering, deleting, and changing customer information.

## INVENTORY INFORMATION

Customer information is very important to any business, but potential customers will only become actual customers if a firm has something to sell them. *Inventory* is a generic term for what firms sell to their customers. Inventory, broadly defined, may include products, services, or both. For example, a hardware store sells products, an accounting firm sells services, and an auto repair shop sells both products and services.

In this revenue cycle discussion of inventory, we are interested only in the goods or services available for sale to customers. We discuss the acquisition of inventory or inventory components in Chapter 7. Firms need information about the inventory they have for sale in the revenue cycle because they must track which inventory items they sell, at what price they sell them, when they sell them, and to whom they sell them.

To ensure that inventory information is consistent wherever they use it, firms try to keep all inventory information in one database table. Any document, report, or transaction that needs inventory information must obtain it from that one inventory table.

## The Inventory Table

The revenue cycle requires an inventory table that contains at least two fields. The first field should be the primary key, a number or code that uniquely identifies the product or service. For products, this field might contain an item number, item code, part number, catalog number, UPC (universal product code), or SKU (stock-keeping unit) number. For services, this field might contain a labor code, task code, or service number. The second field should contain a description of the product or service.

Some firms use a third field to store inventory selling prices in the inventory table. If a firm has fixed selling prices for each inventory item, it can store those selling prices in the inventory table. Firms that sell the same product or service at different prices to different customers must store selling prices in a sales-inventory relationship table. Firms that offer discounts from the list price to certain customers or classes of customers can store the list price in an inventory table and store the discount percentage in their customer table.

One problem that firms face when they store their inventory prices in the inventory table occurs when they change their prices. For example, if a firm recalculates and prints an invoice from last year with this year's prices, they will obtain an incorrect result. Possible solutions to this problem include storing the selling price in a sales-inventory relationship table or creating aggregate records of invoices that include the inventory prices in effect at the time of the transaction. Some firms store prices in an inventory table and copy them to the sales-inventory relationship table when a sale occurs.

Before accounting and inventory control systems were automated, the primary key often contained encoded descriptive information about the inventory item. For example, a women's clothing retailer might have used the mnemonic code *WSk-10-Br-HM* to identify a size 10 brown wool skirt supplied by Hometown Mills. A sales clerk could easily become familiar with many of the codes and not need to look up item descriptions—often a time-consuming task in a manual system. Some firms now assign sequential numbers to their inventory items. However, if employees without easy access to the automated system perform warehousing or shipping tasks, coding inventory items according to some logical mnemonic plan still makes sense.

Let's consider some alternatives for creating a simple inventory coding and description scheme for the Pipefitters Supply Company, a plumbing supply business that sells pipe and fittings. They sell only copper and brass pipe and offer a limited number of pipe lengths, diameters, and types of fittings. The table in Figure 6.8 shows the composition, type, and diameter of the inventory items. The table also shows mnemonic codes that might be used for each inventory attribute.

| Composition | Code | Type | Code | Diameter (Inches) | Code |
|---|---|---|---|---|---|
| Brass | B | 4-foot pipe | 4 | .25 | 025 |
| Copper | C | 8-foot pipe | 8 | .50 | 050 |
| | | Cap fitting | C | 1.00 | 100 |
| | | Elbow | L | 2.00 | 200 |
| | | T-connector | T | 3.00 | 300 |
| | | | | 4.00 | 400 |

**Figure 6.8**  Inventory items.

Note that even this fairly simple inventory will fill 60 rows (2 compositions × 5 types × 6 diameters) in a database table. Therefore, each alternative we consider should accommodate these 60 inventory items and logical additions. For example, the firm might decide to carry plastic pipe and fittings in all types and diameters that they currently sell. This would add another 30 records to the Inventory table.

One coding scheme that might work for the Pipefitters Supply Company inventory is to assign sequential numbers to the inventory items. For example, using a sequential code with a size of three characters and starting with *101* would accommodate up to 899 inventory items. An alternative is to create a code that uses letters and numbers in a systematic way. For example, we could create a coding scheme that would assign *BT-200* to the 2-inch Brass T-connector shown in Figure 6.8. This second coding scheme would help warehouse and shipping employees identify inventory items even if they do not have ready access to the computer system on the warehouse floor or the shipping dock.

Once you have decided on a coding scheme, you must determine how best to store the inventory descriptions in the table. One alternative would be to use one field for the entire inventory description. This field would contain, for example, *2-inch Brass T-connector*. This alternative requires strictly enforced standards for entering the descriptions. For example, you would not want to have one description entered as *2-inch Brass T-connector* and another description entered as *Elbow, 1-inch Copper*. In practice, such standards can be difficult to monitor. A better alternative uses separate fields for each description element. Using separate fields makes it easier to create effective input validity checks. Using separate fields also lets users search, query, and generate reports from the table more easily. In the following exercises, you will learn how to create an inventory table for the Pipefitters data that demonstrates a mnemonic coding scheme and separate description fields.

EXERCISE 6.9: CREATING AN INVENTORY TABLE AND ITS PRIMARY KEY

1. Click the Tables object button in the Database window, click the New button, then double-click Design View in the New Table dialog box.
2. To create the item code field, type *InventoryItemCode* in the first row of the Field Name column. Leave its Data Type set to Text.
3. Click the Primary Key toolbar button.
4. Press F6 to move the cursor to the Field Properties pane of the Table window, set the Field Size to *6*, then press the Tab key twice to move the cursor to the Input Mask property line.
5. Type *>LA\-000;0;_* in the Input Mask property box.
6. Set the InventoryItemCode Caption property to *Item Code*

The Pipefitters mnemonic coding scheme uses the first character to indicate product composition, the second character to indicate product type, and a string of three characters to indicate product diameter. To implement this coding scheme, you can use an Input Mask property that requires the first character to be a letter, capitalizes the first two characters, inserts a hyphen automatically, and requires the last three characters to be numbers.

The > in the input mask converts all subsequent characters to uppercase, the L requires entry of a letter in the first position, the A requires entry of either a letter or a digit in the second position, the \- automatically inserts a literal hyphen, and the 000 requires entry of three digits following the hyphen. The ;0 tells Access to store the hyphen in the Inventory table and the ;_ makes the underscore character the placeholder on input forms.

In Exercise 6.10, you will enter the InventoryComposition field. This is the first of three inventory element description fields. All of Pipefitters' current inventory items are either *Brass* or *Copper*. You can prevent errors and ease data entry by creating a field that accepts only these two field values. Another thing you can do to make data entry easier is to have the form automatically capitalize the first character.

### EXERCISE 6.10: CREATING THE INVENTORYCOMPOSITION FIELD

1. Enter a Field Name of *InventoryComposition* and leave its Data Type set to Text.
2. Press F6 and change the default Field Size to *6*
3. Press Tab twice and set the Input Mask property to *>?<?????*
4. Press Tab and set the Caption property to *Composition*
5. Press Tab twice and set the Validation Rule property to *="Brass" Or ="Copper"*
6. Press Tab and set the Validation Text property to *You must enter either Brass or Copper in this field.*

Thus, the InventoryComposition field uses a combination of input mask and validation properties to control user data entry and reduce errors. The next inventory description field is InventoryType.

### EXERCISE 6.11: CREATING THE INVENTORYTYPE FIELD

1. Enter a Field Name of *InventoryType* and leave its Data Type set to Text.
2. Press F6 and change the Field Size to *11* to accommodate the longest type names that Pipefitters currently has for this field.
3. Enter a Caption property of *Type*
4. Press Tab twice and set the Validation Rule property to *="Cap fitting" Or ="Elbow" Or ="T-connector" Or ="4-foot pipe" Or ="8-foot pipe"*
5. Press Tab and set the Validation Text property to *You must enter one of the following in this field: Cap fitting, Elbow, T-connector, 4-foot pipe, or 8-foot pipe.*

Note that Pipefitters will need to change the validation properties of this field if they add a new type of inventory. Companies that have frequent changes in their inventory must store the inventory descriptions in tables rather than as part of the validation properties. The last element of the inventory description is the InventoryDiameter field.

EXERCISE 6.12: CREATING THE INVENTORYDIAMETER FIELD

1. Enter a Field Name of *InventoryDiameter* and leave its Data Type set to Text.
2. Press F6 and change the Field Size to *8*
3. Press Tab twice and set the Input Mask property to *&&&"-inch";0;_*
4. Press Tab and set the Caption property to *Diameter*
5. Press Tab twice and set the Validation Rule property to *Like ".25-inch" Or Like ".50-inch" Or Like "1.0-inch" Or Like "2.0-inch" Or Like "3.0-inch" Or Like "4.0-inch"* to limit the field so that it accepts only correct values.
6. Press Tab and set the Validation Text property to *You must enter one of the following values in this field: .25-inch, .50-inch, 1.0-inch, 2.0-inch, 3.0-inch, or 4.0-inch.*

Once again, Pipefitters will need to change the validation properties of this field if they add new diameters of pipe stock to their inventory. The Inventory table's structure is now completely defined, so you can save the file by selecting File, Save As and entering a new name for the table of *tblInventory*. Click OK to save the table definition. Close the table for now. Figure 6.9 shows the populated *tblInventory* that is included in the *Ch06.mdb* database on your Companion CD.

To enter data into *tblInventory*, click the Tables object in the Database window and double-click *tblInventory*. The table will open in Datasheet view, ready to accept data. As you enter data, notice how the Validation Rule properties you incorporated in this table make the job easier. You should also try to enter some invalid data. See what types of errors your data input controls detect—and which errors slip through.

## The Inventory Form

Although you can enter data directly into *tblInventory* more easily than you could enter data into *tblCustomer*, you can make data entry and update tasks easier and less error-prone by creating a Data Entry form for *tblInventory*. In our example firm, we restricted the inventory composition, type, and diameter. Although this is somewhat unrealistic for our example firm, it did give us an opportunity to illustrate table-level controls. It also let us illustrate some form design techniques that you will find useful in many different accounting applications.

In Exercise 6.13 you will create an Inventory Data Entry form. Pipefitters employees can use this form to enter new inventory items into their accounting system. Since *tblInventory* has only four small fields, you do not need to use a

| Item Code | Composition | Type | Diameter |
|-----------|-------------|------|----------|
| B4-025 | Brass | 4-foot pipe | .25-inch |
| B4-050 | Brass | 4-foot pipe | .50-inch |
| B4-100 | Brass | 4-foot pipe | 1.0-inch |
| B4-200 | Brass | 4-foot pipe | 2.0-inch |
| B4-300 | Brass | 4-foot pipe | 3.0-inch |
| B4-400 | Brass | 4-foot pipe | 4.0-inch |
| B8-025 | Brass | 8-foot pipe | .25-inch |
| B8-050 | Brass | 8-foot pipe | .50-inch |
| B8-100 | Brass | 8-foot pipe | 1.0-inch |
| B8-200 | Brass | 8-foot pipe | 2.0-inch |
| B8-300 | Brass | 8-foot pipe | 3.0-inch |
| B8-400 | Brass | 8-foot pipe | 4.0-inch |
| BC-025 | Brass | Cap fitting | .25-inch |
| BC-050 | Brass | Cap fitting | .50-inch |
| BC-100 | Brass | Cap fitting | 1.0-inch |
| BC-200 | Brass | Cap fitting | 2.0-inch |
| BC-300 | Brass | Cap fitting | 3.0-inch |
| BC-400 | Brass | Cap fitting | 4.0-inch |
| BL-025 | Brass | Elbow | .25-inch |
| BL-050 | Brass | Elbow | .50-inch |
| BL-100 | Brass | Elbow | 1.0-inch |

Record: 1 of 60

**Figure 6.9** The populated Inventory table in Datasheet view.

columnar form. You can display a number of records at one time by using a tabular form.

## EXERCISE 6.13: CREATING THE INVENTORY DATA ENTRY FORM

1. Click the Forms object in the Database window and click the New button.
2. Select *tblInventory* in the combo box near the bottom of the New Form dialog box, then double click AutoForm: Tabular in the list above the combo box.
3. Select File, Close from the menu, then enter a Form Name of *frmInventory* and click the OK button.

The Access AutoForm tool creates a fairly good-looking form that you can modify to meet Pipefitters' specific needs for entering inventory data efficiently and effectively. This version of the form is included as *frmInventory1* in the *Ch06.mdb* database on your Companion CD.

Of course, we can improve the usefulness of this form. In this section we will provide several exercises that you can follow to improve the appearance and functioning of the form. You can use these techniques in many applications other than inventory forms. Our first exercise includes some general improvements to the form. The results of this exercise, in Form view, appear in Figure 6.10. You can use this figure as a guide while you work through the steps in the next exercise.

EXERCISE 6.14: MAKING GENERAL IMPROVEMENTS TO THE INVENTORY FORM

1. Display the *frmInventory* form in Design view.
2. Select the label controls in the Form Header and click the Bold button on the formatting toolbar.
3. Increase the horizontal spacing between the fields. You can do this by selecting Format, Horizontal Spacing, Increase from the menu with all of the fields selected or by clicking and dragging each control separately.
4. Resize the label controls in the Form Header section to display the larger, bolded text. You can do this manually or use the Format, Size, to Fit menu command.
5. Resize the text box controls in the Detail section to display the full contents of the fields. This will require that you toggle back and forth between Design view and Form view. Be sure to scroll down through all of the table records when checking the width of the controls. You can match the width of the text box controls to the label controls. Click each control while you hold down the Shift key, then select the Format, Size, to Widest menu command.
6. Use the toolbar text align buttons to align the headings and column contents as you see fit. We centered the Item Code and Diameter fields and left-justified the other fields.
7. Choose Edit, Select Form from the menu, then click the Properties toolbar button to open the Properties sheet for the form. Click the Format tab and change the Caption property to Inventory Data Entry. Click the Properties toolbar button to close the Properties sheet.
8. To prepare for the next exercise, open the toolbox by clicking the Toolbox button on the toolbar. The toolbox will open in whatever position in which it was last closed, so you may need to drag it to a more useful position and shape.

You can save your partially completed design by selecting File, Save As, typing the form's name, *frmInventory2*, and then clicking OK. The results of Exercise 6.14 appear in Figure 6.10. This version of the form is also included as *frmInventory2* in the *Ch06.mdb* database on your Companion CD.

Recall that a combo box control is a combination of a text box and a list box. In the next exercise, you will learn how to make the form a more efficient data entry device that also helps prevent input errors by replacing three of the text box controls with combo box controls. You will learn two ways to specify the list of acceptable values for a combo box control. For the InventoryComposition and

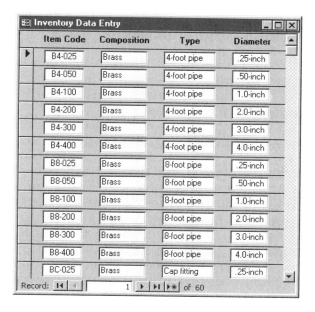

**Figure 6.10**   The improved Inventory Data Entry form in Form view.

InventoryType controls, you will build the acceptable values list directly into each control. In the InventoryDiameter control, you will have the control look up values in another table. Each of these methods has its place in accounting database design.

Entering values into controls works best when the list of acceptable values is short and will not change frequently. When the values list is long, or if the values that are acceptable change frequently, most systems designers find it easier to store the values list in a separate table.

EXERCISE 6.15: ADDING A COMBO BOX
CONTROL FOR INVENTORYCOMPOSITION

1. The first step in this exercise is to remove the text box controls for the three fields that you will be replacing with combo box controls. While holding down the Shift key, click the InventoryComposition, InventoryType, and InventoryDiameter text boxes. Then press the Delete key. Now you can use the Combo Box Wizard to create new controls.
2. Be sure that the Control Wizards button is depressed, then click the Combo Box button in the toolbox. Draw a new control in the Detail section of the form just below the Composition label.
3. In the first Combo Box Wizard dialog box, click the second option button with the caption *I will type in the values that I want*, then click the Next button.

4. Enter *1* in the Number of columns box and then press the Tab key.
5. Type *Brass* in the first row, press Tab, then type *Copper* in the second row.
6. Move the mouse cursor to the right edge of the Col1 column header. When the cursor becomes a thick vertical bar with a horizontal double-arrow, click and drag the right edge of the column to the left. Decrease the column's width so that it accommodates the widest text in the values list, Copper. Click the Next button to open the next dialog box.
7. Click the second option button with the caption *Store that value in this field*, then click the combo box arrow button and select the InventoryComposition field. Click the Next button to open the last dialog box, enter *cboInventoryComposition* as the control's label, then click the Finish button. The Wizard creates a combo box control according to your specifications and places it on the Inventory form.
8. To test the new control, click the Form View button, then click the InventoryComposition combo box arrow button to display the two choices, Brass and Copper. Return to Design view by clicking the Design View toolbar button. The new combo box control should still be selected. Select the combo box label (and only the label) by clicking and dragging a marquee through it. You may want to click the label's handle in its upper left corner and drag it away from other controls if it is overlaying them. Press the Delete key. You can then adjust the size and position of the combo box control to match the text box control it replaced.

### Try it

When you are adding new controls to a form that already has one or more controls, and the controls already on the form are the right size and in the right location, you can use this trick to make sizing and locating the new controls easier. When you create the new control, be sure it is shorter and narrower than the existing control or controls. You can then select both the new and old control (click on each while holding down the Shift key) and use the Format, Size, To Tallest and the Format, Size, To Widest menu commands to match the new control's size to the existing controls. Similarly, you can place the new control a little below or to one side of the existing control and then use the Format, Align menu commands to line up the new control with the existing control or controls.

In the next exercise, you will learn how to create a combo box control for the InventoryType field. You could use the Combo Box Wizard to create a control, but an alternative is to make a copy of the existing combo box, then modify the new control to suit the requirements of its field.

### EXERCISE 6.16: ADDING A COMBO BOX CONTROL FOR INVENTORYTYPE

1. Select the InventoryComposition combo box, press Ctrl+C, then press Ctrl+V.

2. Drag the new combo box into its correct position in the Detail section of the Inventory form.
3. With the new InventoryType combo box selected, click the Properties toolbar button to open the control's Properties sheet and then click the Data tab.
4. Change the Control Source property to *InventoryType* and the Row Source property to *"4-foot pipe"; "8-foot pipe"; "Cap fitting"; "Elbow"; "T-Connector"*. Click the Other tab in the Properties sheet and change the Name setting to *cboInventoryType*. Close the Properties sheet and switch to Form view to test your new InventoryType combo box.

The InventoryDiameter combo box will look up its acceptable values in a separate table, which you must first create. You can take a break from your form-building task—you may close or minimize the Inventory form—and create a simple table that contains the InventoryDiameter values by following the steps in the next exercise.

EXERCISE 6.17: CREATING AN INVENTORY DIAMETER LOOKUP TABLE

1. Click the Tables object in the Database window and click the New button. Double-click Design View in the list that appears in the New Table dialog box.
2. Enter a Field Name of *InventoryDiameter* in the first row and click the Primary Key toolbar button. Change the Field Size to *8* and select View, Datasheet from the menu.
3. Save the table as *tlkpInventoryDiameter* ("tlkp" is the prefix we use for a lookup table).
4. Enter the six valid values in the InventoryDiameter column as shown in Figure 6.11. You can return to the Inventory form by selecting File, Close from the menu.

**Figure 6.11** Entering values in the Inventory Diameter Lookup table.

To continue with the next exercise, reopen *frmInventory2* in Design view. Now you can connect the values in the lookup table to a new combo box control for InventoryDiameter.

EXERCISE 6.18: CREATING AN INVENTORYDIAMETER COMBO BOX

1. Select the InventoryComposition combo box, press Ctrl+C, then press Ctrl+V.
2. Drag the new combo box into its correct position in the Detail section of the Inventory form.
3. With the new InventoryDiameter combo box selected, click the Properties toolbar button to open the control's Properties sheet and change the combo box Control Source property to *InventoryDiameter*, its Row Source Type property to *Table/Query*, and its Row Source property to *tlkpInventoryDiameter*
4. Click on the Properties sheet's Other tab and change the control's name to *cboInventoryDiameter*

At this point, the Inventory Data Entry form should include three functional combo box controls for the three fields that contain the elements of the inventory description. The form should look like the one in Figure 6.12.

**Figure 6.12**   Testing the InventoryType combo box control in Form view.

You can switch to Form view and test the operation of the Inventory Data Entry form. This version of the form is provided as *frmInventory3* in the *Ch06.mdb* database on your Companion CD. When your are finished viewing the form, close it and save the changes.

Note that the Validation Rules you built into the underlying *tblInventory* still operate in the form, no matter how you change the controls. You should always be careful not to create rules in your forms or form controls that conflict with the rules you built into the underlying tables. If you are not paying close attention to these details, it is possible to create a table-form combination that will prevent you from entering any data at all!

## SALES ORDERS

When customers decide to buy products or services, they communicate this desire by sending a purchase order form, sending a letter, making a phone call, or telling a salesperson. Each of these actions is a type of *purchase order*. The firm that receives the purchase order often records it in its own records as a *sales order*.

No matter whether the order arrives as printed paper in the mail, a verbal order over the telephone, or a digital signal through a telecommunications link, all sales orders contain common components that identify when the sales order occurred, which customer placed the order, and which inventory item(s) the customer wishes to purchase.

To record these sales orders for Pipefitters Supply Company, you will need a Sales Order table, *tblSalesOrder*. To identify which customer placed each order, you can include a customer number field in *tblSalesOrder* that is linked to the *tblCustomer* table that you created earlier in this chapter. To track the individual inventory items that the customer has ordered, you can create a link to *tblInventory*. The link between *tblSalesOrder* and *tblInventory* is a many-to-many link since each sales order may contain many items and each inventory item may appear on many different sales orders. Therefore, you cannot use a foreign key link to join the tables. As you learned in Chapter 3, you must create a separate relationship table to model this link. You will learn how to create a relationship table, *tblSalesOrder-Inventory*, that will handle that job here.

## The Sales Order Table

Since each sales order comes from only one customer, and a sales order needs a customer to exist, you can build the customer-sales order link into the Sales Order table. The primary key in *tblCustomer*, CustomerNumber, will become a foreign key in *tblSalesOrder*. Of course, the Sales Order table will need its own primary key and a field for the date of the sales order.

Since customers often send purchase order forms to indicate what items they want to buy, you should consider including a field to store customers' purchase order numbers. We will include a customer purchase order number field in our example. Therefore, *tblSalesOrder* will have four fields: a primary key, a date, a foreign key link to *tblCustomer*, and a record of the customer's purchase order number. Exercise 6.19 shows you how to create this *tblSalesOrder*.

EXERCISE 6.19: CREATING A SALES ORDER TABLE

1. Click the Tables tab in the Database window, then click the New button. Double-click Design View in the New Table dialog box.
2. First, create the primary key field. Enter a Field Name of *SalesOrderNumber* and click the Primary Key toolbar button. Leave the field's Data Type set to Text.
3. Press F6 to move to the Field Properties section of the window and change the Field Size to *6*. This size will accommodate 899,999 sales orders if you use a starting number of 100001.
4. Set the SalesOrderNumber field's Input Mask property to *000000;;_* and its Caption property to *Sales Order Number*
5. Next, create a field for the sales order date by entering a Field Name of *SalesOrderDate* and a Data Type of *Date/Time*
6. Set its Format property to *Short Date* and its Input Mask property to *99/99/99*. If you prefer, you can use the Input Mask wizard by clicking the Build button that appears to the right of the Input Mask property box. If you use the wizard, select the Short Date option. Set its Caption property to *Date*
7. Enter a Field Name of *CustomerNumber* and leave the Data Type set to Text. Set the Field Size to *5*, the Input Mask to *00000*, and the Caption property to *Customer Number*. This field is the foreign key link to *tblCustomer*. Although the field's name in this table need not match its name in *tblCustomer*, it is a good idea to use the same name. We follow this convention in our examples here and on your Companion CD. More important is that the Data Types of these two fields must be compatible. The easiest way to ensure Data Type compatibility is to make the fields an exact match. The primary key in *tblCustomer* is CustomerNumber, a Text field with a Field Size of 5.
8. Enter *CustomerPONumber* as the next Field Name, leave its Data Type set to Text, and set its Field Size property to *15*. Set the Caption property to *Customer PO Number*. This field must allow any combination of numbers, letters, and symbols that customers might decide to use in identifying their purchase orders. Since you cannot anticipate the characteristics of this field, you cannot build any data entry internal controls into the table for this field.

This completes the basic design of *tblSalesOrder*. You will learn how to create the foreign key's referential integrity link to *tblCustomer* later in this chapter. To save your work, select File, Save As from the menu and enter *tblSalesOrder* as the table's name. Click OK to save the table. The table that appears in Datasheet view in Figure 6.13 is included as *tblSalesOrder* in the *Ch06.mdb* database on your Companion CD. Close the table.

| Sales Order Number | Date | Customer Number | Customer PO Number |
|---|---|---|---|
| 100001 | 1/14/01 | 10001 | 101-PR-753979 |
| 100002 | 1/16/01 | 10003 | 26754 |
| 100003 | 1/16/01 | 10007 | BP-8666789 |
| 100004 | 1/17/01 | 10005 | 276-555438 |
| 100005 | 1/17/01 | 10010 | 985553 |
| 100006 | 1/18/01 | 10005 | 276-555497 |
| 100007 | 1/18/01 | 10006 | DD-78725-NC3 |
| 100008 | 1/18/01 | 10001 | 101-PR-754007 |
| 100009 | 1/19/01 | 10002 | 8779465QW |
| 100010 | 1/20/01 | 10004 | B-462-121894 |
| 100011 | 1/20/01 | 10024 | 8675309 |
| 100012 | 1/22/01 | 10035 | ACR-1501 |
| 100013 | 1/22/01 | 10016 | Q-54-2743 |
| 100014 | 1/23/01 | 10017 | 97613 |
| 100015 | 1/23/01 | 10029 | PBR-6905 |
| 100016 | 1/24/01 | 10031 | HZ-37-PZR |
| 100017 | 1/24/01 | 10048 | 5790-808 |
| 100018 | 1/25/01 | 10050 | 212-35P |
| 100019 | 1/26/01 | 10046 | 84-PB-634 |

Record: 1 of 100

**Figure 6.13** The Sales Order table in Datasheet view.

The Sales Order table identifies when an order was received, records which customer placed the order, and assigns the sales order a unique identifying number as its primary key. You can enter only part of the sales order information in this table since *tblSalesOrder* does not store information about which inventory items customers have ordered on specific sales orders. This would require *tblSalesOrder* to have repeating fields, a violation of the normalization rules you learned in Chapter 3. To store this additional information, the database needs a relationship table to link *tblSalesOrder* and *tblInventory*.

## The Sales Order-Inventory Table

If Pipefitters Supply Company accepted orders for only one inventory item at a time, it would not need this table. We could add fields for inventory item code and quantity ordered to *tblSalesOrder*. Most businesses would find this policy to be too restrictive, since it would require their customers to send a separate sales order for each item they wanted to buy.

The Sales Order-Inventory table is a relationship table that records the many-to-many link between *tblSalesOrder* and *tblInventory*. Therefore, the Sales Order-Inventory table needs four fields to store:

• The primary key of *tblSalesOrder*.

• The primary key of *tblInventory*.

- The quantity of each inventory item that appears on each sales order.
- The price of each inventory item that appears on each sales order.

The primary keys from *tblSalesOrder* and *tblInventory* will combine to form the composite primary key in the *tblSalesOrder-Inventory* relationship table. In Microsoft Access, you create a composite primary key by creating two separate fields, one for each entity table's primary key, then designating *both* fields as primary keys. If you are using the Microsoft Access help screens, you may notice that Microsoft uses the term *junction table* instead of *relationship table* in their on-line help and other documentation. Before you begin the next exercise, close any open tables or forms.

EXERCISE 6.20: CREATING THE
*TBLSALESORDER-INVENTORY* RELATIONSHIP TABLE

1. Click the Tables object in the Database window, click the New button, then double-click Design View.
2. Enter a Field Name of *SalesOrderNumber* and leave its Data Type set to Text.
3. Press F6 and change the Field Size property to *6*
4. Set the Input Mask property to *000000;;_*
5. Set the Caption property to *Sales Order Number*, the Required property to *Yes*, and the Indexed property to *Yes (Duplicates OK)*. The Indexed property setting must allow duplicates because a field that is part of a composite primary key may contain duplicate values. Remember that the entity table primary keys that form the composite primary key in a relationship table must always match exactly on Type and Size. These matched fields will allow the database to store values simultaneously in the SalesOrderNumber fields in this table and *tblSalesOrder*. The other half of the composite primary key is the primary key of *tblInventory*, InventoryItemCode.
6. In the second Field Name row, enter *InventoryItemCode* and leave its Data Type set to Text. Press F6 and change the Field Size property to *6*. Set the Input Mask property to *>LA\-000;0;_*, the Caption property to *Item Number*, the Required property to *Yes*, and the Indexed property to *Yes (Duplicates OK)*
7. The next field in *tblSalesOrder-Inventory* will store the quantity of each inventory item a customer orders on a particular sales order. Enter a Field Name of *SOInvQuantity* and set its Data Type to *Number*
8. Set the Field Size property to *Long Integer*, the Decimal Places property to *0*, and the Caption property to *Quantity*. The integer property setting assumes that Pipefitters Supply Company does not accept orders for fractional units. The long integer property setting will allow the company to record a quantity of up to 2 billion units for any one inventory item on any one sales order.
9. The last field in *tblSalesOrder-Inventory* will store the price that the customer agrees to pay for each inventory item on each sales order. To create this field, enter Field Name of *SOInvPrice*, set its Data Type to *Currency*, leave its Field

Size property set to Currency, set its Decimal Places property to *2*, and set its Caption property to *Price*

If you followed the steps in Exercise 6.20 carefully, you will have created most of the structure for *tblSalesOrder-Inventory*. The next step is to set the table's composite primary key. To begin this exercise, you should have *tblSalesOrder-Inventory* open in Design view.

EXERCISE 6.21: CREATING A COMPOSITE
PRIMARY KEY FOR *TBLSALESORDER-INVENTORY*

1. While pressing the Ctrl key, click the row selectors for SalesOrderNumber and for InventoryItemCode.
2. With both fields selected, click the Primary Key toolbar button. The primary key symbol should appear in the row selectors of both fields as shown in Figure 6.14.

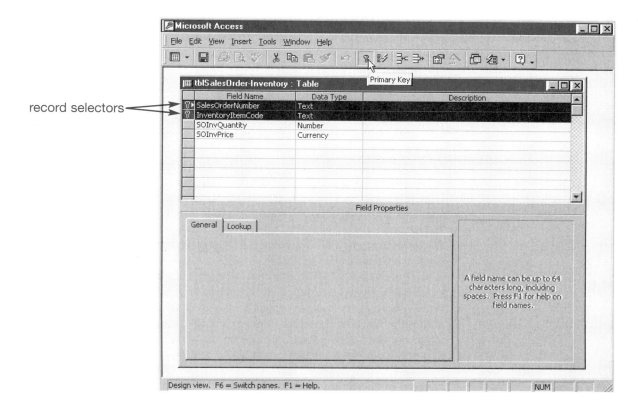

**Figure 6.14** Creating a composite primary key for *tblSalesOrder-Inventory*.

This completes the basic design of *tblSalesOrder-Inventory*. To save your work, select File, Save As from the menu and type **tblSalesOrder-Inventory** as the New Name in the Save As dialog box. Close the table. A version of this table that includes data for the Pipefitters Supply Company is included in the *Ch06.mdb* database on your Companion CD.

You have learned how to create *tblCustomer*, *tblInventory*, *tblSalesOrder*, and *tblSalesOrder-Inventory*. Now you are ready to model the relationships among these tables. In Exercise 6.22, you will establish relationships among these four tables. If your tables do not contain any data, you should not have any problems as you follow the steps. If you have entered data in the tables, you must make sure that the data in key fields are compatible before you begin the exercise. For example, if you have entered any CustomerNumber values in *tblSalesOrder*, those exact values must exist in the CustomerNumber field in *tblCustomer*. Similarly, any values you have entered in the SalesOrderNumber or InventoryItemCode fields in *tblSalesOrder-Inventory* must exist in the corresponding fields of *tblSalesOrder* and *tblInventory*, respectively. If corresponding values do not exist in these fields, Access will not permit you to establish referential integrity on those links.

EXERCISE 6.22: CREATING RELATIONSHIPS AMONG *TBLCUSTOMER*, *TBLINVENTORY*, *TBLSALESORDER*, AND *TBLSALESORDER-INVENTORY*

1. Close any tables or forms that are open on the desktop, then select the menu command Tools, Relationships.
2. In the Show Table dialog box select *tblCustomer*, *tblInventory*, *tblSalesOrder*, and *tblSalesOrder-Inventory* by clicking their names while holding down the Ctrl key.
3. Click the Add button to place the tables you have selected into the Relationships window, then click the Close button.
4. The tables you have chosen should appear in the Relationships window. You may wish to resize and rearrange the tables in the Relationships window using Figure 6.15 as a guide.
5. Click and drag the CustomerNumber field from *tblCustomer* to the CustomerNumber field in *tblSalesOrder*.
6. In the Relationships dialog box that appears, click the Enforce Referential Integrity check box, then click the Create button. Enabling the referential integrity option provides an internal control on the CustomerNumber field in *tblSalesOrder*. This referential integrity link will prevent users from entering customer numbers in *tblSalesOrder* that do not already exist in *tblCustomer*. The nature of the one-to-many link is denoted in the Relationships window by the number *1* that appears on the "one" side of the link and the infinity symbol that appears on the "many" side of the link.
7. Click and drag the InventoryItemCode field from *tblInventory* and drop it on the InventoryItemCode field in *tblSalesOrder-Inventory*. In the Relationships dialog

box that appears, click the Enforce Referential Integrity check box, then click the Create button.

8. Click and drag the SalesOrderNumber field from *tblSalesOrder* and drop it on the SalesOrderNumber field in *tblSalesOrder-Inventory*. In the Relationships dialog box that appears, click the Enforce Referential Integrity check box, then click the Create button.

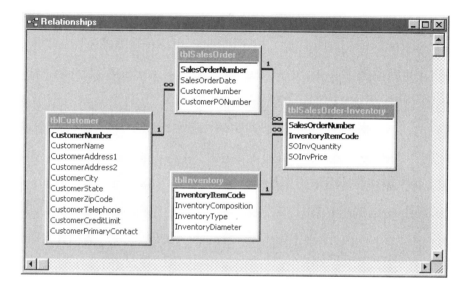

**Figure 6.15** Relationships among *tblCustomer*, *tblInventory*, *tblSalesOrder*, and *tblSalesOrder-Inventory*.

The Relationships window showing all of the links you have created appears in Figure 6.15. We have moved and resized the table representations in the Relationships window to make the table fields and the links easier to see. Select the File, Close menu command to return to the Database window. Click Yes when you are asked if you want to save the changes you have made to the database relationships. Now that you have established the necessary foreign key and relationship table links, you can create a Sales Order Entry form.

## The Sales Order Entry Form

The sales order entry task requires a more complex form than either the tasks of customer information entry or inventory information entry required. To enter all of the information contained in customers' sales orders, we will need a form that links:

- *tblSalesOrder* to *tblCustomer*, to obtain information such as the customer's name and address.

- *tblSalesOrder* to *tblSalesOrder-Inventory*, to obtain a list of the inventory item numbers, quantities, and prices for each item on each sales order.

- *tblSalesOrder-Inventory* to *tblInventory*, to obtain a description for each item on each sales order.

A sales order entry form that meets these objectives will use four tables. The form must read from *tblCustomer* and *tblInventory* and write to *tblSalesOrder* and *tblSalesOrder-Inventory*. Since this form will read data from *tblCustomer* and *tblInventory*, you must have data entered in these tables. The *Ch06.mdb* database on your Companion CD includes populated versions of these tables. If you have not entered data in the tables you have created, you can import the *Ch06.mdb* tables into your database file. Alternatively, you can copy some or all of the individual records from the *Ch06.mdb* and paste them into your database tables. Either of these procedures will save you the time and trouble of entering large amounts of data into tables and will help speed you along to the form-building exercises that follow.

EXERCISE 6.23: CREATING A SALES ORDER ENTRY FORM

1. Be sure that you have closed all tables and forms. Click the Forms object in the Database window, then click the New button.
2. Double-click Form Wizard in the New Form dialog box. Since some of the fields have the same name but appear in different tables, you must be careful to select each field from the correct table. For the Sales Order Entry form, you will want to select the SalesOrderNumber and CustomerNumber fields from *tblSalesOrder* and the InventoryItemNumber field from *tblSalesOrder-Inventory*.
3. Select Table: *tblSalesOrder* from the Tables/Queries combo box in the Form Wizard dialog box and click the >> button to move all of the *tblSalesOrder* fields to the Selected Fields box.
4. Select Table: *tblCustomer* from the Tables/Queries combo box and click the >> button to move all of the *tblCustomer* fields to the Selected Fields box.
5. Scroll up in the Selected Fields box and select *tblCustomer.CustomerNumber*. Click the < button to move that one field back to the Available Fields box. Alternatively, you can select each field in the Available Fields box *except* CustomerNumber and click the > button to place each field into the Selected Fields box individually. No matter which method you use, you should select the CustomerPrimaryContact field in the Selected Fields box before going to the next step. This will ensure that the next field will be added after these fields and will help the Wizard properly create the form. The Wizard places fields on the form it creates in the same order you list the fields in the Selected Fields box here.
6. Select Table: *tblSalesOrder-Inventory* from the Tables/Queries combo box. Select the InventoryItemCode field name in the Available Fields box and click

the > button to place it in the Selected Fields box. Repeat this procedure for SOInvQuantity and SOInvPrice.

7. Select Table: *tblInventory* from the Tables/Queries combo box. Select the InventoryComposition field name in the Available Fields box and click the > button to place it in the Selected Fields box. Repeat this procedure for InventoryType and InventoryDiameter.

8. Now that we have selected the fields that will appear on the form, we can give the Form Wizard further instructions that it can use to create the form. Click the Next button. The Form Wizard should indicate that it has chosen to view data by *tblSalesOrder*, to create a Form with subform(s), and to arrange the fields as shown in Figure 6.16. Click the Next button to accept the Form Wizard's proposed design.

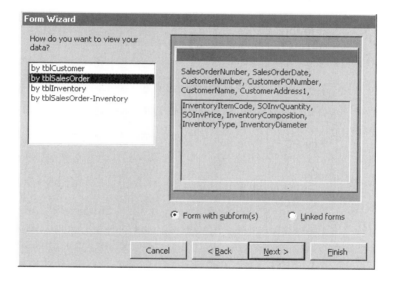

**Figure 6.16**   The Form Wizard's proposed design for the Sales Order Entry form.

9. Move through the next two dialog boxes, selecting the Tabular option in the first and the Standard style in the second.

10. Enter *frmSalesOrder* and *fsubSalesOrder* as the Form and Subform titles, respectively. Click the Finish button to have the Form Wizard create the Sales Order Entry form-subform combination you have specified.

The Form Wizard may take some time—over a minute on slower computers—to generate the forms. When it has completed its work, it will display the finished Sales Order Entry form as shown in Figure 6.17. This figure shows the form connected to tables that are populated with data to show the operation of the form better. Your form will not show any data unless you have populated your tables. Remember that this form is actually two forms, a subform nested inside a form. The Form Wizard has already saved these objects under the names you gave them in the preceding exercise.

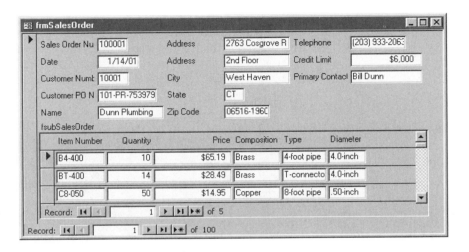

**Figure 6.17**   The Sales Order Entry form generated by the Form Wizard.

Although this Wizard-generated form is certainly usable and includes all of the controls needed to enter, delete, and modify sales order information, you can probably see some ways to improve it. The next two exercises show you how to make improvements that will make the form and subform more effective and easier to use. You might identify other improvements or alternative ways of making the improvements we suggest. We encourage you to experiment, since form design is as much an art as a science. Just remember that you are designing a form for an input clerk to use many hours each day, so avoid bright colors and other design features that might irritate the user.

Whether you have created the Sales Order Entry form using tables that contain data or you have entered data in the form after you created it, you may notice that the form does not scroll through the sales orders in numeric order. The Form Wizard did not include a sorting rule in the query it built behind *frmSalesOrder*. Fortunately, this is fairly easy to change.

EXERCISE 6.24: CHANGING THE SORT ORDER IN FRMSALESORDER

1. Open *frmSalesOrder* in Design view.
2. Click the Properties toolbar button to open the form's Properties sheet if it is not already open on the Access desktop.

3. Click the Properties sheet's Data tab, then click the Record Source property's Build button to open the Query Builder window for the query behind the form.
4. Type *Ascending* in the SalesOrderNumber field's Sort cell in the QBE grid.

While the Query Builder window is open from the previous exercise, you can create a new field, CustomerAddress3, that combines the CustomerCity, CustomerState, and CustomerZipCode fields. Often, combined fields such as this are easier to position on forms because you need not align the individual controls. Follow the steps in Exercise 6.25 to create this combined address field.

EXERCISE 6.25: CREATING THE
CUSTOMERADDRESS3 FIELD IN *FRMSALESORDER*

1. Use the scrollbar at the bottom of the QBE grid to move to next open grid column and press Shift+F2 to open the Zoom box.
2. Type *CustomerAddress3: [CustomerCity] & ", " & [CustomerState] & " " & [CustomerZipCode]* in the Zoom box, then click the OK button to close the Zoom box. Figure 6.18 shows this expression in the Zoom box where you can more easily see the required spacing in the expression (we increased the font size in the Zoom box for this screen capture).

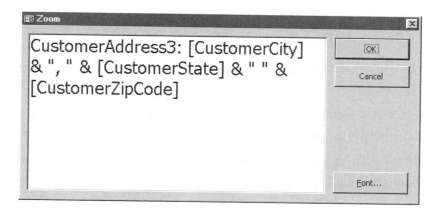

**Figure 6.18**    The CustomerAddress3 expression in the Zoom box.

### Try it

To check your work, click the Run toolbar button (it is the button with the exclamation point) and scroll to the far right of the resulting dynaset. Examine the new field you have created, CustomerAddress3. It should show each customer's city, followed by a comma and a space, state, followed by a space, and zip code.

Exercise 6.26 offers you steps that make cosmetic changes to the form's layout. These improvements can make the form easier to use. These changes are only recommendations; feel free to use your own judgment as you improve the form. You may find it helpful to refer to Figure 6.19, which shows the form modified using the steps in this exercise. You may either close the Properties sheet or drag it to the bottom of the screen so it is out of your way while you perform the steps below.

### EXERCISE 6.26: IMPROVING FRMSALESORDER

1. Select the CustomerCity text box control with the Properties sheet open. Click the Data label and change the Control Source property to *CustomerAddress3*
2. Delete the CustomerState and CustomerZipCode label and text box controls.
3. Delete the *fsubSalesOrder* label on the Subform/Subreport object. Consider deleting the labels for those text box controls that are self-explanatory and in which you will not be entering data on this form. We chose to delete labels for CustomerName, all of the customer address fields, and CustomerTelephone.
4. You can set the properties of the controls that the form will use to display information (rather than allow the user to enter information) so that they blend in with the background of the form. In addition to changing the appearance of these information display controls, you can set their properties to prevent data entry persons from using them to change data in *tblCustomer*. Locking controls to prevent data entry is an important internal control feature that you can build into Access forms. This internal control feature is especially useful in preventing data entry clerks from introducing unintentional errors into the database. With the Properties sheet open, hold down the Shift key and click on the information display text box controls (CustomerName, CustomerAddress1, CustomerAddress2, CustomerAddress3, and CustomerTelephone, CustomerCreditLimit, and CustomerPrimaryContact) and the CustomerCreditLimit and CustomerPrimaryContact label controls to select them.
5. Click the Properties sheet's Format tab and change the Back Style property to *Transparent*, the Special Effect property to *Flat*, and the Border Style property to *Transparent*
6. Hold down the Shift key and click on the two information display label controls (CustomerCreditLimit and CustomerPrimaryContact) to unselect them. Click the Data tab and change the Enabled property to *No* and the Locked property to *Yes*
7. Click the Other tab and change the Tab Stop property to *No*

### Try it

You can make the following appearance adjustments using Figure 6.19 as a guide. As you fine-tune the form, you will find the Format menu commands (Align, Size, Horizontal Spacing, and Vertical Spacing) to be quite helpful. For making small ad-

justments to form controls, the Ctrl+arrow keys and Shift+arrow keys are also useful. The Ctrl+arrow keys move the selected object(s) and the Shift+arrow keys
change the size of the selected object(s).

8. Resize and rearrange the controls so that the data entry controls
   (SalesOrderNumber, SalesOrderDate, CustomerNumber, and
   CustomerPONumber) are separated from the information display controls. Use
   the tools on the Formatting toolbar to set the labels' typefaces to Bold. You can
   also use the Formatting toolbar tools to change the justification of the text box
   control contents.
9. Choose Edit, Select Form from the menu, click the Format tab and change the
   Caption property to *Sales Order Entry* and the Record Selectors property to *No*

The results of these modifications to *frmSalesOrder* appear in Figure 6.19.
This form is included as *frmSalesOrder* in the *Ch06.mdb* database on your
Companion CD. Close the form and save your changes.

**Figure 6.19** The modified *frmSalesOrder* in Form view.

In the next exercise, you will make similar modifications to the subform,
*fsubSalesOrder*. These modifications appear in the subform control portion of the

Sales Order form in Figure 6.19. The modified subform itself appears in Figure 6.20. You can use both figures for guidance as you work through Exercise 6.27. Be sure you have closed all tables and forms before beginning this exercise.

EXERCISE 6.27: IMPROVING FSUBSALESORDER

1. Click the Forms tab in the Database window, select *fsubSalesOrder*, then click the Design button.
2. Delete the InventoryType and InventoryDiameter text box controls (in the Detail section) and the InventoryType and InventoryDiameter label controls (in the Form Header section).
3. Arrange the remaining text box controls and labels in the following left-to-right order on the form: InventoryItemNumber, InventoryComposition, SOInvQuantity, and SOInvPrice.
4. If the Properties sheet is not already open, click the Properties toolbar button. Select the InventoryComposition text box control. Change its properties as follows: click the Format tab and set the Back Style property to *Transparent*, the Special Effect property to *Flat*, and the Border Style property to *Transparent*; click the Data tab and set the Enabled property to *No* and the Locked property to *Yes*; then click the Other tab and set the Tab Stop property to *No*. Next, we will show you how to open the query behind the form and create two new calculated fields that you can use on this form.
5. Choose Edit, Select Form from the menu. Click the Properties sheet's Data tab, select the Record Source property, then click its Build button to open the Query Builder window.
6. Scroll right in the QBE grid, select the first open Field cell, and press Shift+F2 to open the Zoom box. Type *Description: [InventoryDiameter] & " " & [InventoryComposition] & " " & [InventoryType]* in the Zoom box and click the OK button.
7. Click in the next open Field cell in the QBE grid and press Shift+F2. Type *Extension: [SOInvPrice] * [SOInvQuantity]* in the Zoom box and click the OK button. Close the Query Builder window and save your changes.
8. Select the InventoryComposition text box control with the Properties sheet open. Click the Data tab and change the Control Source property to *Description*. Under the Other tab, make the same change to the control's Name property.
9. Select the InventoryComposition label control and change its Caption property under the Format tab to *Description*. Under the Other tab, change the Name property to *Description Label*
10. Click the Field List toolbar button, click and drag the Extension field to the Detail section of the form to the right of the other controls, then click the Field List toolbar button again to close the field list. Select the Extension field's label control, press Ctrl+X to cut the label, click the Form Header section bar, then press Ctrl+V to paste the label in the Form Header. Use the Ctrl+right arrow key to align the label control over the Extension text box control. Using Figure 6.20 as a guide, adjust the font characteristics and alignment of the fields on the form.

**Figure 6.20**  The modified *fsubSalesOrder* in Form view.

The results of these modifications to *fsubSalesOrder* appear in Figure 6.20. This form is included as *fsubSalesOrder* in the *Ch06.mdb* database on your Companion CD. Close the form and save your changes. You should open *frmSalesOrder* and make sure that your revised subform still fits in the *fsubSalesOrder* subform object on *frmSalesOrder*. You can modify either or both forms to obtain a precise fit. Unfortunately, Microsoft Access has not automated this task, so you must do some trial-and-error fitting to get a good result. The Sales Order form in Figure 6.20 has been adjusted to fit the modified *fsubSalesOrder*.

You can further enhance this form by adding buttons that make navigation easier. You can also add error-checking macros to the form. For example, you could write a macro that would test whether a particular sales order would exceed a customer's credit limit. We encourage you to experiment and enhance this form and other sales order forms you create for your own projects or client applications.

## RECORDING SALES

After the credit department approves the sales order and the goods are ready to be shipped, the system must create an invoice and shipping documents. Shipping documents, such as bills of lading or packing slips, vary greatly in appearance and design. However, they always contain a subset of the information that appears on the invoice.

In this section we will show you how to create an invoice report. You can easily modify this invoice to create shipping documents that suit a particular application. The invoice is a very important record in the revenue cycle; it summarizes each sales transaction for accounting and includes valuable marketing information. To create an invoice, you will need two new tables: a Sales table and a Sales-Inventory relationship table. You will also use the *tblCustomer* and *tblInventory* tables that you have already created.

## The Sales Table

Since Pipefitters conducts each sale transaction with only one customer, and the sale transaction needs a customer to exist, you can build the customer-sales link into the Sales table by putting a foreign key field into *tblSales* that corresponds with the primary key field of *tblCustomer*. The Sales table will need fields to store its own primary key and the date the items were shipped. We will also include a SalesOrderNumber field in our example. Therefore, *tblSales* will have four fields: a primary key, a shipment date, a foreign key link to *tblCustomer*, and SalesOrderNumber. In Exercise 6.28 you will create this Sales table.

EXERCISE 6.28: CREATING A SALES TABLE

1. Click the Tables object in the Database window, then click the New button. Double-click Design View in the New Table dialog box.
2. To create the primary key field, enter a Field Name of *InvoiceNumber* and click the Primary Key toolbar button. Leave the field's Data Type set to Text.
3. Set the Field Size property to *6*, the Input Mask property to *000000;;_*, and the Caption property to *Invoice Number*
4. To create a field for the invoice date, enter a Field Name of *InvoiceDate* and a Data Type of *Date/Time*. Set the Format property to *Short Date*
5. Set the Input Mask property to *99/99/99*. If you prefer, you can use the Input Mask Wizard by clicking the Build button that appears to the right of the Input Mask property box. If you use the Wizard, select the Short Date option.
6. Set the Caption property to *Date*
7. Next, enter a Field Name of *CustomerNumber*, leave the Data Type set to Text, set the Field Size to *5*, set the Input Mask to *00000*, and set the Caption property to *Customer Number*
8. Enter *SalesOrderNumber* as the next Field Name, leave its Data Type set to Text, set its Field Size property to *6*, set its Input Mask property to *000000;;_*, and set its Caption property to *Sales Order Number*

This completes the design of *tblSales*. You will add referential integrity links from this table to *tblCustomer* and to the relationship table that connects *tblSales* to *tblInventory* after you create that relationship table in the next exercise. To save your work on the Sales table, select File, Save As from the menu and type *tblSales* as its new name. Click OK to complete the table-save operation. An example *tblSales* is included in the *Ch06.mdb* database on your Companion CD.

## The Sales-Inventory Table

The design and structure of this table is very similar to the design and structure of the *tblSalesOrder-Inventory* table you created earlier in this chapter. The Sales-Inventory table provides the many-to-many link between *tblSales* and *tblInventory* and stores the quantity and price of each inventory item on each invoice. In Exercise 6.29 you will create *tblSales-Inventory* with four fields: InvoiceNumber, InventoryItemNumber, SInvQuantity, and SInvPrice. Before you begin, close all tables and open the Database window.

EXERCISE 6.29: CREATING THE *TBLSALES-INVENTORY* RELATIONSHIP TABLE

1. Click the Tables object in the Database window, click the New button, then double-click Design View.
2. To create the first half of the composite primary key, enter a Field Name of *InvoiceNumber* and leave its Data Type set to Text. Set the Field Size property to *6*, the Input Mask property to *000000;;_*, the Caption property to *Invoice Number*, and the Indexed property to *Yes (Duplicates OK)*
3. To create the second half of the primary key, enter a Field Name of *InventoryItemCode* and leave its Data Type set to Text. Set its Field Size property to *6*, its Input Mask property to *>LA\-000;0;_*, its Caption property to *Item Number*, and its Indexed property to *Yes (Duplicates OK)*
4. While pressing the Ctrl key, click the row selector for InvoiceNumber and then click the row selector for InventoryItemNumber. With both fields selected, click the Primary Key toolbar button. The primary key symbol should appear in the row selectors of both fields.
5. Next, enter a Field Name of *SInvQuantity* and set its Data Type to *Number*
6. Set the Field Size property to *Long Integer*, the Decimal Places property to *0*, and the Caption property to *Quantity*
7. Enter the last Field Name of *SInvPrice* and set its Data Type to *Currency*
8. Leave its Format property set to Currency, set its Decimal Places property to *2*, and set its Caption property to *Price*

This completes *tblSales-Inventory*. To save your work, select File, Save As from the menu and type *tblSales-Inventory* as the table's new name. Click OK to complete the table-save operation. A version of this table that includes data for the Pipefitters Supply Company is included in the *Ch06.mdb* database on your Companion CD for your reference.

In Exercise 6.30 you will model the relationships needed to record sales for the Pipefitters Supply Company. These relationships link *tblCustomer*, *tblInventory*, *tblSales*, and *tblSales-Inventory*. If you have entered data in the tables, be sure that the data in the tables' key fields are compatible, otherwise Access will not permit you to establish referential integrity links on those fields.

EXERCISE 6.30: CREATING RELATIONSHIPS AMONG
*TBLCUSTOMER*, *TBLINVENTORY*, *TBLSALES*, AND *TBLSALES-INVENTORY*

1. Close any tables or forms you have open on the desktop.
2. Select the menu command Tools, Relationships. The Relationships window will appear and display the relationships you established in Exercise 6.22. Since you are going to add more tables to the window in the exercise, you may want to click and drag the edges of the window to make it larger.
3. Select the menu command Relationships, Show Table. Select *tblSales* and *tblSales-Inventory* by clicking their names in the Show Table dialog box while holding down the Ctrl key.
4. Click the Add button, then click the Close button in the Show Table dialog box. The tables you have chosen will appear in the Relationships window. You may wish to resize and rearrange the tables in the Relationships window using Figure 6.21 as a guide.
5. Click and drag the CustomerNumber field from *tblCustomer* to the CustomerNumber field in *tblSales*. In the Relationships dialog box that appears, click the Enforce Referential Integrity check box, then click the Create button.
6. Click and drag InventoryItemCode from *tblInventory* to the InventoryItemCode field in *tblSales-Inventory*. In the Relationships dialog box, click the Enforce Referential Integrity check box, then click the Create button.
7. Click and drag InvoiceNumber from *tblSales* to the InvoiceNumber field in *tblSales-Inventory*. In the Relationships dialog box, click the Enforce Referential Integrity check box, then click the Create button.

The Relationships window showing these links, along with the links you created earlier, appears in Figure 6.21. We have moved and resized the table representations in the Relationships window to make the table fields and the links easier to see.

Close the Relationship window and save your changes. Now that you have established the necessary links, you can create a form in which you can enter sales information.

## The Sales Entry Form

The Sales Entry form closely resembles the Sales Order Entry form you created earlier in this chapter. The Sales Order Entry form lets Pipefitters Supply Company enter the items that their customers order. The Sales Entry form lets Pipefitters enter the items they actually shipped to their customers. If Pipefitters were certain that it would always have all inventory items in stock, they could generate invoices directly from information in the Sales Order table. Unfortunately, this assumption is not realistic for most companies.

To enter sales information for Pipefitters, you will need a separate form that reads from *tblCustomer* and *tblInventory* and writes to *tblSales* and *tblSales-Inventory*. Since the Sales Entry form will read data from *tblCustomer* and

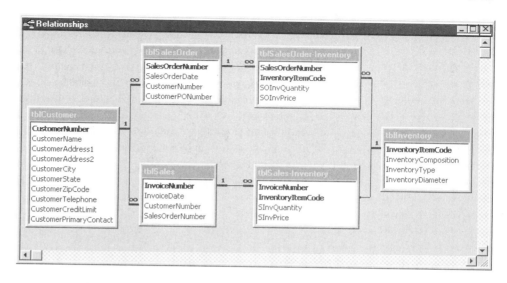

**Figure 6.21** Relationships among *tblCustomer*, *tblInventory*, *tblSales*, and *tblSales-Inventory*.

*tblInventory*, you must have data in these tables before you can build and test the Sales Entry form.

Since the Sales Entry form is so much like the Sales Order Entry form you created earlier in this chapter, you can adapt that form to become the Sales Entry form instead of starting all over. The next two exercises show you how to edit the objects in *frmSalesOrder* and *fsubSalesOrder* to create a sales entry form-subform combination, *frmSales* and *fsubSales*. You will also learn more about how to construct Access forms in general by working through these exercises. The Form Wizard, when it created *frmSalesOrder* and *fsubSalesOrder* for you, hid some of the more interesting details of Access form creation from you.

Whenever you work with form-subform combinations in Access, you should start with the innermost subform and work out from that to the main form. Therefore, you will modify *fsubSalesOrder* in the first of these two exercises.

EXERCISE 6.31: MODIFYING *FSUBSALESORDER* TO CREATE *FSUBSALES*

1. Click the Forms tab in the Database window and select *fsubSalesOrder*. Press Ctrl+C to copy the form object, then press Ctrl+V to paste it back into the Database window. Type *fsubSales* in the Paste As dialog box and click the OK button. Select the new form object and click the Design button to open the form in Design view.
2. To make this form work as a Sales Entry subform, you must replace *tblSalesOrder-Inventory* with *tblSales-Inventory* in the query behind the form

and change the query's field references. Click the Properties toolbar button to open the Properties sheet for the form, then click the Data tab.

3.  Select the Record Source property and click its Build button to open the form's query, then select Query, Show Table from the menu. Double-click *tblSales-Inventory*, then close the Show Table dialog box.

4.  Click anywhere in the *tblSalesOrder-Inventory* object to select it and press the Delete key.

5.  Click and drag InvoiceNumber from *tblSales-Inventory* to the first Field cell in the QBE grid. All of the existing columns will move to the right when you release the mouse button. Set the InvoiceNumber field's Sort order to *Ascending*

6.  Click and drag InventoryItemCode from *tblSales-Inventory* to the second Field cell in the QBE grid. Once again, all of the existing columns will move to the right when you release the mouse button. Be careful to select this field from *tblSales-Inventory* and not from *tblInventory*. If you select the InventoryItemCode field from *tblInventory*, the form will not work properly.

7.  Repeat this procedure by clicking and dragging SInvQuantity and SInvPrice to the third and fourth Field cells, respectively.

8.  Using the scroll bar at the bottom of the QBE grid, move the grid so the Extension field is visible (it should be the last Field cell that contains an entry). Select the Extension field and press Shift+F2 to open the Zoom box. Edit the expression to read *Extension: [SInvPrice]\*[SInvQuantity]* and click OK. Close the Query Builder window and save your changes.

9.  You have changed the underlying query of the form, so you must change the Control Source properties of the text box controls on the form that are bound to fields that you have removed from the query. Select the SOInvQuantity text box control. If the Properties sheet is not open, click the Properties toolbar button. Click the Data tab and change the Control Source property to *SInvQuantity*

10. Select the SOInvPrice text box control. Click the Properties sheet Data tab and change the Control Source property to *SinvPrice*. Close and save the form.

In the next exercise, you will turn *frmSalesOrder* into the main form component of a working Sales Entry form. Be sure you have closed all forms and tables before proceeding.

EXERCISE 6.32: MODIFYING *FRMSALESORDER* TO CREATE *FRMSALES*

1.  Click the Forms tab in the Database window and select *frmSalesOrder*. Press Ctrl+C to copy the form object, then press Ctrl+V to paste it back into the Database window. Type *frmSales* in the Paste As dialog box and click the OK button. With the new form object selected, click the Design button to open the form in Design view.

2.  To make this form work as a Sales Entry subform, you must replace *tblSalesOrder-Inventory* with *tblSales-Inventory* and change the query's field ref-

erences. Open the form in Design view. Then, open the form's Properties sheet and click its Data tab. Select the Record Source property and click its Build button to open the query behind the form.

3. Select the Query, Show Table menu command, then double-click *tblSales*. Click the Show Table dialog box Close button. Click anywhere in the *tblSales-Order* object to select it and press the Delete key.

4. Click and drag InvoiceNumber from *tblSales* to the first Field cell in the QBE grid. The existing columns will move to the right when you release the mouse button. Set the InvoiceNumber field's Sort order to *Ascending*

5. Click and drag InvoiceDate, CustomerNumber, and SalesOrderNumber from *tblSales* to the second, third, and fourth Field cells in the QBE grid, respectively. As in the previous step, the existing columns will move to the right when you release the mouse button.

6. Close the Query Builder window and save your changes.

7. You have changed the underlying query of the form, so you must change the Control Source properties of the text box controls that are bound to fields that you have removed from the query. Either by typing directly in the text box controls on the form or by editing the Control Source properties in each control's Properties sheet, change SalesOrderNumber to *InvoiceNumber*, SalesOrderDate to *InvoiceDate*, and CustomerPONumber to *SalesOrderNumber*

8. Change the Caption properties of the accompanying labels for these controls to match. You may wish to refer to Figure 6.22 as a guide. You should change the Name properties (under the Other tab) for both the text box and label controls, too.

9. Click the *fsubSalesOrder* Subform/Subreport object at the bottom of the form and click the Data tab on the Properties sheet. Change the Source object to *fsubSales*. Change both the Link Child Fields and the Link Master Fields properties to *InvoiceNumber*. You should also change the Subform/Subreport object's Name property to *InvoiceNumber*

You can save your modified *frmSales* form by clicking File, Save. The completed form, showing *fsubSales* nested within *frmSales*, appears in Figure 6.22 in Form view.

## The Invoice Report

The Sales Entry form you just created facilitates the entry of information about sales into the Pipefitters Supply Company revenue cycle accounting system. When Pipefitters ships a customer order, they will want to send an invoice. Although more firms are using electronic data interchange every day, many customers still want an invoice printed on paper. The Access *report* objects help you provide nicely formatted printed output. In this section, you will create a printed invoice. The first step in generating an invoice report is to build a query that will gather the information we have stored about the sales transaction in *tblSales*, *tblCustomer*, *tblInventory*, and *tblSales-Inventory*. In Exercise 6.33, you will build just such an invoice query.

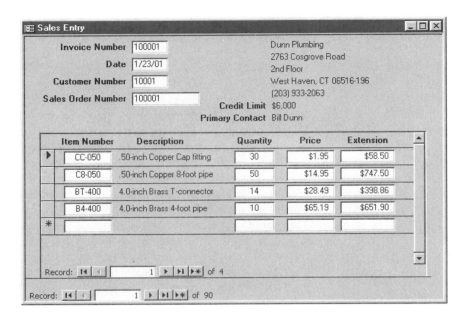

**Figure 6.22**   The completed Sales Entry form in Form view.

EXERCISE 6.33: BUILDING AN INVOICE QUERY

1. In the Database window, click the Queries object, click the New button to open the New Query dialog box, then double-click Simple Query Wizard.
2. Select Table: *tblSales* in the Tables/Queries combo box and click the >> button to move all of that table's fields to the Selected Fields box.
3. Select Table: *tblCustomer* and use the > button to move the CustomerName, CustomerAddress1, CustomerAddress2, CustomerCity, CustomerState, and CustomerZipCode fields to the Selected Fields box.
4. Select Table: *tblSales-Inventory* and move the InventoryItemCode, SInvQuantity, and SInvPrice fields to the Selected Fields box.
5. Select Table: *tblInventory* and move the InventoryComposition field to the Selected Fields box.
6. Click the Next button to move to the next Query Wizard dialog box, then click the Next button in that dialog box to accept the Detail query default.
7. Name the query *qryInvoice*, click the option button to select *Modify the query design*, and click the Finish button. The new query will open in Design view.
8. Set the QBE grid Sort cells for InvoiceNumber and InventoryItemCode to *Ascending*
9. Scroll to the first open column in the QBE grid, select the Field cell, press Shift+F2 to open the Zoom box, type *Description: [InventoryDiameter] & " " & [InventoryComposition] & " " & [InventoryType]* and then click OK.

*Try it*

Note that this is the same expression we used in *fsubSalesOrder* and *fsubSales*. If you prefer, you can copy and paste this expression from one of those forms' queries instead of typing it again. The next two expressions are the same as those we used in *frmSalesOrder* and *frmSales*, so you can copy and paste instead of typing them, too.

10. In the next QBE grid Field cell, open the Zoom box and type *Extension: [SInvPrice]\*[SInvQuantity]* and click OK.
11. In the next QBE grid Field cell, open the Zoom box and type *CustomerAddress3: [CustomerCity] & ", " & [CustomerState] & " " & [CustomerZipCode]* and then click OK.

You can click the Run toolbar button to run the query. Examine the dynaset it produces to check whether you entered the expressions correctly. Close the Query Builder window and save your changes to *qryInvoice*. Next, you will use this query as the basis for the Invoice report.

EXERCISE 6.34: CREATING AN INVOICE REPORT

1. In the Database window, click the Reports tab, then click the New button. In the New Report dialog box, select Report Wizard and choose *qryInvoice* in the combo box. Click the OK button to proceed.
2. Click the >> button to move all of the query's fields from the Available Fields box to the Selected Fields box. Click the Next button to continue.
3. In the next dialog box, click the Next button to accept the default view, by *tblSales*.
4. Click the Next button since you do not need to specify any additional grouping levels for this report.
5. Enter *InventoryItemCode* in the first sorting box, then click the Summary Options button. Click the check box to Sum the Extension field, click OK to return to the previous dialog box, then click the Next button.
6. The next dialog box gives you a choice of Layout options. We used Align Left 1, but you can choose any of the options that you prefer for the look of the printed invoice. Click the Next button to open the styles dialog box. Again, you may choose any one that you prefer. Our choice was the Formal style. Click the Next button to continue.
7. Type *rptInvoice* in the title box and click the option button to select Modify the report's design. Click the Finish button to generate the report.

The report generated by the Report Wizard is fairly close to being a usable document. We have made a number of adjustments to the report's appearance. One page of the finished Invoice report appears in Figure 6.23.

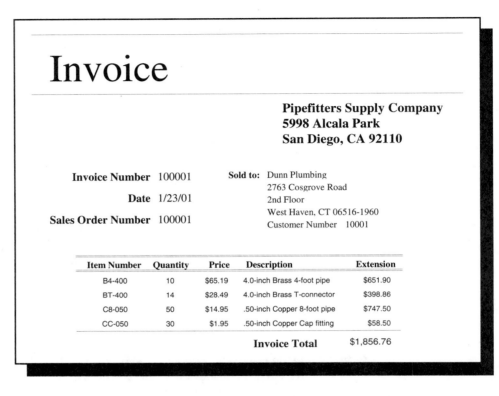

**Figure 6.23**   A printout from *rptInvoice*, the Invoice report.

The design elements appear in the partial image of *rptInvoice* in Report Design view shown in Figure 6.24. We suggest several changes to *rptInvoice* in the next exercise, but we encourage you to use Figure 6.23, Figure 6.24, and your own judgment to create an attractive and useful Invoice report for Pipefitters Supply Company.

EXERCISE 6.35: IMPROVING THE INVOICE REPORT

1. Select of the controls in the InvoiceNumber Header section, then press the Ctrl-down arrow repeatedly to move the controls down and expand the open space at the top of the Header.
2. Move the label control that includes the text *rptInvoice* and the line object from the Report Header section to the InvoiceNumber Header section.

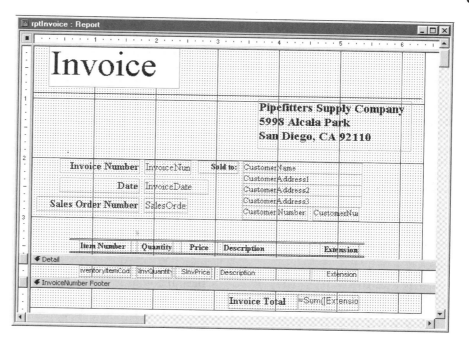

**Figure 6.24**   The bottom portion of *rptInvoice* in Report Design view.

3. Select View, Report Header/Footer from the menu to delete these sections. Click the Yes button to confirm this deletion. Delete the Page Header/Footer using the same procedure.
4. To print one invoice per page, click the InvoiceNumber Footer and click the Properties toolbar button to open its Properties sheet. Click the Format tab and set its Force New Page property to After Section.
5. Click the Toolbox button to open the toolbox. You can use the Label tool to create a label control for Pipefitters Supply Company's name and address.

### Try it

When you are typing text in a label control you will find that the Enter key does not create a carriage return, it just accepts the changes you have made to the control. To place a carriage return in a label control, you must type either Shift+Enter or Ctrl+Enter.

Your Companion CD includes two Invoice report objects in the *Ch06.mdb* file, *rptInvoice1*, which is the report that the Wizard generated, and *rptInvoice2*, which is the report shown in Figures 6.23 and 6.24. These invoices are only two of many possible designs. Different businesses and other organizations use other document designs and include slightly different information items on their invoices. Note that, with a few minor modifications, you could modify this Invoice report for use as a shipping document.

## RECORDING CASH RECEIVED FROM CUSTOMERS

The ultimate objective of the revenue cycle is, of course, to receive customers' payments for the goods or services they have purchased. Firms need to record the amount and date of each incoming customer payment. In this section, you will learn how to construct a simple cash receipts table that tracks cash receipts by customer. A more elaborate system would track cash receipts by invoice number and permit an exact matching of customer payments to specific invoices. Since customers sometimes do not pay by invoice, this matching process can be difficult to design and execute. You can satisfy many business information needs with the basic customer payment tracking procedure described in this section.

## The Cash Receipts Table

The Cash Receipts table includes information about payments received from customers. A tempting candidate for this table's primary key is the preprinted check number that appears on checks that Pipefitters receives from its customers. Unfortunately, this customer check number is not a good primary key because you cannot be certain that the number is unique. Pipefitters could easily receive two different checks from two different customers that have identical preprinted check numbers. Most firms use a *remittance advice number* as the primary key for their Cash Receipts tables. You have probably seen remittance advices, but you may not have known what they were called. For example, the portion of a credit card statement that you tear off and return with your payment is a remittance advice. Businesses usually prepare remittance advices for, or assign remittance advice numbers to, every check they receive.

In addition to the remittance advice number primary key, you will want to include fields for the date that the check was received, the check number, the amount of the check, and the customer number. CustomerNumber will be the foreign key that will link the Cash Receipts table to the Customer table. In this exercise you will build a Cash Receipts table for Pipefitters.

EXERCISE 6.36: BUILDING A CASH RECEIPTS TABLE

1. Click the Tables object in the Database window, then click the New button. Double-click Design View in the New Table dialog box.
2. Enter *RemittanceAdviceNumber* as the first Field Name. Click the Primary Key toolbar button to make this field the table's primary key. Leave the Data Type set to Text, but set the Field Size property to *6*
3. Set the Input Mask property to *000000* and the Caption property to *RA #*
4. Enter *CashReceiptDate* as the next Field Name. Set its Data Type to *Date/Time*. Set its Input Mask property to *99/99/99* and its Caption property to *Date*

5. The next field in the Cash Receipts table will store the customer check number. Although most firms' checks use only numeric characters in their check numbers, some may include other characters. Therefore, this field must allow any combination of numbers, letters, and symbols that might appear on a customer check. Since you cannot anticipate the characteristics of this field, you cannot build any input mask or validation rule data input controls for this field into the Cash Receipts table. Enter *CustomerCheckNumber* as the next Field Name, leave its Data Type set to Text, set its Field Size property to *15*, and set its Caption property to *Customer Check #*

6. To create the foreign key field, enter *CustomerNumber* as the next Field Name with a *Text* Data Type, a Field Size of *5*, and an Input Mask property of *00000*. Set its Caption property to *Customer Number* and its Required property to *Yes*

7. Enter *CashReceiptAmount* as the last Field Name, set its Data Type to *Currency*, its Decimal Places property to *2*, and its Caption property to *Amount*

8. Save the table you have created by selecting File, Save As from the menu and typing *tblCashReceipts* as the table's new name. Click OK and close the Design View window.

Your Companion CD includes *tblCashReceipts* in the *Ch06.mdb* database. Figure 6.25 shows the Cash Receipts table in Datasheet view. Note that the column titles show the text you entered in the Caption properties for each field.

| RA # | Date | Customer Check # | Customer Number | Amount |
|------|------|-----------------|-----------------|--------|
| 100001 | 1/28/01 | 10207 | 10010 | $2,000.00 |
| 100002 | 1/28/01 | 33256 | 10005 | $631.20 |
| 100003 | 1/28/01 | 4927 | 10001 | $1,856.76 |
| 100004 | 1/29/01 | 108755 | 10007 | $781.00 |
| 100005 | 1/30/01 | 10256 | 10010 | $122.50 |
| 100006 | 1/30/01 | 4952 | 10001 | $84.75 |
| 100007 | 1/30/01 | 652 | 10006 | $4,519.80 |
| 100008 | 1/31/01 | 33402 | 10005 | $825.76 |
| 100009 | 2/ 1/01 | 5751 | 10003 | $2,000.00 |
| 100010 | 2/ 2/01 | 1041 | 10004 | $1,417.40 |
| 100011 | 2/ 4/01 | 4970 | 10001 | $641.55 |
| 100012 | 2/ 4/01 | 20122 | 10002 | $739.40 |
| 100013 | 2/ 5/01 | 273255 | 10024 | $1,116.25 |
| 100014 | 2/ 7/01 | 1097 | 10004 | $24.90 |
| 100015 | 2/ 7/01 | 267 | 10050 | $736.07 |
| 100016 | 2/10/01 | 4462 | 10029 | $825.05 |
| 100017 | 2/10/01 | 309152 | 10035 | $708.75 |
| 100018 | 2/12/01 | 991 | 10016 | $485.70 |
| 100019 | 2/13/01 | 8679 | 10048 | $303.90 |

Record: 1 of 80

**Figure 6.25** The Cash Receipts table in Datasheet view.

The final step in creating *tblCashReceipts* is to establish a referential integrity link to *tblCustomer* on the foreign key, CustomerNumber. In the next exercise, you add the Cash Receipts table to the Relationships window and connect it to the Customer table.

EXERCISE 6.37: LINKING THE CASH
RECEIPTS TABLE TO THE CUSTOMER TABLE

1. Click the Relationships toolbar button to open the Relationships window. Click the Show Table toolbar button, select *tblCashReceipts*, click the Add button, then click the Close button.
2. Click and drag CustomerNumber from *tblCustomer* to CustomerNumber in *tblCashReceipts*.
3. Click the Enforce Referential Integrity check box, then click the Create button.
4. Close the Relationships window and save your changes.

The Cash Receipts table, linked to *tblCustomer* on CustomerNumber, is included in the Relationships window that appears in Figure 6.26. The Cash Receipts table is the last table we will include in this chapter's revenue cycle accounting system. Therefore, Figure 6.26 shows a complete picture of the relationships among all revenue cycle tables.

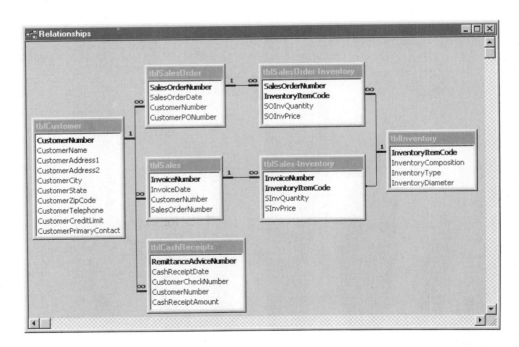

**Figure 6.26**  Relationships among the revenue cycle tables.

You may want to compare the tables and relationships that appear in Figure 6.26 with the data model in Figure 6.1. You can see by comparing these two figures how the data model is the backbone of database design.

## The Cash Receipts Entry Form

The construction of the Cash Receipts form is simple and straightforward. The form works with only one table, *tblCashReceipts*, and that table has few fields. Exercise 6.38 shows you how to create the Cash Receipts form, *frmCashReceipts*.

### EXERCISE 6.38: BUILDING A CASH RECEIPTS FORM

1. Click the Forms object in the Database window and click the New button. In the New Form dialog box, select Form Wizard and choose *tblCashReceipts* in the combo box. Click OK to proceed.
2. Click the >> button to move all of the *tblCashReceipts* fields to the Selected Fields box, then click the Next button.
3. Click the Tabular option button, then click the Next button.
4. In the next dialog box, select the Standard style, then click the Next button.
5. Enter the form name, *frmCashReceipts*, click the *Modify the form's design* option button, then click the Finish button to have the Form Wizard generate the form.
6. With the form in Design view, you can make a few minor adjustments to the form's appearance, such as bolding the titles, increasing the horizontal spacing between the fields, changing the alignment properties of the text box and label controls, typing *Cash Receipts Entry Form* in the form's Caption property, and changing the form's Scroll Bar property to Vertical Only.

The completed *frmCashReceipts* in Form view appears in Figure 6.27. You can use this figure as a guide to fine-tuning your form. Close the form and save your changes.

## Cash Receipts Reports

Standard reporting forms for cash receipts do not exist, so you may create your own report designs to meet the needs of your or your clients' specific businesses. Some firms may want reports of cash receipts by customer, by date, or by geographic region. Although aggregate cash receipts information is important, the details are seldom as interesting as, for example, details of sales transactions.

One useful cash receipts report is the Daily Cash report that you can create by following the steps in the next exercise. Many businesses follow the internal control procedure of depositing all cash receipts intact each day. The Daily Cash report provides the check figures for the bank deposit.

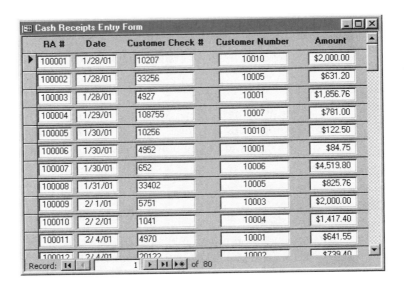

**Figure 6.27** Completed *frmCashReceipts* in Form view.

## EXERCISE 6.39: CREATING A DAILY CASH REPORT

1. In the Database window, click the Reports object and then click the New button. In the New Report dialog box that appears, select Report Wizard and enter *tblCashReceipts* in the combo box. Click the OK button to continue.
2. Click the >> button to move all of the *tblCashReceipts* fields to the Selected Fields box. Click the Next button to continue.
3. Click CashReceiptDate in the list of fields on the left side of the dialog box, then click the > button. The Wizard will insert a second grouping level, titled *CashReceiptDate by Month*, in the report template. Click the up-arrow button above the word *Priority* to move the new grouping to the top of the template.
4. Click CustomerNumber in the report template window, then click the < button to remove CustomerNumber as a grouping level.
5. Click the Grouping Options button. Enter *Day* in the Grouping intervals combo box and click the OK button. The Wizard changes the grouping level *CashReceiptDate by Month* to *CashReceiptDate by Day*. Click the Next button to continue.
6. Enter *CustomerNumber* in the first sort order box, then click the Summary Options button. Click the Sum check box for the CashReceiptAmount field, click the OK button, then click the Next button to continue.
7. Select the Align Left 1 Layout and click the Next button.
8. Select the Corporate style and click the Next button.
9. Enter a report title of *Pipefitters Supply Company Daily Cash Report*, click the option button to *Modify the report's design*, then click the Finish button.

10. Using Figure 6.28 as a guide, make any appearance modifications you would like to see on the form. Select Save As from the menu, enter *rptDailyCash* as its name, then click the OK button. Close the report window.

We have included two Daily Cash report objects on your Companion CD. The *rptDailyCash1* object is the report that the Wizard generated; the *rptDailyCash2* object includes a few modifications to make the report easier to read. We used *rptDailyCash2* to print the report page shown in Figure 6.28.

## OTHER REVENUE CYCLE COMPONENTS

In this chapter, you have created sales order reports, invoice reports, and cash receipts reports. Our purpose was to demonstrate how to generate useful reports from revenue cycle accounting data tables. This section discusses some other revenue cycle reports that you might want to create or adapt to specific business needs.

## Customer Statements

Many firms send their customers a statement of account activity at the end of each month. The statement shows a beginning balance, lists each sale and cash receipt, and calculates an ending balance. This statement lets customers review their purchases and payments regularly. It also lets customers reconcile their accounts payable records with the statement. As we noted earlier in the chapter, many firms now pay from invoices rather than from monthly statements.

Systems designers use two general approaches for combining sales and cash receipts tables in one monthly statement report. One approach requires the use of a common field, such as a sequential transaction number. You can easily modify the *tblSales* and *tblCashReceipts* tables we created in this chapter to include a transaction number field for this purpose. This will, however, de-normalize both tables. A second approach uses queries to summarize and place sales and cash receipts data into an accounts receivable table that has no primary key. This also violates the normalization rules; however, it does so in an aggregate table, rather than the tables that store the originally entered transaction data.

## Sales Analysis

Database accounting information systems include much information that is useful to nonaccountants. Traditional accounting records contained only the date and dollar amount of each sale and cash receipt. A database accounting system contains much more information about each sale and cash receipt. The sales, sales order, inventory, and customer tables we described in this chapter can be combined in many ways to provide useful information to the marketing and strategic management functions.

# *Pipefitters Supply Company Daily Cash Report*

*For Internal Use Only*

*Cash Receipts for:* Sunday, January 28, 2001

| *Customer Number* | *RA #* | *Date* | *Customer Check #* | *Amount* |
|---|---|---|---|---|
| 10001 | 00003 | 1/28/01 | 4927 | $1,856.76 |
| 10005 | 00002 | 1/28/01 | 33256 | $631.20 |
| 10010 | 00001 | 1/28/01 | 10207 | $2,000.00 |
| | | | **Total** | *$4,487.96* |

*Cash Receipts for:* Monday, January 29, 2001

| *Customer Number* | *RA #* | *Date* | *Customer Check #* | *Amount* |
|---|---|---|---|---|
| 10007 | 00004 | 1/29/01 | 108755 | $781.00 |
| | | | **Total** | *$781.00* |

*Cash Receipts for:* Tuesday, January 30, 2001

| *Customer Number* | *RA #* | *Date* | *Customer Check #* | *Amount* |
|---|---|---|---|---|
| 10001 | 00006 | 1/30/01 | 4952 | $84.75 |
| 10006 | 00007 | 1/30/01 | 652 | $4,519.80 |
| 10010 | 00005 | 1/30/01 | 10256 | $122.50 |
| | | | **Total** | *$4,727.05* |

*Cash Receipts for:* Wednesday, January 31, 2001

| *Customer Number* | *RA #* | *Date* | *Customer Check #* | *Amount* |
|---|---|---|---|---|
| 10005 | 00008 | 1/31/01 | 33402 | $825.76 |
| | | | **Total** | *$825.76* |

*Cash Receipts for:* Thursday, February 01, 2001

| *Customer Number* | *RA #* | *Date* | *Customer Check #* | *Amount* |
|---|---|---|---|---|
| 10003 | 00009 | 2/ 1/01 | 5751 | $2,000.00 |
| | | | **Total** | *$2,000.00* |

**Figure 6.28**   First page of the Daily Cash report.

For example, you could combine our Customer, Sales, and Inventory tables to generate reports that show sales by customer, inventory item code, customer city, time period, or any combination of these. If Pipefitters' sales manager wanted to know what dollar amount of brass fittings they sold in North Dakota during last December, you could easily create a query that would provide the answer.

## Sales and Accounts Receivable on the Financial Statements

The traditional function of accounting systems has been to capture and store the information needed to prepare financial statements in accordance with GAAP. You learned a database approach to developing a revenue cycle accounting system that provides much more than the highly aggregated information contained in financial statements.

The database approach also provides basic debit-and-credit accounting information. For example, to obtain the general ledger entry credit to Sales and debit to Accounts Receivable, you can simply add a control to *rptInvoice* that sums the sales totals in its Report Footer. You can create subsidiary ledger debits and credits by adding a CustomerNumber grouping level to *rptInvoice* and including a control that sums the sales totals in the CustomerNumber Footer.

You can follow similar procedures to obtain the general ledger debit to Cash and credit to Accounts Receivable using the numbers generated by the *rptCashReceipts* report we illustrated earlier in this chapter.

## SUMMARY

In this chapter you learned how to construct the tables, forms, queries, and reports commonly used in the revenue cycle of accounting information systems. Tables are the basic building blocks of the revenue cycle. Forms make data entry, editing, and deletion easier. Queries can extract data from several tables at once to help answer complex questions about revenue cycle activities. Reports include invoices and shipping documents; they also may contain summaries of revenue cycle activities for internal management use.

The revenue cycle begins with customer records and finished goods inventory records. As sales orders arrive, we must record information about which customers want to buy which inventory items. When goods are shipped to customers, we create invoices and shipping documents. We record customer payments when we receive them. Finally, we summarize all of these activities and create reports and journal entries that allow the preparation of financial statements.

# QUESTIONS AND PROBLEMS FOR REVIEW

## MULTIPLE-CHOICE QUESTIONS

1. The revenue cycle includes all of the following except
   a. keeping customer information current.
   b. recording the cost of merchandise purchased.
   c. recording payments received from customers.
   d. summarizing sales information.

2. The revenue cycle uses an inventory table to provide
   a. descriptions of products sold.
   b. purchase cost of products sold.
   c. names of vendors that supplied the products sold.
   d. quantity of products sold.
3. The CustomerNumber field in *tblCustomer* is a
   a. composite primary key.
   b. foreign key.
   c. primary key.
   d. relationship key.
4. A good policy would be to delete a record in a customer table only when that customer
   a. files for bankruptcy court protection from creditors.
   b. moves its offices out of the country permanently.
   c. has not made a purchase within the past twelve months.
   d. is no longer related to any other database tables.
5. Fields in data entry forms that only display data should have their Locked and Tab Stop properties set as
   a. Locked = Yes, Tab Stop = Yes.
   b. Locked = Yes, Tab Stop = No.
   c. Locked = No, Tab Stop = Yes.
   d. Locked = No, Tab Stop = No.
6. A mnemonic inventory item coding scheme
   a. helps experienced employees identify inventory quickly.
   b. helps data entry clerks enter inventory codes quickly.
   c. is required by generally accepted accounting principles.
   d. is easier to design than a sequential number coding scheme.
7. A sales order-inventory table would most likely be
   a. an entity table.
   b. a referential integrity table.
   c. a query table.
   d. a relationship table.
8. The link from *tblSales-Inventory* to *tblInventory* on the InventoryItemCode field is a
   a. one-to-one relationship.
   b. one-to-many relationship.
   c. many-to-one relationship.
   d. many-to-many relationship.
9. A slightly modified copy of an invoice report can often serve as a
   a. sales order.
   b. shipping document.
   c. customer record.
   d. cash receipts record.

10. A good primary key for a cash receipts table would be the
    a. customer check number.
    b. invoice number.
    c. cash receipt number.
    d. remittance advice number.

## DISCUSSION QUESTIONS

1. The examples in this chapter assumed that Pipefitters Supply Company was doing business only in the United States. What changes would you make if Pipefitters had many customers from other countries?
2. Service businesses, such as real estate agents, law firms, and accounting firms, do not have inventory. What table would a service business have instead of *tblInventory*?
3. Restaurants do not usually record customers' names and addresses or send out invoices. What tables, forms, queries, and reports might you use in the accounting information system for a restaurant's revenue cycle?
4. How would you decide whether to enforce referential integrity for a foreign key link?
5. Describe how you might create a customer statement that showed sales and cash receipts from customers on one report.

## PROBLEMS

1. Change *tblCustomer* so that the CustomerState field will accept only legal state abbreviations. *Hint:* You should consider adding another table to the revenue cycle system to accomplish this task.
2. Many firms keep track of which salespersons handle particular sales. Modify the revenue cycle system in this chapter to include a salesperson entity.
3. Create a report that shows sales by customer with sales by product grouped under each customer.
4. Modify the revenue cycle system presented in this chapter to include a ship to address on the invoice.
5. Create a report that shows the month-end general ledger entries for sales and cash receipts.

# 7 PURCHASE CYCLE

## OBJECTIVES

Firms' purchase cycle activities include placing orders with vendors, recording purchases, recording payments made to vendors, and maintaining records of these activities. In this chapter, you will learn how to design Microsoft Access tables, queries, forms, and reports that can help you:

- Create and maintain vendor records.
- Create and maintain materials inventory records.
- Print purchase orders.
- Summarize and report purchase order information.
- Record the receipt of ordered materials.
- Print checks and record disbursements to vendors.
- Summarize purchases and accounts payable information.

## INTRODUCTION

This chapter shows how to use Microsoft Access to build the purchase cycle components of accounting information systems. In this book, we define the purchase cycle to include acquisition of goods and services and payment for those goods and services. We cover payroll accounting systems, which accountants sometimes consider to be part of the purchase cycle, in Chapter 8. Payroll record-keeping calculations and record keeping can be quite complex, thus our separate treatment of them.

In manufacturing firms, the main focus of the purchase cycle is ordering, receiving, and paying for materials—including both direct and indirect materials. In a merchandising firm, the main focus of the purchase cycle is the acquisition of goods for resale. Since materials acquisition is not a major concern for service firms, their purchase cycle is somewhat less important to them than it is to manufacturing and merchandising firms. However, all businesses—even service firms—must acquire goods and services that support their selling and administrative functions. This acquisition activity takes place within the purchase cycle. Therefore, all three types of firms need accounting systems that can record purchase cycle activities.

In a manufacturing firm, the purchase cycle process begins when one of the production departments prepares a materials requisition document. In some manufacturing systems, this document is automatically generated by the computer when materials inventory falls below a predetermined reorder point. For example, in a materials requirement planning (MRP) system, the computer can use the master schedule to generate timely materials requisitions without human intervention. In a just-in-time (JIT) production control system, materials requisitions are generated frequently—often daily or weekly. The materials requisition document goes to the purchasing department and is their authorization to prepare a purchase order. In many automated MRP and JIT systems, the computer generates the purchase order directly.

Many merchandising firms, particularly retailers, find that the demand for their goods is highly unpredictable. Manufacturers often have the luxury of planning production; retailers must react quickly to shifts in consumer demand. Ability to accommodate this rapidly fluctuating demand is often the difference between success and failure for a retailer. Therefore, retail merchandisers delegate purchasing decisions to highly skilled buyers who have authority, within a predetermined dollar budget, for purchasing a particular category of merchandise. These buyers use daily sales reports, inventory reports, market research, and their intuitions to make their inventory purchase decisions. To record their purchase decisions, buyers create either purchase requisition documents or purchase orders.

All three types of firms must acquire and pay for goods and services that fall into the category that accountants call selling and administrative expenses. For example, merchandising, manufacturing, and service firms all purchase office supplies, pay for advertising, and reimburse employees for travel expenses. An office manager, department head, or other responsible manager creates the purchase requisition document that authorizes purchase of and payment for such items.

In all three types of firms, the purchasing department uses materials or purchase requisitions as authorization to place purchase orders. Purchasing agents try to find the best prices, terms, and delivery dates offered by approved vendors. In some industries the purchasing agent is a skilled negotiator with considerable latitude in making decisions. Whether it is the result of spirited deal making or is generated automatically, the purchase order is sent to the vendor by the purchasing department. In the past, purchase orders were always paper forms; however, many firms now use electronic data interchange (EDI) to send purchase orders to vendors.

The purchasing department sends a copy of the purchase order, with quantities omitted, to the receiving department or makes similar information available electronically. When shipments of ordered goods arrive, the receiving department completes a receiving report. Accounting must compare the receiving report, the purchase order, and the vendor's invoice. If the details on all these documents match, accounting prepares a check for the amount due. The check is then forwarded to the treasurer with supporting documentation. This documentation typically includes the purchase order, the receiving report, and the vendor's invoice. The package of supporting documents is often called a voucher. The treasurer signs the check, marks or mutilates the voucher and the supporting documents so they cannot be used to authorize a second payment for the same purchase, and sends the check to the vendor.

The purchase cycle system must generate summary reports of purchase and cash disbursement activities for management's use. The system should also generate information that financial accountants can use instead of their traditional double-entry bookkeeping debits and credits to create ledgers, journals, and financial statements.

## ELECTRIC CONTROLS COMPANY PURCHASE CYCLE INFORMATION

In this chapter, you will learn how to build the components of a purchase cycle system for Electric Controls Company, a firm that manufactures custom electrical control panels for industrial customers. You can think of electrical control panels as larger and more complex versions of the metal box that contains the circuit breakers at your house or apartment. Electric Controls buys components such as switches, circuit breakers, and relays to assemble these control panels from a number of different suppliers.

Electric Controls Company contacts vendors to place purchase orders. Each purchase order can include many inventory items. When a shipment arrives at the receiving dock, a receiving clerk counts the inventory items and records which items were received and their quantities as an inventory receipt. The inventory receipt record also includes a notation of the purchaser order on which the inventory items were ordered. Periodically, the accounting department pays for inventory received by writing a check to the vendor. Although Electric Controls Company usually pays for all inventory receipts at the end of each month, they sometimes will pay only part of a large inventory receipt that occurs near the end of the month and pay the balance when it becomes due in the next month, 30 days after the inventory receipt.

The data model for the Electric Controls Company includes five entities: vendor, purchase order, inventory receipt, inventory, and cash disbursement. Each vendor can have many purchase orders. A purchase order can have many inventory items. Vendors can ship inventory items that appear on one purchase order in many shipments, so Electric Controls must be able to record many inventory receipts for a single purchase order. Sometimes vendors will ship inventory from several purchase orders together, but Electric Controls receiving clerks use a separate receiving report for each purchase order to record those inventory receipts. An inventory receipt usually has only one cash disbursement, but it may have more than one if it is large and occurs near month end. A cash disbursement can be in payment of many inventory receipts. The data model for Electric Controls Company's purchase cycle, showing these five entities and the one-to-many and many-to-many relationships among them, appears in Figure 7.1.

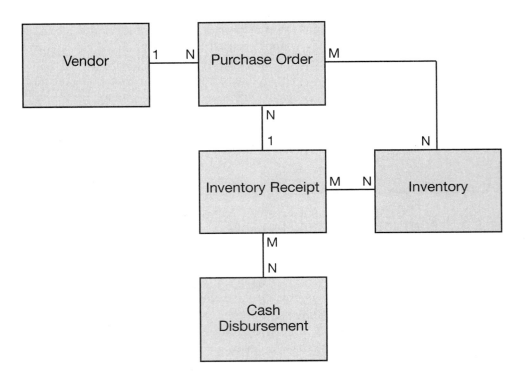

**Figure 7.1**   Electric Controls Company purchase cycle data model.

This chapter will show you how to build elements of the accounting system for Electric Controls' purchase cycle. The design will include five tables for the entities and three additional tables to model the many-to-many relationships. You will learn how to create forms to enter data efficiently, queries that extract information about purchase cycle activities, and reports that Electric Controls can use to print purchase orders, checks, and summary purchase cycle information.

**VENDOR INFORMATION**

Firms need easy and quick access to information about their vendors. Purchasing agents need vendor names, addresses, and telephone numbers. They also need to know for which inventory items a particular vendor has been approved. Vendor information appears on many business documents such as purchase orders and checks. To ensure that vendor information is consistent wherever it is used, firms keep all vendor information in one database table. Any document that needs vendor information obtains it from that one table. If, for example, a vendor moves to a new location, the vendor's address need be changed only once. In a relational database accounting information system, vendor information resides in a vendor table.

## The Vendor Table

The first purchase cycle table that you will build is the vendor table, which will provide a central location for storing all information about each vendor. This makes adding, deleting, or changing vendor information easy and efficient. Many firms also include information about potential vendors—firms they might buy from in the future—in their vendor tables.

Remember that examples of all the tables, forms, queries, and reports that we use in this chapter are included in the *Ch07.mdb* database on your Companion CD. When you are finished with Exercise 7.1, you may want to open this *Ch07.mdb* database and compare your work with the Vendor table we have provided in that database. You can import the vendor information from that table to save you the time of entering data into your Vendor table.

EXERCISE 7.1: CREATING A VENDOR TABLE AND ITS PRIMARY KEY FIELD

1. Start Microsoft Access, click Tables in the Objects bar, then click the New button in the Database window. Double-click Design View in the New Table dialog box.
2. Enter *VendorNumber* as the first Field Name, leave its Data Type set to Text, and click the Primary Key toolbar button to make this field the Vendor table's primary key.
3. Press F6 to switch to the Field Properties pane of the Table window, then set the Field Size property to *4* and the Caption property to *Vendor Number*. Using a sequential number scheme starting with 1001 lets the Electric Controls Company store information for up to 8,999 vendors in the table.
4. Set the Validation Rule property to the expression *Like "####"*. Set the Validation Text property to *Invalid entry. You must enter a Vendor Number of exactly four digits.*

Figure 7.2 shows the Table window displaying the VendorNumber field's property settings at this point.

The Validation Rule property setting will prevent a user from entering anything other than four digits in the VendorNumber field. The Validation Text property makes this internal control feature even more useful. It lets us customize the

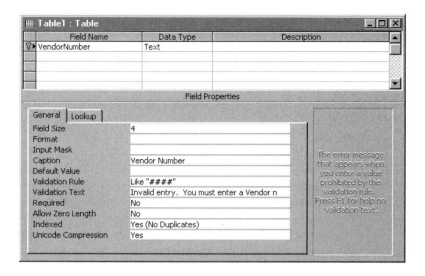

**Figure 7.2**   The VendorNumber field property settings.

error message that will appear in a dialog box whenever a user enters a VendorNumber value of anything other than four digits.

Recall that you can use either an Input Mask property setting or a Validation Rule property setting to control data input. Each method has its strengths and weaknesses. The Input Mask property operates on each character as it is entered, but issues only a standard error message. The Validation Rule property operates on the field as a whole, so it does not warn users of errors until they try to exist the field. A Validation Rule does, however, allow us to customize the error message.

### Try it

You can obtain more information about the Like operator and its syntax by selecting Help, Microsoft Access Help Topics from the menu, then clicking the Index tab and entering *like operator* as the search term. You can also learn more by entering *ValidationRule Property* or *ValidationText Property* in the Help Index window.

The next exercise provides steps you can follow to add fields for vendor address, telephone, and primary contact information. These fields will complete the Vendor table.

EXERCISE 7.2: COMPLETING THE VENDOR TABLE

1. Enter *VendorName* as the next Field Name. Leave its Data Type set to Text and set its Field Size property to *25*. Set the VendorName field's Caption property to

*Name*, since it will usually be obvious from the context on forms and reports that we are referring to a vendor's name.

2. Create *VendorAddress1* and *VendorAddress2* fields to store vendors' street addresses and office or suite numbers, respectively. Use your own judgment in setting the properties of these two fields.

3. Enter *VendorCity* as the next Field Name. Set its Data Type to Text, its Field Size property to *25*, and its Caption property to *City*

4. Enter *VendorState* as the next Field Name. Set its Data Type to Text, its Field Size property to *2*, and its Caption property to *State*

5. Set the Input Mask property for the VendorState field to *>LL*. The > symbol converts lowercase letters to uppercase letters and the LL placeholders in the expression limit entry to two letters. Any other value entered will generate an error message.

6. Enter *VendorZipCode* as the next Field Name. Leave its Data Type set to Text and set its Field Size property to *10*. This setting will accommodate the U.S. Postal Service five-plus-four Zip Code. Set the Caption property for VendorZipCode to *Zip Code*

7. Set an Input Mask property for VendorZipCode of *00000-9999;0;_*. This requires five digits, allows the extra four digits as an option, automatically inserts the hyphen as the user enters the data, stores the hyphen as part of the field contents, and uses the underscore character as a placeholder.

8. Enter *VendorTelephone* as the next Field Name. Leave its Data Type set to Text. Set its Field Size property to *14* (this will provide enough space to store the seven-digit number, a three-digit area code, the two parentheses, one hyphen, and a space) and its Caption property to *Telephone*. Click the Input Mask property Build button to have the Input Mask Wizard create an input mask of *!(999) 000-0000;0;_* for this field as shown in Figure 7.3. Access will require that you save the table before using the Wizard. You can save it with the name *tblVendor* when prompted. Be sure to choose the option of storing the literal characters (the hyphen and the parentheses) with the number.

9. Enter *VendorPrimaryContact* as the last Field Name for *tblVendor*. Leave its Data Type set to Text, and set its Field Size property to *25* and its Caption property to *Primary Contact*

This completes our *tblVendor* design. At this point, you can either close the Table window or open the table in Datasheet view to enter data. If you close the window, a dialog box will appear and ask you if you would like to save your changes. To open the table in Datasheet view, click the first toolbar icon. This icon toggles between Datasheet view and Design view for tables.

If you open the table in Datasheet view, you may notice that the title of each table column is the Caption property value you set. The *Ch07.mdb* database on your Companion CD includes a Vendor table, *tblVendor*, that includes sample data for Electric Controls Company. This table appears in Datasheet view in Figure 7.3.

**Figure 7.3**　The Vendor table, *tblVendor*, in Datasheet view.

Users could enter records directly into *tblVendor* in Datasheet view, but as you can see in Figure 7.3, the *tblVendor* fields do not all appear on the screen at once, even if you display the table in a very small font. Entering data would quickly become a tiresome task, requiring the user to scroll back and forth to view and enter the values in each record. You can make data entry and data viewing tasks much easier by creating a form for *tblVendor*.

## The Vendor Information Form

A form for the Vendor table will make entering, changing, and deleting customer information much easier than using *tblVendor* in Datasheet view. You can use the Access AutoForm tool to create a form and then modify that form to make it more useful. First, close all open windows except the Database window.

EXERCISE 7.3: CREATING A VENDOR
INFORMATION FORM WITH THE AUTOFORM TOOL

1. Click Tables in the Objects bar and select *tblVendor*.
2. Choose Insert, AutoForm from the menu.

The AutoForm tool's result appears in Figure 7.4. This compact form is quite usable. Note that AutoForm examined the fields and determined that a columnar presentation would be necessary for this form. This form is included as *frmVendor1* in the *Ch07.mdb* database on your Companion CD.

Although the AutoForm tool is a handy and quick way to produce a form, some of the form's shortcomings are easy to overcome. The next exercise guides you through some changes that will make the form easier to use. To begin the exercise, have the AutoForm-generated Vendor Information form open on the Access desktop.

**Figure 7.4**    The Vendor Information form created by the AutoForm tool.

EXERCISE 7.4: MODIFYING THE VENDOR INFORMATION FORM

1. Select the View, Design View command from the menu to open the form in Design view, then click and drag its lower-right corner to make it larger in both dimensions. Click and drag the right edge of the gray Detail section background to fill the now-available space.
2. Click and drag a marquee (selection rectangle) around the label controls (and only the label controls) to select them. Click the Bold button on the Formatting toolbar, then click the Align Right button on the Formatting toolbar. Select the Format, Align, Right menu command.
3. Change the text in the VendorAddress1 label control to *Address* and delete the text in the VendorAddress2 label control.
4. Because the form displays one record at a time, the record selector on the left side of the form serves no useful function. To delete it, choose Edit, Select Form from the menu, click the Properties toolbar button to open the form's property sheet, click the Format tab, and change the Record Selectors property to *No*. You can also change the Dividing Lines property to *No*
5. While the property sheet is open for the form, change its Caption property to *Vendor Information Form*
6. Reduce the size of the VendorState text box control, since it only needs to display two letters.

You can make other adjustments to the form's appearance using the completed form shown in Figure 7.5 as a guide. The form displays information for vendor number 1001, the Square P Corporation. To save the form while in Design view, select File, Save As from the menu and enter *frmVendor* in the Save As dialog box. Click OK to complete the save operation. This form is included as *frmVendor2* in the *Ch07.mdb* database on your Companion CD. Close your newly created form.

**Figure 7.5**   The improved Vendor Information form, *frmVendor*.

## Maintaining Vendor Records

You have now built a Vendor table to store vendor information and a Vendor Information form that makes it easy to enter and view data in that table. With the Vendor Information form, you can:

- Create records for new vendors.

- Delete records for vendors that have become inactive or have gone out of business.

- Update Vendor table records as vendors move, get new telephone numbers, and change other items of information you have stored in the Vendor table.

You will want to keep your file of vendor information current. A key advantage of the relational database model is that you add, delete, or change information in only one table. To use the Vendor Information form to add vendors to *tblVendor*, open *frmVendor*. As you enter values, notice how the Input Mask and Validation Rule properties you set in *tblVendor* limit the values you can enter in the VendorNumber, VendorState, VendorZipCode, and VendorTelephone controls. Try entering out-of-range values in these fields to test the internal controls you built into the table.

### Try it

Deleting records from the Vendor table is very easy. Open the Vendor Information form by clicking the Forms tab in the Database window and double-clicking *frmVendor*. To delete a record, move to that record using the navigation buttons at the bottom of the form, then choose Edit, Delete Record from the menu. Microsoft Access gives you a warning message that asks you to confirm the deletion. This deletion is not reversible. You can delete individual fields in a record using the

Delete key in Form view. Individual field deletions are reversible by selecting Edit, Undo delete *before* you move to another field. After you move to another field, you can reverse field deletions in the current record by selecting Edit, Undo Current Field/Record. You can also press Esc repeatedly to reverse deletions.

Be careful when deleting records in accounting databases. Data in one accounting table is usually related to data in other tables. For example, if you examine a record in a purchase order table, it will contain a vendor number. The only place that vendor's name and address is stored is in the related vendor table. If someone deletes that vendor's record in the vendor table, you may never be able to identify the vendor.

Keeping existing vendor records current to reflect address changes, new telephone numbers, and other changes is straightforward. Use the navigation buttons at the bottom of the form to move to the vendor record that you want to change. You can move through the individual fields of the displayed record by using the Enter key or the Tab key. The Shift+Tab key moves backward through the record. The up and down arrow keys also move the cursor through the form. Any changes you make to field contents will be limited by the Input Mask and Validation Rule property settings for *tblVendor*.

## MATERIALS INVENTORY

In Chapter 6 you learned how to track finished goods inventory in the revenue cycle. In this section, you will learn how to build tables and forms that can help you track materials inventories—both the goods that manufacturing firms purchase for resale and the raw materials that manufacturing firms purchase and then convert into finished goods. Firms use materials inventory records to provide inventory descriptions on purchase orders, receiving reports, and other documents. To ensure that materials inventory information is consistent wherever it is used, firms keep all materials inventory information in one database table. Any document, report, or transaction that needs inventory information obtains it from that table.

## The Materials Inventory Table

The purchase cycle requires a materials inventory table that includes at least two fields. The first field must contain the primary key, a number or code that uniquely identifies the inventory item. This primary key field might contain an item number, item code, part number, or catalog number. In some industries, these inventory item identifiers are standardized; for example, some firms use UPC (universal product code) or SKU (stock-keeping unit) numbers as the primary keys in their materials inventory tables. The second field should contain a description of each inventory item. The description may include information about an item's size, weight, shape, color, hardness, or other qualities. A firm may decide to store these inventory item attributes in separate fields.

Electric Controls Company has decided to use a two-field description scheme in its materials inventory table. Electric Controls classifies the parts it uses to build control panels into six categories: circuit breakers, connectors, relays, sheet metal, switches, and wire.

Few firms can store inventory purchase prices in the materials inventory table—that would require the firm to know, in advance, exactly what price it would pay for each item. Thus, Electric Controls Company does not store the prices in its materials inventory table. Each vendor is likely to have its own inventory part number. Since vendors might change their part numbers from time to time, Electric Controls stores the vendor part number for each item as they order it instead of in the materials inventory table.

Electric Controls Company's materials inventory description will include two fields. One field will identify an item's category; the second field will store details about the particular item. The purchasing department personnel who will be using materials inventory information have ready access to Electric Controls Company's computer system. This reduces the benefit of using a mnemonic coding scheme such as the one you created for Pipefitters Supply in Chapter 6. Therefore, you can use a sequential number scheme for the primary key field in the Materials Inventory table for Electric Controls. A three-digit field will allow Electric Controls to maintain records on as many as 899 different materials inventory items. In Exercise 7.5 you will build this table.

EXERCISE 7.5: BUILDING A MATERIALS INVENTORY TABLE

1. In the Database window, click the Tables tab, click the New button, and then double-click Design View in the New Table dialog box.
2. Enter *MaterialsInventoryStockNumber* as the first Field Name and click the Primary Key toolbar button. Leave its Data Type set to Text. Set its Field Size property to *3*, its Input Mask property to *000*, and its Caption property to *Stock Number*
3. Enter a Field Name of *MaterialsInventoryCategory* for the first description field. Leave its Data Type set to Text. Set its Field Size property to *16* to match the number of characters in the longest inventory category name.
4. Set its Input Mask property to *>L<CCCCCCCCCCCCCCC*. This setting will automatically capitalize the first letter entered in the field, thus making data entry easier, and will ensure that any other characters entered are either lowercase letters or spaces.
5. Set the Caption property to *Category*
6. Enter *MaterialsInventoryDescription* as the third Field Name. Leave its Data Type set to Text. Set its Field Size property to *25* and its Caption property to *Description*
7. Save the table, entering *tblMaterialsInventory* in the Save As dialog box. Click OK and then close the table.

Figure 7.6 shows *tblMaterialsInventory* in Datasheet view displaying the data for Electric Controls Company. These data are included in *tblMaterialsInventory* in the *Ch07.mdb* database on your Companion CD.

| Stock Number | Category | Description |
|---|---|---|
| 101 | Sheet metal | 1/8" Steel 4x4 sheet |
| 102 | Switch | DPDT 240v 100a |
| 103 | Wire | 500' Copper #22AWG |
| 104 | Sheet metal | 1/4" Steel 4x4 sheet |
| 105 | Switch | SPDT 240v 100a |
| 106 | Relay | SPDT 120v 40a Silver |
| 107 | Circuit breaker | 240v 40a |
| 108 | Relay | TPST 240v 100a Mercury |
| 109 | Sheet metal | 1/8" Aluminum 4x4 sheet |
| 110 | Wire | 500' Copper Twin #18AWG |
| 111 | Connector | F 240v 100a solderless |
| 112 | Switch | DPST 240v 50a |
| 113 | Connector | M 120v 40a clip |
| 114 | Sheet metal | 1/4" Aluminum 4x4 sheet |
| 115 | Circuit breaker | 120v 40a |

**Figure 7.6** The Electric Controls Company *tblMaterialsInventory* in Datasheet view.

## The Category Table

The Input Mask property setting for the MaterialsInventoryCategory field in *tblMaterialsInventory* capitalizes the first letter and limits the field to 16 characters. However, this setting does not limit the values entered to the six specific categories. As you learned in Chapter 6, a Validation Rule property setting can restrict values entered to the six categories.

An alternative to creating a Validation Rule property that enforces rules about the field's characteristics is to build a separate table that contains the permitted values. You can then enforce referential integrity on a link between the category field in *tblMaterialsInventory* and the category field in the new table. When more than four or five permitted values exist, this separate-table technique can be much more efficient than setting a Validation Rule property. By storing the permitted values in a separate table, the tasks of adding, altering, and deleting values become much easier than if the values are buried in a Validation Rule property setting. In the next two exercises, you will create a category table and enforce referential integrity on a link from that table to *tblMaterialsInventory*.

EXERCISE 7.6: BUILDING A MATERIALS INVENTORY CATEGORY TABLE

1. In the Database window, click the Tables tab, click the New button, and then double-click Design view in the New Table dialog box that appears.
2. Enter *Category* in the first row of the Field Name column and click the Primary Key toolbar button to make this field the primary key.
3. Leave its Data Type set to Text and enter a Field Size property of *16*
4. Select Save As from the menu and enter *tblCategory* as the table's name, then click OK.
5. Select View, Datasheet View from the menu to open the table, then enter the six category values shown in Figure 7.7. When you are finished, close the table.

**Figure 7.7**   The Category table in Datasheet view.

Figure 7.7 shows *tblCategory* in Datasheet view displaying the six categories that Electric Controls Company uses to classify its materials inventory. This table is included in the *Ch07.mdb* database on your Companion CD. Tables like *tblCategory* are sometimes called *lookup tables* because the main table field looks up entered values to determine their validity. You may recall that we used a lookup table in Chapter 6 to store inventory diameter values for use in a combo box control on *frmInventory*. In the next exercise, you will create a lookup link in the Relationships window for the Category table and enforce referential integrity on that link.

EXERCISE 7.7: ENFORCING REFERENTIAL INTEGRITY ON THE CATEGORY LINK

1. Close all open tables. With the Database window displayed, choose the Tools, Relationships menu command.
2. Click the Tables tab in the Show Table dialog box, then select (click while holding down the Ctrl key) *tblCategory* and *tblMaterialsInventory*.

3. Click the Add button, then click the Close button. You can adjust the size and location of the tables displayed in the Relationships window using Figure 7.8 as a guide.

4. Click and drag the Category field from *tblCategory* to the MaterialsInventoryCategory field in *tblMaterialsInventory*. When the Relationships dialog box appears, check it carefully to make certain that you did drag the field to its proper destination.

5. Click the Enforce Referential Integrity check box, then click the Create button.

The Relationships window showing the two linked tables appears in Figure 7.8. To return to the Database window, close the Relationships window and save your changes.

**Figure 7.8**    Linking *tblCategory* and *tblMaterialsInventory*.

## The Materials Inventory Form

The materials inventory form will let users enter inventory records easily and accurately. The form will also provide a convenient way for users to view, update, or delete existing inventory records. In Exercise 7.8 you will create *frmMaterialsInventory*, a materials inventory form.

EXERCISE 7.8: USING AUTOFORM TO CREATE A MATERIALS INVENTORY FORM

1. Click the Forms object in the Database window, then click the New button. Since *tblMaterialsInventory* has only four small fields, you do not need to use a columnar form. You can display a number of records at one time by using a tabular form. Select *tblMaterialsInventory* from the drop-down list in the New Form dialog box.

2. Double-click AutoForm: Tabular in the New Form dialog box.
3. To save the form, press Ctrl+W, click the Yes button to confirm that you want to save changes to the form's design, and enter a Form Name of *frmMaterialsInventory* in the Save As dialog box.
4. Click OK to save the form. Leave the form open, because you will modify it in the next exercise.

As you can see in Figure 7.9, AutoForm creates a fairly good-looking form that we can modify to meet our specific needs for entering the contents of *tblMaterialsInventory* efficiently and effectively. Note how the tabular format lets users view more than one record at a time. This version of the form is included as *frmMaterialsInventory1* in the *Ch07.mdb* database on your Companion CD. This file also includes *tblMaterialsInventory*, which includes the records displayed in Figure 7.9. Your form will show the records, if any, that you entered in your Materials Inventory table.

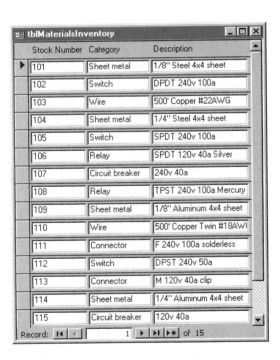

**Figure 7.9** The Materials Inventory form created by the AutoForm tool.

Although the AutoForm tool has made a good start toward creating a usable form, you can improve the appearance and usefulness of the form considerably.

To make the design tools more accessible, you can click the Toolbox toolbar button.

*Try it*

You can click and drag the toolbox around the Design window as you work, but you might find it useful to move the toolbox to the top of the Design window. When you do this, the toolbox icons become slightly larger and arrange themselves across the top of the work area just below the toolbar. You can see this in Figure 7.10, which shows the Materials Inventory form in Design view with the toolbox moved to the top of the Design window, just under the Formatting toolbar. We usually work with the property sheet open, too. To open the property sheet, click the Properties toolbar button. As you can see in Figure 7.10, we often keep the property sheet just partially exposed on the desktop, off to one side or below the form on which we are working.

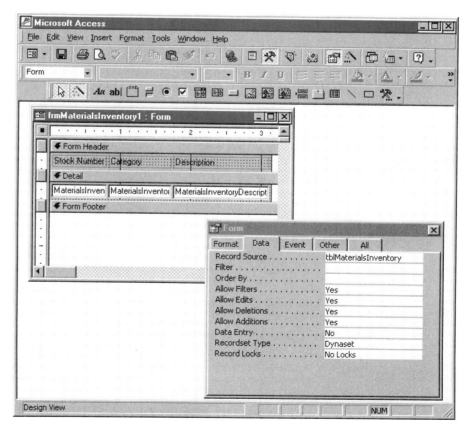

**Figure 7.10** The Materials Inventory form in Design view with the toolbox and property sheet opened.

You can try doing the next two exercises with the toolbox and property sheet open if you wish. In Exercise 7.9 you will improve the design and appearance of *frmMaterialsInventory*.

EXERCISE 7.9: IMPROVING THE MATERIALS INVENTORY FORM

1. Click the Design View toolbar button.
2. Choose Edit, Select Form from the menu, click the Format tab in the property sheet, and change the form's Caption property to *Materials Inventory*
3. Click and drag the right edge of the form to make it wider, then click and drag the edges of the gray Detail section background to fit the enlarged frame.
4. Select the label controls in the Form Header section and click the Bold button on the Formatting toolbar. You may also want to click the Center button on the Formatting toolbar to center-align the labels and use the Shift+right arrow key to make the labels a little wider to expose all of the labels' text.
5. Click and drag a marquee around all of the controls (in both sections of the form) and repeatedly select Format, Horizontal Spacing, Increase from the menu to increase the space between the controls. You can use Figure 7.11 as a guide. Remember, you may need to switch back and forth between Form view and Design view to obtain your desired results.

In the next exercise, you will replace the text box control for the category field with a combo box. By linking this combo box control to *tblCategory*, you can make data entry easier for the employees of Electric Controls Company. You should have the form open in Design view after completing the previous exercise.

EXERCISE 7.10: ADDING A COMBO BOX TO THE MATERIALS INVENTORY FORM

1. Select the MaterialsInventoryCategory text box control in the Detail section and press the Del key.
2. Make sure that the Control Wizards button toolbox tool is depressed.
3. Click the Combo Box tool button in the toolbox and draw a combo box control in the Detail section to replace the MaterialsInventoryCategory text box you just deleted. This will start the Combo Box Wizard.
4. In the first Combo Box Wizard dialog box, click the Next button to accept the default of linking the combo box to a table or query.
5. Double-click *tblCategory* in the list box. This action also moves the Wizard to its next dialog box.
6. Double-click Category, then click the Next button.
7. In the next Combo Box Wizard dialog box, double-click the right edge of the Category column header. This adjusts the column so that it accommodates the widest text, Circuit breaker. Click the Next button.

8. Click the option button to *Store that value in this field*, then select MaterialsInventoryCategory in the combo box. Click the Next button, then click the Finish button.

9. When the Wizard returns you to the Design view desktop, select the new combo box control's label and delete it. The easiest way to do this is to use the Select Object combo box control on the Formatting toolbar to select the new combo box label (it will have a suffix of *_Label*) and press the Del key.

10. You can rename the control (select the control first) by changing its Name property under the Other tab in the property sheet to *cboMaterialsInventoryCategory*

11. Select the File, Save menu command to save the form.

The last step will cause Access to overwrite the form you created earlier. This modified version of the form with the combo box control is included as *frmMaterialsInventory2* in the *Ch07.mdb* database on your Companion CD. To test your new combo box control, select View, Form from the menu, then click the *cboMaterialsInventoryCategory* control's arrow button. The combo box should display the six choices from *tblCategory* as shown in Figure 7.11.

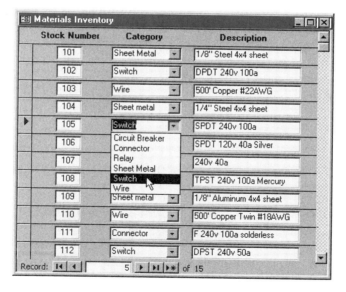

**Figure 7.11**   The operation of the *cboMaterialsInventoryCategory* combo box control.

### Try it

The Combo Box Wizard actually writes a query that accesses tblCategory and inserts the six values from the Category field in that table. To examine this query, click the MaterialsInventoryCategory combo box in Design view with the property sheet open, click the Data tab, select the Row Source property, and click its Build button. It is a simple query, but it does the job. Close all windows except the Database window.

## PURCHASE ORDERS

Now that you have built tables and forms that a firm could use to enter and maintain records of vendors and materials inventory, you can build the system components that facilitate ordering inventory items from vendors. A purchasing department receives materials requisitions from production departments that show materials descriptions and quantities needed. The purchasing department then must:

- Identify vendors that provide these materials.
- Select a vendor.
- Send a purchase order to the chosen vendor.

The format of materials requisitions varies with the firm's industry, size, and the skill level of the production department personnel that prepare materials requisitions. The format also depends on the nature of the firm's production cycle. The form of purchase orders also varies from firm to firm; however, all purchase orders must contain the following:

- Order date.
- Vendor name and address.
- Identification of the inventory item(s) to be purchased.
- Quantities and prices of the inventory item(s) to be purchased.

The purchase order also frequently contains shipping information, including an expected shipping date. You can identify vendors with purchase orders by linking the Vendor table to a new table, the Purchase Order table, because there will only be one vendor for each purchase order. However, connecting purchase orders to the specific inventory items listed on each purchase order requires a separate relationship table to model the many-to-many nature of that link.

## The Purchase Order Table

In this section, you will learn how to create a purchase order table, *tblPurchaseOrder*. Since only one vendor will be associated with any specific purchase order, you can include *tblVendor's* primary key, VendorNumber, as a foreign key in *tblPurchaseOrder* to establish the needed link. Of course, *tblPurchaseOrder* will need its own primary key and a field for the order date.

To keep this example simple, you can omit specific shipping data and just record an expected shipping date. The expected shipping date is the date on which the vendor agrees to ship the items listed on the purchase order. Therefore, *tblPurchaseOrder* needs four fields: a primary key, an order date, a foreign key link to *tblVendor*, and an expected vendor ship date. Exercise 7.11 provides step-by-step procedures you can follow to create a purchase order table for Electric Controls Company.

EXERCISE 7.11: BUILDING A PURCHASE ORDER TABLE

1. In the Database window, click the Tables tab, click the New button, and then double-click Design view in the New Table dialog box that appears.
2. Type *PurchaseOrderNumber* as the first Field Name. Leave its Data Type set to Text and click the Primary Key toolbar button.
3. Set PurchaseOrderNumber's Field Size property to *6* and its Input Mask property to ######, which will accommodate 899,999 purchase orders with a starting number of 100001. Set its Caption property to *P.O. Number*
4. Enter a Field Name of *PurchaseOrderDate* and set its Data Type to *Date/Time*. Set the Input Mask property to *99/99/00;0;_* and the Caption property to *P.O. Date*
5. The next field is the foreign key link to *tblVendor*. In the next exercise, you will establish a referential integrity link on this field to *tblVendor*. Therefore, this field must match the VendorNumber field in *tblVendor*. Enter *VendorNumber* as the Field Name and leave its Data Type set to Text. Set the Field Size property to *4* and the Caption property to *Vendor Number*. You do not need an Input Mask property for VendorNumber because the link to *tblVendor* will ensure that values entered already exist in *tblVendor*.
6. Enter a Field Name of *PurchaseOrderExpectedShipDate* and set its Data Type to *Date/Time*. Set this field's Input Mask property to *99/99/00;0;_* and its Caption property to *Expected Ship Date*
7. Close and save the table as *tblPurchaseOrder*.

In the next exercise, you will connect the Purchase Order table to the Vendor table on the VendorNumber field. Be sure that all tables are closed and the Database window is open on the Access desktop.

EXERCISE 7.12: LINKING THE PURCHASE ORDER TABLE TO THE VENDOR TABLE

1. Click the Relationships toolbar button.
2. Click the Show Table toolbar button, double-click *tblPurchaseOrder*, double-click *tblVendor*, then click the Close button in the Show Table dialog box.
3. Click and drag the VendorNumber field from *tblVendor* to the VendorNumber field in *tblPurchaseOrder*.

4. Click the Enforce Referential Integrity check box, then click the Create button.
5. Close the Relationships window and save the changes you have made.

A copy of *tblPurchaseOrder* is in the *Ch07.mdb* database on your Companion CD. This completes the job of building *tblPurchaseOrder*; however, you cannot enter purchase orders in this table yet. The Purchase Order table does not identify which inventory items are ordered, nor does it identify the quantities and prices of items ordered. In the next section, you will learn how to create a purchase order-materials inventory relationship table to properly store this information.

## The Purchase Order-Materials Inventory Table

If Electric Controls Company ordered only one inventory item on each purchase order, they would not need this table. They could add fields for the inventory item, its quantity, and its price to *tblPurchaseOrder*. Unfortunately, Electric Controls and most other businesses would find themselves drowning in purchase orders if they adopted this approach. The purchase order-materials inventory table is a relationship table that models the many-to-many link between *tblPurchaseOrder* and *tblMaterialsInventory*. That is, each purchase order may have many materials inventory items and each materials inventory item may appear on many purchase orders. The purchase order-materials inventory table needs five fields to store the following values:

- Primary key of tblPurchaseOrder.

- Primary key of tblMaterialsInventory.

- Quantity of specific materials inventory items that appear on specific purchase orders.

- Price of specific materials inventory items that appear on specific purchase orders.

- Vendor inventory stock number for each materials inventory item at the time of a specific purchase order.

In the next exercise, you will learn how to create *tblPurchaseOrder-MaterialsInventory*, a relationship table for Electric Controls Company that will provide these two links and store these five fields. To begin the exercise, close any tables or forms you have open on the desktop and open the Database window.

EXERCISE 7.13: BUILDING A PURCHASE
ORDER-MATERIALS INVENTORY TABLE

1. In the Database window, click the Tables object, click the New button, and double-click Design View in the New Table dialog box that appears.

2. Type *PurchaseOrderNumber* as the first Field Name. Leave its Data Type set to Text.
3. Set PurchaseOrderNumber's Field Size property to *6*, its Input Mask property to ######, its Caption property to *P.O. Number*, and its Indexed property to *Yes (Duplicates OK)*
4. Type *MaterialsInventoryStockNumber* as the next Field Name. Leave its Data Type set to Text. Set its Field Size property to *3* and its Caption property to *Item Number*. Set its Indexed property to *Yes (Duplicates OK)*
5. While holding down the Ctrl key, click the row selectors of the PurchaseOrderNumber field and the MaterialsInventoryStockNumber field. Click the Primary Key toolbar button. The primary key symbol should appear in the row selectors of both fields indicating that you have created a composite primary key for the table.
6. Enter a Field Name of *PurchaseOrder-MaterialsInventoryQuantity* and set its Data Type to *Number*. Set PurchaseOrder-MaterialsInventoryQuantity's Field Size property to *Long Integer*, its Decimal Places property to *0*, and its Caption property to *Quantity*
7. Enter a Field Name of *PurchaseOrder-MaterialsInventoryPrice*, set its Data Type to *Currency*, and set its Caption property to *Price*
8. Enter a Field Name of *PurchaseOrder-MaterialsInventoryVendorStockNumber*, leave its Data Type set to Text, set its Field Size property to *20*, and its Caption Property to *Vendor's Stock Number*
9. Save the table as *tblPurchaseOrder-MaterialsInventory*, then close the table.

We have included a *tblPurchaseOrder-MaterialsInventory* object in the *Ch07.mdb* database on your Companion CD for your reference. Now that the table design is complete, you can create the links to *tblMaterialsInventory* and *tblPurchaseOrder*. The next exercise shows you how. Begin with all tables and forms closed and the Database window open on the Access desktop.

EXERCISE 7.14: LINKING THE PURCHASE ORDER-MATERIALS INVENTORY TABLE

1. Click the Relationships toolbar button.
2. Click the Show Table toolbar button, double-click *tblPurchaseOrder-MaterialsInventory*, then click the Close button.
3. Click and drag the MaterialsInventoryStockNumber field from *tblMaterialsInventory* to the MaterialsInventoryStockNumber field in *tblPurchaseOrder-MaterialsInventory*.
4. Click the Enforce Referential Integrity check box, then click the Create button.
5. Click and drag the PurchaseOrderNumber field from *tblPurchaseOrder* to the PurchaseOrderNumber field in *tblPurchaseOrder-MaterialsInventory*.
6. Click the Enforce Referential Integrity check box, then click the Create button.
7. Close the Relationships window and save your changes.

Figure 7.12 shows the relationships you have created thus far in this chapter. These relationships link Purchase Order to Vendor and to Materials Inventory through the relationship table, *tblPurchaseOrder-MaterialsInventory*.

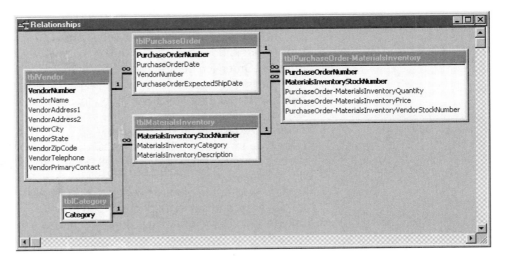

**Figure 7.12**  Relationships between the Purchase Order, Vendor, and Materials Inventory tables.

Now that you have built the necessary tables and linked them, you can create a form that Electric Controls Company can use to enter its purchase orders. The next section shows you how to create such a form.

## The Purchase Order Entry Form

The purchase order entry form is fairly complex. To enter purchase orders, you will create a form that links:

- The Purchase Order table to the Vendor table, to provide the vendor name.

- The Purchase Order table to the Purchase Order-Materials Inventory table, to provide a list of inventory stock numbers, quantities, prices, and vendor stock numbers for each item on each purchase order.

- The Purchase Order-Materials Inventory table to the Materials Inventory table, to provide a description for each item on each purchase order.

A purchase order entry form that meets these objectives will use four tables. The form must read from *tblVendor* and *tblMaterialsInventory* and will write to *tblPurchaseOrder* and *tblPurchaseOrder-MaterialsInventory*. Since the form will read data from *tblVendor* and *tblMaterialsInventory,* you will need to have data in these tables to test the form's operation as you build it. The versions of these two tables that we have included in the *Ch07.mdb* database on your Companion CD contain data. You can use these tables or copy the data from them to your own tables.

The Purchase Order Entry form will allow Electric Controls Company to enter purchase order information simultaneously in *tblPurchaseOrder* and *tblPurchaseOrder-MaterialsInventory*. Microsoft Access handles this simultaneous data entry task best with a form-subform design. This design links *tblPurchaseOrder* to *tblVendor* in the main form and links *tblPurchaseOrder-MaterialsInventory* to *tblMaterialsInventory* in the subform. In Exercise 7.15 you will use the Access Form Wizard to create these two forms.

EXERCISE 7.15: BUILDING THE PURCHASE ORDER ENTRY FORMS

1. Click the Forms object in the Database window and click the New button to open the New Form dialog box. Select *tblPurchaseOrder* in the source table combo box, then double-click Form Wizard in the list box.
2. The Form Wizard dialog box should display Table: *tblPurchaseOrder* in its Tables/Queries combo box. Click the >> button to move all of the fields from the Available Fields list box to the Selected Fields list box.
3. Select Table: *tblVendor* in the Tables/Queries combo box. Select VendorName in the Available Fields list box and click the > button to move it to the Selected Fields list box.
4. Select Table: *tblPurchaseOrder-MaterialsInventory* in the Tables/Queries combo box. Using the > button, move the following fields to the Selected Fields list box: MaterialsInventoryStockNumber, PurchaseOrder-MaterialsInventoryQuantity, PurchaseOrder-MaterialsInventoryPrice, and PurchaseOrder-MaterialsInventoryVendorStockNumber.
5. Select Table: *tblMaterialsInventory* in the Tables/Queries combo box. Using the > button, move the MaterialsInventoryCategory and MaterialsInventoryDescription fields to the Selected Fields list box.
6. Click the Next button to continue. The Form Wizard presents a template of the form-subform design and main sort order in its next dialog box as shown in Figure 7.13.
7. Click the Next button to accept the Form Wizard's design template and continue.
8. Click the Tabular layout option button, then click the Next button.
9. Select the Standard style, then click the Next button.
10. Enter a Form title of *frmPurchaseOrder* and a Subform title of *fsubPurchaseOrder*. Click the Finish button to have the Form Wizard create the two forms.

The Purchase Order Entry form generated by the Form Wizard appears in Figure 7.14 in Form view. We have included the main form and subform that comprise this form in the *Ch07.mdb* database on your Companion CD as *frmPurchaseOrder1* and *fsubPurchaseOrder1*.

**Figure 7.13**   The Form Wizard's proposed template for the Purchase Order Entry form.

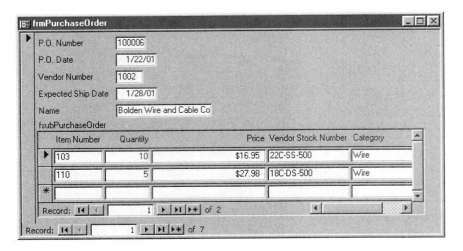

**Figure 7.14**   The Form Wizard-generated Purchase Order Entry form.

Although this design is a good start, you can enhance the form to make it more useful. For example, the first record that appears in the form is purchase order number 100006, not 100001, and the MaterialsInventoryDescription field does not show on the subform because the subform object the Form Wizard created in the purchase order form is not wide enough. You will learn how to fix these problems and identify other ways to improve the form in the next three exercises.

Exercise 7.16 shows you how to make some changes to queries behind the form and subform.

EXERCISE 7.16: EDITING THE PURCHASE
ORDER ENTRY FORM AND SUBFORM QUERIES

1. Open *frmPurchaseOrder* in Design view by selecting the form and clicking the Design button, then click the Properties toolbar button to open the property sheet. We will assume that you have the property sheet open and available in Form Design view throughout this exercise.
2. Select Edit, Select Form from the menu, then click the Data tab in the property sheet. Select the form's Record Source property and click its Build button to open the query that the Form Wizard built behind the form.
3. The form opened with PurchaseOrderNumber 100006, and not PurchaseOrderNumber 100001, because the Form Wizard did not set any sorting options in the query behind *frmPurchaseOrder*. Enter *Ascending* in the PurchaseOrderNumber field's Sort cell in the first QBE grid column to fix this problem. Close the Query Builder window and save your changes.
4. Close *frmPurchaseOrder* and save your changes. Access will display the Database window. Open *fsubPurchaseOrder* in Design view.
5. Click the Data tab in the property sheet, select the Record Source property, then click its Build button to open the query behind the form. Enter *Ascending* in the MaterialsInventoryStockNumber field's Sort cell in the first QBE grid column.
6. Scroll the QBE grid to expose the first open Field cell, select it, then press Shift+F2 to open the Zoom box. Enter *Description: [MaterialsInventoryCategory] & ", " & [MaterialsInventoryDescription]* in the Zoom box, then click the OK button. Close the Query Builder window and save your changes.

In the next exercise, you will make some changes that improve the appearance of the Purchase Order subform. You can use Figure 7.15, which shows the finished subform in Form view, as a guide. Make sure that *fsubPurchaseOrder* is open in Design view before you begin this exercise.

EXERCISE 7.17: ENHANCING THE APPEARANCE
OF THE PURCHASE ORDER SUBFORM

1. Select the MaterialsInventoryCategory text box control and label. Press the Del key to remove them from the form.
2. Move the PurchaseOrder-MaterialsInventoryVendorStockNumber text box control and label to the right of the MaterialsInventoryStockNumber controls. You will

need to move the other controls on the form to the right to make room for this adjustment. See Figure 7.15 for guidance.

3. Select the MaterialsInventoryDescription text box control, click the Data tab in its property sheet, then change its Control Source property to *Description*. Change the Enabled property to *No* and the Locked property to *Yes*

4. Click on the property sheet Format tab and set the control's Back Style to *Transparent*, its Special Effect property to *Flat*, and its Border Style property to *Transparent*. Click the Other tab and enter a Name property of *Description*

5. Select the label controls in the Form Header, then click the Bold button on the Formatting toolbar. Change the size, alignment, and arrangement of the text box and label controls using Figure 7.15 as a guide.

6. Close *fsubPurchaseOrder* and save your changes.

**Figure 7.15**   The enhanced version of *fsubPurchaseOrder*.

Notice that the enhanced version of the subform makes it easy for users to tell which fields require an entry and which do not. In fact, the Description control is locked so that users cannot accidentally change data in the underlying fields. In Exercise 7.18, you will make changes to the main Purchase Order form that will improve its usefulness. You can use Figure 7.16, which shows the finished Purchase Order form, as a guide while you are making these changes.

EXERCISE 7.18: ENHANCING THE APPEARANCE
OF THE PURCHASE ORDER FORM

1. Open *frmPurchaseOrder* in Design view.

2. Select the Subform object label that appears just above the subform and press Ctrl+X to delete it.

3. Select the VendorName label and press Ctrl+X to delete it, then click and drag the VendorName text box control to a position to the right of the VendorNumber

text box control. You may wish to use the Format, Align menu commands to ensure a precise alignment.

4. With the VendorName text box control still selected, click the Data tab in its property sheet, then change its Enabled property to *No* and its Locked property to *Yes*. Click on the property sheet Format tab and set the control's Back Style to *Transparent*, its Special Effect property to *Flat*, and its Border Style property to *Transparent*

5. Select the VendorName text box control and all of the label controls—you can do this by holding down the Shift key as you click each one—and click the Bold button on the Formatting toolbar.

6. Choose the Edit, Select Form command from the menu, click on the form's property sheet Format tab, change its Caption property to *Purchase Order Entry*, and set the Record Selectors property to *No*

7. Using Figure 7.16 as a guide, make any other changes you wish to the form's appearance, then close the form and save your changes.

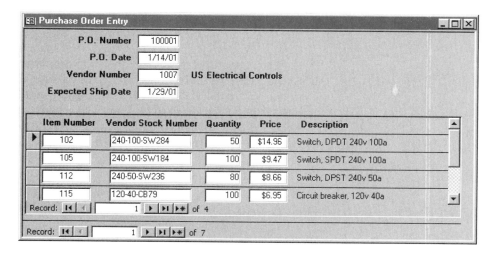

**Figure 7.16**   The completed Purchase Order Entry form.

The Purchase Order form and subform that appear in Figure 7.16 are included in the *Ch07.mdb* database on your Companion CD as *frmPurchaseOrder2* and *fsubPurchaseOrder2*, respectively.

## Printing Purchase Orders

In this section, you will learn how to retrieve and print the purchase cycle information that Electric Controls Company will gather through the forms and store in the tables that you have created. Entering purchase order information is an important step, but sending the printed purchase order to vendors is an important function of the purchase cycle. In Exercise 7.19, you will use the Report Wizard to generate printed purchase orders.

EXERCISE 7.19: BUILDING A PURCHASE ORDER REPORT

1. Click the Reports object in the Database window, then click the New button to open the New Report dialog box. Enter *tblPurchaseOrder* in the source table combo box, then double- click Report Wizard in the list box.
2. The next Report Wizard dialog box should display Table: *tblPurchaseOrder* in its Tables/Queries combo box. Click the >> button to move all of the fields from the Available Fields list box to the Selected Fields list box.
3. Select Table: *tblVendor* in the Tables/Queries combo box. Using the > button, move the following fields to the Selected Fields list box: VendorName, VendorAddress1, VendorAddress2, VendorCity, VendorState, and VendorZipCode.
4. Select Table: *tblPurchaseOrder-MaterialsInventory* in the Tables/Queries combo box. Using the > button, move the following fields to the Selected Fields list box: MaterialsInventoryStockNumber, PurchaseOrder-MaterialsInventoryQuantity, PurchaseOrder-MaterialsInventoryPrice and PurchaseOrder-MaterialsInventoryVendorStockNumber.
5. Select Table: *tblMaterialsInventory* in the Tables/Queries combo box. Using the > button, move the MaterialsInventoryCategory and MaterialsInventoryDescription fields to the Selected Fields list box. Click the Next button to continue. The Report Wizard presents a template of the report-subreport design and main sort order in its next dialog box as shown in Figure 7.17.

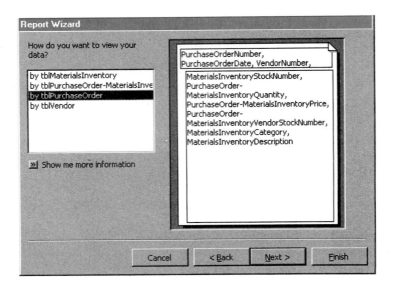

**Figure 7.17**   The Report Wizard's-proposed report template for *rptPurchaseOrder*.

6. To accept the Report Wizard's proposed design, click the Next button. Click the Next button in the dialog box that appears to accept the Report Wizard's grouping on PurchaseOrderNumber.
7. Select MaterialsInventoryStockNumber in the first sort order combo box, then click the Next button.
8. Click the Outline 1 Layout option button, then click the Next button.
9. Select the Bold style, then click the Next button.
10. Enter *rptPurchaseOrder* as the report title, then click the Finish button.
11. Close the report's preview window.

The report generated by the Report Wizard is in very rough form. It does not have a page break at the end of each purchase order, and does not include Electric Controls Company's name or address. In the next three exercises, you will take this report, which is on your Companion CD in the *Ch07.mdb* database as *rptPurchaseOrderCreatedByReportWizard*, and transform it into a useful purchase order report. In Exercise 7.20, you will make changes to the query behind the Purchase Order report.

EXERCISE 7.20: MODIFYING THE QUERY
BEHIND THE PURCHASE ORDER REPORT

1. Open the report you just created (or *rptPurchaseOrderCreatedByReportWizard* on your Companion CD) in Design view. Click the Properties toolbar button to open the property sheet. We will assume that you have the property sheet open throughout this exercise.
2. Click the property sheet Data tab, select the Record Source property, and click on its Build button to open the query behind the report. Type *Ascending* in the first Sort cell in the QBE grid, under the PurchaseOrderNumber Field name.
3. Scroll to the last column in the QBE grid, then choose Insert, Columns from the menu. Select the new column's Field cell, and press Shift+F2 to open the Zoom box. Enter *Description: [MaterialsInventoryCategory] & ", " & [MaterialsInventoryDescription]* in the Zoom box, then click the OK button.
4. Use the procedure in the preceding step to insert another column in the QBE grid, select the new column's Field cell, and press Shift+F2 to open the Zoom box. Enter *Extension: [PurchaseOrder-MaterialsInventoryQuantity]*[PurchaseOrder-MaterialsInventoryPrice]* and click the OK button. This expression calculates the quantity × price extension for each item on the purchase order.
5. Insert another column in the QBE grid, select the new column's Field cell, and press Shift+F2 to open the Zoom box. Enter *VendorNameAndAddress: [VendorName] & Chr(13) & Chr(10) & [VendorAddress1] & Chr(13) & Chr(10) & IIf(IsNull([VendorAddress2]),"",([VendorAddress2] & Chr(13) & Chr(10))) & [VendorCity] & ", " & [VendorState] & " " & [VendorZipCode]* in the Zoom box, then click the OK button.
6. Close the Query Builder window and save your changes.

You may wish to move the property sheet to an unobtrusive location before proceeding. The expression you created for VendorNameAndAddress combines the components of the vendor address into one field that you can print on the purchase order. The expression includes two interesting components. First, the expression uses the Chr() function with the values of 13 and 10 to insert a carriage return and line feeds. Second, the expression uses an IsNull() function nested inside an IIF() function to test whether the VendorAddress2 field contains data. If it does, the expression prints it as the third line of the field.

### Try it

You can learn more about these two functions in Microsoft Access on-line help. You may recall that you used four separate lines for customer name and address information in the Chapter 6 Invoice report. When you print that report, you can see that invoices for customers that did not have second address line information included a blank line in the address. Now that you have seen how to use the Chr(), IsNull(), and IIF() functions, you might want to go back and revise *rptInvoice*.

In Exercise 7.21 you will modify the report's appearance to accommodate the changes you made to its underlying query in Exercise 7.20. As you work through Exercise 7.21, you may want to use the Design view of the finished report, shown in Figure 7.18, and the printout of the finished report, shown in Figure 7.19, as guides to help you with control placement and appearance adjustments. You should have the Purchase Order report open in Design view to begin this exercise.

### EXERCISE 7.21: MODIFYING THE PURCHASE ORDER REPORT'S APPEARANCE

1. Click and drag the top of the Detail section bar down to make room in the PurchaseOrderNumber Header for a title and Electric Controls Company's name and address. Select all of the objects in the PurchaseOrderNumber Header, then click and drag the selected objects down to make room at the top of the section. You may find it easier to use the Ctrl+down arrow key to move the objects straight down.
2. Change the label control text in the Page Header to *Purchase Order*, then select all three objects (the label control and the two line graphics) in the Page Header. The easiest way to select all three objects is to click and drag in the left ruler space from the top of the Page Header section to its bottom. Press Ctrl+X to cut these objects. If any objects remain visible in the Page Header, press Ctrl+Z to undo the cut and try again.
3. Select the PurchaseOrderNumber Header by clicking its Title bar, then press Ctrl+V to paste the objects from the Report Header.
4. Select View, Report Header/Footer from the menu to delete the report's header and footer sections. Select View, Page Header/Footer from the menu to delete

the page header and footer. Click the Yes button to confirm that you want to delete the controls in the Page Footer section.

5. Click the Toolbox button on the toolbar, then select the Label tool. Use it to draw a new label control near the top of the PurchaseOrderNumber Header. Enter Electric Controls Company name and address in that label. Remember to use Ctrl+Enter to insert line breaks when you are typing inside the label control.

6. Select the PurchaseOrderNumber, PurchaseOrderDate, VendorNumber, and PurchaseOrderExpectedShipDate fields, click on the Format tab in the property sheet and change the controls' Border Style to *Transparent*. Select the PurchaseOrderDate and PurchaseOrderExpectedShipDate fields, click the Format tab in the property sheet, and enter a Format property value of *mmmm d ", " yyyy*

7. Change the text of the labels and arrange these controls as they appear in Figures 7.18 and 7.19. You can use the toolbox label control to create the label with the text *Please include this number on all invoices and shipping documents.*

8. Select and delete the six vendor name and address fields. Click the Field List toolbar button to open the Field List, then click and drag VendorNameAndAddress to the PurchaseOrderNumber Header section. Change the label control's text to To: and expand the text box control to accommodate the full vendor name and address. We used a 12-point bold Arial font for this text box in our version of the report.

9. Delete the MaterialsInventoryCategory text box control and its label. Select the MaterialsInventoryDescription text box control in the Detail section, click on the Data tab in the property sheet, and change the Control Source property to *Description*

10. Copy and paste the PurchaseOrder-MaterialsInventoryPrice text box control and label. Change the new text box control's Control Source property to *Extension*, then change the new label's Caption property to match. Using Figures 7.18 and 7.19 as guides, arrange and set the Text Align properties of the report's text box and label controls.

When the Report Wizard created the Purchase Order form, it included a report band for PurchaseOrderNumber. A *report band* groups the report's data by values in one of the report's fields. Report bands in Access can include a variety of sorting and display options, including individual headers and footers for each band. The Report Wizard created a header for the PurchaseOrderNumber report band, but it did not create a footer.

In Exercise 7.22, you will add a footer to the PurchaseOrderNumber report band with controls that will display the total amount of each invoice. You will also set the footer's property to force a new page after it prints. This will print each invoice on a separate page. You should have the Purchase Order report and its property sheet open in Design view to begin this exercise.

EXERCISE 7.22: ADDING A PURCHASEORDERNUMBER
FOOTER TO THE PURCHASE ORDER REPORT

1. Select View, Sorting And Grouping from the menu. In the Sorting and Grouping dialog box that appears, change the PurchaseOrderNumber's Group Footer property to *Yes* and its Keep Together property to *Whole Group*. You can close the dialog box by repeating the menu command you used to open it or by clicking the Sorting And Grouping toolbar button.
2. Click the new PurchaseOrderNumber Footer bar, then click the Format tab in the property sheet. Set the Force New Page property to *After Section*
3. You can copy the line objects from the PurchaseOrderNumber Header section, or create your own footer design. The Footer needs only two controls, a text box control to total the Extension field and an accompanying label control. Copy the Extension text box to this section using the Ctrl+C and Ctrl+V cut-and-paste procedure. Click the Data tab in the property sheet and change the Control Source property to *=Sum([Extension])*. Add a label control with the text *Purchase Order Total* to the Footer section.
4. Close the form and save your changes.

Figure 7.18 shows the completed Purchase Order report in Design view. We turned off the grid (by selecting View, Grid from the menu) for this screen picture so you could see the report's details more clearly.

**Figure 7.18**   The Purchase Order report in Design view.

A copy of purchase order number 100001 for Electric Controls Company, generated as the first page of our Purchase Order report, appears in Figure 7.19. This purchase order, *rptPurchaseOrderExample*, is included in the *Ch07.mdb* database on your Companion CD.

**Figure 7.19**  The purchase order number 100001 printout generated by *rptPurchaseOrderExample*.

**RECORDING MATERIALS INVENTORY RECEIPTS**

After Electric Controls Company enters their purchase order data and mails the printed purchase orders to their vendors, *tblPurchaseOrder-MaterialsInventory* contains detailed line item information about what they expect vendors to ship. When materials arrive on the receiving dock, Electric Controls will want to record the quantity and identity of each item on each shipment. Dock personnel record this information on receiving reports. In the past, the receiving report was a paper form on which the dock worker wrote the information about items received. Today, dock workers can enter the receiving information directly into the firm's accounting database using a database form. This electronic receiving report enters data directly into the Inventory Receipt table.

One advantage of direct data entry into the Inventory Receipt table is that we can assign each item a unique receipt number. Many firms use bar code scanners that read inventory identification codes on inventory packages. These scanners also can date- and time-stamp the inventory receipt record. The accounts payable department collects other information about inventory received, including vendor invoice number and each item's price, from vendor invoices and can enter that information directly into the Inventory Receipt table.

## The Inventory Receipt Table

An inventory receipt table for Electric Controls Company will require seven fields. They store the following information attributes: a primary key for each receipt, the date of the receipt, Electric Control's materials inventory stock number, Electric Control's purchase order number, the vendor's invoice number, the quantity of the item received, and the price billed on the vendor's invoice for the item. In Exercise 7.23, you will create *tblInventoryReceipt*, an inventory receipt table for the Electric Controls Company that meets these data storage requirements.

EXERCISE 7.23: BUILDING AN INVENTORY RECEIPT TABLE

1. In the Database window, click the Tables object, click the New button, and then double-click Design View in the New Table dialog box that appears.
2. Enter the first Field Name, *InventoryReceiptNumber*, and leave its Data Type set to Text. Click on the Primary Key toolbar button to make this field the table's primary key. Set its Field Size property to *6*, its Input Mask Property to ######;;_ and its Caption property to *Inventory Receipt Number*
3. In the next row, enter a Field Name of *InventoryReceiptDate*, set its Data Type to *Date/Time*, its Format Property to *Short Date*, its Input Mask Property to *99/99/00;;_*, and its Caption property to *Date Received*
4. To create the table's first foreign key field, enter a Field Name of *PurchaseOrderNumber* and leave its Data Type set to Text. Set its Field Size to *6*, its Input Mask Property to *000000;;_*, and its Caption property to *Purchase Order Number*
5. To create the table's second foreign key field, enter a Field Name of *MaterialsInventoryStockNumber* and leave its Data Type set to Text. Set its Field Size to *3*, its Input Mask Property to *000;;_*, and its Caption property to *Stock Number*
6. In the next row, enter a Field Name of *InventoryReceiptVendorInvoiceNumber* and leave its Data Type set to Text. Set its Field Size to *20*, and its Caption property to *Vendor Invoice Number*. Since Electric Controls Company cannot control the nature or length of the invoice numbers that their vendors might choose, you must provide sufficient space to hold the longest number a vendor might use.
7. In the next row, enter a Field Name of *InventoryReceiptQuantity* for the next field. Set its Data Type to *Number*, its Field Size property to *Long Integer*, its Decimal Places property to *0*, and its Caption property to *Quantity*
8. In the next row, enter a Field Name of *InventoryReceiptPrice* for the last field. Set its Data Type to *Currency*, its Decimal Places property to *2*, and its Caption property to *Price*

9. Click File, Save As to save your work and close the table. Enter *tblInventoryReceipt* as the Table Name in the Save As dialog box. Click OK, then close the Table window.

In the next exercise, you integrate the Inventory Receipt table with the other purchase cycle tables. You can do this by creating links to the new table and setting referential integrity constraints on those links. Enforcing referential integrity on the links from *tblInventoryReceipt* to the primary keys of *tblPurchaseOrder* and *tblMaterialsInventory* improves internal control in Electric Controls Company's purchasing system. The link to *tblPurchaseOrder* will prevent dock workers from erroneously entering nonexistent purchase order numbers. The link to *tblMaterialsInventory* will prevent entry of nonexistent MaterialsInventoryStockNumbers. To begin the exercise, be sure that all tables, forms, and reports are closed and that the Database window is open on the Access desktop.

### EXERCISE 7.24: LINKING THE INVENTORY RECEIPT TABLE TO EXISTING TABLES

1. Select Tools, Relationships from the menu. The relationships window will appear with a display of the relationships you created earlier in this chapter.
2. Click the Show Table toolbar button.
3. Double-click *tblInventoryReceipt*, then click the Show Table dialog box Close button. You may want to resize and rearrange the tables in the Relationships window using Figure 7.20 as a guide.
4. Click and drag the PurchaseOrderNumber field from *tblPurchaseOrder* to the corresponding field in *tblInventoryReceipt*. Click the Enforce Referential Integrity check box, then click the Create button.
5. Click and drag the MaterialsInventoryStockNumber field from *tblMaterialsInventory* to the corresponding field in *tblInventoryReceipt*. Click the Enforce Referential Integrity check box, then click the Create button. The completed set of relationships appears in Figure 7.20.
6. Close the Relationships window and save your changes.

Figure 7.20 shows the updated relationships among the purchase cycle tables. A copy of the *tblInventoryReceipt* table is included in the *Ch07.mdb* database on your Companion CD. Now that you have a table in which to store information about inventory receipts, your next task is to build a form that will make entering data into the table easy and effective.

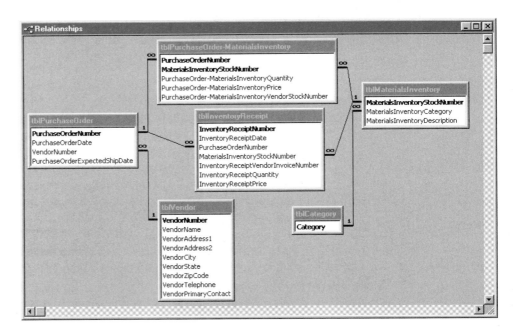

**Figure 7.20**  Connecting *tblInventoryReceipt* with existing purchase cycle tables.

## An Inventory Receipt Form

The inventory receipt form is simple and straightforward. Since you can rely on the referential integrity links to existing values in *tblPurchaseOrder* and *tblMaterialsInventory* for the foreign key fields, PurchaseOrderNumber and MaterialsInventoryStockNumber, you can build the form based on *tblInventoryReceipt* alone. You do not need a complex form design, nor do you need an underlying query. Exercise 7.25 shows you how to create an inventory receipt data entry form for Electric Controls Company.

EXERCISE 7.25: BUILDING AN INVENTORY RECEIPT FORM

1. In the Database window, click the Forms object, then click the New button.
2. Type *tblInventoryReceipt* in the table box or select it from the drop-down list in the New Form dialog box.
3. Double-click AutoForm: Tabular in the New Form dialog box. This AutoForm tool generates a simple tabular form. With a few minor changes, this form will work quite well as Electric Controls Company's Inventory Receipt form.
4. Select View, Design View from the menu, then click the Properties toolbar button to open the property sheet.

5. Select Edit, Select Form from the menu, then click the Format tab in the form's property sheet and enter a Caption property of *Inventory Receipts Data Entry Form*
6. Select all of the label controls in the Form Header, then click the Bold button on the Formatting toolbar.
7. Select the label controls in the Form Header, then press Shift+down arrow repeatedly to increase the height of the controls enough that two lines of text appear in the controls.
8. Using Figure 7.21 as a guide, adjust the arrangement, size, and alignment of the controls on the form. Remember, you can force a line break in a label control by pressing Ctrl+Enter.
9. Close the Inventory Receipt form and save your changes.

The completed form appears in Figure 7.21 in Form view displaying Electric Controls Company's sample data. This Inventory Receipt data entry form is included in the *Ch07.mdb* database on your Companion CD as *frmInventoryReceiptExample*.

**Inventory Receipts Data Entry Form**

| Inventory Receipt Number | Date Received | Purchase Order Number | Stock Number | Vendor Invoice Number | Quantity | Price |
|---|---|---|---|---|---|---|
| 100001 | 1/26/01 | 100006 | 103 | PR-57996-3 | 10 | $16.95 |
| 100002 | 1/26/01 | 100001 | 115 | 3674222 | 100 | $6.95 |
| 100003 | 1/26/01 | 100001 | 105 | 3674222 | 100 | $9.47 |
| 100004 | 1/29/01 | 100003 | 111 | 1294-B173 | 100 | $3.57 |
| 100005 | 1/29/01 | 100003 | 113 | 1294-B173 | 50 | $1.98 |
| 100006 | 1/29/01 | 100005 | 107 | 2719CRT | 50 | $10.27 |
| 100007 | 1/31/01 | 100006 | 110 | PR-58325-9 | 5 | $139.90 |
| 100008 | 1/31/01 | 100004 | 104 | 106599 | 100 | $14.95 |
| 100009 | 1/31/01 | 100001 | 102 | 3675088 | 50 | $14.96 |
| 100010 | 1/31/01 | 100001 | 112 | 3675088 | 80 | $8.66 |

Record: 1 of 11

**Figure 7.21** The completed Inventory Receipt form.

If you test the form, you will find that the foreign key links to *tblPurchaseOrder* and *tblMaterialsInventory* prevent you from entering a value for purchase order number or stock number that does not already exist in the underlying entity table. Note that Electric Controls Company assigns a unique inventory receipt number to each individual stock number received on a purchase order. Many firms still use a receiving report format in which they assign one receiving report number to an entire shipment; a practice that is a holdover from manual record-keeping systems. As computer facilities become increasingly available, even on receiving docks, workers gain the ability to enter atomic-level data directly into the system. In the next section, you learn how to present some of these inventory receipts data.

## Inventory Receipt Reports

Businesses do not use standard reporting forms for inventory receipts, so you may create your own report designs to meet your needs or those of your clients. In this section you will learn how to build an inventory receipt report that calculates the price × quantity extensions for inventory received by the Electric Controls Company.

The report groups inventory receipts by vendor to show what Electric Controls owes their vendors for materials they have received. To be even more useful, the report groups receipts by purchase order number within vendor. Exercise 7.26 shows you how to use the Reports Wizard to select fields from Electric Control's Inventory Receipt, Purchase Order, and Vendor tables. You will also learn how to modify the Report Wizard-generated report to calculate price × quantity extensions for each materials inventory receipt.

EXERCISE 7.26: BUILDING AN INVENTORY RECEIPT REPORT

1. Click the Reports tab in the Database window, then click the New button to open the New Report dialog box. Enter *tblInventoryReceipt* in the source table combo box, then double-click Report Wizard in the list box. The first Report Wizard dialog box should display Table: *tblInventoryReceipt* in its Tables/Queries combo box. Click the >> button to move all of the fields from the Available Fields list box to the Selected Fields list box.
2. Select Table: *tblPurchaseOrder* in the Tables/Queries combo box. Using the > button, move the VendorNumber field to the Selected Fields list box.
3. Enter Table: *tblVendor* in the Tables/Queries combo box. Using the > button, move the VendorName field to the Selected Fields list box. Click the Next button to continue.
4. Since you are going to create your own grouping design for this report, you do not need to give the Report Wizard any instructions about how to view the data. To accept the default design, data organized by *tblInventoryReceipt*, click the Next button.
5. We want the report to group the inventory receipts data by vendor and, within each vendor, by purchase order number. Select VendorName in the grouping levels list box, then click the > button to modify the Report Wizard's template. Next, select PurchaseOrderNumber and click the > button. The wizard will make the changes to the report design template shown in Figure 7.22.
6. To accept the modified design, click the Next button.

**Figure 7.22**   The Report Wizard's-modified template for *rptInventoryReceipt*.

7. Select InventoryReceiptNumber in the first sort order combo box.

### *Try it*

At this point, you are going to play a little trick on the Report Wizard. You want to multiply the price by the quantity to obtain an extension value to include in this report. The Report Wizard does not offer this option, so you will need to add the extension field after the Report Wizard has created the report. You also will want footers in the report that include text box controls with Sum() functions that subtotal the extension amounts for each purchase order and each vendor. To trick the Wizard into generating the footers and text box controls with Sum() functions, you can instruct it to sum the InventoryReceiptPrice fields. You will still need to edit the controls to change InventoryReceiptPrice to Extension, but the Report Wizard will do most of the work for you.

8. Click on the Summary Options button. In the next dialog box, click the Sum checkbox for InventoryReceiptPrice. Be sure that the Show Detail and Summary option button has been selected. Click the OK button to return to the previous dialog box, then click the Next button to proceed.
9. Select the Outline 1 Layout and the Corporate style in the next two dialog boxes, respectively, then enter a report title of *rptInventoryReceipt*. Click the Finish button to generate the report.
10. Open your new form in Design view. Click the Properties toolbar button to open the property sheet.
11. Click the property sheet Data tab, select the Record Source property, and click on its Build button to open the query behind the report.

12. Select the first open Field cell in the QBE grid and press Shift+F2 to open the Zoom box. Enter *Extension: [InventoryReceiptQuantity]* \* *[InventoryReceiptPrice]* and click the OK button. This expression calculates the quantity × price extension for each item received. Close the Query Builder window and save your changes.

13. Make a copy of the InventoryReceiptPrice text box control in the Detail section and its accompanying label control in the PurchaseOrderNumber Header section. Place these new controls, which will contain the Extension field, to the right of the original controls (see Figure 7.23). Change the text box control's Control Source property to Extension. Select the text in the label control, press Ctrl+Enter, then type *Extension*

14. Enter *=Sum(Extension)* in the Control Source property of the controls in the PurchaseOrderNumber Footer, the VendorNumber Footer, and the Report Footer, then change the labels for those controls to match those shown in Figure 7.23.

15. Using Figure 7.23 as a guide, adjust the placement and appearance of the report's controls. Save your new report and close the Report window.

An Inventory Receipt report, *rptInventoryReceiptExample*, is included in the *Ch07.mdb* database on your Companion CD. We encourage you to use Figure 7.23 and the example report on the CD as springboards for experimenting with your own report design ideas.

## CASH DISBURSEMENTS

Thus far in this chapter, you have learned how Electric Controls Company can maintain vendor records, materials inventory records, prepare purchase orders, and record receipts of ordered inventory items. Once they receive materials inventory items, their vendors would like them to pay for the items. This section describes one way to use the information you have gathered in your purchase cycle tables to write checks. The approach we describe here is only one of many possible ways to do this. Since you have a record of materials received in the Inventory Receipts table, you can use that table as a basis for payments.

More elaborate systems might compare purchase order terms to vendor invoice terms before payment. One way to do this is with a voucher system, in which accounting personnel compare purchase orders with vendor invoices, shipping documents, and receiving reports before authorizing payment. You can build on the tables and forms described in this section to create such a system; however, the details of a full voucher system are beyond the scope of this book.

## The Cash Disbursements Table

The cash disbursements table must include fields that store the check number and date of each check. In Exercise 7.27, you will create a cash disbursements table with these fields.

## Inventory Receipts
*By Vendor and by Purchase Order*                    *Electric Controls Company*

*for internal use only*

**VendorNumber 1002    Bolden Wire and Cable Co.**

*Purchase Order Number  100006*

| Inventory Receipt Number | Date Received | Stock Number | Vendor Invoice Number | Quantity | Price | Extension |
|---|---|---|---|---|---|---|
| 100001 | 1/26/01 | 103 | PR-57996-3 | 10 | $16.95 | $169.50 |
| 100007 | 1/31/01 | 110 | PR-58325-9 | 5 | $139.90 | $699.50 |

Total for this Purchase Order  $869.00
Total for this Vendor  $869.00

**VendorNumber 1005    Bomac Sheet Metal Co.**

*Purchase Order Number  100004*

| Inventory Receipt Number | Date Received | Stock Number | Vendor Invoice Number | Quantity | Price | Extension |
|---|---|---|---|---|---|---|
| 100008 | 1/31/01 | 104 | 106599 | 100 | $14.95 | $1,495.00 |

Total for this Purchase Order  $1,495.00
Total for this Vendor  $1,495.00

**VendorNumber 1007    US Electrical Controls**

*Purchase Order Number  100001*

| Inventory Receipt Number | Date Received | Stock Number | Vendor Invoice Number | Quantity | Price | Extension |
|---|---|---|---|---|---|---|
| 100002 | 1/26/01 | 115 | 3674222 | 100 | $6.95 | $695.00 |
| 100003 | 1/26/01 | 105 | 3674222 | 100 | $9.47 | $947.00 |
| 100009 | 1/31/01 | 102 | 3675088 | 50 | $14.96 | $748.00 |
| 100010 | 1/31/01 | 112 | 3675088 | 80 | $8.66 | $692.80 |

Total for this Purchase Order  $3,082.80

*Purchase Order Number  100005*

| Inventory Receipt Number | Date Received | Stock Number | Vendor Invoice Number | Quantity | Price | Extension |
|---|---|---|---|---|---|---|
| 100006 | 1/29/01 | 107 | 2719CRT | 50 | $10.27 | $513.50 |

Total for this Purchase Order  $513.50
Total for this Vendor  $3,596.30

*Page 1 of 2*

**Figure 7.23**  The completed Inventory Receipt report, *rptInventoryReceipt*.

EXERCISE 7.27: BUILDING A CASH DISBURSEMENTS TABLE

1. Open a new table in Design view.
2. Enter *CheckNumber* as the first Field Name and click the Primary Key toolbar button. Leave its Data Type set to Text and set its Field Size property to *5*, its Input Mask property to #####;;_, and its Caption property to *Check Number*
3. Next, enter a Field Name of *CashDisbursementDate*, set its Data Type to *Date/Time*, its Format property to *Short Date*, its Input Mask property to *99/99/00;;_*, and set its Caption property to *Date*
4. Save the table as *tblCashDisbursement*, then close the table.
5. Since *tblCashDisbursement* includes a foreign key link to *tblVendor*, you must establish that link in the Relationships window. You should also enforce referential integrity on the link to ensure that Electric Controls does not erroneously write a check to a supplier that is not in their Vendor table. Select Tools, Relationships from the menu.
6. The Relationships window will appear with a display of the relationships we have already created for the purchase cycle tables. Click the Show Table toolbar button.
7. Double-click *tblCashDisbursement*, then click the Close button.
8. Close the Relationships window and save your changes.

Your Companion CD includes, in its *Ch07.mdb* database, a table object, *tblCashDisbursement*, that we constructed using the steps listed in Exercise 7.27. The last table you need to complete the purchase cycle for the Electric Controls company is a relationship table that will connect the inventory receipts with the checks written to pay for those inventory receipts, the Cash Disbursements-Inventory Receipts table.

## The Cash Disbursements-Inventory Receipts Table

Since Electric Controls Company often pays for more than one materials inventory receipt with each check and sometimes pays for one materials receipt with two or more checks, you need a relationship table to model the many-to-many link between the Cash Disbursements table and the Inventory Receipts table. Exercise 7.28 shows you how to build this Cash Disbursements-Inventory Receipts table. This table only contains two fields, the primary keys of *tblCashDisbursement* and *tblInventoryReceipt*, which combine to form this table's composite primary key.

EXERCISE 7.28: BUILDING A CASH DISBURSEMENTS-INVENTORY RECEIPTS TABLE

1. Open a new table in Design view.
2. Enter a Field Name of *CheckNumber* and leave its Data Type set to Text. Set its Field Size property to *5*, its Input Mask property to #####;;_, its Caption property to *Check Number*, and its Indexed property to *Yes (Duplicates OK)*

3. Enter a second Field Name of *InventoryReceiptNumber* and leave its Data Type set to Text. Set its Field Size property to *6*, its Caption property to Inventory *Receipt Number*, and its Indexed property to *Yes (Duplicates OK)*
4. While pressing the Ctrl key, click the row selectors for each of the two fields. While the two rows are selected, click the Primary Key toolbar button. The primary key symbol should appear in both row selectors.
5. Close and save the table, entering *tblCashDisbursement-InventoryReceipt* as the table name in the Save As dialog box. Click OK to complete the table-save operation.

The *Ch07.mdb* database on your Companion CD includes a *tblCashDisbursement-InventoryReceipt* table. This table contains Electric Controls Company's cash disbursements-inventory receipts information. In the next exercise you will create links back to the entity tables joined by *tblCashDisbursement-InventoryReceipt* and enforce referential integrity on those links. Be sure that all tables, forms, and reports are closed and that the Database window is open on the Access desktop before you begin Exercise 7.29.

### EXERCISE 7.29: LINKING THE CASH DISBURSEMENTS-INVENTORY RECEIPTS TABLE

1. Select Tools, Relationships from the menu.
2. Click the Show Table toolbar button. Double-click *tblCashDisbursement-InventoryReceipt*, then click the Close button. You may want to resize and re-arrange the tables in the Relationships window using Figure 7.24 as a guide.
3. Click and drag the CheckNumber field from *tblCashDisbursement* to the corresponding field in *tblCashDisbursement-InventoryReceipt*. Click the Enforce Referential Integrity check box, then click the Create button.
4. Click and drag the InventoryReceiptNumber from *tblInventoryReceipt* to the corresponding field in *tblCashDisbursement-InventoryReceipt*. Click the Enforce Referential Integrity check box, then click the Create button. The completed set of relationships appears in Figure 7.24.
5. Close the Relationships window and save your changes.

Figure 7.24 shows all of the tables for Electric Controls Company's purchase cycle. Compare this figure to the data model for this cycle that appears in Figure 7.1. You can see how the model provides the basis for the relational tables you created. The five entities and their many-to-many relationships each have a table in the Access implementation. The need for the Category table, which does not appear in the data model, became apparent as you constructed the tables.

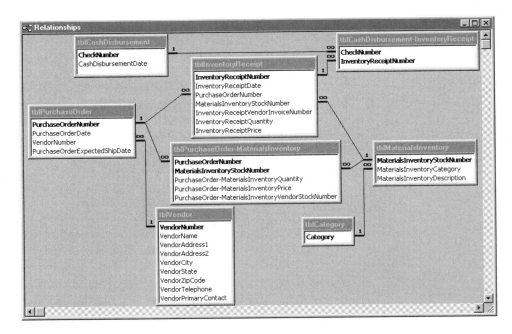

**Figure 7.24**   The complete purchase cycle Relationships window.

## Printing Checks

You can use the cash disbursement information that you have stored to build a report that can print checks. Of course, the report formatting details will vary with the type of check used. Rather than focus your efforts on these formatting details, you will learn how to extract the essential information from the purchase cycle tables that a firm would need no matter what their check format was. In the next exercise, you will learn how to get the data out of the tables and onto paper instead of trying to match a specific check format.

EXERCISE 7.30: EXTRACTING THE INFORMATION NEEDED TO PRINT A CHECK

1. In the Database window, click the Reports object, then click the New button. In the New Report dialog box, select Report Wizard and choose *tblCashDisbursement* in the combo box. Click the OK button to proceed.
2. The Tables/Queries combo box should be displaying Table: *tblCashDisbursement*. Click the >> button to move both of the table's fields from the Available Fields box to the Selected Fields box.
3. Select Table: *tblCashDisbursement-InventoryReceipt* in the Tables/Queries combo box. Select InventoryReceiptNumber in the Available Fields list box, then click the > button to move that field to the Selected Fields list box.

4. Select Table: *tblInventoryReceipt* in the Tables/Queries combo box. Select and use the > button to move the following fields to the Selected fields list box: PurchaseOrderNumber, MaterialsInventoryStockNumber, InventoryReceiptVendorInvoiceNumber, InventoryReceiptQuantity, and InventoryReceiptPrice.

5. Select Table: *tblVendor* in the Tables/Queries combo box. Using the > button, move the following fields to the Selected Fields list box: VendorName, VendorAddress1, VendorAddress2, VendorCity, VendorState, and VendorZipCode. Click the Next button to continue.

6. The Report Wizard design template for the report appears in the next dialog box. It bases this template on the fields selected and the existing relationships among the tables included in earlier Wizard steps. The Wizard placed the PurchaseOrderNumber field in the detail section because Electric Controls Company may write one check for items from several different purchase orders. Click the Next button to continue. Click Next again to accept the grouping levels.

7. Enter or select InventoryReceiptNumber in the first sort order combo box, then click the Next button to continue.

8. Select the Outline 1 Layout and the Corporate style in the next two dialog boxes, respectively. Enter a title of *rptCheck* in the last dialog box, then click the Finish button.

The Report Wizard creates a report that contains most information items that would appear on a check. In the next exercise, you will learn about some modifications that you can make to the form. Remember, each firm will have specific formatting requirements so that the information will appear correctly on its printed checks.

Our main goal here is to show you how to extract the information attributes from the four tables. Other than the information that appears on the Wizard-generated report, Electric Controls Company will need a total dollar amount to print on the check. This amount does not exist in any of our tables because it is a calculation result. Recall that a good database design avoids storing calculation results in relational tables.

In the next exercise you will modify the query behind the report to calculate the check amount and add it to the report. You will also create a single vendor name and address field for use on the printed check. To begin Exercise 7.31, have *rptCheck* open in Design view.

EXERCISE 7.31: CALCULATING THE CHECK AMOUNT

1. Open the property sheet if necessary by clicking the Properties toolbar button.
2. Click the property sheet Data tab, select the Record Source property, and click on its Build button to open the query behind the report.

3. Select the next open Field cell in the QBE grid and press Shift+F2 to open the Zoom box. You will need to scroll right in the QBE grid to find the next open column.

4. Enter *Extension: [InventoryReceiptQuantity] * [InventoryReceiptPrice]* and click the OK button. This expression calculates the quantity × price extension for each inventory receipt.

5. Insert an additional column in the QBE grid, select the new column's Field cell, and press Shift+F2 to open the Zoom box. Enter *VendorNameAndAddress: [VendorName] & Chr(13) & Chr(10) & [VendorAddress1] & Chr(13) & Chr(10) & IIf(IsNull([VendorAddress2]),"",([VendorAddress2] & Chr(13) & Chr(10))) & [VendorCity] & ", " & [VendorState] & " " & [VendorZipCode]* in the Zoom box, then click the OK button. Close the Query Builder window and save your changes.

This expression combines the separately stored elements of the vendor address into one field that you can print on the check. This expression is identical to the one you created for the Purchase Order report earlier in this chapter, so you could open that report's query and copy the text of the expression instead of typing it again.

**Try it**

As you work with Access, you will develop a number of expressions that you use frequently. Since these expressions are all just plain text, you can store them in a word processor file or a text file. Whenever you need one of these expressions, you can simply open your word processor or text editor, make any changes to the expression, then copy and paste the expression into an Access control or property.

The next exercise gives you some general formatting guidelines for improving the check report. You can use the printed check report that appears in Figure 7.25 as you work through Exercise 7.32. You should have *rptCheck* open in Design view as you begin.

EXERCISE 7.32: IMPROVING THE CHECK REPORT

1. Click and drag the top of the Detail section bar down to make room in the CheckNumber Header for the title and Electric Controls Company's name and address. Click and drag a marquee around all of the objects in the CheckNumber Header, then drag the selected objects down.

2. Change the label control text in the Report Header to *Check Report*. Select that label control and the two graphic line objects in the Report Header, then press Ctrl+X to cut these objects. Select the CheckNumber Header by clicking on its

Title bar, then press Ctrl+V to paste the three objects you cut from the Report Header.

3. Select View, Report Header/Footer from the menu to delete the Report Header and Report Footer sections of the report. Select View, Page Header/Footer from the menu to delete the page header and footer. Click the Yes button to confirm that you want to delete the controls in the Page Footer section.

4. Click the Toolbox button on the toolbar, then select the Label tool. Use it to draw a new label control for the Electric Controls Company name and address. Enter the name and address in the new label control.

5. Select the CashDisbursementDate text box control, click the Format tab in its property sheet, and enter a Format property value of *mmmm d ", " yyyy*

6. While holding down the Shift key, select the five vendor address text box controls in the Detail section and the five related label controls in the CheckNumber Header, then press Del.

7. Click the Field List toolbar button to open the Field List, then click and drag VendorNameAndAddress to the PurchaseOrderNumber Header section. Change the label control's text to *Mail Check to:* and expand the text box control to accommodate the full vendor name and address. Click the Field List toolbar button to close the Field List.

8. Move the VendorName text box control to the CheckNumber Header and change the VendorName label control text to *Pay to the Order of*

9. Select the InventoryReceiptPrice text box control in the Detail section and press Ctrl+C to copy the control. We chose to copy this control because it has the currency format settings that we would like to use for our Extension fields.

10. Press Ctrl+V to make a copy of the control in the Detail section. Align the new control as shown in Figure 7.25. Click the Data tab in the property sheet for the control and change its Control Source property to *Extension*. Use the same procedure to make a copy of the label control in the CheckNumber Header section.

11. Create a second copy of the new Extension control using the same procedure; however, paste the control into the CheckNumber Header this time.

12. With the new Extension control selected, click the Data tab in its property sheet and change the Control Source property to *=Sum([Extension])*. This control will calculate and display the total amount of the check. Add a label control with the text *In the Amount of* to the CheckNumber Header section.

13. Click the CheckNumber Header bar, then click the Format tab in its property sheet. Set the Force New Page property to *Before Section*. This will put each check on a new page.

14. Arrange the report's controls as shown in Figure 7.25 or create your own design. Close the report and save your changes.

A printout generated by the Check report that provides sufficient information to permit Electric Controls Company to write check number 10001 appears in Figure 7.25. This report is provided on your Companion CD in the *Ch07.mdb* database as *rptCheckExample*.

**Check Report**

*Electric Controls Company*
*12582 Camino Del Rio*
*San Diego, CA 92110-4264*

Check Number  10001

Date  January 31, 2001

Pay to the Order of  Bolden Wire and Cable Co.

In the Amount of  $869.00

Mail Check to:
Bolden Wire and Cable Co.
2798 Larsen Road
Suite 400
Flint, MI 48502-2966

| Inventory Receipt Number | Purchase Order Number | Stock Number | Vendor Invoice Number | Quantity | Price | Extension |
|---|---|---|---|---|---|---|
| 100001 | 100006 | 103 | PR-57996-3 | 10 | $16.95 | $169.50 |
| 100007 | 100006 | 110 | PR-58325-9 | 5 | $139.90 | $699.50 |

**Figure 7.25**  The Check report for check number 10001.

## PURCHASE CYCLE INFORMATION ON THE FINANCIAL STATEMENTS

In this chapter, you have learned how to use purchase cycle data to create purchase orders, checks, and other useful reports. This section discusses how accountants can extract the purchase cycle information for presentation on financial statements. The two main financial statement items that use purchase cycle information are the purchases account on the income statement and the accounts payable account on the balance sheet.

## Purchases and Accounts Payable on the Financial Statements

The traditional function of an accounting system was to capture and store the information we needed to prepare financial statements and tax returns. The database approach to developing the purchase cycle accounting system that we presented in this chapter provides much more than that minimal level of information. However, the database approach does include the basic debit and credit accounting information that we need to prepare financial statements.

You can calculate the amount of the general ledger debit to Purchases, which is also the amount of the credit to Accounts Payable, by adding one text box control to the Report Footer section of *rptPurchaseOrder*. Set the control's Control Source property to the expression *Sum([Extension])*. A Sum() function in a report footer will provide a grand total for the entire report. To obtain the amount for a particular period, you need to limit the purchase orders included to those that occurred in that period. You can do this in the query behind *rptPurchaseOrder* by setting the Criteria cell value in the QBE grid for the PurchaseOrderDate to a limited set of dates. To obtain the purchases general ledger debit for the year 2001, you would enter an expression of *>=#1/1/01 And <=12/31/01* in the Criteria cell.

You can also generate the amounts to debit the individual vendor accounts in the subsidiary accounts payable ledger. Simply add another grouping level, on VendorNumber to *rptPurchaseOrder* and copy the *Sum([Extension])* control we described in the preceding paragraph to the new VendorNumber Footer. The value in that control will be the debit to the subsidiary account for each vendor. Of course, you would not really need to maintain a subsidiary accounts payable ledger if you had a relational database purchase cycle system such as the one we described in this chapter, but we have seen old accounting habits linger before!

The general ledger and accounts payable subsidiary ledger account credits to Cash and debits to Accounts Payable are just as easy to extract from our purchase cycle relational database tables. Simply add a report footer to *rptCheck* and include a *Sum([Extension])* control in it to calculate the general ledger amounts. To obtain the subsidiary account entry amounts, add a new grouping level on VendorNumber to *rptCheck* and copy the *Sum([Extension])* control to the new VendorNumber Footer.

## SUMMARY

In this chapter, you learned how to construct tables, forms, queries, and reports to use in the purchase cycle of an accounting information system. Tables are the basic building blocks of the purchase cycle and store information about vendors, materials inventories, and purchase cycle transactions. Forms make entering, editing, and deleting transaction information easier. Queries can simultaneously extract data from multiple tables to help answer complex questions about materials inventory, vendors, payments to vendors, and receipts of inventory. Queries also provide a basic building block on which you can construct purchase cycle reports. You learned how to create typical purchase cycle printed outputs such as purchase orders and checks.

The purchase cycle begins with vendor records and materials inventory records. Production departments send materials requisitions to the purchasing department. Using these requisitions, purchasing agents negotiate price and delivery terms, then issue purchase orders to vendors. When materials inventory arrives at the receiving dock, dock workers enter inventory receipts information. Based on this receipts information and its agreement with purchase orders issued and invoices received from vendors, the accounting department prints checks that the treasurer will sign and mail to vendors. Finally, you can summarize all of this activity and create reports and journal entries that facilitate financial statement preparation.

# QUESTIONS AND PROBLEMS FOR REVIEW

## MULTIPLE-CHOICE QUESTIONS

1. The Purchase Order-Materials Inventory table is
    a. a referential integrity table.
    b. a query table.
    c. a relationship table.
    d. an entity table.
2. A good primary key for a Materials Inventory Receipts table would be
    a. remittance advice number.
    b. purchase order number.
    c. vendor invoice number.
    d. receiving report number.
3. The Purchase Order table described in this chapter, *tblPurchaseOrder*, is in first normal form because
    a. its primary key is unique.
    b. it contains no repeating fields.
    c. it contains a valid foreign key.
    d. its primary key exists for every record.
4. Purchase cycle activities include all of the following except
    a. keeping vendor information current.
    b. recording the cost of materials purchased.
    c. recording payments received from customers.
    d. printing purchase orders.
5. The purchase cycle uses a Materials Inventory table to provide
    a. descriptions of materials.
    b. purchase cost of materials.
    c. names of vendors that supply materials.
    d. quantity of materials purchased.
6. The VendorNumber field in *tblVendor* is a
    a. composite primary key.
    b. primary key.
    c. foreign key.
    d. relationship key.
7. In a materials requirements planning system,
    a. the master schedule replaces materials requisitions.
    b. inventory receipts are not recorded.
    c. the computer can generate materials requisitions.
    d. materials requisitions are generated daily.

8. Enforcing referential integrity on VendorNumber from *tblVendor* to *tblPurchaseOrder* is a good way to ensure that
   a. the VendorNumber in *tblVendor* is valid.
   b. the VendorNumber in *tblPurchaseOrder* is valid.
   c. the VendorNumber in both tables contains the right number of characters.
   d. both a and c are correct.

9. The list of materials that production sends to purchasing is called a
   a. request for quote.
   b. purchase order.
   c. bill of materials.
   d. materials requisition.

10. A sequential materials inventory item numbering scheme
    a. is easier to design than a mnemonic coding scheme.
    b. helps experienced employees identify inventory quickly.
    c. prevents data entry clerks from entering inventory codes quickly.
    d. is required by generally accepted accounting principles.

## DISCUSSION QUESTIONS

1. In the Materials Inventory table for Electric Controls Company, you used a Validation Rule property to control input to the MaterialsInventoryCategory field. In the Purchase Orders-Materials Inventory relationship table, you used a foreign key link with referential integrity on the MaterialsInventoryStockNumber field to the Materials Inventory table to accomplish a similar objective. Discuss the advantages and disadvantages of each approach.

2. Describe how you would design the Cash Disbursements Entry form mentioned in the chapter.

3. How would you modify the purchase cycle accounting system described in this chapter if you wished to include vouchers in the system?

4. How could you use the tables in this chapter to measure vendor price and delivery performance? What additional information would you like to add to the system design to make these measurements more effectively?

5. How would you modify the purchase cycle system described in the chapter to include quality measurements?

## PROBLEMS

1. Create a query that identifies those vendors from whom Electric Controls Company has purchased sheet metal products.

2. Create a report that uses tables we designed in this chapter to print a Check Register report. Include check number, check date, payee, and amount in your report.

3. Create a report that lists materials inventory items sorted by category.

4. Modify the purchase cycle system presented in this chapter to include shipping information and freight costs on the Purchase Order form and report.

5. Create a query that will find items on purchase orders that vendors should have shipped seven days before today but that you have not received as of today. *Hint:* Microsoft Access includes a Date() function that you may find helpful.

# 8 Payroll Cycle

Objectives

The payroll cycle system calculates employee earnings, records payments to employees, and maintains payroll records. These records must satisfy a complex array of government regulations pertaining to time and pay records. Firms also use payroll cycle information to create management reports and financial statements. This chapter shows you how to use Microsoft Access tables, queries, forms, and reports to:

- Create and maintain employee records.
- Create and maintain records of time worked.
- Calculate gross and net pay.
- Prepare payroll registers.
- Prepare employee earnings reports.
- Print payroll check information.
- Calculate payroll expense and accruals.
- Calculate payroll tax expense and accruals.

The payroll cycle offers more opportunities to include internal control features than either the revenue cycle or the purchase cycle. Therefore, we will use the payroll cycle system components in this chapter to illustrate a number of data input and review procedure internal controls.

## INTRODUCTION

This chapter shows how to use Access to create the payroll cycle elements of accounting information systems. Many firms chose the payroll cycle to be the first part of their accounting information systems that they automated. The payroll cycle was an ideal first candidate for computerization because it involves complex, yet repetitive, calculations.

Accountants sometimes consider the payroll cycle to be a part of the purchase cycle. The payroll cycle can also be integrated into the production cycle in manufacturing firms. However, treating the payroll cycle as separate from both purchasing and production cycles helps us highlight some of its interesting and unique characteristics. Designing and implementing a full-fledged integrated human resources payroll system is a complex undertaking to which entire books have been devoted. Therefore, we will illustrate only the fundamental payroll cycle system components in this chapter.

All but the very smallest manufacturing, merchandising, and service firms have payroll cycle activity. In this chapter you will learn about payroll activities that virtually all firms undertake. In service and merchandising firms, payroll cost appears as an expense item on the income statement. In manufacturing firms, the portion of payroll expenditures that is related to manufacturing activities becomes a part of the cost of goods manufactured. This cost appears on the financial statements in the cost of goods sold and in the cost of finished goods and work in progress inventories.

## GREENWOOD LUMBER COMPANY PAYROLL CYCLE INFORMATION

In this chapter, you will learn how to build the components of a payroll cycle system for Greenwood Lumber Company. Greenwood is a seller of lumber and related products. It sells primarily to the local construction industry, but in recent years has been increasing its retail sales to homeowners and amateur woodworkers. Because its operations have become more complex, Greenwood is increasingly interested in tracking its payroll costs by department.

Greenwood employs 50 people in nine departments; including four sales departments, three operations departments, and two business management departments. The largest departments are inside sales. Persons in these departments, one for commercial sales and another for retail sales, sell to customers who visit Greenwood's lumberyard or call in their orders. The commercial and retail outside sales staff members travel to customer locations. The three lumberyard operations departments are purchasing, materials handling, and maintenance. The two business management departments are accounting and administration. The administration department handles general management and human resources functions. Greenwood employees are permanently assigned to work for one department.

Greenwood calculates employee pay by the hour—no employees are on a fixed salary—and pays employees on the last day of each month for all hours worked during that month. The normal work week at Greenwood is 40 hours and employees earn overtime at 1.5 times their normal pay rate for any hours they work beyond the normal work week. All employees are paid at the end of each month based on time cards that they submit.

The data model for Greenwood lumber includes only two entities, Employee and Time Worked. A diagram of the data model, showing the two entities and the one-to-many relationship, appears in Figure 8.1.

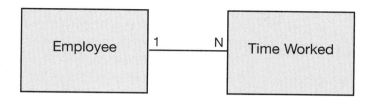

**Figure 8.1**   Greenwood Lumber Company payroll cycle data model.

## EMPLOYEE INFORMATION

The basic building block for any payroll system is employee information. At a minimum, Greenwood will need employee names, social security numbers, and pay rates. To calculate net pay amounts, it will need number of exemptions and marital status information. Greenwood will also need employee addresses for mailing paychecks and employee start dates for determining eligibility for pension and other benefit plans. These are only a few examples of the types of employee information stored in payroll databases. Indeed, some firms track *hundreds* of individual data items for each employee!

Integrated human resources payroll systems are the end product of an evolutionary process. Originally, human resources systems and payroll systems were separate in most companies. When firms began adopting database approaches to reduce data redundancy in their information processing activities, these two systems were ideal targets for integration. However, to enhance internal control, even today's integrated human resources payroll systems limit accounting personnel's access to employee data—additions, deletions, and changes to employee records are typically handled by the human resources department.

## The Employee Table

The first payroll cycle table that we will describe is the Employee table. The Employee table provides a central location for storing all information about each employee. This makes the human resources job of adding, deleting, and updating employee information easy and efficient. It also eliminates data redundancy; human resources creates and maintains data in this table, yet the accounting department can use information stored in the table to calculate payroll and print paychecks. The Employee table will include a fairly large number of fields. You will need to identify a good primary key field, then add fields to store employee names, addresses, social security numbers, pay rates, and start dates. You will also need to store other information in the Employee table such as marital status and number of exemptions that Greenwood will need to calculate withholding taxes.

The first field you will include in the Employee table is its primary key, the employee number. Recall that a table's primary key must be a unique identifier that exists for every record in the table. One tempting primary key candidate for the Employee table is the employee social security number; however, privacy laws discourage firms from using social security numbers to identify employees. Also, large companies have found that the Social Security Administration occasionally assigns the same number to more than one person and sometimes assigns a person more than one number. By creating its own employee numbering scheme, Greenwood can maintain complete control over the integrity of its Employee table's primary key.

Some firms use the employee number to store information implicitly. For example, a firm could make all managers' numbers begin with the digit *4*. This approach breaks down, however, if employees can be promoted or demoted from one job to another. Greenwood has decided to use a simple sequential numbering scheme to ensure that each employee number is unique and that the number contains no implicit information about an employee that might change. In a sequential number scheme, you assign each new employee a number that is one greater than the largest employee number already assigned. You do not reuse old employee numbers after employees leave because the employee number gives us a permanent access path to past employees' records. Although specific rules and practices vary from state to state, employers often are required to keep data about past employees for many years.

As you design the fields that will store employee names, keep in mind what you have learned in earlier chapters about good database design practices. For example, you will store the employee name data in the most atomic form possible; that is, in the smallest possible logical chunks. Greenwood has decided to break employee names into three logical pieces; first name, middle initial, and last name. Other firms might also include separate fields to store titles, such as Mr. and Ms., or surname suffixes, such as Sr., Jr., and III.

The next set of fields in Greenwood's Employee table are the address and telephone number fields. Designing these fields should be a familiar task for you by now, since you have already created address and telephone number fields for customers and vendors in Chapters 6 and 7, respectively. The address and telephone number fields for the Employee table and their properties are similar to those of the Customer and Vendor tables you have already built.

The final group of fields will store information that Greenwood Lumber needs to calculate employees' gross and net pay. This information includes employees' pay rates, number of exemptions claimed, and marital status. You also will need a field to store employees' start dates. Greenwood Lumber organizes its management and supervision by department, so we will include a department identifier in the Employee table. Note that storing the department number in the Employee table works only because Greenwood permanently assigns employees to departments and that employees do not work in more than one department. Other companies that do not have such a policy must store the employee-department link in a relationship table to accommodate the many-to-many relationships that can arise.

In the first exercise, you will create an Employee table for Greenwood Lumber Company. Have the Database window for a new database open on the Access desktop to begin this exercise.

## EXERCISE 8.1: BUILDING AN EMPLOYEE TABLE

1. Click the Tables object in the Database window, then click the New button. Double-click Design View in the New Table dialog box that appears.
2. To create the employee number field, type *EmployeeNumber* in the first row of the Field Name column. Since you will not be using EmployeeNumber in any calculations, we can leave its Data type set to Text. Click the Primary Key toolbar button to make this field the table's primary key. When you use a sequential number coding scheme the size of the EmployeeNumber field will depend on how many employees we expect the business will have. Set the Field Size property to *3*. This will let Greenwood have up to 899 employees if they start with an EmployeeNumber value of 101. Set the Input Mask property to *000* to limit EmployeeNumber entries to numbers and require an entry of exactly three digits. Set the Caption property to *Employee #*
3. Enter *EmployeeLastName* in the second row of the Field Name column and leave its Data Type set to Text. Set its Field Size property to *30* to accommodate the longest employee surname we expect to include in the table, and set its Caption property to *Last Name*
4. Enter *EmployeeFirstName* in the next row of the Field Name column and leave its Data Type set to Text. Set its Field Size property to *15* to accommodate the longest first name we expect to include in the table, and set its Caption property to *First Name*
5. Enter *EmployeeMiddleInitial* in the next row of the Field Name column and leave its Data Type set to Text. Set its Field Size property to *1* and its Input Mask property to >L. This will permit a one-letter middle initial and force it to be capitalized, even if a user enters it in lower case. Set this field's Caption property to *MI*
6. Enter a Field Name of *EmployeeSSN* for the social security number field and leave its Data Type set to Text. Set its Field Size property to *11* to store nine digits and two hyphens for each social security number. Set its Input Mask property to *000\-00\-0000;0;_* to help users enter the field values in the U.S. Social Security System's format, and set its Caption property to *SSN*
7. Enter *EmployeeAddress* in the next row of the Field Name column and leave its Data Type set to Text. Set its Field Size property to *40* and set its Caption property to *Address*

8. Enter *EmployeeCity* in the next row of its Field Name column and leave its Data Type set to Text. Set its Field Size property to *20* and set its Caption property to *City*

9. Enter *EmployeeState* in the next row of the Field Name column and leave its Data Type set to Text. Set its Field Size property to *2*, its Input Mask property to *>LL*, and its Caption property to *State*

10. Enter *EmployeeZipCode* in the next row of the Field Name column and leave its Data Type set to Text. Set its Field Size property to *10*, its Input Mask property to *00000\-9999;0;_*, and its Caption property to *Zip Code*

11. Enter *EmployeeTelephone* in the next row of the Field Name column and leave its Data Type set to Text. Set its Field Size property to *14*, its Input Mask property to *!\(999") "000\-0000;0;_*, and its Caption property to *Phone*. This Input Mask property lets the user enter an area code but does not require that an area code be entered. Remember, you can easily create these complex input masks by using the Build button to invoke the Input Mask Wizard.

12. Enter *EmployeeMaritalStatus* as the next Field Name. Leave its Data Type set to Text, set its Field Size property to *1*, its Input Mask property to *>L*, and its Caption property to *Marital Status*. If an employee does not declare a marital status, U.S. law requires employers to withhold at the single person rate. Therefore, we can set the Default Value property to *S*. Note that Access automatically encloses the value with quotation marks when you leave the Default Value property.

13. Since an employee must be either single or married, the only permissible values for this field are M and S. You can use the Validation properties to limit data entry to these values. Set the Validation Rule property for the EmployeeMaritalStatus field to *=M Or S*. Once again, quotation marks automatically enclose the stated values when you leave the property box.

14. Set the Validation Text property to *Please enter an M for Married or an S for Single.*

15. Another information item that Greenwood needs to calculate its employee's federal income tax withholding amounts is the number of exemptions each employee claims. In the next open row of the Field Name column, type *EmployeeExemptions*

16. Since Greenwood will use the EmployeeExemptions value in calculating net pay, you must store it as a number. The value for this field will always be a whole number (an integer) and will never exceed 255. Set the EmployeeExemptions Data Type to *Number*, its Field Size property to *Byte*, and its Decimal Places property to *0*. Set the field's Input Mask property to *0* and its Caption property to *Exempts*

### Try it

To save storage space and increase database access speed, you should always try to use the smallest storage space on the disk for number fields. In this case, a Byte field size is the most efficient. To learn more about the Field Size property settings that Microsoft Access provides for Number fields, select Help, Microsoft Access

Help Topics from the menu, click the Index tab, enter *FieldSize Property*, double-click on the selection, then double-click on FieldSize Property in the Topics Found dialog box. This Help Topic provides detailed information about the available Field Size property settings including range, decimal precision, and storage requirements.

17. If an employee does not specify a number of exemptions, U.S. tax law requires withholding at the rate for zero exemptions; therefore, set the EmployeeExemptions Default Value property to *0*. Note that Microsoft Access does *not* automatically enclose the 0 in quotation marks because it is a Number Data Type, not a Text Data Type. The quotation marks are only necessary for character values, not number values. When we set the Default Value property for a field with a Number Data Type, Microsoft Access knows to store the default value as a number.

18. To calculate employees' gross pay, we must know what their pay rates are. Greenwood Lumber Company pays all of its employees by the hour, so we can store each employee's pay rate in a field in an EmployeePayRate field. In the next open row of the Field Name column, type *EmployeePayRate*. Set its Data Type to *Currency*, its Decimal Places property to *2*, and its Caption property to *Pay Rate*

19. The U.S. government and many states have established minimum hourly wages. You can use the Validation Rule property to prevent entry of a value in the EmployeePayRate field that is less than the minimum wage. Using the Validation Rule property this way is an example of a *limit check*, an internal control procedure that limits the range of values that a field will accept. You can also use the Validation Rule property to set a maximum value on the field. One way that a data entry person can perpetrate payroll fraud is to change a confederate's pay rate to a large number and issue him or her one paycheck. The confederate then quits and disappears. A data entry person could also commit an unintentional error that overpaid an employee. Although you cannot completely prevent this type of fraud or error, you can reduce the impact by setting a maximum limit on the EmployeePayRate value. If you assume that the legal minimum wage is $5.20 per hour and the highest wage Greenwood expects to pay is $40.00 per hour, you can set minimum and maximum limits on the EmployeePayRate field. Set the EmployeePayRate Validation Rule property to *> 5.19 And < 40.01*, and set its Validation Text property to *The Pay Rate you have entered is not within the allowed range of Pay Rate values.* This Validation Rule property requires that any EmployeePayRate value be within the limit check values. The Validation Text property includes the error message that will appear in a dialog box if a user attempts to enter an out-of-range value.

20. Enter a Field Name of *EmployeeDepartment* and leave its Data Type set to Text. Set its Field Size property to *2*, its Input Mask property to *00*, and its Caption property to *Dept*

21. The last field will store the date each employee began work. Enter a Field Name of *EmployeeStartDate*, set its Data Type to *Date/Time*, its Input Mask property to *99/99/00;0;_*, and its Caption property to *Start Date*

22. To save the Employee table, select the File, Save As menu command and enter *tblEmployee* as the New Name in the Save As dialog box. Close the table.

The *Ch08.mdb* file on your Companion CD includes an Employee table, *tblEmployee*, that includes sample records for the 50 Greenwood Lumber Company employees. This table appears in Figure 8.2 in Datasheet view in a maximized window. This window displays a partial view of the first few Greenwood employee records.

**Figure 8.2**  Greenwood Lumber Company's *tblEmployee* in Datasheet view.

Although the Employee table you just built includes 15 fields, it is actually less complex than the employee tables you will encounter in practice. In addition to the information included in this example, employee tables often include fields that store title, job skill, education level, insurance and pension plan participation codes, direct-deposit bank account information, and even the name of a person to call in case of an emergency.

Many firms associate particular employees with jobs, projects, or departments. For example, Greenwood Lumber Company assigns employees to departments. In the preceding exercise, you used a field to store the department number rather than the department name to avoid wasting storage space. Using a department number makes data entry easier and less error-prone. The next section describes a department table in which you can store department names.

## The Department Table

The Greenwood Lumber Company Department table needs to include two fields. The first field will store a two-digit identifying number for each department. The second field will store the department descriptions. Exercise 8.2 provides step-by-step instructions for building this table.

EXERCISE 8.2 BUILDING A DEPARTMENT TABLE

1. Click the Tables object in the Database window, then click the New button. Double-click Design View in the New Table dialog box.
2. Enter *DepartmentNumber* as the first Field Name and leave its Data Type set to Text.
3. Click the Primary Key toolbar button, then enter the following property values: Field Size, *2*; Input Mask, *00*; and Caption, *Dept #*
4. Enter *DepartmentDescription* as the second Field Name and leave its Data Type set to Text. Enter a Field Size property of *40* and a Caption property of *Description*
5. Select the File, Save As menu command and type *tblDepartment* as the Table Name in the Save As dialog box.
6. Select View, Datasheet to open *tblDepartment* in Datasheet view.

The table shown in Datasheet view in Figure 8.3 is included as *tblDepartment* in the *Ch08.mdb* file on your Companion CD. With the table open in Datasheet view, you can enter Greenwood's department numbers and names. After entering the permitted values, you can follow the steps in Exercise 8.3 to create the link between *tblEmployee* and *tblDepartment*.

EXERCISE 8.3: LINKING *TBLEMPLOYEE* AND *TBLDEPARTMENT*

1. Close *tblEmployee* and *tblDepartment* to return to the Database window.
2. Select the Tools, Relationships menu command to open the Relationships window and the Show Table dialog box.
3. Double-click *tblDepartment* and *tblEmployee* to place them in the Relationships window, then click the Close button.
4. Click and drag the DepartmentNumber field in *tblDepartment* to the EmployeeDepartment field in *tblEmployee*.

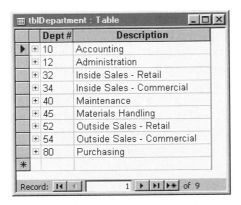

**Figure 8.3**  The Department table in Datasheet view.

5. Click the Enforce Referential Integrity check box, then click the Create button.
6. The Relationship window showing the link appears in Figure 8.4. To return to the Database window, select the File, Close menu command and click the Yes button to save the changes you have made to the table relationships.

**Figure 8.4**  Linking the Employee table and the Department table.

Now that you have completed the brief detour to build *tblDepartment* and link it to *tblEmployee*, you can turn your attention to designing a data entry form for Greenwood's employee information.

## The Employee Information Entry Form

The number and size of the fields in the Employee table make cumbersome the task of entering data directly into the table in Datasheet view. In this section, you will learn how to build a form for the Employee table that will make entering, changing, and deleting employee information much easier.

The Employee Information Entry form must include controls for the 15 fields in *tblEmployee*. One way to make data entry easier in a form with so many fields is to reduce visual clutter. You can do that on this form by grouping related fields into separate sections of the form. Greenwood's Employee table includes information that you can sort into four logical groups: employee identification fields, employee name fields, employee address fields, and payroll calculation information fields.

The employee identification fields are EmployeeNumber, EmployeeDepartment, and EmployeeStartDate. The employee name fields are EmployeeLastName, EmployeeFirstName, and EmployeeMiddleInitial. The employee address fields are EmployeeAddress, EmployeeCity, EmployeeState, EmployeeZipCode, and EmployeeTelephone. The payroll calculation fields are EmployeeSSN, EmployeeMaritalStatus, EmployeeExemptions, and EmployeePayRate.

You will learn how to arrange controls in logical sections for this employee information form in the next three exercises. These exercises will also give you valuable practice in creating a form from scratch—starting with a blank form. You will construct all of the form elements without using the Form Wizard. You can use Figures 8.5 and 8.6 as guides for placing the graphics objects, labels, and controls on the form as you complete the next three exercises. Close all tables and have the Database window open on the Access desktop to begin this exercise.

EXERCISE 8.4: CREATING THE EMPLOYEE INFORMATION ENTRY FORM

1. Click the Forms object in the Database window, then click the New button. Select *tblEmployee* in the combo box control and double-click Design View in the New Form dialog box to open a blank form.
2. Open the toolbox by clicking the Toolbox toolbar button, then open the property sheet by clicking the Properties toolbar button. You should keep the toolbox and the property sheet open on the desktop throughout this exercise.
3. Use the Rectangle toolbox tool to draw a box for the identification fields.
4. Use the Label toolbox tool to create a label for the box and enter the text *Identification* in the label. Set the label's Text Align property to *Center*, its Font Size property to *10*, and its Font Weight to *Bold*
5. Select the box and the label (press the Shift key while clicking each object in succession), click the property sheet Format tab, then set both objects' Special Effect properties to *Raised*
6. Draw a marquee (selection rectangle) around both objects, press Ctrl+C to copy the object group, then press Ctrl+V three times to paste three copies of the object group to the form.

7. Change the label text in the three new groups to *Payroll Calculation*, *Name*, and *Address* as shown in Figure 8.5.

**Figure 8.5**　The Employee Information form under construction.

Note that Figure 8.5 shows the property sheet and the toolbox open. Now that you have a rough layout for the overall form, you can complete the design of each individual section.

EXERCISE 8.5: ADDING FIELDS TO THE EMPLOYEE INFORMATION ENTRY FORM

1. Click the Field List toolbar button to open the *tblEmployee* field list.
2. Click and drag the EmployeeNumber and EmployeeStartDate fields to the first box you created.
3. Use the Combo Box tool from the toolbox to draw a field in the Identification section between the EmployeeNumber and EmployeeStartDate fields. After you draw the combo box control on the form, the first Combo Box Wizard dialog box appears.
4. Click the Next button to accept the default option since you want the combo box control to look up the values for this field in the Department table.

5. Select *tblDepartment* from the list box control, then click the Next button.
6. Click the >> button to move both DepartmentNumber and DepartmentDescription from the Available Fields list box to the Selected Fields list box, then click the Next button.
7. Click the *Hide key column (recommended)* check box to remove the check mark because we *do* want to display *tblDepartment's* key field in our form.
8. Reduce the first column's width and increase the second column's width so that the field values are displayed without extra unused space, then click the Next button.
9. Double-click the DepartmentNumber field name in the Available Fields list box. This selects DepartmentNumber and opens the next Combo Box Wizard dialog box.
10. Click the *Store that value in this field* option button and enter *EmployeeDepartment* in the combo box control, then click the Next button.
11. Enter *Department Number* as the combo box label name and click the Finish button.
12. Using Figure 8.6 as a guide, adjust the size and spacing of the three controls in the Identification Box. You can also set the controls' Font Size, Font Weight, Special Effect, and other properties using Figure 8.6 and your own judgment.

**Figure 8.6**  The completed Employee Information Entry form.

You can follow the same general procedure to click and drag the other *tblEmployee* fields to the appropriate sections of the form, set their properties, and adjust their sizes and spacing. As you refine the appearance of the form, you may find it helpful to toggle between Design and Form view.

**Try it**

You can move between the two view options for forms using the view menu command or the first button on the Form Design toolbar. This button has a drop button to its right, which makes it work much like a combo box control. Clicking on the drop button presents you with a choice of Design view, Form view, and Datasheet view.

EXERCISE 8.6: COMPLETING THE EMPLOYEE INFORMATION ENTRY FORM

1. Choose the Edit, Select Form menu command to select the form. Click the property sheet Format tab and change the form's Caption property to *Employee Information Entry*, its Scroll Bars property to *Neither*, and its Record Selectors property to *No*
2. Click the Detail section bar at the top of the form, then click the property sheet Format tab and change the Detail section's Back Color property to a color that contrasts with the rectangles that contain the text box controls.
3. Select File, Save As from the menu and enter *frmEmployeeInformation* as the form's new name.

**Try it**

When you select any Color property for a form object, a Build button appears to the right of the property box. You can click on this Build button to open a Color palette that offers you a choice of 48 colors and gives you the option of creating your own custom colors. After you choose a color and click the OK button, the number of the color you chose appears as the new property setting. We find this to be much easier than remembering that, for example, maroon is 4194432.

The form shown in Figure 8.6 is included as *frmEmployeeInformationExample* in the *Ch08.mdb* file on your Companion CD. In Figure 8.6, the form is displaying the first record of Greenwood Lumber Company sample data. In addition to learning more about the payroll cycle in this exercise, you learned how to use color, control properties, and object grouping to create a form that contains many fields but is still easy to read and use.

## Maintaining Employee Records

Now that you have an Employee table to store employee information and a form that makes using that table easy, you can efficiently and effectively maintain employee information. With the Employee Information Entry form, Greenwood can enter new employee information easily and update records as employees move, change their number of exemptions or marital status, get new telephone numbers, and change other information items they have entered in the Employee table.

Notice how the combo box control for the EmployeeDepartment field makes data entry easier. When you click the combo box button, a list of all the DepartmentNumber and DepartmentDescription values that are in the Department table appears as shown in Figure 8.7.

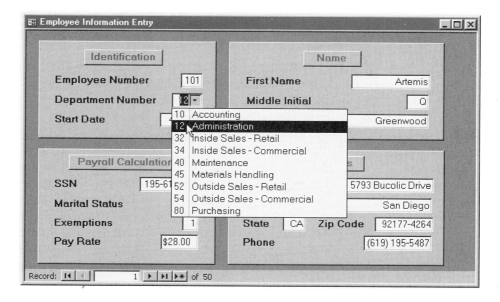

**Figure 8.7**  Using the combo box control to enter a department number.

When a user selects a particular DepartmentDescription value, the combo box control enters the related DepartmentNumber value into the EmployeeDepartment field of the Employee table. The advantages of using a combo box control here include:

• Data entry clerks do not need to memorize lists of department numbers.

• Only valid department numbers can be entered in the Employee table.

• Reduces storage needs in the Employee table by storing department numbers instead of descriptions.

• New departments can be added easily to the Department table and they will automatically appear in the Employee Information Entry form combo box.

Note how the Default Value property settings you incorporated into the Employee table operate in the form. For example, immediately after you create a new record by entering a new EmployeeNumber, the EmployeeMaritalStatus value becomes *S* and the EmployeeExemptions value becomes *0*.

**Try it**

You can test the operation of the other internal control features you built into the table's design. For example, try entering illegal values in the EmployeePayRate field. If you attempt to enter a value less than *5.2* or greater than *40* in the field, a dialog box appears with the error message we entered as the Validation Text property. Note that the form will not permit you to leave the record until you enter an acceptable value in the EmployeePayRate field.

Updating existing employee records to reflect pay rate changes, new addresses, new telephone numbers, and other changes is straightforward. The navigation buttons at the bottom of the form make it easy to find and display any employee record we want to change. The form will let a user move through the individual fields in the displayed record using the Up and Down arrow keys, the Tab and Shift+Tab keys, or the Enter key. Also remember that any internal control features that we built into the table's structure will limit changes to existing field values just as though you were entering new data.

To summarize, you now have a table that contains information about Greenwood Lumber Company's employees. The table relates each piece of information to a particular employee through the employee number—a primary key that uniquely identifies each employee. All information about a particular employee appears in one row of *tblEmployee* and depends on the primary key value for that row. You also have a form that facilitates entering, deleting, and changing employee information. You can use the information in this Employee table to construct payroll cycle forms, queries, and reports for Greenwood Lumber Company.

## Employee Information Reports

You can build a variety of reports using information in *tblEmployee*. The example report that you will build in the next exercise shows one possibility. This example Employee Pay report will list employee names, start dates, and pay rates. The report will group employee records by department and show the average pay rate for each department.

### EXERCISE 8.7 BUILDING AN EMPLOYEE PAY REPORT

1. Click the Reports object in the Database window, then click the New button. Select *tblEmployee* in the combo box control and double-click Design View in the list box control. The report must obtain department names from the Department table. To add the Department table to the report, you must change

the report's Record Source property from *tblEmployee* to a query. You can build this query by opening and editing a query behind the report.

2. Select Edit, Select Report from the menu, click the Properties toolbar button, click the Data tab, select the Record Source property, then click the Build button. Click Yes to open the Query Builder window.
3. Add the Department table using the Show Table toolbar button.
4. Click and drag the DepartmentNumber field from *tblDepartment* to the first Field cell in the QBE grid and enter *Ascending* in its Sort cell.
5. Click and drag the DepartmentDescription field from *tblDepartment* to the second Field cell in the QBE grid.
6. Click and drag the EmployeeNumber field from *tblEmployee* to the third QBE grid Field cell and enter *Ascending* in its Sort cell.
7. Click and drag the asterisk from the Employee table box to the fourth QBE grid Field cell.
8. Click in the fifth QBE grid Field cell and enter *EmployeeName: EmployeeFirstName & " " & EmployeeMiddleInitial & ". " & EmployeeLastName*
9. Return to the Design view window and save your changes when prompted.

Now that you have built the query, you can refine the layout of the report. You will begin by setting up a department group section on the report.

EXERCISE 8.8 REFINING THE LAYOUT OF THE EMPLOYEE PAY REPORT

1. Click the Sorting and Grouping toolbar button and enter *EmployeeDepartment* in the first Field/Expression cell in the Sorting and Grouping dialog box. Press F6 and enter a Group Header property of *Yes*. Enter a Keep Together property of *Whole Group*, then press Alt+F4 to close the dialog box.
2. You should now have four sections on the report: Page Header, EmployeeDepartment Header, Detail, and Page Footer. You can click and drag the bottom edges of these sections to change the size of each. This will give you room to include all of the controls that the report requires. You can refer to Figures 8.8 and 8.9 as you place controls, text boxes, and graphic objects on the report.
3. Click the Field List toolbar button, then click and drag the following fields to the Detail section: *tblEmployee*.EmployeeNumber, EmployeeName, EmployeeStartDate, and EmployeePayRate. Each of these fields will become a control on the report.
4. Draw a selection rectangle around the control labels and press Ctrl+X. This will cut the labels from the text box portion of the control. Click the EmployeeDepartment Header bar, then press Ctrl+V to place the labels in that section. Using Figure 8.8 as a guide, align the labels and controls in two rows.
5. Click and drag the EmployeeDepartment and DepartmentDescription fields to the EmployeeDepartment Header section.

6. To report an average pay rate for each department, you can add a calculating control to the EmployeeDepartment Header. Open the toolbox, then use the Text Box tool to draw a new control in the EmployeeDepartment Header.

7. Change the new control's Name property to *Average Pay Rate*, its Control Source property to *=Avg([EmployeePayRate])*, its Format property to *Fixed*, and its Decimal Places property to *2*

8. Arrange the controls and add label controls and line objects to the Page Header section using Figures 8.8 and 8.9 to guide your judgment. Figure 8.9 shows a printed page from the Employee Pay report for the Greenwood Lumber Company sample data.

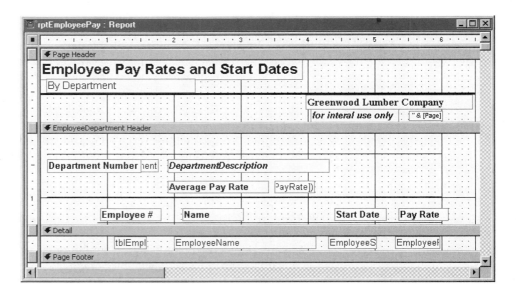

**Figure 8.8**   The Employee Pay report in Design view.

### Try it

As you make fine adjustments to objects' placement on the report, you may find it easier to work with Snap to Grid turned off. You can toggle this desktop setting by selecting Format, Snap to Grid from the menu. You may also find that you have more room to work if you turn the ruler off. You can do this by choosing View, Ruler from the menu.

Save the Employee Pay report by selecting File, Save As from the Design view menu and entering a name of *rptEmployeePay* for the report. The Employee Pay report shown in Figures 8.8 and 8.9 is included in the *Ch08.mdb* file on your Companion CD as *rptEmployeePayExample*.

## Employee Pay Rates and Start Dates
By Department

**Department Number   40   *Maintenance***

| | Average Pay Rate | $16.73 | | |
|---|---|---|---|---|

| Employee # | Name | | Start Date | Pay Rate |
|---|---|---|---|---|
| 111 | Judith F. Ballenger | | 1/21/68 | $18.00 |
| 124 | Louise K. Young | | 7/15/96 | $14.20 |
| 142 | Karl S. Smothers | | 6/15/01 | $18.00 |

**Department Number   45   *Materials Handling***

| | Average Pay Rate | $14.07 | | |
|---|---|---|---|---|

| Employee # | Name | | Start Date | Pay Rate |
|---|---|---|---|---|
| 143 | Byron D. White | | 8/2/01 | $9.10 |
| 106 | Henry X. Wheeler | | 8/3/64 | $15.40 |
| 115 | Esther L. Tufts | | 10/31/80 | $16.60 |
| 126 | Colleen H. Ward | | 4/15/97 | $12.20 |
| 132 | James R. Foster | | 12/1/98 | $14.90 |
| 139 | Edward G. Perciavalle | | 2/2/01 | $16.20 |

**Department Number   52   *Outside Sales - Retail***

| | Average Pay Rate | $9.43 | | |
|---|---|---|---|---|

| Employee # | Name | | Start Date | Pay Rate |
|---|---|---|---|---|
| 149 | Donald T. Forrest | | 12/17/01 | $6.80 |
| 146 | Joel B. Blum | | 11/1/01 | $6.60 |
| 119 | Natalie R. Sherwood | | 9/21/91 | $12.80 |
| 131 | Antonio N. Pelligrini | | 10/15/98 | $11.50 |

**Figure 8.9**   Page 3 of the Employee Pay report.

## RECORDING TIME WORKED

The second main entity in the payroll cycle is usually the time that employees have worked because most employees are paid on that basis. However, not all employees are paid on the basis of time worked. For example, firms may pay salespersons a percentage of their sales as a commission. Similarly, managers may earn a bonus based on their department's profit, production, or efficiency. Even when firms calculate pay using time worked, the methods they use to capture time data vary tremendously, ranging from workers punching a time clock to automated bar code scanners that read employee badges. Regardless of how firms capture time worked data, they must store the data by employee and by pay period before calculating payroll. In the Greenwood Lumber Company payroll database, you will store this information in a time worked table.

## The Time Worked Table

In this section, you will learn how to build a time worked table that stores regular and overtime hours worked by each employee for each pay period. We have made two key simplifying assumptions: that Greenwood calculates all pay on an hourly basis, and that Greenwood pays all of its employees once each month.

You will need a primary key that uniquely identifies each employee's time worked in each pay period. You could create a sequential number for each employee-pay period combination; however, Greenwood already has an employee number for each employee. If you add a field that identifies the pay period for each record, you can build a composite primary key that includes the employee number field and the pay period field that uniquely identifies each pay record.

The Time Worked table will also include two fields that will store the hours employees have worked—one field for regular hours, the other field for overtime hours. Greenwood uses only one overtime pay rate that is one and one-half times the regular pay rate. Further, you can assume that when Greenwood's accounting personnel enter the time worked data in this table, they have already calculated regular and overtime hours from workers' time sheets. You could create a form with controls that calculate regular time and overtime from time record; however, the Access expressions required to do that are beyond the scope of this book.

In exercise 8.9 you will create a Time Worked table for Greenwood Lumber Company that accomplishes the necessary data storage objectives. The Time Worked table also illustrates some internal control features that can help reduce potential losses from errors or irregularities as Greenwood processes its payroll. You should have the Database window open on the Access desktop to begin this exercise.

EXERCISE 8.9 BUILDING A TIME WORKED TABLE

1. Click the Tables object in the Database window, then click the New button. Double-click Design View in the New Table dialog box that appears.
2. Enter a Field Name of *EmployeeNumber*, leave its Data Type set to Text, and set its Field Size to *3*. Enter an Input Mask property of *000*, a Caption property of *Employee #*, and an Indexed property of *Yes (Duplicates OK)*
3. The second part of the primary key must identify the pay period. Since Greenwood pays once each month, you can use the last day of each month as

the value for this field. Enter *TWPayPeriodEnded* in the second Field Name row and enter a Data Type of *Date/Time*. Enter an Input Mask property of *99/99/00;0;_*, a Caption property of *Month Ended*, and an Indexed property of *Yes (Duplicates OK)*

4. To designate these fields as the composite primary key, hold down the Ctrl key and select both fields by clicking their row selectors. With both fields selected, click the Primary Key toolbar button. The primary key symbol should appear in the row selectors of both fields.

5. Enter the next Field Name of *TWRegularTime*. Enter a Data Type of *Number*, a Field Size of *Single*, and a Caption property of *Regular Time*

6. The greatest number of business days that occurs in a calendar month is 23. If Greenwood pays overtime for all hours over eight per day, the TWRegularTime field will never have a legitimate value greater than 184 (23 days × 8 hours per day). You can use the Validation Rule and Text property settings to enforce a limit check internal control on this field. Enter *<185* as the TWRegularTime field's Validation Rule property.

7. Enter *The number of Regular Hours you have entered is too large.* as the TWRegularTime field's Validation Text property.

8. The second hours field, TWOvertime, will store the overtime hours worked. Enter a Field Name of *TWOvertime*, set its Data Type to *Number*, its Field Size to *Single*, and its Caption property to *Overtime*

9. You can establish a limit check internal control on the TWOvertime field, too. However, selecting the limit value is a bit trickier than it was for the TWRegularTime field. Since a Validation Rule property setting will prohibit any greater value, you must set it to accommodate the largest possible number of overtime hours that any employee might ever work. Enter *<200* as the TWOvertime field's Validation Rule property.

10. Enter *The number of Overtime Hours you have entered is too large.* as the TWOvertime field's Validation Text property.

11. Select File, Save As from the menu and enter a name of *tblTimeWorked* in the Save As dialog box.

The table shown in Figure 8.10 is included as *tblTimeWorked* in the *Ch08.mdb* file on your Companion CD. The table in this figure displays the example data as we entered it for Greenwood Lumber Company. Your table will not display any data unless you have entered it or copied it from the version of the table that is on the Companion CD.

Greenwood Lumber's Time Worked table should have a link to *tblEmployee* on the EmployeeNumber field in both tables. If you enforce referential integrity on this link, it will prevent users from entering time worked for employee numbers that do not exist in *tblEmployee*. This internal control feature, called an *existence check* or a *validity check*, can reduce the threat of errors and irregularities in payroll processing. Exercise 8.10 shows you how to create this control feature. Be sure you have closed *tblTimeWorked* and have the Database window open on the Access desktop before you begin this exercise.

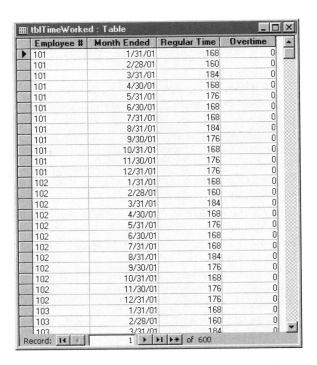

**Figure 8.10**  The Time Worked table in Datasheet view.

EXERCISE 8.10: LINKING *TBLTIMEWORKED* TO *TBLEMPLOYEE*

1. Click the Relationships toolbar button to open the Relationships window. The existing relationship between the Department and Employee tables will appear in the Relationships window.
2. Use the Show Table toolbar button to open the Show Table dialog box. Double-click *tblTimeWorked* to add it to the Relationships window. Close the Show Table dialog box.
3. Click and drag the EmployeeNumber field in *tblEmployee* to the EmployeeNumber field in *tblTimeWorked*.
4. Click the Enforce Referential Integrity check box, then click the Create button. The Relationships window with the new table and link appears in Figure 8.11.

To close the Relationships window and return to the Database window, select the File, Close menu command and click OK to save your changes. Now you can build a data entry form through which you can enter and edit time worked data.

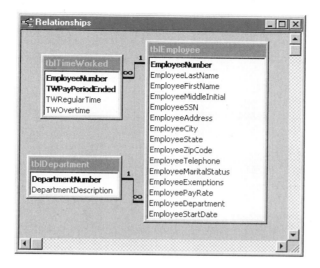

**Figure 8.11**  Linking the Time Worked table to the Employee table.

## The Time Worked Entry Form

You can build a data entry form for the Time Worked table that will ease the task of entering employees' time records. The Time Worked Data Entry form will use the employee name fields in the Employee table to provide another validity check that can help data entry clerks detect errors. You can design the Time Worked Data Entry form so that it displays the employee's name when a user enters an employee number. This lets the user check the displayed name against the employee name on the time sheet source document. In Exercise 8.11 you will create a Time Worked Data Entry form that includes this control feature.

EXERCISE 8.11: BUILDING A DATA ENTRY FORM FOR TIME WORKED

1. In the Database window, click the Forms object, then click the New button. In the New Forms dialog box, enter *tblTimeWorked* in the combo box control and double-click Form Wizard in the list box.
2. The Form Wizard dialog box will open with Table: *tblTimeWorked* selected in the Tables/Queries combo box. Click the >> button to move all of the *tblTimeWorked* fields from the Available Fields list box to the Selected Fields list box.
3. Select or enter *Table: tblEmployee* in the Tables/Queries combo box.
4. Use the > button to move EmployeeFirstName, EmployeeMiddleInitial, and EmployeeLastName from the Available Fields list box to the Selected Fields list box. Figure 8.12 shows the Form Wizard Dialog box at this point. Click the Next button to continue.

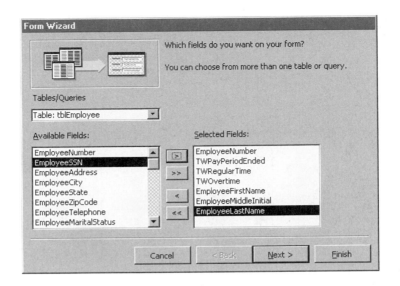

**Figure 8.12**   Selecting Fields in the Form Wizard dialog box.

5.  Click the Next button to accept the default of viewing the data by *tblTimeWorked*.
6.  Click the Tabular option button, then click the Next button to continue.
7.  Click the Standard style, then click the Next button.
8.  Enter *frmTimeWorked* as the form title, then click the Finish button to have the Form Wizard create the form.

The Form Wizard has created a usable form; however, you can make several improvements that will enhance the form's effectiveness and appearance. The next exercise provides steps for doing this. Have the Wizard-generated form open in Design view as you begin this exercise. If the property sheet is not already open on the Access desktop, click the Properties toolbar button to open it.

EXERCISE 8.12: IMPROVING THE WIZARD-
GENERATED TIME WORKED DATA ENTRY FORM

1.  Delete the EmployeeFirstName and EmployeeMiddleInitial text box controls and their labels.
2.  Choose Edit, Select Form from the menu, click the Data tab in the property sheet, then click the Build button for the form's Record Source property to open the query behind the form.
3.  Select the second QBE grid column (the TWPayPeriodEnded field) and press the Delete key.

4. Click and drag the TWPayPeriodEnded field from *tbITimeWorked* to the first QBE grid Field cell and drop it on the EmployeeNumber field name in that cell. The EmployeeNumber field should move one cell to the right, leaving TWPayPeriodEnded in the first cell.

5. Enter *Ascending* in the first two columns' Sort cells. These Sort cell entries will cause the form to sort first by TWPayPeriodEnded and then by EmployeeNumber. This will allow a data entry clerk to add all of the time records for a particular month end in employee number order.

6. Scroll to the right to find the first open QBE grid column and enter *EmployeeName: EmployeeFirstName & " " & EmployeeMiddleInitial & ". " & EmployeeLastName* in its Field cell.

7. Close the Query Builder window and save your changes.

8. Select the EmployeeLastName text box control, click on the Data tab in its property sheet, and change its Control Source property to *EmployeeName*. Click on the property sheet Format tab, then change the Back Style property to *Transparent*, the Special Effect property to *Flat*, and the Border Style property to *Transparent*

9. Using Figure 8.13 as a guide, make the final appearance modifications to the form, which include rearranging the controls, bolding the labels, and entering *Time Worked Data Entry* as the form's Caption property. You can also set the EmployeeName control's Enabled, Locked, and Tab Stop properties to prevent a user from entering data in that field.

**Figure 8.13** The Time Worked Data Entry form displaying sample records in Form view.

When you are satisfied with your form, you can save it as *frmTimeWorkedEntry*. A version of this form is included in the *Ch08.mdb* file on your Companion CD as *frmTimeWorkedEntryExample*. Figure 8.13 shows the Time Worked Entry form displaying records from the Greenwood Lumber Company Time Worked and Employee tables.

The Greenwood Lumber example includes some simplifying assumptions. The sample data includes only one year of data for 50 employees. All employees are paid on an hourly basis that includes regular hours and only one class of over-time hours. A more sophisticated payroll system would track accrual and use of vacation time, paid time off, unpaid time off, and sick days. Payroll systems often must track several types of overtime (for example, over eight hours per day, over forty hours per week, hours worked on holidays) and must calculate pay using measures other than hours. However, even with the limited example components included in this chapter, you can generate some useful and interesting reports.

## Time Reports

Businesses create and use many different reports built on time worked payroll data. The Greenwood Lumber Company example includes only regular and over-time hours in the Time Worked table. However, even in this simple example, the Time Worked table combines with the employee and Department tables to yield a total of 19 different fields that you can use in queries and reports.

To illustrate how you can use these tables to build payroll cycle reports, this section describes a report that displays total regular and overtime hours worked by department. This kind of report can direct managers' attention to departments that might have staffing or work scheduling problems.

You will build this report in two steps. First, you will design a query that links the Time Worked, Employee, and Department tables. In the second step, you will build a report based on the query. Exercise 8.13 shows you how to build the Time Worked query. You should have closed the Time Worked Data Entry form and have the Database window open on the Access desktop to begin.

EXERCISE 8.13: BUILDING THE TIME WORKED QUERY

1. In the Database window, click the Queries object and click the New button. Double-click Design View in the New Query dialog box.
2. In the Show Table box, hold down the Ctrl key and select *tblDepartment*, *tblEmployee*, and *tblTimeWorked*. Click the Add button, then click the Close button.
3. Click and drag the DepartmentDescription field from *tblDepartment* to the first Field cell in the QBE grid.
4. Double-click the TWRegularTime and TWOvertime fields to copy them to the next two QBE grid Field cells.
5. Click the Run toolbar button to test the query.

The dynaset resulting from this query should include the three fields you selected from *tblDepartment* and *tblTimeWorked*. Notice that you included *tblEmployee* in the Query window, but did not use any fields from that table in the query. The Employee table provides the link between *tblDepartment* and *tblTimeWorked*; therefore, you must include it in the query model even though you are not including any Employee table fields in the query.

When you are satisfied that your Time Worked query is operating properly, you can save it as *qryTimeWorked*. Close the query. The *Ch08.mdb* file on your Companion CD includes a *qryTimeWorked* object that you can use as a reference.

Now you can build the Time Worked report using this query. The Time Worked query was a little unusual. The Time Worked report has a twist that makes it interesting, too. To find out more, follow the steps in Exercise 8.14.

EXERCISE 8.14: BUILDING THE TIME WORKED REPORT

1.  In the Database window, click the Reports tab, then click the New button to open the New Report dialog box. Enter or select *qryTimeWorked* in the combo box control, then double-click Design View.
2.  Drag the bottom edge of the Detail section up until the Detail section background grid disappears. The interesting twist to this report is that it contains no detail records! Everything on the form is either a header or a calculated total field.
3.  If the form does not open with a Report Header and Footer, use the Format, Report Header/Footer menu command to create them.
4.  Click the Sorting and Grouping toolbar button and enter *DepartmentDescription* in the first Field/Expression cell in the Sorting and Grouping dialog box. Change the Group Header property to *Yes*, then press Alt+F4 to close the dialog box.
5.  Click the Field List toolbar button, then click and drag the DepartmentDescription field from the Field List to the DepartmentDescription Header. Delete the new control's label.
6.  Open the toolbox and use the Text Box tool to create two controls in the DepartmentDescription Header section. Delete both new controls' labels.
7.  Click the Properties toolbar button and set the Control Source property of the first control to *=Sum([TWRegularTime])*. Set the Control source property of the second control to *=Sum([TWOvertime])*. These controls calculate subtotals of the TWRegularTime and TWOvertime values for each DepartmentDescription value. Using Figure 8.14 as a guide, you can arrange these controls, add label controls to the Page Header section, and add graphic line objects to the report's design.
8.  Close the report, saving it with the name *rptTimeWorked*

The Time Worked report that appears in Figure 8.14 is included in the *Ch08.mdb* file on your Companion CD as *rptTimeWorkedExample*. This report il-

## Time Worked in 2001

| By Department | | Greenwood Lumber Company |
|---|---|---|
| | | *for interal use only* |
| | **Regular Hours** | **Overtime Hours** |
| Accounting | 8,836 | 24 |
| Administration | 5,852 | 8 |
| Inside Sales - Commercial | 10,936 | 33 |
| Inside Sales - Retail | 17,132 | 14 |
| Maintenance | 5,269 | 88 |
| Materials Handling | 11,043 | 110 |
| Outside Sales - Commercial | 8,869 | 32 |
| Outside Sales - Retail | 4,117 | 11 |
| Purchasing | 6,717 | 1 |

**Figure 8.14**   The Time Worked report.

lustrates how you can use the three payroll cycle tables to obtain some interesting information.

The report also demonstrates how you can build a query that uses one table as a link between two other tables that contain data in which you are interested. The Time Worked report is an interesting example of a report that contains no detail records.

By examining the ratio of overtime hours to regular hours shown in this report, managers at Greenwood Lumber Company can identify departments that are improperly staffed or departments that have scheduling problems. Your next task is to use the information in the three payroll cycle tables to calculate payroll.

## CALCULATING PAYROLL

Thus far in this chapter you have learned how to enter and maintain payroll cycle information. You have used this payroll cycle information to produce two useful reports; however, the main transaction processing objective of the payroll cycle is to calculate payroll and print paychecks.

Queries are useful tools for performing payroll calculations. Indeed, if relational database management software lacked a query language, you could not use it to calculate payroll. Because payroll calculations can be very complex, you will learn how to build several queries that each accomplish a step in calculating payroll. Then you will learn how to use these queries to build payroll register reports, employee earnings record reports, and payroll check reports. You can extend this step-by-step approach to more complex payroll systems as you encounter them in your future studies or in your practice of accounting.

## Payroll Calculation Queries

The first payroll calculation is simple, you must compute regular pay. To do this, you need only multiply each employee's pay rate times the number of regular hours he or she worked in the pay period. Since you have pay rates in *tblEmployee* and regular hours by pay period in *tblTimeWorked*, you can query these two tables to calculate regular pay.

You can use the Greenwood Lumber Company sample data to learn how to build these queries. Greenwood's Employee table has 50 employee records and their Time Worked table includes a full year of monthly pay period time data. You will use the January payroll period for the example calculations in these exercises.

### EXERCISE 8.15: CALCULATING GROSS PAY

1. In the Database window, click the Queries object, then click the New button. Click Design View in the New Query dialog box, then click the OK button. The Query Builder window will open along with the Show Table dialog box.
2. Double-click *tblEmployee* and *tblTimeWorked* in the Show Table dialog box, then click the Close button.
3. Click and drag the EmployeeNumber field from *tblTimeWorked* to the first QBE Field cell. Set the Sort cell in the first QBE column to *Ascending*
4. Click and drag the TWPayPeriodEnded field from *tblTimeWorked* to the second QBE Field cell.
5. To have the query obtain only the records for the year's first payroll period, you must set a criterion for the TWPayPeriodEnded field that is equal to the date that the first payroll period ended. Enter *=#1/31/01#* in the second Criteria cell in the QBE grid. The # symbols tell Access to interpret the characters they enclose as a date. To calculate the regular and overtime pay amounts, you can use the pay rate field from *tblEmployee* and the time fields from *tblTimeWorked*.
6. Click in the third QBE Field cell and press Shift+F2 to open the Zoom box. Enter *RegularPay: TWRegularTime * EmployeePayRate* in the Zoom box, then click OK.
7. Click in the fourth QBE Field cell, press Shift+F2, enter *OvertimePay: TWOvertime * EmployeePayRate * 1.5* in the Zoom box, then click OK. These two calculations will compute the amounts of regular pay and overtime pay.
8. To check your work at this point, click the Run toolbar button. The query should produce the dynaset shown in Figure 8.15.
9. Verify that the pay calculations are correct before you continue. The new RegularPay field should be the result of multiplying the TWRegularTime field from *tblTimeWorked* by the EmployeePayRate field from *tblEmployee*. The new OvertimePay field should equal the TWOvertime field times the

| Employee # | Month Ended | RegularPay | OvertimePay |
|---|---|---|---|
| ▶ 101 | 1/31/01 | 4704 | 0 |
| 102 | 1/31/01 | 4704 | 0 |
| 103 | 1/31/01 | 1377.6 | 0 |
| 104 | 1/31/01 | 1579.2 | 56.4 |
| 105 | 1/31/01 | 2066.4 | 147.6 |
| 106 | 1/31/01 | 2587.2 | 254.1 |
| 107 | 1/31/01 | 3763.2 | 0 |
| 108 | 1/31/01 | 1306.4 | 0 |
| 109 | 1/31/01 | 652.5 | 0 |
| 110 | 1/31/01 | 2167.2 | 0 |
| 111 | 1/31/01 | 3024 | 189 |
| 112 | 1/31/01 | 1234.8 | 0 |
| 113 | 1/31/01 | 1558.2 | 0 |
| 114 | 1/31/01 | 1512 | 0 |
| 115 | 1/31/01 | 2788.8 | 74.7 |
| 116 | 1/31/01 | 4033 | 0 |

Record: 1 of 50

**Figure 8.15**  The Gross Pay query calculation intermediate results.

EmployeePayRate field times 1.5 (to pay the overtime rate of one and one-half times the regular rate). For example, employees 104, 105, and 106 had overtime hours in January. You can use a calculator to check the OvertimePay calculations for those three employees. When building complex queries in steps, you should always check results after each step. To create the field that will calculate gross pay, return to the Query window by selecting View, Design View from the menu.

10. Once you have defined a calculated field in a query, Microsoft Access lets you use that new field in further calculations. Click in the fifth QBE grid Field cell, press Shift+F2 to open the Zoom box, enter *GrossPay: RegularPay + OvertimePay*, and click OK.

11. To test the query, click the Run toolbar button. The dynaset resulting from the revised query appears in Figure 8.16.

Once again, you should check the GrossPay field calculations with a calculator before you continue. You can save your query as *qryGrossPay*. The *Ch08.mdb* file on your Companion CD includes *qryGrossPay*, which you can examine if you have trouble getting your query to work properly.

Of course, calculating gross pay is only the first half of the payroll calculation battle. The rest of the challenge is to calculate the deductions from gross pay that determine net pay. Our next step will be to revise *qryGrossPay* so that it calculates deductions and net pay. Payroll deductions include taxes, insurance, profit-sharing contributions, and many other items. The rules for calculating each of these deductions generally fall into one of four categories:

**Figure 8.16** The Gross Pay query final calculation results.

- *Fixed Amount Deductions.* These deductions are easy to calculate because they are a fixed amount each pay period. Examples of these include deductions for health insurance premiums, group life insurance premiums, and employee-approved donations to charitable organizations such as the United Way.

- *Fixed Percentage Deductions.* These deductions are a fixed percentage of gross income each pay period. Examples of these include deductions for employer-withheld city and county earnings taxes in many parts of the United States. Some state income taxes are also calculated as a fixed percentage of all earned income.

- *Varying Percentage Deductions.* These deductions are similar to the fixed percentage deduction except that the percentage changes with variables such as level of income, marital status, and number of exemptions claimed. The U.S. federal income tax that employers must withhold is the best example of this type of tax. Many states have income tax withholding rules that are similar to the federal rules and, therefore, fall into this category.

- *Fixed Percentage Deductions Subject to a Ceiling.* These deductions are a fixed percentage of gross income each pay period until a ceiling amount is reached. The most common example of this deduction type are the deductions under the U.S. Federal Insurance Contributions Act (FICA), commonly called the social security tax. Employers deduct a fixed percentage of gross pay only until the FICA limit for the year is reached. Some states, such as California, require employee contributions to unemployment insurance funds that are calculated this way, too.

The first type of deduction, a fixed amount each pay period, is easy to model. You only need one additional Employee table field, a binary indicator of whether the employee was subject to the deduction, to trigger the calculation. The second type of deduction, a fixed percentage, is even easier to implement. You simply build the fixed percentage into the payroll calculation query. The third type of deduction, a varying percentage, is fairly difficult to implement because it requires one or more additional tables. These tables contain the various percentages and the points at which they change from one to the other. The fourth type of deduction, a fixed percentage subject to a ceiling, is even more difficult to implement. It requires an additional query to calculate year-to-date totals and compare the calculated totals to the ceiling amounts. The ceiling amounts may be stored in a separate table or included in the query.

The Greenwood Lumber Company example payroll calculation includes the second and third types of deductions. The fixed percentage calculation is the social security, or FICA, tax. A deduction for FICA tax is actually the fourth type, since it is a fixed rate up to a maximum pay amount per year. However, we have designed the Greenwood Lumber Company sample data so that none of the employees exceed the FICA ceiling. Therefore, you can model the FICA tax for Greenwood Lumber Company as a fixed percentage deduction. The deduction for the federal income tax that Greenwood must withhold from its employees' pay shows some of the intricacies of modeling the third type of deduction. This deduction is usually called federal withholding tax (FWT) or federal income tax (FIT) withheld.

Please note that the tax deduction calculations we model in this chapter are not intended to be complete or accurate. Employer tax laws change constantly and vary by state. Our purpose here is to give you some practice building tables and queries that you can adapt to specific user needs and to the ever-changing requirements of government regulators.

Before you create the query that will calculate net pay, you will build two tables that contain tax rates and exemption amounts. You could include these rates and amounts in *qryNetPay*, but placing them in separate tables makes updating and modifying the rates and amounts much easier. And remember, tax laws change even more frequently than software versions!

EXERCISE 8.16: BUILDING THE MARITAL STATUS TABLE

1. Click the Tables object in the Database Window, then click the New button. Double-click Design View in the New Table dialog box.
2. Enter *MSMaritalStatus* in the first row of the Field Name column and leave the Data Type set to Text. Click the Primary Key toolbar button.
3. Enter a Field Size property of *1*, an Input Mask property of *>L*, and a Caption property of *Marital Status*

4. Enter =*"M" Or "S"* as the Validation Rule property.
5. Enter *Please enter an M for Married or an S for Single.* as the Validation Text property.
6. Enter *MSFWTRate* in the second row of the Field Name column.
7. Enter a Data Type of *Number*, a Field Size property of *Double*, and a Caption property of *FWT Rate*
8. Save the Marital Status table with the name *tblMaritalStatus*
9. Click the Datasheet toolbar button to change the Marital Status table to Datasheet view to enter the two tax rates shown in Figure 8.17. After you enter the tax rates, close the table.

**Figure 8.17**   The record values in *tblMaritalStatus*.

The table shown in Figure 8.17 is included as *tblMaritalStatus* in the *Ch08.mdb* file on your Companion CD. The Marital Status table stores the percentages that you will use to calculate federal withholding tax for Greenwood Lumber Company. The next exercise shows you how to build a second table that will store the exemption values for the deduction calculation. The exemption values are dollar amounts that the tax withholding calculation will deduct from gross pay before applying the percentages in *tblMaritalStatus*.

EXERCISE 8.17: BUILDING THE EXEMPTION TABLE

1. Click the Tables object in the Database Window, then click the New button. Double-click Design View in the New Table dialog box.
2. Enter *ExemptionNumber* in the first row of the Field Name column and set its Data Type to *Number*. Click the Primary Key toolbar button.
3. Set the ExemptionNumber's Field Size property to *Byte*, its Decimal Places property to *0*, its Input Mask property to *99*, and its Caption property to *Number of Exemptions*
4. Enter *ExemptionAmount* in the second row of the Field Name column.
5. Set its Data Type set to *Number*, its Decimal Places property to *0*, and its Caption property to *Exemption Amount*
6. Save your new table as *tblExemption*

The table shown in Figure 8.18 is included as *tblExemption* in the *Ch08.mdb* file on your Companion CD. You can click the Datasheet toolbar button to open the Exemption table in Datasheet view. Then you can enter the field values shown in Figure 8.18. The simplified tax rules we have assumed for this example allows $200 per monthly pay period for each of the first five exemptions and $100 for each of the next five. Exemptions exceeding 10 do not have an allowance. After you enter the exemption values, close the table and return to the Database window.

| Number of Exemptions | Exemption Amount |
|---|---|
| 0 | 0 |
| 1 | 200 |
| 2 | 400 |
| 3 | 600 |
| 4 | 800 |
| 5 | 1000 |
| 6 | 1100 |
| 7 | 1200 |
| 8 | 1300 |
| 9 | 1400 |
| 10 | 1500 |
| 11 | 1500 |
| 12 | 1500 |
| 13 | 1500 |
| 14 | 1500 |
| 15 | 1500 |

tblExemption : Table — Record: 1 of 16

**Figure 8.18**   The record values in *tblExemption*.

Next, you will create a Net Pay query that can calculate the two sample deductions, FICA and FWT, and net pay. The computation rules for the two simplified deductions are:

- *FICA:* A rate of 7% calculated on gross pay.
- *FWT:* A rate of 20% if married, 30% if single. FWT is calculated on gross pay less allowable exemptions.

In the Net Pay query you will link four tables: Employee, Time Worked, Exemption, and Marital Status. An easy way to create this Net Pay query is to modify the Gross Pay query you built earlier. In the next exercise, you learn how to design a Net Pay query that calculates the two deductions and net pay for Greenwood Lumber's December pay period.

EXERCISE 8.18: CALCULATING NET PAY

1. In the Database window, click the Queries object, click *qryGrossPay* to select it, then click the Design button.
2. Click the Show Table toolbar button, double-click *tblExemption* and *tblMaritalStatus* to add them to the Query Builder window, then click the Close button in the Show Table dialog box.
3. Note that the two tables you just added to the Query window are not linked to either *tblEmployee* or *tblTimeWorked*. To perform the inner joins required by the payroll deduction calculations, you must create links to *tblEmployee*. Click and drag the MSMaritalStatus field from *tblMaritalStatus* to the EmployeeMaritalStatus field in *tblEmployee*.
4. Click and drag the ExemptionNumber field from *tblExemption* to the EmployeeExemptions field in *tblEmployee*.
5. To perform the calculation for the last pay period of the year, change the TWPayPeriodEnded Criteria cell contents to *#12/31/01#*
6. Since you have modified the Gross Pay query, you should save it using the File, Save As menu command. Give the new query a name of *qryNetPay*. The query appears at this stage in Figure 8.19.

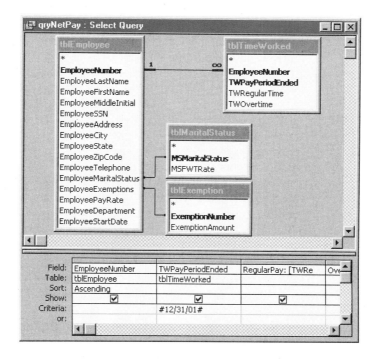

**Figure 8.19** Adding tables and links to *qryNetPay*.

### Try it

When you are modifying an existing query, form, report, or table that you want to keep, it is always a good idea to save the modified object under a new name immediately after making changes to it. Otherwise, you risk accidentally overwriting the existing object with the modified object.

7. Enter *FICA: [GrossPay] * 0.07* in the next open Field cell in the QBE grid.
8. Click the Run toolbar button to test the query.
9. Notice that some of the calculated values for FICA have more than two decimal places. Rounding errors can create many hours of extra work in accounting systems, and payroll calculations are perhaps the most infamous source of those rounding errors. To eliminate rounding errors at the calculation point, accounting systems designers have developed a number of tricks. You can use one of these tricks to make sure FICA values are stored with two decimal places. The trick is to multiply the result by 100, use an integer function to round the value, then divide the rounded value by 100. You can incorporate this rounding procedure into this query by revising the FICA calculation so that it reads *FICA: Int([GrossPay] * 0.07 * 100) / 100*
10. Run the query to test the revised expression. The FICA column values in the resulting dynaset should now have no more than two decimal places. You could have revised the expression to read: *FICA: Int([GrossPay] * 7)* and it would have worked just as well. However, the expression you used has the advantage of being self-documenting—it reveals what you were thinking when you wrote the expression. This can be important if someone else may need to revise the expression in the future—a likely occurrence in payroll systems!
11. The FWT deduction is each employee's gross pay less allowable exemptions multiplied by the tax rate for his or her marital status. Enter *FWT: ([GrossPay] - [ExemptionAmount]) * [MSFWTRate]* in the next open QBE grid Field cell. To test the query, click the Run toolbar button. Because of the values we assumed for the example tax rates and exemption allowances, the rounding problem does not appear in the FWT calculation. Thus, the Int() function trick is not necessary for this calculation.
12. Net pay is the remainder after subtracting FICA and FWT from gross pay. Enter *NetPay: [GrossPay] - [FICA] - [FWT]* in the next open QBE grid Field cell. To test the query, click the Run toolbar button.

As always, you should use a calculator to check a few of the individual employees' net pay calculations. The Net Pay query's dynaset of results appears in Figure 8.20.

The *Ch08.mdb* file on your Companion CD includes a *qryNetPay* object. You can examine this query if you have trouble getting yours to work. Both *qryNetPay* and *qryGrossPay* include complex expressions that are easy to enter in-

**Figure 8.20** The dynaset result of *qryNetPay*.

correctly. You can copy and paste expressions from the example queries to your queries if you wish. This section demonstrated how to calculate gross pay, deductions, and net pay using queries. You can use these queries to create useful payroll cycle reports and accounting entries.

## The Payroll Register

The payroll register is a columnar report that lists each employee's gross pay, deductions, and net pay for a particular pay period. Firms use payroll registers to reconcile paycheck totals to net pay and to support the period's payroll journal entries. Firms can also use information in the payroll register to calculate payroll taxes. You can build a Payroll Register report using the payroll calculation queries and tables that you have created.

You can base the Payroll Register report on a query that does the calculations since Access does not support calculation and summing operations on the same fields in reports. You can modify the *qryNetPay* query to build a Payroll Register query that will extract some of the fields you need from tables and calculate the other fields you need. The data you will need to create Greenwood Lumber Company's payroll register are employee number, employee name, regular pay, overtime pay, gross pay, FWT deduction, FICA deduction, net pay, and payroll period.

In the next exercise you will modify *qryNetPay* and use it to build a Payroll Register query that will extract the information needed for the Payroll Register report.

EXERCISE 8.19: BUILDING A PAYROLL REGISTER QUERY

1. Click the Queries object in the Database window, select *qryNetPay*, then click the Design button.
2. The Net Pay query includes all of the fields you need for the Payroll Register report except employee name. Since you stored the employees' names in three separate fields, you can combine them in different orders to suit different purposes. In this report, Greenwood would like the names to appear in a last-name-first order. Click in the next open QBE Field, press Shift+F2, enter *Name: [EmployeeLastName] & ", " & [EmployeeFirstName] & " " & [EmployeeMiddleInitial] & ". "* in the Zoom box, then click OK.
3. Run the query to test the new field calculation.
4. When you are satisfied that your Payroll Register query operates properly, save it as *qryPayrollRegister*, then close the query.

The *Ch08.mdb* file on your Companion CD includes *qryPayrollRegister* for your reference. The next exercise shows you how to build a Payroll Register report using the Payroll Register query you created in the previous exercise.

EXERCISE 8.20: BUILDING A PAYROLL REGISTER REPORT

1. In the Database window, click the Reports object, and then click the New button. Select *qryPayrollRegister* in the combo box control in the New Report dialog box, then double-click Design View in the list box control.
2. Use the View, Page Header/Footer and the View, Report Header/Footer menu toggles to include a Report Header and Footer instead of the Page Header or Footer on the blank report.
3. Click and drag the right edge of the report to, but not past, the 6.5 inch mark on the top ruler.
4. Click the Field List toolbar button, then click and drag the following fields to the Detail section: EmployeeNumber, Name, RegularPay, OvertimePay, GrossPay, FICA, FWT, and NetPay. Each field will become a text box control with an attached label controls in the Detail section of the report.
5. Click and drag the TWPayPeriodEnded field to the Report Header section of the report.
6. Draw a marquee (selection rectangle) around the label controls that remain in the Detail section and press the Delete key.
7. Open the toolbox and use the Text Box tool to create a control in the Report Footer section. Open the new control's property sheet by clicking the Properties toolbar button and change its Control Source property to *=Sum([RegularPay])*
8. Create similar total controls for the other five calculated fields in the report.

9. Use Figures 8.21 and 8.22 as guides in adding and arranging labels, line objects, and controls on the report.
10. Save the report with the name *rptPayrollRegister*, then close the report.

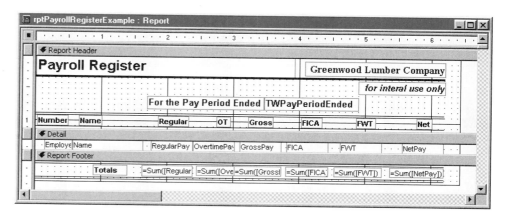

**Figure 8.21** The Payroll Register report in Report Design view.

Figure 8.21 shows the Payroll Register report in Report Design view. Unfortunately, Access does not permit you to adjust the size or spacing of report objects while in Print Preview. Therefore, as you refine the design of the Payroll Register report, you will find it helpful to toggle between Print Preview and Design view using the toolbar button or the View menu commands to move between the two views. Of course, the Payroll Register report shown here is only one way to design the report. You can easily customize this report to meet the needs of specific users. The Payroll Register report shown in Figures 8.21 and 8.22 is included in the *Ch08.mdb* file on your Companion CD as *rptPayrollRegisterExample*.

## The Employee Earnings Report

The Payroll Register report lists *all* employees' earnings for *one* pay period. In contrast, an Employee Earnings report lists *one* employee's earnings for *all* pay periods in a year. The Employee Earnings report provides information for unemployment tax calculations and the year-end W-2 form. You will learn how to build an Employee Earnings report for Esther Tufts, who is employee #115 in the Greenwood Lumber Company sample data. You can extend this example to generate similar reports for other employees, for groups of employees, or even for all employees. One way to build the Employee Earnings report is to modify the Payroll Register query and create the Employee Earnings report based on the new query. You will learn how to do the first step, modifying the Payroll Register query, in the next exercise.

# Payroll Register

### For the Pay Period Ended  December 31, 2001

| Number | Name | Regular | OT | Gross | FICA | FWT | Net |
|---|---|---|---|---|---|---|---|
| 101 | Greenwood, Artemis | $4,928.00 | $0.00 | $4,928.00 | $344.96 | $945.60 | $3,637.44 |
| 102 | Greenwood, Ethel Z. | $4,928.00 | $0.00 | $4,928.00 | $344.96 | $945.60 | $3,637.44 |
| 103 | Baron, Ethel P. | $1,443.20 | $0.00 | $1,443.20 | $101.02 | $312.96 | $1,029.22 |
| 104 | Oppenheim, Cecelia | $1,654.40 | $0.00 | $1,654.40 | $115.80 | $210.88 | $1,327.72 |
| 105 | Washington, Ronald | $2,164.80 | $0.00 | $2,164.80 | $151.53 | $352.96 | $1,660.31 |
| 106 | Wheeler, Henry X. | $2,710.40 | $0.00 | $2,710.40 | $189.72 | $542.08 | $1,978.60 |
| 107 | Surkamp, Elizabeth | $3,942.40 | $0.00 | $3,942.40 | $275.96 | $1,122.72 | $2,543.72 |
| 108 | Diamond, Timothy Y | $1,058.00 | $0.00 | $1,058.00 | $74.06 | $11.60 | $972.34 |
| 109 | Roche, Max E. | $615.00 | $0.00 | $615.00 | $43.05 | $3.00 | $568.95 |
| 110 | Badillo, Lucille B. | $1,754.40 | $0.00 | $1,754.40 | $122.80 | $466.32 | $1,165.28 |
| 111 | Ballenger, Judith F. | $3,168.00 | $27.00 | $3,195.00 | $223.65 | $958.50 | $2,012.85 |
| 112 | Dewar, Melanie C. | $1,019.20 | $0.00 | $1,019.20 | $71.34 | $43.84 | $904.02 |
| 113 | Brown, Alicia K. | $1,431.00 | $0.00 | $1,431.00 | $100.17 | $369.30 | $961.53 |
| 114 | Klusky, Irene R. | $1,566.00 | $0.00 | $1,566.00 | $109.62 | $273.20 | $1,183.18 |
| 115 | Tufts, Esther L. | $2,838.60 | $24.90 | $2,863.50 | $200.44 | $799.05 | $1,864.01 |
| 116 | Thurgood, Margaret | $4,224.00 | $0.00 | $4,224.00 | $295.68 | $764.80 | $3,163.52 |
| 117 | Boldway, Michael B. | $1,366.80 | $0.00 | $1,366.80 | $95.67 | $410.04 | $861.09 |
| 118 | Fenster, Janice S. | $1,204.00 | $0.00 | $1,204.00 | $84.28 | $301.20 | $818.52 |
| 119 | Sherwood, Natalie R | $1,331.20 | $0.00 | $1,331.20 | $93.18 | $226.24 | $1,011.78 |
| 120 | Simon, Arlene P. | $3,150.40 | $0.00 | $3,150.40 | $220.52 | $945.12 | $1,984.76 |
| 121 | Morris, Anne F. | $850.00 | $0.00 | $850.00 | $59.50 | $195.00 | $595.50 |
| 122 | Clark, Carol C. | $1,115.20 | $0.00 | $1,115.20 | $78.06 | $63.04 | $974.10 |
| 123 | Smith, Dierdre R. | $3,784.00 | $0.00 | $3,784.00 | $264.88 | $676.80 | $2,842.32 |
| 124 | Young, Louise K. | $2,499.20 | $0.00 | $2,499.20 | $174.94 | $459.84 | $1,864.42 |
| 125 | Studd, Chester V. | $622.20 | $0.00 | $622.20 | $43.55 | $126.66 | $451.99 |
| 126 | Ward, Colleen H. | $2,147.20 | $18.30 | $2,165.50 | $151.58 | $649.65 | $1,364.27 |
| 127 | Johnson, Travis D. | $3,168.00 | $0.00 | $3,168.00 | $221.76 | $890.40 | $2,055.84 |
| 128 | Gonzales, David G. | $666.00 | $0.00 | $666.00 | $46.62 | $19.80 | $599.58 |
| 129 | Quinn, Charles H. | $1,307.20 | $0.00 | $1,307.20 | $91.50 | $41.44 | $1,174.26 |
| 130 | Flores, Hector L. | $2,868.80 | $0.00 | $2,868.80 | $200.81 | $740.64 | $1,927.35 |
| 131 | Pelligrini, Antonio N. | $2,024.00 | $0.00 | $2,024.00 | $141.68 | $324.80 | $1,557.52 |
| 132 | Foster, James R. | $2,622.40 | $0.00 | $2,622.40 | $183.56 | $726.72 | $1,712.12 |
| 133 | Schwartz, Harold T. | $4,048.00 | $0.00 | $4,048.00 | $283.36 | $1,214.40 | $2,550.24 |
| 134 | Jeffries, Mark T. | $1,276.80 | $0.00 | $1,276.80 | $89.37 | $323.04 | $864.39 |
| 135 | Andrej, Arthur R. | $2,851.20 | $0.00 | $2,851.20 | $199.58 | $795.36 | $1,856.26 |
| 136 | Klippenger, Steven | $1,584.00 | $0.00 | $1,584.00 | $110.88 | $316.80 | $1,156.32 |
| 137 | Beeler, Sheldon O. | $1,734.60 | $0.00 | $1,734.60 | $121.42 | $460.38 | $1,152.80 |
| 138 | Patel, Shantu L. | $2,481.60 | $0.00 | $2,481.60 | $173.71 | $684.48 | $1,623.41 |
| 139 | Perciavalle, Edward | $2,851.20 | $0.00 | $2,851.20 | $199.58 | $330.24 | $2,321.38 |
| 140 | Faumuina, Celestine | $2,205.00 | $0.00 | $2,205.00 | $154.35 | $601.50 | $1,449.15 |
| 141 | Ochoa, Raul V. | $4,576.00 | $0.00 | $4,576.00 | $320.32 | $1,312.80 | $2,942.88 |
| 142 | Smothers, Karl S. | $3,168.00 | $0.00 | $3,168.00 | $221.76 | $950.40 | $1,995.84 |
| 143 | White, Byron D. | $1,601.60 | $0.00 | $1,601.60 | $112.11 | $240.32 | $1,249.17 |
| 144 | Chalfonte, Yves M. | $1,708.00 | $0.00 | $1,708.00 | $119.56 | $452.40 | $1,136.04 |
| 145 | Applegate, Victor N. | $3,819.20 | $0.00 | $3,819.20 | $267.34 | $1,145.76 | $2,406.10 |
| 146 | Blum, Joel B. | $1,161.60 | $0.00 | $1,161.60 | $81.31 | $288.48 | $791.81 |
| 147 | Landers, Myra T. | $1,020.80 | $0.00 | $1,020.80 | $71.45 | $124.16 | $825.19 |
| 148 | Schumacher, Dirk S. | $974.40 | $0.00 | $974.40 | $68.20 | $232.32 | $673.88 |
| 149 | Forrest, Donald T. | $897.60 | $0.00 | $897.60 | $62.83 | $139.52 | $695.25 |
| 150 | Ruvido, Gina C. | $684.40 | $0.00 | $684.40 | $47.90 | $85.32 | $551.18 |
| | **Totals** | $108,816.00 | $70.20 | $108,886.20 | $7,621.88 | $24,617.48 | $76,646.84 |

**Figure 8.22**   The printed Payroll Register report.

## EXERCISE 8.21: MODIFYING *QRYPAYROLLREGISTER* TO CREATE *QRYEMPLOYEEEARNINGS*

1. In the Database window, click the Queries object, click *qryPayrollRegister* to select it, then click the Design button.
2. To avoid accidentally overwriting your Payroll Register query with the modifications you make here, save the query now under its new name. Select the File, Save As menu command and enter *qryEmployeeEarnings* as the query's new name, then click the OK button.
3. Enter *115* in the first QBE grid Criteria cell to select only the payroll information for that EmployeeNumber record. Access automatically encloses the text in quotation marks when you leave the cell because it examines the underlying table's field properties and finds that the EmployeeNumber field has a Data Type of Text.
4. Delete the #12/31/01# entry in the second QBE grid Criteria cell. You want to include all of the pay periods in the Employee Earnings report.
5. Enter *Ascending* in the second QBE grid Sort cell.
6. Save your changes and close the query.

The modified query appears in Figure 8.23. This query will perform the same calculations as the Payroll Register query; however, it will perform the calculations for *all* of the year's pay periods for *one* employee. The dynaset that results from running the Employee Earnings query appears in Figure 8.24. The *Ch08.mdb* file included on your Companion CD includes a query object *qryEmployeeEarnings* that you can use as an example to check your work in the preceding exercise.

Now you can build an Employee Earnings report based on *qryEmployeeEarnings*. This report, which you will create in Exercise 8.22, includes a particularly interesting design feature. It uses the Group On property to generate quarterly subtotals.

## EXERCISE 8.22: BUILDING *RPTEMPLOYEEEARNINGS* BASED ON *QRYEMPLOYEEEARNINGS*

1. In the Database window, click the Reports object, and then click the New button. Enter or select *qryEmployeeEarnings* in the combo box control in the New Report dialog box, then double-click Design View in the list box control.
2. Use the Format, Page Header/Footer menu command to delete the Page Header and Footer, then use the Format, Report Header/Footer menu command to add a Report Header and Footer.
3. Click and drag the right edge of the report's background almost to (but not beyond) the 6.5 inch mark on the top ruler.

**Figure 8.23**   Modifying *qryPayrollRegister* to create *qryEmployeeEarnings*.

| Employee # | Month Ended | RegularPay | OvertimePay | GrossPay | FICA | FWT | NetPay | Name |
|---|---|---|---|---|---|---|---|---|
| 115 | 1/31/01 | 2788.8 | 74.7 | 2863.5 | 200.44 | 799.05 | 1864.01 | Tufts, Esther L. |
| 115 | 2/28/01 | 2622.8 | 0 | 2622.8 | 183.59 | 726.84 | 1712.37 | Tufts, Esther L. |
| 115 | 3/31/01 | 3054.4 | 99.6 | 3154 | 220.78 | 886.2 | 2047.02 | Tufts, Esther L. |
| 115 | 4/30/01 | 2788.8 | 74.7 | 2863.5 | 200.44 | 799.05 | 1864.01 | Tufts, Esther L. |
| 115 | 5/31/01 | 2921.6 | 24.9 | 2946.5 | 206.25 | 823.95 | 1916.3 | Tufts, Esther L. |
| 115 | 6/30/01 | 2788.8 | 74.7 | 2863.5 | 200.44 | 799.05 | 1864.01 | Tufts, Esther L. |
| 115 | 7/31/01 | 2788.8 | 74.7 | 2863.5 | 200.44 | 799.05 | 1864.01 | Tufts, Esther L. |
| 115 | 8/31/01 | 3054.4 | 49.8 | 3104.2 | 217.29 | 871.26 | 2015.65 | Tufts, Esther L. |
| 115 | 9/30/01 | 2921.6 | 49.8 | 2971.4 | 207.99 | 831.42 | 1931.99 | Tufts, Esther L. |
| 115 | 10/31/01 | 2788.8 | 124.5 | 2913.3 | 203.93 | 813.99 | 1895.38 | Tufts, Esther L. |
| 115 | 11/30/01 | 2838.6 | 24.9 | 2863.5 | 200.44 | 799.05 | 1864.01 | Tufts, Esther L. |
| 115 | 12/31/01 | 2838.6 | 24.9 | 2863.5 | 200.44 | 799.05 | 1864.01 | Tufts, Esther L. |

Record: |◄| ◄ | 1 | ► | ►| | ►* | of 12

**Figure 8.24**   The dynaset results for *qryEmployeeEarnings*.

4.  Click the Sorting and Grouping toolbar button and enter *TWPayPeriodEnded* as the first Field; the Sort Order will set itself to Ascending. Enter *Yes* for both the Group Header and Group Footer properties and enter *Qtr* as the Group On property.

5. In the second row of the Field/Expression column, enter *TWPayPeriodEnded* again. Press Alt+F4 to close the Sorting and Grouping dialog box.
6. Click the Field List toolbar button, then click and drag the following fields to the Detail section: TWPayPeriodEnded, RegularPay, OvertimePay, GrossPay, FICA, FWT, and NetPay. When you release the mouse button, each field will become a text box control with an accompanying label control in the Detail section of the report.
7. Click and drag the EmployeeNumber and Name fields to the Report Header section of the report.
8. Select all of the control labels remaining in the Detail section and press Ctrl+X to delete them.
9. Open the toolbox by clicking the Toolbox button on the toolbar.
10. Use the Text Box tool to add a new control in the Report Footer section. With the new control selected, click the Properties toolbar button to open the new control's property sheet and enter *=Sum([RegularPay])* as its Control Source property (under the Data tab).
11. Create text box controls with similar =Sum() expressions for the other five calculated fields in the report.
12. Copy and paste the six total-calculating controls from the Report Footer to the TWPayPeriodEnded Footer. When these controls are placed in the group footer, they will compute quarterly subtotals.

Figure 8.25 shows the Employee Earnings report in Report Design view. You can use Figures 8.25 and 8.26 as guides for positioning line objects and arranging controls on the report.

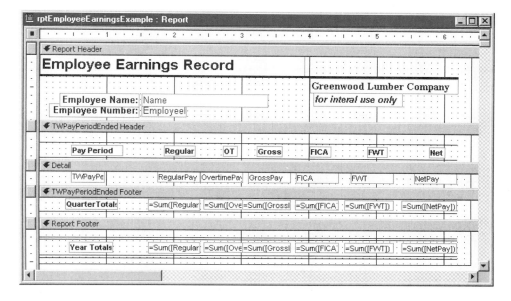

**Figure 8.25** The *rptEmployeeEarnings* in Design view.

Save the report, entering a name of *rptEmployeeEarnings*, then close the report. The Employee Earnings report that appears in Figures 8.25 and 8.26 is included in the *Ch08.mdb* file on your Companion CD as *rptEmployeeEarningsExample*. Figure 8.26 shows the Employee Earnings record that *rptEmployeeEarnings* generates for Greenwood Lumber employee Esther Tufts.

## Employee Earnings Record

Greenwood Lumber Company
*for interal use only*

**Employee Name:** Tufts, Esther L.
**Employee Number:** 115

| Pay Period | Regular | OT | Gross | FICA | FWT | Net |
|---|---|---|---|---|---|---|
| 1/31/01 | $2,788.80 | $74.70 | $2,863.50 | $200.44 | $799.05 | $1,864.01 |
| 2/28/01 | $2,622.80 | $0.00 | $2,622.80 | $183.59 | $726.84 | $1,712.37 |
| 3/31/01 | $3,054.40 | $99.60 | $3,154.00 | $220.78 | $886.20 | $2,047.02 |
| QuarterTotals | $8,466.00 | $174.30 | $8,640.30 | $604.81 | $2,412.09 | $5,623.40 |

| Pay Period | Regular | OT | Gross | FICA | FWT | Net |
|---|---|---|---|---|---|---|
| 4/30/01 | $2,788.80 | $74.70 | $2,863.50 | $200.44 | $799.05 | $1,864.01 |
| 5/31/01 | $2,921.60 | $24.90 | $2,946.50 | $206.25 | $823.95 | $1,916.30 |
| 6/30/01 | $2,788.80 | $74.70 | $2,863.50 | $200.44 | $799.05 | $1,864.01 |
| QuarterTotals | $8,499.20 | $174.30 | $8,673.50 | $607.13 | $2,422.05 | $5,644.32 |

| Pay Period | Regular | OT | Gross | FICA | FWT | Net |
|---|---|---|---|---|---|---|
| 7/31/01 | $2,788.80 | $74.70 | $2,863.50 | $200.44 | $799.05 | $1,864.01 |
| 8/31/01 | $3,054.40 | $49.80 | $3,104.20 | $217.29 | $871.26 | $2,015.65 |
| 9/30/01 | $2,921.60 | $49.80 | $2,971.40 | $207.99 | $831.42 | $1,931.99 |
| QuarterTotals | $8,764.80 | $174.30 | $8,939.10 | $625.72 | $2,501.73 | $5,811.65 |

| Pay Period | Regular | OT | Gross | FICA | FWT | Net |
|---|---|---|---|---|---|---|
| 10/31/01 | $2,788.80 | $124.50 | $2,913.30 | $203.93 | $813.99 | $1,895.38 |
| 11/30/01 | $2,838.60 | $24.90 | $2,863.50 | $200.44 | $799.05 | $1,864.01 |
| 12/31/01 | $2,838.60 | $24.90 | $2,863.50 | $200.44 | $799.05 | $1,864.01 |
| QuarterTotals | $8,466.00 | $174.30 | $8,640.30 | $604.81 | $2,412.09 | $5,623.40 |

| | Regular | OT | Gross | FICA | FWT | Net |
|---|---|---|---|---|---|---|
| Year Totals | $34,196.00 | $697.20 | $34,893.20 | $2,442.47 | $9,747.96 | $22,702.77 |

**Figure 8.26**    The printed *rptEmployeeEarnings*.

## Printing Payroll Checks

The last payroll cycle report we will discuss in this chapter is the payroll check itself. The payroll check should always include an earnings statement or pay stub that shows how the check was calculated. Payroll registers report payroll details for all employees for one pay period. Employee earnings records show one employee's payroll record for the year. The payroll check is one record from each of these reports.

You can use the same queries you built for the Payroll Register report and the Employee Earnings report to generate payroll checks. For example, you can add employee address fields to the information you already have in the Payroll Register query and build a report based on the query that includes page breaks between each employee record. Such a report would print all of the information Greenwood would need to include on a paycheck. The exact form of payroll checks and earnings statements will vary from firm to firm. Since we have already illustrated many report design techniques in this chapter, you are well-equipped to create your own paycheck reports for users or clients.

## PAYROLL CYCLE INFORMATION ON THE FINANCIAL STATEMENTS

In this chapter, we have described how to use payroll cycle data to create data tables, track employee and time worked information, calculate payroll, and print a number of useful reports. This section discusses how payroll cycle information appears on firms' financial statements.

Accountants have always tracked the information needed to prepare financial statements and tax returns. Our database approach to developing payroll cycle accounting system elements provides a variety of information that managers can use to make better decisions. However, the database approach also provides everything that accountants need to calculate payroll cycle debits and credits.

## Payroll Expense, Accruals, and Payables

The general ledger debit to Payroll Expense is the gross payroll total at the bottom of each payroll period's payroll register. The general ledger credit to Cash is included in the same report. By referring to Figure 8.22, the Payroll Register report for Greenwood Lumber Company, you can prepare the December 31, 2001 journal entry. The necessary numbers appear in that report's totals:

| Date | Account | Debit | Credit |
|---|---|---|---|
| Dec. 31, 2001 | Payroll expense | 108,886.20 | |
| | FWT payable | | 24,617.48 |
| | FICA payable | | 7,621.88 |
| | Cash | | 76,646.84 |

Since Greenwood Lumber pays on the last day of each month, our example firm conveniently avoids accruing payroll expenses. However, you could calculate Accrued Payroll using the same information you used to calculate payroll in this chapter. For example, if *tblTimeWorked* had included uncompensated time at the end of a reporting period, you could have run *rptPayrollRegister* to obtain the debits and credits for the accrual entry. This entry would be the same as the journal entry to record Payroll Expense except that the last credit in the entry would be to Accrued Payroll Expense or to Payroll Expense Payable instead of to Cash.

## Payroll Tax Expense, Accruals, and Payables

Payroll tax calculations all use the current period payroll information included in the payroll register. Many payroll taxes require cumulative information, since the tax is payable only on earnings up to a fixed amount per employee each year. State and federal unemployment taxes are good examples of this type of payroll tax.

## SUMMARY

In this chapter, you have learned how to use payroll cycle data to track employee and time worked information, calculate payroll, and print employee information reports, time reports, payroll registers, and employee earnings reports. Many of these reports required you to construct queries and use the queries to build reports.

The payroll cycle begins with employee records and time worked records. Periodically, the firm pays employees and calculates payroll. Payroll calculation can be complex; employers must not only multiply pay rate times hours worked, but must comply with state and federal withholding regulations. Many firms also arrange to deduct charges for insurance and profit sharing contributions from employees' pay. Employers must maintain payroll records to comply with numerous government regulations. Finally, accountants prepare financial statements and tax returns from the payroll cycle information.

# QUESTIONS AND PROBLEMS FOR REVIEW

### MULTIPLE-CHOICE QUESTIONS

1. You can use queries in the payroll cycle to
   a. store time worked data.
   b. store employee pay rates.
   c. calculate payroll deductions.
   d. print an employee earnings report.
2. Payroll cycle activities include all of the following except
   a. recording office supplies expense.
   b. recording changes in employee pay rates.
   c. calculating overtime pay.
   d. keeping employee addresses current.

3. A good primary key for a time worked table in a firm that pays weekly would be
   a. employee number.
   b. week.
   c. employee number *and* week.
   d. employee number *or* week.

4. A good way to make a data entry form that contains many fields easier to use would be to
   a. put the fields in alphabetical order.
   b. right-justify all of the fields.
   c. use a sharply contrasting background color.
   d. group related fields together on the form.

5. Setting the Validation Rule property that limits the minimum value that a user can enter in an employee pay rate field can help prevent
   a. violations of minimum wage laws.
   b. payment for regular hours at the overtime rate.
   c. payment for hours not actually worked.
   d. payroll tax fraud.

6. The EmployeeDepartment field in *tblEmployee* is a
   a. composite primary key.
   b. primary key.
   c. foreign key.
   d. relationship key.

7. A payroll register lists
   a. all wages paid to a single employee for the year.
   b. wages paid to all employees in a single pay period.
   c. all employees who received wages within the past year.
   d. accrued vacation time for all employees.

8. The time worked by department report you built in this chapter could help managers
   a. identify employees that deserved raises.
   b. identify ineffective work scheduling.
   c. both a and b.
   d. neither a nor b.

9. We often design reports based on queries that include calculations because in Microsoft Access
   a. a report cannot include field calculations.
   b. a query cannot include field calculations.
   c. a query cannot compute sums of fields.
   d. a report cannot sum fields that it calculates.

10. Setting a date field's Input Mask property to 99/99/00;1;_
    a. eases data entry by automatically inserting date separators.
    b. prevents entry of future dates in payroll records.
    c. prevents entry of nonexistent dates such as 52/67/88.
    d. requires extra space in the data table to store the date separators.

## DISCUSSION QUESTIONS

1. If you wanted to add employees to whom you pay a percentage commission to the payroll system described in the chapter, you would need to store the commission rate in a table. Discuss which table(s) you might use and why.
2. Describe how you could modify *tblTimeWorked* to include hourly time records. What would be candidate primary keys for the modified table?
3. Why are the purchase cycle and the payroll cycle often discussed separately?
4. How could you modify the time worked by department report to make it more useful to Greenwood Lumber managers?
5. Discuss the advantages and disadvantages of storing employee names in *tblEmployee* in three parts.

## PROBLEMS

1. Write a query that independently verifies the gross pay calculation that *qryGrossPay* performs.
2. Create a report that uses tables from this chapter to print a payroll check and earnings statement for one employee.
3. Create any necessary tables and revise *qryNetPay* to include a deduction for medical insurance. Clearly state any assumptions you must make to accomplish this task.
4. Modify the payroll cycle system presented in this chapter to include employees that earn a fixed salary each pay period.
5. Modify the payroll register report so that it displays only the summary information that Greenwood Lumber Company needs to prepare its general ledger entry for payroll each month.

# 9 PRODUCTION CYCLE

## OBJECTIVES

The production cycle includes all activities that convert raw materials, labor, and overhead into finished products. Therefore, some authors call this cycle the conversion cycle. The production cycle accounting system must trace or allocate manufacturing costs to products produced. The production cycle system must provide managers with information they can use to monitor the manufacturing process. It must also provide financial accountants with information they can use to value inventories and determine the cost of goods sold. This chapter will show you how to use Microsoft Access tables, queries, forms, and reports to:

- Track materials cost.
- Track labor cost.
- Allocate manufacturing overhead cost.
- Create a bill of materials.
- Accumulate costs in a job order cost system.
- Summarize and report job costs.

This chapter also explains how you can adapt the job order cost system examples presented here to build process, hybrid, and activity-based cost systems. Our discussion of the production cycle assumes that you have studied the purchase cycle in Chapter 7 and the payroll cycle in Chapter 8. You will learn how to modify some of the tables you created as you worked through those chapters. You can combine those modified tables with new tables, forms, queries, and reports to build the production cycle system components in this chapter.

## INTRODUCTION

This chapter shows how to use Microsoft Access to create the elements of production cycle accounting systems. Although most accounting information systems textbooks use manufacturing firms to illustrate the production cycle, many service firms are beginning to examine their business processes using a product costing approach. In this approach, a service firm identifies specific components of the services it offers, then tracks and allocates costs to those service components—just as a manufacturing firm tracks and allocates costs to products. Some merchandising firms also track and allocate costs to specific product lines or customers. Therefore, the techniques you learn in this chapter will help you design accounting systems for all three types of firms, even though we use manufacturing examples only.

Chapter 7 showed you how to record the cost of materials purchased. Chapter 8 showed you how to record the cost of paying employees. This chapter describes how you can combine materials and labor costs with other manufacturing costs to determine the total cost of manufactured products. You will modify some of the Chapter 7 and 8 database objects as you work through this chapter. First, however, you need to understand the different ways that firms can accumulate costs in the production cycle.

## COST ACCUMULATION APPROACHES

The goal of the production cycle accounting system is to assign costs to cost objects. If a firm is manufacturing airplanes, the ultimate cost object is *airplane*. If a firm is manufacturing tomato soup, the ultimate cost object is *can of tomato soup*. However, most production cost systems do not allocate costs directly to the ultimate cost object. Instead, they use a three-step approach:

1. Assign costs to intermediate-level cost objects.

2. Assign the intermediate-level cost objects to higher-level cost objects.

3. Assign higher-level cost objects to ultimate cost objects.

Logical intermediate-level cost objects for particular industries or product lines fall into two general categories: jobs and departments. The nature of the manufacturing process usually dictates which category of intermediate-level cost object is appropriate. Therefore, the nature of the manufacturing process typically determines which cost accumulation approach a firm will use.

Firms that manufacture different types or quantities of products use a job order cost accumulation system. The intermediate-level cost objects in job order cost systems are jobs. Firms that manufacture one product or similar types of products that require the same processes and the same mix of labor and overhead use process cost accumulation systems. The intermediate-level cost objects in process cost systems are departments.

## Job Order Cost Accumulation

Firms that produce many different products use *job* as the intermediate-level cost object in their cost accumulation systems. They break down their production processes into jobs, accumulate costs by job, then divide each job's cost by the number of units in each job to determine the cost of each unit. A job order system uses job numbers to track direct costs. Each raw materials inventory item that goes into production is assigned a job number. Each hour or other unit of labor is assigned a job number. Indirect manufacturing overhead costs are allocated to jobs using some rational allocation base, such as direct labor hours or machine hours. Figure 9.1 shows the job order approach to cost accumulation.

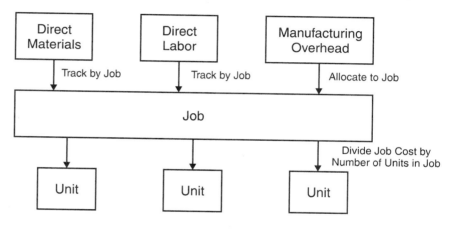

**Figure 9.1**   Job order cost accumulation.

Note that the ultimate cost object, such as *Unit* in Figure 9.1, can be a direct material item with respect to a subsequent job or process. For example, if the task represented in Figure 9.1 was to manufacture computer keyboards, the cost of each unit would include the direct materials, direct labor, and manufacturing overhead cost of one keyboard. If the firm were to then use these keyboards to build computers, the keyboard units would become a direct material in the computer assembly job.

## Process Cost Accumulation

Firms that produce one product or similar products using the same manufacturing processes use *department* as the intermediate-level cost object in their cost accumulation systems. They organize their production processes by departments and accumulate costs by department. To obtain unit cost, they divide each department's monthly total cost by the number of units the department manufactured that month. Therefore, a process cost system uses department numbers to track direct costs. Each raw materials inventory item that enters production is tracked to a specific department.

Some firms assign employees to particular departments. Other firms track each employee-hour worked to a specific department. Firms that use process cost systems allocate indirect manufacturing overhead costs to departments using some rational allocation base. Two common allocation bases are direct labor hours and machine hours. Figure 9.2 describes the process approach to cost accumulation.

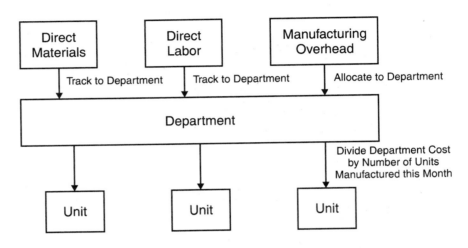

**Figure 9.2**   Process cost accumulation.

The ultimate cost objects in process cost systems, such as *Unit* in Figure 9.2, can be direct materials to a subsequent department. For example, if the job that is diagrammed in Figure 9.2 involved the manufacture of plastic soda bottles, the cost of each unit would include the direct material, direct labor, and manufacturing overhead cost of one bottle. If the firm were to fill these bottles with soda in a subsequent department, the bottles would be accounted for as a direct material in the bottle-filling department.

## Hybrid Cost Accumulation

Some firms produce similar products using the same manufacturing processes, yet use different materials in different batches. For example, a clothing manufacturer may make cotton shirts and silk shirts. The manufacturing processes of cutting, sewing, and attaching buttons is similar for both kinds of shirts. However, the cost of cotton and silk differ considerably. *Department* would be an ineffective intermediate-level cost object for accumulating materials costs—since cloth costs would not be traced to specific batches, all shirts manufactured in a month would have the same cost.

The solution to this problem is a hybrid cost system. The clothing manufacturer can track the cost of direct materials by batch using a job order approach, and can track direct labor and overhead costs by department using a process approach. The job order part of the cost system would track the direct materials cost for each shirt in each batch. The process part of the cost system would track labor and allocate overhead cost for each shirt of either kind manufactured during the month. This particular hybrid system of using a job order approach for direct materials and a process approach for direct labor and manufacturing overhead is called *operation costing*.

## Implications for Production Cycle Accounting Systems

Choosing between job order, process, and hybrid cost accumulation systems is an essential part of production cycle system design. The system must match the nature of the manufacturing process.

Firms that produce a variety of products or provide a variety of services use job order costing systems. These firms need a way to track costs as they flow in different amounts to different customized products or services. Examples of firms that typically use job order costing include aircraft manufacturers, auto repair shops, hospitals, and public accounting firms.

Process costing is the choice of firms that make one or only a few different products that are homogeneous in design and resource use. These firms do essentially the same things the same way every month. Examples of firms that typically use process costing include oil refineries, cement manufacturers, and some chemical manufacturers.

Operation costing is a blend of job order and process costing. Firms that use operation costing have some costs that flow evenly and regularly into their products or services and other costs that vary significantly by job, customer, or production batch. Examples of firms that use operation costing include jewelry manufacturers, garment manufacturers, luggage manufacturers, and auto manufacturers.

Although the meaning of information contained in reports and queries will vary with the accumulation system, table and form designs are surprisingly consistent across system types. In a job order system, all costs are traced or allocated using a job number. In a process system, all costs are traced or allocated using a department number. In both systems, tables and data entry forms must accommodate a number, but the design of the tables and forms is the same whether the number is a job number or a department number.

In this chapter, you will work with a job order cost system example to learn about production cycle accounting system elements; however, remember that you can substitute *department number* for *job number* in a production cycle database design to convert a job order accumulation system to a process accumulation system.

## COST TRACING VS. COST ALLOCATION

Traditionally, accountants have divided manufacturing costs into two categories: direct and indirect. Direct costs are costs that accountants can easily track through the manufacturing process to ultimate cost objects. Accountants usually classify raw materials and labor costs of employees that work in the manufacturing process as direct costs—using the terms *direct materials* and *direct labor*, respectively. All other manufacturing costs are classified as indirect and referred to as *manufacturing overhead*.

## Manufacturing Overhead Allocation

Manufacturing overhead includes all indirect manufacturing costs. Some raw materials costs are not significant enough to warrant the effort and expense of tracking them to jobs or departments. These indirect materials costs are part of manufacturing overhead. The labor costs of employees that do not work directly in the manufacturing process—such as maintenance, materials handling, and supervisory employees—are considered to be indirect labor and included in manufacturing overhead. All other manufacturing costs—for example, insurance, rent, supplies, and utilities—are also included in manufacturing overhead.

To smooth out fluctuations in manufacturing overhead acquisition that might distort product costs, accountants have long followed a practice of normalizing manufacturing overhead costs. The most common normalization procedure is to apply manufacturing overhead costs using a predetermined overhead rate. This normalization procedure requires four steps:

1. Estimate the manufacturing overhead cost for the year.

2. Estimate usage of some activity base that is related to overhead consumption for the year. Common bases include direct labor hours, machine hours, and direct labor cost.

3. Divide the estimated manufacturing overhead cost by an estimate of activity base usage to obtain a predetermined overhead rate.

4. Each period, multiply the predetermined overhead rate by the actual amount of the activity base used in that period by each job or department.

Note that the manufacturing overhead cost for each job or department will vary with the amount of the activity base it consumes during the period. This approach to allocating manufacturing overhead is a *volume-based* approach, since the quantity of the activity base consumed by a particular job or department usually varies with its volume of production.

## Activity-Based Costing

The volume-based approach to allocating manufacturing overhead has been criticized because it can lead to product cost distortions. An alternative procedure for allocating manufacturing costs is to measure activities and track costs for those activities. To perform this activity-based costing procedure, a firm follows four steps:

1. Track individual manufacturing process activities.

2. Record the costs of those activities.

3. Divide the activity cost by a physical measure of the activity to obtain the cost per activity unit.

4. Multiply the cost per activity unit times the quantity of the activity used by the job or department.

Note that these four steps are very similar to those in the normalization process we described earlier. In production cycle systems terms, activity-based costing simply adds another intermediate-level cost object to the cost flow. Figure 9.3 shows the job order cost accumulation system modified to include activity-based cost allocation.

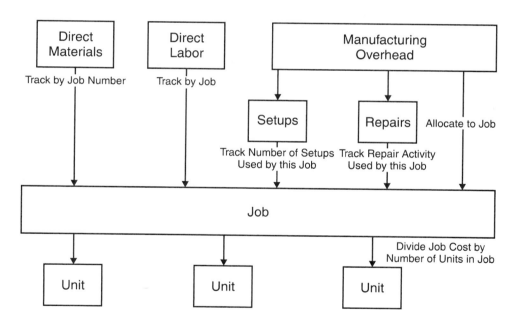

**Figure 9.3** Activity-based job order cost system.

The two activities tracked in this system are machine setups and repairs. This system identifies machine setup and repair costs in the manufacturing overhead cost pool. These identified costs are then traced to the specific activity. Finally, using the number of setups and repair hours that each job requires, the activity costs are allocated to specific jobs. Note that other manufacturing overhead costs are still allocated using direct labor hours or machine hours. Even with activity-based costing firms still have some manufacturing overhead costs that they cannot trace to specific activities.

## Implications for Production Cycle Accounting Systems

Normalizing manufacturing overhead requires the accounting system to do double duty. The system must track the actual overhead costs *and* the applied overhead costs. Fortunately, you have already seen a system for recording and paying actual costs in Chapter 7. Although you used materials acquisition in the Chapter 7 purchase cycle example, those system elements require only minor modifications to include actual manufacturing overhead costs. You learned how to record actual labor costs in Chapter 8. In this chapter, you will learn how to allocate overhead in a database accounting system.

Activity-based costing does not change the nature of cost allocation; it merely adds another layer to the allocation process. Therefore, you can easily extend the examples in this chapter to perform activity-based costing. All you need to do is replicate the cost tracking and allocation systems for each activity center in the system. For example, the cost system described in this chapter allocates manufacturing overhead cost using direct labor hours. You could add activity centers for machine setups and repairs to this system by building two additional tables to track machine setups and repair hours by job number. Similarly, you could extend the job order system described in this chapter to allocate overhead using separate rates for each department instead of one rate for all departments.

## ELECTRIC CONTROLS COMPANY PURCHASE CYCLE INFORMATION

In this chapter, you will learn how to build the components of a production cycle system for Electric Controls Company, the firm for which you developed a purchasing cycle system in Chapter 7. As you may recall, Electric Controls Company manufactures custom electric control panels for industrial customers. Electric Controls buys components of the control panels, then has its employees assemble them. In this manufacturing process, overhead costs are incurred. Electric Controls applies these overhead costs to jobs based on direct labor. Thus Electric Controls tracks the direct materials and direct labor to jobs and allocates overhead to those jobs. This is a standard approach in job order cost systems.

Electric Controls Company creates a job record for each control panel or set of control panels that a customer orders. They use a bill of materials form to organize the direct materials items that are used on each job. Employees record the number of hours that they work on each job.

The data model for Electric Controls Company production cycle includes six entities, job, finished goods, customer, direct materials, time worked (direct labor), and employee. Each job can have many direct materials items and can have many entries in the time worked table. Each entry in the time worked table only has one employee, but an employee can have many time entries in the time worked table. Each job is dedicated to producing a particular type of finished goods item; however, a particular type of finished goods item can be produced in many different jobs. Similarly, each job creates an item for one customer, but a customer may order items that require many jobs.

Although manufacturing overhead is applied to jobs in this system, it does not need its own table. Once an application rate is calculated, the amount of direct labor a job uses determines the manufacturing overhead that will be applied to that job. You will learn how to do this overhead application using a query later in this chapter. The data model for Electric Controls Company production cycle, showing these six entities and the one-to-many and many-to-many relationships among them, appears in Figure 9.4.

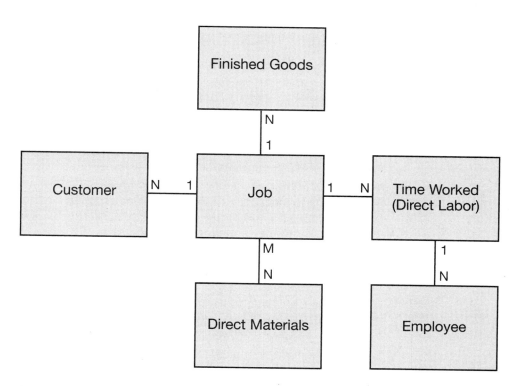

**Figure 9.4**  Electric Controls Company production cycle data model.

The remainder of this chapter will show you how to build elements of the accounting system for Electric Controls' production cycle. The design will include six tables, one for each entity, and one additional table to model the many-to-many relationship. You will learn how to create forms to enter data efficiently, queries that calculate job costs, and reports that Electric Controls can use to print information about jobs and their costs.

## TRACING AND ALLOCATING MANUFACTURING COSTS

To trace and allocate manufacturing costs to jobs, Electric Controls needs a table that will store the individual job records. Each job record will have direct materials, direct labor, and manufacturing overhead costs related to it. Direct materials and direct labor each require a separate table because cost systems track these specific cost flows. Manufacturing overhead does not require its own table because it is an allocated cost.

Although Electric Controls' system is a job order cost system, you can use the same database components in a process accumulation system. You need only substitute *department number* for *job number*. You can also use these system components to perform activity-based costing by adding an additional table for each activity that the system must track or allocate.

## The Job Table

The Job table must have a primary key field that uniquely identifies each job. The Job table must also include fields to store important job dates and foreign key fields that will be different for each firm. For example, one firm may want to relate each job to the customer that ordered the job. You could build such a relationship by including a CustomerNumber foreign key field in the Job table that links to the primary key in the Customer table. Other firms might run jobs as production for inventory rather than for specific customers. These firms would want you to include an InventoryItemCode foreign key field in the Job table that would establish a link to the primary key in the Finished Goods Inventory table. Some firms might use both foreign key links.

Since you have already learned how to build Customer and Inventory tables in Chapter 7, we will not repeat that information here. However, we have included *tblCustomer* and *tblFinishedGoodsInventory* for Electric Controls Company in the *Ch09.mdb* file on your Companion CD. These two tables appear in Datasheet view on the Access desktop in Figure 9.5. They contain the sample data that you will use as you create forms, queries, and reports for Electric Controls in this chapter's examples.

In Exercise 9.1 you will build a Job table that will work with the Finished Goods Inventory table and the Customer table in the production cycle. You should have Access running with the Database window open as you begin the exercise.

EXERCISE 9.1: BUILDING A JOB TABLE

1. To build the Job table, select the Insert, Table menu command and double-click Design View in the New Table dialog box.

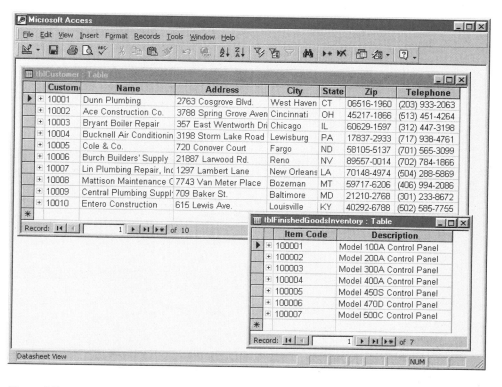

**Figure 9.5** The Customer and Finished Goods Inventory tables in Datasheet view.

2. Enter *JobNumber* in the first row of the Field Name column and leave its Data Type set to Text. Click the Primary Key toolbar button. Enter a Field Size property of *4*, an Input Mask property of *0000*, and a Caption property of *Job #*

3. Enter *JobOrderDate* in the second row of the Field Name column and enter a Data Type of *Date/Time*. Enter *99/99/00;0;_* as the JobOrderDate field's Input Mask property and enter *Order Date* as its Caption property.

4. Enter *JobCompletionDate* in the third row of the Field Name column and enter a Data Type of *Date/Time* for that field. Enter *99/99/00;0;_* as its Input Mask property and *Completion Date* as its Caption property. The JobCompletionDate field will store the expected completion date for each job. Many firms also record an actual completion date to use in generating performance reports.

5. To create the foreign key links to *tblCustomer* and *tblFinishedGoodsInventory*, you can add two fields that match these tables' primary key fields. Enter *CustomerNumber* in the fourth row of the Field Name column and leave its Data Type set to Text. Set its Field Size property to *5*, its Input Mask property to *00000*, and its Caption property to *Customer #*

6. Enter a Field Name of *InventoryItemCode* in the fifth row and leave its Data Type set to Text.

7. Set the InventoryItemCode Field Size property to *6*, its Input Mask property to *000000*, and its Caption property to *Item Code*

Note that you cannot enforce referential integrity on either of the links from these two foreign key fields to their entity tables unless you know that every job will have a customer and a finished goods inventory item code when the job is entered. Save the Job table you have just completed, entering *tblJob* as the table's name in the Save As dialog box. The *Ch09.mdb* file on your Companion CD contains a version of *tblJob* that includes the job records shown in Figure 9.6.

**Figure 9.6**   The *tblJob* records.

You will use these sample job records in queries and reports later in this chapter. Note that the five jobs in *tblJob* include two that were completed in December and three that continue into January.

## The Direct Materials Inventory Table

To track the cost of direct materials, you will need to build a table much like the Materials Inventory table you created and used in Chapter 7 to record materials purchases. In the Chapter 7 purchase cycle system, you stored the cost of each inventory item in the Purchase Order-Materials Inventory table. This design allowed the system to record different costs for the same inventory items purchased from different vendors, or from the same vendors purchased at different times.

In this chapter, we focus on tracing direct materials costs into production. To simplify our example here, you will include the cost of direct materials in the Direct Materials Inventory table. Although a discussion of standard cost systems is beyond the scope of this book, such systems also store the standard cost of each direct materials item in a Direct Materials Inventory table.

Since the Direct Materials Inventory table is so similar to the Materials Inventory table we created in Chapter 7, you can save some work by modifying that table to make a Direct Materials Inventory table instead of starting all over. You can import a copy of the Materials Inventory table from the *Ch07.mdb* file using the procedure you learned earlier in this book.

After you have imported a copy of *tblMaterialsInventory*, it will appear as a Tables object in the *Ch09.mdb* Database window. In Exercise 9.2, you will modify this table for use in the production cycle.

EXERCISE 9.2 : CONVERTING *TBLMATERIALSINVENTORY*
TO *TBLDIRECTMATERIALSINVENTORY*

1. In the Database window, click the Tables object and click *tblMaterialsInventory*. Press Ctrl+C to make a copy of the table.
2. Press Ctrl+V to paste the copy of the table. Enter *tblDirectMaterialsInventory* as the Table Name in the Paste Table As dialog box. Be sure the Structure and Data option button is selected in the Paste Options section, then click OK.
3. Select *tblDirectMaterialsInventory* in the Database window and click the Design button to open the table in Design view.
4. Change the names of the three fields to *DMStockNumber*, *DMCategory*, and *DMDescription*, respectively.
5. In the fourth row of the Field Name column, enter *DMCost*
6. Set the new field's Data Type to *Currency*, its Decimal Places property to *2*, and its Caption property to *DM Cost*
7. Select View, Datasheet View to open the table in Datasheet view. Click Yes when prompted to save the changes you have made thus far to the table.
8. In Datasheet view, the table should display values in the first three fields. You can enter the DMCost values using Figure 9.7 as a guide. The *Ch09.mdb* file on your Companion CD includes a version of *tblDirectMaterialsInventory* that includes the sample job records shown in Figure 9.7.
9. Select File, Close to close the table.

| Stock # | Category | Description | DM Cost |
|---|---|---|---|
| 101 | Sheet metal | 1/8" Steel 4x4 sheet | $8.45 |
| 102 | Switch | DPDT 240v 100a | $14.96 |
| 103 | Wire | 500' Copper #22AWG | $16.95 |
| 104 | Sheet metal | 1/4" Steel 4x4 sheet | $14.95 |
| 105 | Switch | SPDT 240v 100a | $9.47 |
| 106 | Relay | SPDT 120v 40a Silver | $32.89 |
| 107 | Circuit breaker | 240v 40a | $10.27 |
| 108 | Relay | TPST 240v 100a Mercury | $18.96 |
| 109 | Sheet metal | 1/8" Aluminum 4x4 sheet | $12.68 |
| 110 | Wire | 500' Copper Twin #18AWG | $27.98 |
| 111 | Connector | F 240v 100a solderless | $3.57 |
| 112 | Switch | DPST 240v 50a | $8.66 |
| 113 | Connector | M 120v 40a clip | $1.98 |
| 114 | Sheet metal | 1/4" Aluminum 4x4 sheet | $19.49 |
| 115 | Circuit breaker | 120v 40a | $6.95 |
| | | | $0.00 |

Record: 1 of 15

**Figure 9.7** The populated Direct Materials Inventory table in Datasheet view.

Now you have a Job table with a record for each job and a Direct Materials Inventory table with a record for each materials inventory item that Electric

Controls Company might use in a particular job. To link these two tables and track the direct materials used on each job, you need a relationship table, the Job-Direct Materials Inventory table.

## The Job-Direct Materials Inventory Table

Since each job can include many different direct materials and each direct materials item can be used in many different jobs, the Job table and the Direct Materials Inventory table have a many-to-many relationship. The Job-Direct Materials Inventory table is the relationship table that models this relation. The composite primary key for this relationship table will require two fields, the primary key fields of the two entity tables: the Job table and the Direct Materials Inventory table. The table also needs a field to store the quantity of each inventory item used on each job. In the next exercise you will build the Job-Direct Materials Inventory table for the production cycle.

EXERCISE 9.3: BUILDING A JOB-DIRECT MATERIALS INVENTORY TABLE

1. With the Database window open, select Insert, Table from the menu, then double-click Design View.
2. Enter the name of *tblJob's* primary key field, *JobNumber*, as the first Field Name. Leave its Data Type set to Text and set its Field Size to *4*. Remember, when using entity table primary keys as part of the composite primary key in a relationship table, you always want to match Data Type and Field Size exactly.
3. Set JobNumber's Input Mask property to *0000*, its Caption property to *Job #*, and its Indexed property to *Yes (Duplicates OK)*
4. Enter *DMStockNumber* in the second row of the Field Name column. Leave its Data Type set to Text. Set its Field Size property to *3*, its Input Mask property to *000*, its Caption property to *Stock #*, and its Indexed property to *Yes (Duplicates OK)*
5. While pressing the Ctrl key, select both fields by clicking the row selectors for each field. With both fields selected, click the Primary Key toolbar button. The Primary key symbol should appear in the row selectors of both fields.
6. The third field will store the quantity of each materials item used on each job. Enter *JobDMQuantity* on the third Field Name line. Set its Data Type to *Number* and its Caption property to *Quantity*
7. Select the File, Save As menu command. Type *tblJob-DirectMaterialsInventory* as the name for your new table in the Save As dialog box.
8. Select the File, Close menu command to close the table.

A copy of this table that includes the sample records you will use later in this chapter is included as *tblJob-DirectMaterialsInventory* in *Ch09.mdb* on your Companion CD. To ensure that any JobNumber value entered in the Job-Direct

Materials Inventory table exists in *tblJob*, you can establish referential integrity between *tblJob-DirectMaterialsInventory* and *tblJob* on the JobNumber field. You can also ensure that each record in *tblJob-DirectMaterialsInventory* refers to an existing materials stock number by establishing referential integrity with *tblDirectMaterialsInventory* on the DMStockNumber field. To create these two links and enforce referential integrity on them, follow the steps in Exercise 9.4. To begin the exercise, you should close all tables and have the Database window open on the desktop.

EXERCISE 9.4: LINKING JOB AND DIRECT MATERIALS RECORDS

1. Click the Relationships toolbar button to open the Relationships window and the Show Table dialog box.
2. Double-click *tblDirectMaterialsInventory*, *tblJob*, and *tblJob-DirectMaterialsInventory* to place them in the Relationships window. Close the Show Table dialog box.
3. Click and drag the JobNumber field in *tblJob* to the JobNumber field in *tblJob-DirectMaterialsInventory*. Click the Enforce Referential Integrity check box, then click the Create button.
4. Click and drag the DMStockNumber field in *tblDirectMaterialsInventory* to the DMStockNumber field in *tblJob-DirectMaterialsInventory*.
5. Click the Enforce Referential Integrity check box, then click the Create button.
6. The Relationship window showing these links appears in Figure 9.8. To return to the Database window, select the File, Close menu command. Click the Yes button to save your changes to the Relationships layout.

**Figure 9.8** Creating referential integrity links for *tblJob-DirectMaterialsInventory*.

## The Bill of Materials Form

Many firms use a bill of materials to organize the list of direct materials for each job. We can use this idea to create a form that will make entering records into *tblJob-DirectMaterialsInventory* easier and less prone to error. The Bill of Materials form is fairly complex. It must write records to *tblJob-DirectMaterialsInventory* and read records from:

- *tblJob*—to obtain the job order and completion dates.
- *tblDirectMaterialsInventory*—to obtain the category, description and cost of each materials item.
- *tblCustomer*—to obtain the customer name.
- *tblFinishedGoodsInventory*—to obtain the description of the finished goods inventory item that the job produces.

Since the Bill of Materials form will read data from *tblCustomer* and *tblMaterialsInventory*, it is very important to have data in these tables before you build the form. If you have not entered data in these tables yet, you can copy the sample records from the tables that we have included in the *Ch09.mdb* file on your Companion CD.

You will use the Bill of Materials form to enter job information simultaneously in both *tblJob* and *tblJob-DirectMaterialsInventory*. As you have seen in earlier chapters, Access handles this task best with a form-subform design. In this Bill of Materials form design, you will link *tblJob* to *tblCustomer* in the main form section. The link from *tblJob-DirectMaterialsInventory*, the relationship table, to *tblDirectMaterialsInventory* will occur in the subform section.

Since you have had experience working with complex forms in Chapters 7 and 8, you will not use the Form Wizard to construct this form. Instead, you will learn how to build a form-subform combination from blank forms. When you build complex forms in Access, you should always create the subform first. If you have a multiple subform design, you should start with the most deeply nested subform. In Exercise 9.5, you will create the query behind the Bill of Materials subform.

EXERCISE 9.5: BUILDING THE BILL OF MATERIALS SUBFORM QUERY

1. Click the Forms object in the Database window, then click the New button. Enter *tblJob-DirectMaterialsInventory* in the combo box control of the New Form dialog box, then double-click Design View in the list box control.
2. Select the View, Form Header/Footer menu command.
3. Select the Edit, Select Form menu command.
4. Click the Properties toolbar button, click the Data tab in the form's property sheet, then click the Record Source property's Build button. Click Yes to open the form's Query Builder window.
5. Click the Show Table toolbar button, then double-click tblDirectMaterialsInventory. Click the Close button. The Direct Materials

Inventory table, linked on DMStockNumber to *tblJob-DirectMaterialsInventory*, should now appear in the top section of the Query Builder window.

6. Click and drag the JobNumber field from tblJob-DirectMaterialsInventory to the first QBE grid Field cell, then set its Sort order to *Ascending*

7. Click and drag the DMStockNumber field from *tblJob-DirectMaterialsInventory* to the second QBE grid Field cell, then set its Sort order to *Ascending*

8. Click and drag the JobDMQuantity field from *tblJob-DirectMaterialsInventory* to the next open QBE grid Field cell.

9. Enter *Description: [DMCategory] & " - " & [DMDescription]* in the next open QBE grid Field cell (you may want to press Shift+F2 to open the Zoom box to make entering this expression easier).

10. Click and drag the DMCost field from *tblDirectMaterialsInventory to the next* open QBE grid Field cell.

11. Close the Query Builder window and save your changes.

Figure 9.9 shows the Bill of Materials subform query in the Query Builder window Design view.

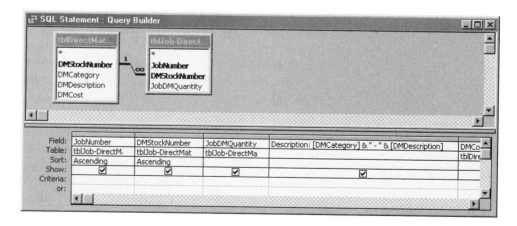

**Figure 9.9**   The Bill of Materials subform query.

The Bill of Materials Subform should be open in Design view as you begin the next exercise.

EXERCISE 9.6: COMPLETING THE BILL OF MATERIALS SUBFORM

1. Click the Field List toolbar button, then click and drag the DMStockNumber, JobDMQuantity, Description, and DMCost fields to the Detail section of the form.

2. Using Figure 9.10 as a guide, arrange the controls and labels on the form.
3. You can also change the form and control appearance properties as shown in the figure. Remember to set the Enabled, Locked, and Tab Stop properties for the Description and DMCost controls to prevent users from changing values in those fields.
4. Save the subform by choosing the menu command File, Save As. Enter a name of *fsubBillOfMaterials* for the form.
5. Select File, Close from the menu to close the form.

**Figure 9.10**  The Bill of Materials subform in Design view.

In the next two exercises, you will build the main part of the Bill of Materials form. Since you have had considerable experience in designing and building forms as you worked through the exercises in the earlier chapters of this book, we encourage you to use your own ideas as you create this form. We do have an example form for your reference on the Companion CD, but we encourage you to explore in this exercise.

To have the form automatically look up the CustomerName when a user enters a CustomerNumber, you must include *tblCustomer* in the form's design structure. You will also need to include *tblFinishedGoodsInventory* to obtain the description of the item being manufactured on the job. The first step in building the main form is to open a new form and create its underlying query.

EXERCISE 9.7: CREATING A QUERY FOR THE BILL OF MATERIALS MAIN FORM

1. Click the Forms object in the Database window, then click the New button. Enter *tblJob* in the New Form combo box control, then double-click Design View.
2. Open the form's property sheet by selecting the form, then clicking the Properties toolbar button.
3. Click the form's Record Source property Build button, then click Yes to open a new query behind the form.

4. Click the Show Table toolbar button and add *tblCustomer*, *tblJob-DirectMaterialsInventory*, and *tblFinishedGoodsInventory* to the top pane of the Query Builder window. Close the Show Table dialog box.
5. Note that *tblCustomer*, linked on CustomerNumber to *tblJob*, and *tblFinishedGoodsInventory*, linked on InventoryItemCode, now appear in the Query Builder window. Also appearing in the window is *tblJob-DirectMaterialsInventory* with its referential integrity link on JobNumber to *tblJob*. Click and drag the JobNumber field from *tblJob-DirectMaterialsInventory* to the first Field cell in the QBE grid, then enter *Ascending* in the first Sort cell.
6. Double-click the asterisk in *tblJob* to include all of *tblJob* fields in the next QBE grid Field cell.
7. Double-click the CustomerName field in *tblCustomer*, then double-click the InventoryDescription field in *tblFinishedGoodsInventory* to include those fields in the next two QBE grid Field cells, respectively.
8. Close the Query Builder window to return to the form, open in Design view.

Now that you have created the form and built a query behind the form, you can complete the form design. The next exercise provides guidance for that task.

EXERCISE 9.8: COMPLETING THE BILL OF MATERIALS MAIN FORM

1. Click the Field List toolbar button, then click and drag the following fields to the form: JobNumber, JobOrderDate, InventoryDescription, CustomerName, and JobCompletionDate.
2. If the toolbox is not already open, click the Toolbox toolbar button. If the property sheet is not open, click the Properties toolbar button.
3. Click the Subform/Subreport toolbox button. If the Subform Wizard opens, click the Cancel button.
4. Using Figure 9.11 as a guide, draw the outline of the subform at the bottom of the Detail section.
5. Select the subform's label and press Ctrl+X to delete it.
6. Click the Data tab in the subform's property sheet. Enter a Source Object property for the subform object of *fsubBillOfMaterials*
7. Enter *JobNumber* in both the Link Child Fields property and the Link Master Fields property.
8. Using Figures 9.11 and 9.12 as guides, modify the controls' properties and add labels to the Bill of Materials form. Remember to set the Enabled, Locked, and Tab Stop properties for the CustomerName and InventoryDescription controls to prevent users from changing values in those fields.
9. To save your Bill of Materials form, select File, Save As from the menu and enter *frmBillOfMaterials* as the form's new name in the Save As dialog box.

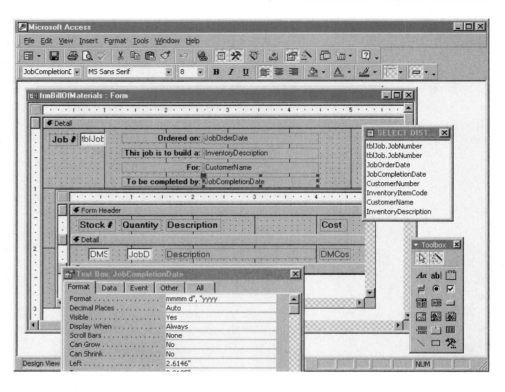

**Figure 9.11**   The Bill of Materials form in Design view.

The *Ch09.mdb* file on your Companion CD includes two forms, *frmBillOfMaterials* and *fsubBillOfMaterials*, that you can use as aids in designing your forms. Figure 9.12 shows the Bill of Materials form in Form view after a user has entered the materials for job number 1001 in the sample data. In addition to its role as a data entry tool, this form provides a convenient way for managers to review the materials that have been charged to a job—although most firms would design a report for that purpose.

## The Time Worked Table

To track labor costs into the production process, you need to know the number of hours each employee works on each job. Then you can multiply the hours times each employee's pay rate to determine the direct labor cost for the job. In Chapter 8, you created two tables that contain most of the information you will need to track direct labor cost in the production cycle. Since you constructed an Employee table in Chapter 8, we will not ask you to recreate your work here. However, we have included an Employee table, *tblEmployee*, in *Ch09.mdb* on your Companion CD. The *tblEmployee* object contains the employee data you will use in this chapter. The Employee table structure appears in Figure 9.13.

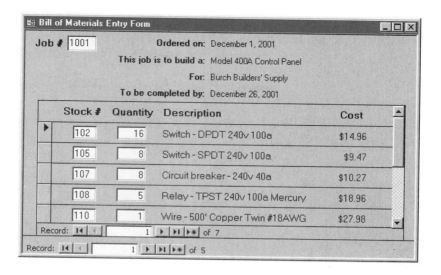

**Figure 9.12**   The Bill of Materials form in Form View.

**Figure 9.13**   The Chapter 9 *tblEmployee* structure.

Note that we have simplified the table structure so that you can focus more easily on cost flow issues. For example, we have omitted the EmployeeDepartmentNumber field because Electric Controls is tracking costs by job rather than by department in this chapter. This Chapter 9 version of *tblEmployee* includes only five employee records.

The Time Worked table requires such substantial modifications that creating a new table is easier than adapting *tblTimeWorked* from Chapter 8. To record time worked on each job in one-hour increments, the table will need a primary key that uniquely identifies each block of time that each employee works on each job—certainly a more difficult challenge than creating a primary key for the Chapter 8 Time Worked table. To avoid the details of time arithmetic, we will assume that each employee completes one time card for each week. Further, we will assume that each time card has preprinted sequential numbers for job time entries. An example of such a time card appears in Figure 9.14. You will use the sequence numbers on the time card as part of the unique identifier for each record in *tblTimeWorked*.

| Name | Employee Number | Pay Period Ending |
| --- | --- | --- |
| *Ethel Baron* | *103* | *12/16/01* |

| | Hours | Job Number |
| --- | --- | --- |
| 1 | *14* | *1002* |
| 2 | *8* | *1005* |
| 3 | *9* | *1001* |
| 4 | *6* | *1002* |
| 5 | *3* | *1005* |
| 6 | | |
| 7 | | |
| 8 | | |
| 9 | | |
| 10 | | |

**Figure 9.14**   A sequentially numbered time card.

In the next exercise you will create *tblTimeWorked*. The primary key for the table will be a composite of three fields: pay period ended date, time card sequence number, and employee number. The Time Worked table must include these three fields to uniquely identify each bit of time worked by each employee on each job. The table will also need fields for number of hours and job number for each record. The JobNumber field is a foreign key and will link *tblTimeWorked* to *tblJob*. Close all database objects and have the Database window open to begin the exercise.

EXERCISE 9.9: BUILDING THE PRODUCTION CYCLE TIME WORKED TABLE

1. Select the Insert, Table menu command and double-click Design View in the New Table dialog box.
2. Enter *EmployeeNumber* as the first Field Name. Leave its Data Type set to Text.
3. Set its Field Size to *3*, its Input Mask property to *000*, its Caption property to *Employee #*, and its Indexed property to *Yes (Duplicates OK)*

4.  The second part of the composite primary key must identify the pay period. You can use the last day of each weekly pay period as the value for this field. Enter *TWPayPeriodEnded* in the second row of the Field Name column and set its Data Type to *Date/Time*

5.  Set the field's Input Mask property to *99/99/00;0;_*, its Caption property to *Week Ended*, and its Indexed property to *Yes (Duplicates OK)*

6.  The third part of the composite primary key will identify the line on the time card using the preprinted sequence number. Enter *TWSequenceNumber* in the third row of the Field Name column and set the Data Type to *Number*. Since the time cards have only ten lines, you can enter a Field Size property of *Byte*

7.  Set the field's Decimal Places property to *0*, its Input Mask property to *99*, its Caption property to *Sequence #*, and its Indexed property to *Yes (Duplicates OK)*

8.  While pressing the Ctrl key, select all three fields by clicking the row selectors for each field.

9.  With the fields selected, click the Primary Key toolbar button. The primary key symbol should appear in the row selectors of all three fields.

10. Next, you can create a field that will store the number of hours recorded on the time card for each sequence number and create the foreign key field for job number. Enter *TWHours* on the fourth row of the Field Name column. Set its Data Type to *Number*, and its Caption property to *Hours*

11. Enter *JobNumber* in the Field Name column. Leave its Data Type set to Text. Set its Field Size property to *4*, its Input Mask property to *0000*, and its Caption property to *Job #*

12. To save the table, select the File, Save As menu command and enter *tblTimeWorked* as the table's new name. Close the table.

The *Ch09.mdb* file on your Companion CD includes *tblTimeWorked*, which contains the sample data you will use later in this chapter. To ensure that each employee number entered in *tblTimeWorked* is for an employee that actually exists, you can build a referential integrity link to *tblEmployee*. You can also enforce referential integrity on the table's foreign key link to *tblJob*. This will ensure that any job number entered in *tblTimeWorked* is a valid job number that already exists in *tblJob*. In the next exercise you will add these links to *tblTimeWorked*.

EXERCISE 9.10: LINKING *TBLTIMEWORKED* TO *TBLJOB* AND *TBLEMPLOYEE*

1.  Click the Relationships toolbar button to open the Relationships window, then click the Show Table toolbar button. Double-click *tblEmployee* and *tblTimeWorked* to add these tables to the Relationships window, then close the Show Table dialog box.

2.  Click and drag the JobNumber field in *tblJob* to the JobNumber field in *tblTimeWorked*.

3.  Click the Enforce Referential Integrity check box, then click the Create button.

4. Click and drag the EmployeeNumber field in *tblEmployee* to the EmployeeNumber field in *tblTimeWorked*.
5. Click the Enforce Referential Integrity check box, then click the Create button.
6. Select File, Close from the menu to close the Relationships window and return to the Database window. Click the Yes button to save your changes. The Relationship window showing these links added to the existing production cycle system links appears in Figure 9.15.

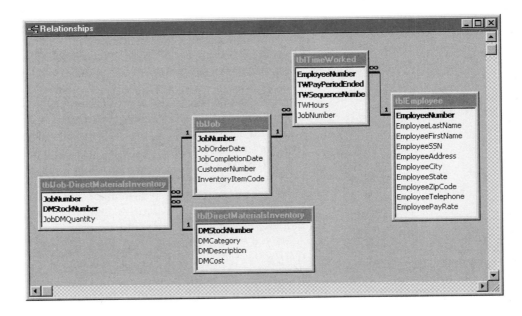

**Figure 9.15**   Adding referential integrity links to *tblTimeWorked*.

Electric Controls Company can use the records in *tblTimeWorked* in many ways. For example, by multiplying the hours for a particular job from *tblTimeWorked* by the employee pay rates from *tblEmployee* for the employees who worked on that job, they can calculate the direct labor cost for a particular job. Exercise 9.11 shows you how you can build a query that calculates the direct labor cost for job number 1001 in the sample data.

EXERCISE 9.11: CALCULATING THE
DIRECT LABOR COST FOR JOB NUMBER 1001

1. Select the Insert, Query menu command, then double-click Design View in the New Query dialog box.
2. Double-click *tblEmployee* and *tblTimeWorked* in the Show Table dialog box, then click the Close button.

3. Click and drag the JobNumber field from *tblTimeWorked* to the first QBE grid Field cell.
4. Enter *1001* in the first QBE grid Criteria cell. Microsoft Access encloses your entry with quotation marks as you leave the cell.
5. Enter *DLCost: [EmployeePayRate] * [TWHours]* in the second QBE grid Field cell. This field multiplies the employee pay rates times the hours that employee worked on job number 1001 and places the answer in a new field, DLCost.
6. Click the Run toolbar button to test the query. The resulting dynaset, which shows the direct labor costs for job number 1001, appears in Figure 9.16.

| Job # | DL Cost |
|---|---|
| 1001 | 168 |
| 1001 | 252 |
| 1001 | 131.2 |
| 1001 | 49.2 |
| 1001 | 73.8 |
| 1001 | 16.4 |
| 1001 | 47 |
| 1001 | 28.2 |
| 1001 | 150.4 |
| 1001 | 122.2 |
| 1001 | 9.4 |
| 1001 | 184.5 |
| 1001 | 36.9 |
| 1001 | 147.6 |
| 1001 | 61.5 |
| 1001 | 135.3 |

**Figure 9.16** Direct labor costs for job number 1001.

Of course, if you really wanted to know the direct labor cost for job number 1001, the result shown in Figure 9.16 is probably not exactly the answer you had hoped to get. You would more likely want a single dollar amount rather than a column of numbers that you must enter into a calculator to obtain a total. Fortunately, you can modify the query slightly to get the answer in a more useful form. Follow the steps in the next exercise to see how.

EXERCISE 9.12: CALCULATING THE TOTAL DIRECT LABOR COST FOR JOB NUMBER 1001

1. Return the desktop to Query Design view. Select View, Totals from the menu or click the Totals toolbar button. This adds a row of Total cells to the QBE grid between the Table cells row and the Sort cells row.

2. Enter *Group By* in the first Total cell, then enter *Sum* in the second Total cell. Figure 9.17 shows the Query window with these changes.
3. Click the Run toolbar button to test the modified query.

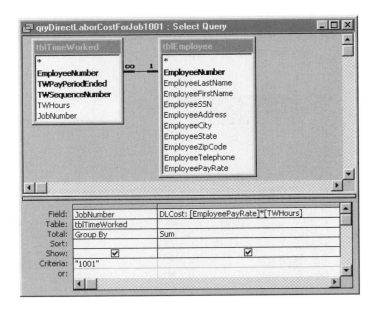

**Figure 9.17**   Summing the DLCost field.

The query's dynaset, shown in Figure 9.18, now contains only one row with one number, 1613.60, which is the total of all the DLCost calculations for job number 1001 that are displayed in Figure 9.16. This query is included in *Ch09.mdb* on your Companion CD as *qryDirectLaborCostForJob1001*. This query is just one example of how you can use queries on various combinations of the Job, Time Worked, and Employee tables to answer a variety of questions about the use and cost of direct labor resources.

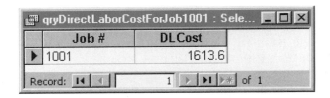

**Figure 9.18**   The dynaset result of summing DLCost field.

## Allocating Manufacturing Overhead

Cost accounting systems do not track manufacturing overhead costs into production as they track direct materials and direct labor costs. At the beginning of the year, accountants and production managers get together and estimate the total manufacturing overhead costs they expect to incur during the upcoming year. They also estimate the manufacturing activity level for the year. The activity measure is usually volume based; that is, the activity measure is expected to increase with higher manufacturing volume.

Firms often use direct labor hours, direct labor cost, or machine hours as activity measures. The labor-based activity measures work well for manufacturing operations in which human beings do most of the work. Machine hours work well for manufacturing operations in which machines do most of the work.

Cost accountants divide the estimated manufacturing cost by the estimated activity measure to calculate a predetermined overhead rate. They use this rate to apply overhead to production throughout the year. Assume that Electric Controls' estimates for this year are:

| | |
|---|---|
| Estimated manufacturing overhead cost | $78,000 |
| Estimated direct labor hours | 4,800 |

The predetermined overhead rate is:

$78,000 ÷ 4,800 direct labor hours = $16.25 per direct labor hour

Therefore, Electric Controls' production cycle accounting system must allocate $16.25 per direct labor hour to each job.

You have already captured the direct labor hours per job in *tblTimeWorked*. Production cycle systems that allocate manufacturing overhead using other allocation bases may need additional tables. For example, a firm that allocates manufacturing overhead using machine hours would need a machine hours table to store the number of machine hours used by each job. The structure of this machine hours table would be very similar to the structure of *tblTimeWorked*.

At this point, you have created tables that will track direct materials and direct labor costs. You have also seen how accountants allocate manufacturing overhead costs. Your next step is to use these tables to calculate job costs.

## REPORTING JOB COSTS

The goal of tracking and allocating manufacturing costs is to provide information for calculating job or department costs. Since Electric Controls uses a job order cost accumulation system, you must now calculate job costs. The Job Cost report that you will create in this section summarizes direct materials, direct labor, and manufacturing overhead costs by job.

This task requires a series of four queries and a report. The first three queries calculate and sum the direct materials, direct labor, and manufacturing overhead costs for each job. The fourth query combines these three summation queries and provides a basis for the Job Cost report.

## Direct Materials Cost

The first step in building the Job Cost report is to calculate the total direct materials cost for each job. You will perform this calculation with a Direct Materials Cost query in the next exercise.

EXERCISE 9.13: BUILDING THE DIRECT MATERIALS COST QUERY

1. Click the Queries object in the Database window, then click the New button. Double-click Design View in the New Query dialog box.
2. In the Show Table dialog box, double-click *tblDirectMaterialsInventory*, *tblJob*, and *tblJob-DirectMaterialsInventory* to add these tables to the query. Click the Close button.
3. Click and drag the JobNumber field from *tblJob* to the first QBE grid Field cell.
4. Enter *DM Cost: [DMCost] * [JobDMQuantity]* in the second QBE grid Field cell.
5. Click the Totals toolbar button to open the Total line in the QBE grid.
6. Change the second QBE grid Total cell to *Sum*
7. Select the File, Save As menu command and enter *qryDirectMaterialsCost* as the query's new name.
8. Close the query. Figure 9.19 shows the query in Design view.

**Figure 9.19** The Direct Materials Cost query in Design view.

When you run this query, it should return a dynaset with five direct materials cost values, one for each job. The *Ch09.mdb* file on your Companion CD includes this query, named *qryDirectMaterialsCost*, for your reference.

## Direct Labor Cost

The second step in building the Job Cost report is to calculate the total direct labor cost for each job. In Exercise 9.14, you will do this with a Direct Labor Cost query.

EXERCISE 9.14: BUILDING THE DIRECT LABOR COST QUERY

1. Click the Queries object in the Database window, then click the New button. Double-click Design View in the New Query dialog box.
2. In the Show Table dialog box, double-click *tblEmployee*, *tblJob*, and *tblTimeWorked* to add these tables to the query. Click the Close button.
3. Click and drag the JobNumber field from *tblJob* to the first QBE grid Field cell.
4. Enter **DL Cost: [EmployeePayRate] * [TWHours]** in the second QBE grid Field cell.
5. Click the Totals toolbar button to open the Total line in the QBE grid.
6. Change the second QBE grid Total cell to *Sum*
7. Select the File, Save As menu command and enter *qryDirectLaborCost* as the query's name. Close the query.

When you run the query, it should return a dynaset with direct labor values for the five jobs in *tblJob*. The *Ch09.mdb* file on your Companion CD includes a Direct Labor Cost query, *qryDirectLaborCost*, for your reference.

## Manufacturing Overhead Cost

The next step in building the Job Cost report is to calculate the total manufacturing overhead cost for each job. The manufacturing overhead calculation needs the hours worked on each job from *tblTimeWorked* because Electric Controls Company applies overhead using direct labor hours as the activity base. To use a different activity base, such as machine hours, you would need to include a table that contained information about how each job consumed that activity base. In the next exercise, you will create a Manufacturing Overhead Cost query that uses the predetermined overhead rate we calculated earlier in this chapter.

EXERCISE 9.15: BUILDING THE MANUFACTURING OVERHEAD COST QUERY

1. Click the Queries object in the Database window, then click the New button. Double-click Design View in the New Query dialog box.
2. In the Show Table dialog box, double-click *tblJob* and *tblTimeWorked* to add these tables to the query. Click the Close button.
3. Click and drag the JobNumber field from *tblJob* to the first QBE grid Field cell.

4. Enter *MOH Cost: [TWHours] * 16.25* in the second QBE grid Field cell. This multiplies direct labor hours times the $16.25 per hour predetermined manufacturing overhead rate.
5. Click the Totals toolbar button to open the Total line in the QBE grid.
6. Change the second QBE grid Total cell to *Sum*
7. Select the File, Save As menu command and enter *qryManufacturingOverheadCost* as the query's name. Close the query.

Figure 9.20 shows the query in Design view. When you run the query, it should return a dynaset with manufacturing overhead values for the five jobs in the Job table. The *Ch09.mdb* file on your Companion CD includes a Manufacturing Overhead Cost query for your reference named *qryManufacturingOverheadCost*.

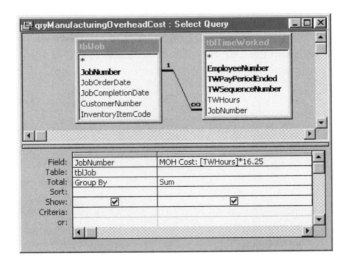

**Figure 9.20**   The Manufacturing Overhead Cost query in Design view.

## Job Cost Calculation

Now you can build the summary query that will combine the results of the direct materials, direct labor, and manufacturing overhead queries. This procedure of using one query to summarize other queries is sometimes called *nesting* queries. In the next exercise you will build a Job Cost query.

EXERCISE 9.16: BUILDING THE JOB COST QUERY

1. Click the Queries object in the Database window, then click the New button. Double-click Design view in the New Query dialog box.

2. In the Show table dialog box, double-click *tblJob* to add the Job table to the upper pane of the Query Builder window. Click the Queries tab of the Show Table dialog box.

3. Double-click *qryDirectMaterialsCost*, *qryDirectLaborCost*, and *qryManufacturingOverheadCost* to add these queries to the Job Cost query. Close the Show Table dialog box.

4. Click and drag the JobNumber field from *tblJob* to the first QBE grid Field cell.

5. Click and drag the DM Cost, DL Cost, and MOH Cost fields to the next three open QBE grid Field cells.

6. Click the Totals toolbar button to open the Total line in the QBE grid.

7. Enter *Sum* in each of the three QBE grid Total cells for DM Cost, DL Cost, and MOH Cost.

8. Select the File, Save As menu command and enter *qryJobCost* as the query's name. Figure 9.21 shows the query in Design view. Close the query.

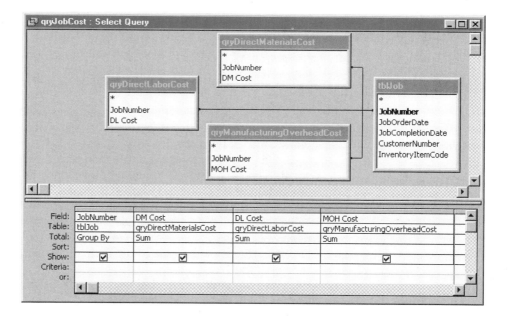

**Figure 9.21** The Job Cost query in Design view.

When you run the query, it should return a dynaset with direct materials, direct labor, and manufacturing overhead values for the five jobs in *tblJob*. The query results appear in Figure 9.22. The *Ch09.mdb* file on your Companion CD includes *qryJobCost* for your reference.

## The Job Cost Report

The Job Cost query provides useful results, but you can create a better-looking printout than the Datasheet view results of the query by creating a report in

**Figure 9.22** The Job Cost query results in Datasheet view.

Access. In the next two exercises, you will create a report that uses the *qryJobCost* calculations in a report design. To begin the first exercise, in which you will build the query behind the form, close all tables, forms, and queries and have the Database window open on the Access desktop.

EXERCISE 9.17: BUILDING THE QUERY BEHIND THE JOB COST REPORT

1.  Click the Reports object in the Database window, then click the New button.
2.  Select *tblJob* in the New Report combo box control, then double-click Design View in the list box control.
3.  Click the Properties toolbar button, then click the Data tab in the form's property sheet. Select the Record Source property, then click its Build button. Click the Yes button when prompted to open the Query Builder window.
4.  The Query Builder window will open with *tblJob* in the top pane. Click the Show Table button, then double-click *tblFinishedGoodsInventory* to include it in the query.
5.  Click the Queries tab on the Show Table dialog box. Double-click *qryJobCost*, then click the Close button.
6.  Click and drag the JobNumber field from *tblJob* to the first QBE grid Field cell. Set the Sort cell to *Ascending*. Click the check box in the Show cell to remove the selection.
7.  Click and drag the asterisk from *qryJobCost* to the second QBE grid Field cell.
8.  Enter *Total: [SumOfDM Cost]+[SumOfDL Cost]+[SumOfMOH Cost]* in the third QBE grid Field cell.
9.  Click and drag the InventoryDescription field from *tblFinishedGoodsInventory* to the fourth QBE grid Field cell.

The Job Cost report's query design appears in the Query Builder window shown in Figure 9.23. Notice that this is a query that includes a query, *qryJobCost*, which in turn is a query that includes three other queries. This query nesting occurs often in production cycle databases and can be many levels deep. The nesting of queries within queries can become quite complex for systems that calculate costs for manufactured products with many subassemblies and component parts.

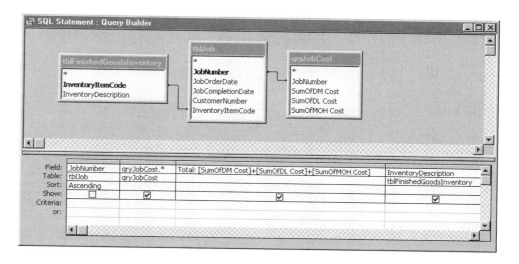

**Figure 9.23** The query behind the Job Cost report.

You can click the Run toolbar button to test your query. When you are satisfied that the query is operating properly, close the Query Builder window, save your changes, and return to the report in Design view. Next you will complete the Job Cost report design. You can use Figures 9.24 and 9.25 as guides while you follow the steps in the next exercise.

EXERCISE 9.18: COMPLETING THE JOB COST REPORT

1. Click the Field List toolbar button, then click and drag all six fields to the Detail Section of the report.
2. Delete the label controls.
3. Use the View menu command to delete the Page Header/Footer and add a Report Header/Footer.
4. Add descriptive labels for the column totals and the report title to the Report Header section.
5. Use the Text Box tool to create controls in the Report Footer.
6. You can use the Sum() function to have these controls in the Report Footer sum the column amounts. For example, the Direct Materials total text box control contains the expression =Sum([SumOfDM Cost]). The square brackets are impor-

tant here because the field names include a space. Figure 9.24 shows *rptJobCost* in Design view.

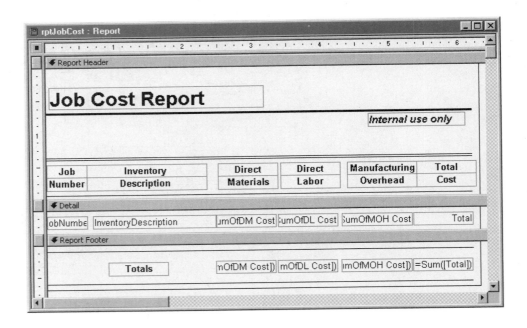

**Figure 9.24**   The Job Cost report in Design view.

We have turned off the Design view grid in the screen shown in Figure 9.24 so you can better see the details of the text box controls and the line objects in the report's design. When you are satisfied with your report design, you can save and close the report. The *Ch09.mdb* file on your Companion CD includes *rptJobCost*, which you can examine for details of the report's formatting and layout. A printout of the Job Cost report appears in Figure 9.25.

## Production Cycle Relationships

The production cycle is unusual in that many of its most useful elements are not stored in tables, but are calculated with queries. The Electric Controls Company example you worked through in this chapter is no exception. Although important information is stored in the production cycle tables, the job cost accumulations occur in queries and reports based on those queries. Figure 9.26 shows the complete set of entity tables and their relationships for the production cycle.

Notice that we have added links from the Job table to the Customer table and the Finished Goods table. These links do not have referential integrity constraints because Electric Controls Company wanted to enter jobs that had not yet been as-

# Job Cost Report

*Internal use only*

| Job Number | Inventory Description | Direct Materials | Direct Labor | Manufacturing Overhead | Total Cost |
|---|---|---|---|---|---|
| 1001 | Model 400A Control Panel | $1,133.52 | $1,613.60 | $2,145.00 | $4,892.12 |
| 1002 | Model 500C Control Panel | $2,055.48 | $3,680.80 | $4,160.00 | $9,896.28 |
| 1003 | Model 300A Control Panel | $884.14 | $970.50 | $877.50 | $2,732.14 |
| 1004 | Model 100A Control Panel | $335.33 | $806.40 | $1,170.00 | $2,311.73 |
| 1005 | Model 470D Control Panel | $1,158.91 | $1,267.70 | $2,031.25 | $4,457.86 |
| **Totals** | | $5,567.38 | $8,339.00 | $10,383.75 | $24,290.13 |

**Figure 9.25**  The Job Cost report printout.

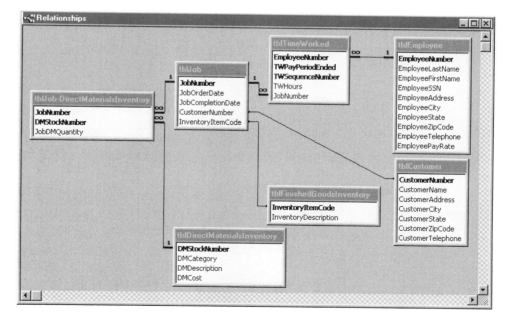

**Figure 9.26**  Production cycle entity tables and their relationships.

sociated with either a specific customer or a specific completed part number. You can compare the tables and relationships with the data model for Electric Controls' production cycle that we presented in Figure 9.1 at the beginning of the chapter to see how the implementation follows the model in the production cycle.

**SUMMARY**

In this chapter you learned how production cycle activities convert raw materials, labor, and overhead into finished products. You learned how production cycle accounting traces and allocates manufacturing costs to products. The production cycle system elements you built as you worked through this chapter can provide managers with information for monitoring manufacturing processes. The production cycle system also provides financial accountants with information they need to value inventories and determine the cost of goods sold.

Although this chapter explained how to use Access database management software in a manufacturing setting, a growing number of merchandising and service firms are examining their business processes using a product costing approach. Therefore, the techniques you learned in this chapter can help you design accounting systems for all three types of firms: manufacturing, merchandising, and service.

# QUESTIONS AND PROBLEMS FOR REVIEW

## MULTIPLE-CHOICE QUESTIONS

1. You can use queries in the production cycle to
   a. calculate direct materials cost.
   b. calculate the predetermined overhead rate.
   c. store employee pay rates.
   d. store hours worked by job.
2. Production cycle activities include all of the following except
   a. allocating manufacturing overhead.
   b. calculating job costs.
   c. calculating payroll deductions.
   d. tracing direct materials costs to jobs.
3. In a process cost accumulation system
   a. direct materials costs are traced to departments.
   b. manufacturing overhead costs are traced to departments.
   c. both a and b.
   d. neither a nor b.

4. The InventoryItemCode field in *tblJob* is a
   a. composite primary key.
   b. relationship key.
   c. primary key.
   d. foreign key.
5. A time worked table's composite primary key that combines an employee number field with a job number field may not be a unique identifier because an employee may
   a. work on several jobs in a pay period.
   b. work on the same job more than once in a pay period.
   c. change employee numbers during the year.
   d. work on several jobs in different pay periods.
6. To measure the timeliness of job completions, you would need to add
   a. a time field to the Direct Materials Inventory table.
   b. a Standard Cost table.
   c. a date completed field to *tblJob*.
   d. an estimated time field to *tblJob*.
7. The Direct Materials Inventory table includes switches, relays, and connectors rated at 120 and 240 volts. You could improve this table by
   a. placing the voltage rating at the beginning of the description field.
   b. placing the voltage rating at the end of the description field.
   c. placing the voltage rating in a separate table.
   d. placing the voltage rating in a separate field in the same table.
8. The Employee table in this chapter does not include a field for employee department because we accumulated costs using a
   a. job order system.
   b. process cost system.
   c. operation cost system.
   d. hybrid cost system.
9. Calculating job costs required a series of queries because in Microsoft Access
   a. a report cannot multiply by a constant.
   b. a report cannot compute sums of calculated fields.
   c. both a and b.
   d. neither a nor b.
10. In an activity-based job order cost system
    a. some manufacturing overhead costs are allocated to departments.
    b. all manufacturing overhead costs are traced to departments.
    c. some manufacturing costs are traced to activities then allocated to departments.
    d. some manufacturing costs are traced to activities then allocated to jobs.

## DISCUSSION QUESTIONS

1. Describe the changes you would make to the production cycle system described in this chapter to convert it to a process cost accumulation system.
2. What tables and queries would you add to those described in this chapter to convert it to an activity-based job order cost system?
3. Compare the Employee table in this chapter to the Employee table in Chapter 8. Explain the differences in the tables' structures.
4. Compare the Time Worked table in this chapter to the Time Worked table in Chapter 8. Explain the differences in the tables' structures.
5. Describe the modifications you would make to the production cycle elements described in this chapter to accommodate an operation cost accumulation system.

## PROBLEMS

1. Add a field to *tblJob* for budgeted cost. Create queries and a report that use this field to compute budget vs. actual differences by job.
2. Create a data entry form that would help persons enter time card data into the Time Worked table. Model the form after the time card shown in Figure 9.14 to make the data entry task easier.
3. Modify *rptJobCost* to display the customer name for each job.
4. Work-in-process inventory includes all jobs that have not been completed at month end. Modify the Job Cost queries and report to calculate the cost of December's work-in-process inventory.
5. Create a Job Cost Card form that facilitates the input of *budgeted* direct materials and direct labor cost data into Budgeted Direct Materials and Budgeted Time tables.

# 10 AUTOMATING DATABASE PROCEDURES

## OBJECTIVES

Chapter 10 explains the art of automating database procedures with macros and Visual Basic for Applications (VBA) code. You will learn how to write macros and attach them to command buttons. You will learn how to use VBA to create powerful, small code segments to produce database objects that automatically react to changes. Though it sounds like you are in for a lot of programming in this chapter, this is not the case. You will learn to create small code segments that are both easy to understand and that provide powerful features. Several of the sub procedures are products of the Access Control Wizard, which help you create command buttons backed by VBA code and error-checking routines. This chapter teaches you how to create useful and professional-looking enhancements that will make using your forms and reports even easier. In particular, you will learn:

- What events are and how they propagate throughout your application.
- How actions are recognized and triggered by events.
- How to write a macro and attach it to a command button that activates the macro.
- How to write Visual Basic for Applications (VBA) code and attach the code to event procedures.
- How to create form navigation buttons.
- How to incorporate small code segments that reside behind a form and that provide data validity, range, and reasonableness checks on form fields.

## MACROS AND VISUAL BASIC FOR APPLICATIONS (VBA)

Access contains two powerful tools that provide you with the capability of taking your database to a full-scale, automated, easy-to-use application. The tools are Access macro programming and Visual Basic for Applications (VBA). Both tools allow you to write code that takes action when selected events occur. Access macros provide simple tools to automate many kinds of tasks. For instance, you can easily create a navigation macro, attached to a button, that goes to the next record in a table when the button is clicked. When a user clicks the button, that action triggers the *click event*, one of several events that a button recognizes. This causes the navigation button macro code to execute. Visual Basic for Applications, while similar to Access macro programming in many ways, is a full-featured programming language that extends the macro language and provides tools that are not available in Access macros. For example, VBA allows you to handle error conditions, while macros do not. VBA has several looping structures that permit code to be executed repeatedly until the code recognizes some stopping condition. Macros do not provide repetitive processing (looping). Macros are easier to write and understand, so we will start by writing a macro or two. Then, you will take what you learned about macros and jump into VBA. This chapter is not a substitute for a thorough discussion of either macro programming or VBA programming. The intention here is to give you a good, fundamental understanding of both macros and VBA code. You can extend your knowledge of both by enhancing your database applications and reading books on the topic.

## Automating Database Applications

A macro or VBA—known collectively as *code*—is a single action or a series of actions stored with a form or stored independently as an object in the Macros or Modules collection of the Database window. Code automates an application and simplifies the use of tables, queries, forms, and reports. You can automate many database tasks with either a macro or VBA, reducing a task to just a few mouse clicks. Code can be used to create complete turnkey applications, or it can be used to simply enhance an application with small code segments performing specialized duties. Our objective is to introduce you to a few useful language elements that can simplify the use of your applications and automate procedures. Then you can use these representative examples in your applications, applying and extending the techniques you learned in the textbook to specific situations you encounter.

## States, Events, and Event Properties

When you click a button on the Access toolbar, you change the state of that button. It changes from unclicked to clicked. Similarly, whenever you use a keyboard or a mouse, you are changing the state of something within the computer. An object's state is its list of characteristics, or properties, and their values. Access keeps track of each object's set of possible states. For instance, a button can be in the *enabled* state. If it is not, then it is in the *not enabled* state. Access automatically recognizes that a user cannot click a button (also known as a *command button*) when it is in the disabled state. This is a built-in behavior of a button. Furthermore, Access indicates that a button's state is not enabled by making it appear dim—making the label appear light gray instead of dark black. The importance of knowing that objects have states is that you can take advantage of objects' states by interrupt processing or by taking an alternative action whenever an object is in a certain state. For instance, Access recognizes when a user clicks a button and then automatically transfers execution to the user-written code that is assigned to react to the button click event.

Any change of an object's state is called an *event*. A macro or VBA code can react to an event by performing a series of program steps. Steps of code assigned to react to a button click, for example, are known as *code behind the button*. The code can cause any number of actions to occur and can determine how an object behaves after a triggering event occurs. As a database designer, you indicate which code reacts to which event by naming the code and placing its name in the object's *event property*. Similar to other properties, most objects have several event properties. Each event property is either empty or contains the name of the bit of code that handles that particular event. If an event property is empty, then the event causes nothing to happen—the event goes unnoticed. Otherwise, the code that is named in the event property "listens" for its assigned event to occur on that object and then reacts to the event in a prescribed way.

Figure 10.1 shows the Event tab of a button's property sheet. Notice the names of the event properties listed. Two event properties have been assigned code to perform prescribed duties when the associated events occur. The On Click event property currently has VBA code assigned to it ("[Event Procedure]" indicates VBA code is assigned). Also called an *event handler*, the assigned event property code responds whenever someone clicks the button to which the property is associated. The only other event handler is a macro named CheckIt. A specific name appearing in an event property indicates the assigned code is a macro and not VBA code. Associated with the event "On Dbl Click" (shorthand for "on double click"), the CheckIt macro jumps into action when anyone double-clicks the command button called *cmdExit* (see the property sheet Title bar for an object's type and name).

**Figure 10.1** A command button's event properties.

Here's an example in which a macro simplifies a process for anyone using a data entry form. You know that in order to delete data stored in the tables constituting the Sales Order system shown in Chapter 5 (Figure 5.8), you must first delete the order lines from the subform. Once you delete the individual order lines, then you can delete the main order record (the main form is shown in Figure 5.8 also). However, someone using your accounting system may not know much about database systems generally or the referential integrity rules in particular that preclude deleting master form records before deleting subform records. Therefore, you cannot expect those using your accounting system to realize, for example, which keys to press to delete a record or even that you must delete the subform data first.

You can reduce these kinds of difficulties by creating intuitively labeled buttons that carry out the required actions in the correct sequence. A button might execute a series of steps to accomplish an activity such as editing a data field or searching a database for a particular item. For instance, you can simplify the process of deleting information by creating a button labeled *Delete Record* and placing it on a form. When a user clicks the command button, it invokes a macro or VBA code. The code automatically selects a complete record, executes the Select Record command, and then executes the Delete command. By automating frequently used procedures with buttons, you minimize users' keystrokes, remove their need to make complicated menu and command choices, and greatly reduce the probability that they will make an error. One button performs a series of steps that accomplish a complete task. Those using your accounting system will be happy that they do not have to study and learn the database commands. Instead, they can concentrate on the accounting task at hand.

Figure 10.2 shows an example of a form containing buttons with code invisibly attached to the buttons. When a user clicks the Save Record button, the database is updated with the altered record. Similarly, the Cancel Changes button is attached to code that cancels the most recent changes made to the data.

An example of the value of a command button and its attached code (a macro in this particular example) is the record navigation button labeled "First" found on The Coffee Merchant's Customer form. The macro that is behind the First button consists of three steps. Figure 10.3 shows the First macro in the Macro design window.

What is the macro doing? The Macro window shows three columns: Macro Name, Action, and Comment. The Macro Name column contains the macro's name. The Action column contains one or more steps or actions that the macro performs. In this example, the macro contains three actions: Echo, GoToRecord, and GoToControl. Access executes a macro beginning with the first step, which also contains the macro's name in the Macro Name step of the same row. The Echo command freezes the screen while the macro is running to suppress displaying messages and actions as they occur in quick sequence. The next statement, GoToRecord, moves to the first record in the table. The third statement, GoToControl, moves the focus to the first field in the form, CustomerID. (When

**Figure 10.2** Example of a form with command buttons.

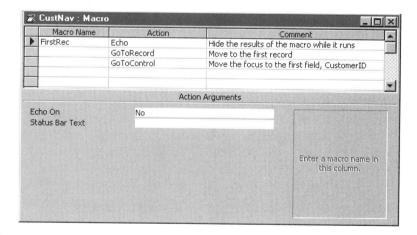

**Figure 10.3** The macro that responds when the First command button is clicked.

an object—a field or button, for example—has the *focus* you can affect the object by typing something on the keyboard or by clicking the mouse. Only one object at a time can have the focus.)

Do not be concerned if the meanings of the lines in Figure 10.3 are not apparent to you. You will learn more about these later in this chapter. The example merely illustrates a typical macro.

Macros or VBA code can be attached to objects other than buttons. You can attach code to a form itself. For instance, you can embellish a form with a macro that prompts users for a password whenever the form is opened and before displaying database information. Form fields can have macros attached to them as well. You can modify a form field so its value is validated before the cursor is allowed to pass to the next field.

In the next section, you will learn about how to attach a macro to a button's click event. Following the explanation, you will learn how to create more versatile code to attach to buttons' events using Visual Basic. Once you see the power of VBA, we think you will agree that VBA is the best and most efficient way to write code to perform tasks in response to events. First, let's look at a simple macro and build a button to launch it.

## AUTOMATING FORMS WITH COMMAND BUTTONS

You develop macros and VBA code by planning them, attaching them to the objects whose behaviors are to be affected, and then testing them to ensure that they work correctly. To understand both macros and VBA code and their usefulness, we will add a few buttons to the Customer form, *frmCustomer*. This form displays The Coffee Merchant's customer information and allows you to update customer information. To set the stage for this chapter, first start Windows and copy the database *Ch10.mdb* found in the Ch10 folder on your Companion CD to your hard drive. Remember to clear the Read-only property of the copied database before you attempt to open it. Once the database is copied, open *Ch10.mdb*.

## Creating a Command Button

Let's make things a bit easier for your users by placing database navigation buttons on the form displaying customer information. Though navigation buttons are available in the Form window, the ones we design will be larger and easier to locate. Later, we will add some safeguards that are not available with the Access-supplied, standard navigation buttons. (We have set one of the form properties specifically to *not* display the usual navigation buttons.) Together, we will create a button that will move to the first customer record in the database and display it. After we create that button, you can create three other navigation buttons using the first one as a model. The other buttons move to the next record, the previous record, and the last record. First we create a button (command button). Then we create a macro that causes an action to occur when the button is clicked. Follow the steps in the next exercise to create a button object and place it on the Customer form, *frmCustomer*.

EXERCISE 10.1: CREATING A COMMAND BUTTON

1. Click Forms on the Objects bar to display the form names in the Database window.

2. Select the form *frmCustomer* and then click the Design View button to display the form in Design view. Maximize the form so it fills the window.
3. Select Toolbox from the View menu to place the toolbox on the screen. Drag the toolbox to the right edge of the window so it is out of the way.
4. If the Control Wizards tool is selected (see Figure 10.4; the tool has a light background and appears pressed in), then click it so that the Control Wizard does not interfere with your work as you build a command button.
5. Click the Command Button tool in the toolbox (see Figure 10.4). Then move the mouse pointer below the Credit Limit field in an open area. Click the mouse to drop the button onto the form. If the Command Button Wizard opens, then simply click the Cancel button located near the bottom of the dialog box.
6. Click the newly created button twice *slowly* until a vertical bar (the *insertion point*) appears within the button's label.
7. Using the Backspace and Delete keys, remove the command button's current label (*Command25*, for example) and type *&First* in its place. Click outside the button to deselect it. The ampersand precedes any letter in the command button's label to indicate which key is the button's access key. An *access key* is a keyboard shortcut. Pressing Alt and typing the access key (*f* in this example) is the equivalent to clicking the command button with your mouse.
8. Select Save As from the File menu and type *frmCustomer1* in the upper text box of the Save As dialog box.
9. Click OK to save the form under the new name. (Leave the form on your screen because you will continue to make changes to it.)

Control Wizards tool (not selected)

Command Button tool

**Figure 10.4** Access Toolbox showing some of its many tools.

With the new button in place, switch to Form view and try it out. Click the First button with your mouse or press Alt+F. Notice that it seems to do nothing except appear sunken when you click it. The sunken appearance is one of a command button's *built-in* behaviors. The reason nothing else happens is that you have not yet associated any code—a macro or VBA code—to the button's *On Click event*. You do that next.

## Creating a Macro and Attaching It to a Command Button

To change the way a button behaves when you click it, you can attach a macro to one of the button's event properties (it has several). Because you want the button to react and do a series of actions when it is clicked, you associate code (a macro in this example) with the button's On Click event. You do this by displaying the command button's property sheet and writing the macro's name into the text of the On Click property. First, though, you must *create* a macro that performs the duties of going to the first record in the database displayed by the form. Once the macro is created and saved, you can then attach it to an event property.

In the next exercise, you create a macro that is attached to the First navigation button (see Figure 10.2) and executed when the button is clicked. Ensure that the form *frmCustomer1* is still loaded and displayed in Design view.

### EXERCISE 10.2: CREATING A DATABASE NAVIGATION MACRO

1.  Maximize the form, close the toolbox, click the First button to select it (selection handles appear around the button), and display the button's property sheet (View, Properties). Drag the property sheet to a location where you can see both it and the navigation button labeled First.
2.  Click the property sheet's Other tab, double-click the Name property, and type *cmdFirst* (this changes the button's internal name).
3.  Click the property sheet's Event tab to display the button's event properties. Click inside the On Click property text box. An arrow and a Build button (...) are displayed on the right side of the text box.
4.  Click the Build button. When the Choose Builder dialog box is displayed, double-click the Macro Builder choice. The Save As dialog box is displayed.
5.  Type the macro name *CustNav* and click OK. The Macro Design window opens.
6.  Click Macro Names in the View menu to display the Macro Name column in the Design view window.
7.  Move the insertion point to the first row, Macro Name column and type the name *FirstRec* to mark the macro's first line of code.
8.  Move the insertion point to the Action column. Click the drop-down list box arrow to display the *action list*.
9.  Scroll the list until the action Echo appears. Click that action to place it into the Action column.
10. Click the comment column to the right in the same row and enter the comment *Hide the results of the macro while it runs* in that cell.
11. Click the Echo On text box in the Action Arguments panel and select No from the drop-down list.
12. Move the insertion point to the Action column of the second row. Click the drop-down list box arrow, scroll the list until the action GoToRecord appears, and click that action to place it in the Action column.
13. Click the comment column to the right in the same row and enter the comment *Move to the first record* in that cell.

14. In the Action Arguments panel, click the Record row in the argument list, click the drop-down list box arrow, and select First from the list. The hint box to the right gives you information on what to specify for the action argument.
15. Move the insertion point to the Action column of the third row. Click the drop-down list box arrow, scroll the list until the action GoToControl appears, and click that action to place it in the Action column.
16. Click the comment column to the right in the same row and enter the comment *Move the focus to the first field, CustomerID* in that comment cell.
17. In the Action Arguments panel, click the Control Name text box and type *CustomerID*
18. Click the Macro window Close button and click the Yes button when you are asked if you want to save the changes.

The completed macro is called FirstRec. It has appeared previously in Figure 10.3. Your macro should look like that one.

You have just created a macro group. A *macro group* is a collection of macros. When you use a macro group, it is easier to keep track of related macros such as the navigation button macros. They are contained in one macro group rather than stored as several separate macros. Over time, creating individual macros causes their numbers to soar and makes them very difficult to manage. Creating macro groups is no different from creating single macros. The advantage of a group is organization. Related macros can be placed under one "roof" so they can be easily located later. This is especially helpful when you have an application with hundreds of macros.

Although you have attached the CustNav macro—a *group* macro name—to the First button's On Click event, the actual name that appears in the On Click property must be changed to FirstRec before you can execute the macro by clicking the First button. After all, FirstRec is the name appearing in the Macro Name column of the CustNav macro group. FirstRec contains the code to move to the first database record, so let's change the macro name associated with the First button's On Click event. The next exercise shows you how to make this simple change.

EXERCISE 10.3: ATTACHING A MACRO TO A BUTTON'S ON CLICK EVENT

1. With the form in Design view, select the First button and display its Event properties.
2. Click within the On Click text box and then click the down arrow that appears on the right side of the text box (see Figure 10.5). (Be careful to not click the Build button, because that will display the macro itself, not the list of macro names.)

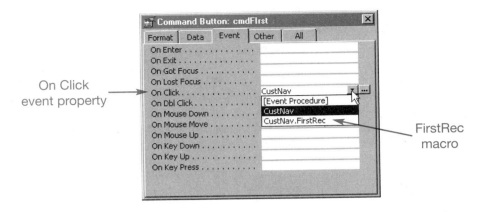

**On Click event property**

**FirstRec macro**

**Figure 10.5** Selecting a macro to attach to the On Click event.

3. Click the choice *CustNav.FirstRec* in the selection list. (You refer to a particular macro that is part of a macro group by specifying the macro group name, a dot, followed by the macro name.)
4. Click the property sheet's Close button.
5. Select Save from the File menu to save your changes.
6. Click the form's Close button.

**Try it**

Try out the new button. First, return to Form view and then select Edit, GoTo, Last to move to the last customer record. Now, click the First button. The form displays the first record in the table.

In the next section, you create the remaining three navigation buttons by building Visual Basic for Applications code and attaching the code to the remaining navigation buttons.

## Creating Other Form Navigation Buttons with VBA

Creating the remaining navigation buttons that perform the duties of a form's traditional navigation buttons is relatively simple. You have created the first of these already. The procedure is similar for the Previous, Next, and Last navigation buttons. This time, however, you will use a Wizard to help you build the command buttons and the code that they invoke when they are clicked. Let's create a command button to go to the previous record in the database. In preparation for the exercise, open the *Ch10.mdb* database, click Forms on the Objects bar, and open *frmCustomer1* in Design view. Execute the steps in the following exercise to create a new navigation button backed by VBA code.

## EXERCISE 10.4: CREATING A COMMAND BUTTON USING THE CONTROL WIZARDS TOOL

1. Select Toolbox from the View menu, if necessary, to display the toolbox and click the Control Wizards tool (see Figure 10.4) so that it is pressed in. (With the Control Wizards tool engaged, the Wizard helps us build a command button complete with VBA code behind the button.)
2. Click the Command Button tool in the toolbox and click on the *frmCustomer1* form just to the right of the existing First command button. The command button is placed on the form and the Control Wizard starts by asking what actions you want the new button to perform.
3. In the Categories list, select Record Navigation.
4. In the Actions list, select GoTo Previous Record and then click the Next button.
5. Select the Text option button so that a label appears on the button instead of a graphic. Type *&Previous* in the text box to the right of the Text option button. Click the Next button. When you create your own buttons in other projects, you may wish to use pictures provided for your use. There is a large library of icons from which you can choose.
6. Type *cmdPrevious* in the text box to rename the button a meaningful name that follows programming guidelines for naming objects.
7. Click Finish to complete the button-building process. The Wizard finishes creating the command button. Simultaneously and invisibly, the Wizard also writes several lines of VBA code and automatically attaches them to the On Click event property for you.
8. Close the property sheet, if necessary, and save the altered form, *frmCustomer1*. Leave the form open in Design view.

Let's look at the code that the Control Wizard created and attached to the Previous button's On Click event. The next exercise shows you how to view the code attached to an object's event property.

## EXERCISE 10.5: VIEWING THE VBA CODE ATTACHED TO A BUTTON'S EVENT PROPERTY

1. Right-click the Previous button and click Build Event from the pop-up command list. The Build Event command tells Access to open the Visual Basic window and to display the *default* event procedure for the selected object. In this case, the command button is the object and its default event procedure is the On Click event. Thus, Visual Basic displays the code window showing VBA code behind the On Click procedure (see Figure 10.6).
2. Look around the Visual Basic window and notice the menus it contains. Hover the mouse over the toolbar buttons and observe the ToolTips. Don't worry right now about what the code means. We'll examine code in more detail later in this chapter.

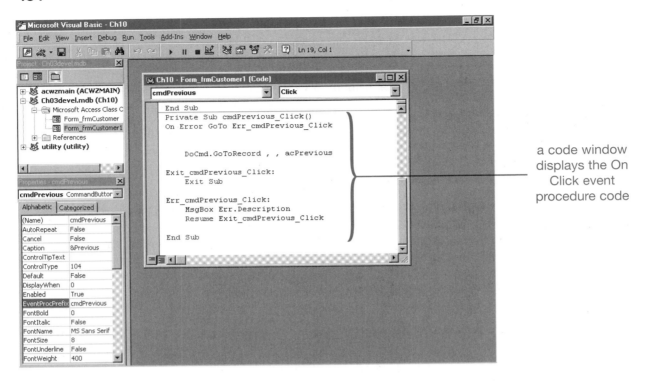

**Figure 10.6**   Examining a command button's code in the Visual Basic window.

3. After you have spent a few minutes observing the Visual Basic window, click the File menu and then click Close and Return to Microsoft Access. The Visual Basic window closes and the familiar Access Database window reappears.

Creating the missing two navigation buttons, Next and Last, is straightforward. To create the Next navigation button that goes to the next record in the customer table, repeat Exercise 10.4 but make these changes to the exercise's steps:

- Step 4: Select GoTo Next Record.
- Step 5: Type *Ne&xt* in the text box to the right of the Text option button. (The ampersand precedes the letter you want to serve as the command's quick access key.)
- Step 6: Type *cmdNext* to rename the button.

To create the Last navigation button that goes to the last record in the customer table, repeat Exercise 10.4 once again but make these changes to the exercise's steps:

- Step 4: Select GoTo Last Record.
- Step 5: Type *&Last* in the text box to the right of the Text option button.
- Step 6: Type *cmdLast* to rename the button.

If you want to size the navigation buttons so that they more closely match those shown in Figure 10.2, then take a moment to complete the next exercise.

EXERCISE 10.6: OPTIMIZING BUTTON SIZES

1. In Design view, select all four database navigation buttons. (Press and hold the Shift key and then click each navigation button.)
2. Select Format, Size, To Fit. This optimizes the button lengths to be just long enough to display the buttons' names.
3. With the four buttons still selected, make them all the same length but no longer than the longest button by selecting Format, Size, To Widest. This step sizes the buttons to a uniform width.
4. Finally, (with all buttons selected) grab one of the handles in the middle, top edge of a button and drag it toward the bottom edge to reduce the height of all the buttons slightly. Ensure that you can still see the buttons' labels, however.
5. Rearrange the buttons so that they appear side by side as shown in Figure 10.2.
6. To make the buttons line up perfectly and have equal space between them, select all four buttons again, select Format, Align, Bottom and then select Format, Horizontal Spacing, Make Equal.
7. Click Save from the File menu to save the form.

Now that you have created four navigation buttons of your own, you can eliminate Access' built-in navigation buttons. There's no need for two sets of navigation buttons. Eliminate Access' navigation buttons by executing the steps that follow.

EXERCISE 10.7: ELIMINATE THE DEFAULT
NAVIGATION BUTTONS AND RECORD SELECTORS

1. With *frmCustomer1* still in Design view, click the Select Form command from the Edit menu.
2. Open the property sheet, click the Format tab, and set the Navigation Buttons property to No.
3. Set the Record Selectors property to No. (You can double-click any Yes/No property to toggle its value.) When the Record Selectors property is set to No, the record selector arrow disappears from a form's left edge of a form.

4. Close the property sheet and toolbox, if open.
5. Select File and then Save to save the form.
6. Close the form.

**Try it**

Try out the new form navigation buttons. Open the form in Form view, click the Last button, click the Previous button, and then click the First button. What happens if you click the First navigation button and then click the Previous navigation button?

## Printing a Macro, Macro Group, or VBA Code

You should always save your code prior to testing it. When you closed the Macro window, Access prompted you about saving the macro. By clicking the Yes button, you saved the *cmdFirst* macro that you created in Exercise 10.2. Similarly, if you were to make changes to the Wizard-generated VBA code like the code in Figure 10.6, then Access will prompt you to save your changes when you attempt to close the Visual Basic window. If you do not save your code prior to testing it, an errant bit of VBA code can execute incorrectly and make it impossible to save the changes. For instance, suppose you alter the code in the Last navigation button, return to Form view, and click the Last button to test the changes. If an error in execution of the VBA code occurs, then you can be left staring at an error message in the Visual Basic window and have no easy way to save your latest version of your code.

Part of the process of developing a database system is documenting your work. One part of documenting your developing or completed system is maintaining a printout of all the code—macros and VBA—that you have written. You may want to keep these documents in a notebook along with printouts of forms, reports, queries, and tables. To print a macro, click Macros in the Objects bar of the Database window to display the list of macro names. Then click the macro name you want to print and select Print from the File menu. Select the items you want to include in the printout from the list in the Print Macro Definition dialog box. Then click OK. That's all there is to it. You must repeat this process for every macro you want to print because, unfortunately, there is no way to print more than one macro at a time.

To print VBA code for *all* the procedures attached to any objects on a particular form, click Forms on the Objects bar of the Database window. Then, select the form name containing the VBA code that you want to print. Click Code from the View menu and then click Print from the File menu. Click the Current Module option (or Current Project to print the code for the entire database) and click the OK button on the Print dialog box. Figure 10.7 shows an example of the code you created for three of the navigation buttons.

```
Form_frmCustomer1 - 1

Option Compare Database
Option Explicit

Private Sub cmdPrevious_Click()
On Error GoTo Err_cmdPrevious_Click


    DoCmd.GoToRecord , , acPrevious

Exit_cmdPrevious_Click:
    Exit Sub

Err_cmdPrevious_Click:
    MsgBox Err.Description
    Resume Exit_cmdPrevious_Click

End Sub
Private Sub cmdNext_Click()
On Error GoTo Err_cmdNext_Click


    DoCmd.GoToRecord , , acNext

Exit_cmdNext_Click:
    Exit Sub

Err_cmdNext_Click:
    MsgBox Err.Description
    Resume Exit_cmdNext_Click

End Sub
Private Sub cmdLast_Click()
On Error GoTo Err_cmdLast_Click


    DoCmd.GoToRecord , , acLast

Exit_cmdLast_Click:
    Exit Sub

Err_cmdLast_Click:
    MsgBox Err.Description
    Resume Exit_cmdLast_Click

End Sub
```

**Figure 10.7**  Example code printout.

## Access Events

So far, we have looked at one event property, called On Click, which occurs whenever the object having that property is clicked. Objects besides command buttons have On Click event properties. For example, you can click a form, a text box, or a label. Though clicking such objects is uncommon, they respond by launching the macro or VBA code that is attached to the On Click event property, if any. There are many other events to which various Access objects can respond. Figure 10.8 lists several event properties, when they spring into action, and why you might want to know when the event occurs.

There are more event properties than those listed in Figure 10.8, but the figure contains important event properties that you will need for this chapter. On Change is an event property that occurs when the On Change event occurs. Entering a new value, or changing an existing value, in an object such as a text

| Event Property | Occurs When | Use the Event To |
| --- | --- | --- |
| On Change | A control's value changes | Update any other related controls |
| On Click | A user clicks the mouse on an object | Do anything. It is the most used of all events |
| On Current | A form is opened or requeried | Create more intelligent form navigation buttons |
| On Delete | A record is about to be deleted | Ensure it is okay to delete the selected record |
| On Exit | A control loses the focus to another control | Validate the data in a control |
| On Open | A form is displayed but before the first record is displayed | Initialize form messages and default values |

**Figure 10.8**   Selected event properties and examples of their uses.

box triggers the On Change event, which launches the code attached to the On Change event property. The On Current event property is particularly handy whenever you use a form to view or change a table's contents. If you move to and display another record in a form, the On Current event occurs. (Developers sometimes say that an event *fires* or that some action *triggers* an event.)

## Improving Navigation Buttons

One way to improve the four navigation buttons on the customer form is to change their behavior slightly to help the user. For instance, removing choices that are inapplicable helps users understand which actions are available and which are not. Specifically, when a user clicks the Last button, Access moves to the last record in the customer table. In this case, the Next button has no meaning, because there is no "next" record in the table—you are viewing the last record. Thus it would help users to disable the Next button so that they understand that button is inapplicable in the current content. On the other hand, when a user then clicks the Previous navigation button, Access moves to the record just before the last one. In this case, the Next button should be available because there is a *next* record.

Well-designed Windows applications disable and enable commands and buttons to help the user and indicate when they can and cannot be used. For example, if there is nothing on the Clipboard, then the Paste command in the Edit menu of most Microsoft products is dimmed (light gray), which indicates that you cannot paste anything. You will add similar user convenience features to your four-button customer form. The next exercise takes advantage of a convenient event property for forms called On Current. The On Current event invokes the On Current form event property whenever the form on which you are working is opened or a new record is displayed in the form. This is handy, because all four of the navigation buttons cause a new record to display in the form and thus cause the On Current event to occur. The next exercise shows you how to write a general-purpose VBA procedure that is attached to the On Current event property and monitors every record change or form-opening event. It is there that your event procedure can gain control and determine if any of the navigation buttons should be disabled or enabled. In preparation for this exercise, open the *Ch10.mdb* database, if necessary, and close all windows except the Database window.

## EXERCISE 10.8: CREATING BETTER NAVIGATION BUTTONS

1. Open *frmCustomer1* in Design view.
2. Click Select Form in the Edit menu to select the entire form and click the Properties button on the Design view toolbar to display the property sheet. The property sheet displays "Form" in the Title bar if you have selected the form. If the property sheet Title bar displays "Section: Detail" for example, then press the shortcut Ctrl+R to select the entire form.
3. Click the Event tab.
4. Click the On Current event property text box and then click the Build button that appears on the right side of the On Current property.
5. Click Code Builder in the Choose Builder dialog box and click OK. The Current event procedure opens in a Visual Basic window.
6. Add the following code to the form's Current event procedure. Be careful to type all new code between the statements *Private Sub Form_Current()* and *End Sub*. Figure 10.9 shows the Visual Basic window with the following code already entered:

    *'If the CustomerID control is empty, then a new record is being displayed.*
    *'In this case, shift the focus to the Previous button*
    *'and disable the Next button.*
    *'If there is a value in CustomerID, then enable the Next button.*

    *If IsNull (Me.CustomerID) Then*
      *cmdPrevious.SetFocus*
      *cmdNext.Enabled = False*
    *Else*
      *cmdNext.Enabled = True*
    *End If*

7. Click Close and Return to Microsoft Access in the File menu to close the Visual Basic code window.
8. Close the form and save it when Access prompts you.

### Try it

Open the form in Form view. Try out the new safeguard built into the form. Click the Last button to go to the last record in the customer table. Now, click the Next button to open the empty record beyond the last actual table record. If you entered the

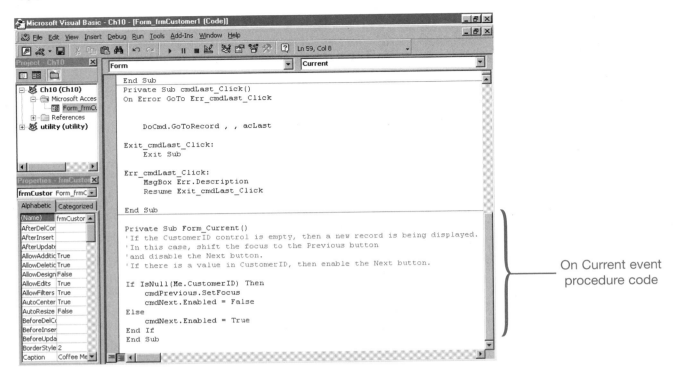

**Figure 10.9**    Completed On Current event procedure.

code correctly in the preceding exercise, notice that the Next button is dimmed and you cannot click it. Finally, click the First navigation button and observe that the Next button is enabled again.

What is the code doing? The first four lines of code you typed all begin with apostrophes. This is the way you write Visual Basic comment lines. Everything following an apostrophe on a line is ignored by Visual Basic. The blank line following the comments provides needed visual separation between comments and code.

By using the On Current event property, you gain control of a form whenever the user moves from one record to another—including moving to the last record in the table and the empty record beyond that. You know that the user has pressed the Next button to reach the empty record beyond the last record in the customer table by inspecting the CustomerID control on the form. If the user has moved to a new record, the CustomerID control will be empty. The expression in the first line examines CustomerID to determine if it is empty:

If IsNull (Me.CustomerID)

IsNull is a built-in function available in Access that tests to see if the enclosed object (a control in this case) is empty (Null) or not. We get the value of the CustomerID control of the first record using the reference Me.CustomerID. The keyword "Me" indicates to Access that we want to refer to the current object's set of records—in this case, the current object is the form *frmCustomer1*. If the value of CustomerID is empty, or null, then we know that we have reached an empty record.

The expression following the If statement—the statement described previously—is evaluated. It can be either true or false. If it is true, then the statements following "Then" and before the "Else" phrases are executed. If the statement is false, then only the statement(s) between the "Else" and the "End If" are executed. In other words, the If/Then/Else structure provides two mutually exclusive choices, meaning Access will execute one or the other but not both.

What happens if the expression following the If phrase is true? Two statements are executed:

```
cmdPrevious.SetFocus
cmdNext.Enabled = False
```

Using the object.method notation, the statement "cmdPrevious.SetFocus" moves the focus to the cmdPrevious button. SetFocus is called a *method* and cmdPrevious is an object on which the method operates. The result is that the focus first moves off the Next button and to the Previous button. (Recall that an object having the focus is the only object that can accept input—be clicked in this case.) The next statement sets the Enabled property of the cmdNext object to the value of False. Simply stated, the cmdNext button becomes unavailable and appears dimmed on the form.

What happens if the user had pressed the Next button and the second record in the customer display became available in the *frmCustomer1* form? First, the Current event would occur, triggering the code you entered for the On Current event property. The If statement evaluates the expression IsNull (Me.CustomerID) and returns the value False—the CustomerID control is not empty because the second record has a value for CustomerID. Continuing with the code (examine Figure 10.9), only the statement following Else in the If/Then/Else structure is executed: cmdNext.Enabled = True. That statement sets the cmdNext's enabled property to True. This means that the button is available and a user can click it. If you were to omit that statement, then the Next button would remain forever unavailable (dimmed) after the first time a user goes to the new record beyond the last actual record in the customer table.

The statement "End If" marks the end of the If statement. Following the End If statement is the automatically supplied "End Sub" statement, which marks the end of the entire event procedure that responds to the On Current event. One formatting convention is worth noting. Statements on the Then and Else sides of the If statement are indented for readability. It helps you to visually identify which statements belong with which parts of the structure.

## IMPLEMENTING DATABASE MANIPULATION BUTTONS

Other useful buttons that can save time for your users and simplify their work include those that update a record, insert a new record in the database, delete an unwanted record, post all changes to a record to the database, and cancel (negate) any changes made to a record. While these tasks can be accomplished by using the Access menus, those menus can be intimidating to anyone not familiar with Microsoft Access. So, we show you how to create the buttons and associated macros to accomplish these important database tasks. We continue to use The Coffee Merchant's Customer form. When you are done with this section, your form (*frmCustomer1*) should resemble Figure 10.2, and all the form's buttons should work correctly.

## Creating the Save Record and New Record Buttons

Users want to be able to easily save an edited record and add a new record to a database. You can facilitate these two operations by providing buttons that perform those functions. You can implement saving a record with a very small piece of VBA code. The Save Record button saves all changes to the current record by executing the Save Record command on the Records menu. It does this with the VBA DoMenuItem command, which invokes existing menu commands to do the work. It is as simple as that.

Let's build the VBA code to be attached to the Save Record button. As with creating the navigation buttons, you can use a Wizard or you can build it yourself. If you choose to build it yourself, then there are two major steps involved. First, place a button on the form; second, create the On Click event property's VBA code to carry out the action. Create the Save Record button by completing the following exercise.

EXERCISE 10.9: CREATING THE SAVEREC BUTTON AND VBA CODE

1. Open *frmCustomer1* in Design view, open the toolbox, and click the Control Wizard tool so that it is pressed in—we want the Control Wizard to help us again.
2. Click the Command Button tool in the toolbox and click on the *frmCustomer1* form on the right side of the form (see Figure 10.2). Access places the command button on the form and the Control Wizard starts displaying dialog boxes.
3. In the Categories list, select Record Operations.
4. In the Actions list, select Save Record and then click the Next button.
5. Select the Text option button so that a label appears on the button instead of a graphic.
6. Type *&Save Record* in the text box to the right of the Text option button. (Alternatively, you can simply move to the left side of the text box—so that the insertion point is to the left of Save—and type *&* only.) Click the Next button.
7. Type *cmdSaveRecord* in the text box to give the button a meaningful name.

8. Click Finish to complete the button-building process. The Wizard creates the button and attaches VBA code to the button's On Click event property.

9. Save the altered form, *frmCustomer1*. Leave the form open in Design view.

If you want to see the VBA code that Access built for you, then right-click the Save Record button and select Build Event from the pop-up menu. The Visual Basic window opens. All the VBA code you or the Control Wizard created so far is found in this window. Simply scroll to the top or bottom to view various event procedures. You can display a particular procedure, such as the cmdSaveRecord_Click event procedure you created in the preceding exercise, by clicking inside the procedure you want to view and then clicking the Procedure View button in the lower left corner of the Visual Basic window (see Figure 10.10). Click the Full Module View button to view all the event procedures in the module.

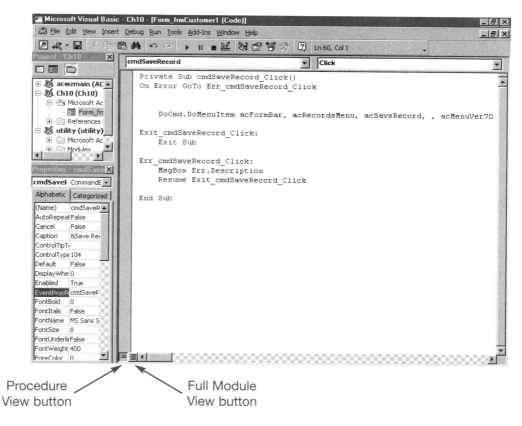

Procedure View button

Full Module View button

**Figure 10.10** Completed Save Record event procedure.

### Try it

To test the new Save Record button, let's create a new customer record. First, display *frmCustomer1* in Form view. Select Data Entry from the Records menu to display an empty form. Enter any data you want, but be sure to assign a CustomerID value that is greater than 36000. This way, you will not inadvertently change an existing customer record. Now click the Save Record button.

Satisfy yourself that the record was actually posted to the database by alternately clicking the First and Last navigation buttons. After you click the Last button, your new record will be displayed. Figure 10.11 shows an example of a new record after the Save Record button has been clicked. (Soon, we will create and use a Delete Record button to remove the record you entered so that the Customer database remains unchanged.)

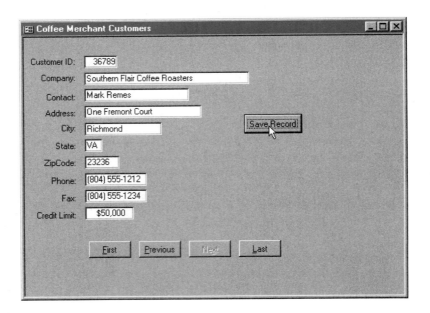

**Figure 10.11**   Adding a record and saving it with the Save Record button.

The New Record button and associated procedure is equally simple to implement. Repeat Exercise 10.9 but make the following changes in the steps:

- Step 4: Select Add New Record in the Actions list.

- Step 6: Type *&New Record*.

- Step 7: Type *cmdNewRecord* in the text box.

Leave the Toolbox and Design view window open, because you will be adding two more buttons in rapid succession. Recall that the ampersand designates the button's access key. Keyboard users can press Alt+N to click the button. Do not be concerned if the Save Record and New Record buttons are not the exact same size or are not aligned correctly. You will take care of all that soon.

Figure 10.12 shows the VBA code that the Control Wizard generated. Here's what the lines of the code accomplish. Execution begins with the first line of code following the statement "Private Sub…" The On Error statement simply tells Access that if any type of error occurs, continue execution at the label Err_cmdNewRecord_Click. That label is near the bottom of the sub procedure. The workhorse of the sub procedure is the line

    DoCmd.GoToRecord , , acNewRec

DoCmd is called an object. Following the object is a period and "GoToRecord." GoToRecord is a *method*, which is an action affecting the object to which it is attached. Following the object and its method are one or more arguments. *Arguments* to a method supply additional information about how the method should operate. Commas separate method arguments from one another. You indicate omitted or unneeded arguments by a blank space and a comma. Following the two omitted arguments is the very important intrinsic constant, "acNewRec." An *intrinsic constant* is a character string that has an unchanging value. The intrinsic constant shown in Figure 10.12, acNewRec, indicates that Access should display a new,

**Figure 10.12**   VBA code behind the New Record button.

blank record. The last line that Access executes during normal processing is "Exit Sub." That command terminates the sub procedure and returns control back to Access. Above Exit Sub is a label, "Exit_cmdNewRecord_Click," which is required so that the procedure can pass control to the Exit Sub command if it detects an error and passes control to the error processing portion of the sub procedure.

## Modifying VBA Code

While the Control Wizard does a good job of building VBA code for a variety of predefined tasks, the code can use some refinement. Open *frmCustomer1* in Form view and try this. Click the New Record button. Access opens a new record, clearing all the form's controls. Notice that the focus is on the button labeled Previous. We programmed the On Current event to place the focus on the Previous button whenever Access detects that the record displayed has an empty CustomerID. This happens when you click the New Record button, too. What is the user's next action after clicking the New Record button? He or she will probably click in the Customer ID text box to begin entering information. Simplify things for users by placing the insertion point in the Customer ID field for them. That action is called *setting the focus*. You may remember that we used the SetFocus method in the On Current form property event to move the focus to the Previous button. Let's modify the code behind the New Record button.

EXERCISE 10.10: MODIFYING THE NEW RECORD VBA CODE

1. Display *frmCustomer1* in Design view, right-click the New Record button, and click Build Event in the pop-up list. The Visual Basic window opens and displays the sub procedure attached to the On Click event property.
2. Click the Procedure View button in the corner of the Visual Basic window to zoom in on the cmdNewRecord_Click sub procedure.
3. Click the empty line below the one with DoCmd.GoToRecord, press Tab to indent the line just like the one above it, type *CustomerID.setfocus*, and press Enter. As you type, you notice that you get help from Access (see Figure 10.13). Notice that Access capitalizes *setfocus* after you press Enter. You do not need to match the capitalization of objects or methods, because Access will do that for you automatically when you move to a new line. This is an excellent way to ensure you have spelled words correctly—type objects' names in lower case. If Access does not capitalize selected letters to match the spelling of an object, then you have misspelled the name.
4. Press Alt+Q to save the VBA code and close the Visual Basic window.
5. Save the altered form.

In step 3 you noticed that as soon as you typed *set*, Visual Basic displayed a list of an object's methods and properties in a list. As you continue typing, the list automatically scrolls down to the first list member that matches what you have

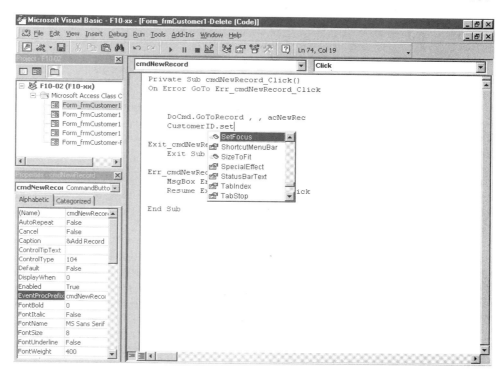

**Figure 10.13** Modifying a sub procedure.

typed so far. If the list highlights the correct item in the list, you do not need to continue typing. Pressing the spacebar when Visual Basic highlights the correct method or property will enter the remainder for you and close the list. You may find this the easiest way to write code. Using this method guarantees that you will not misspell the method.

---

**Try it**

Observe the changed New Record button. Open *frmCustomer1* in Form view and click the New Record button. Where is the focus now? If you did Exercise 10.10, the focus will be in the Customer ID text box.

---

**Creating the Delete Record and Cancel Changes Buttons**

The Delete Record button deletes the currently displayed record from the database. In contrast, the Cancel Changes button discards any changes made to the current record, restoring the original record. The difference between the two actions is that the Cancel Changes button restores the original values of a record that has not been posted (saved) in the database. In other words, Cancel Changes allows you to rescind any changes to the current record *before* the record is saved to the database. On the other hand, the Delete Record button irrevocably *removes* a record from the database.

Build the two buttons again by using the Control Wizard. First, you will build the Delete Record button by following the steps of an exercise. Next, you will build the Cancel Changes button by hand without using the Control Wizard (gasp!). Finally, with all four database manipulation buttons in place, you will align them and make them a uniform size.

Prepare for the exercise by displaying *frmCustomer1* in Design view and opening the toolbox, if it is not already open. Follow the steps in the next exercise to create the Delete Record button and associated VBA code.

### EXERCISE 10.11: CREATING THE DELETE RECORD BUTTON AND CODE

1. Click the Command Button tool in the toolbox and click on the *frmCustomer1* form on the right side of the form, just below the New Record button (see Figure 10.2). Access places the command button on the form and the Control Wizard starts displaying dialog boxes.
2. In the Categories list, select Record Operations.
3. In the Actions list, select Delete Record and then click the Next button.
4. Select the Text option button so that a label appears on the button instead of a graphic.
5. Type *&Delete Record* in the text box to the right of the Text option button. Click the Next button.
6. Type *cmdDeleteRecord* in the text box to give the button a meaningful name.
7. Click Finish to complete the button-building process. The Wizard creates the button and attaches VBA code to the button's On Click event property.
8. Save the altered form, *frmCustomer1*. Leave the form open in Design view.

The last database manipulation button you will create is Cancel Changes. This button's code is simple enough to not need the help of the Control Wizard. Besides, it's good to practice building VBA code from scratch to get an idea of how it works. Two general steps are required: Create a button control and place it on the form, and create the code that executes when the On Click event occurs and attach it to the button's On Click event property. Execute the following exercise to build the Cancel Changes button.

### EXERCISE 10.12: MANUALLY CREATING THE CANCEL CHANGES BUTTON AND CODE

1. With the toolbox open, click the Control Wizard tool so it is *not* selected. This time we do not want the Wizard's help.

2. Place the command button on the form below the Delete Record button.
3. Right-click the new command button, select Properties from the pop-up list, and click the All tab.
4. Double-click the Name property, if necessary, to highlight the entire name and type *cmdCancel* to replace the existing name. The Name property is an internal name used by VBA code to refer to the button.
5. Type *&Cancel Changes* in the Caption property, which is found just below the Name property. The Caption property contains the text that is on the button's surface—the label that users see on the button.
6. Click the Event tab of the property sheet, click the On Click event property, and click the button to the right with the three dots. (This button is called the *Build button*.) The Choose Builder dialog box opens.
7. Click Code Builder in the left panel and click the OK button. The Visual Basic window opens. Access conveniently places the insertion point between the first and last statements of the cmdCancel_Click sub procedure. It is at that position that you will type code that carries out the undo operation.
8. Press Tab to indent the code line and then type:

   *DoCmd.DoMenuItem acFormBar, acEditMenu, acUndo*

   and press Enter.
9. Next, type *CustomerID.setfocus* and press Enter. (See Figure 10.14.)
10. Select Close and Return to Microsoft Access on the File menu.
11. Select File, Save to save your form and its new command button.

### Try it

Check out the new Cancel Changes button. Switch *frmCustomer1* to Form view, make a few changes to the current record, and click the Cancel Changes button. All the changes you have made will be rescinded, and the record will be restored to its original form.

As you created the four data manipulation buttons, you may not have bothered with making them all the same size or even aligning them—rightly so. We believe that you should save cosmetic work such as this until after you have done the "heavy lifting" involved with creating buttons and their associated event procedures. Once this is done, you can fix any visual problems. Now is a good time to make the four data manipulation buttons the same size, align them, and make the space between them equal. Simply repeat Exercise 10.6 using the four data manipulations in place of the four navigation buttons. Change step 6: Align the buttons on their *left* sides by selecting Format, Align, Left (instead of Format, Align, Bottom); secondly, select Format, Vertical Spacing (rather than Horizontal Spacing), Make Equal. When you've completed this exercise, your customer form should resemble Figure 10.2. The only features that your form may not have when

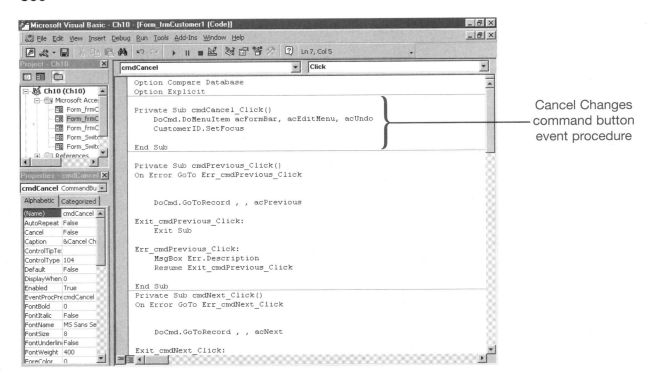

**Figure 10.14** Cancel Changes event procedure.

compared to Figure 10.2 are the rectangles that appear around the two groups of buttons. If you want to add the rectangles, then follow the next Try it.

### Try it

With *frmCustomer1* in Design view, open the toolbox, click the Rectangle tool, and drag the rectangle on the form so that it surrounds the four navigation buttons. Release the mouse. Repeat this for the data manipulation buttons.

## AUTOMATING INTERNAL CONTROL FEATURES

Most database systems provide some built-in validity checking whereby input values are checked to ensure they are acceptable. Microsoft Access is no exception, providing a Validation Rule for tables, forms, and controls. For example, Access can prevent you from entering a number such as 67.89 in a date field on a form, because Access automatically applies data validation based on a field's data type. If you attempt to enter data that does not match the field data type, Access displays an error message. Other control features built into Access tables include a field's Input Mask, Required, and Validation Rule properties. Although Access' built-in validity checks are powerful in a general way, they simply cannot handle more specific and rigorous data checks. A form's date field is an example. What do you suppose Access would do if you entered an invoice date such as 10/17/2020 and pressed Enter or Tab? Although that date is probably not reasonable for most applications, Access allows you to enter it without issuing an error message.

You *can* detect and prevent erroneous dates as well as prevent other types of data entry errors that would pass Access' fundamental validity tests. Central to validating data are macros attached to events associated with a field or form to be validated. Access macro statements and VBA code provide powerful features that make elaborate, interfield validity checking easy to implement.

Data validation implemented with VBA code is particularly useful in automating internal controls involving databases that are external to the application. For example, it is not difficult to write a small code block that checks available inventory of an item as the sales order quantity is being entered. When the input quantity exceeds available supplies of an item, a VBA sub procedure can detect the condition and issue a warning message. In other circumstances, VBA code can reduce on-hand quantities to the appropriate value based on the quantity that is entered into an order form. This stock-checking internal control is a business rule that can be enforced best by writing VBA code and associating it with one of a field's several event properties.

We show examples of validating a field and enforcing business rules in the two sections that follow. You can use these as models to create your own validity checking and rule enforcement procedures for your accounting applications.

## Validating User Input

One example of application-specific data validation is checking data that a user enters on a form *before* you allow the user to post that changed information to the database's tables. For instance, you might want to validate a purchase order date immediately after a user enters it on a form to ensure that the value is reasonable. In the case of any date field, the term "reasonable" is a temporal measure that depends on the application. Though we might implement this type of date validation at the root—with the built-in Validation Rule property available for each field in the table itself—code to test values *before* they make it into a table makes more sense. This is particularly true when you want to *share* the validation procedure across forms and applications within the same database. You can create small VBA sub procedures that can detect certain errors immediately. Frequently, Access does not identify a mistake until you move off the current record. Depending on automatic validity checks provided by Access can delay recognizing mistakes, which can frustrate users who have keyed a lot of data in the meantime.

Chapter 5 introduced you to an Order Entry form, which is shown in Figure 10.15. Recall that the form fields Customer (customer number) and Salesperson (sales representative) use a combo box to look up and display a list of acceptable values for their respective fields.

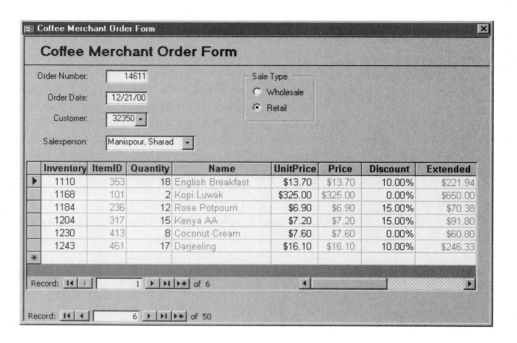

**Figure 10.15**    The Coffee Merchant Order form.

Let's create a VBA event procedure that checks the Order Date field on The Coffee Merchant Order form to ensure that the date is acceptable. We will attach the code to the Before Update event property of the Order Date field control. By associating the VBA code with the Before Update event property for the field, Access will automatically execute the code just after the user moves from the Order Date to another control on the form. Triggering the Before Update property means that Access will not move the value that the user typed into the Order Date text box to an internal storage area until the procedure checks the value. When the last value is entered on The Coffee Merchant form, Access then moves all form data from memory where it is temporarily housed into the various tables in the database. The Before Update property is an ideal way to check any field's contents before permitting the change to post to a database.

The ValidDateCheck VBA sub procedure checks the Order Date field to ensure it is valid. If it is, then the code permits the focus to move to any form field that the user clicks. On the other hand, the code does not allow the cursor to move from the Order Date control if the date value does not conform to the rules you have established. You will attach the date validation code only to the Order Date control (internally named txtOrderDate). If this type of date validation is something you find yourself doing for other controls, then you may want to write a general-purpose date-check code and place it in the Modules collection. Any code listed in the Modules collection is available for use by *any* object in the entire database. Code created for and attached to any form, like all the code we have created so far in this chapter, is available only to the form to which it is attached.

The date validation rule we wish to implement is this: Any order date entered into The Coffee Merchant's Order form must be plus or minus 14 days of today's date (inclusive). All other dates (those outside that range) are invalid. This rule, though arbitrary, allows data entry persons the flexibility of backdating or post-dating the order up to 14 days. When an invalid date is recognized, an information message is displayed and then the user is allowed to correct the date. This may not always be a good policy, but we implement the rule simply to show you how to enforce it. You are free to tweak such rules as you see fit.

Prepare for the next exercise by closing all Access windows except the Database window for *Ch10.mdb*. Next, open *frmOrder* in Design view.

EXERCISE 10.13: WRITING VBA CODE
FOR THE BEFORE UPDATE EVENT PROPERTY

1. Right-click the Order Date text box control (*not* the Order Date label control), select Properties from the pop-up menu to display the control's property sheet, click the Before Update event property, and click the Build button (the ellipsis) on the right side of the property. The Choose Builder dialog box opens.
2. Select Code Builder from the list of three choices and click the OK button to begin writing code for the Before Update event property of the Order Date text box control.
3. Press Tab to indent the first line of code, then type *'Validate Order Date* and press Enter. That is how you enter a comment line; begin the line with an apostrophe and then type the text. Notice that Access changes the color of comment lines to green. That makes comments easy to distinguish from code.
4. Enter the following code beneath the comment you just typed, pressing Enter at the end of each line. Press Tab as needed to match the indenting shown here. Be aware that the second line in the following code ends with a comma, a space, and an underscore character—in that order.

```
If txtOrderDate < Date - 14 Or txtOrderDate > Date + 14 Then
    MsgBox "Date is incorrect. Please reenter.", _
        vbOKOnly + vbExclamation, "Error"
    Cancel = True          'reenter data
Else
    Cancel = False         'data is fine as entered
End If
```

5. Press Alt+Q to close the Visual Basic code window.
6. Save the altered form by clicking Save in the File menu. Figure 10.16 shows the Before Update event property VBA code. Your code should match it exactly.

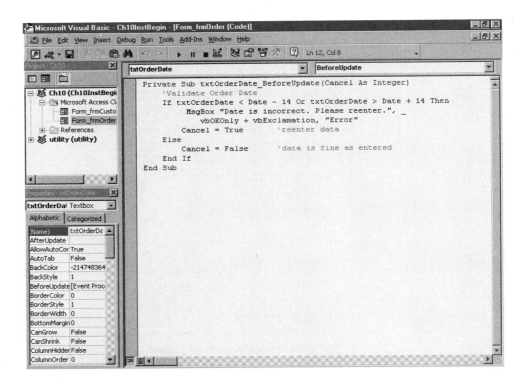

**Figure 10.16**   VBA code to check user-input order dates.

Before you learn exactly what the code does, let's see if the code works. Always test your work thoroughly before you release it. Follow the next Try it to test the VBA code.

**Try it**

Display *frmOrder* in Form view. Select Data Entry in the Records menu to display an empty order form. Type *77777* in the Order Number text box. Press Tab to move to the Order Date field. Type the date *10/17/04* in the text box and press Tab. The error dialog box shown in Figure 10.17 should appear warning you that the date you entered is incorrect. The VBA code you wrote tests the input date to make sure it is within four weeks (two before and two after) of the current date—based on the current date stored on the computer you are using. Click the OK button on the dialog box to remove the dialog box. Next, drag the mouse over the entire Order Date text box, press the Delete key to erase the incorrect date, and type in today's date. Press Tab to move to the Customer list box. Click the list arrow and select any customer's name. Press Tab to move to the Salesperson's text box, click the drop-down arrow, and select any salesperson from the drop-down list. Click the Form View window Close button to close the form.

invalid date entered
in order date field

error warning

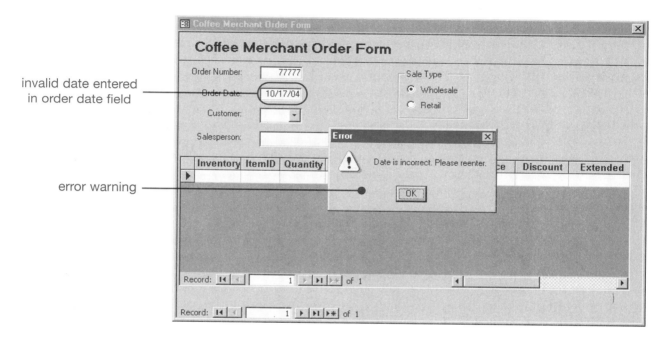

**Figure 10.17**   Example of an attempt to enter an invalid order date.

What do the lines of the sub procedure mean? First, notice that the name of the procedure includes both the form control name (txtOrderDate) and the event procedure (Before Update) to which it is attached. The sub procedure has one argument, on the same line as the Sub statement, enclosed in parentheses. A sub procedure *argument* is a name used to pass information into and out of a sub procedure—a sort of communication pipe linking the inside of the procedure to the code outside the procedure. The sub procedure's argument is called *Cancel* and is an integer. (Arguments are declared in the argument list on the Sub statement.) The second line contains a comment describing what the procedure does. Here, we used a very brief comment. You may want to include multiple line comments to fully explain the purpose of any sub procedures you write. The remainder of the sub procedure is a single statement, believe it or not. The If statement provides three parts as follows:

```
If <conditional expression> Then
     <statements1>
Else
     <statements2>
End If
```

The <conditional expression> is an arbitrarily complex expression that evaluates to true or false. To validate the date a user enters in the txtOrderDate field, the expression tests whether the value of the date in the control txtOrderDate is prior to today's date (Date) minus 14 days or later than today's date plus 14 days. The word "Date" that appears in the conditional expression is a VBA built-in function that returns the current date, which it gets by interrogating the computer system's clock. Either the expression is true or false. If the expression is true, then that means the date entered is out of range (too old or in the future). If the expression is true—indicating an error—then the first statement(s) (<statements1> in the preceding syntax) are executed in the If/Then/Else statement and none others. If the expression is false, that means the date is reasonable based on your arbitrary constraints. In that case, any statements between the Else and End If phrases are executed.

What happens if the order date is out of range? Access executes the MsgBox statement and then executes the Cancel statement. The MsgBox statement displays a message box on the screen informing the user about an unusual condition or providing an informational message. The message you want to display follows the MsgBox statement in quotation marks. The second argument, separated from the first by a comma, is a bit more complicated. It tells Access which buttons and icons to display on the message box. Because the line is long, we use a *statement continuation* indicator—a blank followed by an underline—to indicate that the statement continues uninterrupted on the next line. (Normally, a statement must be written on a single line, no matter how long it is.) Using *intrinsic constants*, which are constants that appear to be variables, vbOKOnly tells Access to display the OK button only. To display other buttons, you can simply use a plus sign to mathematically "add" other buttons or icons to the message box. For example, the intrinsic value vbExclamation displays a standard Windows exclamation point in the message box. The third argument, "Error" is the text you want to appear in the Title bar of the message box. After displaying a message box using the MsgBox built-in procedure, Access encounters the statement

```
Cancel = True       'reenter date
```

That sets the value of the Cancel argument—the variable named in the argument list of the sub procedure—to the value of true. There is a comment in the right part of the line to document the statement. Like the full-line comment, it begins with an apostrophe. The remainder of a line with an apostrophe is commentary. When control returns to the Access form, it causes the cursor to remain in the txtOrderDate control rather than moving to another control on the form. In other words, it cancels the input value and keeps the focus on the control that is in error. Once the code on the "Then" side of the If/Then/Else is executed, control jumps over the rest of the statement and to the End Sub statement. That returns control from the sub procedure back to the Access form.

Suppose the order date value *is* valid. Then what happens? The conditional expression evaluates to false and the statement after the Else phrase is executed. The statement

```
Cancel = False        'data is fine as entered
```

executes. It accepts the user-input order date and allows Access to move to whatever field the user reaches by clicking the mouse or pressing the Tab key. A comment follows the expression and begins with an apostrophe.

The date range we chose to illustrate validity checking is arbitrary. What we want to illustrate is how to write a simple data validation sub procedure. You can choose to validate dates, numeric values, and even character strings for any number of form fields using the same techniques shown here. Use the date validation method as an example to create similar form field validation tests.

## Enforcing Business Rules

Access VBA code is essential for enforcing the many obvious and sometimes subtle business rules. These rules vary from company to company, department to department within a company, and among programs for a single department or division within a company. Business rules might include the stipulation that a sales order that a clerk is entering must be checked against the customer's payment history file before it is approved. Another rule might require that a sales representative's number be included on each sales order form so that the order's origin is easily traced if necessary. Neither of the preceding rules validates data input, because the form fields involved are not subject to range or reasonableness tests. Rather, the tests performed are more subtle and involve information that is not linked to the current form. We show you in this section how to construct these types of business rule tests.

It is important, when entering a sales order, to check that there is sufficient stock to be able to supply the item being entered. Look at Figure 10.15 for a moment. When you enter "18" in the Quantity column for English Breakfast, an automatic procedure should engage and check the stock on hand to ensure the order can be filled. If less than 18 pounds of the requested item are in stock, then some action should be started to handle the situation. At the very least, a message should appear on the screen warning the order entry person that insufficient stock exists for the particular item. Then the order entry person can note on the order form that the item is back-ordered. Alternatively, he or she can attempt to locate the requested item in an alternate inventory source. Ideally, the system should also automatically generate a purchase request for additional stock. That purchase request could be an entry in another table that is printed daily to see what stock should be ordered.

We will show you how and where to place a check to ensure stock ordered is available while the order is being processed. For illustration purposes, we will keep the reaction to a stock shortage brief: the process merely warns the data entry person of the shortage. Later, you can embellish the procedure to include a mechanism that creates a purchase order or to simply insert an appropriately identified row in a purchase table.

The exercise that follows shows you how to build a simple VBA procedure that checks each line item quantity value just after it is entered (but before it is placed into the order table). Checking is conceptually simple, the quantity ordered is compared to the item's OnHand value stored in the *tblInventory* table. If the ordered amount just entered exceeds available stock, a warning message displays on the screen. The VBA code that performs the comparison between requested quantity and the actual quantity available is attached to the Quantity column's Before Update event procedure. The Quantity column is part of the *fsubOrder* subform. The subform is embedded in the master form, *frmOrder* (see Figure 10.15). Prepare for Exercise 10.14 by closing all windows in the Ch10 database except the Database window.

We begin by writing the VBA code that performs the stock check. In writing the code, we will use an Access built-in function called DLookup to look up and return the amount of stock on hand for a particular item. The DLookup function interrogates the *tblInventory* table and locates the Quantity value for a user-specified inventory item. The VBA code will display a warning message if the code determines that the amount of the item in stock is less than the quantity requested in the order. Otherwise, the macro returns control to the Order Entry form. (Clearly, you will also want to *decrease* the stock on hand quantity in inventory by the amount ordered so that the inventory counts remain accurate. That is left as an exercise to the student.)

EXERCISE 10.14: WRITING VBA CODE TO CHECK AVAILABLE STOCK

1. Click Forms on the *Ch10.mdb* Objects bar and open *fsubOrder* in Design view.
2. Right-click the Quantity control, click Properties from the pop-up menu to display the control's property sheet, click the Before Update event property, and click the Build button (the ellipsis button) on the right side of the property. The Choose Builder dialog box opens.
3. Select Code Builder from the list of choices and click the OK button to begin writing code.

4. Press Tab to indent the first line of code, then type *'Check available stock quantity* and press Enter.
5. Enter the following code beneath the comment you just typed, pressing Enter at the end of each line and pressing Tab as needed to match the line indent shown below. Remember to continue the first line by terminating it with a comma, a space, and the underscore character (in that order).

> *If Quantity > DLookup("[OnHand]", "[tblInventory]", _*
>       *"[ItemID]=Forms![frmOrder]![fsubOrder].Form![ItemID]") Then*
>     *MsgBox "Quantity requested greater than available stock", vbOKOnly*
>     *Cancel = True    'quantity requested not available*
> *Else*
>     *Cancel = False    'quantity available to satisfy request*
> *End If*

6. Press Alt+Q to close the Visual Basic code window.
7. Save the altered form by clicking Save in the File menu. Figure 10.18 shows the Before Update event property VBA code. Your code should match it.

object for which code is being written

object's event property to which the code is attached

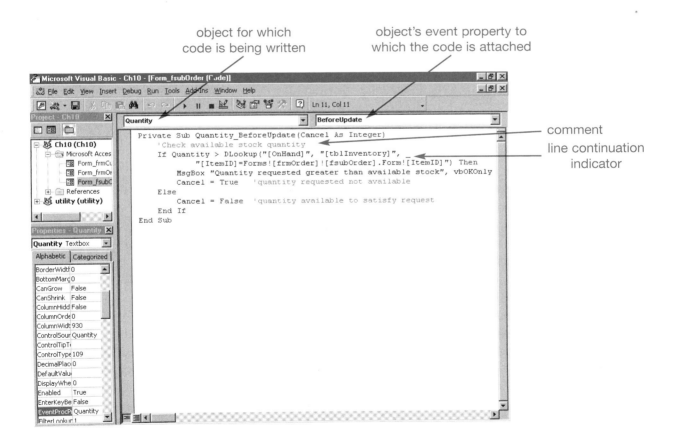

comment

line continuation indicator

**Figure 10.18** VBA code to check order quantity against available quantity.

Here's an explanation of the VBA code you just entered. Whenever someone enters into the *frmOrder* subform an item quantity value and then attempts to move to the next field in the order entry detail line, the Before Update event triggers. This causes the Before Update VBA code to take control. Like the previous VBA code you wrote, this sub procedure consists of an If/Then/Else statement that contains two alternative actions. The DLookup built-in function, part of the conditional expression that is tested, has this general form:

DLookup(expression, domain, criteria)

The actual expression used in your code contains "[OnHand]" for the expression argument. This is the column value that is located and returned from the *tblInventory* table. The *tblInventory* table name is the second argument of the DLookup function. It names the table to be searched for the stock quantity. Finally, the third argument indicates which row of the *tblInventory* table to look for. A match between the ItemID of the *fsubOrder* form and the same item in the *tblInventory* table contains the inventory row containing the stock on hand we seek. That criteria argument is the rather lengthy expression:

"[ItemID]=Forms![frmOrder]![fsubOrder].Form![ItemID]"

The notation beginning after the equal sign is the standard way to name a subform field embedded within a form. It requests a match between the order line item identification in the order entry and the inventory item whose primary key is also ItemID.

After DLookup returns a single number—the OnHand value for the chosen inventory item—it is compared to the Quantity value that the user entered. The entire "expression" portion of the DLookup function in a simplified form is this:

[Quantity]>quantity retrieved from the inventory by DLookup

If the preceding condition is true—a larger quantity is requested than is available—then the statements following the word *Then* are executed. In such a case, the MsgBox statement issues a warning message. Notice the lengthy IF statement continues on a second line. Recall that you indicate a line continues by typing a space followed by the underscore character. Continue typing the remainder of the statement on a new line. (It is best to break a statement in a blank space and not in the middle of a character string enclosed in quotation marks.) The second statement, "Cancel = True" passes a true value back to Access when the sub procedure completes. This causes the focus to not move and gives the user a chance to read the warning message and reenter a corrected quantity value. If the quantity requested by the user is *less than* the quantity available in inventory, then the Cancel variable is set to false. Normal processing of the order entry continues when false is returned from the sub procedure.

There are alternative actions that you could take if there were not sufficient stock to fulfill the current order. You could update the OnHand column of the *tblInventory* table to reflect how much of the item was taken from stock (negative amounts mean a back-order situation exists). Or you could halt processing. We have shown you one way to deal with the situation—display a warning message.

Now that you have a fundamental understanding of the VBA code attached to the Quantity control's Before Update event property, let's test the code. Experiencing the code in action (triggering a warning message) really drives home how this process enforces a fundamental business rule.

### Try it

Display the *frmOrder* form in Form view and click the First Record navigation button. The first sales order displays. Execute each of the following steps to see exactly how your newly created business rule catches an attempt to order more of an item than currently exists in stock. Move the mouse pointer to the Quantity column in the last row of the subform corresponding to the *Ethiopia Sidamo* entry. Double-click the current Quantity entry to highlight it. Type the new quantity value, *5000*, and press Tab to enter the value. A warning message is displayed because there are only 3,440 pounds of Ethiopia Sidamo (item 167) in stock, not the requested 5,000 pounds (see Figure 10.19). Click OK to remove the message box and change the quantity back to its original value, *4*. Close the form.

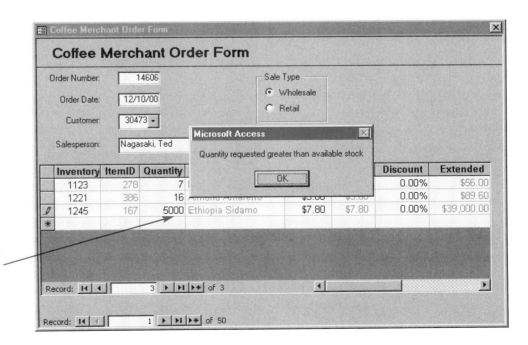

requested quantity exceeds available stock

**Figure 10.19** The stock-check VBA code in action.

**USING A
SWITCHBOARD
FORM**

To add polish to your database application, consider creating a database startup form. A *startup form* opens automatically when a user double-clicks a database application file name to open it. The most common way to provide a simple yet helpful opening screen is to create a form that serves as a main menu. From the opening form, users can click various buttons to print reports, open forms, or examine individual tables. We have included a preliminary example of a startup form in your *Ch10.mdb* database. Called *Switchboard*, the opening form contains three buttons, a graphic, and a bit of text. Figure 10.20 shows the completed Switchboard form. You will begin with a Switchboard form that is almost complete and finish it.

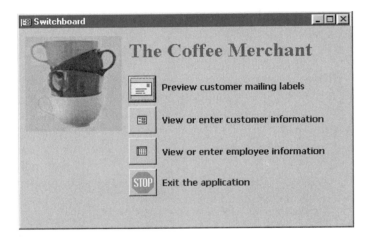

**Figure 10.20**   Example database application startup (switchboard) form.

Database designers frequently use the term *switchboard* for this type of startup form because it contains buttons that allow a user to switch from one part of a database application to just about any other. Like a telephone switchboard, the startup form provides a switching function. Your database contains a preliminary version of the Switchboard form that is stored in the Forms collection of your *Ch10.mdb* database. The only difference between your Switchboard form and the one shown in Figure 10.20 is that the bottom button and accompanying text are omitted on your form. Otherwise, the two forms behave identically. The functional heart of your Switchboard form consists of the three buttons that open selected forms and reports in your database. Clicking the top button opens a customer mailing label report in a Preview window. When you click the button containing an icon of a form—just below the preview customer command button—it displays a Customer form in Form view. With the Customer form, you can review the customers or make changes to them. The third and last button on your pre-liminary form displays an Employee form. Like the Customer form, the Employee form provides your users a convenient way to either review the employee infor-mation or make changes to it.

---

**Try it**

Before going on, open the Switchboard form to see how it works. First, hover the mouse pointer over the large label "The Coffee Merchant." Within a few seconds, a ControlTip displays the owner's name and date when the company was estab-lished. Hover the mouse pointer over the button next to the label "View or enter customer information." What does the button's ControlTip display? Finally, try out a switchboard button: Click the middle button to open up a customer form. When you are done examining the customer form, close it by clicking the Form view Close button. The Switchboard form comes to the foreground. Close the Switchboard form.

---

## Adding an Exit Button to the Switchboard Form

A switchboard-style startup form should also sport a button or menu that exits the application. This provides a non-expert a simple way of halting an application and makes the application more polished. You will add another button to the Switchboard form that will exit Access when the user clicks it. To the right of the new command button you will add a label that indicates the purpose of the but-ton. Finally, you will set several form-level properties so that the startup form looks more like a switchboard-style form and less like a record-displaying type of form.

In preparation for the next exercise, open *Ch10.mdb* (if necessary) and close all windows except the Database window. Click Forms on the Objects bar and dis-play Switchboard in Design view.

---

EXERCISE 10.15: ADDING AN EXIT BUTTON TO THE SWITCHBOARD FORM

1. Open the toolbox, make sure that the Control Wizard tool is selected, and then click the Command Button tool.
2. Click the form just beneath and aligned with the left edge of the bottom button of the three. The Command Button Wizard begins displaying a series of dialog boxes.
3. Select Application from the Categories list. Quit Application is already selected in the Actions list.
4. Click Next. The Control Wizard asks if you want text or a picture. Unlike other command buttons you created in other chapters, you want a picture on this command button. The Picture option button and the Stop Sign are already se-lected. Those are good choices.

5. Click Next to go to the next dialog box. Type *cmdExitApplication* in the text box to assign the button a meaningful, internal name.
6. Click Finish. The Control Wizard completes its work and places a new button on your form.

You may wish to align the new button with the existing ones by executing the Align command of the Format menu. In addition, you may want to ensure that there is equal spacing between the buttons by executing Vertical Spacing in the Format menu. Of course, you want to select all four buttons before both of the previous formatting operations.

## Adding a Label to the Switchboard Form

The next step to modify the Switchboard form is to add text to the right of the command button you just added. Users will understand exactly what the button does if there is accompanying text on the form to the right of the button. With the form still in Design view, do the following.

EXERCISE 10.16: ADDING A LABEL TO THE SWITCHBOARD FORM

1. Close the toolbox and click the label above and to the right of your new button— the label with the text "View or enter customer information." Selection handles appear around the selected label.
2. Press Ctrl+C to copy the label to the Clipboard. Press Ctrl+V to paste the label onto the form. The pasted label, which is identical to the label you selected in step 1, is enclosed in selection handles.
3. Move the mouse inside the selected label. When the mouse cursor changes to a full hand (thumb and four fingers), click and move the label so that it is to the right of your new button and approximately aligned on its left side with the labels above it.
4. Click inside the label again so that a vertical bar appears. Then drag across the letters in the label to select all of them.
5. Type *Exit the application* to replace the selected text and click outside the label to view the results. The text should now match the text shown in Figure 10.20.
6. Select Save As from the File menu and type *Switchboard2* in the text box and click OK to save the modified form. Saving the changed form under a new name provides you the opportunity to save the original Switchboard form in case you want to work with it.

The last step in modifying the Switchboard form is to change particular form properties. You will set several properties that are assigned to the form as a unit. Changes you will make enhance the form's function and appearance.

## Modifying a Form's Properties

Several properties of the Switchboard form are designed to help display database records but are not well suited for a switchboard-style form. The properties are all form-level properties—those attached to the form as a whole. Form properties that you will change on the Switchboard form include these (listed in the order that they occur in the form's property sheet): Caption, ViewsAllowed, ScrollBars, RecordSelectors, NavigationButtons, Dividing Lines, AutoCenter, and BorderStyle.

### EXERCISE 10.17: MODIFYING A FORM'S PROPERTIES

1. With the Switchboard2 form displayed in Design view, open the property sheet and click Select Form in the Edit menu (or click the shortcut, Ctrl+R). The property sheet Title bar displays "Form," which assures you that you have selected the form rather than a particular object on the form.
2. Click the Format tab on the property sheet.
3. Set the following properties to the values indicated. After you set the form properties as shown, your switchboard form will look like a dialog box instead of a database form. Your form's property sheet should match the properties shown in Figure 10.21.

| Property | Value |
|---|---|
| Caption | Switchboard |
| ViewsAllowed | Form |
| ScrollBars | Neither |
| RecordSelectors | No |
| NavigationButtons | No |
| Dividing Lines | No |
| AutoCenter | Yes |
| BorderStyle | Thin |

4. Close the property sheet.
5. Close the Switchboard2 form and click Yes when Access asks you if you want to save your changes.

### Try it

Test your form by opening Switchboard2 in Form view. Then, click the exit button you just created. Access will close both the database and itself, returning control to Windows.

"Form" indicates that the
form object is selected

**Figure 10.21**  Switchboard form property settings.

## Making a Switchboard Form Open Automatically

A switchboard-style form does not automatically display when a user opens your database. The name "Switchboard" does not impart some special significance to the Access database program. You do not want your database users wondering how to start your elegant database application. Automatically launching a switchboard form—providing an entryway to your application—is a terrific way to help your database users.

The last step in completing your database application is to tell Access to launch your Switchboard form automatically, making it the startup form for your entire database application. The following exercise tells you how to do this.

EXERCISE 10.18: ESTABLISHING A DATABASE APPLICATION STARTUP FORM

1. With the *Ch10.mdb* Database window open, click Startup on the Tools menu.
2. Type *The Coffee Merchant Database* in the Application Title text box. This text appears in the Access application window Title bar in place of "Microsoft Access."
3. Click the Display Form/Page list box and then select Switchboard2 from the list of forms.
4. Clear the Display Database Window check box. From now on, when users open your database, the Database window will not appear. They do not need it because your Switchboard form replaces it.

5. Clear the Allow Toolbar/Menu changes check box (see Figure 10.22). This prevents users from changing any custom toolbars or menus you might create for your application.
6. Click OK to finalize your choices.

database Title bar text      startup form's name

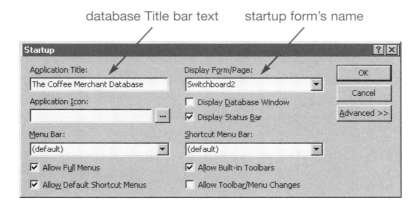

**Figure 10.22**   Designating a database startup form.

### Try it

Close the *Ch10.mdb* database and Access simultaneously by clicking the Access Title bar's Close button. Now, use Windows Explorer to locate *Ch10.mdb* on your hard disk and double-click the database file name. What is different about the way Access behaves? If you made all the changes correctly, then your Switchboard form opens, but the Database window does not. Notice that the application Title bar contains the text you typed in step 2 of Exercise 18 (see Figure 10.23).

**SUMMARY**   You have learned how to use Access macros and VBA code to automate database procedures to provide form navigation and to perform data tests. You created buttons and linked macros or VBA code to them so that they perform a series of steps. With navigation buttons, you simplified moving around the database rows displayed on a form. You discovered that other database activities can be simplified by making buttons that modify database rows, create new rows, save changes, and cancel changes. Though creating buttons is more work initially, these buttons spare users from learning details about the database system and its interaction language and provide built-in error detection.

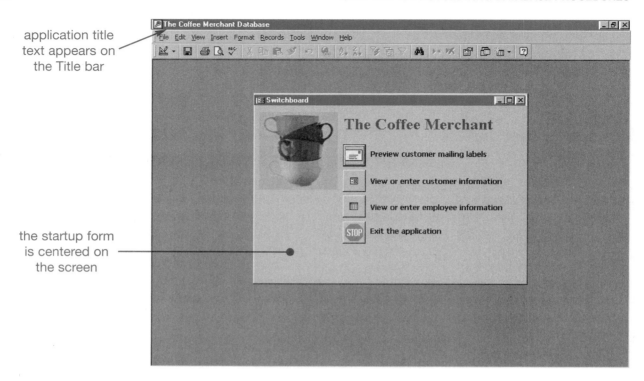

application title text appears on the Title bar

the startup form is centered on the screen

**Figure 10.23**  Automatically displaying the startup form.

Access databases, like other database management systems, support events. Events are recognized when particular conditions exist. A button click is an event, the mouse moving over a form control is an event, and leaving a control by pressing the Tab key is an event. Each of the many events that can occur to an object—a form, a list box, or command button, for example—has an associated event property. You can write VBA code or macros that are assigned to an individual object's event properties that spring into action when appropriate. For example, you can write an arbitrarily complicated bit of VBA code that executes whenever a user clicks a particular command button. The code is attached to the command button's On Click event procedure. Other events such as a form's On Current event provide convenient ways to gain control over a process to validate form fields before Access posts changes to the database.

Data validation and internal controls are important in maintaining a robust database that is free from errors. Creating data validation VBA code is one way to preserve the integrity of your database. You also learned that you could use behind-the-scenes code to automate internal control features. The controls you read about and implemented included validating dates entered in orders and checking stock on hand to ensure that an order can be filled.

# QUESTIONS AND PROBLEMS FOR REVIEW

## MULTIPLE-CHOICE QUESTIONS

1. You can create small program segments that alter the behavior of objects. These program segments are known by what general name?
   a. event properties
   b. events
   c. actions
   d. sub procedures or macros

2. When you click a button on a form, it causes which of the following events to occur?
   a. Open
   b. GetFocus
   c. MouseOpen
   d. Click

3. A macro containing other macros is called a
   a. procedure macro.
   b. group menu.
   c. macro group.
   d. menu cluster.

4. You can display a dialog box with an informative or warning message with which of the following macros?
   a. MessInfo
   b. InfoBox
   c. MessageBox
   d. MsgBox

5. When creating a VBA procedure to check the contents of a form, you attach the VBA code to which form event property so that it can check a record each time a new record is displayed?
   a. Pop Up
   b. On Current
   c. On Load
   d. Before Update

6. You can attach a validation code (a macro or VBA code) to what event property to prevent the cursor from moving off the current form field just prior to Access updating the data?
   a. canMove
   b. Before Update
   c. After Update
   d. After Focus

7. What VBA statement provides for two distinct statement groups to be executed depending on whether a statement is true or false?
   a. comment
   b. End Sub
   c. If/Then/Else
   d. MsgBox

8. What is the name of the symbol that indicates a VBA statement is continued on the line that follows it?
   a. hyphen
   b. colon
   c. semicolon
   d. underscore

9. What VBA statement tests the control txtLastName on the current form to determine if it is empty?
   a. IsEmpty(Me.txtLastName)
   b. IsNull(Me.txtLastName)
   c. IsEmpty(txtLastName.Me)
   d. Me.txtLastName.Null = True

10. The name of the special VBA variables, such as vbOkOnly, that are actually numeric constants, are _____ values.
    a. real
    b. event procedure
    c. intrinsic
    d. startup

## DISCUSSION QUESTIONS

1. What are the advantages, if any, of using custom-designed buttons to automate a procedure that can be executed by using existing Microsoft Access menus?

2. Describe what advantages, if any, would accrue by attaching field validation code to check whether a field is empty or not. After all, you can check the Required property in the table's Design view to accomplish the same thing. What is the difference in these two approaches?

3. Discuss the meaning and relationship between events and event properties. List at least five form event properties and briefly describe the event properties. Use Access Help and search for the definition or use of the event properties you choose to describe.

4. Discuss why you might want to disable a command button. For example, under what circumstances would you disable the Next database navigation button? Discuss the exact way you would write a segment of VBA code to disable a button whose name is cmdNext. Also mention the difference between a button's Caption property and its Name property. Which displays on the button's surface? Can you refer to a button by its Caption property?

5. Describe in detail the DLookup function (three or four sentences will do). Start by defining its general format: What are its arguments? Then, describe concisely the purpose of the function and where it might prove useful.

## PROBLEMS

1. Create a form that allows you to view information in both of the inventory tables *tblInventory* and *tblInventoryDescription* simultaneously. Then create four navigation buttons labeled *First Record*, *Previous Record*, *Next Record*, and *Last Record* and with associated VBA code that implements the record navigation. Create a group macro that contains all four macros. Print an example of the form (choose any inventory item) and print the VBA code for the four navigation buttons. Be sure to write your name on each page of output.

2. Modify The Coffee Merchant's Order form (*frmOrder*) so that the Order Number and Order Date fields are validated by VBA code. The validation rule for the Order Number field is that the Order Number must be between 15000 and 48000, inclusive. The validation rule for the Order Date field should be changed. Valid dates are between 30 days ago and today's date, inclusive. Both validation routines should display a message box indicating the problem. In no case should the user be permitted to continue filling out the rest of the form until the mistake is corrected. Print the two validation sub procedures and the form.

3. Write an event procedure that validates the ZipCode field in the customer form, *frmCustomer*. The VBA code prevents the cursor from leaving the ZipCode field unless a valid, existing Zipcode is found in the *Zipcodes.mdb* database found in the folder named *Supplement* on your Companion CD. Ensure that the entered Zipcode corresponds to the correct city and state abbreviation by consulting the *Zipcodes.mdb* database. Include a warning message dialog box that displays if an invalid Zipcode value is entered. The warning dialog box should display the message *Incorrect Zipcode entered*. Print the VBA sub procedure. Be prepared to demonstrate this code to your instructor.

4. Write an event procedure (VBA code) that uses a message box to display the quantity on hand of an inventory item. Attach the code to the After Update event procedure of the InventoryID field found on the subform, *fsubOrder*. The code executes the moment that the mouse pointer enters the InventoryID control. It displays the *total* quantity on hand of the inventory item—just in time for the user to determine if the item is in sufficient quantity *before* he or she enters a quantity value. (Hint: Use the DLookup function identical to the one shown in the text to look up the inventory in stock. Put the entire function in the first argument of the MsgBox function. The second argument of the MsgBox function should be at least an OK button.)

5. Add another button to the Switchboard2 form to display the order form (*frmOrder* and *fsubOrder*). Add an appropriate label to the right of the new

button. Be sure to implement ControlTips both for the new button and the text to the right of the button. The ControlTip for the button can contain a phrase about what the button does. The ControlTip for the label to the right of the new button should display your first and last names.

# INDEX